W9-CBT-805

THE DOG ENCYCLOPEDIA

THE DOG ENCYCLOPEDIA

LONDON, NEW YORK, MELBOURNE, MUNICH, AND DELHI

DORLING KINDERSLEY
Senior Editor Kathryn Hennessy
Project Art Editor Amy Orsborne
Editorial Assistant Alexandra Beeden
US Senior Editor Rebecca Warren
US Editors Kate Johnsen, Margaret Parrish
Jacket Designer Laura Brim
Jacket Editor Manisha Majithia
Jacket Design Development Manager Sophia Tampakopoulos
Producer, Pre-Production Adam Stoneham
Producer Gemma Sharpe
Photographer Tracy Morgan
Managing Art Editor Karen Self
Managing Editor Esther Ripley
Publisher Sarah Larter
Art Director Phil Ormerod
Associate Publishing Director Liz Wheeler
Publishing Director Jonathan Metcalf

Consultant Editor Kim Dennis-Bryan
Contributors Ann Baggaley, Katie John

DK INDIA
Senior Editor Monica Saigal
Senior Art Editors Chhaya Sajwan, Ranjita Bhattacharji
Editors Antara Moitra, Suparna Sengupta
Art Editors Devan Das, Supriya Mahajan, Pooja Pawwar, Pooja Pipil, Neha Sharma, Priyanka Singh, Amit Varma
Assistant Editor Archana Ramachandran
Assistant Art Editors Payal Rosalind Malik, Ankita Mukherjee, Astha Singh, Dhirendra Singh
Managing Editor Pakshalika Jayaprakash
Managing Art Editor Arunesh Talapatra
Senior DTP Designer Jagtar Singh
DTP Designers Arvind Kumar, Sachin Singh, Mohammad Usman, Tanveer Abbas Zaidi
Pre-production Manager Balwant Singh
Picture Research Surya Sankash Sarangi

First American Edition, 2013
Published in the United States by DK Publishing, 345 Hudson Street, New York, New York 10014

10 9
019 - 185332 - July/2013

Published in Great Britain by Dorling Kindersley Limited.
A catalog record for this book is available from the Library of Congress.

ISBN: 978-1-4654-0844-0

DK books are available at special discounts when purchased in bulk for sales, promotion, premiums, fund-raising, or educational use. For details, contact: DK Publishing Special Markets, 345 Hudson Street, New York, New York 10014 or SpecialSales@dk.com.

Printed and bound in China by Leo

Discover more at
www.dk.com

Disclaimer

Every effort has been made to ensure that the information in this book is accurate. Neither the publishers or the authors accept any legal responsibility for any personal injury or injuries to dogs or other damage or loss arising from the undertaking of any of the activities or exercises presented in this book, or from the reliance on any advice in this book. If your dog is ill or has behavioral problems, please seek the advice of a qualified professional, such as a vet or behavioral expert.

CONTENTS

1 INTRODUCTION TO DOGS

2 GUIDE TO BREEDS

3 CARE AND TRAINING

CHAPTER 1

INTRODUCTION TO DOGS

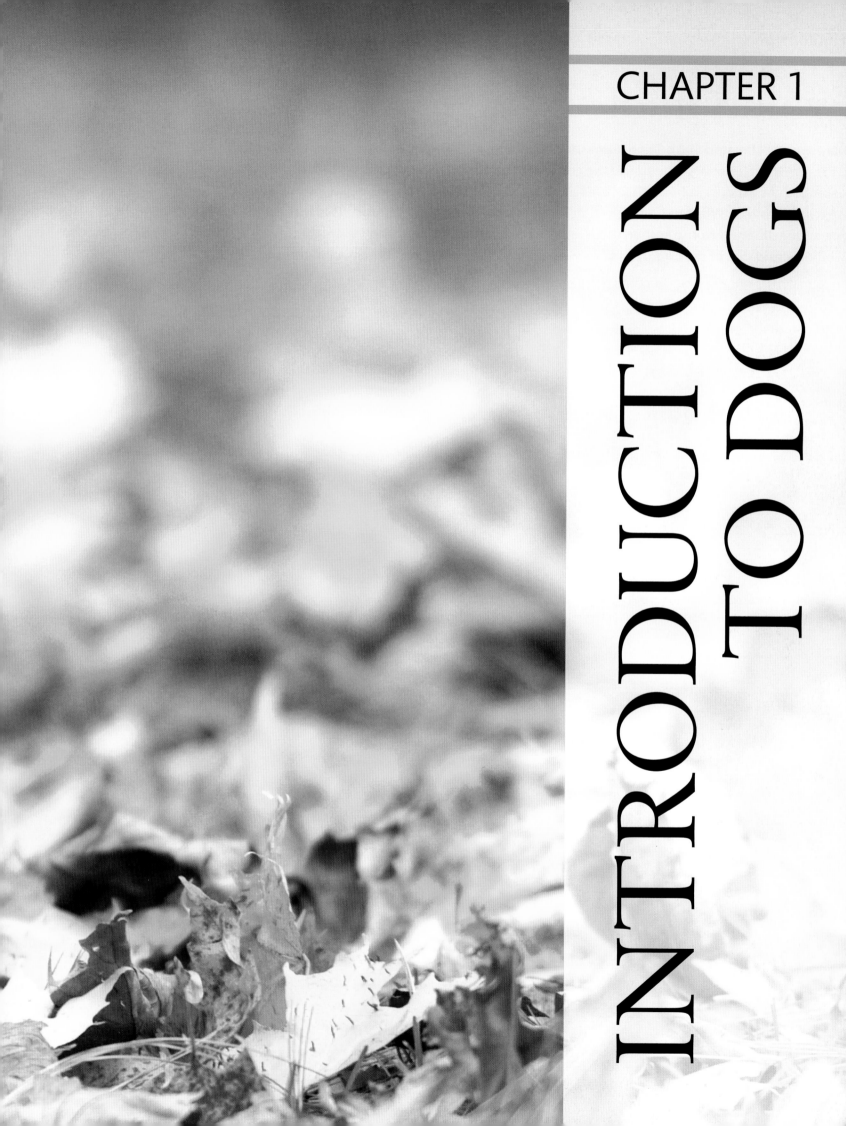

Evolution of the dog

There are an estimated 500 million domestic dogs worldwide, and all of them are related. At the base of their evolutionary tree stands the gray wolf, from which every type and breed of dog has descended. As geneticists have discovered, in terms of DNA, the difference between wolf and dog is infinitesimal. While natural selection has produced some of the changes that make one type of dog different from another, the effect of human influence has been far greater. It could be said that of the hundreds of modern dogs known today, all of them are man-made.

DAWN OF THE DOG

The history of the dog, and its transformation from wolf to domestic companion, goes back deep in prehistory, to the settlements of early hunter-gatherer peoples. In these primitive communities, wolves would scavenge among the litter around the camp site and were a useful source of hides and meat. The wolves might also, inadvertently, raise the alarm should an intruder or outsider approach the camp. Just why people first brought wolves into the domestic circle can perhaps be partly explained by the fact that humans in general seem programmed to adopt animals, either as playmates or status symbols. Possibly a small furry wolf cub appealed to our ancestors as much as it would to anyone today. Being social animals, wolves that became campside hangers-on may have readily made the transition between bonding with their pack and bonding with humans, particularly if there were advantages in terms of food and shelter.

As hunters themselves, early people would have been familiar with the behavior of wolves and appreciative of their persistence and skill when working as a team to track and bring down prey. Once tribespeople realized that a tame wolf with a sharp nose and a strong killing instinct would be an asset as a hunting companion, the human and dog partnership was born. If, as seems likely, the most promising animals were picked out for such use, this would also have been the very beginning of a selection process for desirable traits that still continues among dog breeders today.

Archeological evidence
Evidence, such as these 12,000-year-old skeletal remains of a human and a dog (top right) found in Israel, suggests that dogs may have been among the first animals to be domesticated.

Working together
Wolves live in packs cooperating with one another to hunt and rear their young. This pack lifestyle made it relatively easy for early humans to domesticate them. Instead of bonding with other wolves, selected wolf cubs happily adapted to living with a group of people.

The domestication of wolves is not likely to have occurred as an isolated incident, but repeatedly at different times and in widely separated regions. Archeological evidence of dogs buried alongside humans has turned up in areas as far apart as the Middle East (thought to be possibly one of the original sites of domestication), China, Germany, Scandinavia, and North America. Until recently the earliest of these remains was dated at approximately 14,000 years old, but the results of research into a fossilized canine skull found in Siberia, published in 2011, suggest that dogs were already domesticated as long as 30,000 years ago.

Whenever and wherever it happened, as wolves were domesticated, both their appearance and temperament began to change. New types of canid emerged, and their diversity was increased by crossbreeding between different dog populations. Depending on availability of food and climatic conditions, some hunter-gatherer tribes were isolated for generations, but others were migratory, which meant that the dogs following at their heels met and mated with others outside

RELATIONSHIPS OF THE DOG FAMILY (CANIDS)

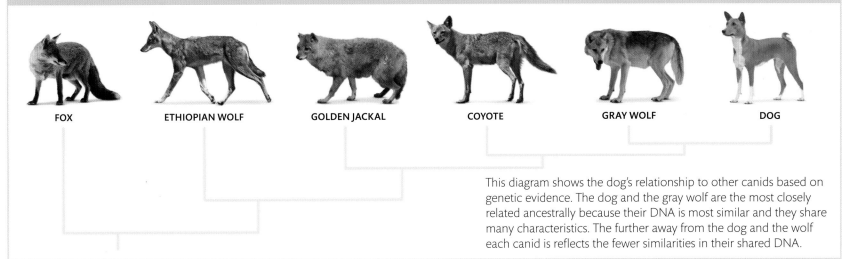

FOX

ETHIOPIAN WOLF

GOLDEN JACKAL

COYOTE

GRAY WOLF

DOG

This diagram shows the dog's relationship to other canids based on genetic evidence. The dog and the gray wolf are the most closely related ancestrally because their DNA is most similar and they share many characteristics. The further away from the dog and the wolf each canid is reflects the fewer similarities in their shared DNA.

their "clan." These early exchanges of traits and characters laid the foundation for the development of many different types of dog, but thousands of years were still to pass before anything like true breeds were established.

MODERN BREEDS

Initially people began to develop distinct types of dog for particular jobs—hounds to hunt game, mastiffs to guard property, and shepherd dogs to herd livestock. They selectively bred these dogs to be physically and temperamentally suited for their role—keen noses for hunting, long legs for racing, strength and stamina for hard outdoor work, and a strong protective instinct in dogs needed for guard duties. Later came the terriers and companion dogs. When humans better understood the laws of inheritance, and were able to manipulate them, the process of change was greatly accelerated. Then once dogs started to be kept more for companionship and as pets than for practical purposes, their appearance began to take precedence over function. Since the founding of the first breed societies in the late 19th century, rigorous standards have been compiled for pedigree dogs. These set out the ideal type, color, and conformation for each breed, and cover every imaginable point, from the set of the ears on a spaniel to the distribution of spots on a Dalmatian (see p.286).

The explosion in the variety of domestic dogs has taken place over a relatively short time, especially from the 20th century onward. Modern dogs may sometimes seem in danger of becoming fashion accessories, but human interference has caused other, greater concerns. Creating the "right" look has in some breeds been to the detriment of the dog's health. Flattened noses that cause breathing problems, too-large heads in puppies leading to whelping difficulties, and over-long backs combined with spinal disorders are just some of the built-in faults that responsible breeders now seek to mitigate. In the most recent experiments, planned crosses between one breed and another have produced a range of novelty dogs that mix and match inherited characteristics, such as the curly coat of one parent and the biddable temperament of the other.

Dogs have come a long way in appearance and character since they were wolves, and while people continue to desire the company of canines, they are also likely to want to go on changing them. In some breeds, most obviously in dogs such as the husky types and the German Shepherd (see p.42), wolflike characteristics still linger, in others the original template has been altered out of all recognition. An early hunter confronted with, say, a Pekingese (see p.270), would probably not realize at first that he was looking at a dog.

Varying looks
Many types of dog were established by the 1800s, including the Saint Bernard and English Toy Spaniel seen in this illustration. Until breed standards were established, however, types continued to change.

Skeleton and muscle

All mammals have a skeleton that is stabilized and given mobility by ligaments, tendons, and muscles. In dogs, this system evolved to serve their ancestral needs as fast-running carnivores. However, once domesticated, humans created different dogs for different tasks and in doing so altered their skeletons, too. Although some changes, such as dwarfism, result naturally from mutations, deliberate selection has created most of the variety seen in modern breeds today.

SPECIALIZED SKELETON

Speed and agility are of prime importance for a predator. The prey sets the pace and direction of the chase and, for a successful outcome, a hunting dog has to be ready to move fast and turn within a split second.

Much of a dog's speed relies on an extremely flexible spine, which bends and stretches easily with every stride. The powerful hindquarters provide forward propulsion, while adaptations to the forelegs increase stride length. Traction is created by the nonretractile claws, which act like the running spikes on an athlete's shoes.

As a quadruped, a dog has four weight-bearing legs. The forelegs have no bony attachment, like the human collarbone (clavicle), and are connected to the body only by muscles. This allows them to slide back and forth over the rib cage, increasing stride length. The long bones of the forelegs—the radius and ulna—fit tightly together, unlike the equivalent bones in the human forearm. This is an essential adaptation in an animal that may need to change direction rapidly in pursuit of prey. The tight fit prevents rotation of the bones and reduces the risk of fracture. For extra stability, some of the small bones in the dog's wrist joint are fused together, restricting rotation of the foot and minimizing the likelihood of injury. For a hunter, this is important, since injury will reduce hunting success and in serious cases would lead to starvation.

Dogs have a characteristic "tiptoe" gait. There are four weight-bearing toes on each foot and a vestigial dewclaw on the inside of

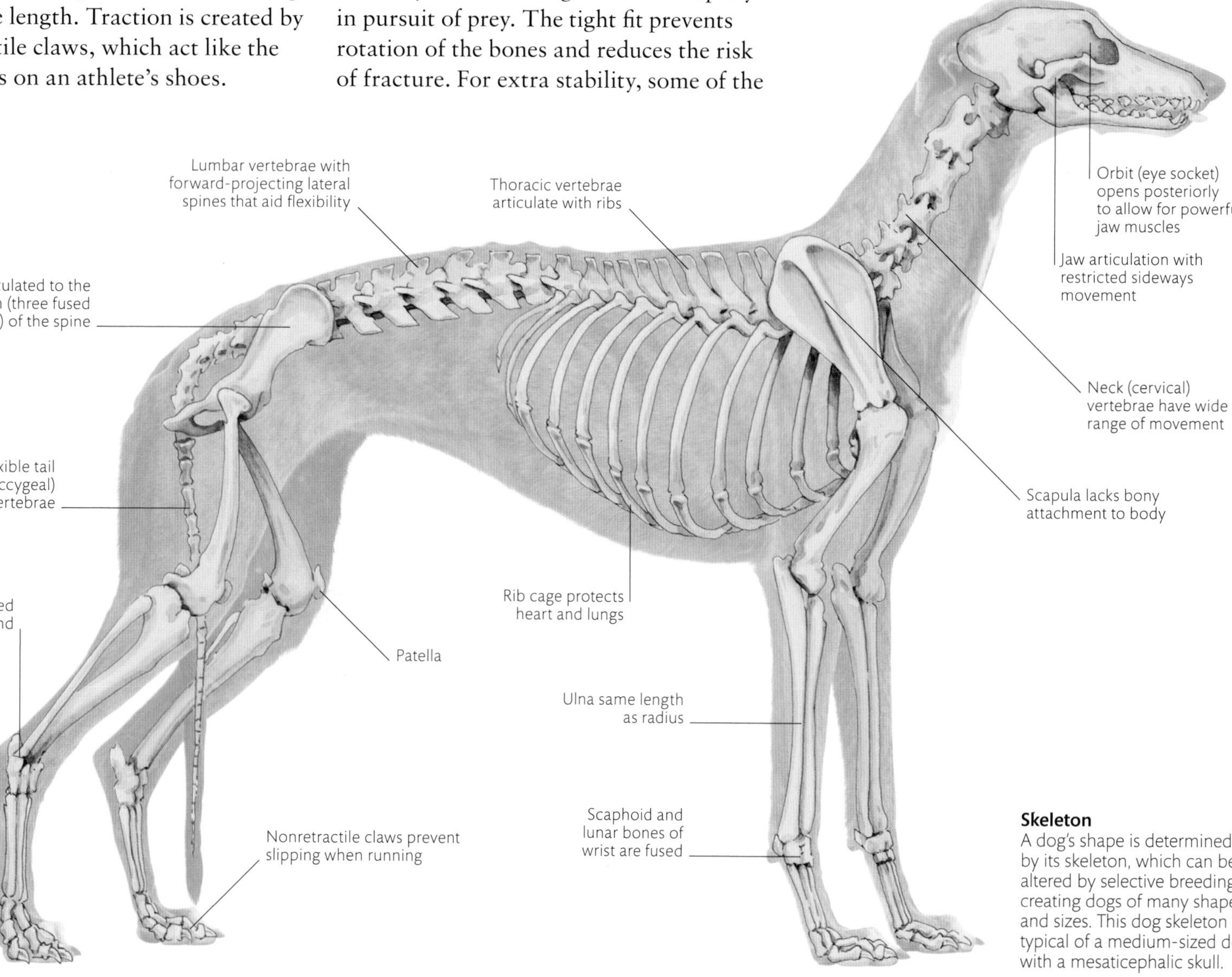

Lumbar vertebrae with forward-projecting lateral spines that aid flexibility

Thoracic vertebrae articulate with ribs

Orbit (eye socket) opens posteriorly to allow for powerful jaw muscles

Jaw articulation with restricted sideways movement

Pelvis articulated to the sacrum (three fused vertebrae) of the spine

Neck (cervical) vertebrae have wide range of movement

Flexible tail (coccygeal) vertebrae

Scapula lacks bony attachment to body

Rib cage protects heart and lungs

Hock (heel) raised off the ground

Patella

Ulna same length as radius

Scaphoid and lunar bones of wrist are fused

Nonretractile claws prevent slipping when running

Skeleton
A dog's shape is determined by its skeleton, which can be altered by selective breeding, creating dogs of many shapes and sizes. This dog skeleton is typical of a medium-sized dog with a mesaticephalic skull.

SKULL SHAPES

The canine skull has three basic variations: dolichocephalic (long and narrow); mesaticephalic (wolflike, being equally proportioned in terms of cranium width and length of nasal cavity); and brachycephalic (short and broad). The diversity of skull shapes in the domestic dog is the result of changes made to the original canine template by selective breeding.

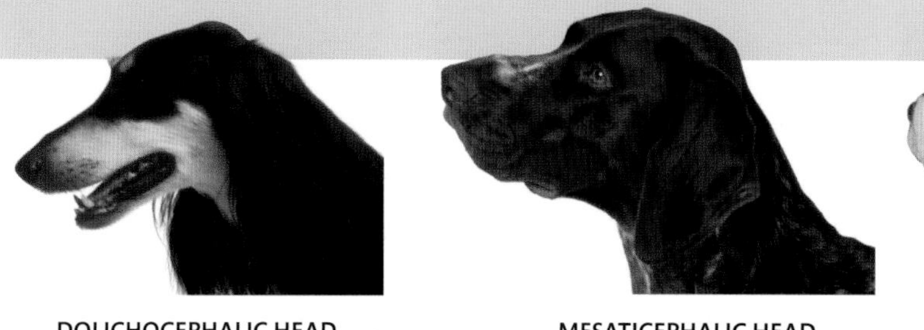

DOLICHOCEPHALIC HEAD (SALUKI)

MESATICEPHALIC HEAD (GERMAN SHORTHAIRED POINTER)

BRACHYCEPHALIC HEAD (BULLDOG)

each front leg, equivalent to the human thumb. However, in a few dogs, such as the Tibetan Mastiff (see p.80) there are dewclaws on the hind feet, too, while in others, such as the Great Pyrenees (see p.78), there are double dewclaws. The occurrence of extra toes is known as polydactyly.

Bone size can be manipulated relatively easily by selective breeding, so humans have been able to alter the proportions of the canine skeleton to create miniature or outsize versions of dogs, from Chihuahuas (see p.282) to Great Danes (see p.96). Significant changes have also been made to the shape of the canine skull (see box above).

MUSCLE POWER

A dog's limbs are controlled mainly by muscles in their upper parts. The lower legs have more tendons than muscles, which saves weight and reduces energy expenditure. Very fast dogs, such as Greyhounds (see p.126), have a high proportion of what are known as "fast" twitch muscle fibers, which, because of the way they obtain their energy, allow brief bursts of great speed; in dogs built for endurance, like huskies and retrievers, "slow" twitch fibers that keep them going longer are more numerous.

A hunting dog not only needs to outrun prey, but to seize and hold it. As in all carnivores, the canine skull is modified for the attachment of massive muscles that operate the jaw and help to prevent it from moving sideways, possibly even dislocating, in the effort to grip a struggling victim. Large neck muscles provide the strength for lifting and carrying the kill.

The dog also makes use of more subtle muscle power than humans do. Relying a good deal on body language to communicate with each other, a dog constantly twitches with muscle activity: curling a lip in a snarl, pricking up ears to show attention, or wagging a tail as a sign of welcome or conciliation.

Muscles that open jaw
Muscular sling supports and stabilizes foreleg from below
Neck muscles control head movements, which are important in visual and auditory orientation, and for grooming and predation
Powerful upper foreleg muscles extend and retract leg
Muscles in the tail allow movement of the tip or of the entire length—for example, when it is wagged
Forearm muscles stabilize, protect, support, and control the paws and toes
Thin muscle layer covers abdomen
Achilles tendon is most prominent tendon on dog's body
Lower limbs have little muscle mass, only tendons and ligaments

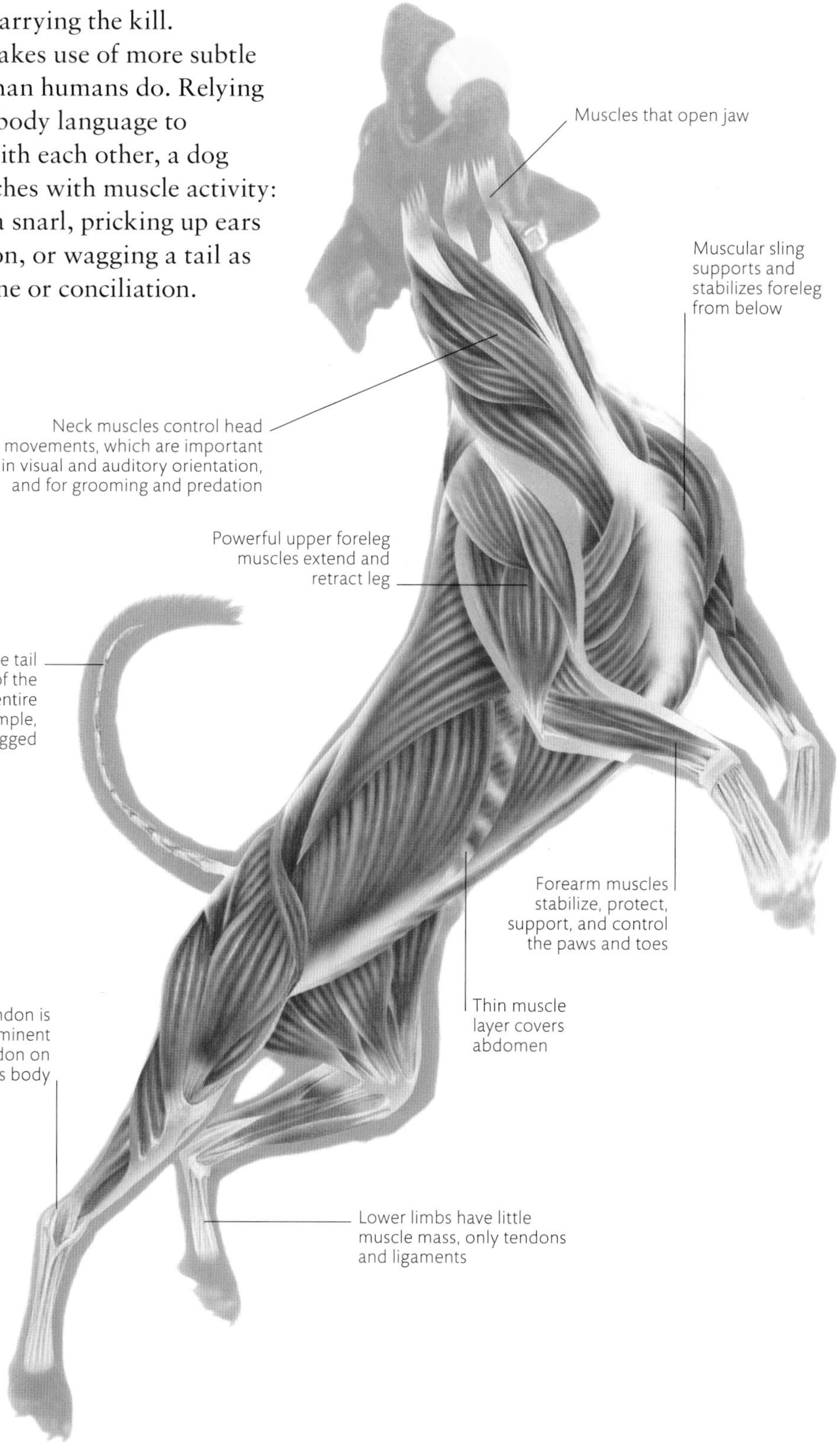

Muscles
All dogs have the same muscles. They allow a dog to move and also play an important part in communication. Some of the limb muscles act in antagonistic pairs, one extending the leg and the other retracting it.

Senses

Dogs are very alert to their surroundings and highly responsive to sensory information. They look and listen to interpret their surroundings, just as we do. Although we see things with greater clarity—except at night, when canine vision is an advantage—dogs hear much more and possess a superbly developed sense of smell. A dog's nose is his best asset and he relies on it to provide him with a detailed account of the world.

SIGHT

Although dogs cannot see the range of color that humans can, they do see some colors. This limited range is because a dog only has two types of color-responsive cells (dichromatic vision) in the retina—the light-sensitive layer at the back of the eye—instead of three (trichromatic vision) as humans have. The canine world is viewed in shades of gray, blue, and yellow, without red, orange, or green—in much the same way as a person with red-green color-blindness. Dogs do, however, have excellent long-distance vision. They are particularly quick to pick up movement and can even detect lameness, a useful adaptation in a predatory animal seeking an easy kill. Canines see best in the low light of dawn and dusk—prime times for hunting in the wild. With less acute close vision, a dog relies more on scent, or touch through his sensitive whiskers, to investigate nearby objects.

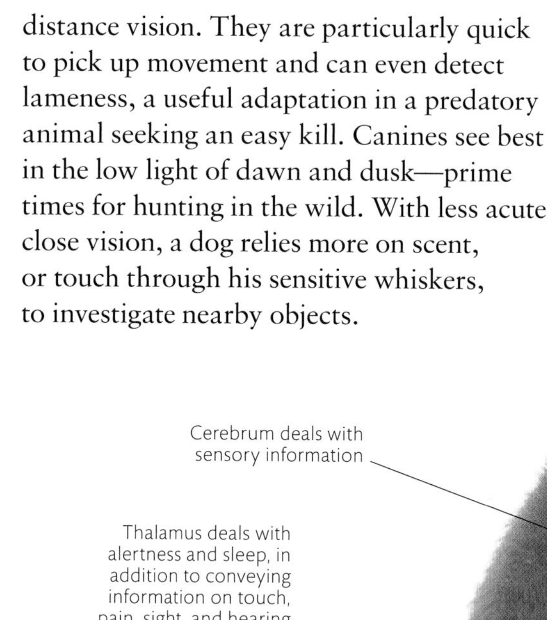

Cerebrum deals with sensory information
Thalamus deals with alertness and sleep, in addition to conveying information on touch, pain, sight, and hearing
Pineal gland is situated at the base of the brain and coordinates the dog's body clock
Pituitary gland produces several hormones and also serves as a link between the nervous system and other endocrine glands
Hypothalamus regulates eating and drinking and controls pituitary gland
Cerebellum controls movement
Some areas of the brain stem control salivation, others relay information about hearing, taste, and balance
Spinal cord connects with the peripheral nervous system network that carries sensory information over the entire body

EAR SHAPES

ERECT (ALASKAN MALAMUTE)

CANDLE-FLAME (ENGLISH TOY TERRIER)

ROSE (GREYHOUND)

BUTTON (PUG)

DROP (BROHOLMER)

PENDANT (BLOODHOUND)

Ear types
There are three main types of ear—erect (top row), semierect (middle row), and drop (bottom row)—but each includes a variety of different forms. Ears strongly influence a dog's overall appearance and so in many breeds the correct set, shape, and carriage of the ears is carefully detailed in their respective breed standards.

HEARING

Puppies are born deaf, but as dogs mature they develop a sense of hearing that is about four times as acute as ours. They can hear sounds too low or too high in pitch to be audible to humans and are also good at detecting the direction the sounds come from. Breeds with erect ears—the best design for funneling sound—usually have sharper hearing than those with drop or pendant ears. A dog's ears are also highly mobile and frequently used to communicate with others: slightly pulled back to signal friendship; dropped or flattened in fear or submission; or raised in aggression.

SMELL

Dogs take in most information through their noses, receiving complex messages from odors that are undetectable to humans. Sampling a smell can tell a dog about the readiness of a bitch for mating, the age, sex, and condition of a prey animal, and possibly the mood of his owner.

Even more remarkable, dogs can detect and interpret who or what has crossed their path before, which is why they are so good at tracking. With training, dogs can be taught to sniff out drugs and even detect disease.

The area of a dog's brain that interprets scent messages is estimated to be about 40 times larger than ours. Although scenting ability depends to some extent on the size of the dog and the shape of his muzzle, the average canine nose has somewhere in the region of 200 million scent receptors, compared to about 5 million in humans.

TASTE

In mammals, the senses of taste and smell are closely linked. But although a dog's nose tells him a great deal about what he is eating, his sense of taste is less well developed. A human has an estimated 10,000 taste buds receptive to the basic tastes of bitter, sour, salty, and sweet, but canines have probably fewer than 2,000. Unlike us, dogs do not have a strong response to the taste of salt; this is probably because their wild ancestors evolved to eat meat, which has a high salt content, and so there was no need to discriminate between foods. Possibly to provide a balance to this salty diet, dogs have taste receptors on the tips of their tongues that are highly receptive to water.

Choroid membrane prevents reflection of light within the eye and carries nutrients and oxygen to retina

Lachrymal gland produces tears

Pupil controls amount of light entering eye

Transparent cornea covers iris and pupil

Iris (colored part of eye)

Optic nerve carries information to brain

Lens

Third eyelid protects front of eye and spreads tears over surface

Light-sensitive retina contains two types of color-responsive cells

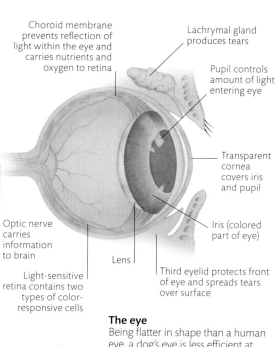

The eye
Being flatter in shape than a human eye, a dog's eye is less efficient at adjusting the focal length of the lens. But while a dog's vision may lack fine detail, it is much more sensitive to light and movement.

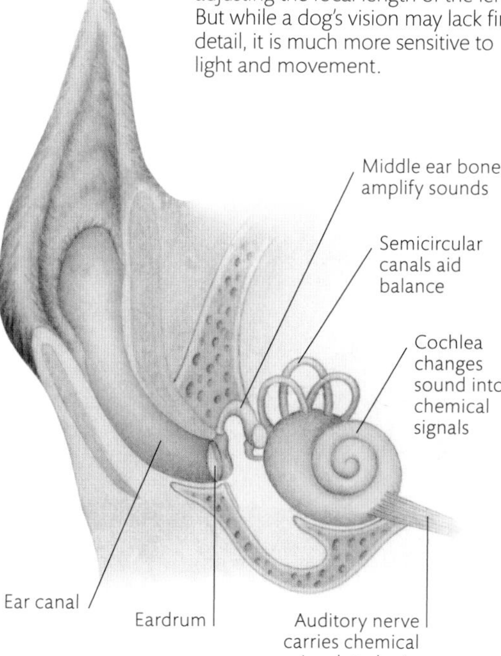

The ear
The mobile external part of the ear scans for and funnels sound waves toward the middle and inner ear, where they are amplified and transformed into chemical signals that can be interpreted by the brain.

Brain

Tongue rather insensitive to salt

Position of vomeronasal organ

Nasal membranes have around 200 million scent receptors

Thin, convoluted turbinal bones covered with nasal membranes capture scent molecules

Water receptors concentrated on tip of tongue

The brain
All the sensory information that a dog receives is carried along nerves to the brain, where it is interpreted and then acted upon in an appropriate way. The speed at which this happens can be extremely rapid: for example, the source of a sound can be pinpointed about six-hundredths of a second after it is heard.

Nose and tongue
Scent and taste are chemical senses located in the dog's muzzle. Additional scent receptors in the vomeronasal organ at the base of the nasal cavity are important for gathering information about other dogs.

Cardiovascular and digestive systems

The major body systems that keep a dog, and all other mammals, up and running can function only by working together. Oxygen drawn in by the lungs and nutrients contributed by the digestive system are the essential fuels of life and must be transported to every part of the body. Circulating blood, driven through a network of arteries and veins by the steady beating of the heart, provides the vital supply line.

CIRCULATION AND RESPIRATION

A dog's heart functions in the same way as our own, pumping with a regular rhythm to keep blood moving around the body. Inside the muscular walls of the heart there are four chambers that contract and relax in a sequence with each heartbeat. This forces blood out of the heart through the arteries and into circulation and allows the heart to refill with blood returning via the veins.

This circulatory, or cardiovascular, system operates in conjunction with the respiratory system to bring oxygen to every cell in the body and to remove waste, such as carbon dioxide, produced by cell activity. Blood flows in a continuous circuit, picking up oxygen from inhaled air in the lungs, and then carrying it, together with nutrients absorbed through the intestinal walls, around the entire body. At the same time that oxygen is collected in the lungs, carbon dioxide diffuses out of the bloodstream and is expelled from the body in exhaled breath.

The respiratory system also has a vital role in preventing a dog's body from overheating. Because a dog has only a few sweat glands, mostly in its paws, it cannot keep cool by perspiring. Instead, a dog pants, exhaling warm air that causes saliva in its mouth to evaporate—latent heat is lost, and the dog's body temperature decreases as a result.

Also invaluable for dogs, especially cold-climate spitz breeds, is an adaptation to the cardiovascular system that prevents excessive loss of body heat through the paws when in contact with cold ground.

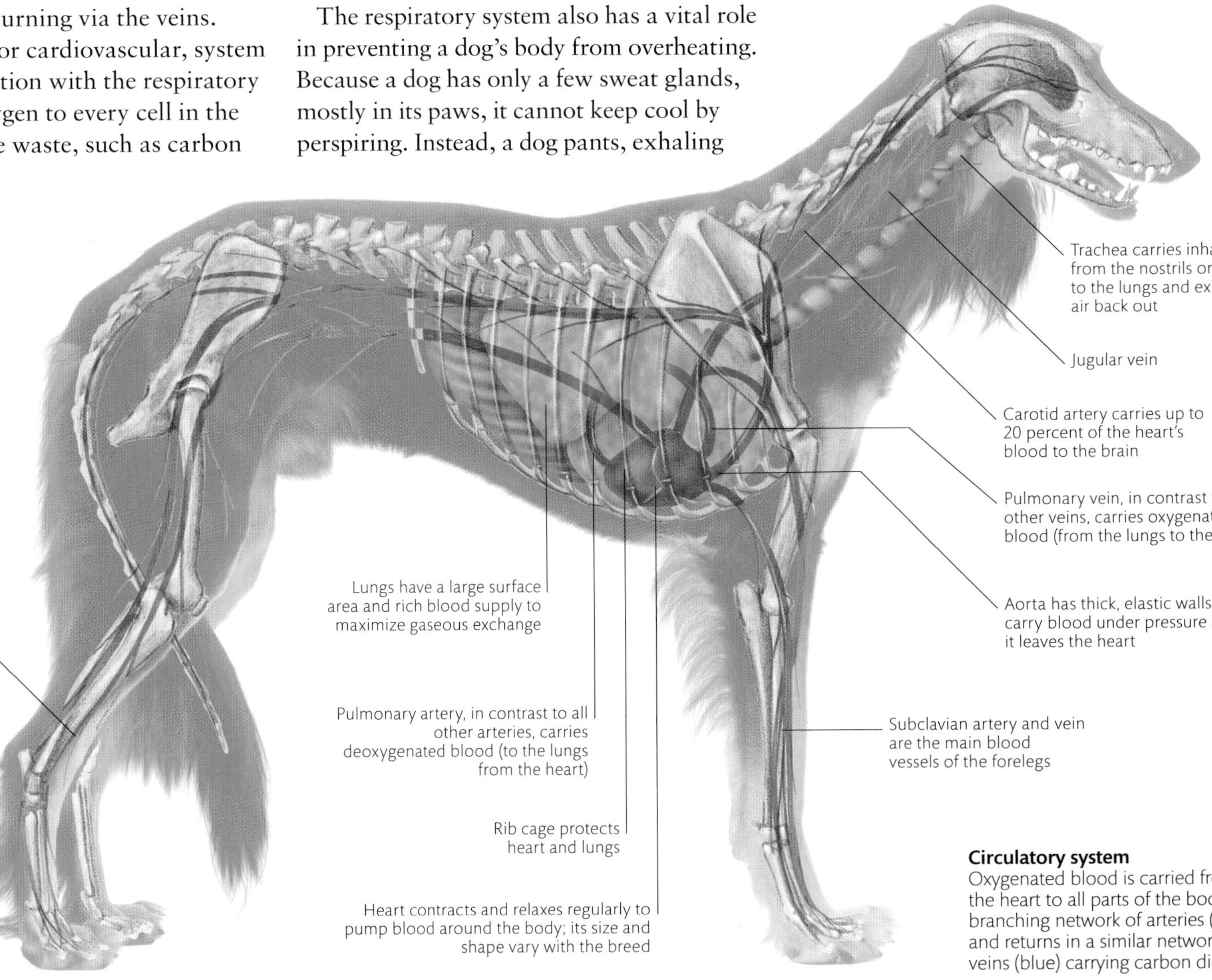

Trachea carries inhaled air from the nostrils or mouth to the lungs and exhaled air back out

Jugular vein

Carotid artery carries up to 20 percent of the heart's blood to the brain

Pulmonary vein, in contrast to all other veins, carries oxygenated blood (from the lungs to the heart)

Aorta has thick, elastic walls to carry blood under pressure as it leaves the heart

Subclavian artery and vein are the main blood vessels of the forelegs

Femoral artery and vein are the main blood vessels of the hind legs

Lungs have a large surface area and rich blood supply to maximize gaseous exchange

Pulmonary artery, in contrast to all other arteries, carries deoxygenated blood (to the lungs from the heart)

Rib cage protects heart and lungs

Heart contracts and relaxes regularly to pump blood around the body; its size and shape vary with the breed

Circulatory system
Oxygenated blood is carried from the heart to all parts of the body in a branching network of arteries (red), and returns in a similar network of veins (blue) carrying carbon dioxide.

Where the blood flows in and out of the paws, the arteries and veins are in very close proximity. As warm arterial blood passes into the paws, it transfers its heat to the cooler returning venous blood, so the heat is retained in the body rather than lost to the environment. Known as counter-current heat exchange, the same mechanism operates in the skin of walruses and in penguins' feet, allowing them to survive in freezing polar environments.

TEETH

By the age of 7 to 8 months, most dogs have a full set of 42 adult teeth, all adapted for eating meat. At the front, the upper and lower jaws have six incisors flanked at either side by a single large canine tooth that was once used for grasping, holding, and piercing prey. Along the sides of the jaws are the premolars and molars. The fourth upper premolar and lower first molar on each side of the jaw are called carnassial teeth and are a feature of all mammals belonging to the Carnivora order. These teeth act like a pair of scissors and are used for cutting and shearing through hide and bone.

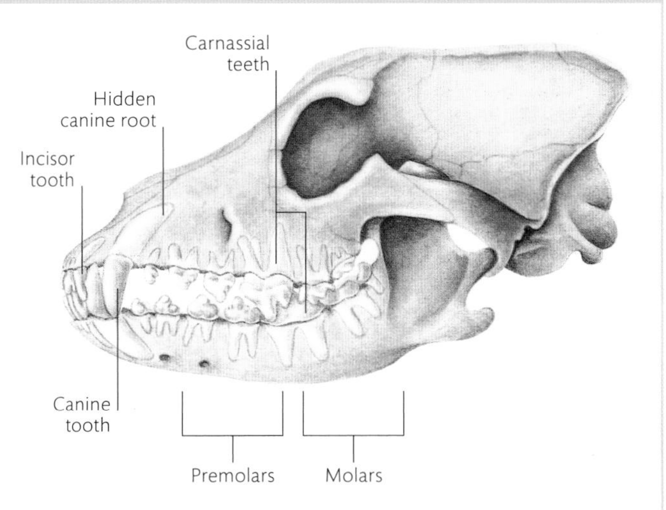
Carnassial teeth
Hidden canine root
Incisor tooth
Canine tooth
Premolars
Molars

DIGESTING FOOD

A healthy dog wastes no time in clearing its food bowl, gulping down one mouthful after another without stopping to chew anything. Canids are programmed to eat fast, not out of greed but out of necessity—in the wild the slowest feeder risks losing its meal to ravenous pack mates. Humans tend to savor the food in their mouths, chewing it and mixing it well with saliva, which starts the process of digestion even before swallowing. Dogs, which have relatively few taste buds compared to humans, simply grab large chunks of food and swallow them whole. To mitigate this, they also have an excellent gag reflex. If they eat something unpleasant they can simply throw it up.

The canine digestive tract is short and designed specifically for processing meat, which is much more quickly and easily digested than plant material. A dog's stomach contains high levels of digestive acids that break down meat, bone, and fat rapidly, reducing food to a liquid that then passes into the small intestine. Once there, digestive enzymes produced by the liver and pancreas aid the breakdown of food into nutrients that can be absorbed into the bloodstream through the intestinal walls. Any undigested material moves through the large intestine to be eliminated as feces. In dogs, the transit time of food through the digestive tract, from eating to elimination, takes around 8 to 9 hours, compared with an average of 36 to 48 hours in humans.

Sharp teeth bite off lumps of meat, which are mixed with saliva and swallowed whole without chewing
Muscular contractions of the esophagus move the lumps of food down into the stomach
Stomach has rings of muscle at its entrance (cardiac sphincter) and exit (pyloric sphincter) and produces enzymes, and mucus that coats its walls, protecting them from the acid it produces to break down the fibrous tissue in meat
Liver produces bile to help break down fat into molecules that can then be absorbed by the blood
Pancreas produces more enzymes and substances that neutralize the stomach acid on entering the duodenum
Nutrients are absorbed through the walls of the small intestine into the bloodstream
Large intestine absorbs excess liquid. Feces are formed and are passed from the body

Digestive system
Structurally simple—essentially the gut is a long tube—but functionally complex, the digestive system processes food, releasing its nutrients so they can be absorbed into the blood stream.

Urinary, reproductive, and hormonal systems

In dogs, as in mammals generally, the urinary and reproductive systems share much of the same area in the hind part of the abdominal cavity. Their tracts become linked together in the male, where urine and sperm have a combined exit point through the penis. Like all body functions, both these systems are fine-tuned by hormonal action. Hormones control the production and volume of urine, and they ensure that a female dog's reproductive periods occur at optimum times.

URINARY SYSTEM

The function of the urinary system is to remove waste from the blood and expel it from the body, along with excess water, as urine. The urinary organs comprise the kidneys, which work as filtering units and make urine; the ureters, tubes that carry urine away from the kidneys; the bladder, which acts as a reservoir; and the urethra, the tube through which urine is excreted. The process is regulated by hormones acting on the kidneys to maintain the correct balance of salts and other chemicals in the body.

Dogs urinate not just to relieve their bladders but also to mark territory and communicate with other dogs. Hormones and chemicals carried in the urine have an odor that provides a sniffing dog with information, including whether a recent passer-by is male or female. The smell fades quickly in the open air, which is why male dogs constantly mark spots with small amounts of urine, often returning to the same place to refresh the message. Bitches tend to empty their bladders completely in just one place. Urine of either sex contains nitrogen and it is this that is responsible for the brown patches that appear on lawns where dogs have been.

Brain controls most hypothalamic activity

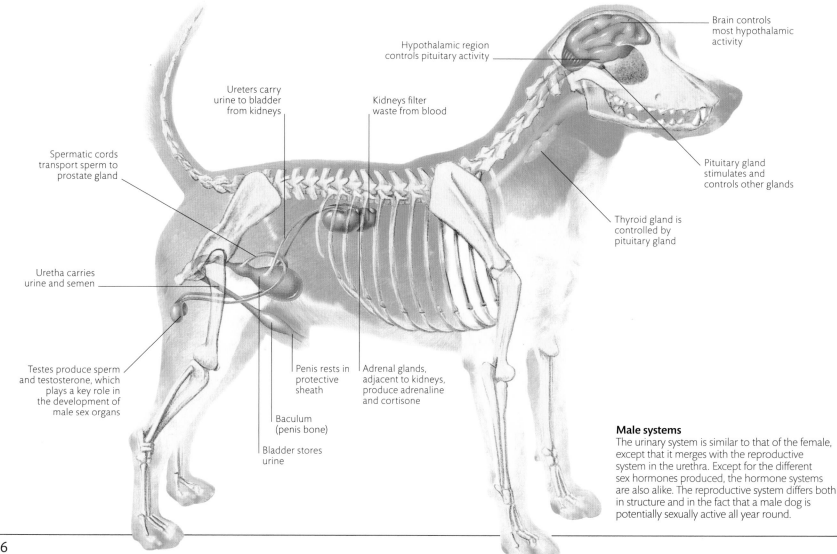

Hypothalamic region controls pituitary activity

Ureters carry urine to bladder from kidneys

Kidneys filter waste from blood

Spermatic cords transport sperm to prostate gland

Pituitary gland stimulates and controls other glands

Thyroid gland is controlled by pituitary gland

Uretha carries urine and semen

Testes produce sperm and testosterone, which plays a key role in the development of male sex organs

Penis rests in protective sheath

Adrenal glands, adjacent to kidneys, produce adrenaline and cortisone

Baculum (penis bone)

Bladder stores urine

Male systems
The urinary system is similar to that of the female, except that it merges with the reproductive system in the urethra. Except for the different sex hormones produced, the hormone systems are also alike. The reproductive system differs both in structure and in the fact that a male dog is potentially sexually active all year round.

REPRODUCTION

Dogs usually reach sexual maturity somewhere between 6 and 12 months of age. In wild canines such as the wolf, females normally have one period of estrus a year (known as "coming into season," or being "in heat"), during which they ovulate and are ready to breed. With a few exceptions, the Basenji being one, domestic dogs usually have two seasons a year. The onset of estrus is marked by a small discharge of blood, which lasts for around nine days, after which the bitch will be willing to mate.

Male dogs have a bone within the penis called the baculum. During mating, the area around the bone enlarges, locking the penis inside the female and creating what is known as the "tie," which can last for some minutes. If mating leads to fertilization of the female ova (eggs), the pregnancy that follows will last between 60 to 68 days. The size of the litter depends on the type of dog, with larger breeds tending to have larger litters. Anything from one to fourteen or more puppies may be born, but a litter of six to eight is the average.

HORMONES

Produced by specialized glands and tissues and released into the bloodstream, hormones are chemicals that affect specific cells. Hormonal activity controls many body functions, including growth, metabolism, sexual development, and reproduction.

Neutering dogs removes the production sites of the sex hormones—testosterone in males, and estrogen in females—and prevents unwanted pregnancies. As a result of the loss of testosterone, male dogs lose the urge to wander in search of females and are less likely to show aggression. Neutering also affects coat shedding in bitches, which usually have their heaviest coat loss twice a year, triggered by the hormone that brings them into season. Spayed (neutered) females tend to shed all year round. Neutering may also increase the probability of obesity in later life.

HORMONES IN PREGNANCY

During pregnancy, rising levels of hormones such as estrogen help to prepare a bitch for giving birth and also, by stimulating development of the milk glands, for feeding her puppies. In a lactating (nursing) bitch, milk production is maintained by an increase in the hormone prolactin, which also influences maternal behavior, arousing strong protective instincts and ensuring that the mother will not desert her puppies while they are still totally dependent on her for survival.

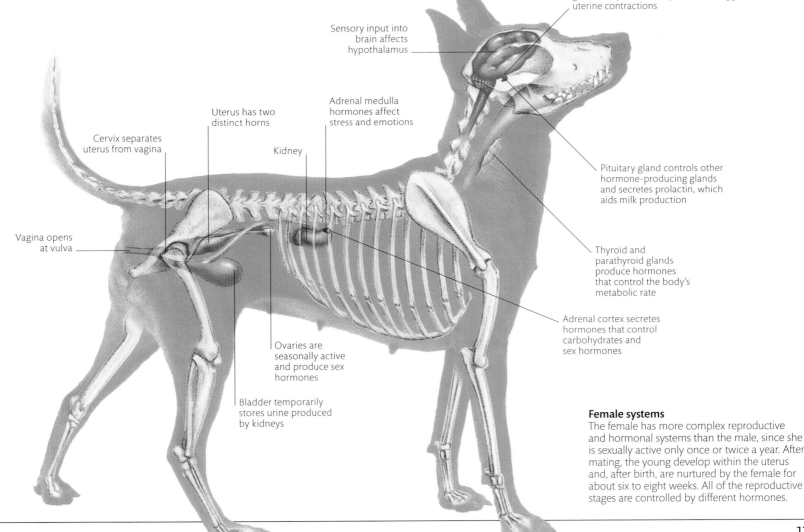

Hypothalamus gland stimulates pituitary gland and produces oxytocin that triggers uterine contractions

Sensory input into brain affects hypothalamus

Adrenal medulla hormones affect stress and emotions

Uterus has two distinct horns

Cervix separates uterus from vagina

Kidney

Pituitary gland controls other hormone-producing glands and secretes prolactin, which aids milk production

Vagina opens at vulva

Thyroid and parathyroid glands produce hormones that control the body's metabolic rate

Adrenal cortex secretes hormones that control carbohydrates and sex hormones

Ovaries are seasonally active and produce sex hormones

Bladder temporarily stores urine produced by kidneys

Female systems
The female has more complex reproductive and hormonal systems than the male, since she is sexually active only once or twice a year. After mating, the young develop within the uterus and, after birth, are nurtured by the female for about six to eight weeks. All of the reproductive stages are controlled by different hormones.

Skin and coat

Dogs are thin-skinned, but for the majority their covering of hair provides sufficient warmth and protection. Canine coats come in many types: some dogs have "big hair," others are short, wiry, curly, or corded. A handful of breeds have bare skins, with perhaps a sprinkling of hairs on their extremities. While natural selection is responsible for some variation in dogs' coats, humans have introduced most changes, partly for utility but more often for fashion.

SKIN STRUCTURE

In common with all mammals, dogs have three layers of skin: the epidermis, or outer layer; the dermis, or middle layer; and the subcutaneous layer, consisting largely of fat cells. Compared with humans, dogs have only a thin epidermis as, with the exception of the few hairless breeds, they have fur coats to provide protection and insulation.

Dogs' hair grows from complex follicles, consisting of a central guard hair and several, finer undercoat hairs, which all project through the same skin pore in the epidermis. Dogs also have sensitive facial hairs, called tactile hairs, which are deeply rooted and well supplied with blood and nerves. These include whiskers, eyebrows, and hairs on the ears.

Oil glands (known as sebaceous glands) are linked to the hair follicles, into which they secrete a substance called sebum. This acts as a skin lubricant and helps to keep the coat glossy and waterproof. Most follicles also have an attached muscle that can raise the hair to trap warm air or, more noticeably, lift the hackles along a dog's back: for example, when he is afraid or angry. Unlike humans, dogs do not perspire through their skin and have functional sweat glands mainly in the pads of their feet.

COAT TYPES

Some of the main coat types are shown below. Most breeds of dog have only one coat type, but some, such as the Pyrenean Sheepdog (see p.50), have several. Many types of dog have a double coat, consisting of a top coat of guard hairs, which provides waterproofing, and a shorter, softer undercoat. In Spitz dogs, such

HAIRLESS

SHORT, SINGLE COAT

CURLY COAT

WIRE-HAIRED COAT

FULL, DOUBLE COAT

SEMI-LONG COAT

LONG-HAIRED, SILKY COAT

CORDED COAT

as the Chow Chow (see p.112), this dual layer can be immensely thick. With such insulation, traditional sled dogs of the northern hemisphere, such as the Greenland Dog (see p.100) remain impervious to the most bitter cold. Even the feet of these dogs are protected by long hairs between the toes, which also give them excellent traction on snow and ice—and adaptations of the blood vessels in the feet (see p.14) help to prevent heat loss, too.

Dogs with extravagantly long hair are bred today for appearance alone, although some originally needed their heavy coats for an outdoor life. For example, the Afghan Hound (see p.136) is a sight hound from the cold, high mountains of Afghanistan, and the Bearded Collie (see p.57) has a working background as a herding dog. On the other hand, the silky, flowing coat of the diminutive Yorkshire Terrier (see p.190) has probably always been more decorative than functional, despite the breed's long history. Some very attractive dogs, such as the Cocker Spaniel (see p.222) and English Setter (see p.241), have semi-long coats combining silky-textured body hair of moderate length with longer feathering on the tail, underside, and legs.

Some short-haired dogs have sleek, firm-textured coats that often consist of guard hairs only. The Dalmatian (see p.286) and some pointers and hounds are typical. In wire-haired dogs, largely the terrier group, the guard hairs are kinked, giving a coarse, springy texture. These coats are serviceable in cold weather and stand up well to an energetic terrier lifestyle of digging or delving through undergrowth. Breeds with curly coats are uncommon, the best known being the Poodle (see p.229, 276), sometimes seen clipped in fantastic style for the show ring. In a few rare breeds, including the Komondor (see p.66) and Puli (see p.65), curls are taken to extremes, developing into long cords resembling dreadlocks that virtually obscure the dog's entire body. Natural genetic mutations have resulted in several hairless breeds. Dogs like the Xoloitzcuintli (see p.37) and the Chinese Crested (see p.280) have been around for centuries, but it is only in modern times that hairlessness has been deliberately perpetuated by selective breeding. Some hairless dogs have a few wisps of hair on the head and feet, and sometimes a plume on the tail.

As any owner can testify, all dogs shed a certain amount of hair. Shedding is a natural seasonal response to the hours of daylight, and reaches a peak in the spring as the coat thins in readiness for warmer weather. In double-coated dogs, whether long- or short-haired, hair loss can be considerable as the thick undercoat falls out. When dogs live largely indoors in well-heated houses, the shedding pattern may change, with the dog losing a little hair throughout the year.

COAT COLORS

Some dogs have just one color or one color combination, but many have two or three color variations, or more. Where applicable, the breed descriptions in this book include color swatches that match as closely as possible the coat colors recognized in a breed. These are in addition to the colors that can be seen in the photographs of the dog.

A swatch may represent a range of colors. The swatches listed in the key are as specified in the various breed standards but different names may be given for the same color: for example, while red is used to describe many breeds, ruby is used for English Toy Spaniels and Cavalier King Charles Spaniels. A final generic swatch is used to represent breeds that have a limited variety of colors, or those that can have any color.

Cream; white; white-beige; blonde; yellow

Gray; ashen-gray; slate-gray; steel-gray; gray brindle; wolf-gray; silver

Gold; russet-gold; apricot; biscuit; wheaten; sandy; light sand; mustard; straw; straw-bracken; Isabella; all shades of fawn; pale brown; yellow-red; sable

Red; red merle; ruby; stag-red; deep red ginger; sandy-red; red-fawn; red-brown; chestnut-brown; lion; orange; orange roan

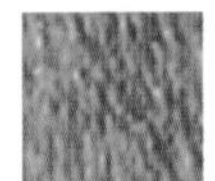
Liver; bronze

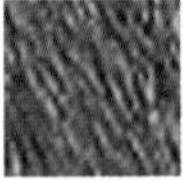
Blue; blue merle (blue-gray); ash

Dark brown; bos (brown); chocolate; dead leaf; havana

Black; nearly black; dark gray

Black and tan; vieräugl; karamis; King Charles; black grizzle and tan; black and brown

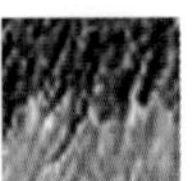
Blue mottled with tan; blue and tan

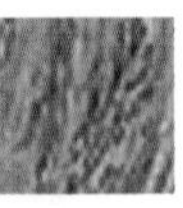
Liver and tan

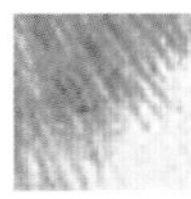
Gold and white (either color may predominate); white and chestnut; yellow and white; white with orange; sable and white; orange belton; lemon belton

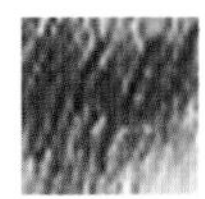
Chestnut, red, and white; red and white; red and white spotted

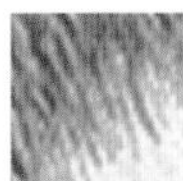
Liver and white; liver belton; brown and white (either color may predominate); red roan; roan; white with liver spots

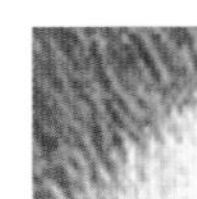
Tan and white (either color may predominate)

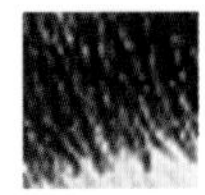
Black and white (either color may predominate); piebald; black and white spotted; sesame; black sesame; black and silver

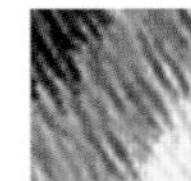
Black, tan, and white; gray, black, and tan; white, chocolate, and tan; Prince Charles; (all also known as tricolor)

Brindle; black brindle; dark brindle; fawn brindle; pepper and salt; range of red brindles

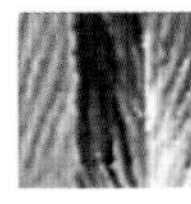
Variety of colors or any color

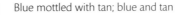

Dogs in religion, myth, and culture

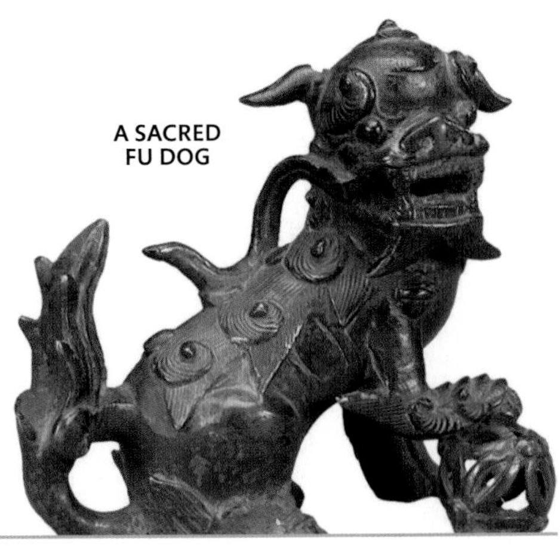

A SACRED FU DOG

With a relationship that began before the dawn of civilization, it is not surprising that, over millennia, dogs and humans have developed strong cultural links. From being servants of man in the material world, dogs crossed the spiritual divide to become servants of heaven and hell. And as the bond between humans and canines strengthened into one of love and loyalty, dogs were finally seen as characters—which has made them indispensable role-players in popular literature and entertainment for adults and children alike.

DOGS IN RELIGION

With dogs seen as traditional protectors, it was natural that they should be given symbolic duties as guardians in many belief systems. In ancient Egypt, as tomb paintings and hieroglyphs reveal, dogs were associated with the jackal-headed god Anubis, guide of spirits in the Underworld. Similar evidence of the religious significance of dogs has been found at burial sites of the Mayan Classic era (c.300–900CE), where sculptures and mummies suggest that dogs were buried with their owners to lead their souls in the afterlife. The Aztecs (14th–16th century) buried pottery figures of dogs with their dead and probably used dogs as sacrifices in religious ceremonies. In China statues of Fu dogs, also known as guardian lions, are seen at the entrances of many Buddhist temples—their lionlike appearance giving them sacred significance.

Most major religions practiced today are largely dismissive of dogs, and some shun them as unclean. But to Hindus in parts of present-day India and Nepal, dogs are regarded as guardians of the gates to heaven and are associated with the god Vishnu, whose four dogs are said to represent the four Vedas, the ancient holy texts of the Hindus. At an annual religious festival dogs are decorated with flower garlands and marked with the sacred red dot (*tika*) on their foreheads.

Argos, the great dog
In Homer's *The Odyssey*, Argos is Odysseus's faithful dog. When Odysseus arrives back to his homeland, Ithaca, in disguise after 20 years, Argos is the first to recognize him.

CANINE MYTHS AND LEGENDS

Dogs both faithful and frightening have featured in classical myths, legends, and folk tales throughout the ages and in all countries. None is more loyal than Argos, Odysseus's hunting dog, who waits 20 years to welcome his master home and then dies with a final wag of his tail. And possibly none is more monstrous than the three-headed hound Cerberus, keeper of the entrance to Hades, whose capture was the 12th and most dangerous Labor of Hercules.

The concept of the phantom dog occurs time and again in stories of the supernatural. Malevolent dogs are part of the folklore of peoples across the world, from North and South America to Asia. Many legends originate in Britain and Ireland, where ghostly dogs, usually large and black, frightened people by haunting graveyards or lonely crossroads. Phantom dogs were given various regional names, such as the Barghest and the Grim. On a dark and deserted road, Charlotte Bronte's usually strong-minded heroine Jane Eyre is briefly spooked into thinking she has seen the Gytrash, the spirit-hound of northern England. Sir Arthur Conan Doyle picked up on the black dog legend in *The Hound of the Baskervilles* (1901), his eerie tale of a fiery-eyed hound visiting terror on Dartmoor in Britain.

DOGS IN LITERATURE

People have been writing about dogs for around 2,000 years, but the earliest books were practical guides for people who kept dogs for working, primarily hunting. Fictional dogs certainly appear in dozens of Aesop's Fables, written around 500 years BCE, but here the Greek moralizer was using dogs as a way of illustrating human characteristics and failings, such as greed or gullibility. It was only in much later centuries, when dogs became pets and companions, that they began to be treated as personalities in their own right.

White Fang
The 1906 novel *White Fang* by Jack London tells the story of a dog-wolf crossbreed. After successfully fighting several other dogs, he is matched with a bulldog that nearly kills him.

An early fictional dog with enduring appeal is "Crab," from Shakespeare's *The Two Gentlemen of Verona* (c.1592), whose owner, the servant Launce, mournfully describes him as "the sourest-natured dog that lives." This heartless hound, usually played on stage for laughs by a real dog, may have been less than a "best friend," but in most dog stories devotion has always been the keynote.

Typical of a genre more popular a century ago than today are the books of Jack London, such as *The Call of the Wild* (1903) and *White Fang* (1906)—tales told partly from the dog's point of view, combined with rip-roaring action. Despite their undeniable elements of brutality, these books survive as classics.

Among cozier storybook canines that have stayed the course, one of the best loved is Nana, a sad-eyed Newfoundland (see p.78) dog, nurse to the Darling children in *Peter Pan*, who marches her charges to school and nags them into the bathtub. Also familiar to millions of children is Timmy, the rough-coated mongrel who features as the fifth member of the *Famous Five* in a stream of stories written by Enid Blyton between the 1940s and 1960s. Timmy helps to save the day in all kinds of improbable adventures, but he is nonetheless a more believable dog than Nana, and one that children can readily imagine as a companion. Other old faithfuls include Snowy the white terrier, sidekick to the boy detective Tintin (see p.209), and Dorothy's dog Toto in *The Wizard of Oz*.

DOGS ON SCREEN

Since the 20th century dog stories have been a huge success in movies. Walt Disney's cartoon dogs have delighted moviegoers for decades—hapless Pluto; well-bred Lady and street-wise Tramp; the 101 Dalmatians (see p.286). Real-life dogs have appeared in other popular films, such as *Lassie* (see p.52), *Old Yeller*, *Big Red*, and *The Incredible Journey*. In the tradition of Shakespeare's "Crab," dogs make good film comedians and many leading actors have allowed themselves to be upstaged by a canine costar; such memorable screen dogs include the lugubrious mastiff helping with police investigations in *Turner and Hooch* (1989), the delinquent Labrador in *Marley and Me* (2008), and the scene-stealing Jack Russell in *The Artist* (2011).

The Incredible Journey
One of the biggest tearjerkers of the 1960s, *The Incredible Journey* was based on a book of the same name and told the story of Luath, the Labrador, Bodger, the Bull Terrier, and Tao, an indomitable Siamese cat, as they journey across hundreds of miles of dangerous wilderness to reach home.

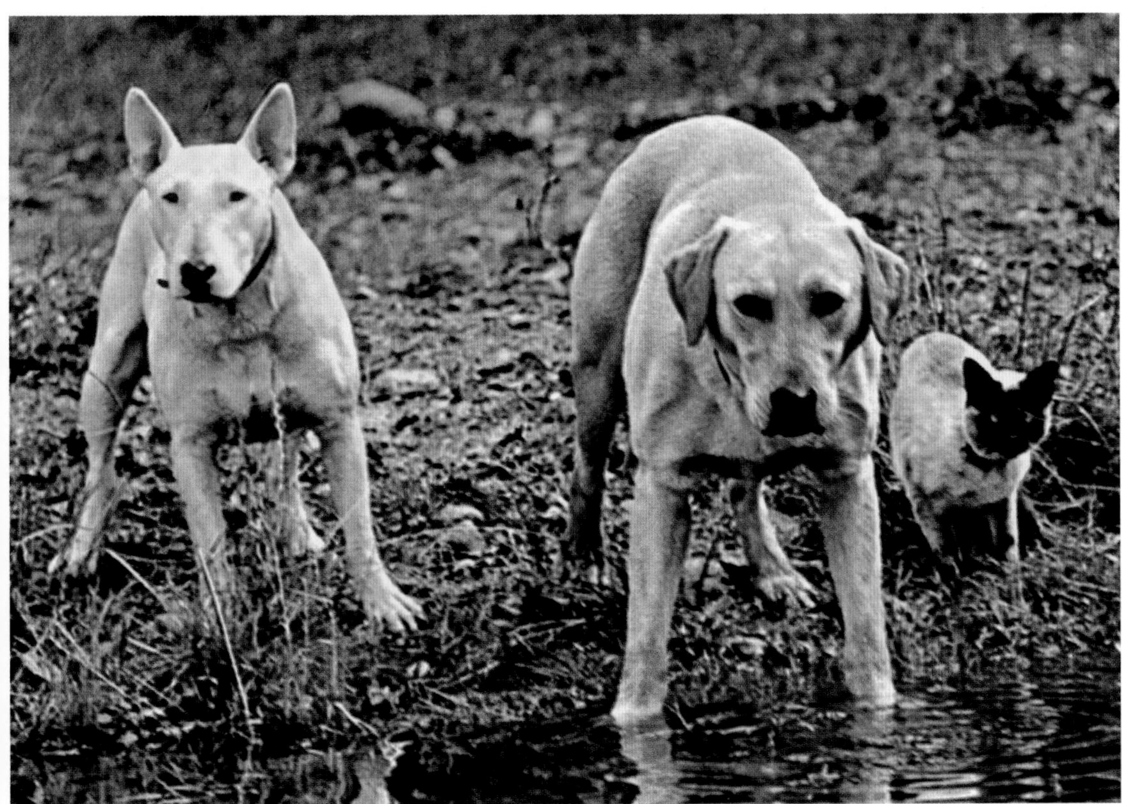

The Artist
Uggie is a Jack Russell Terrier famous for his roles in *Mr. Fix It*, *Water for Elephants*, and *The Artist*. Uggie's role in *The Artist* (a still from the movie above) drew great acclaim worldwide and the film went on to win multiple awards.

Dogs in art and advertising

Drawn and painted, sculpted, woven into tapestries, photographed, used as company logos: dogs have had visual appeal for the entire span of their association with humans. In almost every type of medium, they tell stories without words, say something about their owners or the people who portray them, and reflect the lifestyles and tastes of different ages. Most people like dogs and enjoy them as subjects in art. Commercial organizations have long relied on this unfailing attraction by using dog images to promote goods and services.

HOGARTH WITH HIS PET PUG, TRUMP

PORTRAYING DOGS

A history of the domestic dog can be traced through the development of art. Probably some of the earliest depictions of dogs, in their original role as hunting companions, are prehistoric rock paintings discovered in Saharan Africa, believed by some authorities to be more than 5,000 years old. Dogs, similar in appearance to today's greyhounds, hunted on through the Classical ages of Greece and Rome in superbly rendered sculptures, especially associated with the Greek goddess Artemis (Roman Diana). The best-known Classical dogs are not hunters, though, but the fierce, chained guard dogs in lifelike mosaics retrieved from the ashes of Pompeii. In later ages slender sight hounds pursued deer and unicorns across medieval tapestries; an estimated 35 dogs appear in the famous Bayeux Tapestry illustrating the Norman Conquest of Britain, albeit largely confined to the fringes of the main action. The hunting dog theme continued into the sporting prints of the 18th century, with their packs of foxhounds in full cry, and the portraits of gundogs, dead game hanging limply from their jaws, favored by the 19th-century landed shooting fraternity.

Before dogs became accepted as the norm in ordinary homes during the 19th century, they were usually painted as pets only in portraits commissioned by the wealthy—as companions of aristocrats or in the arms of small beribboned children. But dogs

Rock carving
From the Neolithic period to the 21st century, dogs have been enjoyed as art subjects. This petroglyph in Youf Ahakit Tassili Ahaggar, Sahara Desert, Algeria, is one of the earliest depictions.

Ringwood, a Brocklesby Foxhound
This anatomically accurate portrait of a Foxhound painted by English painter George Stubbs in 1792 reveals how Foxhounds looked at the time.

Bayeux Tapestry
This section of the Bayeux Tapestry from the 11th century depicts three large dogs and two smaller ones running ahead of a huntsman.

A king's companion
This portrait of Emperor Charles V by Tiziano Vecelli (Titian) subtly suggests the emperor's power as he is depicted restraining one of his large dogs.

portrayed as a fact of life, desirable or otherwise, have been common in art for centuries. William Hogarth (1697–1764), who posed with his pet pug, Trump, in a self-portrait, included dogs as part of the social commentary implicit in his work. Hogarth's dogs go about their canine affairs largely unregarded, stealing food scraps or lifting a leg to urinate. Dogs began to be painted as a subject in their own right in the late 18th century by painters such as George Stubbs. A more sentimental attitude to dogs crept in with the Victorian artists, famously Sir Edwin Landseer (1802–73), whose portraits of self-sacrificing Newfoundlands (see p.79), pert terriers, and noble deerhounds embody the virtues and emotions of his era.

Some of the greatest pictures in the world include a dog or two—variously interpreted by impressionists, post-impressionists, surrealists, modernists, and others. Renoir painted dogs innumerable times, sitting on laps, going for walks, and at picnics. Amid the crowded scene of one of his most famous works, *The Boating Party* (1880–81), a small dog shares the limelight in the foreground. Another artist who enjoyed painting dogs was Pierre Bonnard (1867–1947); from street mutts to family pets, he showed them bursting with real character.

More disturbing are the dogs used as obscure symbols in the surreal paintings of Salvador Dali. The starving hound chewing a carcass in Dali's *Metamorphosis of Narcissis* (1937) possibly reflects death and decay. Just as enigmatic is fellow surrealist Joan Miro's cartoonish little dog baying at an uncaring Moon in a largely barren canvas (*Dog Barking at the Moon*, 1926). Dog-lover Picasso's simple sketch of his dog, Lump, captures the essence of the Dachshund (see p.170) in a few graceful lines and has become one of his most popular prints.

Lucien Freud included his beloved whippets, Eli and Pluto, in several of his powerful human portraits—in his *Girl with a White Dog* (1950–51) the bull terrier is as much a focal point of the picture as the female model, Freud's first wife.

COMMERCIAL ICONS

Dog appeal has proved immensely valuable in the field of commercial advertising. In much the same way as artists sometimes portray dogs symbolically, so marketing managers find dogs useful for putting their messages across: bulldogs, strong and reliable, sell insurance; large, shaggy dogs suggest a family-friendly product; small, fluffy breeds have the right image for beauty aids.

One of the best-known advertising icons of all time is the painting of the terrier "Nipper," used as a logo since 1899 by the music company HMV (His Master's Voice). Equally long survivors are the black Scottie (see p.189) and the West Highland White Terrier (see p.188), famous since the 1890s as the trademark for a brand of Scotch whisky. Original bar figurines, jugs, and ashtrays featuring the "Black and White" pair are now collectors' items.

With the arrival of commercial television, dogs started appearing on screen in advertisements promoting almost anything from cans of paint to credit cards. Since the 1970s, hundreds of huggable Labrador Retriever (see pp.260) puppies have taken on the role as mascot for a best-selling toilet tissue, gamboling amid unraveling toilet-paper rolls. Naturally, dogs are used to advertise their own products, too. Bright-eyed and bouncing, they testify to the excellence of various canned and packaged pet foods—although the biggest hit, Henry the bloodhound in a much-loved television advertisement of the 1960s and 70s, simply sat and looked doleful.

In the world of fashion, dogs are also often used on the principle that "cute sells." Alongside leggy models in haute couture clothes or advertising luxury goods, dogs work particularly well as accessories. Today's upmarket fashion magazines are full of photoshoots featuring Pugs (see p.268) and Chihuahuas (see p.282) wearing a small fortune in designer jewelry around their necks or poking their heads out of expensive handbags.

His Master's Voice
Used as a logo since 1899 by the music company HMV, Nipper, the terrier gazing transfixed into the trumpet of a windup gramophone, has survived into the 21st century despite the advent of new technology.

Dogs in sports and service

From the dawn of their relationship, dogs and humans have worked and played together successfully. Most dogs are natural enthusiasts for chasing and running, and people the world over learned early on how to exploit these inclinations for hunting and sports. Canine intelligence has also proved more than equal to the numerous demands made on dogs as work partners. Most are eager to please and have readily taken on duties as guardians, herders, guides, trackers, and even home helpers.

HUNTING FOR PLEASURE

Primitive peoples used dogs to help them catch game for food, but with the rise of civilizations, hunting with dogs developed into a sport as well, although usually only for the wealthier members of society. As paintings dating back nearly 3,000 years depict, the Ancient Egyptians hunted with dogs very similar to some of today's big-eared sight hounds, such as the Pharaoh Hound (see p.32) and Ibizan Hound (see p.33) In China the tombs of the Han dynasty (206BCE–220CE), have yielded realistic figurines of heftily built mastiff-type hunting dogs that appear to be "pointing" at game.

By medieval times in Europe, hunting with dogs of various types was the passion of kings and landowning nobility. Swift-running hounds, resembling modern greyhounds and harriers, were sent after smaller game; but dangerous quarry such as bear and wild boar required larger hounds, hunting in varied packs that included the now-extinct types known as alaunts and lymers, which were broadly similar to mastiffs and bloodhounds.

In later centuries, pack-hunting dogs developed into distinctly recognizable breeds, such as foxhounds, staghounds, and otterhounds. Hunting of live game with hounds is now illegal in some countries, but the excitement of the chase lives on in drag-hunting, in which the pack follows a trail of artificial scent. Hunting dogs with highly specialized roles were developed when the invention of guns led to the growth of sports shooting of waterfowl and game birds such as pheasant and grouse. Among the breeds still bred and trained today are pointers and setters that direct the guns to their targets, spaniels for working in undergrowth to flush out game, and retrievers to bring back fallen birds.

Tracking and chasing
Early hunters appreciated the ability of hounds to follow a scent as well as their speed when chasing quarry so worked with them to increase their hunting success, as seen in this Roman relief of Hercules hunting.

SPORTING DOGS

Hunting is by no means the only way humans have used dogs for their own amusement. One of the earliest, and most brutal, "entertainments" was pit fighting, in which powerful dogs, such as the mastiffs once seen in the arenas of Ancient Rome, were set against bears, bulls, and sometimes each other. The battles were bloody, and victory for one combatant meant death or mutilation for the other. On a smaller scale, pit fights between terriers and rats once had a widespread following.

People have come up with many other ways of using dogs in sports, among which trials of speed have been the most enduring. Coursing, in which competing pairs of fast sight hounds such as Greyhounds, Whippets, or Salukis are sent in pursuit of hares, was popular for nearly 2,000 years before being made illegal in most European countries. Greyhound racing has attracted big crowds for hundreds of years; and since the 20th century some of the most challenging races in terms of speed and endurance have been for teams of sled dogs—tough, cold-weather breeds such as Greenland Dogs (see p.100) and Siberian Huskies (see p.101)—competing over hundreds of miles in harsh northern territories.

Afghan Hounds racing
Dog racing has been a popular means of entertainment for centuries. Several breeds, including Afghan Hounds, race as they chase an artificial lure around a track until they cross the finish line.

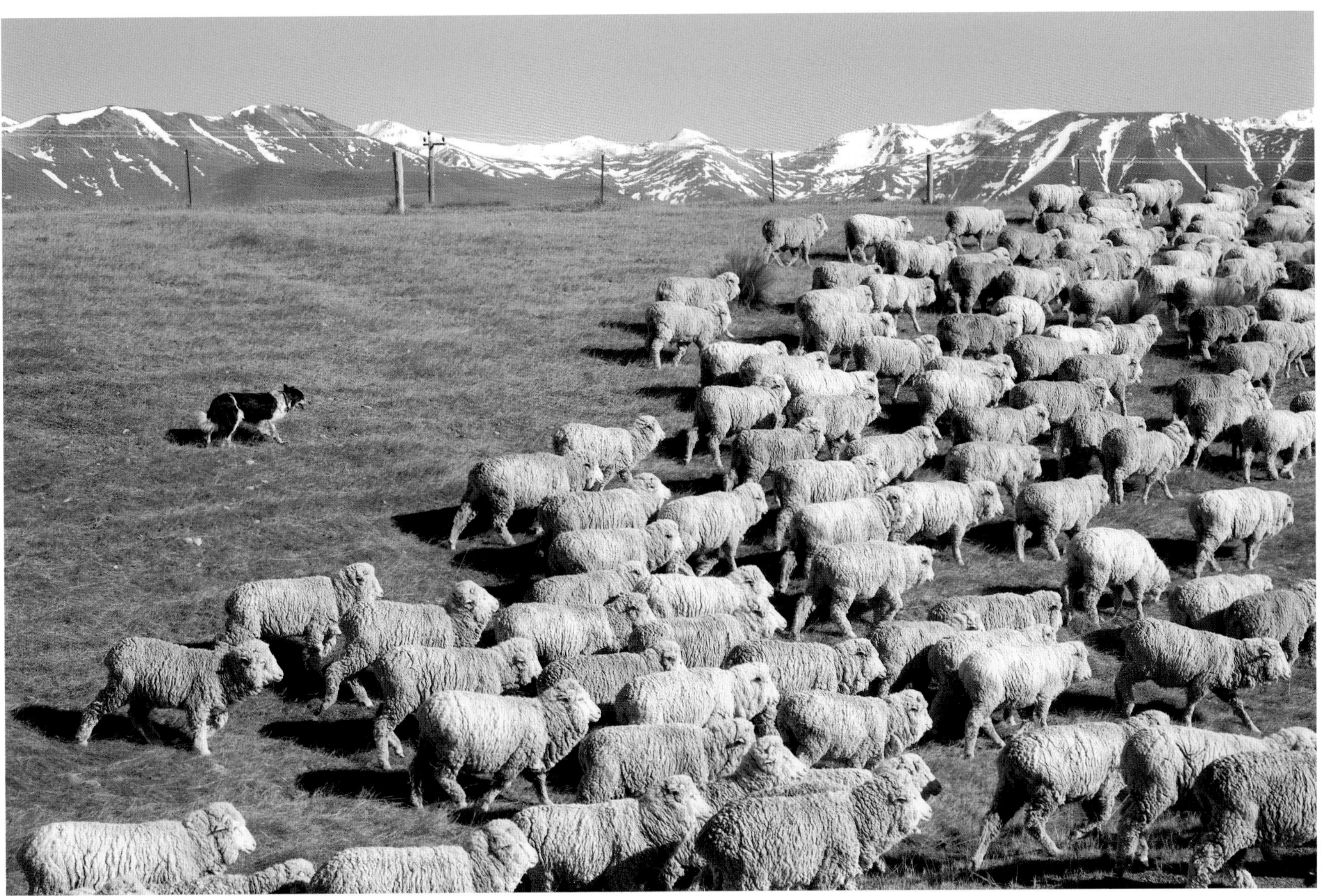

Gathering the flock
Sheepdogs are trained to round up and herd flocks and are hardy enough to work in severe climate conditions. Here a Border Collie herds sheep in Twizel, New Zealand.

Among the gentler sports are trials in which dogs display their agility, intelligence, and obedience by negotiating tricky obstacle courses. Agility trials are often highly competitive affairs; but many are no more than low-key local events, in which anyone's pet with a zest for leaping over jumps or wriggling through pipes can take part.

DOGS IN SERVICE

Another of the early occupations for dogs in the service of humans was as guardians and herders of livestock, and the tradition continues in many parts of the world. Pastoral work is not always peaceful where bears and wolves live, and so large, powerful breeds with fiercely protective instincts, such as the thick-coated shepherd dogs still seen in eastern Europe, were developed to deal with dangerous predators.

Harnessing canine strength has sometimes been taken literally, with larger dogs used as draft animals, whether for hauling sleds over polar ice, drawing milk carts, or taking small children for rides in traps. In the past even small dogs were sometimes used for providing motive power: unfortunate terriers could be found in the sweltering kitchens of large houses and inns, running endlessly in treadwheels to turn roasting spits.

Dogs have gone to war for centuries, and in World Wars I and II were employed to carry messages, first aid, and ammunition across no-go zones. Today dogs trained to sniff out explosive devices are important members of the armed forces. A dog's ability to scent trouble has also proved helpful to police and security forces. Baying bloodhounds pursue fleeing suspects, and specially trained dogs are also invaluable in such work as detecting drugs or locating survivors in areas of devastation.

Dogs have often made life in the home easier, too. The Ancient Aztecs used hairless dogs as hot-water bottles on cold nights, but in the modern world canine partners sometimes have to be more active. Guide dogs help people with impaired sight to safely negotiate hazards such as traffic and stairs. Many people with other disabilities or illnesses also rely on dogs trained to perform such tasks as warning of impending epileptic seizures or even loading the washing machine. In hospitals, hospices, and nursing homes dogs chosen carefully for their amenable temperaments are brought in to provide comfort and distraction, and their services as a very real form of therapy are widely acknowledged.

CHAPTER 2

GUIDE TO BREEDS

A primitive dog of many talents
Today the Peruvian Hairless is kept mainly as a pet, but for hundreds of years this athletic breed was used for hunting and guarding as well as for therapeutic purposes and companionship.

PRIMITIVE DOGS

Many modern dog breeds are the result of hundreds of years of breeding for particular characteristics, but a few, commonly regarded as primitive dogs, have remained close to the original "blueprint" of their wolf ancestors. As a group, primitive dogs are not clearly defined, and not all authorities agree that such a category should be recognized.

As variously listed, primitive dogs are a diverse group, but many of them share typically wolflike characteristics. These include erect ears, a wedge-shaped head with a pointed muzzle, and a tendency to howl rather than bark. Their coats are usually short but vary in color and density according to the region from which the dog originates. Most primitive dogs come into season only once a year, unlike other domestic dogs, which have two cycles of estrus a year.

Canine specialists are now taking an interest in dogs that have had little to do with humans and nothing to do with breed development programs. These primitive dogs, which come from various parts of the world, include the Carolina Dog (see p.35) of North America and the rare New Guinea Singing Dog (see p.32), which is genetically very close to the dingo of Australia. Such dogs have evolved naturally rather than through breeding for temperament or appearance and cannot be considered completely domesticated. The New Guinea Singing Dog, which is on the verge of extinction, is more likely to be seen in zoos than in homes.

Several dogs are included in the primitive group because they are believed to be uninfluenced by any other types over thousands of years. Among them is the Basenji (see p.30) from Africa, long used for hunting in its native country before becoming a popular pet. Other examples are hairless dogs from Mexico and South America, genetic mutations of coated breeds that resemble dogs depicted in the art and artifacts of ancient civilizations.

Recent genetic investigations suggest that two dogs included in this section—the Pharaoh Hound (see p.32) and the Ibizan Hound (see p.33)—should no longer be considered primitive. These breeds are popularly supposed to be the direct descendants of big-eared Egyptian hounds pictured in drawings dating back 3,000 years. However, there is genetic evidence that the line of descent may not have remained unbroken down the centuries. It is probable that the Pharaoh and Ibizan Hounds are in fact modern re-creations of ancient breeds.

Basenji

HEIGHT	WEIGHT	LIFE SPAN	Variety of colors
16–17in (40–43cm)	22–24lb (10–11kg)	Over 10 years	White markings may appear on chest, feet, and tail tip.

This neat and graceful dog is always on the alert and ready to protect, but instead of barking it yodels

One of the most primitive breeds, the Basenji is a hunting dog from Central Africa. Like the Canaan Dog (see p.32), it belongs to a group known as Schensi dogs—breeds that have not been completely domesticated. Basenjis are traditionally used by pygmy hunters; they live semi-independently in a pack alongside the tribe, but are employed for driving big game into nets. The dogs are fitted with bells around their necks to scare their prey. Western explorers originally encountered these dogs in the 17th century and used names such as "Congo Terrier" or "Bush Dog" to describe them. In the 1930s the first dogs were imported into the UK, and the breed was named *basenji* (meaning "little things from the bush" or "villagers' dogs" in one of the languages of the Congo region of Africa).

An unusual feature of the Basenji is that it does not bark—the larynx (voice box) is shaped differently from that of most other dogs. Instead, the dogs howl or yodel; some of the African tribespeople who use them refer to them as "talking dogs." Another notable feature is that the females come into season only once a year, like wolves, rather than twice, as with domestic dogs.

The Basenji is affectionate and fun-loving, and is a popular house dog. Although loyal to its family, it is rather independent-minded, so may need careful training to follow orders. These dogs are fast, agile, and intelligent; they locate their prey by both sight and scent, and enjoy chasing and tracking activities. They need plenty of mental and physical exercise if they are not to become bored.

DEDICATED BREEDER

Veronica Tudor-Williams (below) was one of the first people to import the Basenji to the UK from Africa in the late 1930s. She continued breeding her dogs during the food shortages of World War II and exported puppies to North America, helping to establish the breed there. In 1959 she traveled to southern Sudan in search of native Basenji dogs that could be used to improve the breed. She returned with two. One of them, a red and white female named Fula, was never presented at shows but was still extremely influential and appears in the pedigrees of nearly all registered Basenjis.

Tail carried in tight curl over back

Forehead wrinkles when alert

Finely chiseled features

Very long forearms

Red

Flat-topped skull

Smooth, short coat

Long, elegant neck

PUPPY

New Guinea Singing Dog

HEIGHT 16–18in (40–45cm)
WEIGHT 18–31lb (8–14kg)
LIFE SPAN 15–20 years

Sable | Black and tan
White markings are common with all color types.

This rare dingolike breed is a native of New Guinea, where it lives feral or in semidomestication. The Singing Dog is kept as a curiosity in zoos worldwide but has become a challenging pet for a few dedicated owners. It has the extraordinary ability to vary the notes of its howl, hence the name.

Canaan Dog

HEIGHT 20–24in (50–60cm)
WEIGHT 40–55lb (18–25kg)
LIFE SPAN Over 10 years

White | Black
Red and white spotted | Black and white spotted

Bred in Israel as a watchdog and herder, the Canaan Dog has strong protective instincts that do not usually turn into aggression. It is highly intelligent, and with steady training makes a reliable and affectionate companion. Not a common breed, it has yet to achieve widespread popularity.

Dark, slightly slanting eyes
Brushlike, thick tail, carried high and curled
Dense, harsh coat
Low-set, broad ears
Tucked-up belly
Sandy
White chest markings

Pharaoh Hound

HEIGHT 21–25in (53–63cm)
WEIGHT 44–55lb (20–25kg)
LIFE SPAN Over 10 years

Although the modern Pharaoh Hound was developed in Malta, this graceful breed bears a strong resemblance to the prick-eared hunting dogs illustrated in the art and artifacts of Ancient Egypt. The Pharaoh Hound is calm-tempered but needs a lot of exercise and unless restrained outdoors will fly off in pursuit of small animals, including other pets.

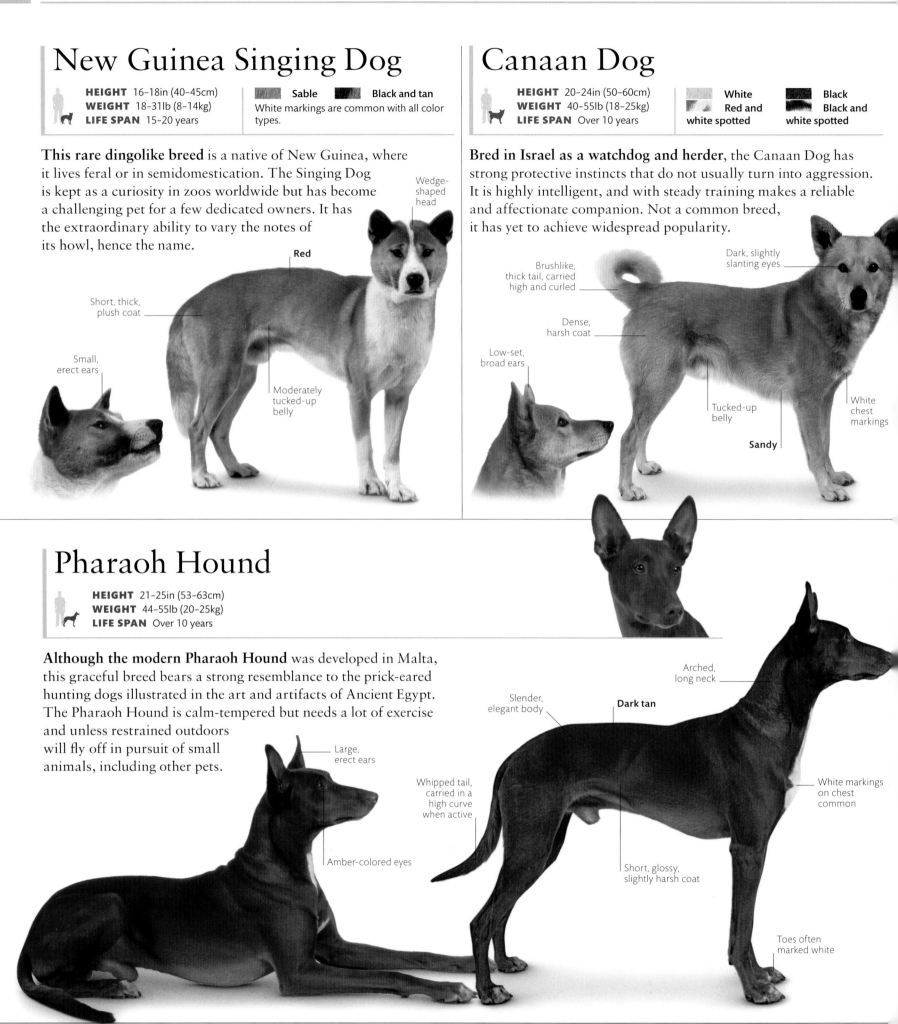

Canarian Warren Hound

HEIGHT 21-25in (53-64cm)
WEIGHT 35-49lb (16-22kg)
LIFE SPAN 12-13 years

Also known as the Podenco Canario, this hound—found on all the Canary Islands—has Egyptian roots dating back thousands of years. The breed is used as a rabbit-hunter and is highly valued for its speed, keen sight, and excellent nose. Sensitive and restless, it is unlikely to adapt well to a quiet life indoors.

Red
Flesh-colored nose
Low-set, slightly tapered tail
Small, amber-colored eyes
Slender, athletic body
White markings on chest
Sleek, smooth coat

Cirneco dell'Etna

HEIGHT 17-20in (42-52cm)
WEIGHT 18-26lb (8-12kg)
LIFE SPAN 12-14 years

Isabella, light sand

This Sicilian breed, which may have originated in the area immediately around Mount Etna, is rare outside its native country. Lithe and strong, the Cirneco dell'Etna is built to run and hunt. Although good-natured, this dog is not an ideal option for owners who want a placid house pet.

Ibizan Hound

HEIGHT 22-29in (56-74cm)
WEIGHT 44-51lb (20-23kg)
LIFE SPAN 10-12 years

Lion

Used in Spain as a pack dog for hunting rabbits, the Ibizan Hound can cover the roughest ground at a "raking trot" characteristic of the breed. This dog also has an enormous jump and can easily leap over a garden fence. As long as an owner bears security in mind, the Ibizan Hound is not difficult to keep, but it is an all-action dog that needs relentless exercise. The breed has a charming temperament and fits in well with family life. There are two coat types—smooth and rough—both of which are easy to maintain.

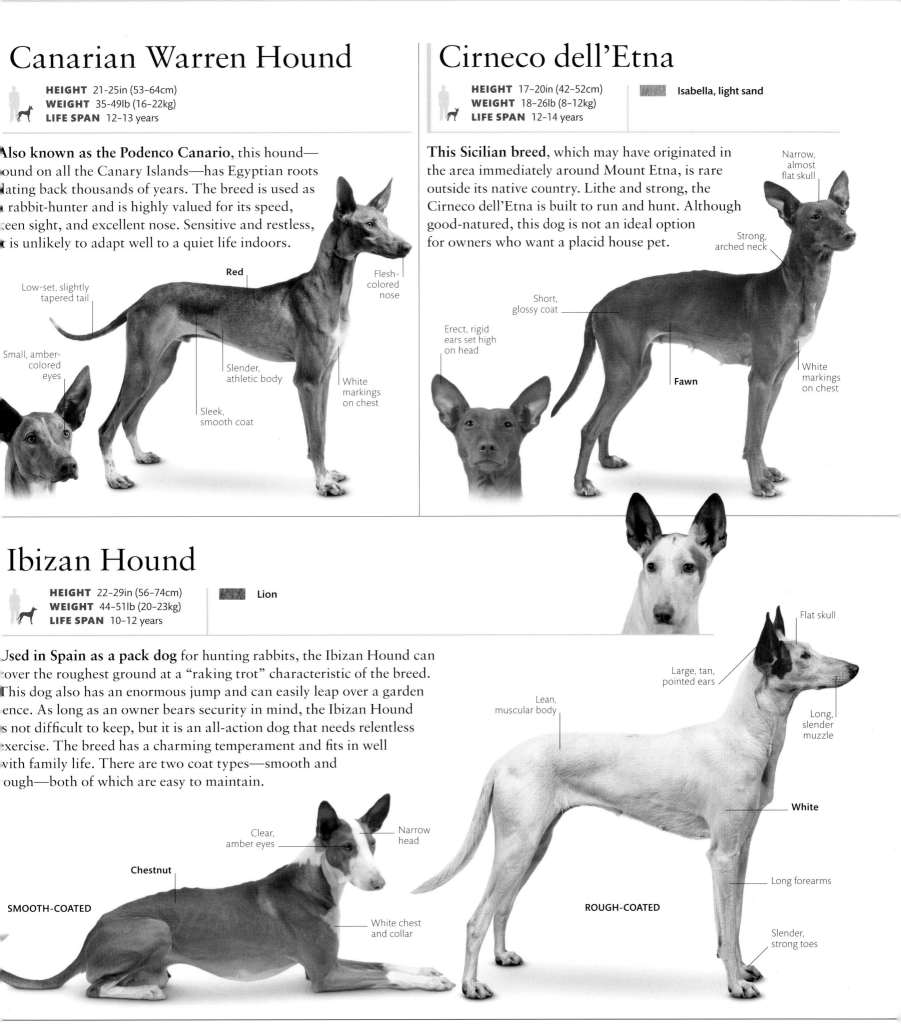

SMOOTH-COATED

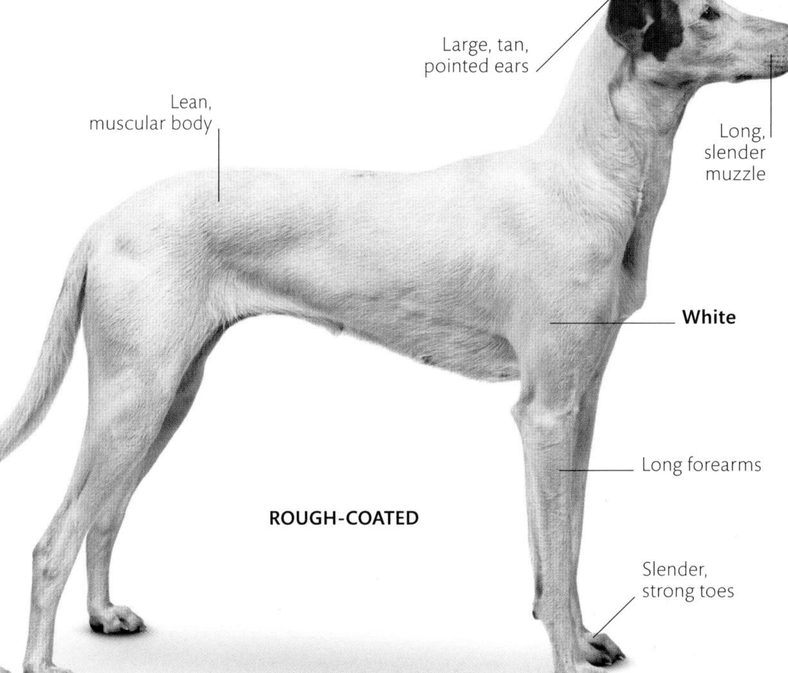

ROUGH-COATED

Portuguese Podengo

WIREHAIRED PEQUENO

HEIGHT
Pequeno: 8–12in (20–30cm)
Medio: 16–21in (40–54cm)
Grande: 22–28in (55–70cm)

WEIGHT
Pequeno: 9–11lb (4–5kg)
Medio: 35–44lb (16–20kg)
Grande: 44–66lb (20–30kg)

LIFE SPAN
Over 12 years

White, yellow
Black
White dogs have patches of yellow, black, or fawn. Pequeno dogs may be brown.

An all-purpose hunter that makes an entertaining companion given sufficient mental and physical activity

The national dog of Portugal, the Portuguese Podengo is said to have originated from dogs brought to the Iberian Peninsula by the Phoenicians over 2,000 years ago. Today there are three different varieties: small (Pequeno), medium (Medio), and large (Grande). Smooth-haired Podengos are more commonly found in the north of the country where the climate is damp, since their quick-drying coat is suited to wet weather. Wirehaired types are more commonly found in the drier south. All varieties were traditionally bred for hunting, and in Portugal some are still used for that purpose.

The Portuguese, being seafaring people, were among the first Europeans to explore and colonize the Americas in the 15th and 16th centuries, laying claim to parts of Canada and Brazil. It is said that the ships used for these explorations carried Podengos, a useful asset because they helped to control vermin during the voyages. On reaching new lands, the dogs were put back to their usual work. However, as *podengo* is a general Portuguese term that refers to any prick-eared hound, these early exports were probably very different from the breed recognized today.

The modern Portuguese Podengo, and in particular the Pequeno variety, is rapidly growing in popularity as a companion dog, having been imported to both the UK and the US. In contrast, the Podengo Grande has become increasingly rare since the 1970s, although efforts are being made to increase its numbers again. Regardless of size, the Podengo's intelligence and alertness make it an excellent watchdog.

SUITABLY SIZED

Bred primarily to hunt hare and rabbit, the Portuguese Podengo is a primitive sight hound. It was bred in three sizes so it could work in any type of terrain. The Grande dog was developed in south central Portugal to hunt in open areas where speed is important. The Medio, being a smaller and more maneuverable dog, was found farther north where there is more cover for game. The smallest, the Pequeno, hunts in very dense undergrowth that would be too difficult for larger dogs to work in effectively.

White blaze on face

Fawn with white markings

Strong hindquarters

Rounded feet with well arched toes

SMOOTH-HAIRED MEDIO

Large, triangular, erect ears

Short coat

Fawn

SMOOTH-HAIRED PEQUENO

Carolina Dog

HEIGHT 18–20in (45–50cm)
WEIGHT 33–44lb (15–20kg)
LIFE SPAN 12–14 years

Deep red-ginger
Black and tan

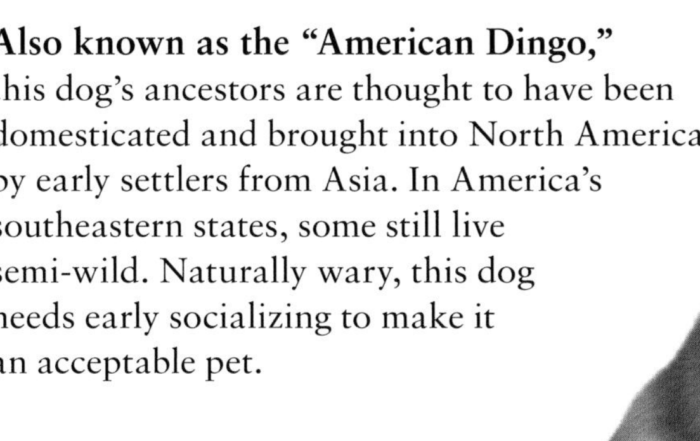

Also known as the "American Dingo," this dog's ancestors are thought to have been domesticated and brought into North America by early settlers from Asia. In America's southeastern states, some still live semi-wild. Naturally wary, this dog needs early socializing to make it an acceptable pet.

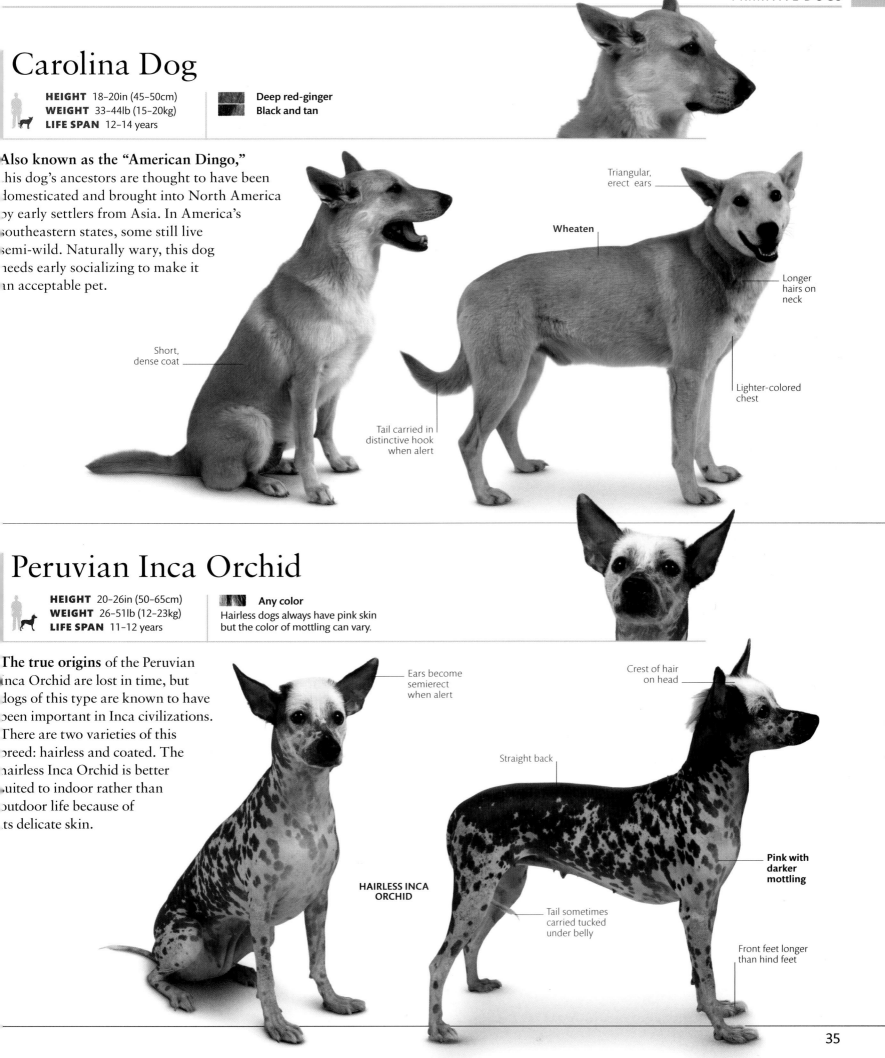

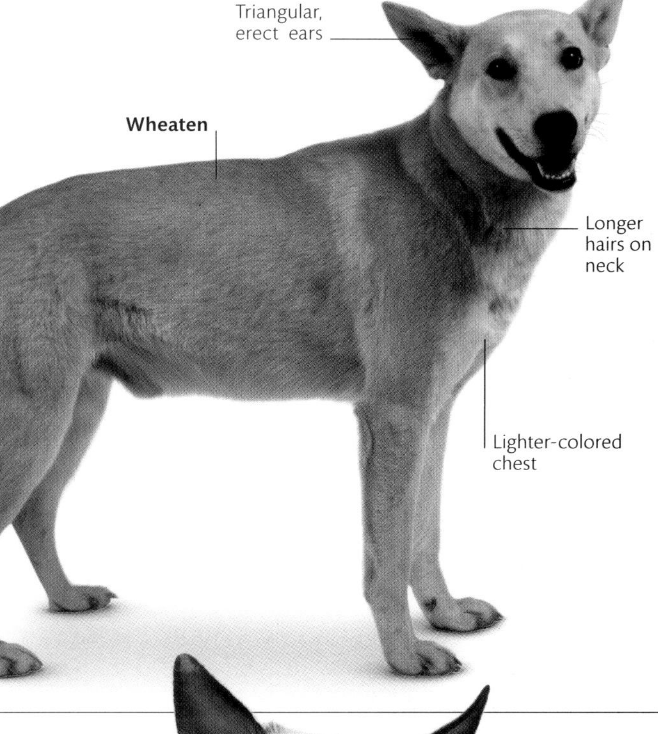

Peruvian Inca Orchid

HEIGHT 20–26in (50–65cm)
WEIGHT 26–51lb (12–23kg)
LIFE SPAN 11–12 years

Any color
Hairless dogs always have pink skin but the color of mottling can vary.

The true origins of the Peruvian Inca Orchid are lost in time, but dogs of this type are known to have been important in Inca civilizations. There are two varieties of this breed: hairless and coated. The hairless Inca Orchid is better suited to indoor rather than outdoor life because of its delicate skin.

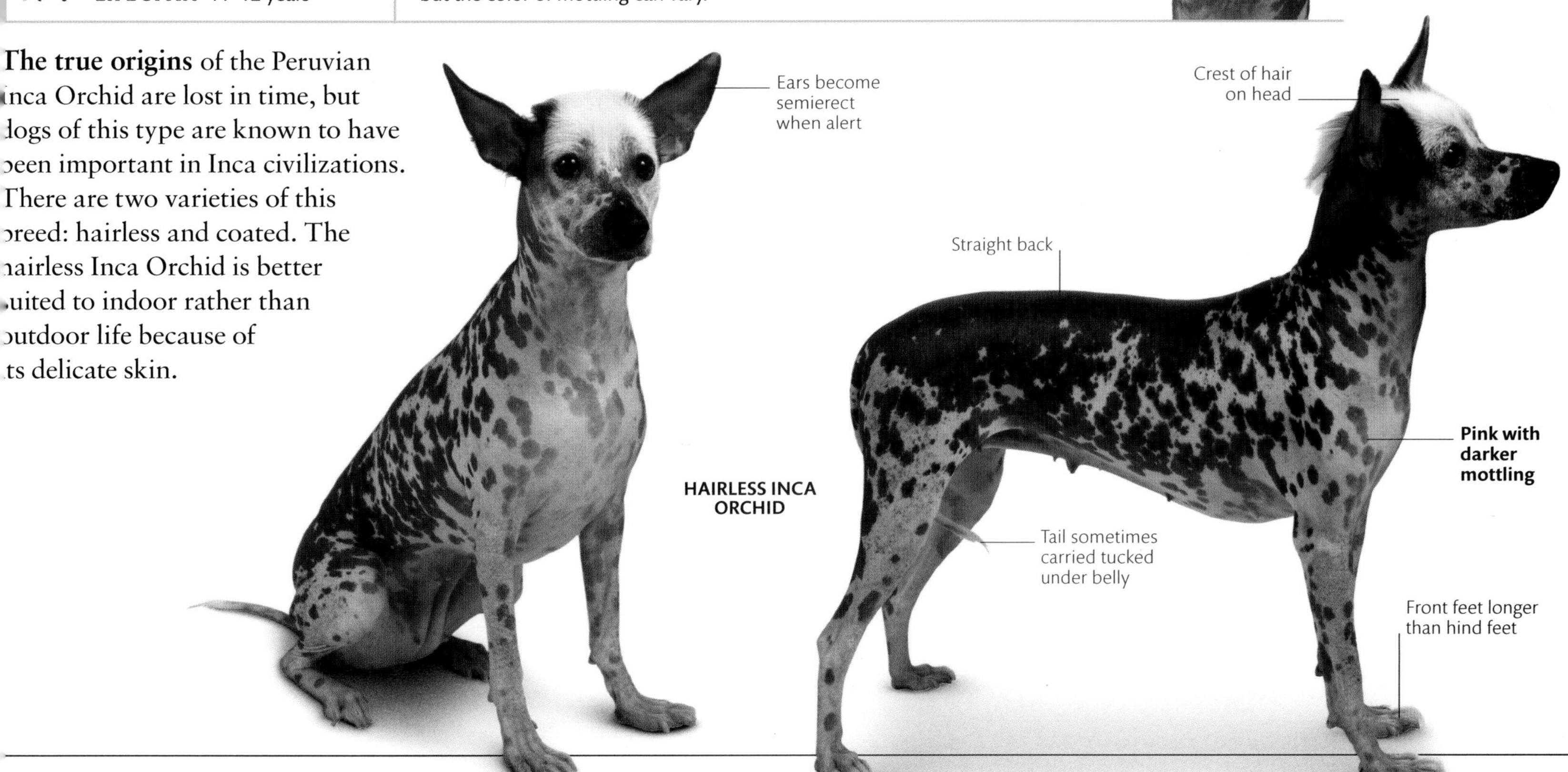

Peruvian Hairless

HEIGHT
Miniature: 10–16in (25–40cm)
Medio: 16–20in (40–50cm)
Grande: 20–26in (50–65cm)

WEIGHT
Miniature: 9–18lb (4–8kg)
Medio: 18–26lb (8–12kg)
Grande: 26–55lb (12–25kg)

LIFE SPAN
11–12 years

Blonde
Dark brown
Black

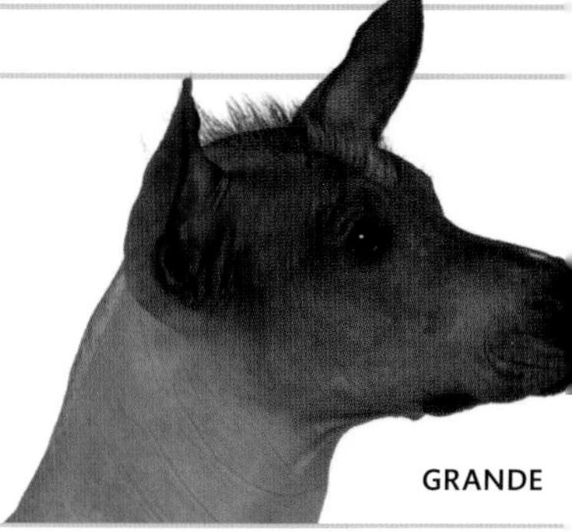

GRANDE

This gentle, bright, and agile dog is affectionate with owners but may be shy when around strangers

Records of hairless dogs in South America date back to pre-Inca times; images of them are found on pottery dating from 750BCE. These lively and graceful dogs were often seen in the homes of Incan nobility.

The Andean peoples believed these companion dogs brought good luck and promoted health, and would hug them to relieve aches and pains. The dogs' urine and feces may have been used in medicines. When a person died, artifacts of hairless dogs were sometimes buried with them to keep the person company in the afterlife.

After the Spanish Conquest of Peru in the 16th century, hairless dogs were persecuted almost to extinction. However, some did survive and since 2001 the Peruvian Hairless has been a protected breed—part of the National Patrimony of Peru. In 2008 a Peruvian Hairless was offered to President Obama as a family pet.

Peruvian Hairless dogs come in three sizes—miniature, medio, and grande. Hairlessness—often accompanied by the absence of some molar and premolar teeth—is produced by a particular recessive gene, but occasionally dogs with coats do occur in litters. The fine skin needs some protection since these dogs are susceptible to the cold and easily sunburned.

LOST IN TIME

The pre-Inca Nazca civilization of coastal Peru is famous for producing the massive geoglyphs, known collectively as the Nazca Lines. Among the various designs and shapes, there are over 70 different animals, including a dog. Created between 100–800CE and measuring 167ft (51m) in length, the dog's outline was produced by removing surface gravel to expose the lighter rocks below. It is possible that the dog depicted (below) represents an ancestor of the Peruvian Hairless.

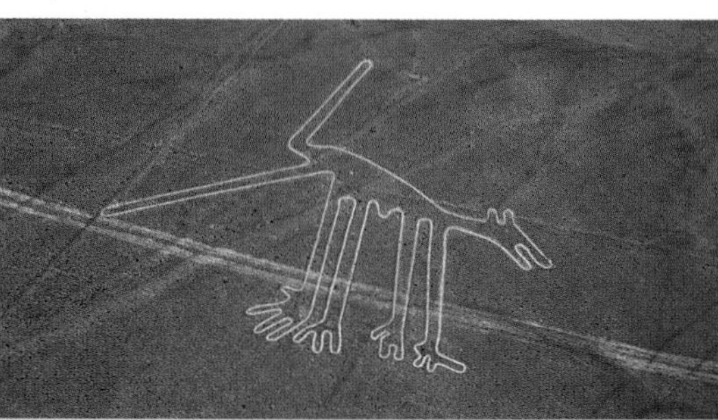

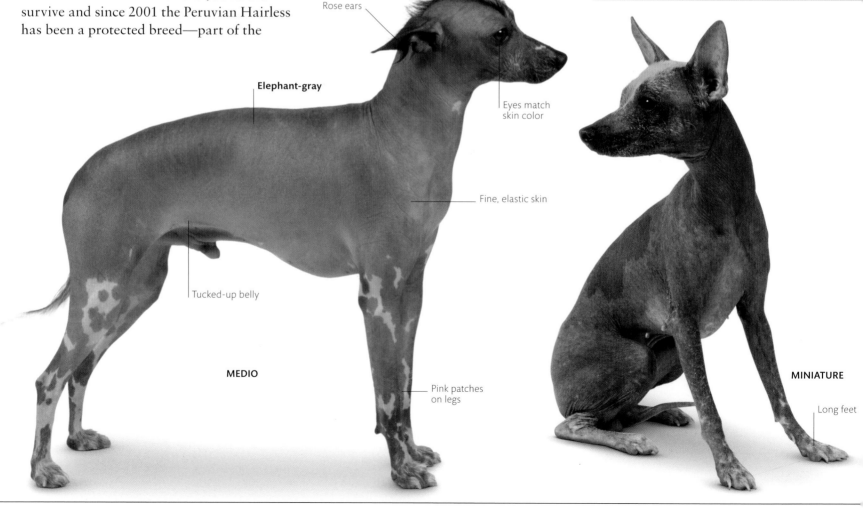

Crest of hairs

Rose ears

Elephant-gray

Eyes match skin color

Fine, elastic skin

Tucked-up belly

MEDIO

Pink patches on legs

MINIATURE

Long feet

Xoloitzcuintli

HEIGHT	WEIGHT	LIFE SPAN	
Miniature: 10–14in (25–35cm) Intermediate: 14–18in (36–45cm) Standard: 18–24in (46–60cm)	Miniature: 5–15lb (2–7kg) Intermediate: 15–31lb (7–14kg) Standard: 24–40lb (11–18kg)	Over 10 years	 **Red** **Liver or Bronze** (right)

MINIATURE (PUPPY)

This calm-natured, alert dog is easy to care for and makes a delightful and entertaining companion

Also known as the Mexican Hairless or Xolo (pronounced sholo), hairless dogs have featured in ceramic paintings and figurines dating from over 3,000 years ago and been found in the tombs of Aztec, Mayan, and other Central American peoples.

In pre-Conquest Mexico hairless dogs were valued companions and bed-warmers. In addition, the dogs had sacred significance. The animals were used as guard dogs to protect the home from evil spirits as well as intruders, and they were thought to guide the soul through the underworld. Some dogs were sacrificed or ritually eaten in religious ceremonies; because of these practices, hairless dogs barely escaped extinction. It was not until the mid-20th century that breeders began to work toward the dog's recovery.

Three sizes are now recognized: miniature, intermediate, and standard. Like all hairless dogs, this breed has limited general appeal and remains a rarity. Nonetheless, the Mexican Hairless is good-tempered, affectionate, and highly intelligent. The dogs are good companions and watchdogs, and are starting to be used as service dogs to provide relief for chronic pain—an echo of their traditional role. In addition, being hairless makes them good pets for allergy sufferers.

USEFUL COMPANION

Mexican Hairless dogs feel warm to the touch because, lacking fur, they radiate their body heat. In the past this attribute was appreciated by farmers who used the dogs as bed-warmers. The practice supposedly gave rise to the phrase "three dog nights" for very cold evenings. The dog's body heat was also thought to have healing properties and it would be held against painful areas of the body to provide a warm compress.

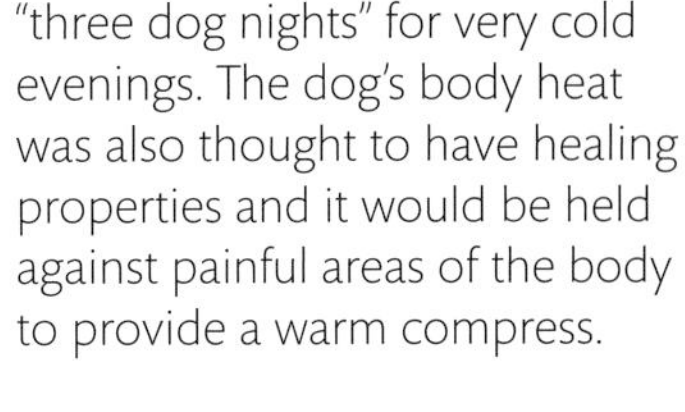

MEXICAN EARTHENWARE DOG 100BCE–300CE

INTERMEDIATE

STANDARD

Rescue work
Baerli, a German Shepherd Dog, explores a hole in the snow as part of his training for avalanche search and rescue work.

WORKING DOGS

The list of jobs that humans ask dogs to perform is almost endless. In the thousands of years since dogs were domesticated, canine helpers have guarded homes, rescued people in danger, gone to war, and looked after the sick and disabled—to give just a few examples. In this book the working group is represented by breeds traditionally developed for pastoral work and guard duties.

In general, the dogs in this highly diverse group tend to be large, though there are a few small but nonetheless robust exceptions. Working dogs are bred for strength and stamina, and many of them are capable of living outdoors in all weathers.

A collie rounding up its flock is for most people the archetypal shepherd dog, but many other types of dog are used to work with livestock. These pastoral breeds, as they are known, are used for both herding and guarding. Herding dogs have a natural instinct for driving stock, though not all of them work in the same way. Border Collies (see p.51), for example, keep their sheep in order by stalking and staring, while the traditional cattle herders such as Welsh Corgis (see pp.58, 60) and the Australian Cattle Dog (see p.62) nip at heels, and some herders bark as they work. Guardian sheepdogs, which include mountain breeds such as the Maremma (see p.69) and the Great Pyrenees (see p.78), are designed to protect their flocks from predators such as wolves. Usually very large, many of these dogs are white, heavy-coated, and scarcely distinguishable from the sheep they live with and protect all their lives.

Guard duties of another kind are often carried out by dogs of the mastiff type, recognizable as descendants of the enormous molossus dogs seen in friezes and artifacts from the ancient world. Such breeds as the Bullmastiff (see p.94), the Dogue de Bordeaux (see p.89), and the Neapolitan Mastiff (see p.92) are used worldwide by security forces and for guarding property. Typically, these dogs are massively built and powerful, with small ears (often cropped in countries where the practice is still legal) and pendulous flews (lips).

Many working breeds are excellent as companion dogs. Pastoral herders are extremely intelligent and generally easy to train, and often enjoy using their skills in agility trials and other canine competitions. Livestock guardian dogs, because of their size and protective nature, are less likely to be suited to family life. In recent decades a number of the mastiff-type breeds have achieved great popularity as companions. Although some were produced originally for fighting, if reared in the home and socialized early they adapt to life as a pet.

Saarloos Wolfdog

HEIGHT 24–30in (60–75cm)
WEIGHT 77–88lb (35–40kg)
LIFE SPAN Over 10 years

Cream
Bos (brown)

The Saarloos Wolfdog is the result of selective crossbreeding to produce a German Shepherd-type dog with natural traits closer to those of its wolf ancestors. Although it was suggested that this new breed could be useful as a guide dog, the Saarloos Wolfdog has proved better suited to life as a pet and companion. However, it needs sensitive handling.

Czechoslovakian Wolfdog

HEIGHT 24–26in (60–65cm)
WEIGHT 44–57lb (20–26kg)
LIFE SPAN 12–16 years

Created through breeding programs that initially crossed German Shepherd Dogs with wolves, the Czechoslovakian Wolfdog has inherited many of the traits of its wild ancestors. This breed is quick, fearless, resilient, and wary of strangers. It is also faithful and obedient with familiar handlers, qualities that make it an excellent house dog.

King Shepherd

HEIGHT 25–29in (64–74cm)
WEIGHT 90–145lb (41–66kg)
LIFE SPAN 10–11 years

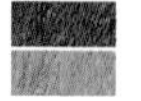

Black
Sable with black markings

Black dogs may have red, gold, or cream markings.

Developed in the US and recognized since the late 1990s, this large and handsome dog clearly shows the German Shepherd Dog (see p.42) in its breeding history. King Shepherds love to work as herders or guard dogs, but have a placid and tolerant nature that allows them to fit in well with a family. There are two coat types: smooth and rough.

ROUGH-COATED

Laekenois

HEIGHT 22–26in (56–66cm)
WEIGHT 55–65lb (25–29kg)
LIFE SPAN Over 10 years

Of the four breeds of Belgian Shepherd Dog, this wiry-coated variety was the first to be developed, in the 1880s. The Laekenois is named after the Château de Laeken, near Antwerp, and was once much favored by the Belgian royal family. Rarely seen, this delightful dog deserves to be more widely appreciated.

Belgian Sheepdog

HEIGHT 22–26in (56–66cm)
WEIGHT 51–75lb (23–34kg)
LIFE SPAN Over 10 years

From 1893 black-coated Belgian Sheepdogs were selectively bred at a kennel in the village of Groenendael, near Brussels. This handsome variety is now extremely popular. Like most herding dogs, the Belgian Sheepdog needs an owner who understands the importance of early socializing and firm but kindly control.

Belgian Malinois

HEIGHT 22–26in (56–66cm)
WEIGHT 60–65lb (27–29kg)
LIFE SPAN Over 10 years

All colors have black overlay.

Believed to have originated in Malines, in Belgium, the Malinois is a short-haired variety of the Belgian Shepherd Dog. Like its fellow breeds, it is a natural guard dog. Although its behavior may be unpredictable, with responsible training the Malinois socializes well and makes a loyal companion.

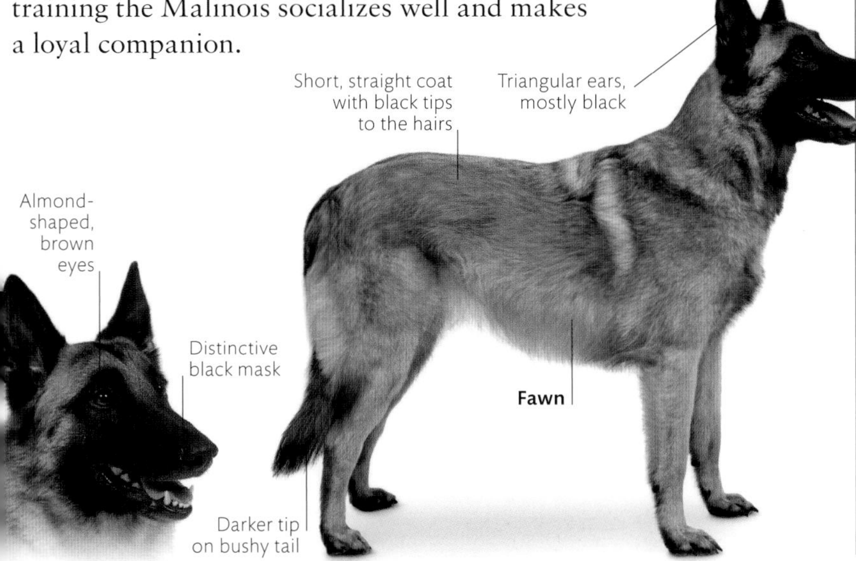

Belgian Tervuren

HEIGHT 22–26in (56–66cm)
WEIGHT 40–65lb (18–29kg)
LIFE SPAN Over 10 years

Gray
All colors have black overlay.

The most popular of the Belgian Shepherd Dogs worldwide, this variety was named after the village where it was developed by a local breeder. The Belgian Tervuren has strong protective instincts and is frequently used for guarding and police work. Its beautiful, black-tipped coat sheds regularly and needs plenty of grooming.

German Shepherd Dog

HEIGHT	WEIGHT	LIFE SPAN	
23–25in (58–63cm)	49–88lb (22–40kg)	Over 10 years	 Sable Black

One of the most popular breeds worldwide, this intelligent and versatile herding dog makes a faithful companion

This breed was developed by a German cavalry captain, Max von Stephanitz, from dogs used to guard and herd livestock. The first examples appeared in the 1880s, and the breed was registered in Germany as the Deutsche Schäferhund (German Shepherd Dog) in 1899; the first registered individual dog was a male named Horand von Grafrath.

During World War I the dog's name was changed in the UK to Alsatian. This new name was chosen because the first dogs were brought back from Alsace-Lorraine by soldiers that had served there, and also because the name avoided reference to Germany; for the same reason, in the US its name was changed to Shepherd Dog. Soldiers from both countries were impressed by the breed's abilities.

Highly adaptable and obedient, the German Shepherd Dog has proved valuable as a guard dog and tracker, and is used by police and armed forces worldwide. It is also employed as a search and rescue dog and as a guide dog for blind people.

The modern breed has a coat that can vary from long to short. The German Shepherd Dog has a reputation for being fierce, but dogs produced by reputable breeders usually have a steady temperament. These dogs need to be handled in a calm, authoritative way so that they will not become overly dominant, but they are brave and willing to learn. They need plenty of exercise and do well at jobs such as protecting the home. If responsibly handled, they will become loyal, faithful members of the family.

CANINE SUPERSTAR

Rescued from a WWI battlefield by US Marine Lee Duncan, Rin Tin Tin (below) was taken to California where Duncan trained him for film work. He starred in 28 Hollywood films and became so popular that in 1929 he received the most votes for the Best Actor Oscar. However, the Academy, fearing that giving the award to an animal would undermine their credibility, instead gave it to the runner-up. Rin Tin Tin died in 1932, but some of his descendants, trained by Duncan, also appeared in movies.

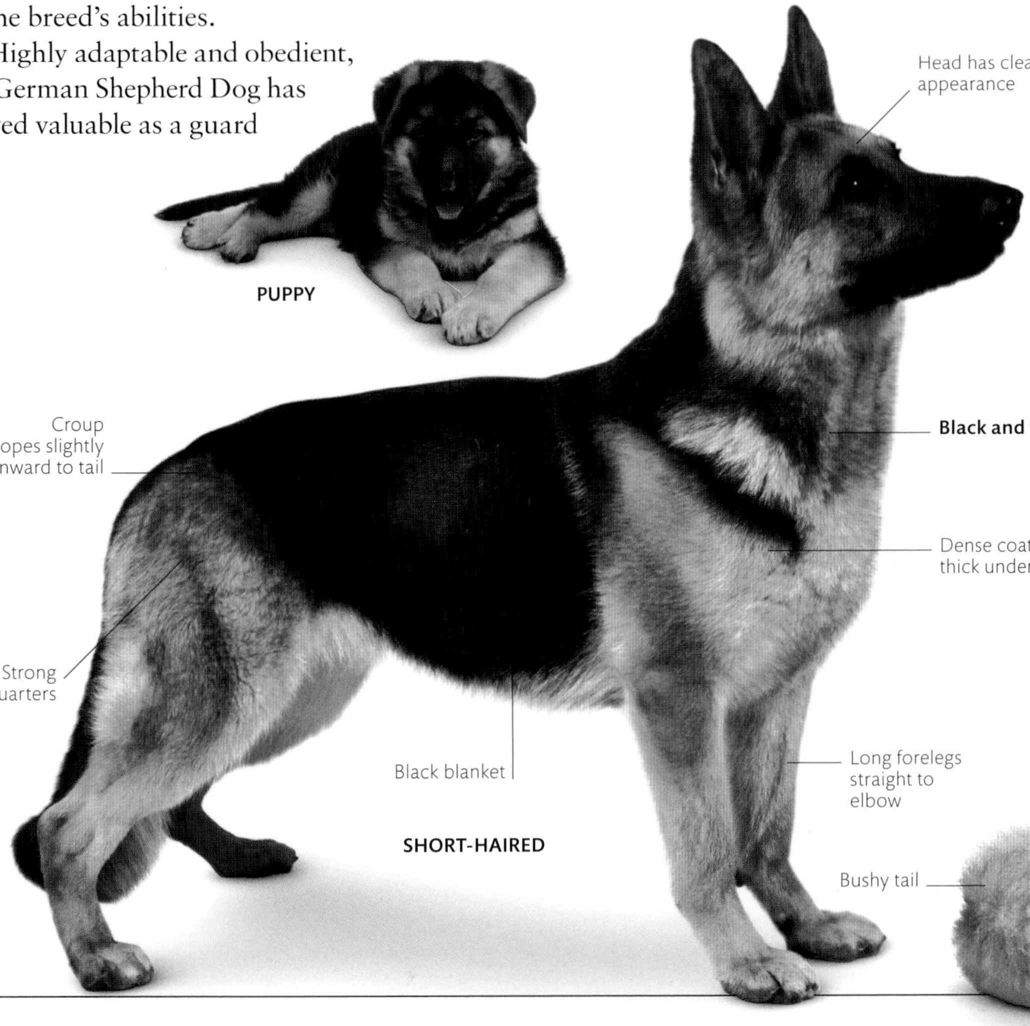

PUPPY

Head has clean-cut appearance

Croup slopes slightly downward to tail

Black and tan

Dense coat with thick undercoat

Strong hindquarters

Black blanket

Long forelegs straight to elbow

SHORT-HAIRED

Large, firm, erect ears

Bicolor

Bushy tail

LONG-HAIRED

Picardy Sheepdog

HEIGHT 22–26in (55–65cm)
WEIGHT 51–71lb (23–32kg)
LIFE SPAN 13–14 years

Dark gray
Fawn-brindle
May have white markings.

The history of the Picardy Sheepdog is uncertain, but this tough-looking breed may have originated over a century ago in the Picardy region of northeastern France. With quiet and patient training, this dog makes a sociable companion and a good playmate for children. The rugged coat is relatively easy to groom.

Dutch Shepherd Dog

HEIGHT 22–24in (55–62cm)
WEIGHT 66–68lb (30–31kg)
LIFE SPAN 12–14 years

Fawn-brindle

Not often seen outside the Netherlands, and relatively uncommon even there, in the last 200 years this breed has become far more than an all-purpose farm dog. The breed has been used for security and police work, as a guide dog, and in obedience trials. Reliable and affectionate with family members, it has a natural wariness of strangers. There are three varieties of the Dutch Shepherd Dog: long-haired, short-haired, and rough-haired.

SHORT-HAIRED

LONG-HAIRED

ROUGH-HAIRED

Mudi

HEIGHT 15–19in (38–47cm)
WEIGHT 18–29lb (8–13kg)
LIFE SPAN 13–14 years

Fawn
Blue merle, ash
Brown
May have white markings.

Originally used as a working dog by Hungarian sheep- and cattle-herders, this rare breed is tough, bold, and energetic. With its friendly and adaptable nature, the Mudi makes a good house dog. It needs plenty of exercise to stay fit and healthy, and responds well to sympathetic training.

Standard Schnauzer

HEIGHT 18–20in (45–50cm)
WEIGHT 31–44lb (14–20kg)
LIFE SPAN Over 10 years

Black

The medium-sized Standard Schnauzer was established as a breed in the 1880s in southern Germany. Alert and agile, the Standard Schnauzer was used primarily as a versatile farm dog with a formidable reputation for rat hunting. Placid and affectionate, but with a lively sense of fun, the breed is now popular as a family dog.

Giant Schnauzer

HEIGHT	WEIGHT	LIFE SPAN	
24–28in (60–70cm)	65–90lb (29–41kg)	Over 10 years	Pepper and salt

Even-tempered, intelligent, and easy to train, this powerful dog has strong guarding instincts

Robust and powerfully built, the Giant Schnauzer from southern Germany was developed from the standard Schnauzer (see p.45) by crossing with larger local dogs and, it is thought, with breeds such as the Great Dane (see p.96) and the Bouvier des Flandres (opposite).

The Giant Schnauzer, with its powerful frame and weather-resistant coat, was originally used for farm work and for herding and driving cattle. By the early 20th century the breed's intelligence, trainability, and impressive appearance had been recognized as ideal qualities for a guard dog. Giant Schnauzers were first brought to the US in the 1930s and to the UK in the 1960s. The breed has become more popular in the US and Europe since the 1970s.

The Giant Schnauzer is now widely used by security forces in Europe as a police dog and for tracking and search and rescue duties. An equable temperament also makes it suitable as a home watchdog and family pet. Despite its size, the Giant Schnauzer is easy to manage if given plenty of exercise. A quick learner, it excels at obedience and agility activities. Its dense, wiry, double-layered coat needs regular maintenance, with daily grooming and trimming (shaping) every few months.

SAFE AND SOUND

This stamp, issued in East Germany in the late 1970s, shows a typical working Giant Schnauzer with clipped ears and a docked tail. In the years leading up to World War I, the Giant Schnauzer was found to be well suited to police work—its large size and impressive bark proving an excellent deterrent to trouble. Despite the breed's popularity in Germany, the preferred choice for this type of work in other countries tended to be the German Shepherd.

EAST GERMAN STAMP ISSUED LATE 1970S

Tail carried high

Black

Dense, wiry coat

Drop ears with rounded tips

Dark eyes

Bearded muzzle

Deep chest

Slight feathering on back of forelegs

Bushy eyebrows overhang eyes

Strong, graceful neck

Bouvier des Flandres

HEIGHT	WEIGHT	LIFE SPAN	Variety of colors
23–27in (59–68cm)	60–88lb (27–40kg)	Over 10 years	May have small, white star on chest.

PRESIDENTIAL DOGS

One of the largest dogs to live at the White House was Lucky, a Bouvier des Flandres puppy given to Nancy Reagan in December 1984. As Lucky matured, she also became stronger and more boisterous. She started to drag the president around during press photo shoots (below), which did not give the impression of a leader in control. In November 1985 Lucky was sent to live at the Reagans' California ranch and was replaced by a smaller, more manageable English Toy Spaniel named Rex.

Loyal and fearless, this independent dog does well in town or country but needs plenty of space and an experienced owner

The Bouvier breeds were developed in Belgium and northern France for herding, guarding, and driving cattle; the French word *bouvier* means cowherd. Of the various Bouviers, the Bouvier des Flandres is the most commonly encountered.

During World War I they were used as messenger dogs and ambulance dogs (guiding medical helpers to wounded men), but Flanders was devastated by the fighting, and the breed itself was almost destroyed. One dog that survived was a male named Nic, which became a founding sire of the modern breed. When Nic was presented at the Olympic Show in Antwerp, Belgium, in 1920, he was recognized as the ideal type of Bouvier. During the 1920s breeders worked to resurrect the Bouvier des Flandres.

Today the breed is valued as a guard dog and a family pet. Calm and easy to train, it nevertheless has strong protective instincts and is still used for military and police work, and as a search and rescue dog. Despite originally being an outdoor dog, the Bouvier des Flandres can adjust to an urban home, as long as it has plenty of exercise every day. The coat needs to be groomed several times a week and trimmed every three months.

Heavily feathered tail

Silver-brindle

Long, coarse beard

Very thick coat, coarse to touch

High-set, drop ears

Dense coat extends over feet

Bouvier des Ardennes

HEIGHT 20–24in (52–62cm)
WEIGHT 49–77lb (22–35kg)
LIFE SPAN Over 10 years

Variety of colors

This hardy, active, former cattle herder from the Belgian Ardennes is now rarely seen, either as a working dog or a house dog. A handful of enthusiasts have kept the breed in existence, and with its adaptable temperament and zest for life the Bouvier des Ardennes has the potential for future popularity.

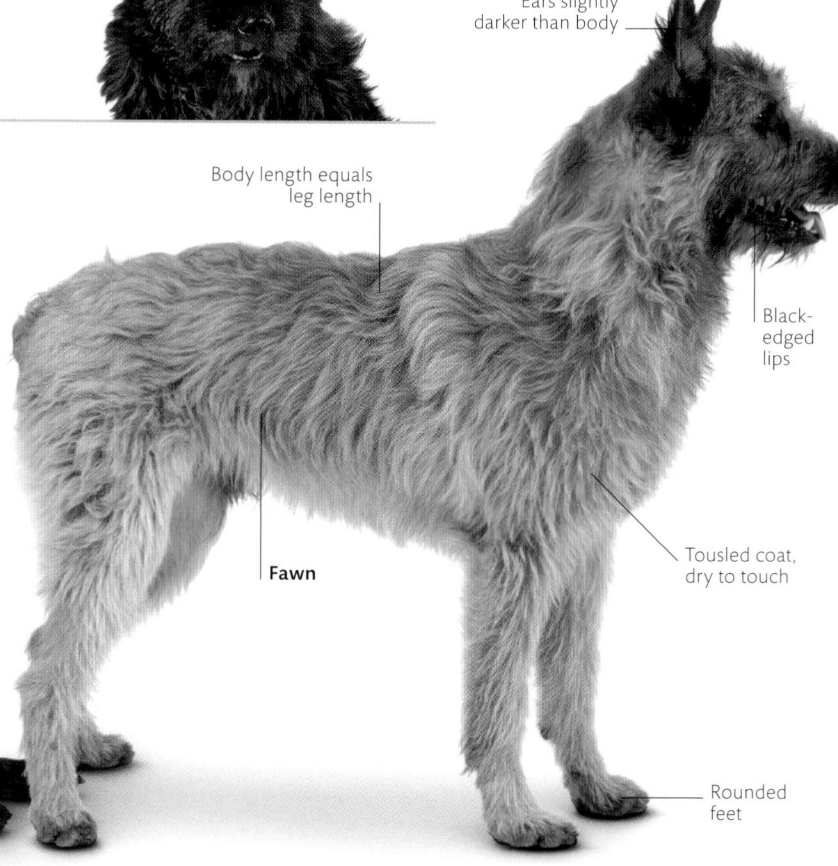

Croatian Shepherd Dog

HEIGHT 16–20in (40–50cm)
WEIGHT 29–44lb (13–20kg)
LIFE SPAN 13–14 years

Relatively small and lightly built for a shepherd dog, this breed is active and alert. Easy to train for work, the Croatian Shepherd Dog may be harder to handle as a house dog because of its natural herding and guarding instincts. Its unusually wavy or curly coat is a distinctive feature.

Sarplaninac

HEIGHT Over 23in (58cm)
WEIGHT 66–99lb (30–45kg)
LIFE SPAN 11–13 years

Any solid color

Formerly known as the Illyrian Shepherd Dog, this impressive breed is now named after the Sarplanina Mountains of Macedonia where it originated. The Sarplaninac is very much an outdoor, working dog. Although it has a sociable though protective temperament, its size and energy levels make it impractical as a family pet.

Karst Shepherd Dog

HEIGHT 21–25in (54–63cm)
WEIGHT 55–93lb (25–42kg)
LIFE SPAN 11–12 years

ormerly known as the Illyrian Shepherd Dog, this dog was eparated from another breed of the same name and renamed he Karst, or Istrian, Shepherd Dog in the 1960s. Used for erding and guarding in the alpine Karst region of lovenia, this excellent working dog can make good companion with careful training nd early socialization.

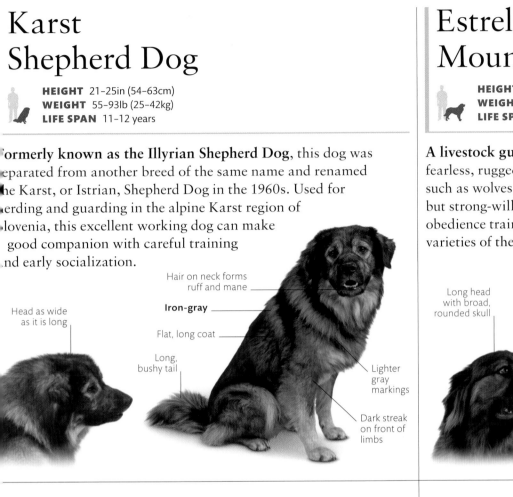

Estrela Mountain Dog

HEIGHT 24–28in (62–72cm)
WEIGHT 77–132lb (35–60kg)
LIFE SPAN Over 10 years

Wolf-gray or Black brindle
Underside and extremities may have white markings.

A livestock guardian from the Estrela Mountains of Portugal, this fearless, rugged dog was bred to protect flocks against predators such as wolves. The Estrela Mountain Dog is a loyal and friendly but strong-willed companion that needs consistent and patient obedience training. There are long-coated and short-coated varieties of the breed.

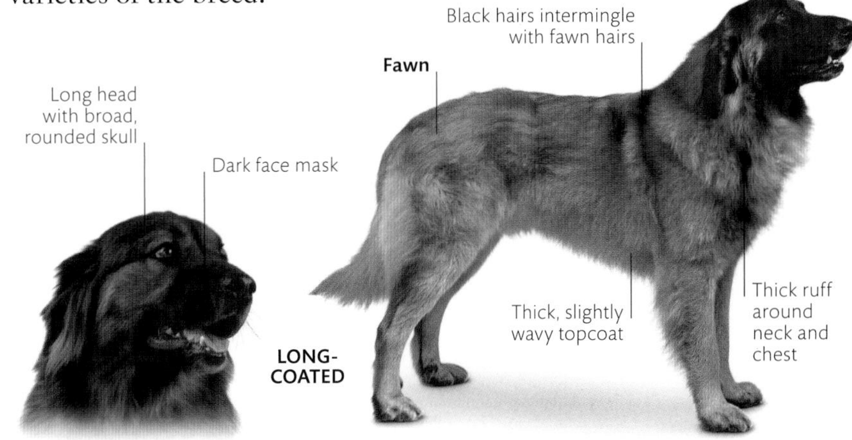

Portuguese Watchdog

HEIGHT 25–29in (64–74cm)
WEIGHT 77–132lb (35–60kg)
LIFE SPAN 12 years

Wolf-gray **Black**
Coat may be brindled; white coats have colored patches.

ossibly descended from the powerful mastiffs brought into urope from Asia by nomadic herders, this breed is also known s the Rafeiro de Alentejo, named after the Alentejo region f Portugal. Traditionally used for guarding, the ortuguese Watchdog is vigilant and suspicious f strangers. Formidable in size and strength, hough not aggressive, this dog is unsuitable or novice handlers.

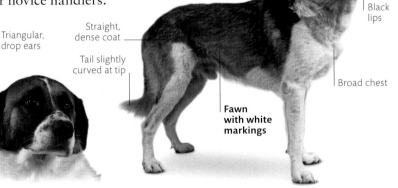

Castro Laboreiro Dog

HEIGHT 21–25in (55–64cm)
WEIGHT 55–88lb (25–40kg)
LIFE SPAN 12–13 years

Wolf-gray
May have a small white spot on chest.

Named after its home village in the mountains of northern Portugal, this dog, sometimes known as the Portuguese Cattle Dog, was bred to work as a livestock-guardian. Its distinctive alarm bark starts low and ends high-pitched. This dog develops a strong bond with family members but may be hostile to strangers.

Portuguese Sheepdog

HEIGHT 17–22in (42–55cm)
WEIGHT 37–60lb (17–27kg)
LIFE SPAN 12–13 years

Variety of colors
May have a small amount of white on chest.

In its native country this shaggy, agile dog is sometimes known as the monkey dog. The Portuguese Sheepdog loves to be outdoors, herding. Lively and extremely intelligent, the breed has also gained popularity as a companion and sporting dog in Portugal, although it is little known elsewhere.

Catalan Sheepdog

HEIGHT 18–22in (45–55cm)
WEIGHT 44–60lb (20–27kg)
LIFE SPAN 12–14 years

Gray
Sable
Black and ta
May have white markings.

Bred in Catalonia, Spain, as a flock-herder and guard, this hardy dog has an attractive weatherproof coat that allows it to work in almost any conditions. With high intelligence, a quiet temperament and a readiness to please, the Catalan Sheepdog is relatively easy to train and makes an excellent family companion.

Pyrenean Sheepdog

HEIGHT 15–19in (38–48cm)
WEIGHT 15–31lb (7–14kg)
LIFE SPAN 12–13 years

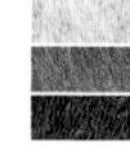

Gray
Blue
Black
Black and white
Blue coats may be merle, slate, or brindle. Unmixed colors are preferred.

Small and lightly built for a sheepdog, this breed has long been used for herding flocks in the French Pyrenees. It remained almost unknown beyond its native mountain regions until the beginning of the 20th century. Lithe, energetic, and ready to join in any interesting activity, the Pyrenean Sheepdog does well in canine sports such as agility trials. For an active family, the Pyrenean Sheepdog is an excellent pet. The breed comes in two coat varieties—long or semi-long—and may have a rough or smooth face.

Border Collie

HEIGHT	WEIGHT	LIFE SPAN	
20–21in (50–53cm)	26–44lb (12–20kg)	Over 10 years	Variety of colors

This superintelligent dog needs an experienced owner and plenty of physical and mental activity

The Border Collie's reputation as the quintessential sheepdog reaches far beyond the English-Scottish border where it originated. Almost all Border Collies are descended from a dog named Old Hemp, born in Northumbria (northern England) in 1894. Old Hemp was such a good sheepdog that many other farmers wanted pups sired by him; he had more than 200 offspring.

When herding sheep a Border Collie works quickly and silently, responding immediately to voice, whistle, or hand commands from the shepherd. The dogs are used to round up sheep, to move them from pasture to pasture or pen, and to isolate individual animals, if necessary.

Primarily a working dog, the Border Collie was not officially recognized as a breed by the Kennel Club in the UK until 1976.

Tireless energy, a low boredom threshold, and an independent spirit mean that the Border Collie needs plenty of physical and mental challenges every day if kept as a pet. Many take part in dog agility competitions. These competitions, which started in the UK in 1978, require owners to train and direct their dogs to pass through a course of obstacles. Border Collies excel in this activity as, just like when herding sheep, they rapidly follow their owner's commands. There are two varieties of coat: moderately long and smooth.

FOREVER FAITHFUL

The town of Benton, Montana, is perhaps best known for a dog that kept a six-year vigil for his shepherd owner. The shepherd became sick and died after coming to the town hospital for treatment in 1936. The dog saw his coffin loaded on to a train and from that point the dog—named Old Shep by station staff—met each incoming train, looking for his master. His devotion became famous. In 1942 Old Shep was killed by a train. He was buried on the bluff overlooking the station, where a memorial to him was erected.

BRONZE STATUE OF OLD SHEP IN FORT BENTON, MONTANA

Low-set tail reaches hock

Muscular, athletic body

Black and white

Distinct stop

Ears set well apart

MODERATELY LONG COAT

Feathering on forelegs

Collie

HEIGHT	WEIGHT	LIFE SPAN		
20–24in (51–61cm)	51–75lb (23–34kg)	12–14 years	 Gold Blue merle Gold and white	 Black, tan, and white

This proud and beautiful, sweet-tempered dog makes a loyal family companion but needs plenty of exercise

This rich-coated breed, a descendant of the rather less-refined Scottish working shepherd dogs, is much admired today as a pet and in the show ring. The Collie's history may go back as far as Roman Britain, but dogs recognizably of this type did not attract wide attention until the 19th century. Queen Victoria is credited with popularizing the breed both in Europe and the US. Later, Lassie, the highly intelligent star of film and television, confirmed the Collie's status as one of the best-loved dogs of all time.

This breed is mild-tempered and tolerant of other dogs and pets. It is highly responsive to training and makes an affectionate and protective companion. However, the people-loving Collie readily accepts visitors to the home and therefore does not make a good guard dog. An athletic breed, it is eager for fun and will take part eagerly in canine sports such as agility trials.

The herding instinct has not been entirely bred out of Collies; their sharp awareness of movement may trigger an impulse to "round up" friends and family. Early socializing can prevent this trait from becoming a nuisance.

Like all breeds originally intended as working dogs, the Collie becomes restless when underexercised or left alone for long periods, and may start to bark excessively. However, given an energetic daily run, it can be kept in a modest-sized house or even an apartment.

This dog's long, thick coat needs regular grooming to prevent tangles and matting. More frequent grooming sessions may be needed when the dense undercoat is being shed, which occurs twice a year.

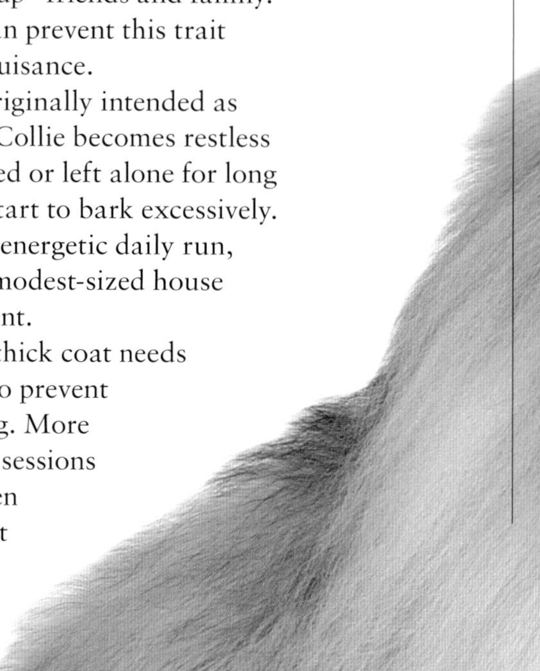

LASSIE—THE FAITHFUL FRIEND

The first Lassie film, *Lassie Come Home*, was based on a book in which Lassie's poor owners sell her to a rich duke, but the dog escapes and makes a long, dangerous trek to return to her family home. Several more films and a TV series followed, showing Lassie's bravery and loyalty to her human friends. Despite the girl's name, all of the canine actors were male. The original dog, Pal, was actually rather badly behaved before he was trained for his life in the movies.

A POSTER FROM THE 1994 FILM

PUPPY

Sable and white

Smooth Collie

HEIGHT	WEIGHT	LIFE SPAN	
20–24in (51–61cm)	40–66lb (18–30kg)	Over 10 years	Sable and white Black, tan, and white

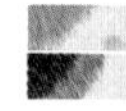

A HELPING HAND

Dogs have been used for many years to assist blind, deaf, and disabled people, but there is now a new way to help those suffering with Alzheimer's Disease. Choosing Smooth Collies to do this work has proved enormously successful. The dogs are trained to guide their owner home or remain with them until help arrives (below)—they carry a GPS on their harness to locate them. Loyal and devoted, these trained dogs are unusual because they often work without any commands from their owner and are also able to cope with the mood swings associated with the condition.

This increasingly rare collie is calm and friendly, making it ideal for the elderly or families with young children

Recognized as a breed in its own right, the Smooth Collie shares many physical features with the Collie (see p.52). Both breeds are descended from Scottish farm and herding dogs. Early Collies were smaller than today's dogs, with shorter muzzles, but during the 19th century breeders created a taller, more elegant animal for the show ring. As with the Collie, the breed was promoted by Queen Victoria who kept both Collies and Smooth Collies in her kennels.

Today the Smooth Collie is less well-known than its rough-haired counterpart. In the UK the Kennel Club has listed it as a Vulnerable Native Breed, signifying a breed that registers fewer than 300 new animals per year; in 2010 just 54 new dogs were registered. The breed is even less familiar in other countries.

The Smooth Collie is sometimes used as a sheepdog or watchdog but is also a good house dog that enjoys being with people. Mild-mannered and friendly, it needs plenty of company, exercise, and mental stimulation. The breed, like the Collie, does well in agility and obedience competitions. The short-haired coat is easy to maintain, needing little more than regular brushing.

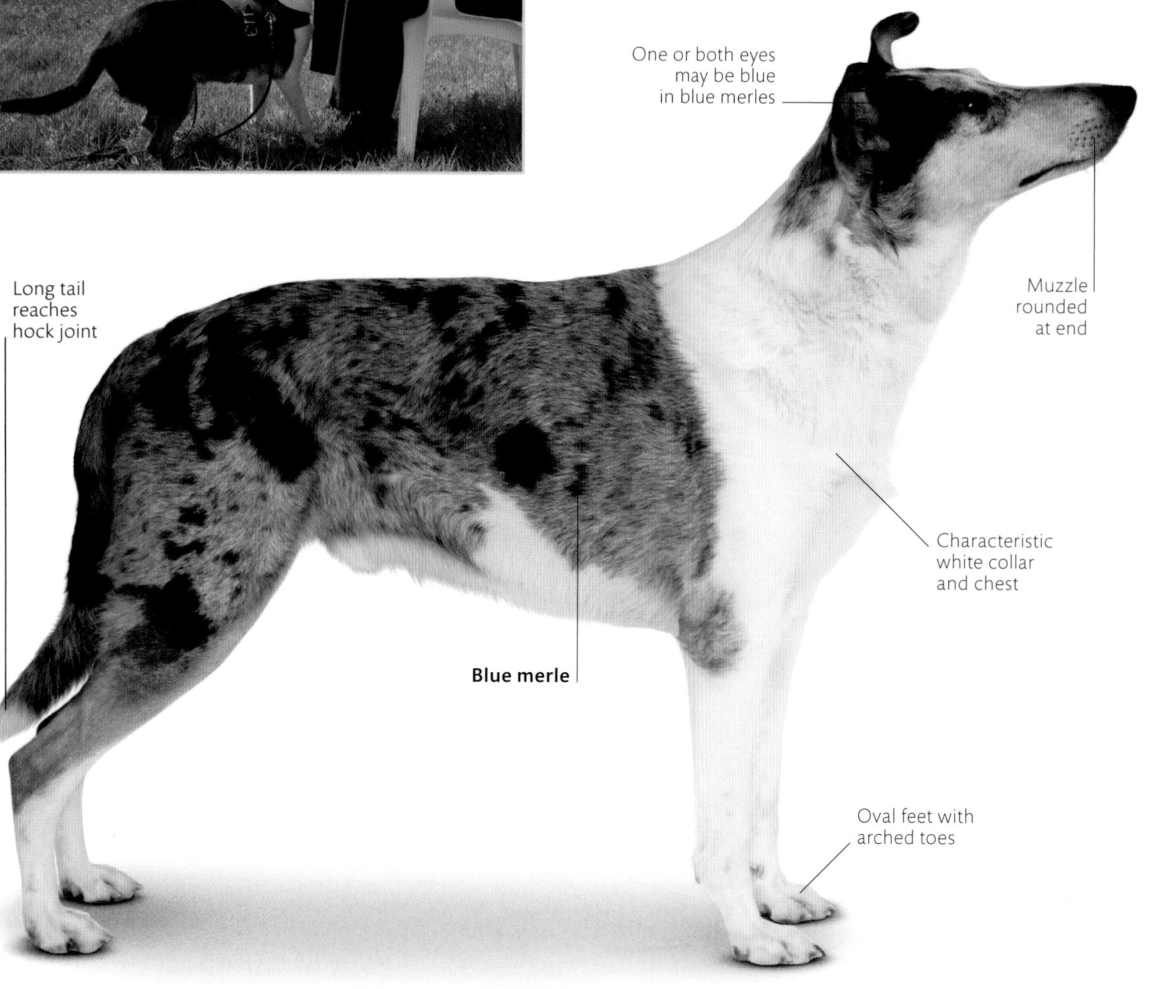

Shetland Sheepdog

HEIGHT 14–15in (35–38cm)
WEIGHT 13–37lb (6–17kg)
LIFE SPAN Over 10 years

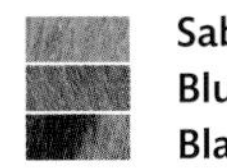

Sable
Blue merle
Black and tan
Black and white

'irst bred in the rugged Shetland Islands, ›eyond the northern coast of mainland ›cotland, this miniature collie is ›ardy and resilient. Bursting with ›nergy but easily trained and ›ffectionate, the Shetland ›heepdog adapts well to ›amily life and is a loyal ›et. Regular grooming ›essions are necessary ›o maintain the ›eautiful coat.

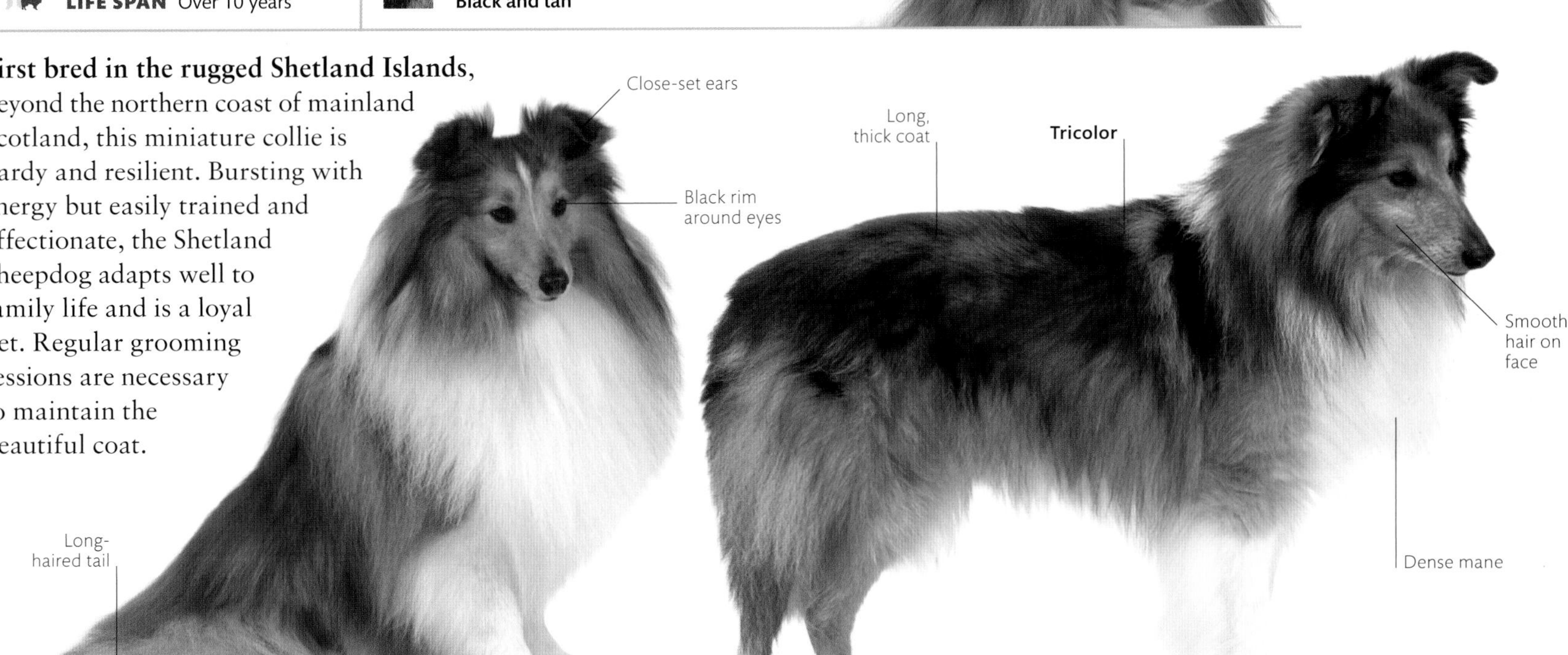

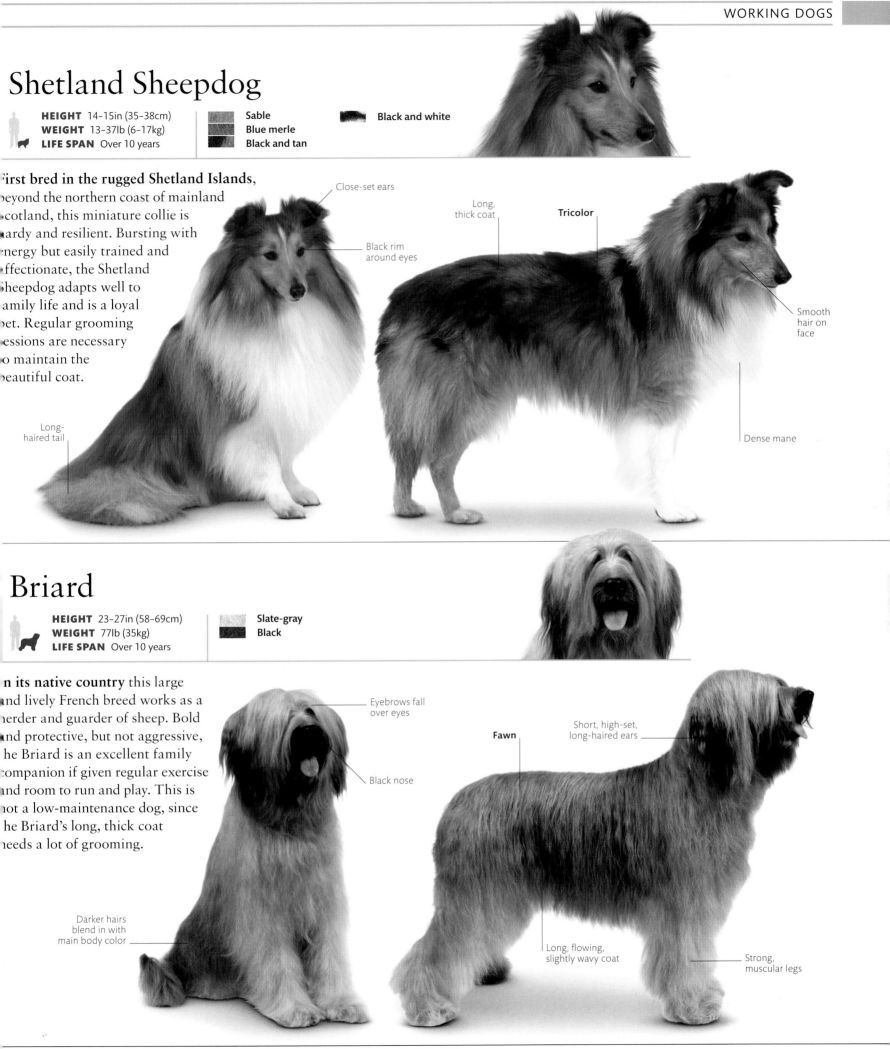

Briard

HEIGHT 23–27in (58–69cm)
WEIGHT 77lb (35kg)
LIFE SPAN Over 10 years

Slate-gray
Black

n its native country this large ›nd lively French breed works as a ›erder and guarder of sheep. Bold ›nd protective, but not aggressive, ›he Briard is an excellent family ›ompanion if given regular exercise ›nd room to run and play. This is ›ot a low-maintenance dog, since ›he Briard's long, thick coat ›eeds a lot of grooming.

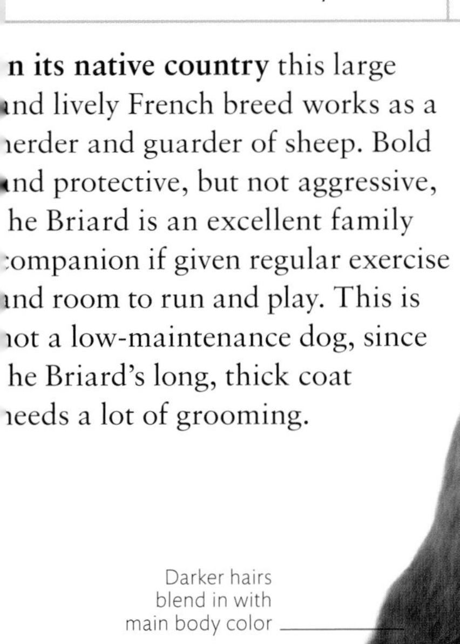

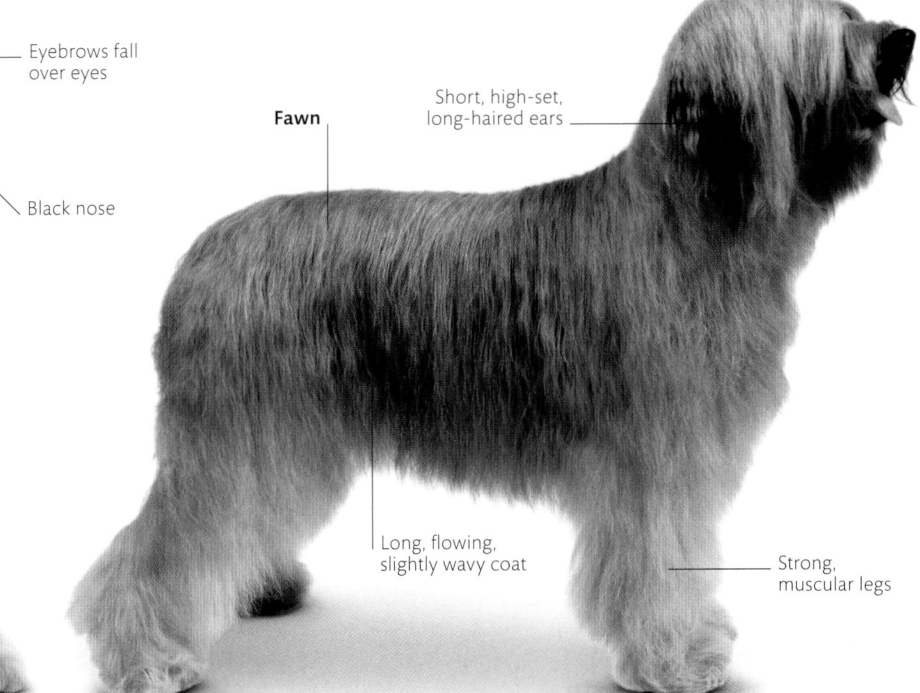

Old English Sheepdog

HEIGHT	WEIGHT	LIFE SPAN	Gray
22–24in (56–61cm)	60–99lb (27–45kg)	Over 10 years	Any shade of gray or blue. Body and hindquarters of solid color, with no white patches.

THE DULUX DOG

To many English-speaking people around the world, the Old English Sheepdog has become synonymous with Dulux, the international paint brand. The first Dulux advertisements featuring the dog appeared in 1961; it was felt that the big, fluffy dog would give the film sets an appealing family home feel. The dogs have been the stars of the shows for over 50 years, and some even had their own chauffeurs. They and the brand made each other world famous; today, Old English Sheepdogs are often recognized as "Dulux dogs."

This good-tempered and intelligent dog needs frequent grooming to maintain its shaggy coat

Native to southwest England, the Old English Sheepdog is descended from large, strong dogs used to guard livestock against wolves, as well as from the Bearded Collie (opposite), and, possibly, breeds such as the South Russian Shepherd Dog (opposite). By the mid-19th century the dogs were being used to drive livestock to market. It was customary to dock the tail (bob it), to show that the animal was a working dog and thus exempt from tax; the alternative name of Bobtail Sheepdog is still sometimes used.

The breed was highly popular in the 1970s and 80s, due to its use in movies and advertisements, but more recently it has fallen out of favor; in 2012 only 316 new dogs were registered with the UK's Kennel Club, prompting the Club to put the Old English Sheepdog on its watch list of endangered breeds.

This big, strong dog requires a great deal of exercise. The coat always has been dense and shaggy; in the old days shepherds would shear their dogs as well as the sheep and use the hair to make cloth. However, modern animals' coats have become so thick that they need constant care to prevent them from becoming tangled and matted.

Eyes obscured by coat
Small ears covered by coat
Deep, relatively short body
Longer coat on hindquarters
Very thick, shaggy coat with white markings
Blue
White markings on head, neck, and chest

Bearded Collie

HEIGHT 20–22in (51–56cm)
WEIGHT 44–55lb (20–25kg)
LIFE SPAN Over 10 years

Sandy
Red-brown
Blue
Black

Until the middle of the 20th century the Bearded Collie was familiar only in Scotland and the north of England, where it was valued as a sheepdog. Now widely appreciated for its attractive appearance, compact size, and gentle nature, this breed has great appeal as a pet. However, it is more likely to enjoy the space of a rural home than a compact urban environment.

Polish Lowland Sheepdog

HEIGHT 17–20in (42–50cm)
WEIGHT 31–35lb (14–16kg)
LIFE SPAN 12–15 years

Any color

Bred to work on the plainlands of Northern Europe as a herder and a guard dog, this delightfully shaggy dog is both rugged and agile. The breed has brains as well as brawn and responds readily to training for a variety of purposes. Exercise and grooming should be high on its owner's agenda.

Dutch Schapendoes

HEIGHT 16–20in (40–50cm)
WEIGHT 26–44lb (12–20kg)
LIFE SPAN 13–14 years

Any color

Swift, tireless, and intelligent, this breed is the perfect natural sheep herder. Moving as if on springs, a working Dutch Schapendoes can run at high speed and bound lightly over almost any obstacle in its path. The breed has the temperament to make a good companion but will not thrive without activity.

South Russian Shepherd Dog

HEIGHT 24–26in (62–65cm)
WEIGHT 106–110lb (48–50kg)
LIFE SPAN 9–11 years

Ashen gray
Straw
Yellow and white

This big sheepdog from the Russian steppes was bred not to round up flocks but to guard them against fierce predators. Quick to react, naturally dominant, and highly protective, this breed, also known as the Ovtcharka (sheep herder in Russian), needs an owner who can establish authority early on.

Pembroke Welsh Corgi

HEIGHT	WEIGHT	LIFE SPAN	
10–12in (25–30cm)	20–26lb (9–12kg)	12–15 years	Fawn and sable

A sharp and confident watchdog with a big bark for its size, this dog makes a good family pet if given enough exercise

The more widely known of the two Corgi breeds, the Pembroke Welsh Corgi is distinguished from the Cardigan Welsh Corgi (see p.60) by its slightly smaller ears, lighter build, finer features, and, in some dogs, lack of tail. The Pembroke Welsh Corgi is the younger of the two, even though its ancestry has been traced back to 1107, when Flemish weavers and farmers first imported dogs from Europe into western Wales. The two breeds were crossed for a time in the 19th century, but the Pembroke Welsh Corgi was recognized as a separate breed in 1934.

Corgis have a long history as cattle herders and guard dogs in Wales. Their low-slung shape and general agility made them ideally suited to driving cattle, sheep, and ponies to market by nipping at their heels. Today, these alert and active little dogs are still used occasionally in herding and dog agility events. Pembroke Welsh Corgis make excellent watchdogs and enjoy family life, but they may revert to their herding instincts and nip ankles, a tendency that can be minimized by early training. Corgis have a tendency to gain weight easily so need a regulated regime of diet and exercise.

The Pembroke Welsh Corgi is notable for having a feature called a "fairy saddle"—an area over the shoulders where the fur grows in a different thickness and direction from the rest of the coat. The name derives from the legend that fairies used these dogs as their steeds.

FIT FOR A QUEEN

The British royal family is well known for its love of dogs—and no breed is more closely associated with the Windsors than the Pembroke Welsh Corgi. King George VI, father of the reigning monarch, Queen Elizabeth II, acquired the first royal corgi, Rozavel Golden Eagle ("Dookie"), in 1933. The Queen has owned and bred Pembroke Welsh Corgis since she was 18 years old. One of her dogs, Monty (now deceased), starred with her in a James Bond movie sequence at the opening ceremony of the 2012 London Olympics.

Cardigan Welsh Corgi

HEIGHT 11–12in (28–31cm)
WEIGHT 24–37lb (11–17kg)
LIFE SPAN 12–15 years

Any color

White markings, if present, should not dominate.

The two varieties of Welsh Corgi were classified as separate breeds in the 1930s. Less popular as a house dog than its relative, the Pembroke Welsh Corgi (see p.58), the Cardigan Welsh Corgi can be distinguished by its larger round ears and longer body. Full of character, it fits well into a small home.

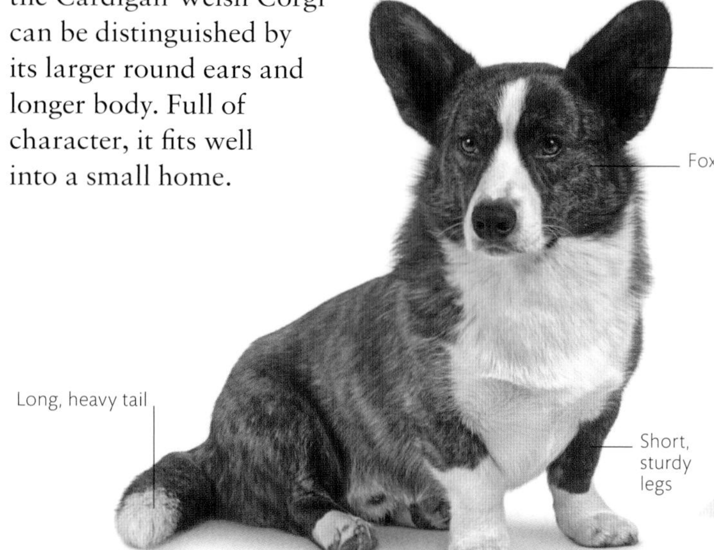

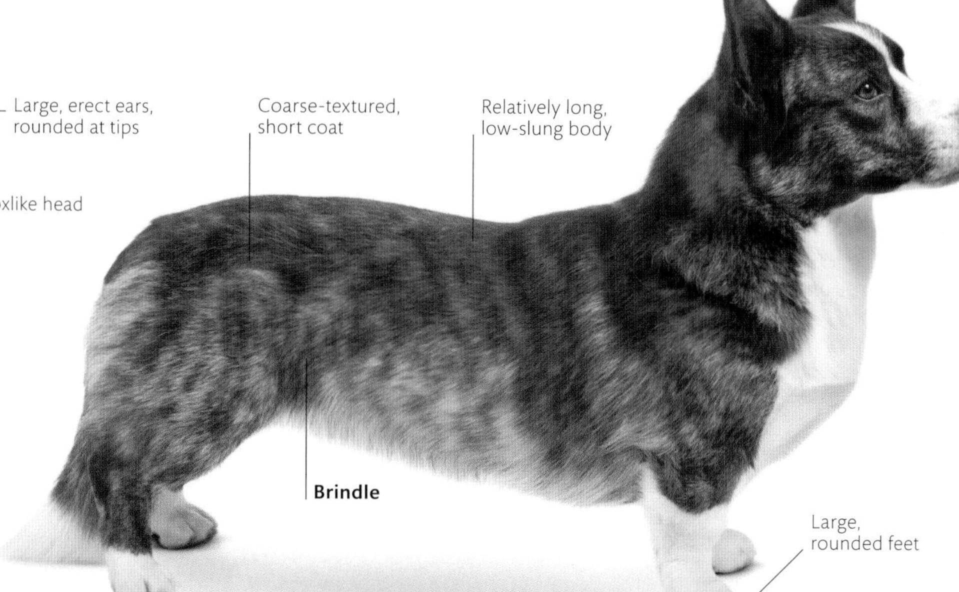

Swedish Vallhund

HEIGHT 12–14in (31–35cm)
WEIGHT 26–35lb (12–16kg)
LIFE SPAN 12–14 years

Steel-gray
Red
Red and gray coats may be mixed with brown or yellow.

Like the Welsh Corgis (above and p.58), which at first glance it closely resembles, the Swedish Vallhund was used as a cattle-herding dog. This tough and workmanlike breed continues to make itself useful on Swedish farms. Uncommon as a house dog, it is gradually becoming more widely known and appreciated for its happy personality.

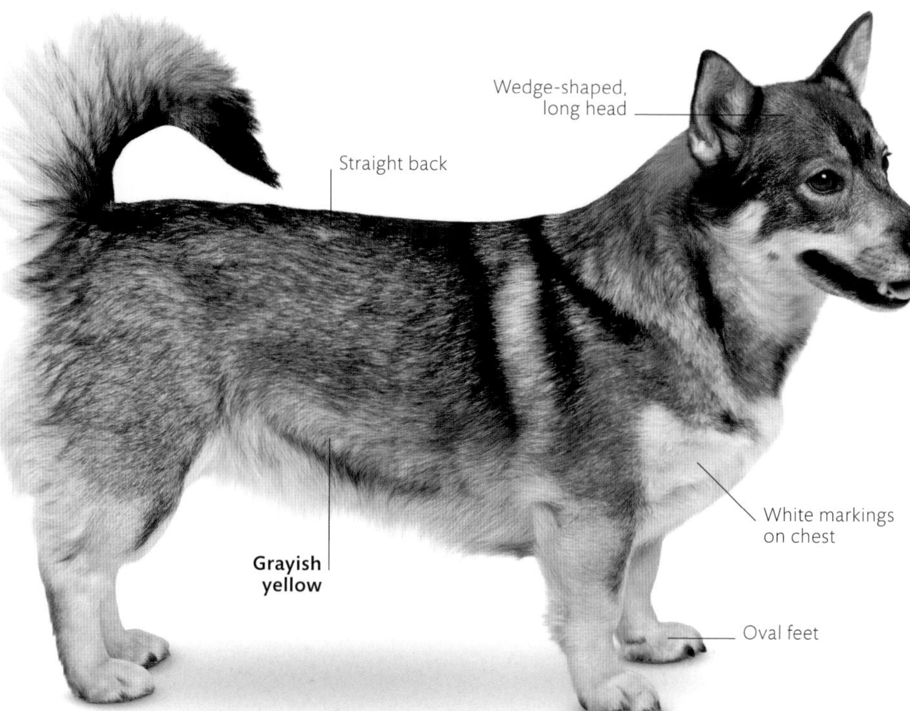

New Zealand Huntaway

HEIGHT 20–24in (50–61cm)
WEIGHT 40–66lb (18–30kg)
LIFE SPAN 12–14 years

Tricolor
Dark brindle
Currently may still appear in other colors.

The New Zealand Huntaway lacks a breed standard and is not recognized by any kennel club due to its mixed breeding, which may include German Shepherd (see p.42), Rottweiler (see p.83), and Border Collie (see p.51). Developed in New Zealand to be a working sheepdog, it is an excellent worker and is also gaining popularity as a house dog.

Australian Kelpie

HEIGHT 17–20in (43–51cm)
WEIGHT 24–44lb (11–20kg)
LIFE SPAN 10–14 years

Variety of colors

The Australian Kelpie was developed to work as a sheepdog in the vast open expanses of Australia. Energetic and agile, the breed has seemingly endless reserves of stamina and a low boredom threshold. An all-action dog, it is best suited to a working life where its herding skills can be put to full use.

Australian Cattle Dog

HEIGHT	WEIGHT	LIFE SPAN
17–20in (43–51cm)	31–40lb (14–18kg)	Over 10 years

Strong, hardy, and workmanlike, this trustworthy herding dog is a little wary of strangers

Once widely used for cattle driving and guarding, this breed is also called the Australian Heeler. It originated in the 19th century when herdsmen needed a dog that could manage semi-wild cattle on vast ranches and run for long distances in rough terrain and intense heat. In the 1840s a rancher named Thomas Hall crossed some collies with dingos, creating the "Hall's heeler" (the name "heeler" referring to the dogs' tendency to drive cattle by nipping at their heels). These dogs were, in turn, crossed with Dalmatians (see p.286), Bull Terriers (see p.197), and Kelpies (a black-and-tan herding breed). The Australian Cattle Dog breed finally became established in the 1890s.

The crossbreeding had resulted in a dog with strong herding instincts, the tough, quiet nature of a dingo, and the Dalmatian's ability to work alongside horses. Many still have the blue-merle coloring of their collie ancestors. The breed is notable for its tireless, easy gait and ability to produce sudden bursts of speed.

The Australian Cattle Dog has many merits as a family dog, being hardy, alert, and loyal to its owner. An ancestry that includes the dingo has, however, made the breed naturally suspicious of strangers. Bred to work strenuous days and cover long distances, it requires plenty of exercise. Ideally, the dog needs firm handling and work to make use of its mental and physical energy, otherwise it will become bored and stubborn. Training is not difficult because the dog is highly intelligent and willing to please; it excels in herding, obedience, and agility activities.

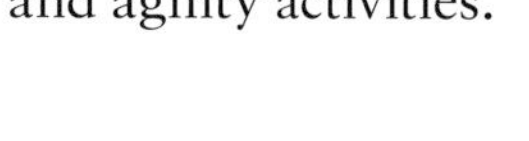

Coat longer and thicker on neck

Red speckle

LONGEST-LIVED DOG

Australian Cattle Dogs are known for being robust and healthy—but one, called Bluey, holds the Guinness World Record as the longest-lived dog. Bluey was born in June 1910 and was owned by Australian couple Les and Esma Hall. The dog worked for more than 20 years herding sheep and cattle (as below) on a diet of kangaroo and emu meat. He was finally put down in November 1939, at the age of 29 years, 5 months, and 7 days.

Lancashire Heeler

HEIGHT 10–12in (25–30cm)
WEIGHT 9–15lb (4–7kg)
LIFE SPAN 15 years

Liver and tan

Intelligent, tough, and workmanlike, the Lancashire Heeler is well suited to its original use as a cattle herder in the north of England. The breed may have been the result of crosses between the Pembroke Welsh Corgi (see p.58) and the Manchester Terrier (see p.212). Less inclined to be "nippy" than other heelers, this good-looking little dog fits well with families if trained carefully.

Bergamasco

HEIGHT 21–24in (54–62cm)
WEIGHT 57–84lb (26–38kg)
LIFE SPAN Over 10 years

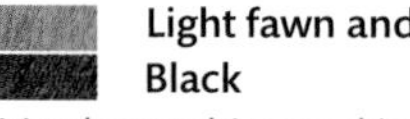

Light fawn and Isabella
Black
May have white markings.

A sheepdog and guard dog, the powerful Bergamasco was bred for a tough, outdoor life in the northern Italian mountains. Its weatherproof coat is thick, greasy to the touch, and easily becomes matted, but once the coat becomes flocked, grooming time is greatly reduced. The Bergamasco is companionable and loyal but needs firm control.

Pronounced stop on skull covered by hair

Tail carried low

Broad, straight back

Gray

Flocked coat

Pumi

HEIGHT 15–19in (38–47cm)
WEIGHT 18–33lb (8–15kg)
LIFE SPAN 12–13 years

Cream
Gray
Gold

Small, white markings may occur on chest and toes.

Developed in Hungary during the 18th century, the Pumi is a cross between the Hungarian Puli (below) and terrier-type dogs from Germany and France. An excellent herder of livestock and a good all-around farm dog, the Pumi has proved to be equally successful as a house dog. Bold and restless, this breed thrives on action.

Hungarian Puli

HEIGHT 14–17in (36–44cm)
WEIGHT 22–33lb (10–15kg)
LIFE SPAN Over 12 years

White
Gray
Fawn

May have small, white markings on chest and feet.

Thought to have been brought into central Europe by the nomadic Magyar tribes of Asia, the Hungarian Puli was traditionally used as a herding dog. Affectionate and quick to learn, it makes a good family pet but gets bored easily without fun and company. Its corded coat needs special attention.

Komondor

HEIGHT	WEIGHT	LIFE SPAN
24–31in (60–80cm)	79–135lb (36–61kg)	Under 10 years

Not for novices, this large, powerful dog needs an experienced owner who will give it time and attention

The Komondor is descended from guard dogs brought to Hungary by a people called the Cumans, as they migrated westward from what is now China to the Danube basin. The earliest written evidence of dogs of this type dates from the mid-16th century, but they may have existed for centuries earlier. It was not until the early 20th century that the breed became known outside Hungary.

The Komondor was traditionally used to protect sheep, goats, and cattle from wolves and bears. Left by their human owners, they lived among the flocks and worked independently to guard the livestock from predators. Many were used to guard military installations during World War II and were killed in service, and as a result the breed nearly died out. However, a number of dogs were saved by a few dedicated breeders. Today the largest populations are in Hungary and the US, where dogs have been used to guard livestock from coyotes and other predators. Although generally quiet and reserved in nature, the Komondor will fearlessly act to tackle anything it sees as a threat. The breed has strong guarding instincts and can be loyal protectors of their home, although they are more suited to being outdoor or farm dogs than family pets. The Komondor's independent nature and instincts, combined with considerable size and strength, mean that ownership should be considered only by those with plenty of dog-handling experience and space. Daily grooming is essential to maintain the Komondor's extraordinary tasseled coat.

PUPPY

IN SHEEP'S CLOTHING

Not only does the Komondor look like the native Hungarian sheep it is bred to protect, it is treated like one. The puppies are raised with sheep from infancy and live with them all year round so the sheep are not afraid of them. The dogs in turn treat the sheep as members of their pack and protect them. Raised in human company they have similar protective habits toward family members. The Komondor is even shorn like a sheep each summer to remove the long, woolly coat that protects it from the cold in winter.

Aidi

HEIGHT 21–24in (53–61cm)
WEIGHT 51–55lb (23–25kg)
LIFE SPAN About 12 years

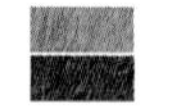

Fawn **Brown** (right)
Black
Fawn, brown, and black coats may be spotted with white.

Also known as the Atlas Mountain Dog, this type of dog has been used for centuries as a guard dog by the nomadic peoples of Morocco. The Aidi is faithful, fearless, and always on the alert to protect its owners and their possessions. But its strong guarding instincts mean that this dog is not always suited to a domestic lifestyle.

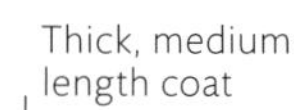

Australian Shepherd

HEIGHT 18–23in (46–58cm)
WEIGHT 40–65lb (18–29kg)
LIFE SPAN Over 10 years

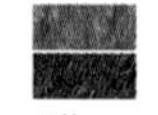

Red, red merle
Black
All coats may have tan markings.

Not an "Aussie" at all, this shepherd dog was bred in the US. Its name derives from its ancestors, which were worked by Basque shepherds who emigrated to Australia in the late 19th century and then later moved on to the US. The Australian Shepherd, still useful as a ranch dog and tracker, is becoming increasingly valued as a pet.

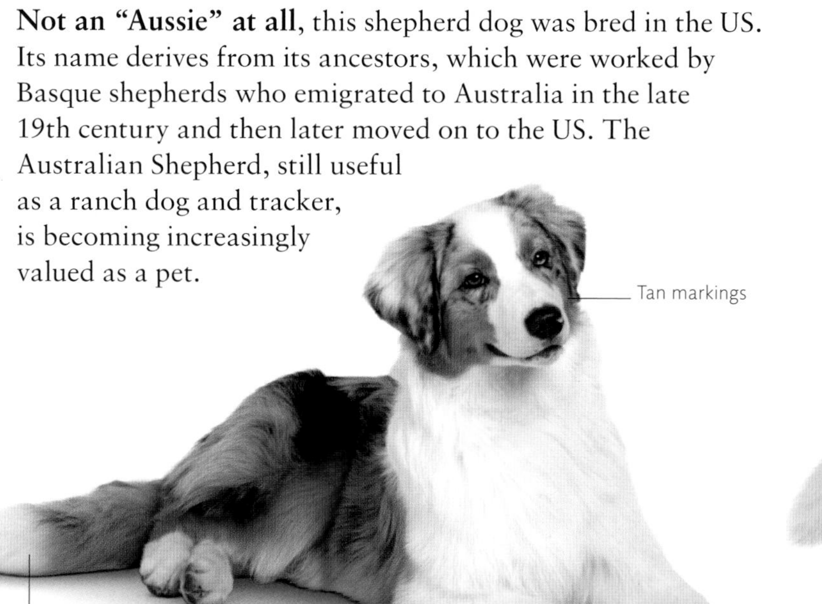

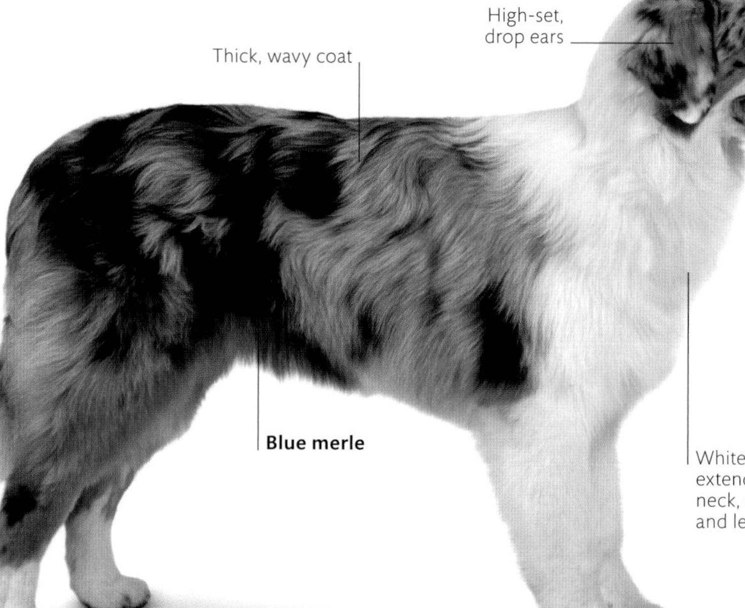

Hellenic Shepherd Dog

HEIGHT 24–30in (60–75cm)
WEIGHT 71–110lb (32–50kg)
LIFE SPAN 12 years

Variety of colors

The ancestors of this breed, which is also known as the Greek Sheepdog, may have been the sheepdogs brought into Greece many centuries ago by Turkish migrants. Tough, brave, and a natural guardian and flock leader, the Hellenic Shepherd Dog has excellent qualities for a working dog, but is too dominant in temperament to make a reliable family companion. There are two coat types: long-haired and short-haired.

Maremma Sheepdog

HEIGHT 24–29in (60–73cm)
WEIGHT 66–99lb (30–45kg)
LIFE SPAN Over 10 years

The sheep herders of the central Italian plains have long used the Maremma Sheepdog to guard their flocks. With an imposing stance and a magnificent, thick, white coat, this handsome dog has obvious attractions but needs expert handling. Like many dogs bred for outdoor work, this sheepdog is not the ideal choice for the home.

Cursinu

HEIGHT 18–23in (46–58cm)
WEIGHT Not known
LIFE SPAN Over 10 years

Dogs of this type have existed on the island of Corsica for over a hundred years, although the Cursinu has only been recognized in France since 2003. Energetic, fast-moving, and versatile, it is used for both hunting and herding and, although it can adapt to home life, it is probably at its best as a working dog.

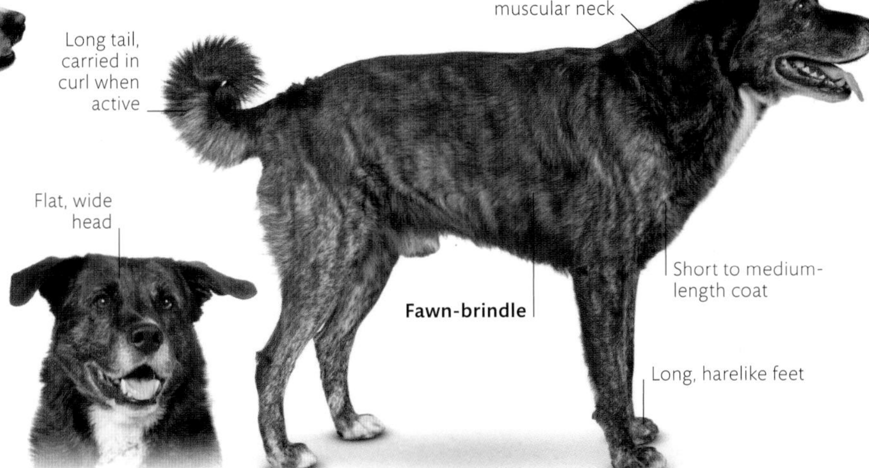

Romanian Shepherd Dogs

HEIGHT	WEIGHT	LIFE SPAN		
23–31in (59–78cm)	77–154lb (35–70kg)	12–14 years	White-beige Black	Bucovina only may appear as white, white-beige, black, or ashen-gray and may have patches of color.

CARPATIN

MOLOSSUS DOGS

Said to be descendants of ancient molossus dogs that were crossed with local domestic dogs, the Romanian Shepherd Dog is an impressive animal. The ancient molossus dogs were used in battle, for hunting (as seen in this frieze from c.645BCE), and for guarding property and working with livestock. Those used for herding were said by Aristotle (384–322BCE) to be "superior to others in size, and in the courage with which they face the attacks of wild animals." These attributes are essential for the Romanian Shepherd Dogs that are used to guard livestock today.

These watchful and courageous dogs need space and freedom to run and may be wary of strangers

In the mountainous Carpathian region of Romania, shepherds rely on large, robust dogs to guard their flocks in all weather. Regional breeding has resulted in several distinct types: the three main forms are the Carpatin, the Bucovina, and the Mioritic. The lean, wolflike Carpatin originated in the lower Carpathian-Danube area of eastern Romania; the heavier Molossoid Bucovina was developed in the northeastern mountains; and the shaggy-haired Mioritic arose in the north. All types have to be strong and courageous to defend livestock against predators such as wolves, bears, and lynxes. From the 1930s onward efforts were made to preserve all three types. The different Romanian Shepherd Dog breeds were provisionally recognized by the FCI in the early years of this century.

Romanian Shepherd Dogs are little known outside their native country. All types are better suited to outdoor rather than indoor life, and none is widely known as a companion dog. With strong watchdog instincts, Romanian Shepherd Dogs are highly territorial and suspicious of strangers. They need plenty of activity, as well as early socialization and firm training.

CARPATIN

MIORITIC

Appenzell Cattle Dog

HEIGHT 20–22in (50–56cm)
WEIGHT 49–71lb (22–32kg)
LIFE SPAN 12–13 years

Bred for herding and guarding on Alpine farms, the Appenzell Cattle Dog has also taken well to urban life. The breed has a firm following in Switzerland but is not yet widely known elsewhere. Keen, alert, and full of energy, this dog is at its best when kept occupied.

Entlebucher Mountain Dog

HEIGHT 17–20in (42–50cm)
WEIGHT 46–62lb (21–28kg)
LIFE SPAN 11–15 years

The smallest of several long-established Swiss mountain dogs, this cattle-driving breed from the Entlebuch valley is gaining popularity as a house dog. Bouncing with high spirits, the Entlebucher Mountain Dog is confident and well behaved within the family, but has strong protective instincts and is inclined to be wary around strangers.

Bernese Mountain Dog

HEIGHT	WEIGHT	LIFE SPAN
23–28in (58–70cm)	71–120lb (32–54kg)	Under 10 years

A beautifully marked, versatile breed with an attractive personality and kind nature, this dog enjoys family life

This lovely dog takes its name from the Swiss canton of Berne, where it traditionally worked as an all-purpose farm dog; it was also used to pull carts to transport goods such as milk and cheese to market. The breed began to decline in the 19th century as other types of dog were imported to Switzerland. Initial work on restoring the breed was done by Franz Schertenlieb who traveled all over Switzerland looking for dogs and, later, a Swiss professor called Albert Heim began working to preserve and promote the breed too. A breed club was formed in 1907, and during the 20th century the breed became popular worldwide.

The Bernese Mountain Dog is attractive in both looks and nature, and has become popular as a family dog. Slow to mature, these dogs keep their puppyish tendencies for longer than other breeds. Although large and strong, the dogs are not overly dominant. They enjoy human company and need to spend a lot of time around people, rather than be confined to a kennel or yard. The breed is affectionate and reliable with children. In recent years it has become popular as a therapy dog for older people, sick children, or those with special needs. It is also still used for farm work as well as search and rescue work.

The eye-catching tricolor coat needs plenty of grooming to maintain its silky texture and characteristic soft sheen. The coat is heavy, so this dog is not suited to extremely warm climates.

CART DOGS

In the past, people who couldn't afford a horse would use dogs to pull carts, leading to the development of breeds such as the Bernese Mountain Dog. This breed was used in the summer to transport milk, and later cheese, from the mountains where the cattle grazed to the valleys below. Because of this practice, dogs were sometimes referred to locally as Cheese Dogs. When not working as a draft animal, the Bernese Mountain Dog was used to control stock and guard property.

PUPPY

Tricolor

Triangular, drop ears

White blaze on head

Broad, deep chest with white markings

Long, bushy, jet-black tail

Long, silky, slightly wavy coat

Reddish brown markings extend down to feet

Broad head with well-defined stop

Greater Swiss Mountain Dog

HEIGHT 24–28in (60–72cm)
WEIGHT 79–130lb (36–59kg)
LIFE SPAN 8–11 years

Bred in the Swiss Alps, this huge, strong, striking dog was once used to haul carts full of dairy produce, for cattle herding, and for guard duties. The dog had all but disappeared by the beginning of the 20th century, but breeding by enthusiasts saved it from extinction; however, it is still rare. A true working dog, its agreeable temperament makes it a sociable family companion for those with room to spare.

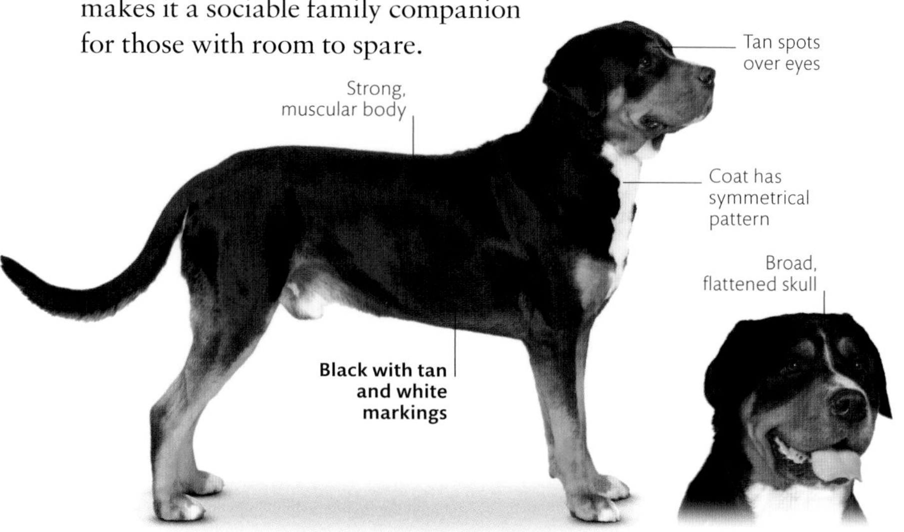

White Swiss Shepherd Dog

HEIGHT 21–26in (53–66cm)
WEIGHT 55–88lb (25–40kg)
LIFE SPAN 8–11 years

Pure white shepherd dogs were first brought into Switzerland from North America in the 1970s. Developed over the next two decades, it was recognized in Switzerland as a breed in 1991. Good-tempered and intelligent, it is suitable for both work and companionship. There are two coat types: medium-haired and long-haired.

Anatolian Shepherd Dog

HEIGHT 28–32in (71–81cm)
WEIGHT 90–141lb (41–64kg)
LIFE SPAN 12–15 years

 Any color

After a long history as a livestock guardian, this hardy and powerful breed is still used in Turkey as a working dog. Bred for its courage and independence of spirit, the Anatolian Shepherd Dog respects the authority of a firm and loving owner. If kept as a companion dog, training and socializing should begin early.

Kangal Dog

HEIGHT 28–31in (70–80cm)
WEIGHT 88–143lb (40–65kg)
LIFE SPAN 12–15 years

Pale brown
Pale gray
White markings on feet and chest only.

Known as the national dog of Turkey, the Kangal Dog is a mastiff-type mountain dog bred in central Turkey to guard flocks against wolves, jackals, and bears. The breed is strongly protective toward its human family. It is independent-minded and needs experienced handling and a lot of exercise.

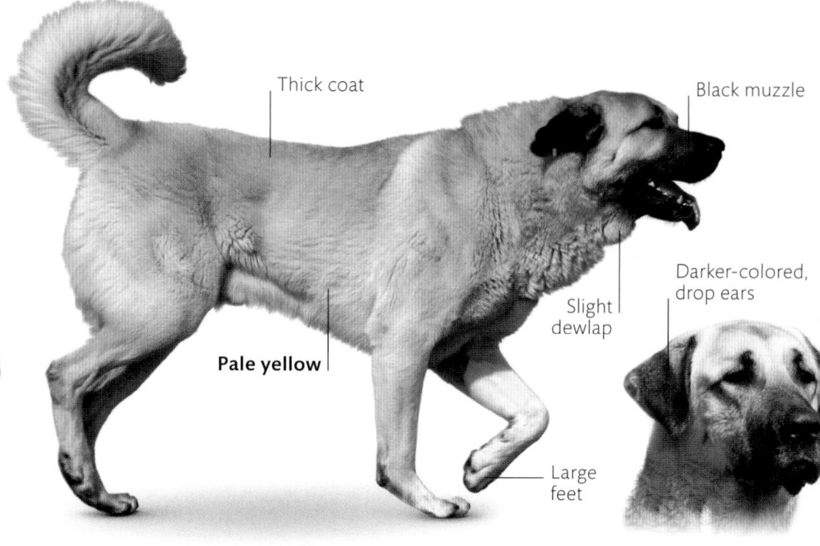

Akbash

HEIGHT 27–31in (69–79cm)
WEIGHT 75–130lb (34–59kg)
LIFE SPAN 10–11 years

A powerful Turkish breed developed for guarding flocks, Akbash-ype dogs have probably been around for several thousands of years. Jsed on ranches in North America as a livestock and property guard, the Akbash is best suited to a working life and needs skilled andling to prevent behavior problems. There are two coat types: nedium-haired and long-haired.

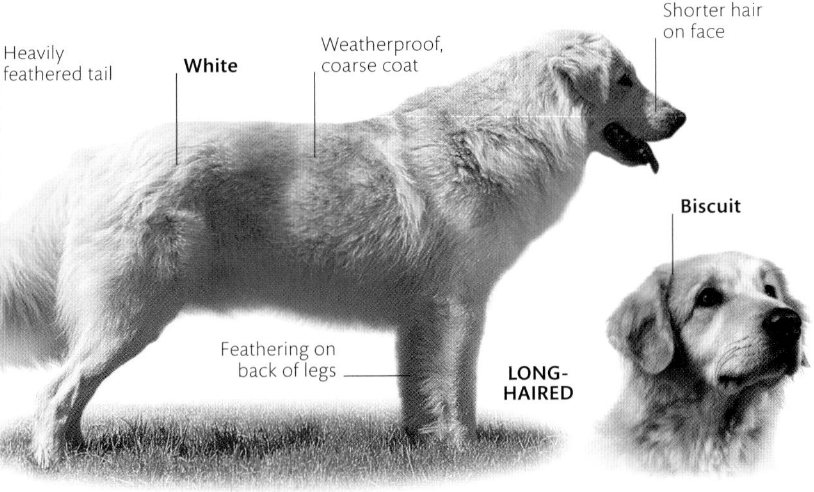

Central Asian Shepherd Dog

HEIGHT 26–31in (65–78cm)
WEIGHT 88–174lb (40–79kg)
LIFE SPAN 12–14 years

Variety of colors

The nomadic herdsmen of Central Asia—the regions now known as Kazakhstan, Turkmenistan, Tajikistan, Uzbekistan, and Kyrgyzstan—have used dogs of this type to protect their flocks for hundreds of years. Once bred selectively in the former USSR, this rare breed needs early socialization. There are two coat types: short-haired and long-haired.

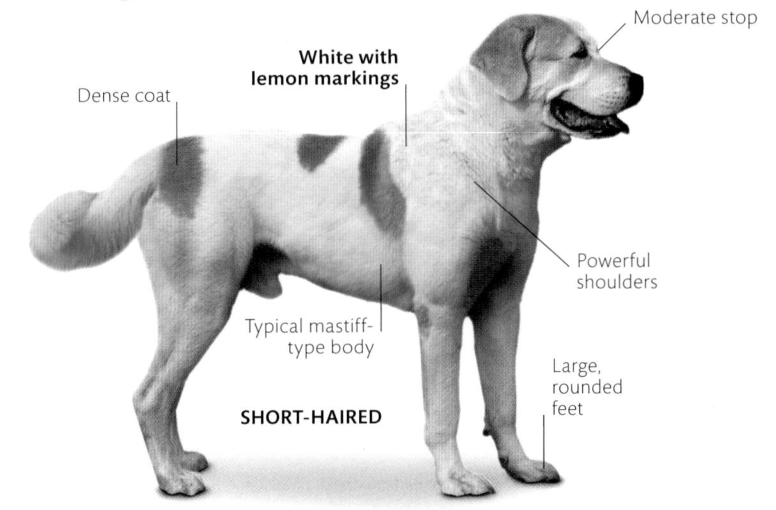

Caucasian Shepherd Dog

HEIGHT 26–30in (67–75cm)
WEIGHT 99–154lb (45–70kg)
LIFE SPAN 10–11 years

Variety of colors

Developed from various large dogs, this shepherd dog was once used to guard flocks in the Caucasian regions. In the 1920s selective breeding of this dog began in the former USSR and continued later in Germany. An excellent watchdog, it requires careful handling if it is to be a good companion.

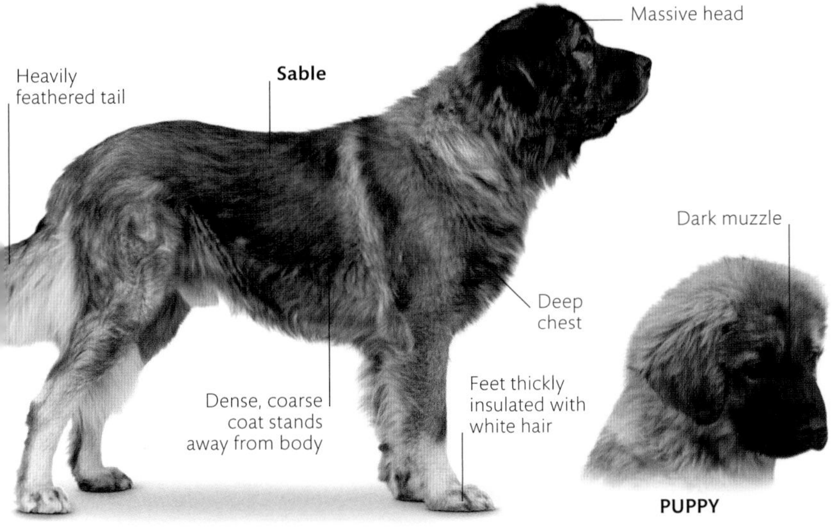

Leonberger

HEIGHT 28–31in (72–80cm)
WEIGHT 99–170lb (45–77kg)
LIFE SPAN Over 10 years

Sandy
Red
May have white markings.

Named after the Bavarian town of Leonberg, this breed was developed in the mid-19th century by crossing a St. Bernard (see p.76) with a Newfoundland (see p.79). After the two World Wars, Leonbergers had almost disappeared, but the breed has recovered and is popular for its splendid looks and friendly nature.

Saint Bernard

HEIGHT	WEIGHT	LIFE SPAN	
28–30in (70–75cm)	130–180lb (59–81kg)	8–10 years	Brindle

This kindly giant has a delightful temperament but its unrivaled size prohibits it from being a pet for many

Originating in the 18th century, this breed was created by the monks of St. Bernard's Hospice in the Swiss Alps. The monks crossbred the various mastiff-type dogs that had existed in the Swiss valleys for centuries, probably for use as watchdogs and companions. The dogs' unique rescue duties date from the late 18th century. The animals could smell people hidden under snow and sense impending avalanches. The monks sent the dogs out in groups to find lost travelers; one dog would lie beside a casualty to keep the person warm while another would return to the monastery to alert the monks. However, the image of the rescuing Saint Bernard carrying a cask of medicinal brandy around his neck is apochryphal.

During the severe winters of 1816–18 many dogs died doing rescue work, and numbers fell dangerously low. In the 1830s some crosses were made with Newfoundland dogs (see p.78), but the crossbreeds' long hair picked up too much snow and ice, making them unsuitable for rescue work. The crosses were given away and the monks returned to breeding the shorter-haired dogs. During the 19th century the breed became popular outside Switzerland, particularly in England where the Saint Bernard was crossed with English Mastiffs to produce a larger, heavier dog.

The Saint Bernard is calm and affectionate, and is especially good with children. It is relatively rare as a house dog due to its giant size and its need for plenty of space and food. There are two coat types: smooth-haired and rough-haired.

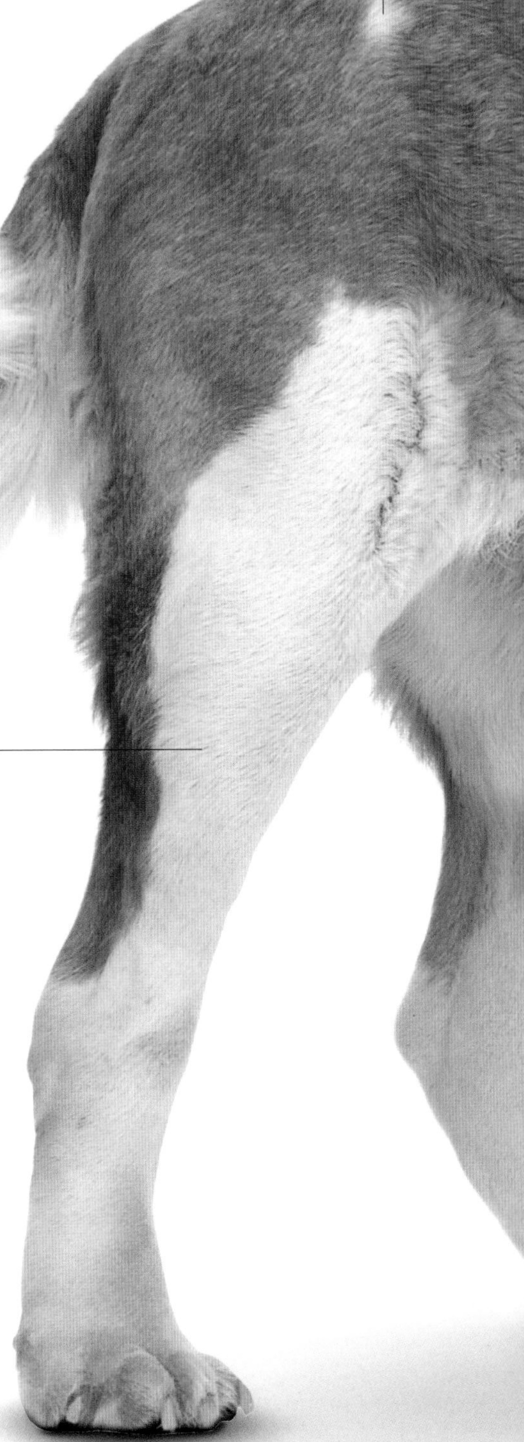

BARRY THE MOUNTAIN RESCUE DOG

The most famous Saint Bernard rescue dog was a male named Barry, who lived from 1800 to 1814. He was owned by the monks of St. Bernard's Hospice. Barry is said to have rescued more than 40 people, including a young boy whom he found in a cavern of ice; the dog revived the boy by licking him, and then carried him back to the monks. Since then, the hospice has always named one of their dogs Barry in his honor. A monument to the original Barry (right) can be found in the Paris dog cemetery.

CIMETIÈRE DES CHIENS D'ASNIÉRES-SUR-SEINE, PARIS, FRANCE

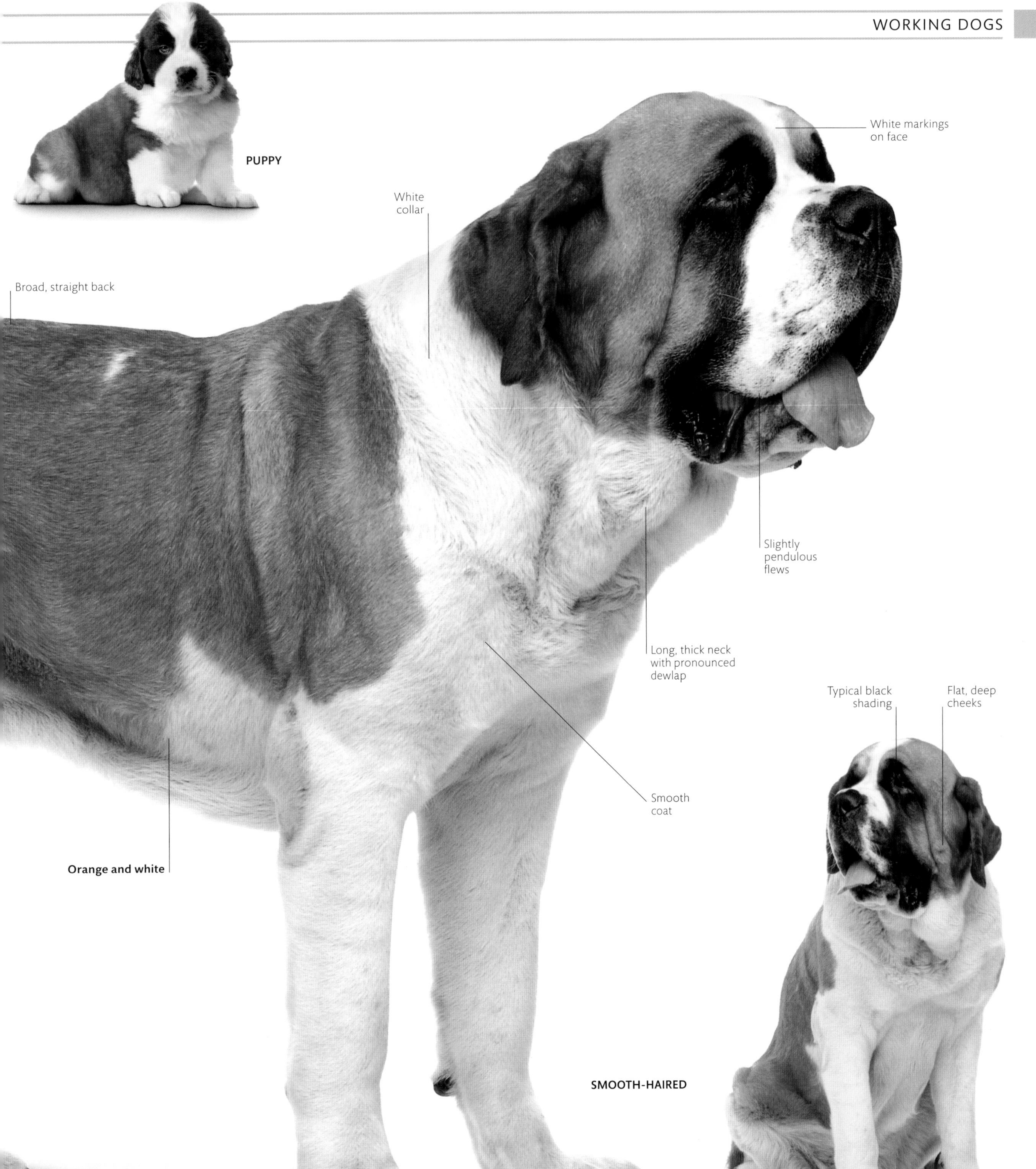

PUPPY

White collar

White markings on face

Broad, straight back

Slightly pendulous flews

Long, thick neck with pronounced dewlap

Typical black shading

Flat, deep cheeks

Smooth coat

Orange and white

SMOOTH-HAIRED

Tatra Shepherd Dog

HEIGHT 24–28in (60–70cm)
WEIGHT 79–130lb (36–59kg)
LIFE SPAN 10–12 years

Still used for protecting and herding flocks in the high Tatra mountains of Poland, this huge and handsome dog takes its duties just as seriously when guarding home and household. Usually gentle with those it knows, this breed requires an experienced owner with a watchful eye for potential aggression if it is to be kept as a companion.

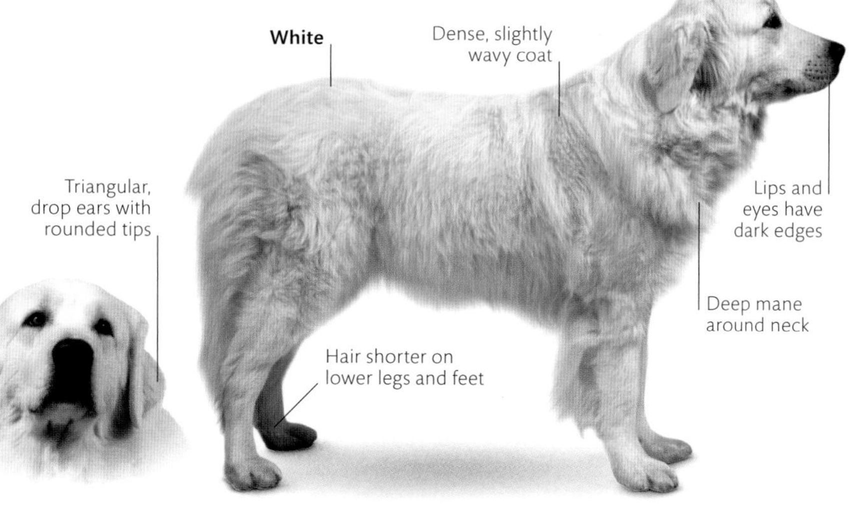

Pyrenean Mastiff

HEIGHT 28–32in (72–81cm)
WEIGHT 120–154lb (54–70kg)
LIFE SPAN 10 years

A native of Spain, the Pyrenean Mastiff was originally kept for guarding mountain flocks. Large and courageous enough to take on a bear or a wolf, this breed is now often used as a house guard. Intelligent and calm, it can also be a good companion dog if it has the right training.

Great Pyrenees

HEIGHT 26–28in (65–70cm)
WEIGHT 88–110lb (40–50kg)
LIFE SPAN 9–11 years

Pure white

One of the most imposing of all dogs, this breed comes from the French Pyrenees, where its traditional role was as a guarder of flocks. Thoroughly assimilated into modern family life, the Great Pyrenees is calm-natured and unaggressive, reliable in the home, and good with children. Despite the dog's huge size and strength, it does not need an excessive amount of exercise. Owners should, however, be prepared to put their energies into grooming.

Newfoundland

HEIGHT 26–28in (66–71cm)
WEIGHT 110–152lb (50–69kg)
LIFE SPAN 9–11 years

Dark brown

Although the Newfoundland is associated with the Canadian province of the same name, the dog's true origins are uncertain. Historically employed by fishermen to retrieve nets, it is sometimes used today for sea rescues. The breed has a protective nature and is renowned for being gentle with children. Its large size rules this dog out as a pet for a small home.

Landseer

HEIGHT 26–28in (66–71cm)
WEIGHT 110–152lb (50–69kg)
LIFE SPAN 9–11 years

This color variant of the Newfoundland (above) is regarded as a distinct breed in some countries. The Landseer is named after the mid-Victorian British painter Sir Edwin Landseer, who often painted these dogs. Aside from its bicolored coat, this dog shares all the attributes of solid-colored Newfoundlands, being placid, friendly, and dependable.

Tibetan Mastiff

HEIGHT	WEIGHT	LIFE SPAN		
24–26in (61–66cm)	80–220lb (36–100kg)	Over 10 years	Slate-gray Gold Black	Black and slate-gray dogs may have tan markings.

)ne of the smaller mastiffs, this independent dog is ›xtremely loyal but may take time to train and socialize

)**ne of the world's oldest dog breeds**, the 'ibetan Mastiff was traditionally used to uard livestock by nomadic shepherds in the Iimalayas, as well as to protect villages and ıonasteries. The dogs were often left to oam free at night to guard villages, or left ›ehind to guard shepherds' families when the ıen moved their flocks to higher pastures.

Ancestors of these dogs were brought vestward with the armies of Attila the Hun nd Genghis Khan, laying the foundations for some of today's giant Molossus breeds.

Since the 18th century small numbers of Tibetan Mastiffs have been exported to the West, but the breed only started to become well-known in the UK from the 1970s onward. Tibetan Mastiffs are also becoming popular in China, where they are regarded as bringers of health and prosperity.

In its native country, the Tibetan Mastiff can still be rather large and fierce. However, in the West, selective breeding and training have greatly reduced any aggressive tendencies. The Tibetan Mastiff has strong protective instincts, especially with children. It is a good house dog and companion, although it is fairly independent-minded and not overtly affectionate. The breed takes time to reach full maturity and needs thorough, steady training.

Tibetan Mastiff bitches come into season once a year rather than twice, as is usual for dogs. The coat needs plenty of grooming and is not suited for hot, humid climates, but it does not have dander, which reduces the risk of allergic reactions.

PUPPY

THE WORLD'S MOST EXPENSIVE DOG

The Tibetan Mastiff is still uncommon beyond its native land, but this ancient breed has become something of a status symbol in China. In 2011 a young dog named *Hong Dong* (Big Splash) was sold to a Chinese coal baron for 10 million yuan (just over $1.5 million), so becoming the world's most expensive dog. Big Splash was prized not only for being a perfect physical specimen, but also because his coat was red—a lucky color in China.

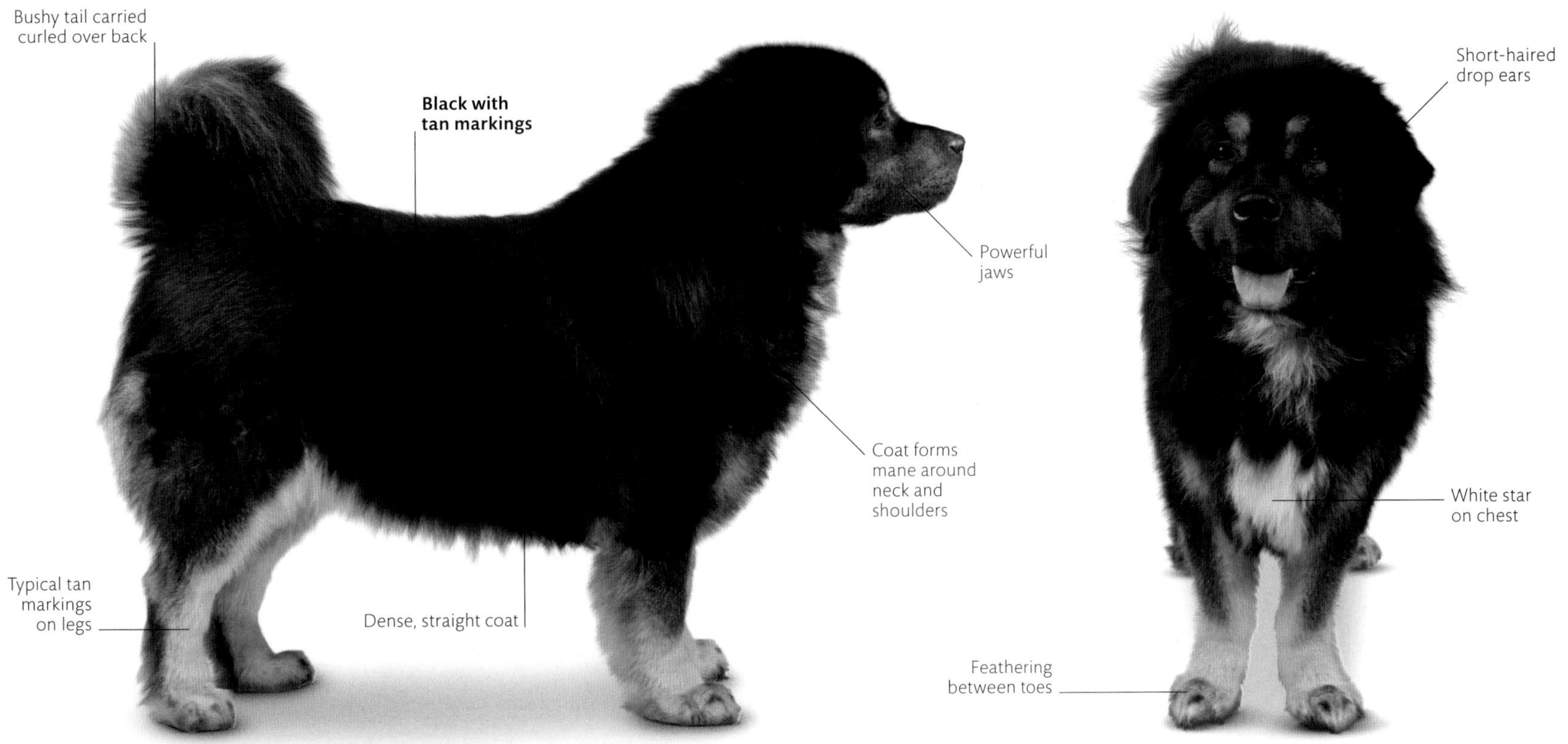

Tibetan Kyi Apso

HEIGHT 22–28in (56–71cm)
WEIGHT 68–84lb (31–38kg)
LIFE SPAN 7–10 years

Any color

Only a handful of Kyi Apsos have appeared outside Tibet and the breed is elusive even in its own country. Traditionally, this dog is a guard of flocks and homes. The Tibetan Kyi Apso has a characteristic springy gait, and is agile and capable of rapid bursts of speed.

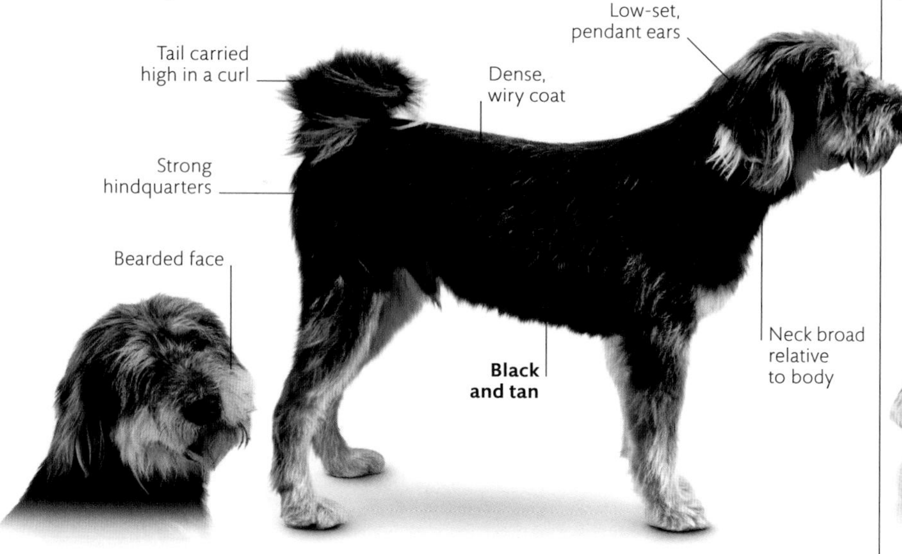

Slovakian Chuvach

HEIGHT 23–28in (59–70cm)
WEIGHT 68–97lb (31–44kg)
LIFE SPAN 11–13 years

Originally a shepherd's guard dog from the Slovakian Alps, the Slovakian Chuvach has been developed successfully into a good house dog. This large, powerful breed retains the alertness and watchfulness that made it a superb defender of farms and livestock. Tactful training is needed to achieve the best results.

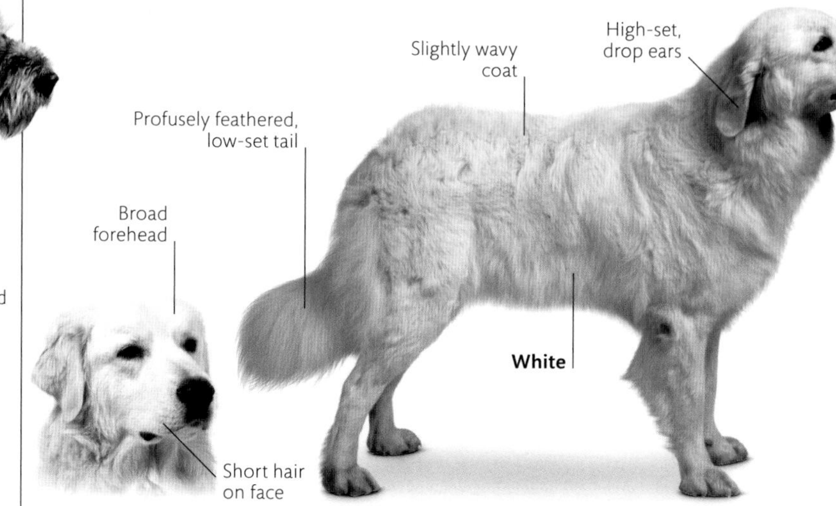

Kuvasz

HEIGHT 26–30in (66–75cm)
WEIGHT 71–115lb (32–52kg)
LIFE SPAN 10–12 years

Probably the oldest and best known of Hungary's breeds, the Kuvasz was once used as a shepherd's guard dog. The breed's naturally protective instincts may lead to aggressiveness, and it takes firm training to make the Kuvasz an acceptable house dog.

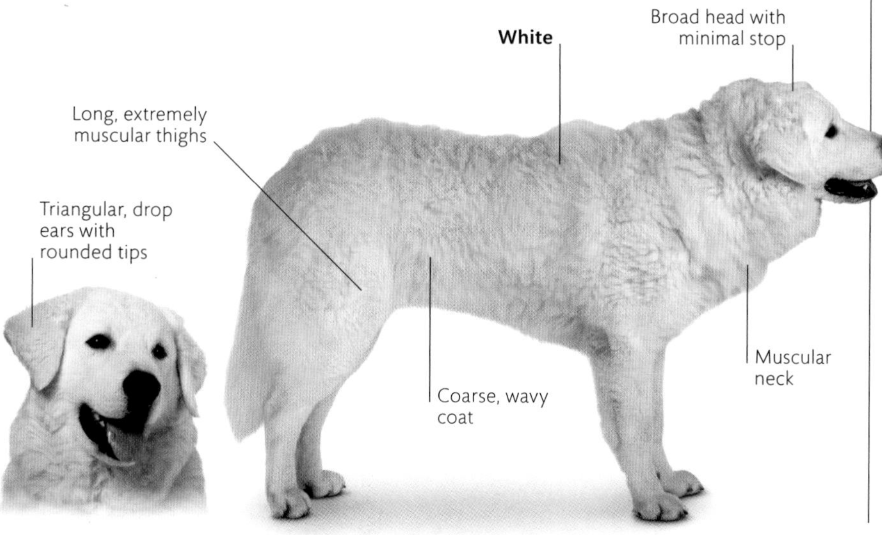

Hovawart

HEIGHT 23–28in (58–70cm)
WEIGHT 62–99lb (28–45kg)
LIFE SPAN 10–14 years

Blonde

Little known as a companion dog but growing in popularity, the Hovawart's forerunners were used as farm dogs in the 13th century. The modern breed was developed in Germany in the first half of the 20th century. Very hardy and ready to go outdoors in any weather, it is a friendly and faithful house dog. The Hovawart is not difficult to train but may need careful handling around other dogs.

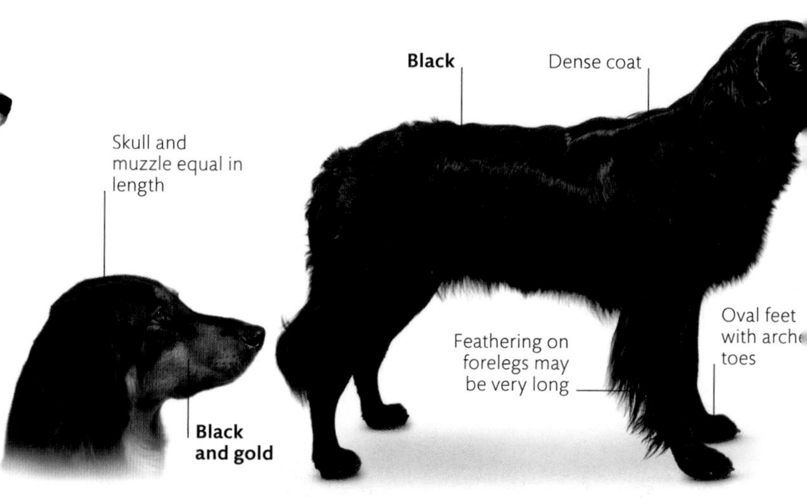

Rottweiler

HEIGHT	WEIGHT	LIFE SPAN
23–27in (58–69cm)	84–130lb (38–59kg)	10–11 years

This big, burly, protective dog makes a good companion if well socialized by an experienced owner

The Rottweiler is descended from dogs used by Roman armies to drive cattle on long marches. Some of the drovers and their dogs settled in southern Germany, where the dogs were interbred with local cattle dogs. The breed was centered in the livestock-trading town of Rottweil in southern Germany, where they were used to herd and drive cattle, hunt bear, and pull carts as butchers' dogs. During the 19th century these jobs died out and the breed dwindled almost to extinction. It was revived in the early 20th century, particularly for work as a police dog because of its guarding and fighting instinct. Today, Rottweilers are extensively used by military and police forces, as guard dogs, and in search and rescue work.

The Rottweiler has acquired an image as a vicious guard dog and an intimidating status symbol. However, despite the breed's great strength, impressive swagger, and easily aroused protective responses, it is not naturally ill-tempered. With thoughtful training from a firm and experienced owner who is alert to potential triggers of aggression, this dog makes a calm and obedient companion. Rottweilers are more agile than their size and sturdy build might suggest, and appreciate plenty of vigorous exercise.

IN SAFE HANDS

The eagerness of a Rottweiler to please its owner makes it an easy and rewarding dog to train. This quality combined with its size and strength makes it an ideal dog for law enforcement and security work. Quick to react, and obedient to its handler, it has sufficient strength to restrain even the most persistent of law breakers. Employed extensively by the military and police in Germany during WWI, the Rottweiler was introduced to the US and the UK in the 1930s. They are now the police dog of choice in several countries.

Broad head with well-defined stop

Small, drop ears

Short, smooth, shiny coat

Deep muzzle with firm flews

Tan chest markings

Black and tan

Tan markings on legs

Tan markings clearly defined on head

Broad, deep chest

Chinese Shar-Pei

HEIGHT
18–20in
(46–51cm)

WEIGHT
40–55lb
(18–25kg)

LIFE SPAN
Over 10 years

Variety of colors

A generally friendly temperament is hidden behind this dog's scowling face

The origins of this native Chinese breed are not known, but dogs of this type are shown on pottery dating from the Han dynasty (206BCE–220CE) and are mentioned in manuscripts dating from the 13th century. The Chinese Shar-Pei's traditional jobs included herding and guarding livestock, hunting, and fighting; the dog's wrinkled skin and bristly coat made it difficult for other dogs to grab hold of the animal. (The name Shar-Pei roughly means "sandy coat," referring to the rough texture of the hair).

During the 20th century the numbers dwindled almost to extinction in mainland China, although the Shar-Pei was still being bred in Hong Kong and Taiwan. In the 1970s the breed became popular in the US, and, at least for a while, owning a Chinese Shar-Pei became a fashion statement due to its rarity. People started breeding the dogs to accentuate their wrinkled faces, producing what the Chinese called the meat-mouth type (as opposed to the traditional, cleaner-faced bone-mouth form). However, breeding for excessively loose and folded facial skin caused the dogs to develop entropion (a painful condition in which the eyelashes turn inward), and so this practice has now largely stopped.

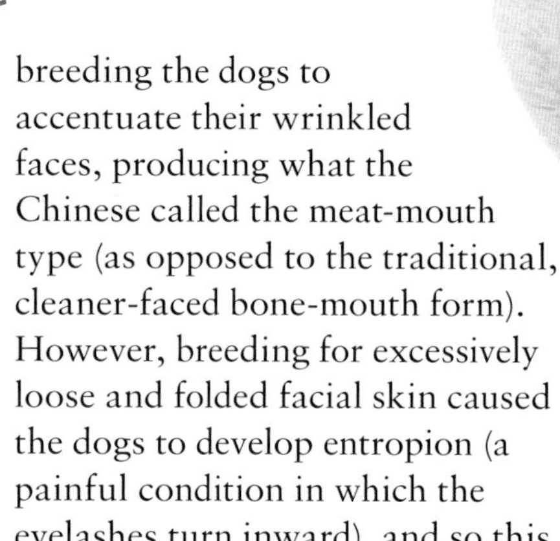

PUPPY

The Chinese Shar-Pei's amiable nature and compact size make it suitable for a town or country home. The dog's distinctive appearance includes the famous wrinkles, which are limited to the head and shoulders on adults; a blue tongue; small, triangular ears; and a snub nose, which some Chinese people call a butterfly-cookie nose. The coat varies in length from very short and prickly to the touch (the horse coat) to slightly longer and smoother hair (the brush coat).

Tail carried high and curved over

FIT FOR THE TASK

The similarity between dog artifacts of the Han dynasty (206BCE–220CE) and the Shar-Pei are very striking, despite the drop ears and much looser, wrinkled skin of the modern dog. It is thought that these features were developed when the Shar-Pei was used as a fighting dog. Small, drop ears minimized the chance of injury, and the loose skin prevented its adversary from getting a firm grip, allowing the Chinese Shar-Pei to maneuver and defend itself.

EARTHENWARE STATUE, EASTERN HAN DYNASTY

Wrinkles on forehead give frowning expression
Small, high-set, button ears
Wrinkled skin over shoulders and neck
Typical flews of a meat-mouth type
Back dips slightly behind withers
Short, velvety, "horse" coat
Square, sturdily built body
Broad muzzle with fleshy flews
Fawn
Loose skin on back and legs wrinkles when dog is seated

Beauceron

HEIGHT 25–28in (63–70cm)
WEIGHT 65–85lb (29–39kg)
LIFE SPAN 10–15 years

Gray, black, and tan

May have a few white chest hairs.

A herding and guard dog from the flatlands of the Beauce region in central France, the Beauceron is an excellent worker and, in the right situation, a gentle family companion. This big, strong dog can be intolerant of other dogs; early training is needed to minimize potential problems.

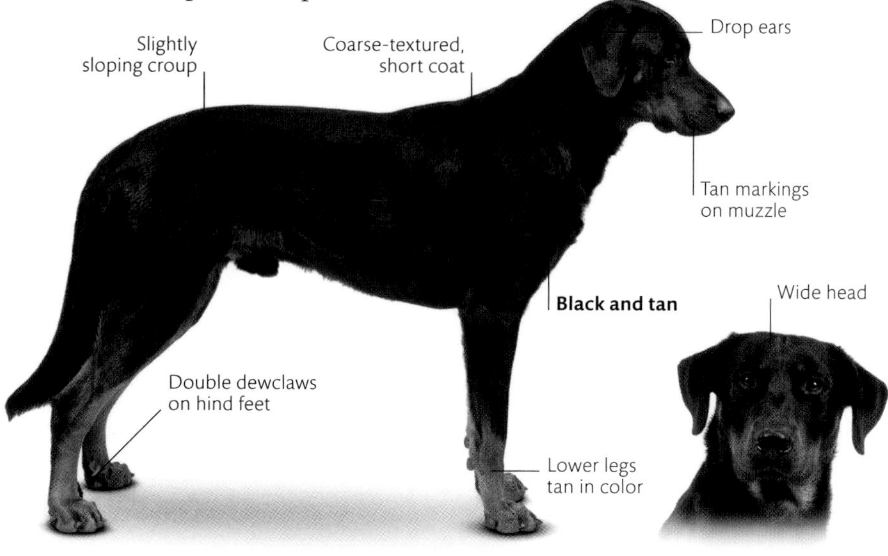

Majorca Shepherd Dog

HEIGHT 24–29in (62–73cm)
WEIGHT 77–88lb (35–40kg)
LIFE SPAN 11–13 years

Comparatively rare worldwide, the Majorca Shepherd Dog is regarded with pride in Majorca, where it was once widely used as a shepherd dog, and is now popular as a show dog. Although usually willing to obey, this breed has strong herding instincts and can be defensive with strangers and other dogs.

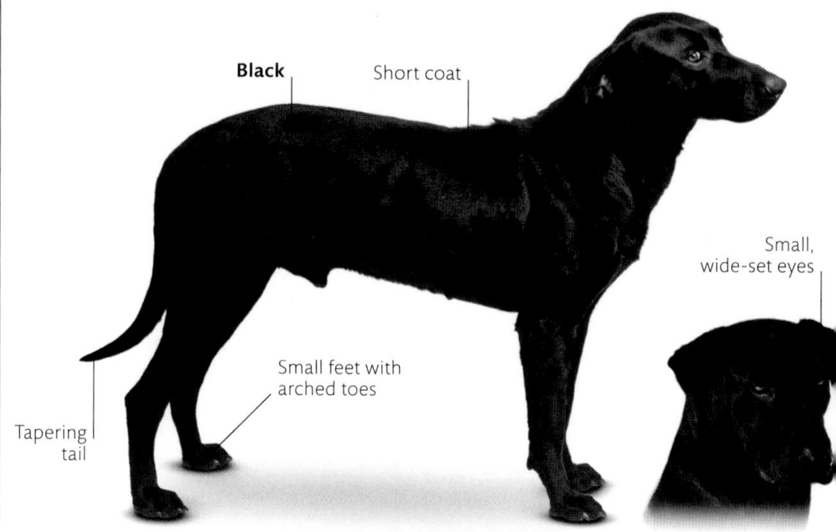

Taiwan Dog

HEIGHT 17–20in (43–52cm)
WEIGHT 26–40lb (12–18kg)
LIFE SPAN Over 10 years

Variety of colors

The Taiwan Dog, formerly known as the Formosan Mountain Dog, is something of a rarity, even in its native country. It is believed to have descended from the semi-wild dogs once used for hunting in the interior of Taiwan. The breed makes an intelligent family dog, but its hunting instincts need to be kept in check.

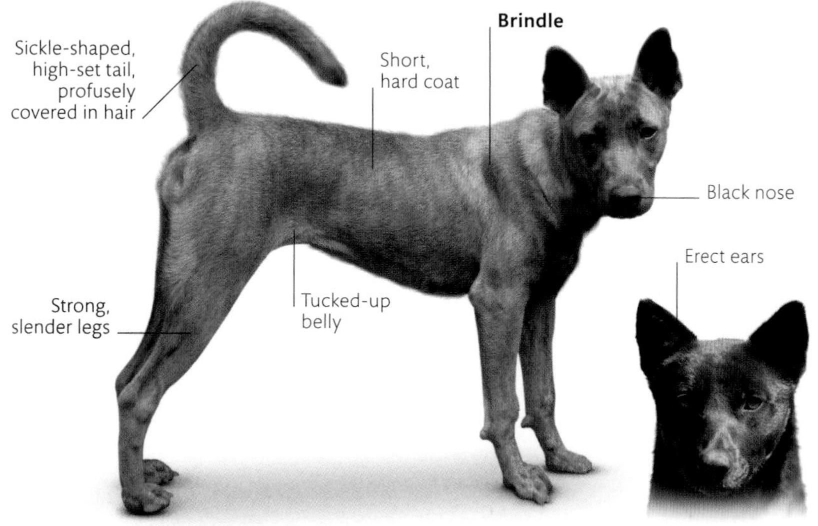

Mallorca Mastiff

HEIGHT 20–23in (52–58cm)
WEIGHT 66–84lb (30–38kg)
LIFE SPAN 10–12 years

Black

The Mallorca Mastiff, also known as the Ca de Bou, has a background that includes fighting and bullbaiting. A powerful breed, it has the typical mastiff-type build and watchful nature. When handled firmly but quietly, this dog socializes well, but it is probably better suited to life as a guard dog rather than as a family pet.

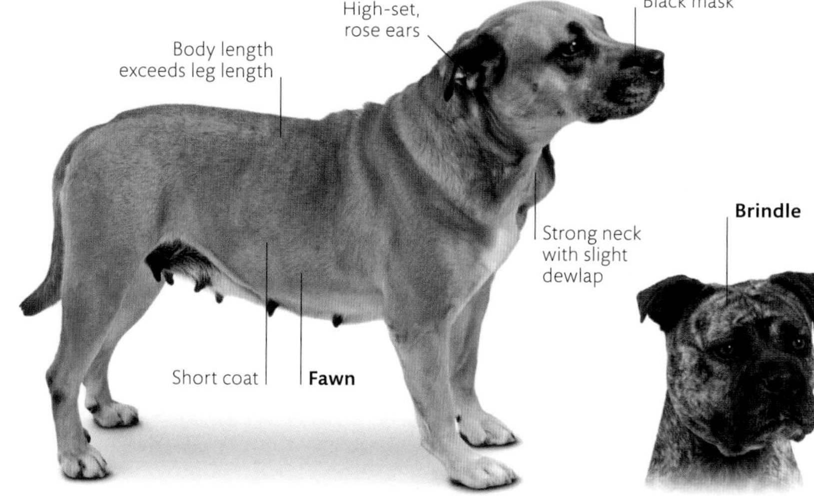

Dogo Canario

HEIGHT 22–26in (56–66cm)
WEIGHT 88–143lb (40–65kg)
LIFE SPAN 9–11 years

Brindle

May have white markings.

Bred in the Canary Islands in the early 19th century as a fighting dog, the Dogo Canario is believed to include the Mastiff (see p.93) in its ancestry. Difficult to train and socialize, a Dogo Canario is manageable if the owner understands and controls the dog's dominant nature. Early socialization is essential.

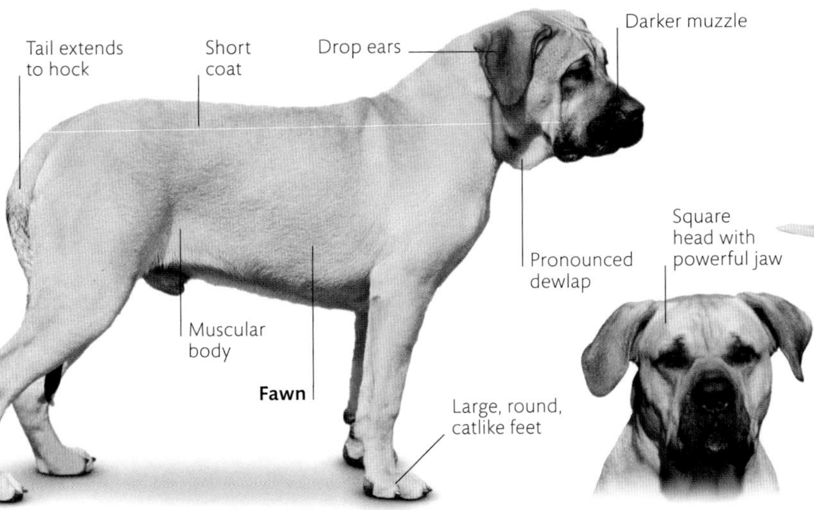

Dogo Argentino

HEIGHT 24–27in (60–68cm)
WEIGHT 79–99lb (36–45kg)
LIFE SPAN 10–12 years

Originating in the 1920s in Cordoba, Argentina, the Dogo Argentino was the creation of a local doctor who wanted a dog for hunting large game. Breeding from old fighting dogs such as mastiffs and the Bulldog (see p.95) produced this new dog. The Dogo Argentino has a kind temperament but can be overprotective.

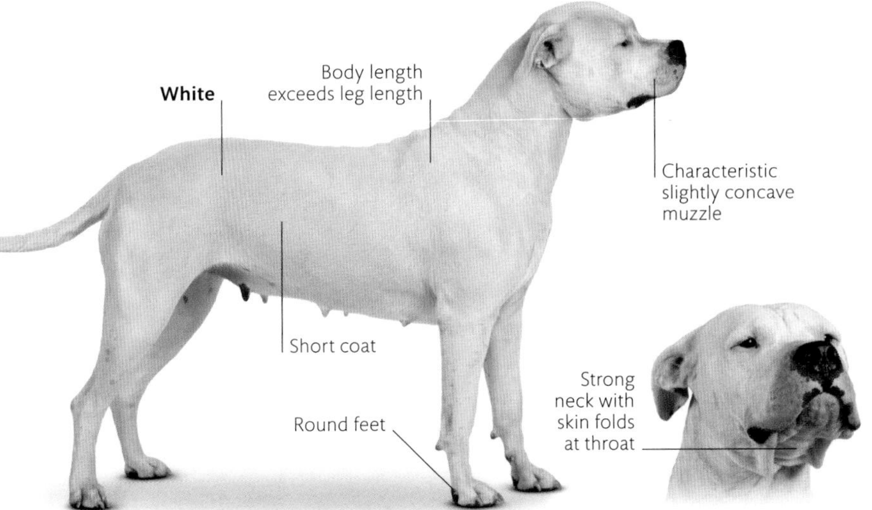

Fila Brasileiro

HEIGHT 24–30in (60–75cm)
WEIGHT Over 88lb (40kg)
LIFE SPAN 9–11years

Any solid color

Bred to guard large estates and livestock, the Fila Brasileiro does not fear intruders of any kind. Huge but beautifully proportioned, this dog exudes confidence and determination. Although the Fila Brasileiro is kind and quiet within a family, the average owner may find the breed's hunting and protective instincts difficult to manage.

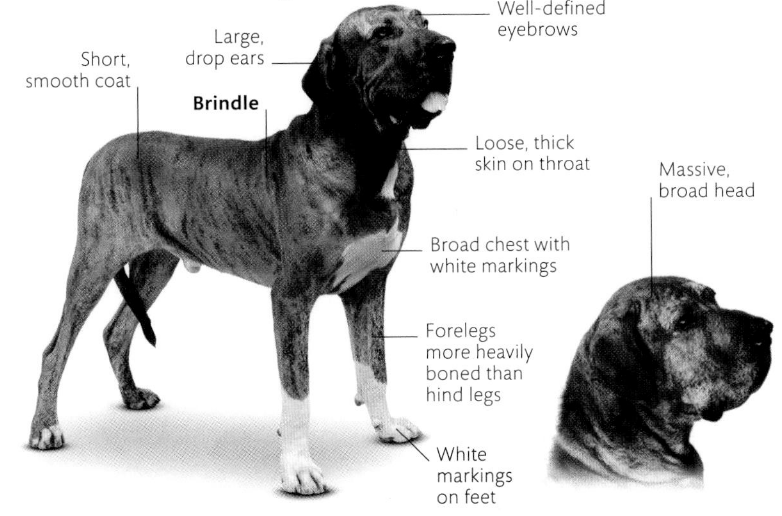

Uruguayan Cimarron

HEIGHT 22–24in (55–61cm)
WEIGHT 73–99lb (33–45kg)
LIFE SPAN 10–13 years

Fawn

Fawn coats may have black shading.

The ancestors of this breed were dogs brought into Uruguay by Spanish and Portuguese colonists and crossed with local dog breeds. Bred by farmers in the remote area of Cerro Largo, the Uruguayan Cimarron was used for guarding and herding. Like many working dogs, a Uruguayan Cimarron kept as a companion needs an experienced owner.

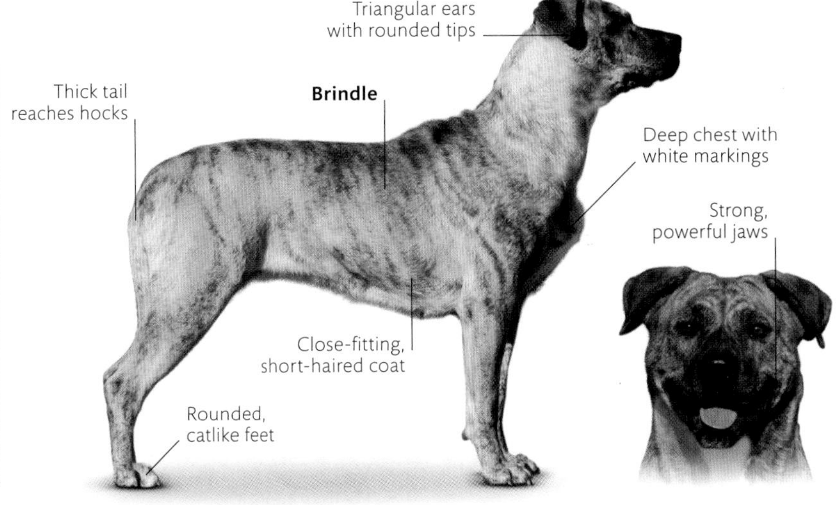

Alapaha Blue Blood Bulldog

HEIGHT 18–24in (46–61cm)
WEIGHT 55–90lb (25–41kg)
LIFE SPAN 12–15 years.

White

Dogs may have patches of any color.

Bulldog-type dogs were once commonly used as guards in the plantations of southern Georgia. By the early 19th century such dogs were almost extinct, but dedicated breeding over the next 200 years regenerated the type and produced the Alapaha Blue Blood Bulldog. This dog is still rare and not widely known outside the US. Muscular and intrepid, an Alapaha Blue Blood Bulldog has strong protective instincts, but it is easy to train to be a well behaved and affectionate companion. Energetic outdoors, this dog is happiest when given plenty of exercise.

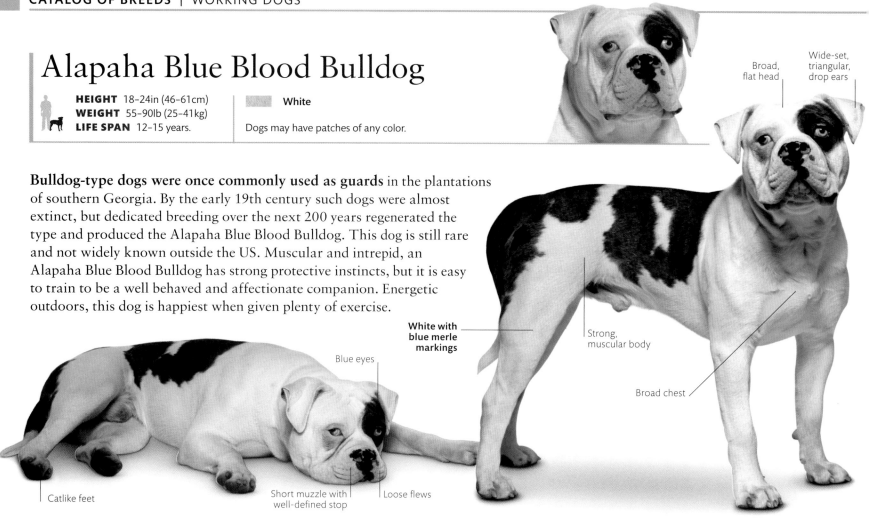

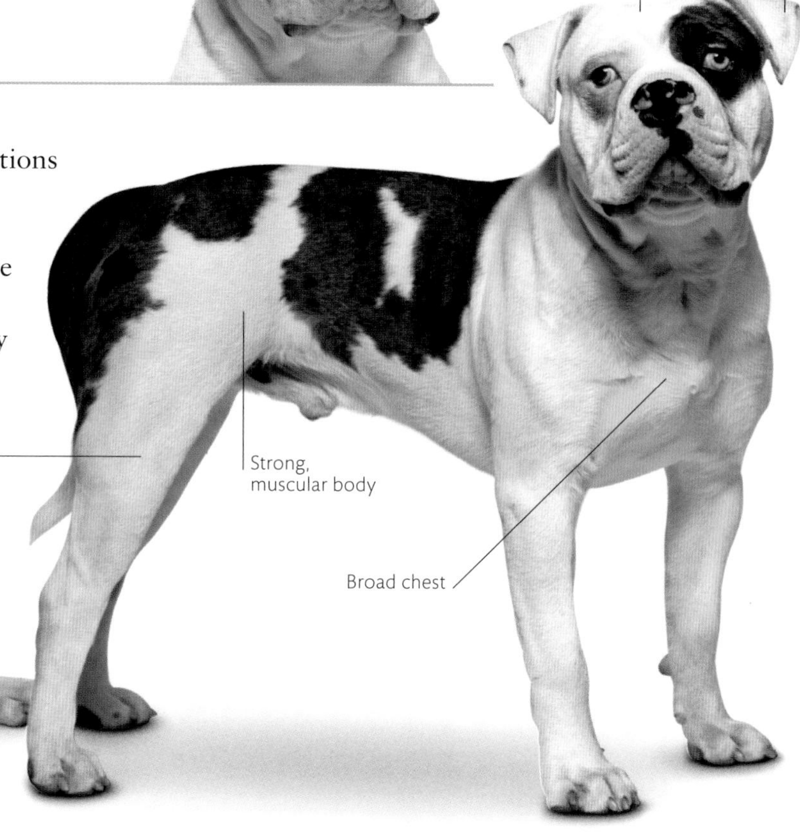

Boerboel

HEIGHT 22–26in (55–66cm)
WEIGHT 165–198lb (75–90kg)
LIFE SPAN 12–15 years

Variety of colors

May have darker face mask.

The Boerboel was developed from the large, mastiff-type dogs brought, from the 17th century onward, by settlers to the Cape area of South Africa. Affectionate with family and friends, the Boerboel is a formidable guard dog of huge size and strength. An experienced owner and early socialization are very important.

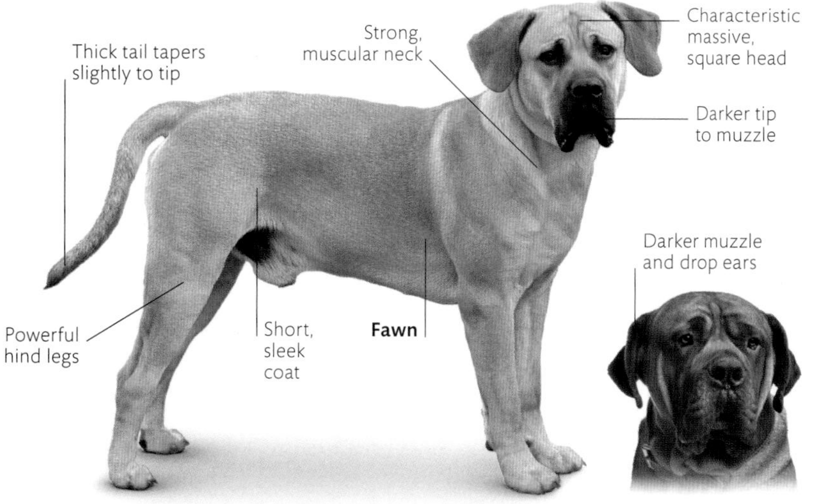

Spanish Mastiff

HEIGHT 28–31in (72–80cm)
WEIGHT 115–221lb (52–100kg)
LIFE SPAN 10–11 years

Any color

Once used for guarding livestock and homes in Spain, the Spanish Mastiff still carries out its traditional duties. The breed is also popular in its native country as a companion dog. Kind and loyal within the family, this breed can be aggressive with strangers and other dogs.

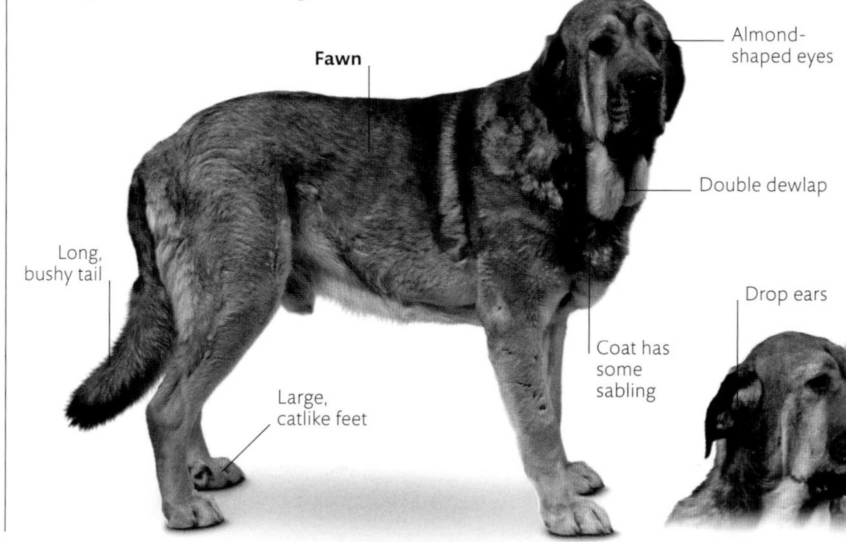

St. Miguel Cattle Dog

HEIGHT 19–24in (48–60cm)
WEIGHT 44–77lb (20–35kg)
LIFE SPAN About 15 years

Gray brindle

Also known as the Azores Cattle Dog, this robust cattle herder and guard dog originally came from the Azorean island of São Miguel. The breed is quiet and obedient with a trusted owner but needs careful handling where children or strangers are concerned.

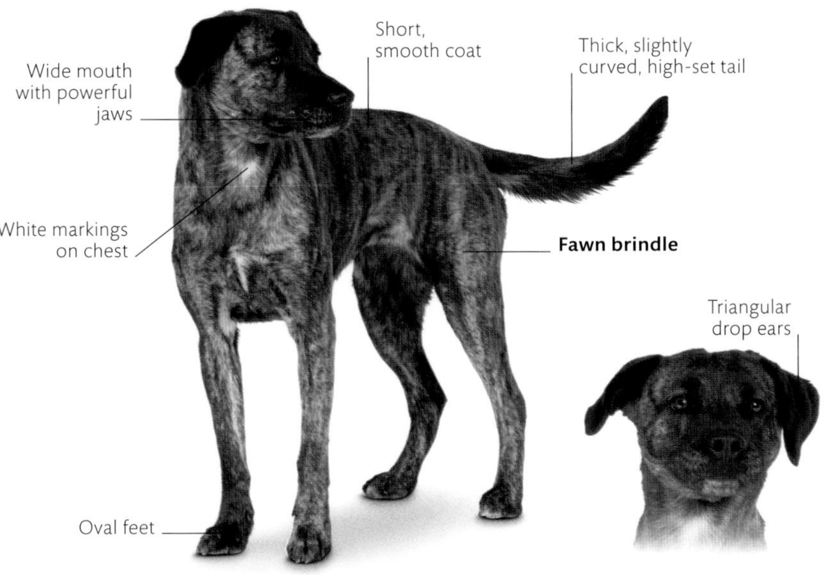

Cane Corso

HEIGHT 24–27in (60–68cm)
WEIGHT 88–110lb (40–50kg)
LIFE SPAN 10–11 years

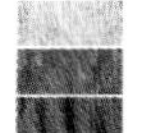

Gray
Stag-red
Brindle

May have white markings.

Descended from Roman fighting dogs, the Cane Corso is now used mainly for guarding and tracking. More graceful in build than many types of mastiff, this is nonetheless an extremely strong and robust breed. It can make a good house dog, but experienced and responsible ownership is essential.

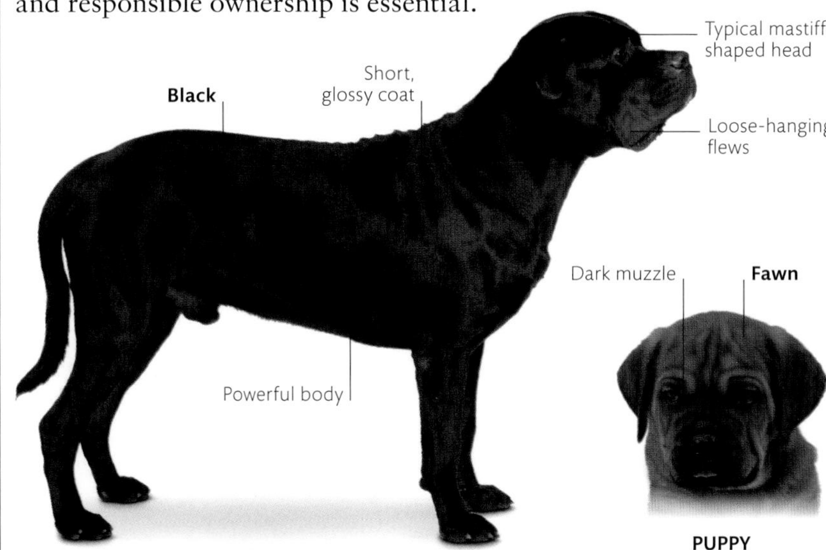

Dogue De Bordeaux

HEIGHT 23–27in (58–68cm)
WEIGHT 99–110lb (45–50kg)
LIFE SPAN 10–12 years

This old French breed was once used for hunting and fighting. The Dogue de Bordeaux's instincts make it a natural guard dog but, lacking aggression, it is easier to train and socialize than some mastiff types. Experienced handling is still necessary, however, if this powerful and athletic dog is to fit comfortably into a family home.

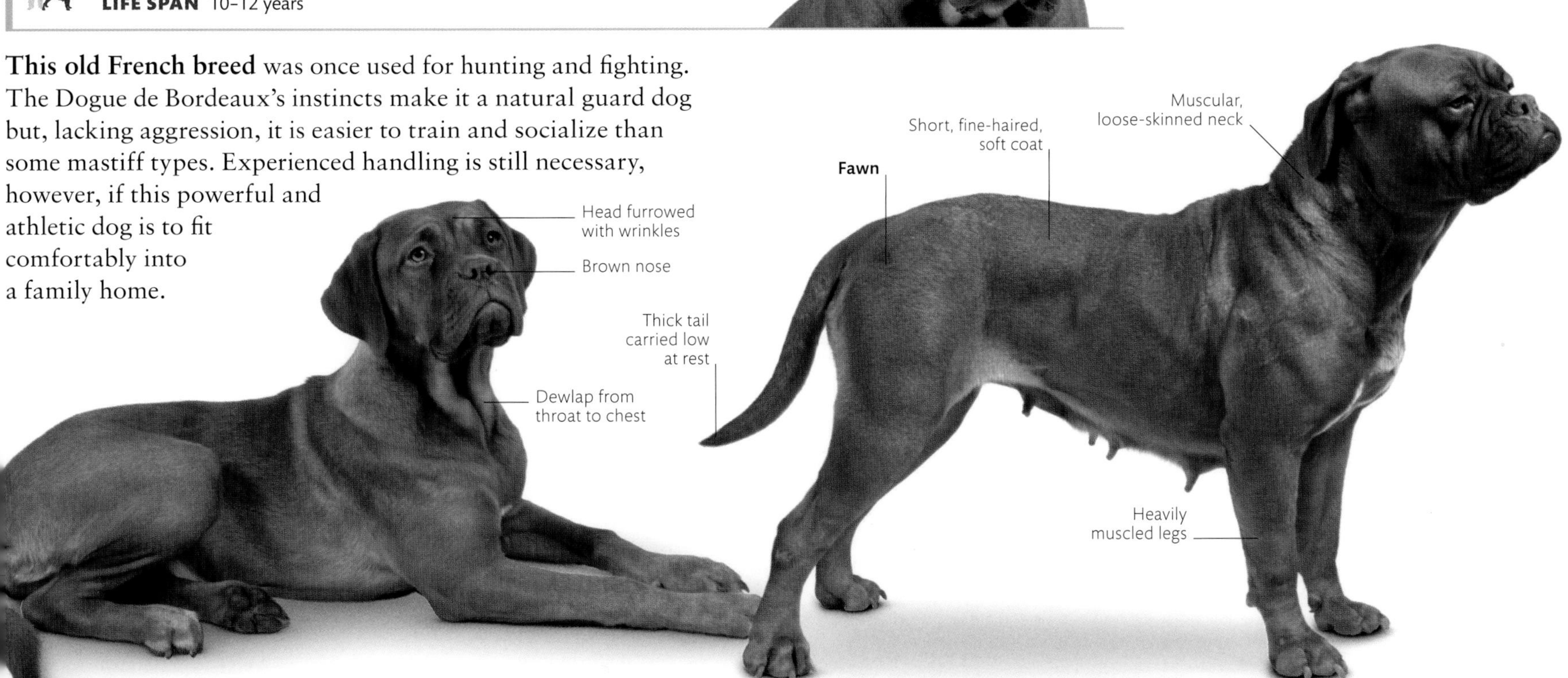

Boxer

HEIGHT	WEIGHT	LIFE SPAN	
21–25in (53–63cm)	55–71lb (25–32kg)	10–14 years	**Gold** **Black brindle** White markings should not exceed a third of coat color.

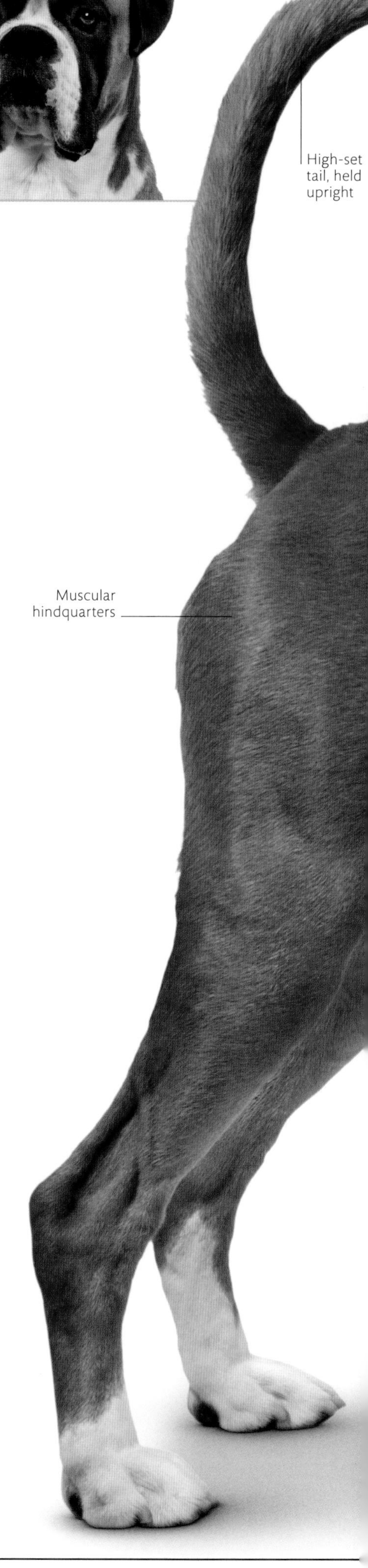

This clever, loyal, exuberant, and fun-loving dog is ideal for an energetic owner who enjoys an outdoor life

Once a Boxer-owner, always a Boxer-owner—this German breed is so big on personality that few who live with it ever look at another type of dog. The Boxer in its modern form was developed in the 19th century, and its ancestry is thought to include mastiff-type dogs such as the Great Dane (see p.96) and the Bulldog (see p.95). Powerful and athletic, it was bred primarily for fighting and bullbaiting, but was also used for farm work, hauling, and for hunting and holding down large game such as wild boar. Because of its endurance and courage, the breed is used today as a police and military search and rescue dog and for guard work.

The Boxer's history, its proud, upstanding attitude, and forward-thrusting jaw give the impression of an intimidating dog, and certainly it can be protective of home and family, but it makes a wonderful companion. It is loyal, affectionate, endearingly attention-seeking, and a boisterous but tolerant friend for children. This energetic breed suits fit, active owners since it keeps its high spirits and playfulness into late maturity. Almost any sort of fun keeps a Boxer happy but, ideally, it needs a good two-hour walk every day with plenty of room for romping around in the open. At home, given its stamina and curiosity, a Boxer enjoys a large yard where it has space to roam and interesting corners to explore.

This highly intelligent dog can be a handful to train but is obedient provided it receives calm and consistent commands and clear leadership. With early socializing, a Boxer is likely to get along well with any other pets in the family, although out on walks its hunting instincts may be aroused if there are birds or small animals to chase.

PUPPY

WHAT'S IN A NAME?

There are several stories about how the Boxer got its name—the most charming, but also the most unlikely, is based on the observation that these dogs, when meeting, often stand on their hind legs and use their front feet to push against one another. An Englishman, upon seeing this, said it reminded him of prize fighters sparring and so called the dogs "Boxers." Historically, the dogs were used as fighting dogs and it is this fact that is more likely to account for their name.

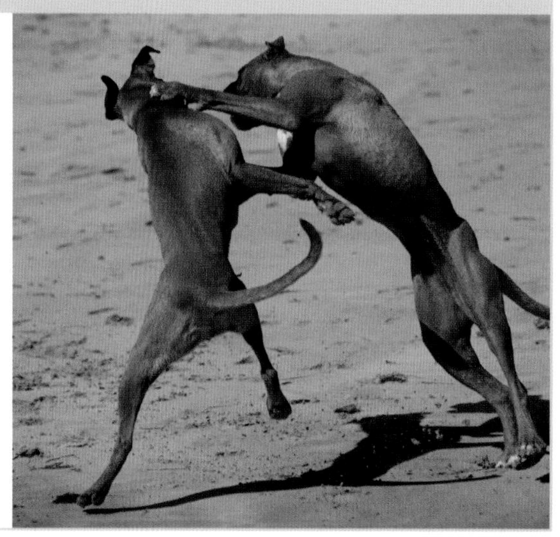

High-set, drop ears with rounded tips
Distinct stop
Arched neck
Body square in profile
Fawn
Short, broad muzzle
White chest
Smooth coat
Expressive face with dark brown eyes and wrinkled forehead
Tucked-up belly
Lower jaw longer than upper jaw (undershot)
White feet and lower legs

Neapolitan Mastiff

HEIGHT	WEIGHT	LIFE SPAN	
24–30in (60–75cm)	110–154lb (50–70kg)	Up to 10 years	Variety of colors

HAGRID'S GIANT PET

In the stories about Harry Potter, the boy wizard, Fang is a dog belonging to the half-giant Rubeus Hagrid, keeper of the grounds for Hogwarts School. Despite his scary exterior, Hagrid has a kind heart. He is noted for keeping dangerous pets and lovingly overlooking their ferocity. Like his master, Fang looks fierce but is friendly, with a bark a lot worse than his bite. Although he is called a "boarhound" in the books, Neapolitan Mastiffs were chosen for the films; their size and appearance matches Fang's character exactly. Fang is seen below on the red carpet at the premiere of *Harry Potter and the Half-Blood Prince* held at the Gard du Nord, Paris.

This canine heavyweight makes a loyal companion for a responsible owner with plenty of space

The ancestors of this imposing breed were the Molossus fighting dogs used in the Roman amphitheater and as dogs of war in the Roman armies. The armies took the dogs with them across Europe, thus giving rise to the various mastiff breeds. In the area around Naples, these dogs survived as guard dogs, produced by breeders known as *Mastinari*. Although highly prized, their numbers dwindled, until, in the 1940s, they became primarily known through enthusiasts, including the writer Piero Scanziani who had his own breeding kennels. The dog is now honored as the national mastiff of Italy. The breed has an intimidating appearance: huge, heavy-headed, and with a stern expression. Despite its heavy frame, the Neapolitan Mastiff can be quick and agile when taking action against threats to its owners or territory. The breed is now employed by the Italian armed forces and police force, and is used as a guard dog on farms and country estates.

The Neapolitan Mastiff can be calm, friendly, and devoted to its family, but it needs a confident and capable owner to socialize it effectively. Because of its size, this dog needs lots of living space and can be expensive to maintain.

Drop ears set well apart on broad skull

Gray

Tail thick at base, tapers to tip

Deep muzzle with pendulous flews

Moderate dewlap

Short coat with harsh texture

White patch on tip of toe

Large head with loose-fitting skin

Mastiff

HEIGHT	WEIGHT	LIFE SPAN	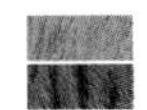
28–30in (70–77cm)	175–190lb (79–86kg)	Under 10 years	Apricot Brindle May have some white on body, chest, and feet.

ʒtrong and imposing, but calm and affectionate, this ntelligent guard dog thrives on human company

Ͻne of the oldest British breeds, he Mastiff is another breed that was leveloped from Molossus dogs that vere probably brought to Britain during Ɽoman occupation. In later centuries, hey were the "dogs of war" mentioned n William Shakespeare's *Henry V*: one Mastiff defended its wounded owner, Sir Piers Legh, against French soldiers during he Battle of Agincourt in 1415. Mastiff-ike dogs were also used in medieval Britain or guarding homes and protecting livestock rom wolves, as well as in dogfighting, ɔullbaiting, and bearbaiting. When these ports were banned the breed declined.

Pure-bred Mastiffs first appeared in the 19th century on large country estates, but by the end of World War II numbers had fallen drastically in Britain. The breed was revived by importing dogs from the US, and has gradually risen in popularity.

Despite its violent history, the Mastiff is even-tempered, amiable, and likes company, preferably human. Sheer size is probably the most serious drawback to housing, feeding, and exercising this breed. It is intelligent and trainable, but needs an owner with the experience and physical strength to exert firm control and ensure that its guarding instinct does not get out of hand.

MASTIFF IN MOTION

Historically, Mastiffs looked somewhat different, being more lightly built and about 3in (10cm) taller than the dogs seen today. This series of pioneering photographs taken by Eadweard Muybridge in the late 19th century were part of his extensive study on animal locomotion. It allowed people to observe how a breed like the Mastiff, not known to be overly energetic, moved. It could then be compared with athletic dog breeds, such as the Greyhound (see p.126), which Muybridge also filmed running.

Long, broad body

Fawn

Small, flat, black ears, set high on head

Wide-set, small eyes

Black muzzle

Forehead wrinkles when alert

Pendulous flews

Short coat, thickest over neck and shoulders

Straight, big-boned legs

Bullmastiff

HEIGHT 24–27in (61–69cm)
WEIGHT 90–130lb (41–59kg)
LIFE SPAN Under 10 years

Red
Brindle

A cross between the Old English Mastiff and the Bulldog (opposite), the Bullmastiff was developed to be a gamekeeper's guard dog. With a more reliable temperament than many other mastiff types, this breed makes an intelligent and faithful house dog. The Bullmastiff's square and solid frame houses a lively spirit and boundless energy.

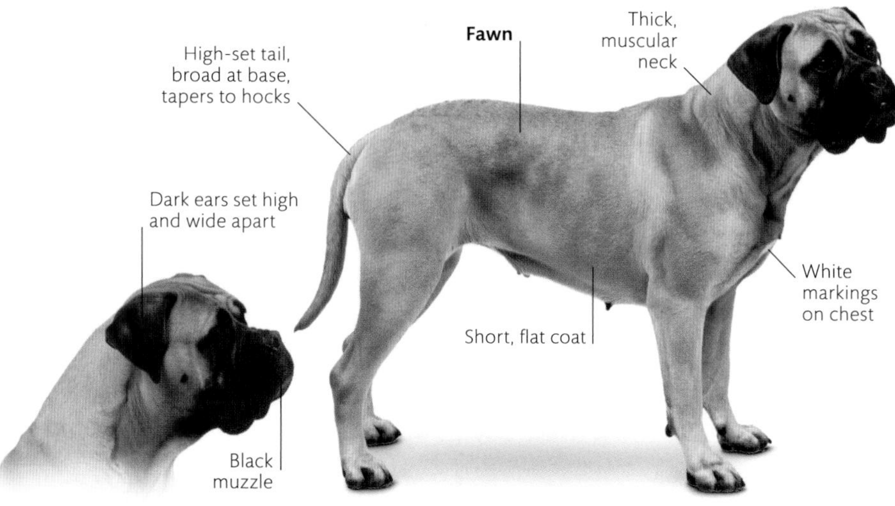

Broholmer

HEIGHT 28–30in (70–75cm)
WEIGHT 88–154lb (40–70kg)
LIFE SPAN 6–11 years

Black

Historically a hunting dog, and later a farm guard dog, the Broholmer is now almost exclusively kept at home. The breed had all but disappeared by the mid-20th century but was revived and "reconstructed" by enthusiasts, though it is rarely seen outside its native Denmark.

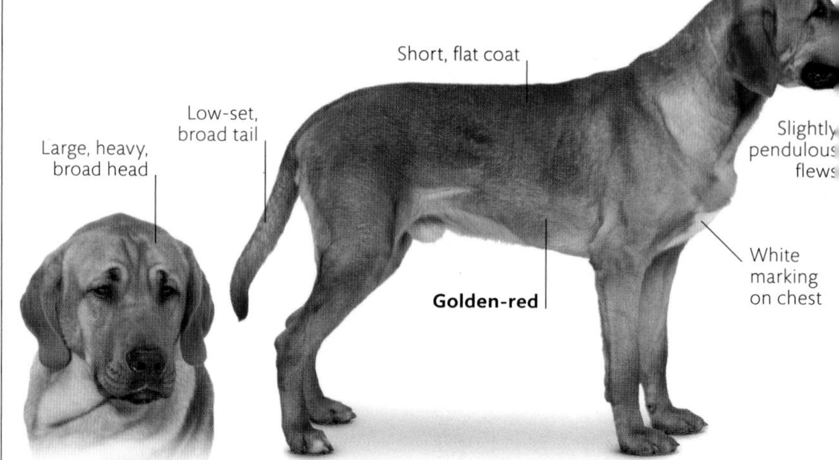

Tosa

HEIGHT 22–24in (55–60cm)
WEIGHT 82–198lb (37–90kg)
LIFE SPAN Over 10 years

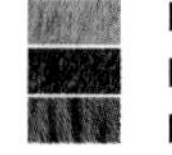

Fawn
Black
Brindle

The Tosa was developed from progressive crossbreeding between Japanese fighting dogs and Western breeds such as the Bulldog (opposite), Mastiff (see p.93), and Great Dane (see p.96). Very large, strongly built, and possessing a latent fighting instinct, the Tosa is considered to be a dog that should only be owned by expert handlers.

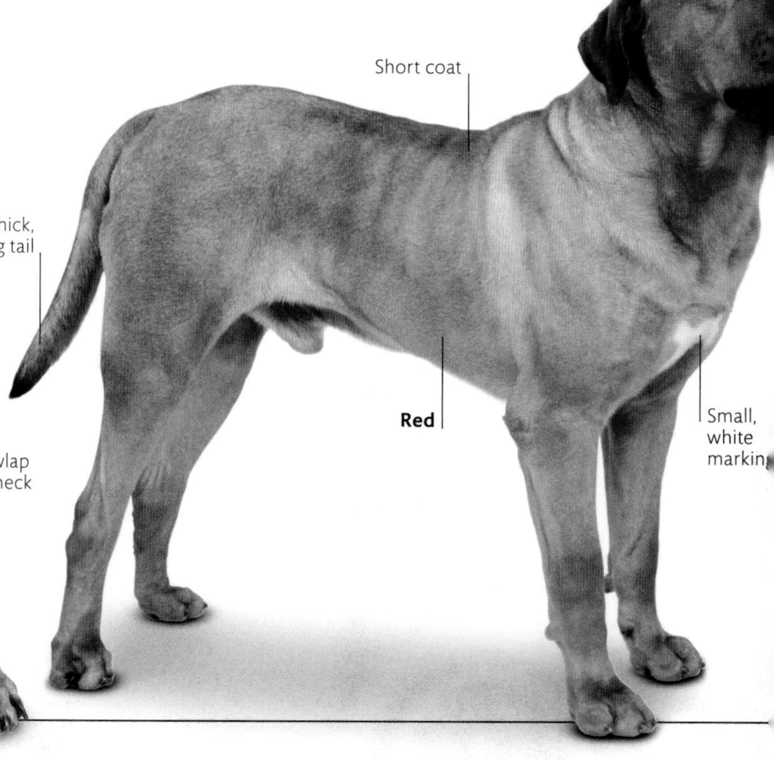

Bulldog

HEIGHT	WEIGHT	LIFE SPAN	Variety of colors
15–16in (38–40cm)	51–55lb (23–25kg)	Under 10 years	

Full of character, this dog has become the symbol for courage, determination, and tenacity

A traditional British breed, the Bulldog has descended from small Mastiffs. The name comes from the dog's original use in bullbaiting, during which the dog would attack the bull from below and hang on to its nose or throat. The wide head and protruding lower jaw gave the Bulldog its legendary grip, while the position of the nose, tipped back behind the mouth, allowed the dog to keep breathing without relaxing its bite.

Bullbaiting was banned in Britain in 1835, but from the mid-19th century the dogs began to be featured in the show ring. Breeders started producing dogs with more exaggerated physical features while minimizing the aggression in their nature, so the modern breed is very different from its fierce predecessor.

The Bulldog is now known as a good-natured and lovable companion. It does have a stubborn streak as well as a protective instinct, and these traits need to be handled with tact, although they rarely develop into aggression. With a squat and massively muscled body, wrinkled head, and upturned nose, this breed has character rather than beauty. Despite its waddling gait, the Bulldog needs plenty of exercise to prevent it from gaining too much weight.

THE ENGLISH BULLDOG

The Bulldog has come to exemplify traditional Englishness. The 18th-century fictional character John Bull, made famous by cartoonists such as James Gillray, was shown with a Bulldog by his side; both man and dog stood for the plain, honest Englishman who was fond of his food and not averse to a fight. The tenacious bulldog spirit became associated with World Wars I and II (shown below in a WWI postcard), and is perhaps most closely linked with Prime Minister Winston Churchill and his speech in 1940 rousing the embattled nation to defend itself against its enemies.

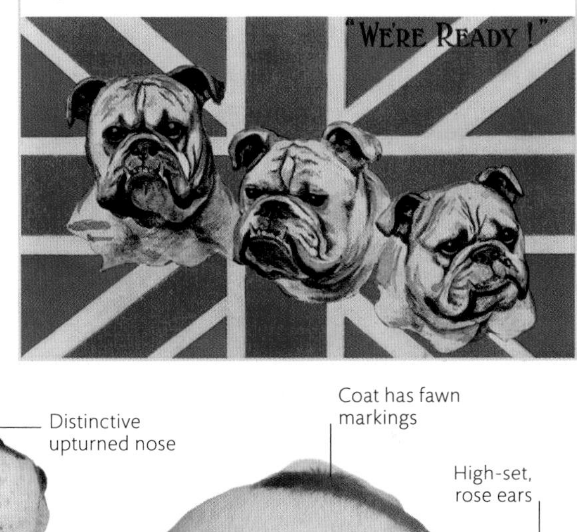

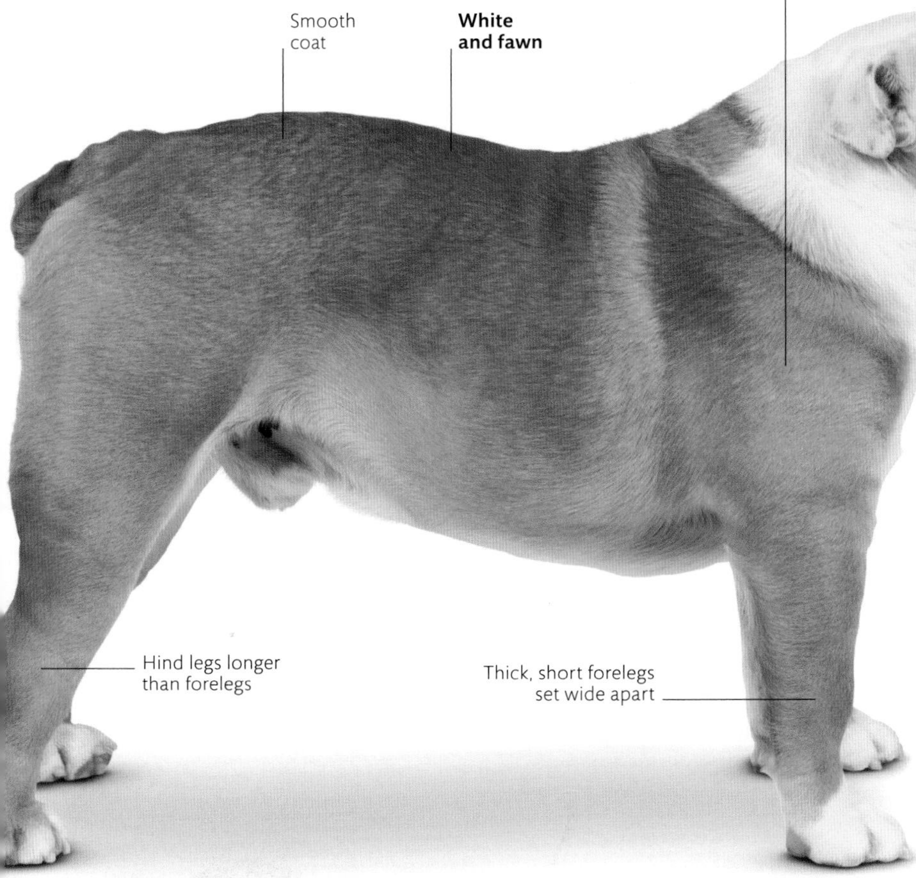

Sloping, muscular shoulders

Smooth coat

White and fawn

Distinctive upturned nose

Thick, pendant lips

Hind legs longer than forelegs

Thick, short forelegs set wide apart

Coat has fawn markings

High-set, rose ears

Lower jaw longer than upper jaw (undershot)

Broad, round, deep chest

Great Dane

HEIGHT	WEIGHT	LIFE SPAN	
28–30in (71–76cm)	101–120lb (46–54kg)	Under 10 years	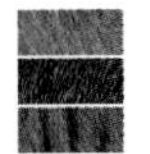 Blue Black Brindle

\ colossal but gentle and affectionate family pet, this dog s easy to maintain but needs plenty of room

ometimes called "the Apollo of dogs" fter the Greek god, the Great Dane exhibits legance and dignity with tall stature, to nake for a truly impressive animal. In fact, ogs resembling the Great Dane can be seen n ancient Egyptian and ancient Greek art. 'he modern breed first appeared in the 18th entury in Germany—not Denmark, as its ame suggests—where it was developed o hunt bear and wild boar. The original Ferman boarhounds, thought to have been mixture of mastiff-type dogs and Irish Nolfhounds, were crossed with Greyhounds o create a tall, agile, long-striding dog, vith the speed and strength to bring down large quarry.

Great Danes are one of the tallest of all dog breeds, and several individuals have held the Guinness World Record for being the tallest dog in the world. The record holder in 2012, a dog named Zeus, was measured at 3ft 8in (1.12m) from the ground to his withers—the same height as a child's pony.

Despite its imposing appearance, the easy-going Great Dane is a gentle giant, usually friendly toward people and other animals. These dogs need a lot of human company, and can be costly to keep, but are rewarding family pets. They are content to be house dogs, provided there is enough space for them to move around freely and lie comfortably. They are also effective guard dogs. The Great Dane needs plenty of exercise, but young pups should not be allowed to run around too much—their fast-growing bones cannot cope with the strain.

A HERO NAMED SCOOBY DOO

The cartoon dog Scooby Doo is the hero of a long-running TV series created by Hanna-Barbera. His creator, artist Iwao Takamoto, was inspired by a woman he knew who bred Great Danes. After she had described to him the ideal pedigree dog, Takamoto comically distorted these features to create a gangling, chicken-hearted character with a dopey face. Yet despite being frightened of everything, Scooby Doo and his hapless human friend Shaggy (below) rescue their friends and defeat villains, triumphing every time!

PUPPY

Deep, long body

Long, arched neck with no loose skin

Dark shading on head and ears

Triangular, drop ears

Broad muzzle

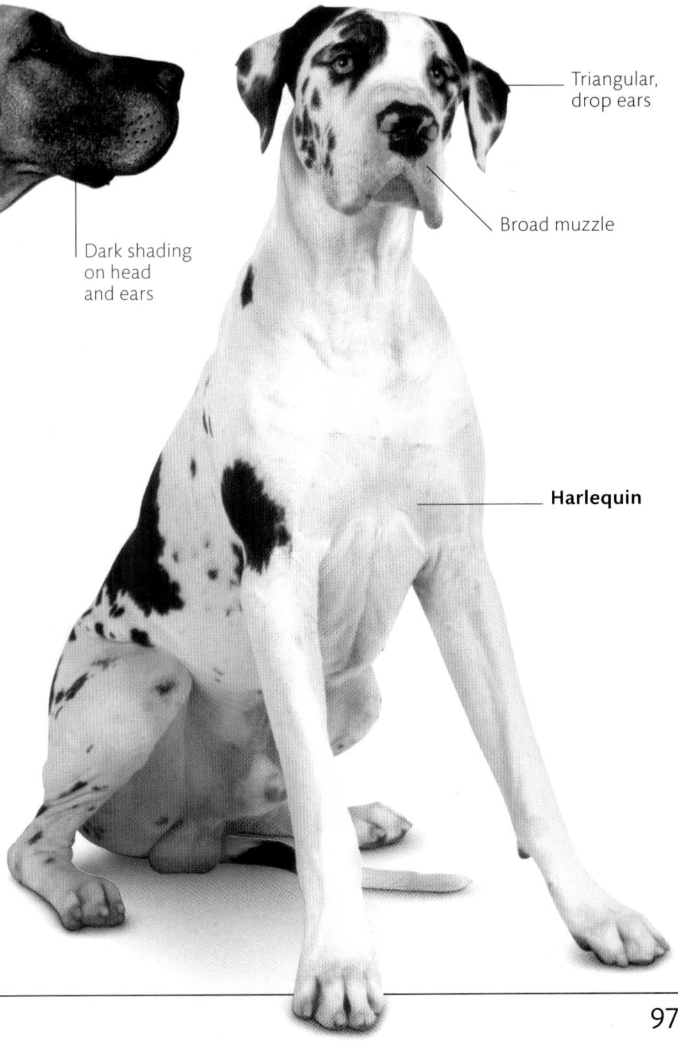

Harlequin

Slightly tucked-up belly

Fawn

Straight forelegs

Catlike feet

Pulling together
A team of Siberian Huskies plows effortlessly through deep snow. With an experienced handler, these hardy and tireless dogs work together superbly.

SPITZ-TYPE DOGS

A team of huskies pulling a sled over icy wastelands epitomizes the type of dog known as a Spitz. In fact, this group has diverse uses, including herding, hunting, and guarding; many smaller types are kept solely as pets. Descent from wolves is apparent in most spitz-type dogs: the shape of the head, the typical wolf coloring, and an alert expression.

Many of the modern spitz-type dogs seen today originated centuries ago in Arctic regions, although a number, including the Chow Chow (see p.112) and Akita (see p.111), come from East Asia. The more ancient history of the spitz group remains uncertain. One theory currently being explored is that spitz-type dogs all have their earliest origins in Asia, some migrating alongside tribal movements into Africa and others across the Bering Strait to North America.

Breeds such as the Greenland Dog (see p.100) and Siberian Husky (see p.101) were used most famously for sled-hauling by the polar explorers of the 19th and early 20th centuries. These tough dogs worked in appalling weather conditions, often on a diet of poor food, and not infrequently ended up being eaten themselves when the explorers ran out of rations. Such spitz-type sled dogs were also once widely used by North American hunters and fur trappers. Today the sled-hauling spitz breeds are popular for endurance racing and with tourists who want to try their hand at dog-driving. Other spitz dogs have been bred for hunting large game such as wolf and bear, and for herding caribou. The Akita, originally from Japan, was developed as a fighter and bear hunter and now often works as a guard dog. Among the small, nonworking spitz dogs are the Pomeranian (see p.118), selectively bred down in size from a larger type of dog, and the newly created Alaskan Klee Kai (see p.104), a miniature husky.

Spitz dogs, both large and small, have the characteristics of animals bred specifically for living in extremely cold climates. Typically, they have a very thick double coat, which varies in length and density according to the origin of a breed. Other features for preventing heat loss in low temperatures are small, pointed, furry ears, and heavily furred feet. An attractive addition to many breeds is the distinctive "spitz" tail that curls upward over the back.

As house dogs, most spitz breeds are happy with family life, but they are not the easiest of dogs to train. Without sufficient exercise and amusement they can resort to disruptive behavior such as digging holes and barking.

Greenland Dog

HEIGHT	WEIGHT	LIFE SPAN	
20–27in (51–68cm)	60–106lb (27–48kg)	Over 10 years	Any color

This friendly dog has great strength and endurance and loves outdoor action but needs firm handling

The classic sled dog of polar expeditions, the Greenland Dog was used by indigenous peoples long before European and American explorers discovered its worth. Dogs of this type were brought to Greenland from Siberia with migrating people 5,000 years ago.

The dogs need endurance to work hard in temperatures as low as -69°F (-56°C) and are trained to pull sleds of up to 1,000lb (450kg). The hunters also train their dogs to hunt seals and walruses and even take on polar bears. The animals work as a pack but semi-independently: when pulling a sled, they are hitched on separate lines so that each dog can pick its own way across the terrain.

The Greenland Dog needs careful training and handling because it is both powerful and stubborn, and has a strong drive for dominance (although more with other dogs than with people). The breed also needs physical and mental challenges to keep it busy, so does best in the hands of an experienced owner. With the right owner, the Greenland Dog is a cheerful extrovert and affectionate companion.

POLAR EXPLORER

The Greenland Dog has played a vital role in expeditions to the North and South Poles. The explorers Robert Peary (1856–1920) and Roald Amundsen (1872–1928) used the sled dogs and handling methods of indigenous Arctic peoples. Amundsen (below) took Greenland Dogs on his attempt to conquer the South Pole in 1911, and 11 of these survived to reach the Pole with him. Greenland Dogs were used for working on Antarctic bases until they were banned from Antarctica as a non-native species in 1992.

Bushy tail curls loosely over back

Black and fawn

Hair forms long breeches on hindquarters

Sturdy, heavily boned legs

Thick, weatherproof, double coat

Large feet with thick hair between toes

Small, erect, wide-set ears

Lighter markings on face

Muscular, compact body

Siberian Husky

HEIGHT	WEIGHT	LIFE SPAN	
20–24in (51–60cm)	35–60lb (16–27kg)	Over 10 years	Any color

This versatile and sociable dog enjoys being a part of a human "pack," but its urge to chase needs to be controlled

Long used as a sled dog by the Chukchi people of northeastern Siberia, the Siberian Husky has great endurance and an appetite for work. The thick double coat protects against extreme cold; at night the dog uses its bushy tail to keep its face warm.

In 1908 Huskies from Siberia were introduced to Alaska for dogsled racing, notably the 408-mile (657-km) All-Alaska Sweepstakes. In 1930 the Soviets stopped the export of Siberian Huskies, but that year the American Kennel Club recognized the breed. The Siberian Husky proved itself in polar expeditions, and in the US Army's Arctic Search and Rescue Unit during World War II. The breed remains popular in sports such as dogsled racing.

Siberian Huskies make peaceable, lovable companions but need plenty of exercise. They are independent-minded, and their instinct to pull means that they need careful training on the leash. Siberian Huskies have a strong pack instinct and need to be with both people and other dogs. They tend to see small animals as prey, so owners should socialize their puppy with other pets early on. The coat should be groomed once or twice a week.

BALTO—A DOGSLED HERO

Born in 1919, Balto was originally bred for dogsled racing in Alaska, but in 1925 relay teams of sled dogs were urgently needed to help carry diphtheria vaccine from Anchorage to Nome to prevent an epidemic. Balto led the last team, braving a fierce blizzard and a freezing river to cover the final leg and deliver the vaccine safely. The team received a hero's welcome from the press. A statue of Balto was erected in Central Park, New York City, and a Hollywood movie was made about his deeds.

BALTO STATUE, NEW YORK

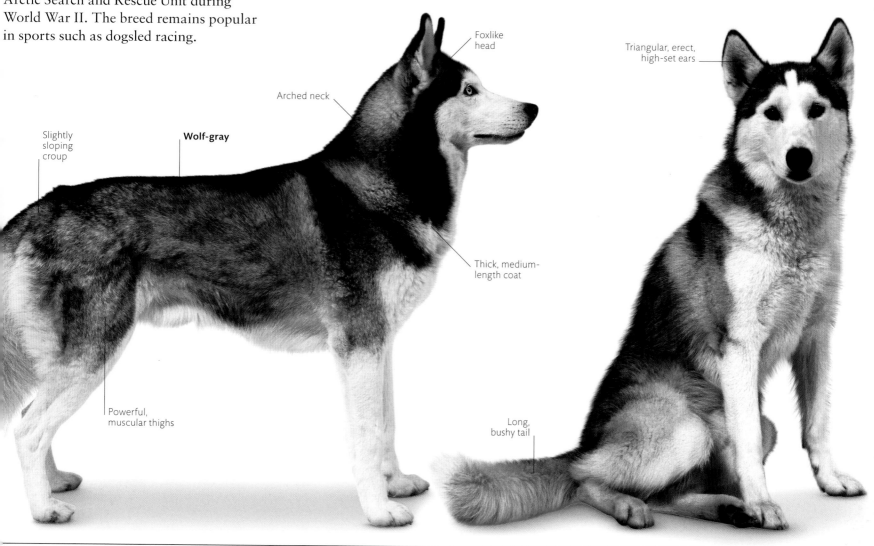

Foxlike head

Arched neck

Slightly sloping croup

Wolf-gray

Thick, medium-length coat

Powerful, muscular thighs

Triangular, erect, high-set ears

Long, bushy tail

Alaskan Malamute

HEIGHT	WEIGHT	LIFE SPAN	Variety of colors
23–28in (58–71cm)	84–123lb (38–56kg)	12–15 years	All dogs have white underparts.

A large, sled-pulling dog that can adapt well to family life given sufficient space and exercise

The wolflike Alaskan Malamute is named after the Native American Mahlemut people who bred these dogs to pull heavy loads and travel great distances across the snow when sleds were the only mode of transport. Today it is still used to haul freight in remote North American locations, and successfully takes part in dogsled racing competitions. Also used on polar expeditions, this breed has staggering amounts of stamina, strength, and tenacity combined with a highly tuned sense of direction and smell.

For all its toughness, the Alaskan Malamute is a friendly dog, at least toward people, which means that it cannot be relied on as a guard dog. It likes children but is too big and boisterous to be left alone with a small child. The Alaskan Malamute, especially the male, tends to be intolerant of strange dogs, and without thorough socializing can quickly become aggressive. The breed also has a strong chasing instinct and can disappear far and fast in pursuit of small animals that it sees as prey. Owners should be cautious about where and when to exercise this dog off the leash. A quick learner, the Alaskan Malamute has a strong will, so needs firm handling and training in good habits right from the start.

The Alaskan Malamute settles well into domestic life as long as it has at least two hours of exercise each day and a yard to roam in. A bored dog, with energy to spare, can be destructive if left at home without supervision. Although its thick coat sheds in spring, there is a risk of overheating if the dog is overexercised in hot weather, and so needs access to shade. The hardy Alaskan Malamute is happy to sleep outdoors, provided it has a companion.

WORTH THEIR WEIGHT IN GOLD

During the 1896–99 Klondike Gold Rush, prospectors would pay huge prices, up to $1,500, for a team of Malamute dogs to transport their equipment from supply towns such as Skagway and Dawson City to the gold fields. Each man was required to carry enough supplies to last him for one year, including 1,000lb (454kg) of food. In winter a team of Malamutes could haul half a ton of equipment over the snow-covered terrain in subzero temperatures. In summer, used as pack animals, they could carry a 50lb (23kg) load over a distance of 20 miles (32km).

PUPPY

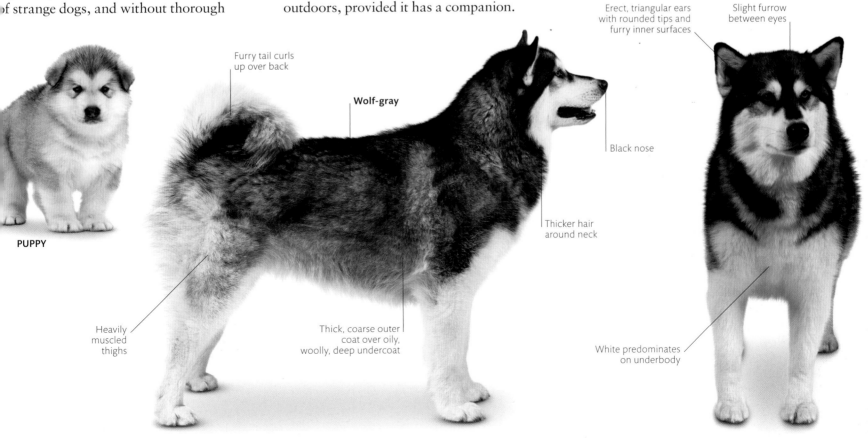

Furry tail curls up over back

Wolf-gray

Black nose

Thicker hair around neck

Heavily muscled thighs

Thick, coarse outer coat over oily, woolly, deep undercoat

Erect, triangular ears with rounded tips and furry inner surfaces

Slight furrow between eyes

White predominates on underbody

Alaskan Klee Kai

HEIGHT
Toy: Up to 13in (33cm)
Miniature: 13–15in (33–38cm)
Standard: 15–17in (38–44cm)

WEIGHT
Toy: Up to 9lb (4kg)
Miniature: 9–15lb (4–7kg)
Standard: 15–22lb (7–10kg)

LIFE SPAN
Over 10 years

 **Any color**

A NEW BREED

This companion Spitz was created in Alaska by Linda Spurlin and her family. The family mated Alaskan and Siberian huskies with small dogs to create a mini husky and gave their new breed the name Klee Kai, derived from Inuit words meaning little dog. Although the Alaskan Klee Kai remains rare, the breed has been recognized by some organizations and there are now breeders' groups in the US and several other countries.

This energetic and inquisitive mini husky is confident with owners but wary of strangers

This miniature version of the Siberian Husky (see p.101) was developed in the 1970s to be a house dog. The Alaskan Klee Kai is found in three sizes: toy, miniature, and standard. There are two forms of coat: standard (short) and full (slightly longer and thicker).

The Alaskan Klee Kai appreciates company and likes to be treated as a pack member within a family. However, unlike its larger Husky cousins, it is reserved with strangers, so requires careful training and early socializing. Any children in the family need to be taught to treat the dog gently, as the Alaskan Klee Kai can snap if teased. It is highly intelligent and curious, so enjoys obedience and agility contests, and some Alaskan Klee Kais have been trained as therapy dogs.

The Alaskan Klee Kai fits well in a modest-sized home but, like its larger relative, has a great deal of energy and needs plenty of exercise, including a long walk each day, to stay in good physical and mental health. In addition, it is highly vocal, especially when "talking" to its family (this trait also makes Alaskan Klee Kais good watchdogs). The dogs molt twice a year, and the full-coated type needs regular grooming.

Heavy-coated, brushlike tail

Dense, moderately long coat

Triangular, erect ears

Distinct stop

Tapering muzzle

Characteristic facial mask

Wolf-gray

Lighter-colored underparts

MINIATURE, STANDARD COAT

Eyes of this dog are different colors

Black and white

STANDARD, STANDARD COAT

Canadian Eskimo Dog

HEIGHT 20–28in (50–70cm)
WEIGHT 40–88lb (18–40kg)
LIFE SPAN Over 10 years

Any color

Any markings allowed.

One of the oldest breeds of sled dog in the world, the Canadian Eskimo Dog, or Inuit Dog, is built for survival in the harshest conditions. This breed has a natural instinct for running with a pack and enjoys company, either canine or human. Training should be firm, ideally with plenty of fun.

Chinook

HEIGHT 22–26in (55–66cm)
WEIGHT 55–71lb (25–32kg)
LIFE SPAN 10–15 years

Developed as a sled dog at the beginning of the 20th century in the US, the Chinook is the result of various crosses between mastiffs, the Greenland Dog (see p.100), and shepherd dogs. Active but gentle-natured, this is a fun-loving breed and makes an excellent all-around family dog.

Karelian Bear Dog

HEIGHT 20–22in (52–57cm)
WEIGHT 44–51lb (20–23kg)
LIFE SPAN 10–12 years

Developed in Finland, this fearless hunting dog was bred to challenge big game, particularly bear and elk. The Karelian Bear Dog has a strong fighting instinct, which does not turn into aggression against people but may cause problems with other dogs. This breed is unlikely to settle well into domestic life.

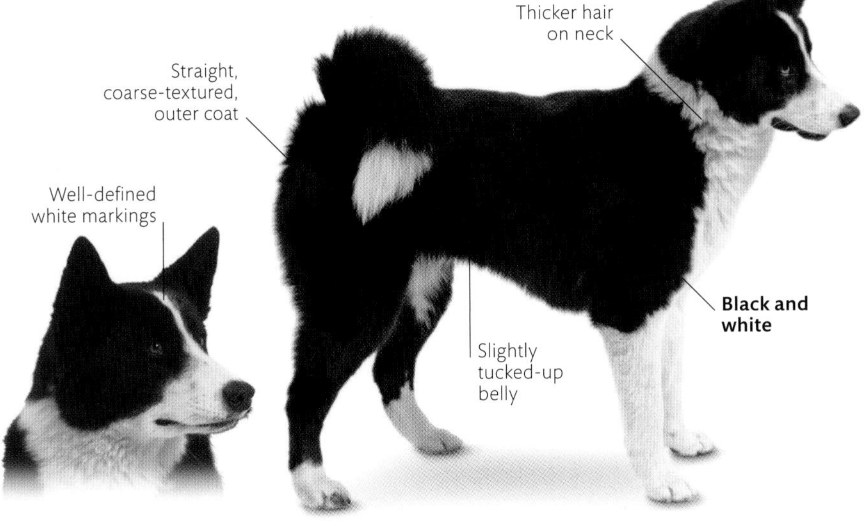

Samoyed

HEIGHT	WEIGHT	LIFE SPAN
18–22in (46–56cm)	35–66lb (16–30kg)	Over 12 years

This strikingly attractive dog has a high-maintenance coat, but its cheerful disposition makes it an excellent family pet

Developed by the nomadic Samoyedic people of Siberia, this beautiful dog was used for herding and guarding reindeer and for sled-hauling. Although a tough, outdoor worker, it was also very much a family dog, taking its place in its owner's tent and enjoying human companionship. These dogs were brought to England in the 1800s and were first seen in the US around a decade later. Numerous myths and unsubstantiated stories link the Samoyeds to the polar expeditions of the late 19th and early 20th centuries, but it appears likely that this breed was included among sled teams taken to the Antarctic during the heyday of polar exploration.

The modern Samoyed retains the sociable and easygoing temperament that made it so valued as part of a nomadic family. Behind the smiling expression characteristic of the breed is an affectionate nature and a desire to be friends with everyone. However, the Samoyed retains the watchdog instincts for which it was bred. Although never aggressive, it will bark at anything that arouses its suspicion.

This dog craves company and likes to be kept occupied mentally and physically. Intelligent and spirited, a bored or lonely Samoyed will resort to mischief—whether it is digging holes or finding a way to escape through a fence. The breed responds well to thoughtful handling, but training requires patience and persistence on the part of its owner.

Daily grooming is essential to keep the Samoyed's magnificent, stand-out coat in order and maintain its distinctive silvery sheen. Seasonal shedding of the undercoat can be very heavy but, except in very warm conditions, normally occurs only once a year.

PUPPY

Long, bushy tail carried over back, falls to one side

THE NOMADS' COMPANION

Traditionally, the Samoyed dog has played a central part in the lives of its Siberian owners, and for some remote communities it still does today (right). The nomads depended on their dogs for guarding their reindeer herds and encampments. These working dogs were also members of the family; Samoyeds were allowed free access to the *choom* (family tent), shared the family's food, and would sleep with the children to keep them warm. The Samoyedic people revered their dogs, and in return the dogs developed a notable gentleness and sympathy toward humans.

Erect, round-tipped ears
thickly lined with hair
Dark eyes rimmed
with black
Muscular, broad back
Ruff of longer,
denser hair
around neck
White
Broad, wedge-
shaped head
Thick, soft coat
with silver-tipped
outer hairs
Typical smiling
expression
Feathering on
back of front legs

West Siberian Laika

HEIGHT 20–24in (51–62cm)
WEIGHT 40–49lb (18–22kg)
LIFE SPAN 10–12 years

Variety of colors

Bred for hunting in the forests of Siberia, this handsome dog is very popular in its native country. The breed is strong and confident and eager to follow game, either large or small. Although the West Siberian Laika has a steady temperament, its readiness to hunt makes it unsuitable as a house dog for most families.

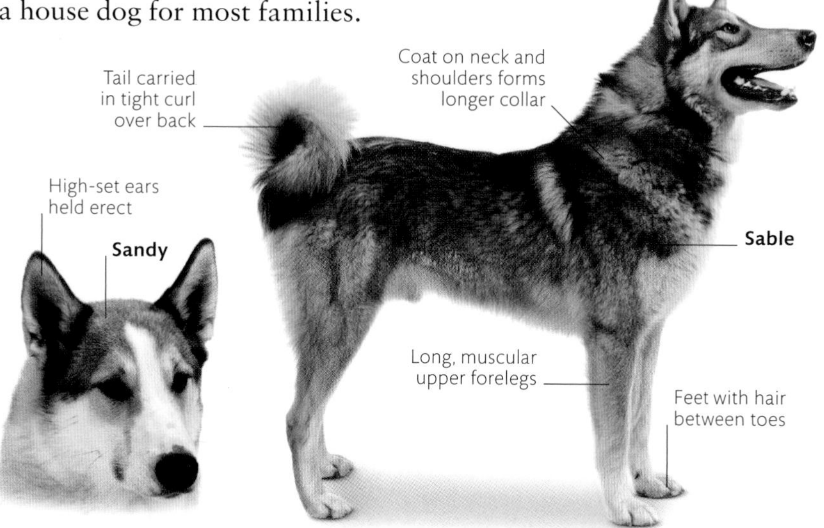

East Siberian Laika

HEIGHT 21–25in (53–64cm)
WEIGHT 40–51lb (18–23kg)
LIFE SPAN 10–12 years

White
Karamis
Piebald

The popularity of this Russian hunting dog is widespread in its own country and also reaches into Scandinavia. Bred for work, the East Siberian Laika is tough, active, and confident. Although it has a strong instinct for following big game, it is controllable, steady-tempered, and friendly with people.

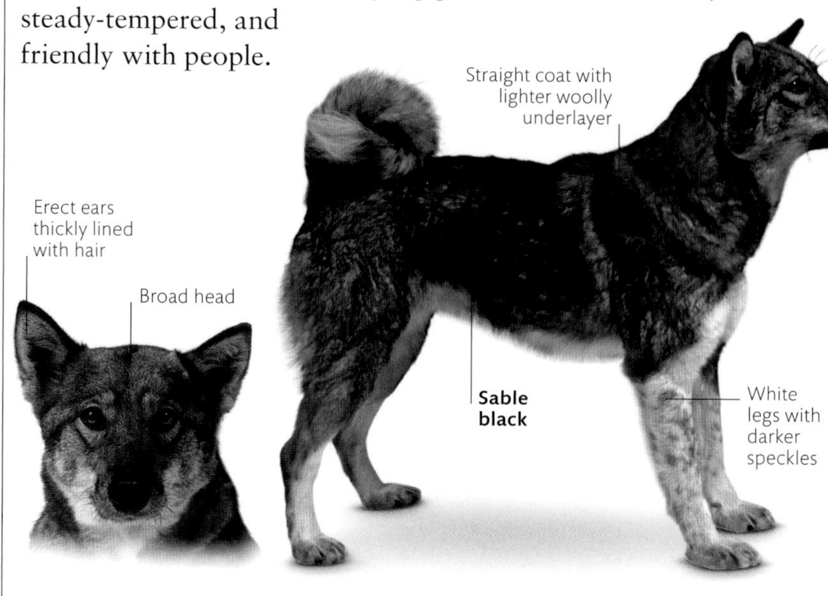

Russian-European Laika

HEIGHT 19–23in (48–58cm)
WEIGHT 44–51lb (20–23kg)
LIFE SPAN 10–12 years

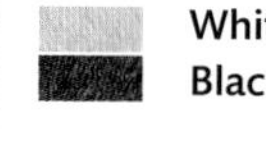

White
Black

This Laika was only acknowledged as a distinct breed in the early 1940s. Strong but lean-limbed, the Russian-European Laika has been used mainly for hunting in Russia's northern forests. A steady worker, this dog is excellent when used for its traditional purpose but does not adapt well to a domestic lifestyle.

Finnish Spitz

HEIGHT 15–20in (39–50cm)
WEIGHT 31–35lb (14–16kg)
LIFE SPAN 12–15 years

Finland's national dog was bred for hunting small game and is still used for sports in Scandinavia. With its pert, foxlike appearance, luxuriant coat, and enthusiasm for play, the Finnish Spitz makes an appealing family pet. The breed has a tendency to bark a great deal; this should be discouraged at an early age.

Finnish Lapphund

HEIGHT 17–19in (44–49cm)
WEIGHT 33–53lb (15–24kg)
LIFE SPAN 12–15 years

Any color

Developed from the dogs used as caribou herders and guards by the Sami people of Lapland, the Finnish Lapphund is enjoying growing popularity, both in Finland and elsewhere. Affectionate and faithful, this adaptable breed is willing to work, but is equally happy as a family pet and watchdog.

Lapponian Herder

HEIGHT 18–20in (46–51cm)
WEIGHT Up to 66lb (30kg)
LIFE SPAN 11–12 years

Originally bred from Finnish Lapphunds (left), German Shepherd Dogs (see p.42), and working collies, this dog was recognized as a separate breed in the 1960s. The Lapponian Herder, or Lapinporokoira, is still kept for work by caribou hunters, and sometimes as a house dog. This breed has a calm and friendly nature.

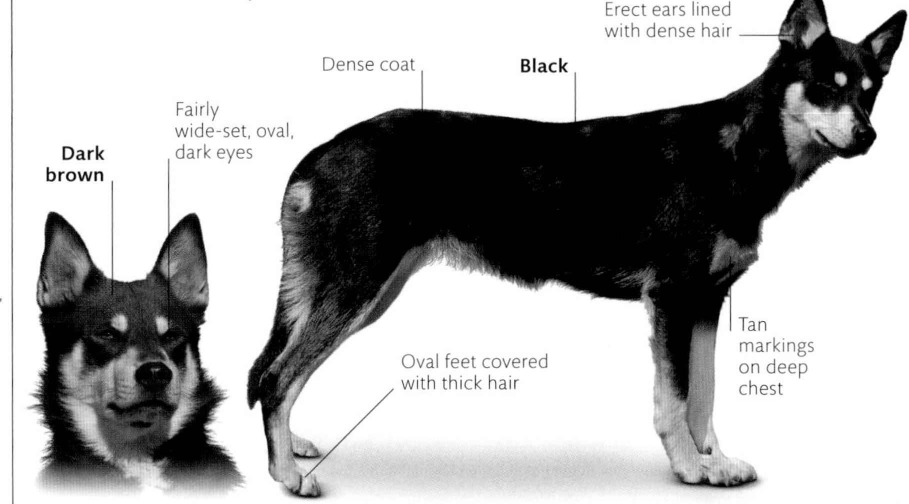

Swedish Lapphund

HEIGHT 16–20in (40–51cm)
WEIGHT 42–46lb (19–21kg)
LIFE SPAN 9–15 years

Brown
Black and brown
May have white mark on chest, feet, and tip of tail.

Similar to the Finnish Lapphund (above) in all but color, the Swedish Lapphund was once used as a caribou herder by the nomadic Sami people. This breed is popular in Sweden as a house dog but remains uncommon elsewhere. It enjoys company and tends to bark if left alone for long periods.

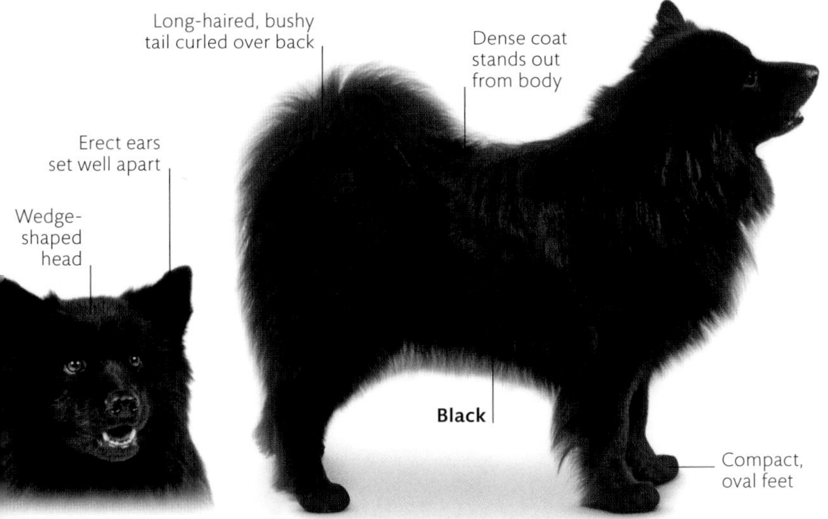

Swedish Elkhound

HEIGHT 20–26in (52–65cm)
WEIGHT Up to 66lb (30kg)
LIFE SPAN 12–13 years

Developed in Sweden's northern forest regions, this large, upstanding dog, also known as the Jämthund, was once kept for hunting elk, bear, and lynx. Popular with Sweden's military forces, this breed is the country's national dog. Although good with families, the Swedish Elkhound needs careful handling when around other dogs or pets.

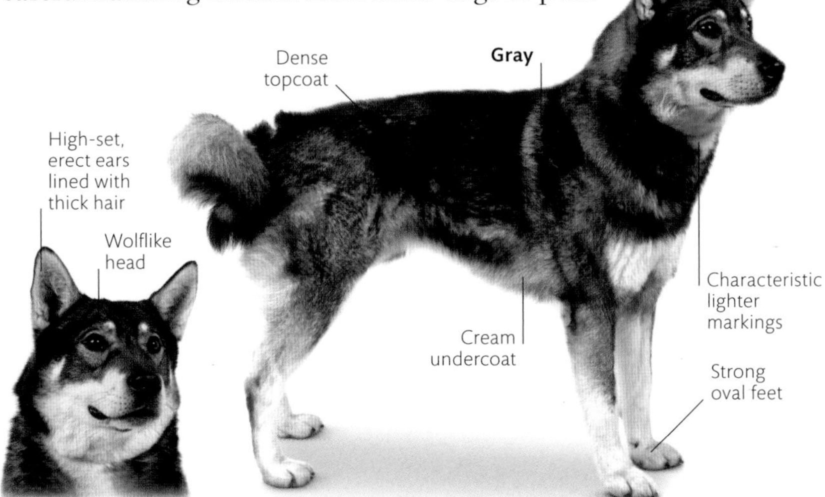

Norwegian Elkhound

HEIGHT 19–20in (49–52cm)
WEIGHT 44–51lb (20–23kg)
LIFE SPAN 12–15 years

Believed to have existed in Scandinavia for many hundreds of years, the Norwegian Elkhound was once used for tracking game, and is sturdy enough for sled hauling. Impervious to cold and wet weather, this dog likes to be outdoors. The breed has a strong hunting instinct and needs patient training.

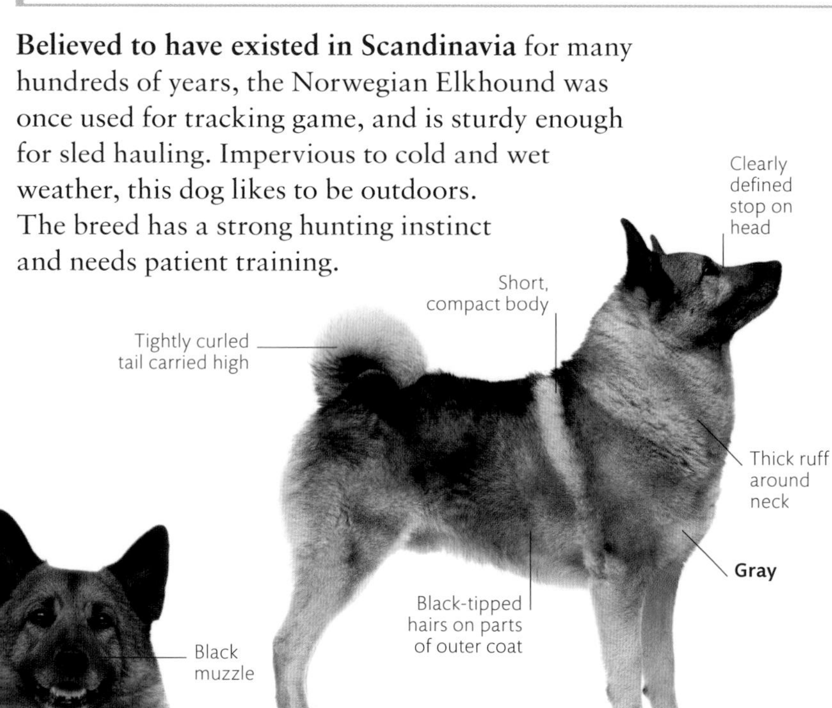

Black Norwegian Elkhound

HEIGHT 17–19in (43–49cm)
WEIGHT 40–60lb (18–27kg)
LIFE SPAN 12–15 years

This breed is a smaller, rarer version of the gray-coated Norwegian Elkhound (left). Originally bred for tracking game, it is versatile enough to be a sled dog, herder, watchdog, or family companion. It tends to bark readily but can be taught to stop on command.

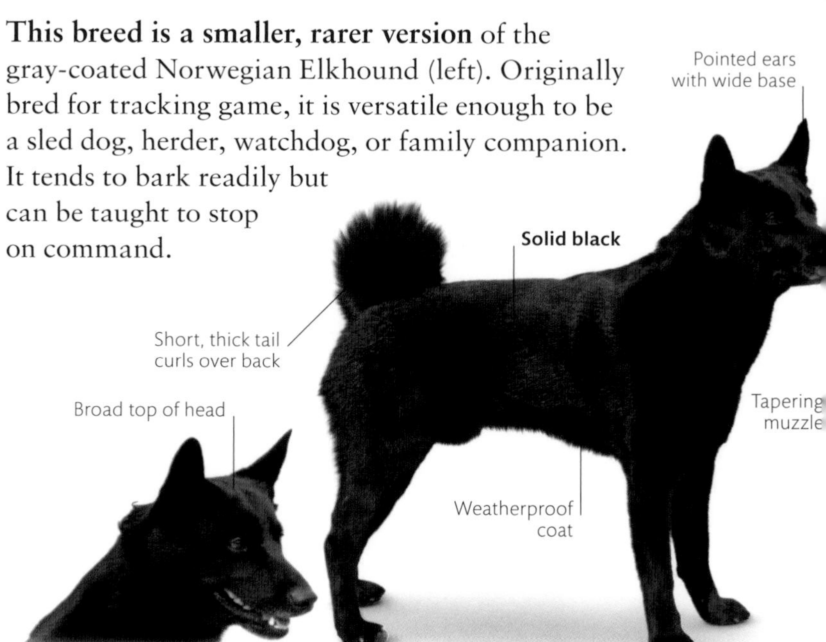

Hokkaido Dog

HEIGHT 18–20in (46–52cm)
WEIGHT 44–66lb (20–30kg)
LIFE SPAN 11–13 years

 **Variety of colors**

Dogs of this type were brought to the Japanese island of Hokkaido by the migrating Ainu people (Ainu Dog is the breed's alternative name). Although medium-sized, the Hokkaido Dog was bold and tough enough to hunt bear. Careful training and socializing can make this dog a good companion and home guardian.

Akita

HEIGHT	WEIGHT	LIFE SPAN	
American: 24–28in (61–71cm) Japanese: 23–28in (58–70cm)	American: 65–115lb (29–52kg) Japanese: 75–99lb (34–45kg)	10–12 years	Any color

This strong dog has a variable temperament and requires experienced handling to avoid wayward behavior

This big, powerful breed is descended rom hunting dogs bred in the rugged Akita Prefecture, on the island of Honshu n Japan, to hunt large quarry such as deer, pear, and wild boar. The Japanese Akita, or Akita Inu, was first developed in the 19th century as a fighting and hunting dog. The breed is a national treasure of Japan, and the dogs are seen as symbols of good luck.

The first Akita Inu was brought to the US in 1937 by Helen Keller. American servicemen returning home after World War II brought more Akitas with them, and these formed the basis of the American Akita, which is the breed now known as Akita today. The American Akita is recognized in many countries as a separate breed from the Akita Inu, and is larger and more imposing than its Japanese forebear.

The Akita is a substantial and strikingly handsome dog. It has a quiet dignity, is loyal and protective toward its human family, and is especially good with children. However, it tends to be domineering with other dogs. This breed needs an experienced owner and clear rules set at a young age to prevent bad behavior.

THE FAITHFUL HACHI-KO

Born in 1923, Hachi-ko was an Akita Inu. Each day when his owner, Professor Ueno, went to work, Hachi-ko accompanied him to Tokyo's Shibuya Station, then waited all day to walk home with him. In 1925 Professor Ueno died at work. Hachi-ko waited for him—for more than 10 years. He became a national hero for his loyalty, and when he died, Japan held a day of mourning. A statue of Hachi-ko was erected at Shibuya Station (below), and each year a ceremony is held to honor him.

Thick, bushy tail curls over back

Fawn

Black overlay

Black face mask

Deep, wide chest

Coarse outer coat stands away from body

Well developed muscular hindquarters

White chest markings extend down to feet

AMERICAN AKITA

Red-fawn

Triangular, erect ears

White markings

JAPANESE AKITA INU

Chow Chow

HEIGHT	WEIGHT	LIFE SPAN		
18–22in (46–56 cm)	46–71lb (21–32kg)	8–12 years	Cream Gold Red	Blue Black

This handsome dog with a coat like a teddy bear is loyal to its owner but can be reserved with strangers

Dogs of this type have been known in China for at least 2,000 years; one bas-relief carving from about 150BCE shows hunters with dogs resembling Chow Chows. The dogs' original uses included hunting birds, guarding livestock, and, in winter, pulling sleds. In addition, some of these dogs were raised as a source of meat and fur. They were prized by emperors and the nobility; in the 8th century CE one Tang dynasty emperor had 5,000 chowlike dogs in his kennels.

The first few dogs reached the West in the late 18th century. They acquired the name Chow Chow in England, where the term simply referred to curios brought back from East Asia. The breed's name in Chinese is actually *Songshi Quan*, often translated as "puffy lion dog." Larger numbers were imported to the UK in the late 19th century, and when Queen Victoria obtained one, their popularity was assured. The dogs were first shown in the US in 1890 but were not popular there until the 1920s.

The Chow Chow is now usually kept as a pet. Rather aloof in nature, the breed is devoted to its family but may be wary of strangers. It can have a dominant character, so needs firm training and early socializing. It requires only moderate exercise but benefits from the mental stimulation of a daily walk. The breed is notable for its thick coat and lionlike ruff, its furrowed face, and its blue-black tongue. There are two varieties: rough-coated with an immensely thick, upstanding coat, and smooth-coated, with short, dense hair.

THE PET THERAPY PIONEER

Today many different dogs are used as "therapy dogs" to comfort troubled or stressed people. The first canine therapy assistant was a Chow Chow named Jo-Fi, who worked with the father of psychoanalysis himself: Sigmund Freud (below, in Austria c.1935). During therapy sessions, Jo-Fi would remain in the room with Freud and was given clues to the clients' mental state. Jo-Fi would stay close to quiet or depressed people, but move away from those who were tense. Freud noted that Jo-Fi had a calming, reassuring influence on his clients, particularly children.

PUPPY

ROUGH-COATED

Shikoku

HEIGHT 18–20in (46–52cm)
WEIGHT 35–57lb (16–26kg)
LIFE SPAN 10–12 years

Sesame and black sesame

Once used as a boar hunter in remote mountain regions of Japan, the Shikoku remained largely inaccessible for crossbreeding. As a result, this breed is very true to its origins. Resilient, agile, and keen to chase other animals, the Shikoku is challenging to train but forms a close bond with people it loves and trusts.

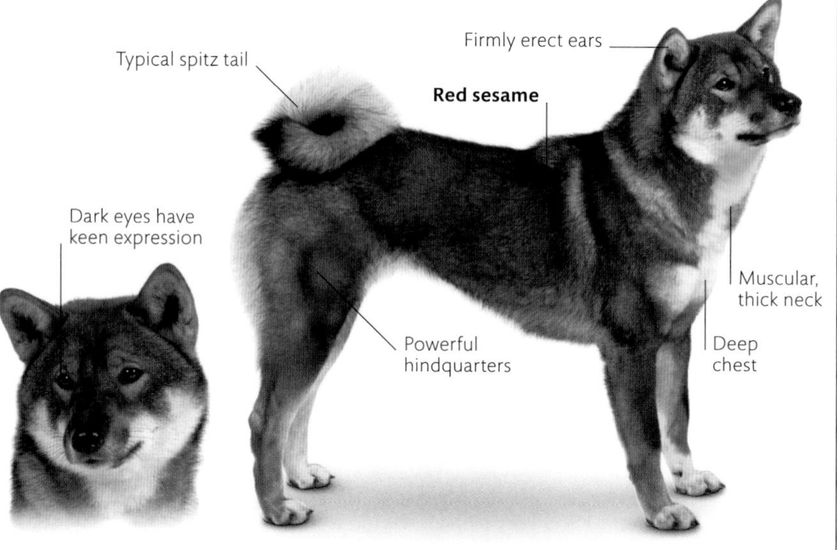

Korean Jindo

HEIGHT 18–21in (46–53cm)
WEIGHT 20–51lb (9–23kg)
LIFE SPAN 12–15 years

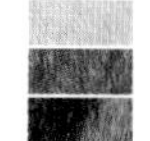

White
Red
Black and tan

Named after the Korean island of Jindo where it originated, the breed is popular in Korea but something of a rarity elsewhere. Used to hunt game, both large and small, the Korean Jindo's keen instinct for chasing other animals may be difficult to curb.

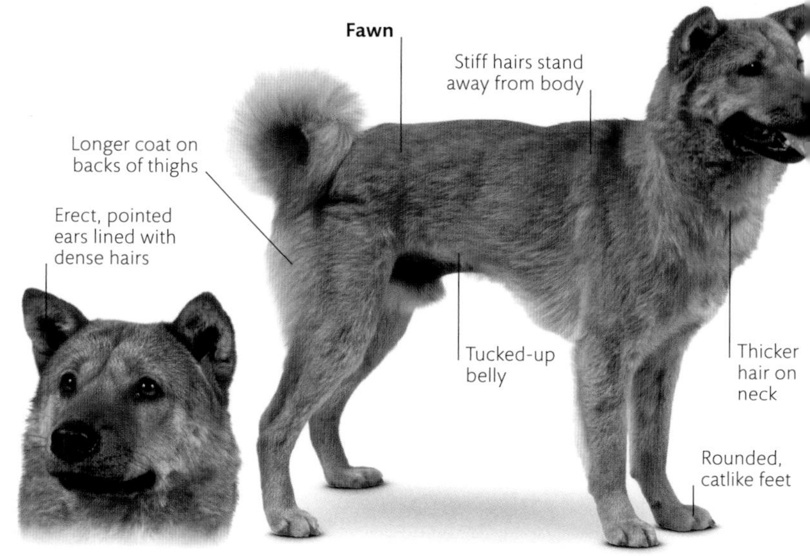

Shiba Inu

HEIGHT 15–16in (37–40cm)
WEIGHT 15–24lb (7–11kg)
LIFE SPAN 12–15 years

White | Black and tan
Red dogs may have a black overlay (red sesame).

Japan's smallest hunting dog, the Shiba Inu is a national treasure and has been known in its native country for hundreds of years. Bold and lively, the Shiba Inu makes a happy family dog, but can be unreliable if not socialized early on, and needs to have its hunting instinct controlled outdoors.

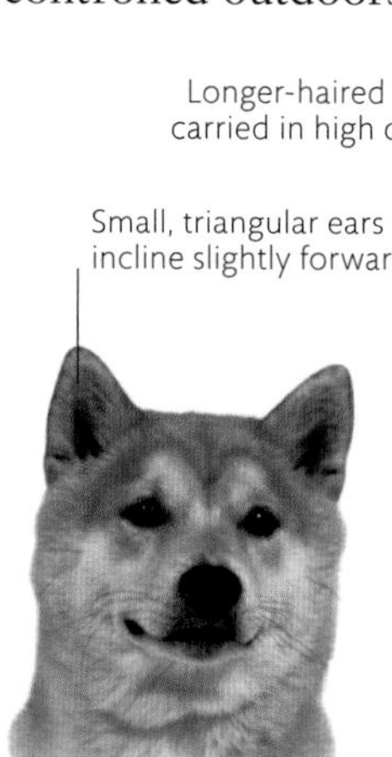

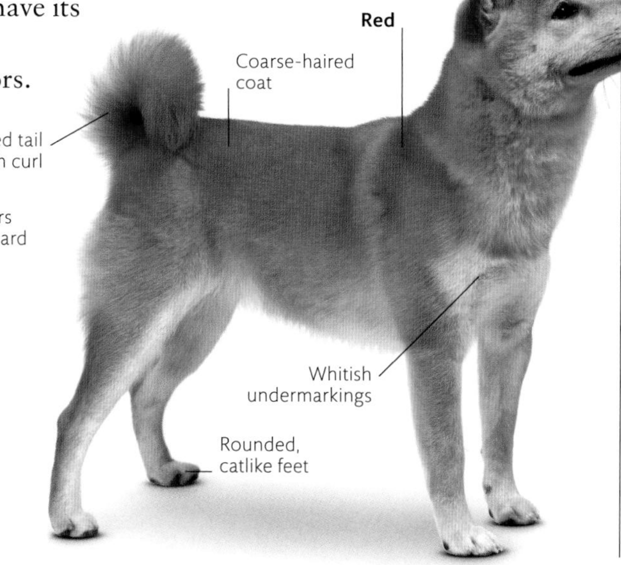

Kai

HEIGHT 19–21in (48–53cm)
WEIGHT 24–55lb (11–25kg)
LIFE SPAN 12–15 years

Range of red brindles

One of the oldest and purest of Japan's native dog breeds, the Kai was given the status of national treasure in 1934. An active and athletic hunter, used to running in packs, this dog may settle reasonably well into being a home companion but is not recommended for a novice owner.

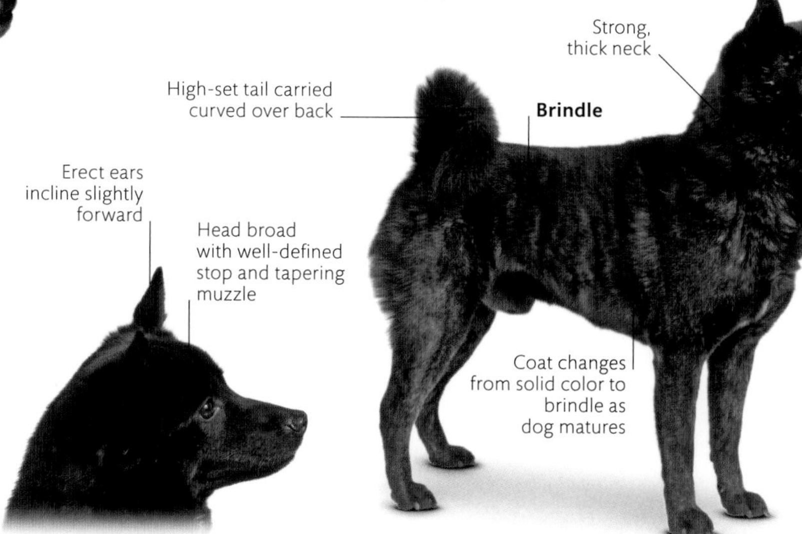

Kishu

HEIGHT 18–20in (46–52cm)
WEIGHT 29–60lb (13–27kg)
LIFE SPAN 11–13 years

Now rare but much prized, the Kishu was possibly bred hundreds of years ago for hunting large game in Japan's mountainous Kyushu region. A national treasure, this dog is quiet and faithful but can be a handful as a companion because of its strong instinct to chase.

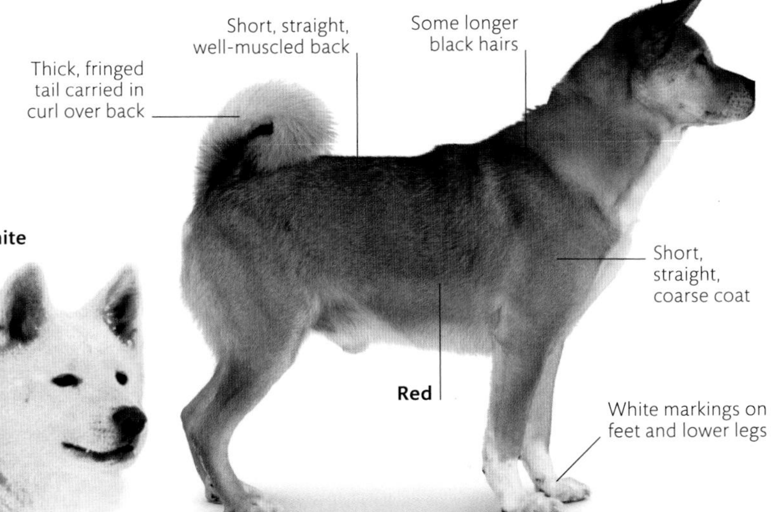

Japanese Spitz

HEIGHT 12–15in (30–37cm)
WEIGHT 11–22lb (5–10kg)
LIFE SPAN Over 12 years

Although the Japanese Spitz looks like a miniature version of the Samoyed (see p.106), there is no evidence that the two have a common descent. The breed was developed in Japan, and the popularity of this bright and energetic little dog has spread worldwide. Persistent barking is characteristic but can be controlled with training.

Eurasier

HEIGHT 19–24in (48–60cm)
WEIGHT 40–71lb (18–32kg)
LIFE SPAN Over 12 years

Any color
Coats should not be all white, liver, or with white patches.

A modern and still rare breed, the Eurasier was created in Germany in the 1960s from crossing the Chow Chow (see p.112), German Wolfspitz (see p.117), and Samoyed (see p.106). A good companion dog, it is even-tempered and calm but watchful. It readily forms close family bonds.

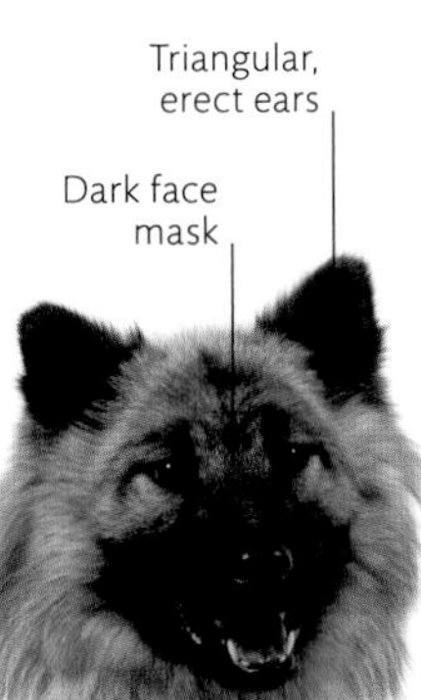

Italian Volpino

HEIGHT 10–12in (25–30cm)
WEIGHT 9–11lb (4–5kg)
LIFE SPAN Up to 16 years

Red

A favorite in Italy for over a century, this appealing little dog was kept by nobility as a pampered pet, and by farmers as a watchdog. Quick to bark at strangers, the Italian Volpino alerted bigger guard dogs to potential trouble. Lively and fun-loving, the breed is suitable for almost any type of home.

German Spitz

HEIGHT	WEIGHT	LIFE SPAN	
Klein: 9–11in (23–29cm)	Klein: 18–22lb (8–10kg)	14–15 years	Variety of colors
Mittel: 12–15in (30–38cm)	Mittel: 24–26lb (11–12kg)		
Gross: 17–20in (42–50cm)	Gross: 37–40lb (17–18kg)		

GROSS

A bustling and happy dog, with good watchdog instincts, the German Spitz is quick to learn and suitable for any home

There are three sizes of the German Spitz—Klein (small) and Mittel (medium) are both recognized by the KC, and Gross (giant) is recognized by the FCI. They are all descendants of the herding dogs once used by nomadic tribes of the Arctic.

Traditionally, German Spitz dogs were used for hunting and livestock herding, and as watchdogs; their thick undercoat and tough outer coat protected them in the cold and wet. During the 19th century the dogs became more popular as companion and show dogs. Some of these dogs were also exported to the US and gave rise to the American Eskimo Dog (see p.121). All varieties of German Spitz are relatively rare.

German Spitzes enjoy lots of human attention, but they need careful training because they have an independent spirit that can turn into willfulness without firm leadership. The dogs can get along well with children if they are taught to respect them. Once their place in the family has been established, these cheerful, affectionate dogs are excellent companions for owners of all ages. The immensely thick coat must be groomed thoroughly every day to keep it from becoming matted.

AGE AND WISDOM?

In a 19th-century German fable, illustrated below, a Spitz dog outwits a Pug that is trying to steal its bone. Whether Spitz breeds really are more intelligent than Pugs is not known, but Spitz breeds were considered to be one of the oldest breeds. In 1750, based on his knowledge of the German Spitz, German naturalist Count Buffon suggested that the Spitz was the ancestor of all domestic dogs. Modern genetic evidence supports Buffon's idea that some Spitz dogs originated early, but today no one breed is considered ancestral to all others, and comparative intelligence is still a matter of debate.

Tail curls over back

Compact, square body

Short hair on face

Moderately broad head

Wolf-sable

Thick frill around neck and shoulders

Profuse double coat with long outer hair

Long feathering on back of legs

Orange-sable

MITTEL

KLEIN

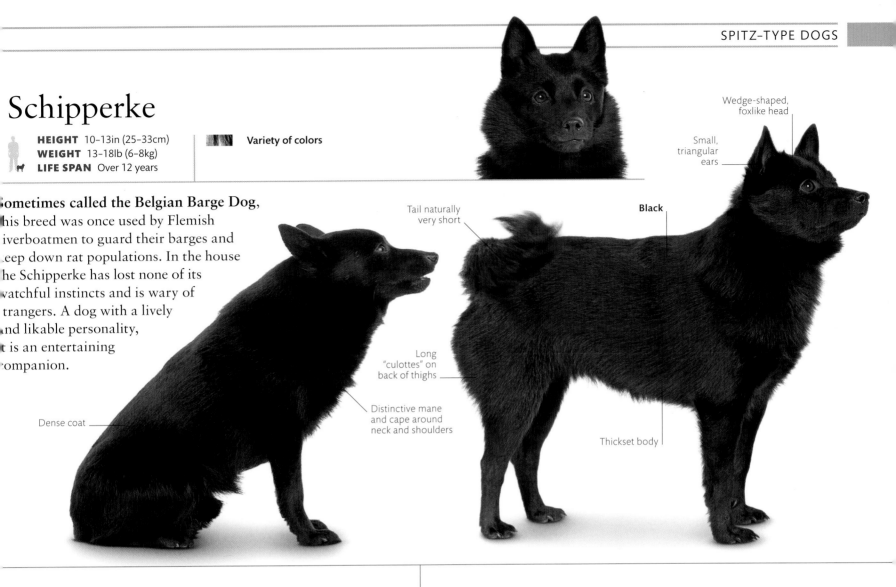

Schipperke

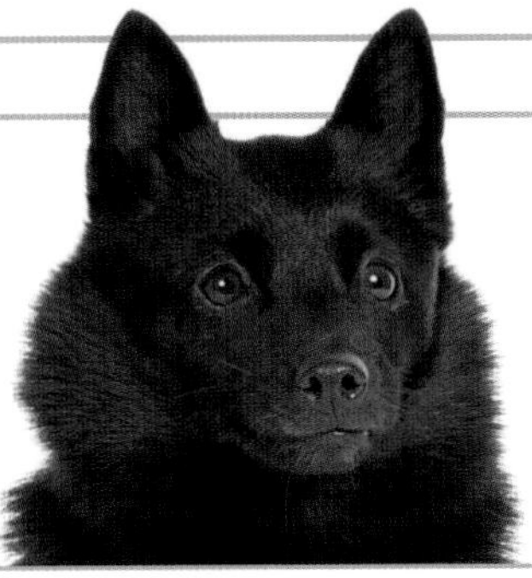

HEIGHT 10–13in (25–33cm)
WEIGHT 13–18lb (6–8kg)
LIFE SPAN Over 12 years

Variety of colors

ometimes called the Belgian Barge Dog, his breed was once used by Flemish iverboatmen to guard their barges and eep down rat populations. In the house he Schipperke has lost none of its vatchful instincts and is wary of trangers. A dog with a lively nd likable personality, t is an entertaining ompanion.

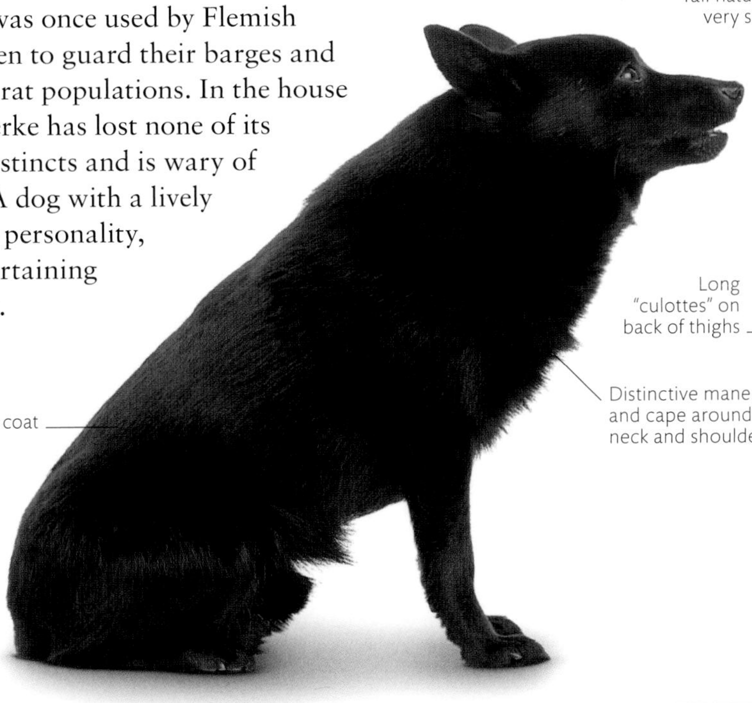

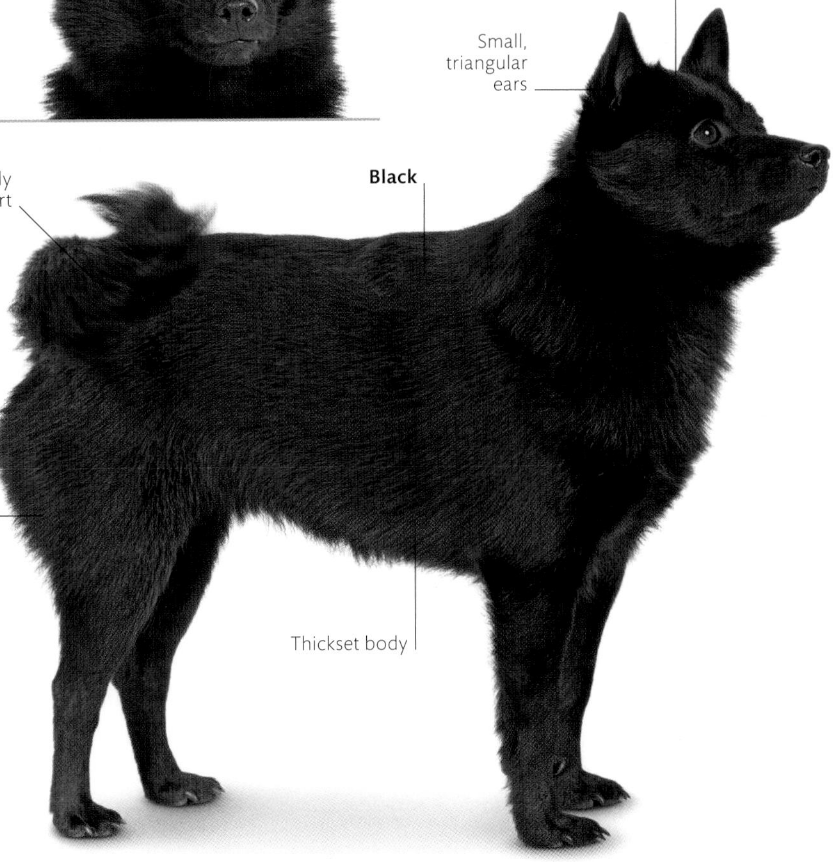

Wedge-shaped, foxlike head
Small, triangular ears
Tail naturally very short
Black
Long "culottes" on back of thighs
Distinctive mane and cape around neck and shoulders
Dense coat
Thickset body

Keeshond

HEIGHT 17–18in (43–46cm)
WEIGHT 33–44lb (15–20kg)
LIFE SPAN 12–15 years

The Keeshond was used in the 18th century by the riverboatmen and farmers of Holland as a watchdog. Not aggressive, this ntelligent and outgoing breed has an amiable nature that nakes it a much-loved companion dog. The Keeshond s willing to learn, and it mixes well with people and other pets.

German Wolfspitz

HEIGHT 17–22in (43–55cm)
WEIGHT 60–71lb (27–32kg)
LIFE SPAN 12–15 years

The German Wolfspitz is one of the oldest-known European dogs. It has given rise to the Keeshond (left) and in some countries the two are not regarded as separate breeds. Highly trainable, it is eager to be a part of family life. Suspicious of strangers, this dog barks readily but is not aggressive.

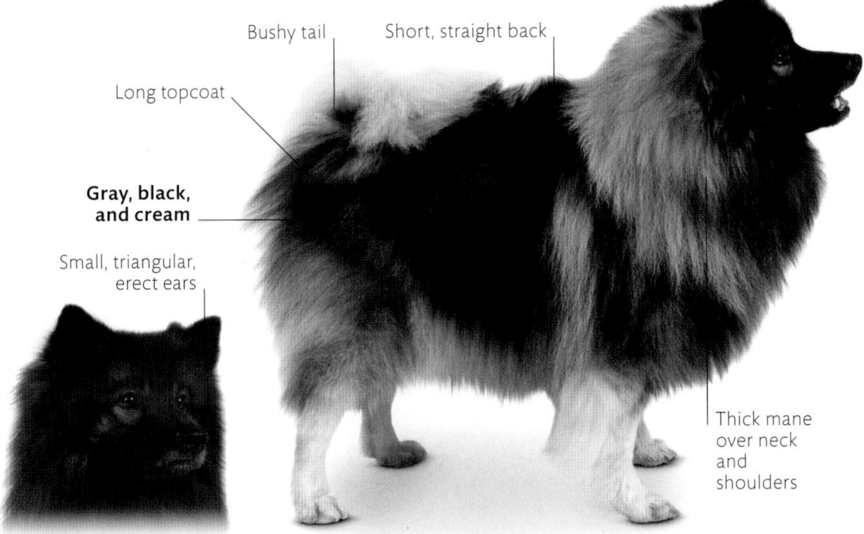

Pomeranian

HEIGHT	WEIGHT	LIFE SPAN	Any solid color
9–11in (22–28cm)	5–7lb (2–3kg)	12–15 years	Should be free from black or white shading.

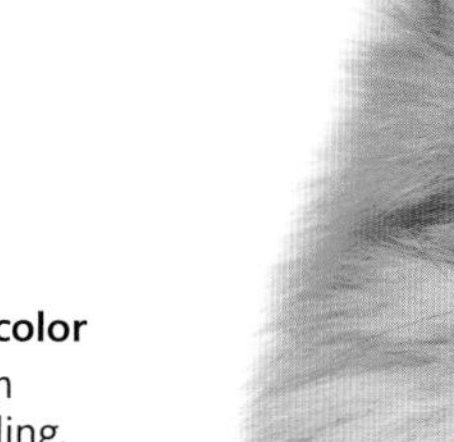

This affectionate miniature dog is brave and protective despite its small size, and it makes an excellent family pet

This breed, the smallest of the German Spitz-type dogs (see p.116), is known in some countries as the "dwarf Spitz" (Zwergspitz or Spitz nain). The Pomeranian takes its name from the region of Pomerania (now in northern Poland/northeast Germany), where its ancestors were bred as sheepdogs.

The original dogs from Pomerania were much larger than today's dogs, weighing as much as 31lb (14kg), and were usually white. These Spitz-type dogs were imported from Europe into the UK from the 1760s onward; all dogs of this type were generally known as "Pomeranians," whatever their country of origin.

During the late 19th century the Pomeranian was selectively bred down to "toy" size, partly due to Queen Victoria's enthusiasm for smaller dogs. Small Spitz-type dogs of different colors were imported from Germany and Italy to develop the breed (and to eliminate the old Pomeranians' tendency to be snappy). Breeders' clubs were set up in the UK in 1891 and in the US in 1900. During the 20th century the breed's main characteristics—its small size, luxuriant "puffball" coat, and cheerful nature—were further refined.

The intelligent, lively Pomeranian is an affectionate pet. It enjoys human company and will become devoted to its owner. However, the breed needs firm but gentle training so that it will not become overly dominant. Amazingly fast for their size, these dogs should be supervised if running loose. The thick coat is not difficult to groom but needs to be brushed every few days.

PUPPY

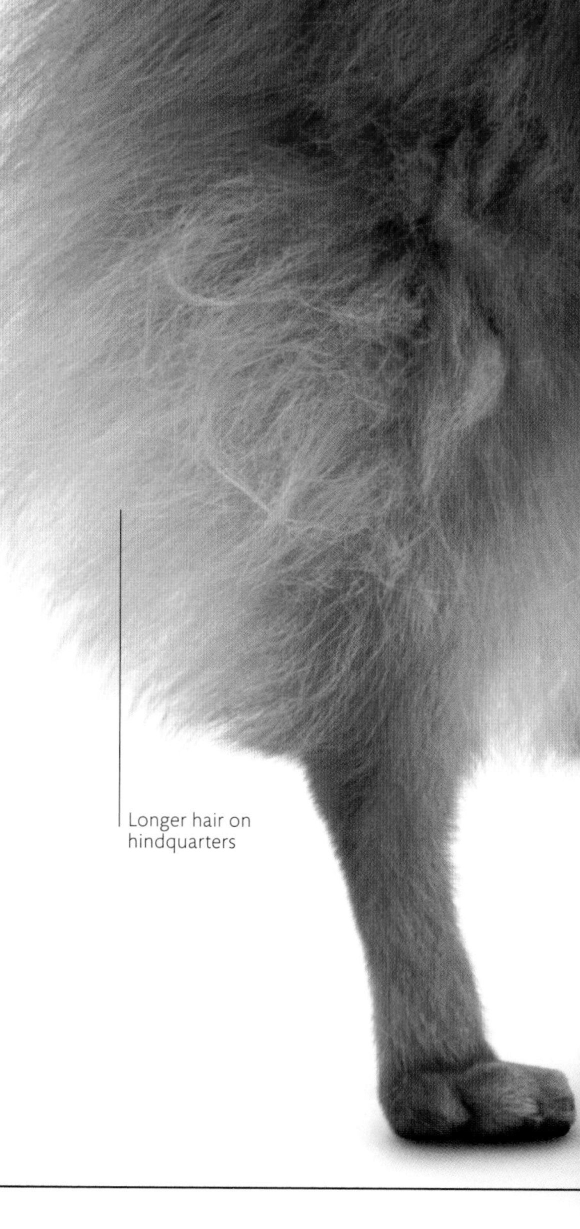

Longer hair on hindquarters

ROYAL PATRONAGE

When Queen Charlotte, wife of George III, came to Britain in 1761 she was accompanied by several white spitz dogs. These dogs were much larger than Pomeranians are today but were nevertheless the favored companion of German courtiers of the time. The dogs rapidly became popular in Britain and feature in several paintings by Gainsborough, such as *The Morning Walk* (right). The popularity of the breed increased further when Queen Victoria acquired several smaller Pomeranians on a trip to Italy in 1888.

MR. AND MRS. WILLIAM HALLETT ("THE MORNING WALK") BY THOMAS GAINSBOROUGH, 1785

Heavily plumed tail carried over back
Small, erect ears
Orange
Slightly oval, black-rimmed, dark eyes
Abundant frill around neck, shoulders, and chest
Smooth-haired, foxlike face
Soft, fluffy coat
Shorter hair on lower legs

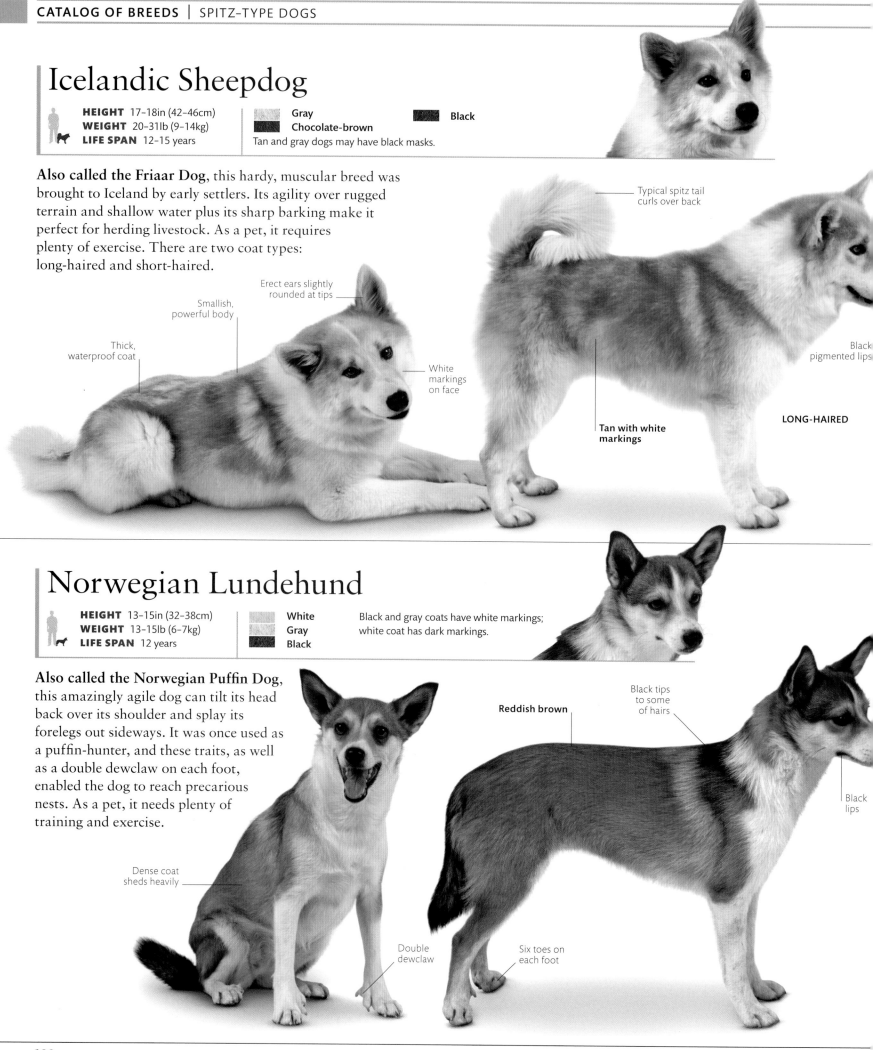

Icelandic Sheepdog

HEIGHT 17–18in (42–46cm)
WEIGHT 20–31lb (9–14kg)
LIFE SPAN 12–15 years

Gray
Chocolate-brown
Black

Tan and gray dogs may have black masks.

Also called the Friaar Dog, this hardy, muscular breed was brought to Iceland by early settlers. Its agility over rugged terrain and shallow water plus its sharp barking make it perfect for herding livestock. As a pet, it requires plenty of exercise. There are two coat types: long-haired and short-haired.

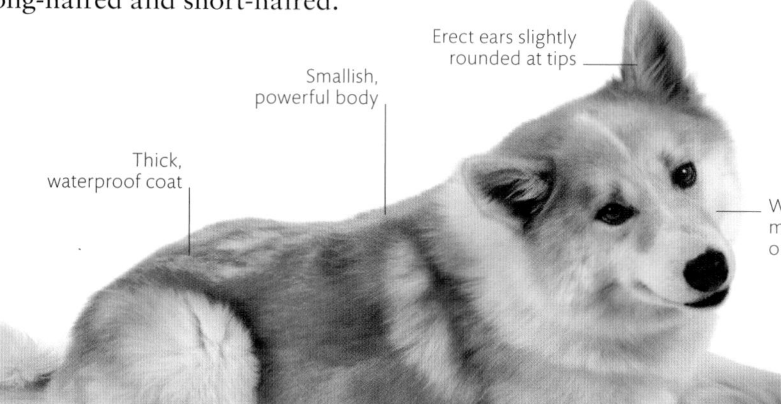

Norwegian Lundehund

HEIGHT 13–15in (32–38cm)
WEIGHT 13–15lb (6–7kg)
LIFE SPAN 12 years

White
Gray
Black

Black and gray coats have white markings; white coat has dark markings.

Also called the Norwegian Puffin Dog, this amazingly agile dog can tilt its head back over its shoulder and splay its forelegs out sideways. It was once used as a puffin-hunter, and these traits, as well as a double dewclaw on each foot, enabled the dog to reach precarious nests. As a pet, it needs plenty of training and exercise.

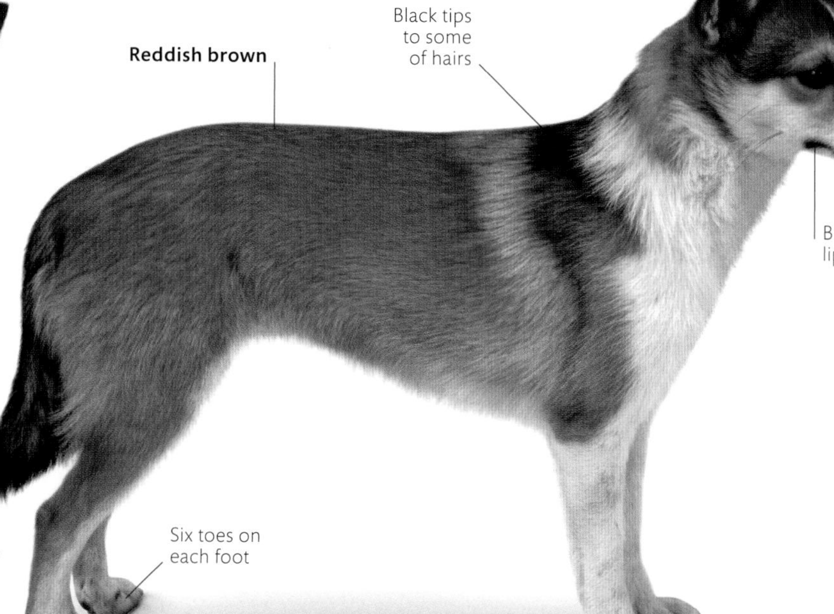

Nordic Spitz

HEIGHT 17–18in (42–45cm)
WEIGHT 18–33lb (8–15kg)
LIFE SPAN 15–20 years

This small, light spitz is Sweden's national dog. Its local name, Norbottenspets, means spitz from the county of Bothnia. It was once used to hunt squirrels and, more recently, game birds. A bright-eyed, bushy-tailed dog, the Nordic Spitz is not difficult to train, but requires regular exercise.

Foxlike head with typical tan markings
Compact body
Erect, black ears
White
Short, straight coat
Well-defined tan patch on hindquarters

Norwegian Buhund

HEIGHT 16–18in (41–46cm)
WEIGHT 26–40lb (12–18kg)
LIFE SPAN 12–15 years

Red
Red, wheaten, and wolf-sable coats may have black mask, ears, and tip to tail.

This medium-sized, agile farm dog was once used to guard against bears and wolves. Today the breed thrives when it has plenty of exercise and constant training. A sharp barker that molts heavily twice a year, this dog may not be ideal for a house-proud owner.

American Eskimo Dog

HEIGHT Miniature: 9–12in (23–30cm); Toy: 12–15in (30–38cm); Standard: Over 15–19in (38–48cm)
WEIGHT Miniature: 7–11lb (3–5kg); Toy: 11–20lb (5–9kg); Standard: 20–40lb (9–18kg)
LIFE SPAN 12–13 years

Despite its name, this is not a true Eskimo breed, but was developed in Germany and probably brought to the US by German settlers in the 19th century. Once seen performing tricks in traveling circuses, the American Eskimo Dog is a fast learner and eager to please. The breed comes in three sizes: toy, miniature, and standard.

White
Long guard hairs form topcoat

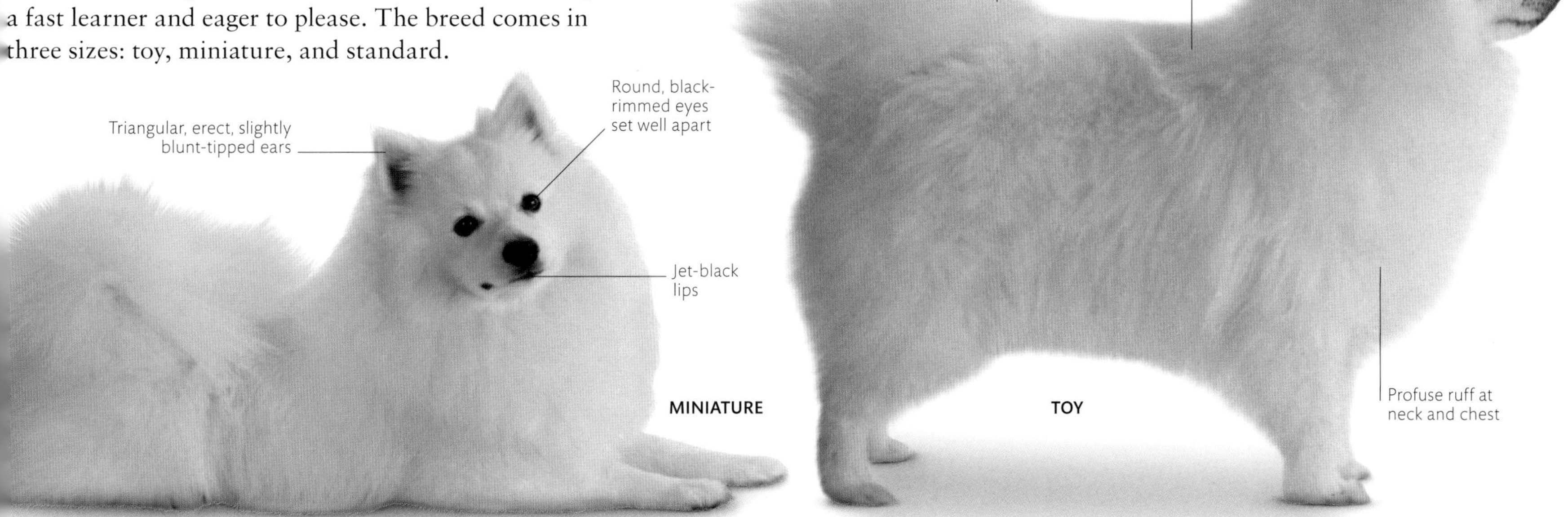

Papillon

HEIGHT	WEIGHT	LIFE SPAN	
8–11in (20–28cm)	5–11lb (2–5kg)	14 years	White  Black and white White coats may have any color patches except liver.

Dainty and delightful, but definitely not delicate, this dog makes a fun-loving and intelligent companion

The Papillon is named for its erect, fringed ears, resembling butterfly wings (the word *papillon* is French for "butterfly"). The breed is descended from the "dwarf spaniels" that were popular in the royal courts of Europe from the Renaissance onward. This type of dog was often portrayed in paintings of and for the nobility, such as the 1538 *Venus of Urbino* by Titian. In 17th-century France similar dogs were imported and bred at the court of Louis XIV, and in the 18th century they were the pampered favorites of Madame de Pompadour and Marie Antoinette.

The earliest form of the Papillon had drop ears; this type still exists and is known as the Phalène (French for "moth"). Toward the end of the 19th century the modern Papillon with its erect ears began to appear, and this version is now much more commonly seen. In both types the ears are notable for their long, silky fringes.

In the UK and the US, both the Papillon and the Phalène are regarded as the same breed, since the two types can occur in the same litter. The FCI refers to both types as Continental Toy Spaniels.

Today the Papillon is most often seen as a pet or in the show ring. These lively, intelligent dogs love human companionship and enjoy plenty of play and exercise. They require early socializing with other dogs and strangers, since some individuals can be nervous. The long, fine, silky coat needs daily grooming to prevent mats from forming.

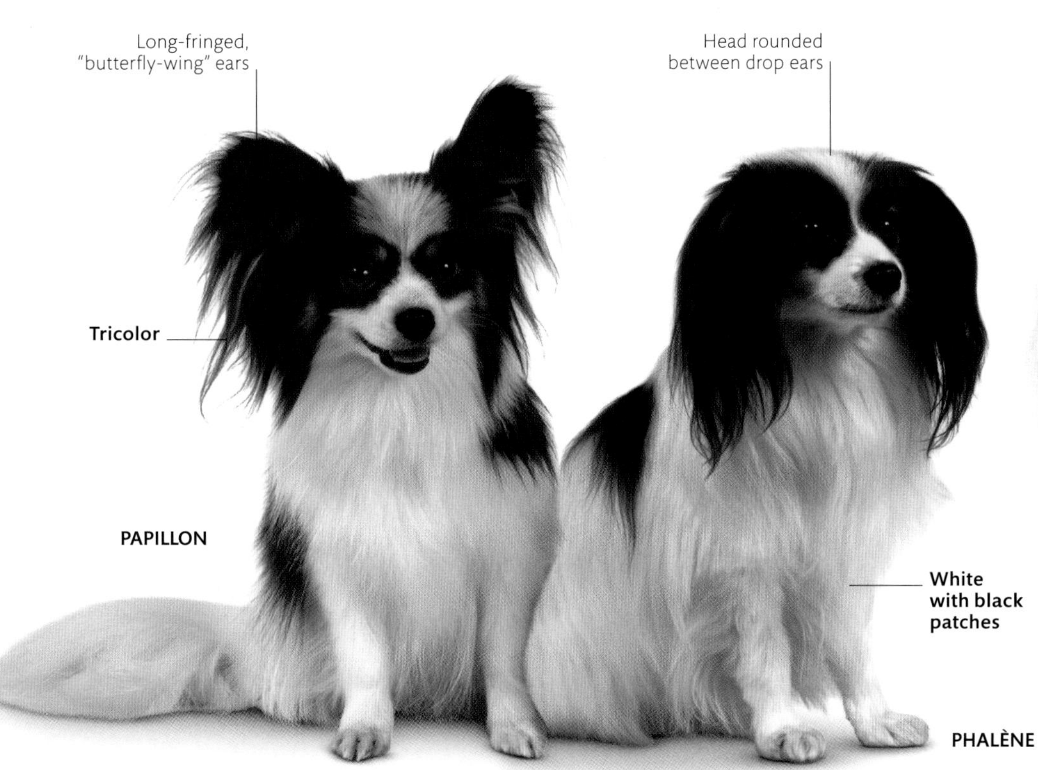

FRENCH COURT LAPDOG

In the past lapdogs were luxuries that only the wealthy could afford. Small, spaniel-like dogs, resembling the Papillon, start to appear alongside their owners in portraits painted around 1500. Their popularity in Continental Europe continued to increase, and by the 18th century the Papillon had become a firm favorite of the French court (as can be seen in Jean Baptiste Greuze's 1774 portrait of Madame de Porcin, below). Marie Antoinette kept them as boudoir dogs and it is said that, in 1793, she carried her dog Thisbe with her to the guillotine.

High speed
On the racetrack, greyhounds have been recorded as reaching top speeds of around 45mph (72km/h). They are one of the fastest living animals.

SIGHT HOUNDS

Canine speed merchants, the sight hounds—or gazehounds as they are sometimes called—are hunting dogs that locate and follow their prey primarily by using their keen eyesight. Streamlined, lightly framed, but powerful, a sight hound in pursuit of quarry moves rapidly and turns with great flexibility. Many dogs in this group were bred to hunt specific prey.

As shown by archeological evidence, lean, leggy dogs have been hunting alongside humans for thousands of years, but the early development of modern sight hounds is not entirely clear. It is likely that many crosses involving a diversity of other breeds, including terriers, went into the creation of classic sight hounds such as the Greyhound (see p.126) and the Whippet (see p.128).

Most sight hounds are easily recognizable as a type. Selective breeding has developed characteristics designed to promote speed: strong, supple backs and an athletic build enable the body to stretch out at full gallop; long-striding, elastic limbs, and powerful hindquarters to provide impulsion. Another characteristic is a long, narrow head that either lacks a pronounced stop or, as in the case of the Borzoi (see p.132), has no stop at all. Typically in a sight hound bred to hunt and snap up small prey, the head is carried low when the dog runs at full stretch. Another common feature of sight hounds is a deep chest accommodating a larger than usual heart and allowing for good lung capacity. Short or fine, silky coats tend to be the norm among this group of dogs; only the Afghan Hound (see p.136) is very long-haired.

Graceful and aristocratic, sight hounds during their history have been the favored hunting dogs of the wealthy and well born. Greyhounds, or at least coursing dogs very similar to the modern breed, were kept by the pharaohs of ancient Egypt. For centuries Salukis (see p.131) were, and occasionally still are, used by sheikhs for hunting gazelle in the desert. In pre-Soviet Russia the spectacular Borzoi was the dog of choice for the nobility and even royalty, specifically bred for running down and killing wolves.

Today sight hounds are used for racing and coursing and are very often kept as pets. Usually non-aggressive, although sometimes a little aloof, sight hounds make attractive family dogs but need to be handled with caution when outdoors and may be best exercised on a leash. Their instinct to pursue small animals can be strong enough to override all obedience training. A sight hound chasing after what it perceives to be prey is almost impossible to stop.

Greyhound

HEIGHT	WEIGHT	LIFE SPAN	
27–30in (69–76cm)	60–66lb (27–30kg)	11–12 years	Any color

Capable of astonishing speed, this dog makes a docile and gentle family pet and is content with short bursts of exercise

Developed in the UK, the greyhound's earliest ancestors were once thought to have been the slender hounds depicted in Egyptian tombs dating from around 4000BCE. However, DNA evidence has suggested that, despite appearances, the breed is more closely related to herding dogs. Another possible ancestor is an ancient Celtic dog called the Vertragus, used for hunting and hare coursing.

Large, athletic sight hounds were known in Britain by 1000CE. At first they were commonly used for hunting, but during the Middle Ages only the aristocracy could afford to keep them. In the 18th century hare coursing became popular among the upper classes, and the first Greyhound stud books were opened.

Capable of reaching 45mph (72km/h) in short bursts, the sleek and powerful Greyhound is built for running. It is still used for hare coursing but is more commonly seen at dog races. Some Greyhounds are also bred for the show ring; these are larger than racing dogs.

Retired racing Greyhounds are becoming popular as pets. They are gentle and easy to keep, requiring only moderate exercise, but their slender frame and thin coat mean that they need protection from the cold.

MICK THE MILLER

The UK's first great racing Greyhound was an Irish dog belonging to a priest. Born in 1926, Mick the Miller was sickly as a pup but won 15 races in Ireland. He then triumphed at the 1929 Derby at London's White City, breaking the world speed record over 525 yards. From 1929 to 1931 Mick the Miller (right) won an array of major races, and he became a firm favorite with the public. Once retired, he earned $90,000 in stud fees, and also appeared in a movie. He died in 1939.

MICK BEING MASSAGED WHILE IN TRAINING AT WALTON-ON-THAMES

Long and narrow head

Muscular, long, slightly arched neck

Brindle

Short, smooth coat

Deep chest housing powerful lungs and heart

Long, low-set, tapering tail

Small, ros ears, fine in texture

Straight long forelegs

Italian Greyhound

HEIGHT	WEIGHT	LIFE SPAN	Variety of colors
13–15in (32–38cm)	9–11lb (4–5kg)	14 years	Black and blue with tan markings, and brindle not permitted.

Ihis miniature, satin-skinned greyhound enjoys creature comforts but needs more exercise than its size might suggest

Ihis mini-greyhound originated in Aediterranean countries—small ;reyhound-type dogs feature in Turkish and Greek art dating from 2,000 years ago, and similar dog was found in the lava flows at ompeii. By the time of the Renaissance, niniature greyhounds were much favored ets in the Italian court. They were brought o England in the 17th century and became ighly popular there and in the other royal ourts of Europe.

The Italian Greyhound needs daily xercise and mental stimulation. Despite ts small size, the breed is fast and can each 40mph (64km/h) in a sudden burst. t is highly energetic and intelligent, with strong chasing instinct. As suggested by its noble past, the Italian Greyhound loves to be pampered. Usually devoted to its human family, the breed needs plenty of interaction with people, otherwise it may become bored and wayward. It is more hardy than its delicate frame would suggest, but it can still be injured by active children or other, larger dogs.

The breed's short coat and thin skin make it susceptible to cold and wet weather, so it will need a jacket when going outdoors in wintry conditions.

A KING'S BEST FRIEND

Frederick the Great of Prussia (seen below, right, in a wood engraving after an 18th century drawing) was said to have owned more than 50 miniature greyhounds and even took one to battle in his saddlebag during the Seven Years' War (1756–63). When this dog died, Frederick had it buried at his favorite residence, the Sanssouci Palace, in Potsdam. Frederick had wished to be buried after death alongside his dog, but his successor did not allow it. Frederick died in 1786 but it was only in 1991 that his remains were moved and his wish granted.

Large eyes

Short, satin-soft coat

Red-fawn

Long, slender, gracefully arched neck

Fine, supple skin

Very fine-boned legs

Long, fine tail set very low

Very fine muzzle

Rose ears placed well back

Long, flat, narrow head

ADULT AND PUPPIES

Whippet

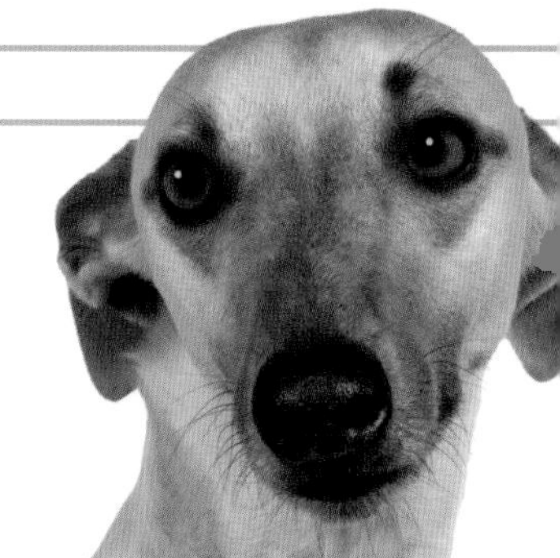

HEIGHT	WEIGHT	LIFE SPAN	Any color
17–20in (44–51cm)	24–40lb (11–18kg)	12–15 years	

The ultimate sprinter, this dog is calm, sweet-natured, and adoring at home but remains an avid hunter

The fastest domesticated animal for its weight, the Whippet is capable of speeds of up to 35mph (56km/h). It has impressive powers of acceleration, and can twist and turn at speed with dexterity. This elegant little dog was developed in the north of England in the late 19th century by crossing the Greyhound (see p.126) with various terriers. Originally bred for hunting hare, rabbit, and other small game, the Whippet soon became popular as an affordable sporting dog. Whippet racing, held wherever there was enough space for dogs to sprint a couple of hundred yards, became a regular fixture for working men of mill and mining towns. Today the breed is still used for racing, as well as lure coursing and agility trials, but is mostly kept as a pet.

Quiet, docile, and affectionate, the Whippet behaves well in the house and is gentle with children. A sensitive breed, it needs tactful handling and is easily distressed by rough play or harsh commands. With its delicate skin and short, fine hair, the Whippet needs to wear a coat in cold weather. Its own coat is almost odor-free, without a doggy smell even when wet. Puppies with long coats are occasionally born but are not officially recognized.

The Whippet has abundant energy and should be given regular exercise and, in safe areas, plenty of opportunity to run free. It is generally good with other dogs but has a strong hunting instinct and chases cats and small animals if given the chance.

A Whippet will tolerate, or at least ignore, a household cat if the two are raised together, but it should not be left unsupervised with other family pets such as rabbits or guinea pigs. This breed is wary of strangers, so it makes a reasonable watchdog. Toward its owners, the Whippet shows unswerving loyalty.

THE POOR MAN'S RACEHORSE

In the industrial areas of 19th-century England, rag racing with Whippets, in which the dogs chased a lure made of cloth, was immensely popular. Working families took great pride in their racing Whippets and valued the extra income that winning dogs could earn. The breed came to be known as the "poor man's racehorse." The owners lavished care on their dogs, allowing them to share the family's food and even the children's beds.

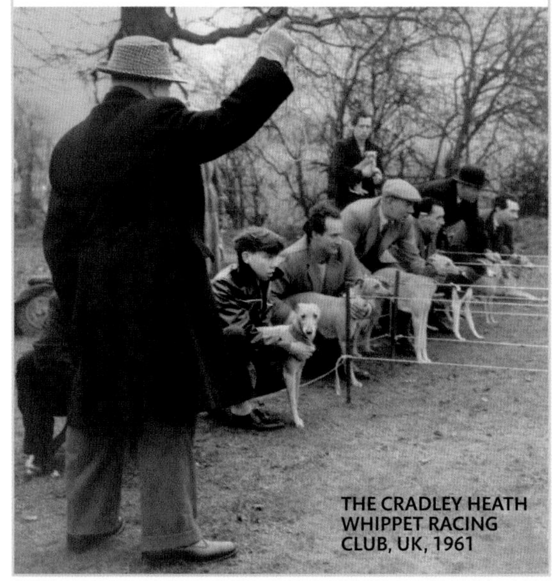

THE CRADLEY HEATH WHIPPET RACING CLUB, UK, 1961

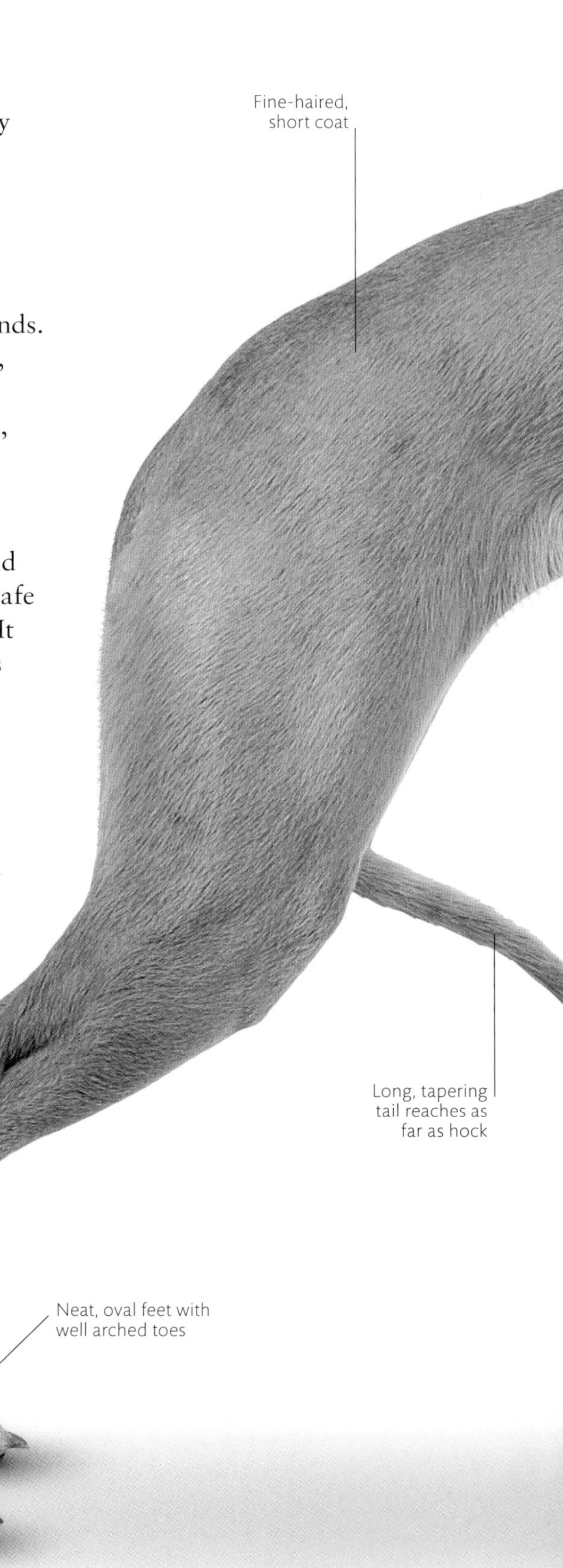

Fine-haired, short coat

Long, tapering tail reaches as far as hock

Neat, oval feet with well arched toes

Brindle
and white
Rose ears
Muscular,
elegant outline
Darker muzzle
Silver-fawn
Expressive,
oval eyes
Tucked-up
belly
Deep chest
Well muscled
hindquarters

Rampur Greyhound

HEIGHT 22–30in (56–75cm)
WEIGHT 59–66lb (27–30kg)
LIFE SPAN 8–10 years

Any color

Now rare, the Rampur Greyhound was once the favorite sporting companion of Indian princes. Used mainly to hunt jackal and deer, this powerful dog was also capable of bringing down wild boar. The breed's origins are uncertain, but may include crosses between the English Greyhound and native Indian breeds chosen for their strength and tenacity.

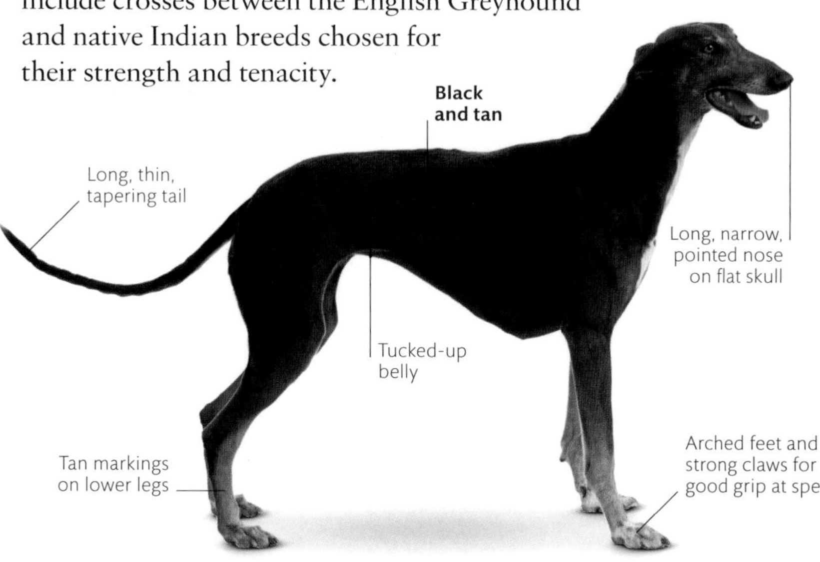

Hungarian Greyhound

HEIGHT 24–28in (62–70cm)
WEIGHT 55–88lb (25–40kg)
LIFE SPAN 12–14 years

Any color

This dog, once used for hunting rabbit and fox, may have entered Hungary with the Magyars over 1,000 years ago. Not as fast as a Greyhound (see p.126) but tougher and tireless, the Hungarian Greyhound (or Magyar Agar) needs a regular run. It makes a faithful and protective companion.

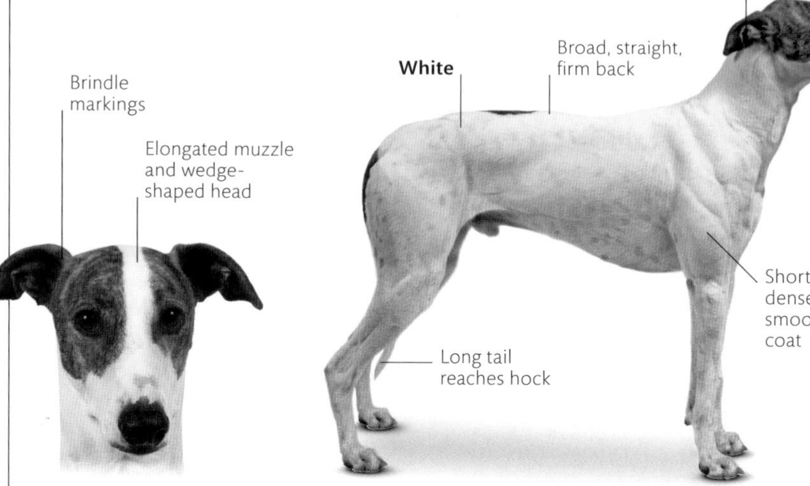

Polish Greyhound

HEIGHT 27–31in (68–80cm)
WEIGHT 143–187lb (65–85kg)
LIFE SPAN 12–15 years

All colors

Possibly a mix of the Greyhound (see p.126) and the Borzoi (see p.132) in origin, the Polish Greyhound is stronger and sturdier than other sight hounds. It is bred to hunt bustard (a large, cranelike bird) and wolves, and is a popular track racer. The Polish Greyhound requires firm training, plenty of exercise, and regular brushing.

Saluki

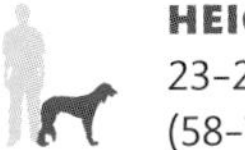

HEIGHT	WEIGHT	LIFE SPAN	
23–28in (58–71cm)	35–65lb (16–29kg)	12 years	Variety of colors

This slim-framed, sleek, and intelligent gazelle hunter makes a loyal and courageous family companion

)ne of the oldest breeds in existence, aluki-type dogs have been used as unting dogs for thousands of years. They are shown on wall carvings from he Sumerian empire (in what is now raq), dating from 7000–6000BCE, and n paintings in ancient Egyptian tombs; heir mummified bodies have been found uried with pharaohs. Similar dogs were nown in China in the Tang dynasty 618–907CE), and were first brought to urope by Crusaders in the 12th century.

The Saluki is esteemed in the Middle ast for its swiftness; over long distances, t can be faster than a Greyhound (see p.126). Although Muslims traditionally viewed dogs as unclean, they made an exception for the Saluki, allowing it to live in the family tent. Salukis were never sold, but they might be presented to people as a mark of honor.

The Saluki is gentle but may seem aloof to strangers, although it is more loving to its owners. It is highly intelligent, so needs plenty of mental and physical challenges if it is not to become bored and willful. Its strong chasing instinct needs to be kept under control. There are two coat types: smooth and feathered.

PRIZED HUNTER

Early drawings of the Saluki (as in the illustration from the early 1840s below) show dogs with well developed feathering on legs and tail. However, they are depicted without the long feathering on the ears that is typical of the feathered-coat variety today. The Bedouin traditionally prize these dogs for their hunting prowess rather than their appearance. Salukis are used to hunt fast-moving prey such as gazelles (giving rise to the alternative name "gazelle-hound"), as well as fox and rabbit.

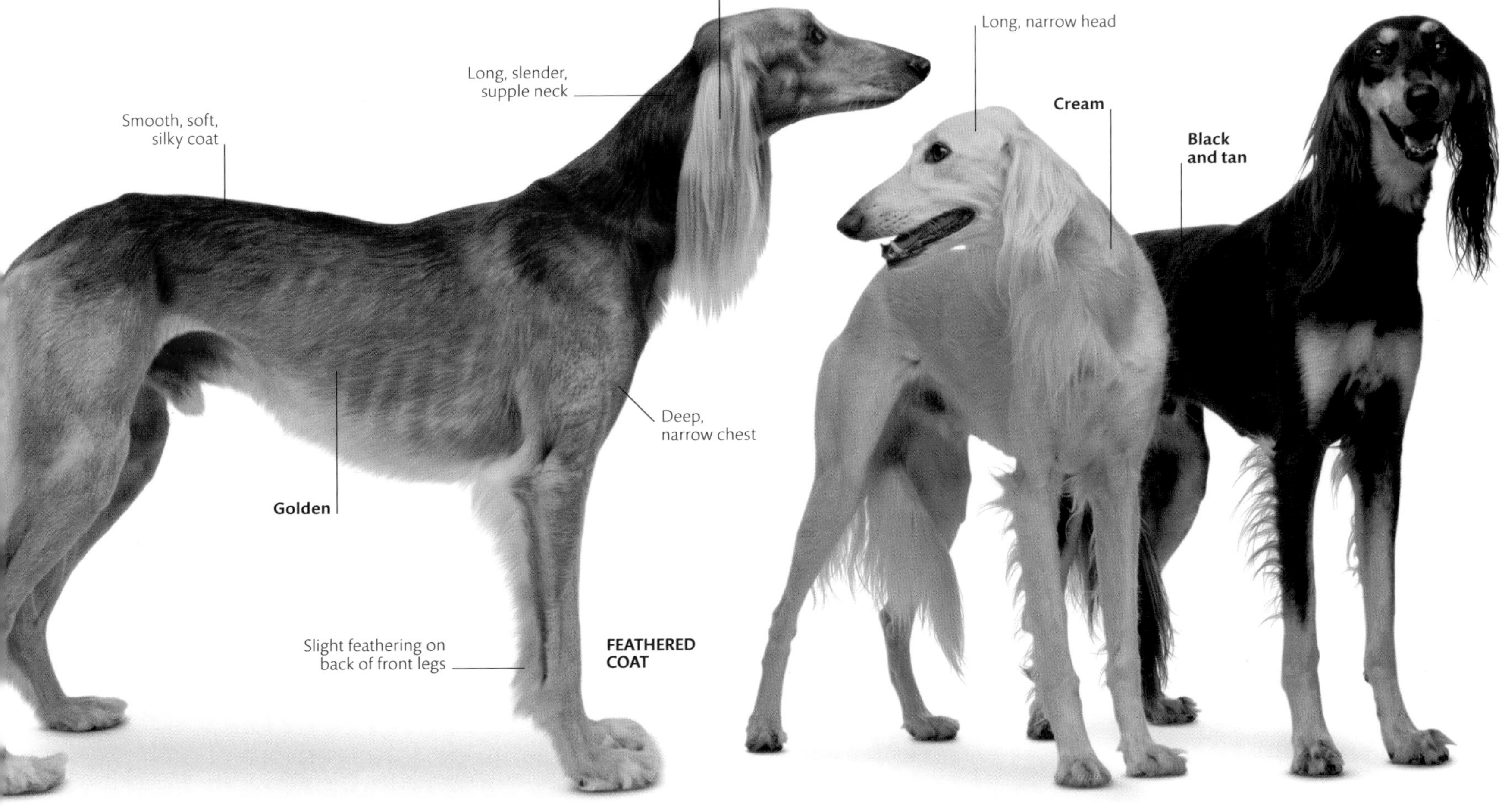

Pendant ears with long, silky hair

Long, narrow head

Long, slender, supple neck

Smooth, soft, silky coat

Cream

Black and tan

Deep, narrow chest

Golden

Slight feathering on back of front legs

FEATHERED COAT

Borzoi

HEIGHT	WEIGHT	LIFE SPAN	
27–29in (68–74cm)	60–106lb (27–48kg)	11–13 years	Variety of colors

A CULTURAL ICON

The powerful, glamorous Borzoi has won itself a place in literature and film. Leo Tolstoy's epic novel *War and Peace* contains a powerful description of a Borzoi pack hunting a wolf. In F. Scott Fitzgerald's *The Beautiful and Damned*, the main character's girlfriend compares him to a "Russian wolfhound"; he is flattered because they are "usually photographed with princesses and dukes." The Borzoi was a favorite subject in Art Deco art and has featured in many movies—in addition to being an elegant companion for movie stars.

ALEXANDRA, WIFE OF EDWARD VII, WITH HER PET BORZOI

This noble Russian hound combines speed, elegance, and a desire to chase with a certain nonchalance

Descended from Central Asian sight hounds, this tall, elegant dog was brought westwards by traders. Once known as the Russian Wolfhound, the Borzoi was bred to hunt wolves for Russian tsars and nobility; the original dogs were crossed with Greyhounds (see p.126) for speed, and with native Russian dogs for strength and resistance to cold. The nobles would take as many as 100 dogs on a hunt, releasing them in groups of three to bring down a wolf; one dog would attack the wolf's hind quarters, while the other two caught its neck.

After the Russian Revolution in 1917, many of these "aristocratic" dogs were killed, but during the 1940s a soldier named Constantin Esmont persuaded the Soviet government to preserve the Borzoi for use by hunters in the fur trade. In Russia the Borzoi is still valued mainly for its hunting abilities, but outside the country it has been bred for many years as a show dog and companion dog.

Today the Borzoi is happy in a regular home environment but needs plenty of long walks and runs as well as training to control its strong chasing instinct. It also requires a routine of brushing and bathing to keep its long, wavy coat in top condition.

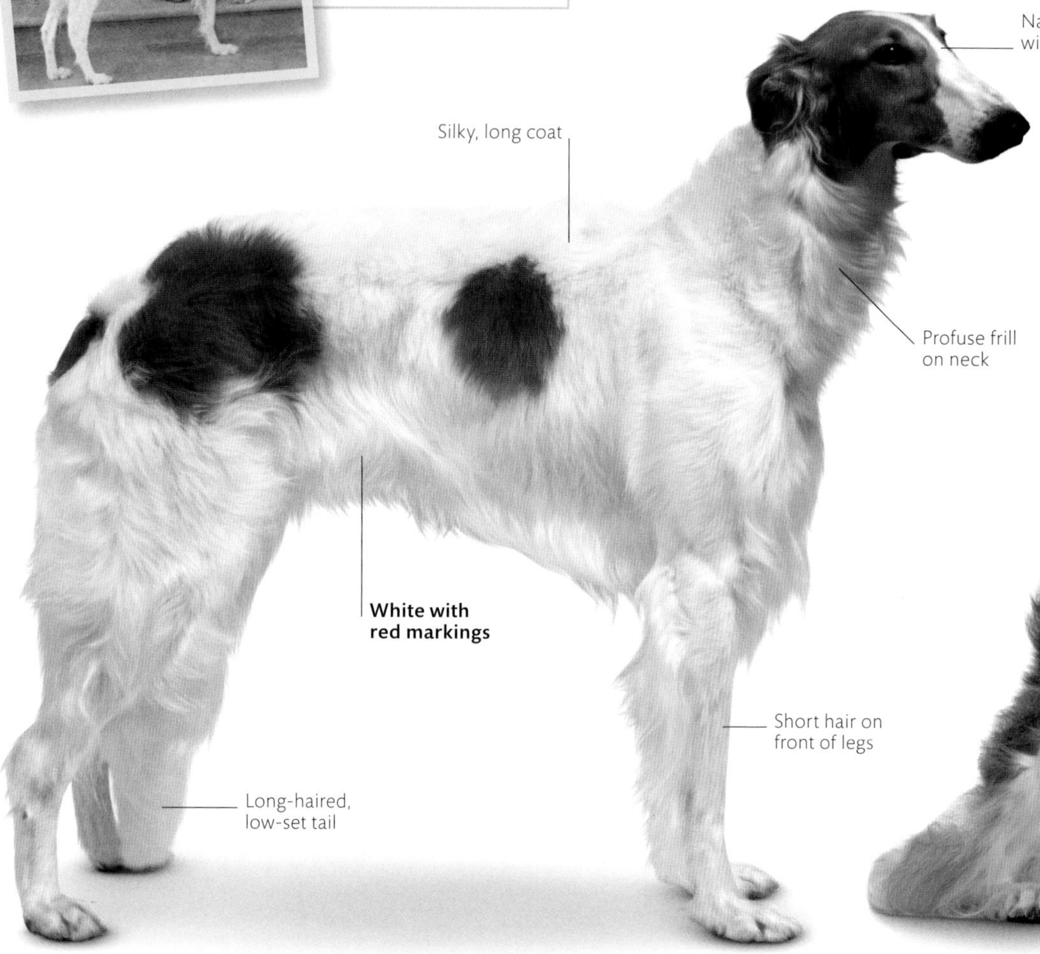

Narrow, refined head with imperceptible stop

Silky, long coat

Profuse frill on neck

White with red markings

Short hair on front of legs

Long-haired, low-set tail

Short, smooth coat on head

Black mask

Hare-shaped feet with well padded toes

Deerhound

HEIGHT 28–30in (71–76cm)
WEIGHT 82–101lb (37–46kg)
LIFE SPAN 10–11 years

Red-fawn or sandy red
Black brindle

)nce the preserve of Scottish stag-hunting nobility, this haggier version of the Irish Wolfhound (see p.134) is now as nuch at home in a cozy living room as it is by a baronial og fire. It is lazy and companionable indoors, s long as it has a strenuous walk every ay and plenty of outdoor space.

Spanish Greyhound

HEIGHT 23–28in (58–72cm)
WEIGHT 44–66lb (20–30kg)
LIFE SPAN 12 years

Any color

Thought to be a descendant of dogs that came into the berian Peninsula with the Celts around 500BCE, he Spanish Greyhound is a fast-footed hunter.)nce kept only by royalty, the breed ecame widely popular for oursing and racing. Spanish Greyhounds are not hard o train as house dogs ut have high exercise equirements. There re two coat varieties: mooth-haired and vire-haired.

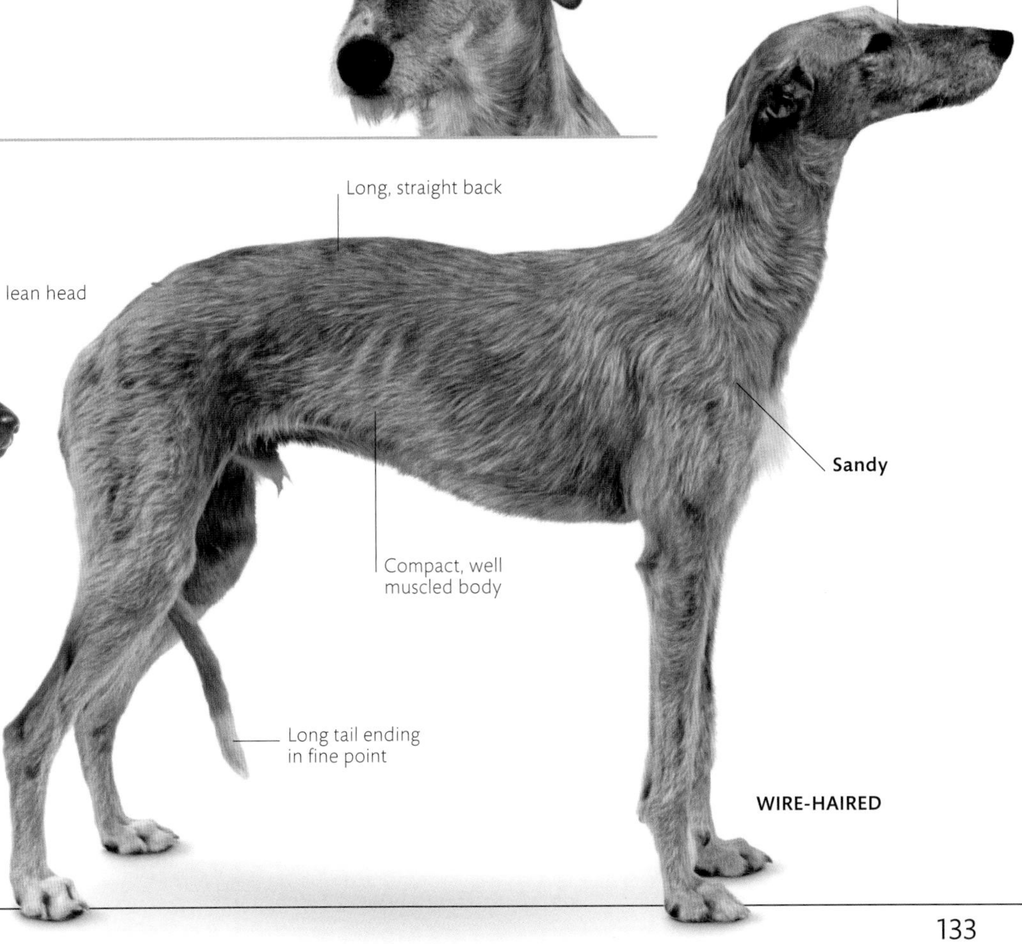

Irish Wolfhound

HEIGHT	WEIGHT	LIFE SPAN	
28–34in (71–86cm)	105–150lb (48–68kg)	8–10 years	Variety of colors

\ loyal, dignified, and docile hound, this gentle giant is the vorld's tallest breed and needs room to relax and run

'his breed derives its name from its 'aditional use in hunting wolves. Dogs f this type have been known in Ireland or thousands of years; Irish chieftains and ings used them as dogs of war, as well s for hunting wolves and elk. The "great ound," or *cu*, is mentioned in Irish laws and terature, and was known to the Romans, too. For centuries the dogs were reserved for oyalty and the nobility and were given as resents to important foreigners; so many were given away that their export was prohibited in 1652 so that Ireland would not be overrun with wolves. However, once the last wolf was killed in 1786, the Irish Wolfhound lost its traditional purpose and the dogs became very scarce. In the 1870s a British Army officer, Captain George A. Graham, started a program to revive it, using outcrosses to breeds such as the Scottish Deerhound (see p.133) and the Great Dane (see p.96). In 1902 an Irish Wolfhound was presented to the Irish Guards as a regimental mascot, and the breed still performs this role today.

Despite its imposing appearance—this giant, heavy breed can reach well over 6ft (1.8m) tall when standing on its hind legs—the Irish Wolfhound has a calm, gentle nature. It is often kept as a companion dog and needs and enjoys human company. However, it is best suited to owners who can afford substantial food bills and who have sufficient indoor and outdoor space to keep such a large, heavy dog. The coarse coat requires regular brushing and combing.

GELERT

In Welsh legend, Gelert was the favorite hound of Prince Llewellyn the Great. One day Llewellyn went hunting, leaving Gelert behind, and on his return was horrified to find his baby son missing and Gelert with blood on his jaws. Believing that Gelert had killed the baby, Llewellyn ran the dog through with his sword. Just then the baby cried; Llewellyn found him lying on a wolf, which Gelert had clearly killed. Stricken with remorse, Llewellyn buried Gelert with a memorial stone in honor of his dog. Today a sculpture of Gelert (below) stands near his grave in Beddgelert, Wales.

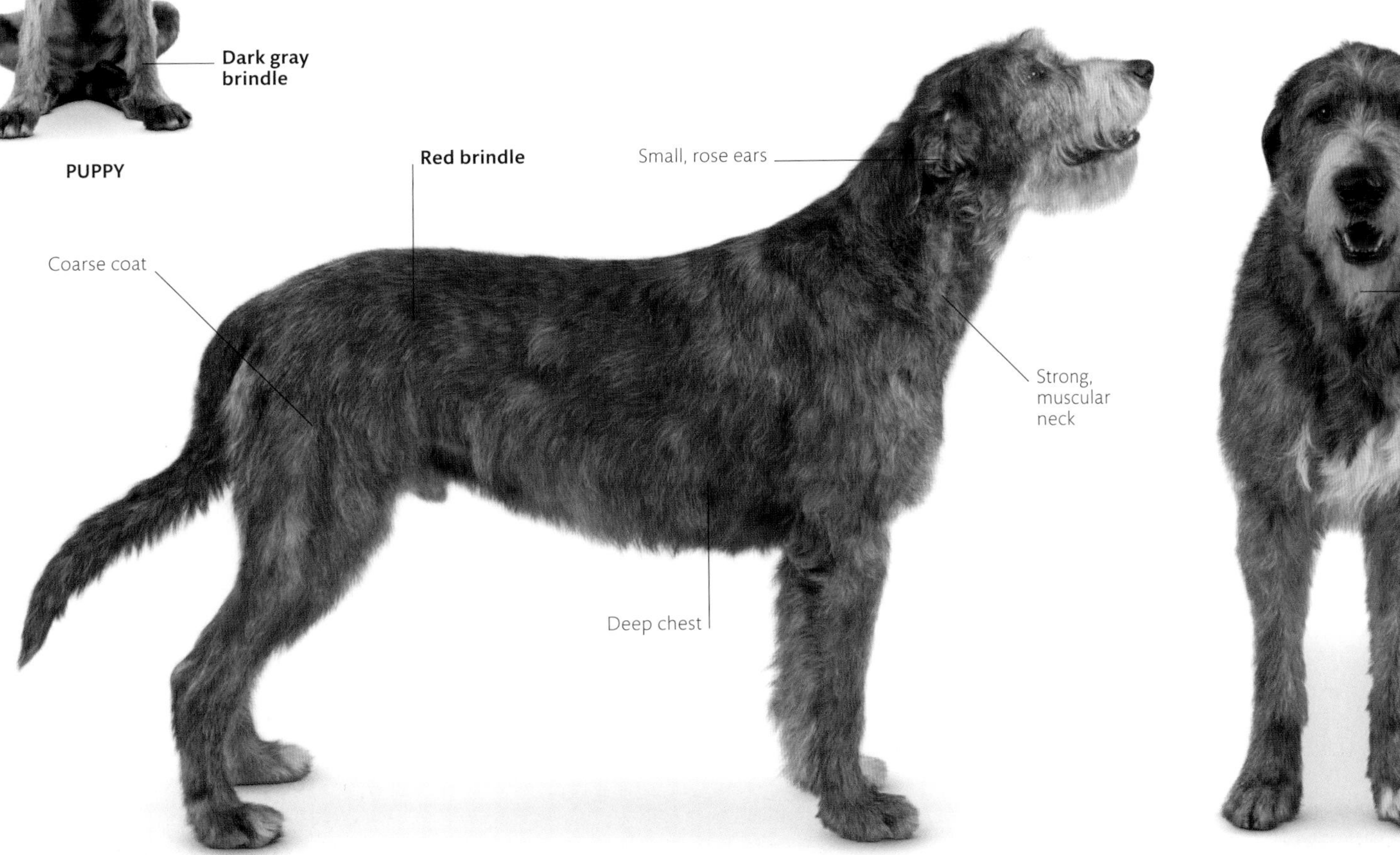

Afghan Hound

HEIGHT	WEIGHT	LIFE SPAN	
25–29in (63–74cm)	50–64lb (23–29kg)	12–14 years	Any color

WORLD'S FIRST CLONED DOG

In 2005 Seoul National University in South Korea amazed the world by revealing Snuppy, the first cloned dog. Snuppy was created using DNA from an adult Afghan Hound's ear cells, inserted into eggs from female dogs. A total of 123 surrogate mothers were used, and three pups were born, of which Snuppy was the sole survivor—genetically identical to his father. In 2008 Snuppy became a father himself, with ten puppies being born to two cloned mothers.

SNUPPY (RIGHT) SITS NEXT TO THE DOG FROM WHICH HE WAS CLONED

The supermodel of dogs, this breed makes a glamorous, aloof, and high-maintenance but affectionate pet

The origin of the Afghan Hound is unknown, but its ancestors are thought to have been brought along trade routes to Afghanistan. There, people used it to hunt hare, deer, and wild goat, as well as wolves and snow leopards. The dogs were suited to such work since they had agility and stamina, and were adept at running fast over rough terrain, turning quickly, and leaping up mountain slopes. The long, silky coat gave protection from cold, while the large feet could grip well and were resistant to injury. Various types existed in Afghanistan; dogs from desert areas were lighter in build, with a finer coat, while those from the mountains were more heavy-coated.

The Afghan Hound was not known outside Afghanistan until the late 19th century wher British soldiers first brought it to England. In the 1930s Marx Brother Zeppo introduced this breed to the US, and it has been popular since with celebrities.

Today, the Afghan Hound is a spectacula show dog and a loving, if occasionally wayward, family pet. It also excels at lure coursing (chasing a mechanical lure) and obedience events. The dog needs plenty of exercise, including chances to run freely. The Afghan Hound's long show coat needs a great deal of regular grooming.

Gold

Long muzzle and skull

Pendant ears covered with long, silky hair

Tail is relatively bare, carried in a ring and raised when moving

Long, silky coat has fine texture except along short, close saddle

Feet strong and covered with thick, long hair

Red

Dark eyes, almost triangular-looking, slanting slightly upward

Darker hair on ear tips

Sloughi

HEIGHT 24–28in (61–72cm)
WEIGHT 44–60lb (20–27kg)
LIFE SPAN 12 years

ong established in North Africa, here it is much prized as a hunting og, the Sloughi has only recently ecome known in the US and urope. This quiet-natured breed is pleasant companion and likes ome life. A Sloughi needs early ocializing with other household ets since its urge to chase small nimals is strong.

Azawakh

HEIGHT 24–29in (60–74cm)
WEIGHT 33–55lb (15–25kg)
LIFE SPAN 12–13 years

This long-legged hound comes from the desert areas of the southern ahara. The Azawakh is used by nomadic tribes for hunting, guarding, nd as a companion dog. It has exceptionally fine skin. With careful andling and a daily run, he Azawakh settles well s a house pet.

Pack hunting
Foxhunting with pack hounds was once a familiar sight in rural UK. The modern alternative is drag hunting—where hounds follow an artificial scent.

SCENT HOUNDS

keen sense of smell is an essential part of being a dog. The sharpest noses belong to the scent ounds, which track prey more by following scent than by using their eyes, as the sight hounds o (see pp.124–25). These dogs, which often hunt in packs, have a natural ability to pick up a trail, ven if it is days old, and will follow it single-mindedly.

t is not known exactly when ertain dogs were first recognized or their exceptional ability to hunt y scent. The origins of the modern cent hound possibly date back to he mastiff-type dogs of the ancient vorld, brought into Europe by traders rom the region that is now Syria. By he Middle Ages hunting with packs f scent hounds was a widespread and opular sport, the quarry including ox, hare, deer, and wild boar. Pack unting arrived in North America in he 17th century with English settlers, vho brought their own foxhounds vith them.

Scent hounds come in all sizes, but ypically have substantial muzzles acked with odor-detecting sensors, oose, moist lips that also aid scent detection, and long, pendant ears. Bred for staying power rather than speed, they are strong-bodied, especially in the forequarters. The breeds of scent hound known today were selectively developed not only according to the size of prey that they followed but also the countryside that the hunts covered. The English Foxhound (see p.158), for example, is comparatively fleet and lightly built for accompanying a mounted hunt over mostly open terrain. Similar in general appearance but much smaller, the Beagle (see p.152) hunted hare, sometimes in thick undergrowth, with followers on foot. Some short-legged dogs were bred to follow or dig out quarry below ground. The best known of these small scent hounds is the Dachshund (see p.170), an agile little dog, adept at getting in and out of tight spots. The Otterhound (see p.142), which hunted its quarry in rivers and streams, sometimes swimming for much of the time, has a water-repellent coat and more extensive webbing between its toes than most dogs.

With a ban on hunting with hounds in the UK, the future of British breeds such as the English Foxhound or Harrier (see p.154) is uncertain. Although usually gregarious and good with other dogs, pack hounds rarely make satisfactory house pets. They need space, are often vocal, and their eagerness to follow any scent trail can make them difficult to train.

Bruno Jura Hound

HEIGHT 18–22in (45–57cm)
WEIGHT 35–44lb (16–20kg)
LIFE SPAN 10–11 years

One of two similar breeds of hound developed in the Swiss Jura mountain region, this is one of four laufhunds (see p.173) that probably descended from older, heavier French breeds. Used mainly for rabbit hunting, it has a powerful nose and great strength and agility when working on steep terrain. Restless and ever on the go, this breed does not enjoy indoor confinement.

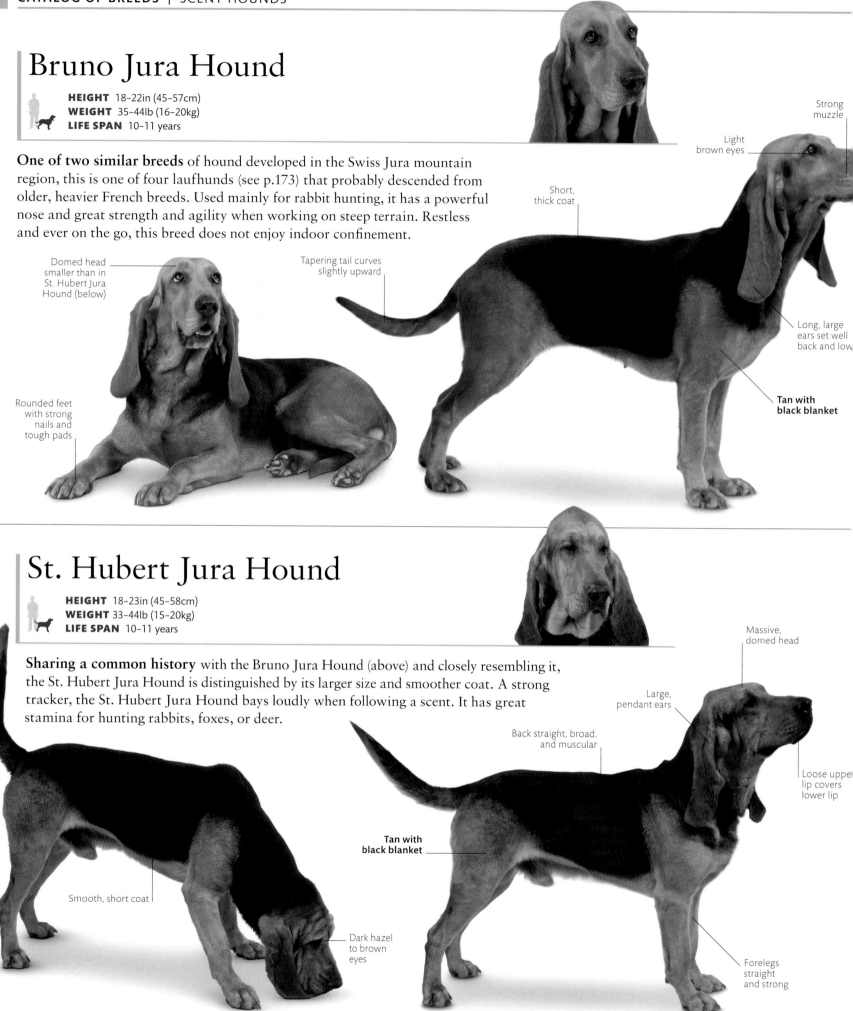

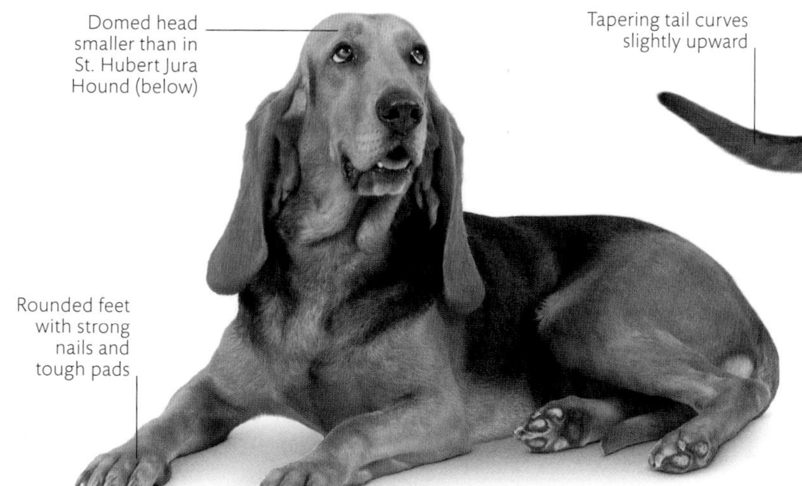

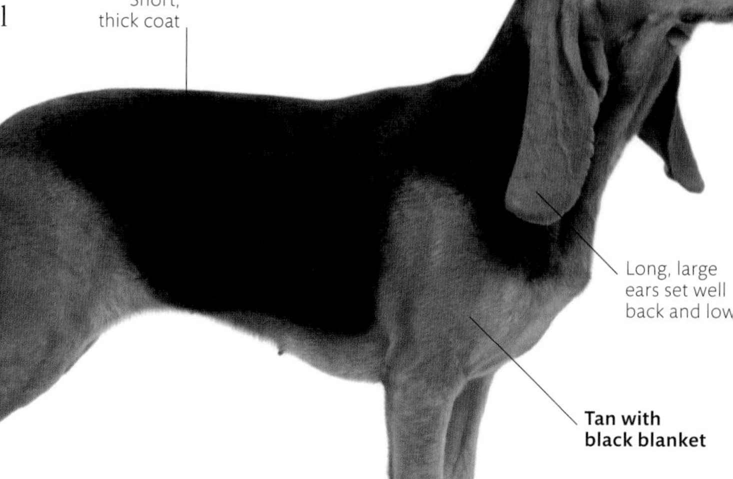

St. Hubert Jura Hound

HEIGHT 18–23in (45–58cm)
WEIGHT 33–44lb (15–20kg)
LIFE SPAN 10–11 years

Sharing a common history with the Bruno Jura Hound (above) and closely resembling it, the St. Hubert Jura Hound is distinguished by its larger size and smoother coat. A strong tracker, the St. Hubert Jura Hound bays loudly when following a scent. It has great stamina for hunting rabbits, foxes, or deer.

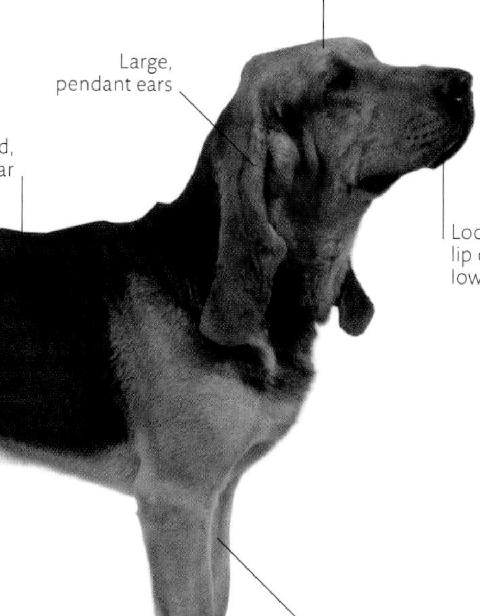

Bloodhound

HEIGHT	WEIGHT	LIFE SPAN	
23–27in (58–69cm)	79–110lb (36–50kg)	10–12 years	Black and tan Liver and tan

Gentle and sociable despite its size, this dog has a deep bellowing voice and a strong desire to hunt

The ultimate scent hound, the Bloodhound is sometimes called a nose with a dog attached. Dogs of this type have appeared in written records since the 14th century, although they are thought to be even older. The dogs were used to hunt deer and wild boar and to follow people. In Scotland sleuthhounds were used to track the raiders and cattle thieves who operated along the English-Scottish border. In the 17th century the eminent scientist Sir Robert Boyle told of a Bloodhound that tracked a man over seven miles and through two busy towns, tracing the man to the very room where he was concealed. During the 19th century French breeders imported some Bloodhounds to resurrect the old Chien de St. Hubert breed. Later in the 19th century people began to breed pure Bloodhounds in the US; Americans have used the dogs for tracking criminals and missing people, and evidence from a Bloodhound can be admissible in a court of law.

The tracking instinct is so strong that it can make obedience training difficult, since the dog will be easily distracted by scents around it. Nevertheless, this good-natured dog is an excellent family companion for those with room to spare.

THE CANINE SUPER-SLEUTH

Historically used in Britain for stag hunting, Bloodhounds are superb tracking dogs, as depicted in the 17th century engraving below. As deer numbers fell, the Bloodhound became somewhat redundant, though a few were kept on large estates to track down poachers. Early settlers in the US used Bloodhounds to track people, too. As recently as 1977, two 14-month-old Bloodhounds—Sandy and Little Red—tracked down prison escapee James Earl Ray, the man who shot Civil Rights leader Martin Luther King.

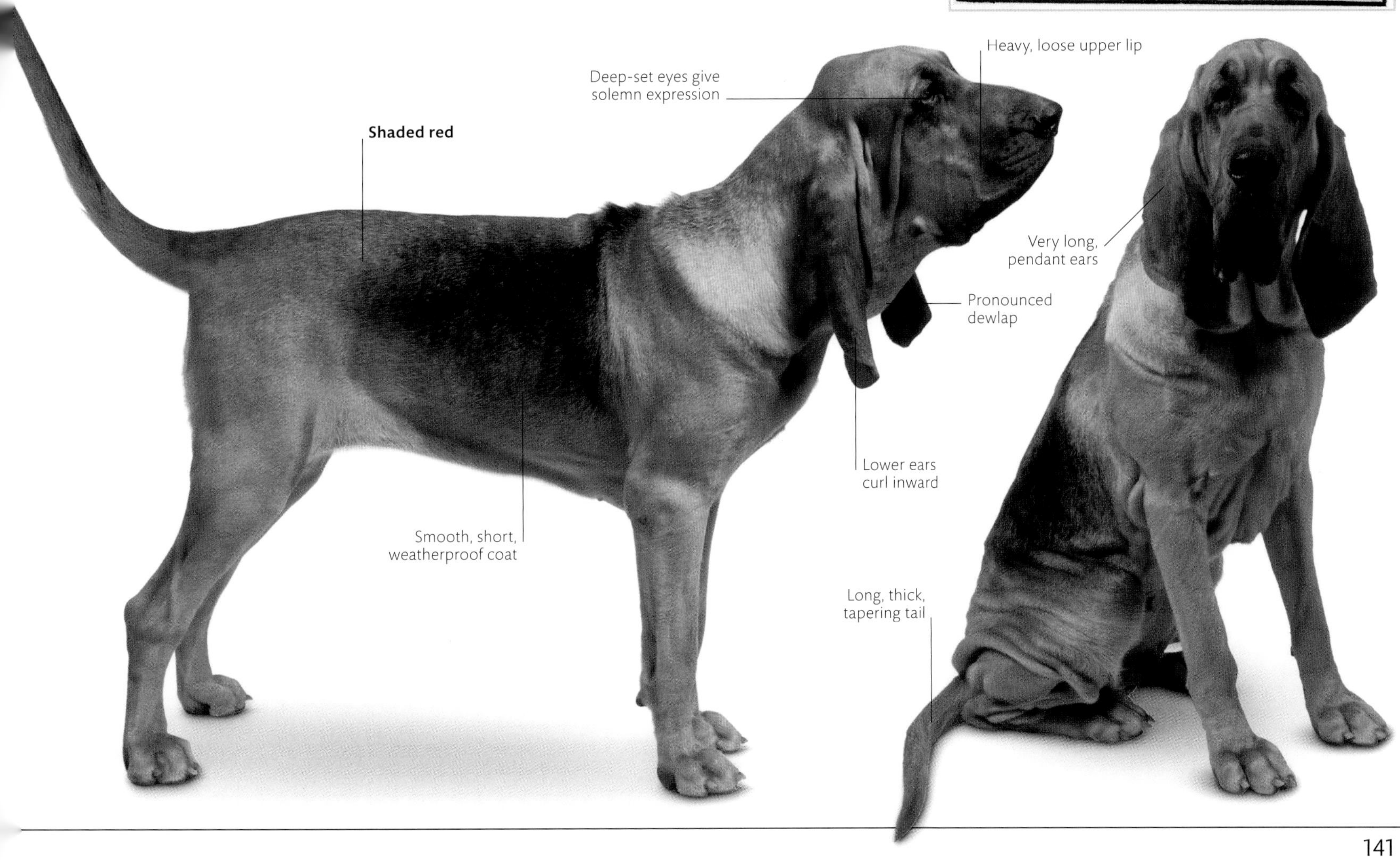

Shaded red

Deep-set eyes give solemn expression

Heavy, loose upper lip

Very long, pendant ears

Pronounced dewlap

Lower ears curl inward

Smooth, short, weatherproof coat

Long, thick, tapering tail

Otterhound

HEIGHT	WEIGHT	LIFE SPAN	
24–27in (61–69cm)	66–115lb (30–52kg)	10–12 years	Any hound color

Easy-going and affectionate, this boisterous dog has retained a strong hunting instinct and needs plenty of exercise

As its name suggests, this shaggy-coated hound was once used for hunting otters. Though its exact origins are uncertain, dogs of a similar type, working in packs, were known in England from about the 18th century, and there are records of otter-hunting with pack hounds as far back as the 12th century. When otters became a protected species, and otter hunting was banned in the UK in 1978, the number of Otterhounds declined sharply. The breed is now considered rare, with fewer than 60 puppies being registered by the Kennel Club each year. Small numbers of Otterhounds are found in other countries, including the US, Canada, and New Zealand.

The Otterhound is a strong, energetic dog that, given sufficient exercise, readily adapts to life in the home. It is intelligent and good-natured but, as is the case with many former pack hounds, can be difficult to train. Being large and boisterous, the breed is not recommended for small homes or families with elderly members or young children, since there is a risk of them being knocked over. The Otterhound is best suited to owners who enjoy outdoor activities and have a large yard or access to open spaces where the dog can run safely. Bred for hunting in water, this hound loves swimming and will splash around happily in streams for hours if given the opportunity.

The Otterhound's dense, coarse coat is slightly oily, and therefore water-repellent. Regular grooming is usually enough to keep the long topcoat free from tangles; the longer facial hair may need washing occasionally.

AN ENDANGERED BREED

The Otterhound is the most vulnerable dog breed in the UK; in 2011 only 38 new dogs were registered. Their decline in popularity can be linked to a number of events. In the late 1920s the breed's reputation suffered with the publication of *Tarka the Otter*, which features a hunting Otterhound named Deadlock as the enemy of the otter hero, Tarka. Then in 1978 otter hunting was made illegal, although this did not have a great effect, since packs were simply switched to hunting mink. Finally, all hunting with packs of dogs was banned in the early 2000s.

Head well covered
with hair
Black and tan
Rough,
waterproof coat
Long, pendant
ears fold in on
leading edge
Deep chest
Large, round feet
with well-developed
webbing between toes

Grand Griffon Vendéen

HEIGHT	WEIGHT	LIFE SPAN	
24–27in (60–68cm)	66–77lb (30–35kg)	12–13 years	Fawn, Black and tan, Black and white, Tricolor. Fawn dogs can have black overlay

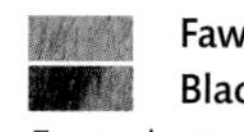

THE CLERK'S DOG

The name "griffon" comes from the French word *greffier*, meaning "clerk." The ancestors of the Grand Griffon Vendéen (and of other griffon breeds) were white, wire-haired hunting dogs. One of the first people to breed this type of dog, in the 15th century, was a French clerk. For this reason, the early name for the dog was "greffier dog," which became shortened to "griffon." Later, the word "griffon" became more widely used to denote various types of rough-haired hunting dog.

This well proportioned, passionate hunter is intelligent and family-friendly but is best-suited to a rural lifestyle

There are four varieties of Griffon Vendéen, all originating in the Vendée area of western France. The Grand Griffon Vendéen, as its name implies, is the largest; it is also the longest established. Its ancestry includes the 15th-century "greffier dog," the Griffon Fauve de Bretagne (see p.149), and the now extinct Griffon de Bresse, as well as rough-coated hunting dogs from Italy.

The breed was historically used for hunting large game such as deer and wild boar, and is still used for these purposes today. It works as a pack hound or on a leash. It is willing to follow trails even in thick undergrowth; the double-layered coat, with its dense undercoat and wiry topcoat, gives protection against all types of vegetation and weather.

Coat colors include mixtures of black, white, tan, and fawn. There are several varieties of fawn with black-tipped hairs, known traditionally as "hare color," "wolf color," "badger color," or "boar color."

This dog has a beautiful musical voice and an appealing personality. It also has a strong tracking instinct and is rather independent-minded, so requires careful training and firm handling. In addition, the dog needs plenty of space and daily exercise

White and orange

Long, feathered tail

Narrow, inward-turning ears covered in fine hair

Rough, bushy coat

Eyebrows pronounced but not covering eyes

Front of muzzle has square appearance

Griffon Nivernais

HEIGHT 21–24in (53–62cm)
WEIGHT 51–55lb (23–25kg)
LIFE SPAN 12–15 years

ne of the oldest French sporting dogs, this breed has oodlines that include the English Foxhound (see p.158) and e Otterhound (see p.142). Used for tracking wild boar, the riffon Nivernais has great endurance. It may work dividually but usually hunts in pack. The rough, tousled coat rovides protection against ick vegetation.

Briquet Griffon Vendéen

HEIGHT 19–22in (48–55cm)
WEIGHT 35–53lb (16–24kg)
LIFE SPAN 12 years

Fawn with black overlay
Black and tan
White and black
Black, tan, and white

riquet means "medium sized"—an apt description for this ell proportioned hound. A handsome and determined chaser f wild boar and roe deer, it is a scaled-down version of the rand Griffon Vendéen (opposite), from which it was bred. his hound hunts in a pack ut can adapt to urban fe if introduced to early on.

Basset Hound

HEIGHT	WEIGHT	LIFE SPAN	Variety of colors
13–15in (33–38cm)	40–60lb (18–27kg)	10–13 years	Any recognized hound color.

This low-slung, floppy-eared dog is a superb tracker but, despite its strong hunting instinct, makes an affectionate pet

The "Basset" breeds of dog originated in France; the name is derived from the French word *bas*, meaning "low," and refers to their low-slung, short-legged shape. Dogs of this type had existed in France for centuries, but the first actual mention of "basset" dogs appeared in a French hunting text written in 1585. These dogs were ideal for men who hunted on foot because they followed trails at a slow pace. After the French Revolution in 1789, Basset breeds became more popular as a common man's dog and were typically used to hunt rabbit and hare.

The Basset Hound first attracted great attention at a dog show in Paris in 1863. English people began to import the dogs in the 1870s, and the first breed standard for the Basset Hound was established in the UK at the end of the 19th century.

Today some Basset Hounds are still used for hunting and tracking, either in packs or alone. The breed is well suited for small game such as fox, hare, opossum, and pheasant, and for working in heavy cover. This consummate sniffer dog has a very keen sense of smell and a strong tracking instinct; once it has picked up a scent it may follow the trail tenaciously, immune to all distraction.

Most Basset Hounds are kept as family pets. The breed is intelligent, calm, loyal, and affectionate, but can be stubborn, so needs kind and firm training.

THE HUSH PUPPIES® DOG

The Basset Hound is famous as the symbol of the Hush Puppies® brand of shoe. The shoes and the name both originate from 1950s America. "Barking dogs" at the time was slang for tired feet, and as real-life barking dogs were sometimes quietened with corn fritters called "hush puppies," one of the sales managers saw the potential of the name for the comfortable range of shoes. The Basset Hound with its relaxed look was quickly adopted for the logo. In the 1980s a dog named Jason featured in several witty print and TV advertisements, making the brand hugely popular worldwide.

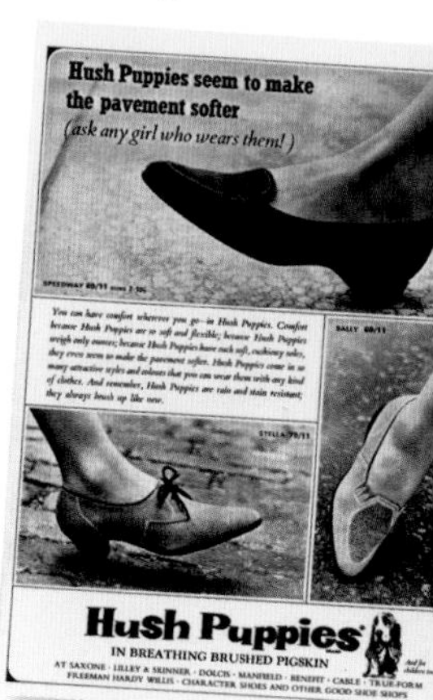

A 1965 MAGAZINE ADVERTISEMENT FOR HUSH PUPPIES®

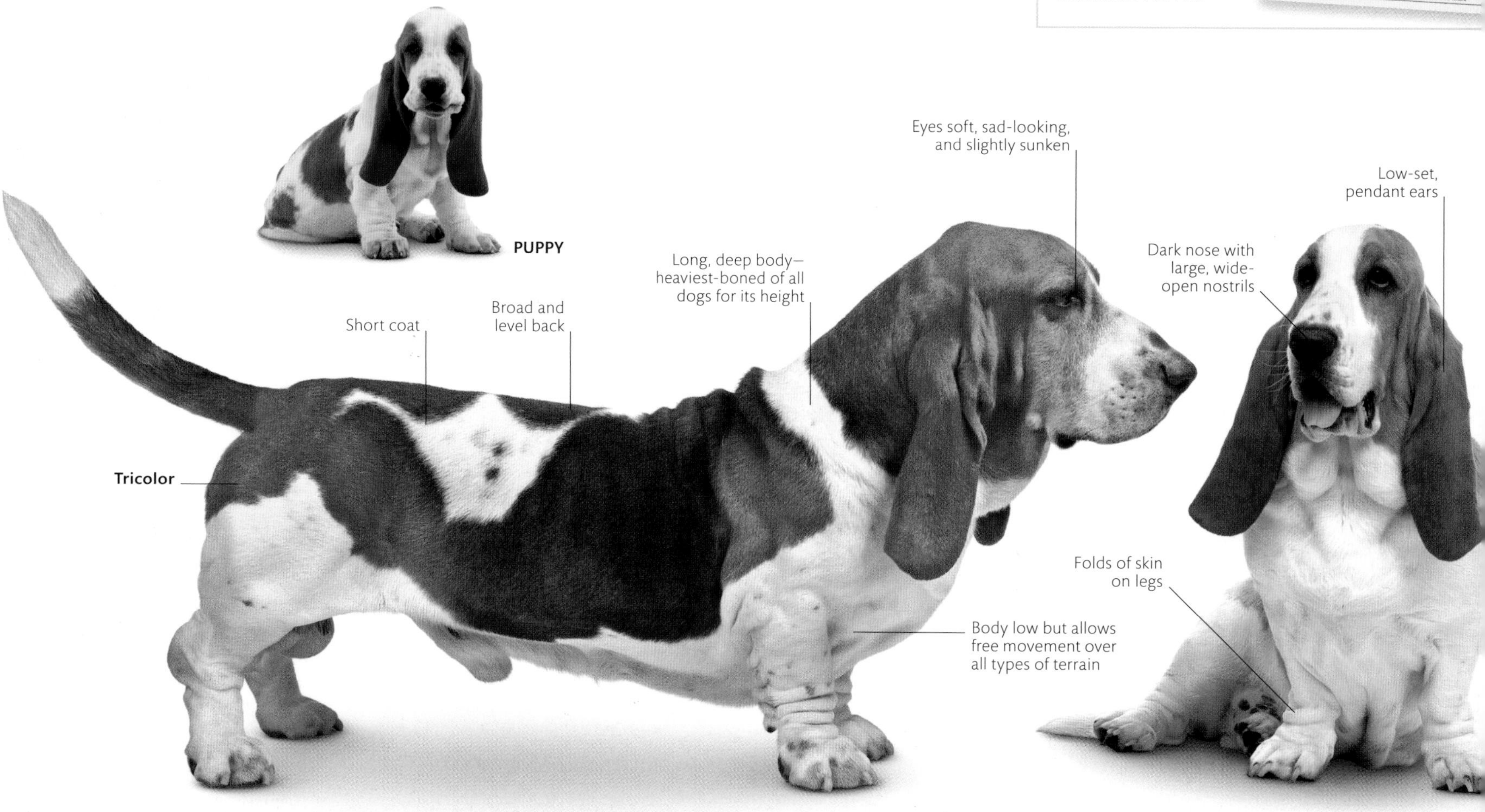

PUPPY

Short coat

Broad and level back

Long, deep body—heaviest-boned of all dogs for its height

Eyes soft, sad-looking, and slightly sunken

Low-set, pendant ears

Dark nose with large, wide-open nostrils

Tricolor

Folds of skin on legs

Body low but allows free movement over all types of terrain

The Bloodhound in all but size!
The short legs of the Basset Hound result from a genetic condition that also causes limb distortion, typically producing a cabriolelike shape. Slower than its larger cousins, but nonetheless effective at following a scent, it can be easily followed by hunters on foot.

Grand Basset Griffon Vendéen

HEIGHT 15–17in (38–44cm)
WEIGHT 40–44lb (18–20kg)
LIFE SPAN 12 years

White and orange

This basset-type Griffon Vendéen hound was originally developed in France for hunting rabbit. Today it is used for tracking all types of game, from rabbit to wild boar. Brave and tenacious when on the trail, the short-legged Grand Basset Griffon Vendéen is adept at working in difficult countryside such as dense scrub.

White with black grizzle and orange markings

Long, pendant ears

Prominent nose with wide nostrils

Flat, hard hair with thick undercoat

Petit Basset Griffon Vendéen

HEIGHT 13–15in (33–38cm)
WEIGHT 24–42lb (11–19kg)
LIFE SPAN 12–14 years

Smallest of the Griffon Vendéen breeds of France, the Petit Basset Griffon Vendéen is an alert, active, and vigorous hound, capable of a long day's hunting. Short legs, a body twice the dog's height, and a thick, rough coat make this breed ideal for work in dense, brambly undergrowth. Full of restless energy, the Petit Basset Griffon Vendéen is a family dog for people who enjoy spending time outdoors.

Long eyebrows, beard, and mustache

White, black and orange

Basset Artesien Normand

HEIGHT 12–14in (30–36cm)
WEIGHT 33–44lb (15–20kg)
LIFE SPAN 13–15 years

Tan and white

his low-slung, long-bodied dog from the Artois and Normandy
gions of France is renowned for searching, tracking, flushing
ut, and pursuing hare, rabbit, and deer—either individually
r in small packs. An elegant hound, it has a very deep
ark that is perhaps surprising for its size. Like many
ounds, it requires experienced training.

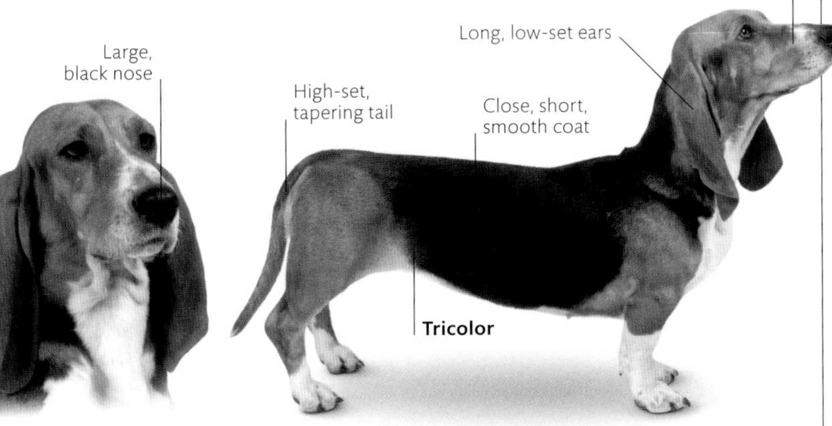

Basset Fauve de Bretagne

HEIGHT 13–15in (32–38cm)
WEIGHT 35–40lb (16–18kg)
LIFE SPAN 12–14 years

This versatile and nimble French hound has the same qualities as the breed from which it is derived: the Griffon Fauve de Bretagne (below). It is courageous and has a well developed sense of smell, which makes it ideal for tracking and search and rescue. Although wiry, a weekly brush and comb is all that its coat requires.

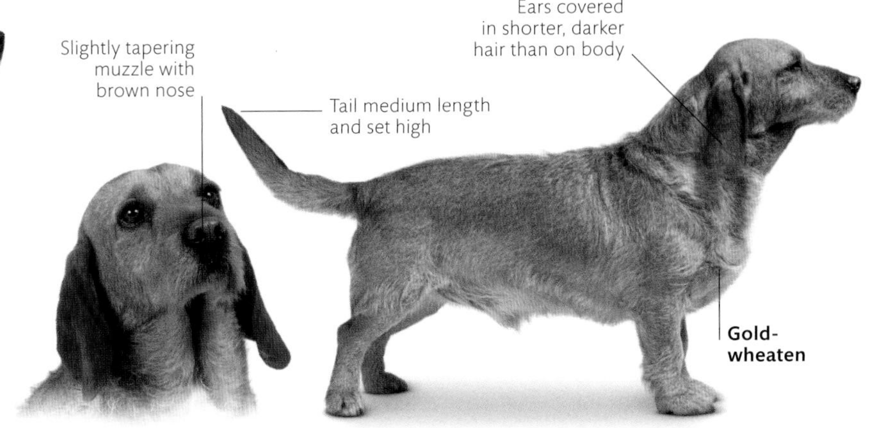

Griffon Fauve de Bretagne

HEIGHT 19–22in (47–56cm)
WEIGHT 40–49lb (18–22kg)
LIFE SPAN 12–13 years

)ne of the oldest French hounds, with ancestors dating
ack to the 1500s, the Griffon Fauve de Bretagne was bred in
rittany to guard against wolves. Today it is a versatile hunter
nd lively house dog. Its short-legged cousin is the Basset
auve de Bretagne (above).

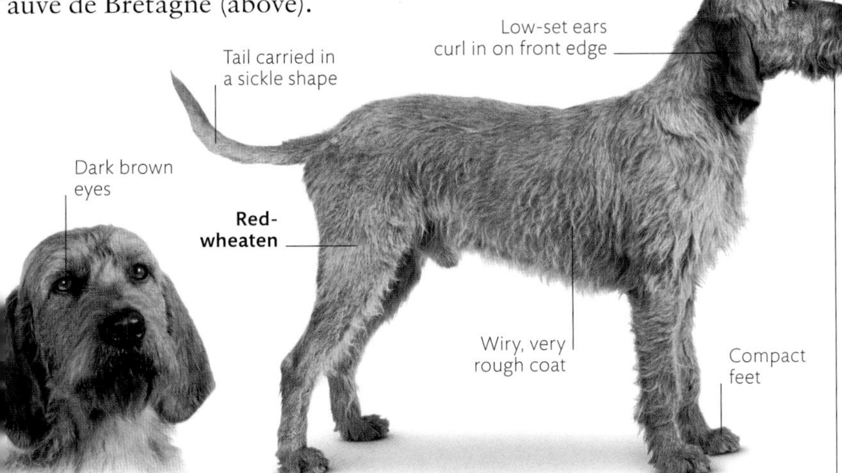

Istrian Wire-haired Hound

HEIGHT 18–23in (46–58cm)
WEIGHT 35–53lb (16–24kg)
LIFE SPAN 12 years

With its boundless tenacity and passion for hunting, the Istrian Wire-haired Hound is similar to the smooth-coated variety (see p.150). Due to its stubborn nature it can be difficult to train, so is not an ideal pet. It is known as the Istarski Oštrodlaki Gonic in its homeland on the Istrian peninsula of Croatia.

Istrian Smooth-coated Hound

HEIGHT 17–22in (44–56cm)
WEIGHT 31–44lb (14–20kg)
LIFE SPAN 12 years

Bred for hunting rabbit and fox in the vast open terrain of Croatia, the handsome and well-built Istarski Kratkodlaki Gonic, as it is known in its native land, displays a stunning snow-white coat. It is kept across the Istrian peninsula as a working dog but also makes a contented house dog in a rural household.

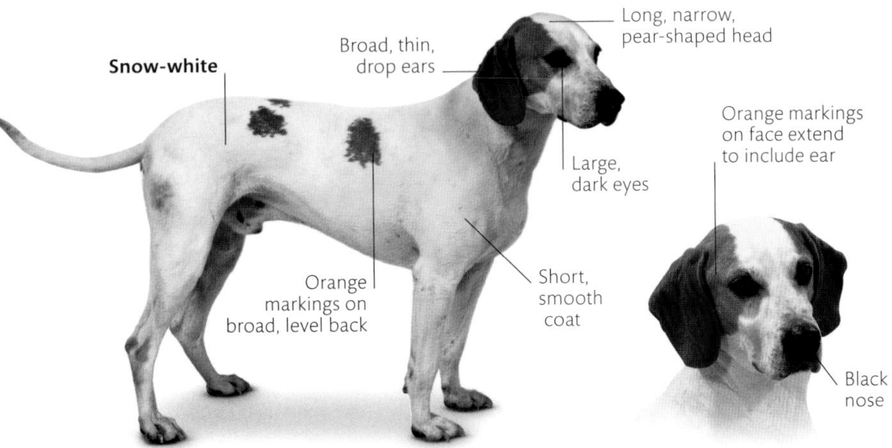

Styrian Coarse-haired Mountain Hound

HEIGHT 18–21in (45–53cm)
WEIGHT 33–40lb (15–18kg)
LIFE SPAN 12 years

Red

This medium-sized dog is agile on difficult, steep terrain, having developed its hunting skills in the mountains of Austria and Slovenia. It can make a calm and good-natured pet. It is also known as the Peintingen Hound after its 18th-century developer, who started by crossing a Hanoverian Scent Hound (see p.175) with an Istrian Wire-haired Hound (see p.149).

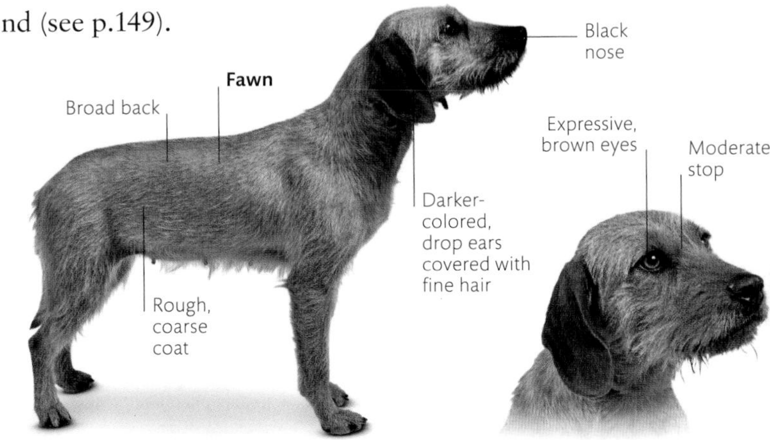

Austrian Black and Tan Hound

HEIGHT 19–22in (48–56cm)
WEIGHT 33–51lb (15–23kg)
LIFE SPAN 12–14 years

Sometimes known as the Brandlbracke, the Austrian Black and Tan Hound has descended from the Celtic Hound. Popular locally, it was bred to seek out rabbits and track down wounded animals with its highly tuned senses of smell and direction. It works eagerly and has a calm temperament.

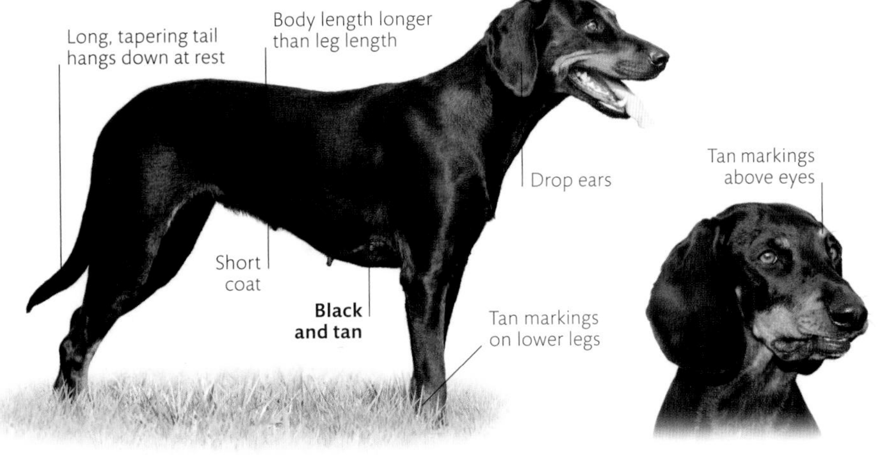

Spanish Hound

HEIGHT 19–22in (48–57cm)
WEIGHT 44–55lb (20–25kg)
LIFE SPAN 11–13 years

The ancestors of the Spanish Hound date back to the Middle Ages. Also known as the Sabueso Español, this dog is a specialized, lone rabbit hunter that will track its prey all day, following the commands of an experienced owner. There is considerable variation in the height of this breed: males being much larger than females.

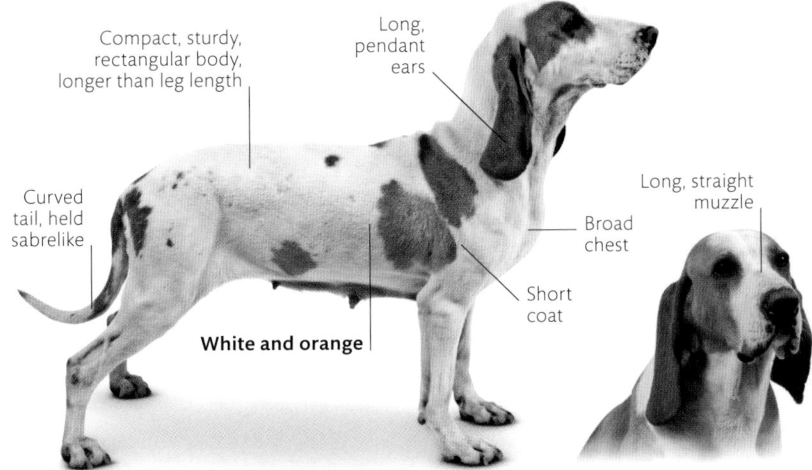

Segugio Italiano

HEIGHT	WEIGHT	LIFE SPAN	
19–23in (48–59cm)	40–62lb (18–28kg)	10–14 years	Wheaten Black and tan

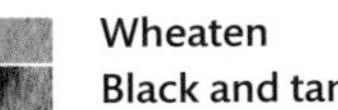

RENAISSANCE HOUND

The Segugio Italiano's distinct appearance—body of a sight hound, head of a scent hound—reflects its combined skills of speed, endurance, and tracking. Dogs with a similar look are seen in European paintings (below, a scene from a Flemish illuminated manuscript c.1515–20) and sculptures, from the 16th and 17th centuries, when wild boar hunts were extravagant affairs involving noblemen on horseback, liveried musicians, and hundreds of dogs. By the end of the Renaissance period the popularity of this grand style of hunting declined and these dogs were not needed in such large numbers.

This intelligent and sweet-natured hound makes a good companion for a family that enjoys the outdoors

Italian hounds of this type are thought to date from pre-Roman times and to be descended from Egyptian hounds. Originally bred as a boar hunter, the bread is now more often used by farmers to track rabbit, and is appreciated for its versatility. A fast sprinter, it also has the stamina for running long distances, and is tenacious in following a scent. In addition, it has an unusual hunting technique in which it follows rabbits (the breed name comes from the Italian word *seguire*, meaning to follow) and drives them toward the hunter, thus enabling a hunter to work alone.

The Segugio Italiano is usually calm and quiet, but when at work emits a distinctive, excited, high-pitched bark. Primarily kept as a working dog, the breed is good with children and other dogs, provided it is well-trained. It needs access to open spaces and plenty of daily exercise in order to work off its physical and mental energy. Although the Segugio Italiano is usually cautious in temperament, even a well-trained dog is likely to take off if it spots a rabbit. There are two coat varieties: wire-haired and short-haired.

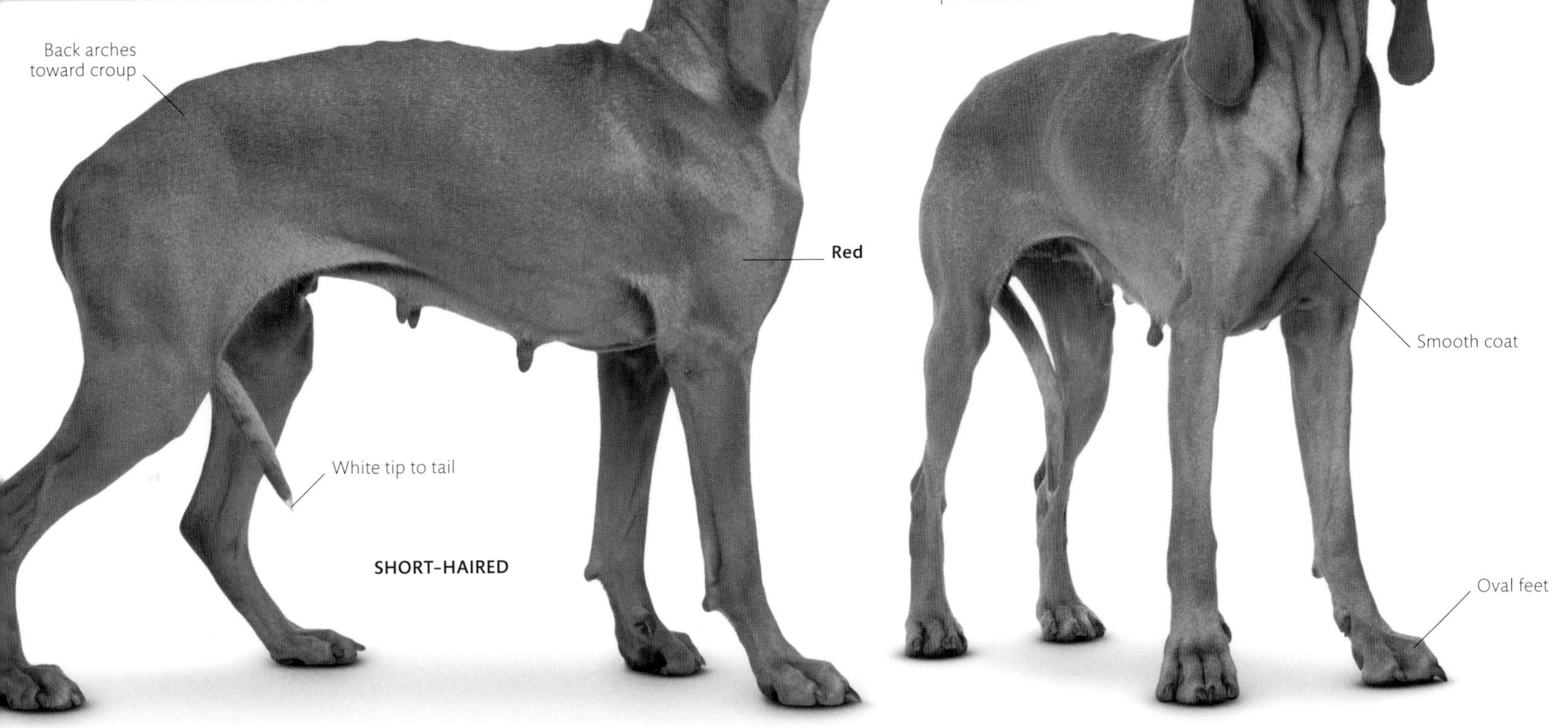

Elongated head with small stop

Large, dark, oval eyes

Black nose

Low-set, pendant ears

Back arches toward croup

Red

Smooth coat

White tip to tail

SHORT-HAIRED

Oval feet

Beagle

HEIGHT	WEIGHT	LIFE SPAN	
13–16in (33–40cm)	20–24lb (9–11kg)	13 years	Variety of colors

One of the most popular scent hounds, this active, happy-go-lucky dog has a strong chasing instinct

A sturdy, compact dog with a cheerful disposition, the Beagle looks similar to an English Foxhound (see p.158) in miniature. The Beagle's origins are unclear, but it appears to have a long history, possibly being developed from other English scent hounds such as the Harrier (see p.154). In England, from the 16th century onward, packs of small Beagle-type hounds were kept to hunt hare and rabbit, but it was not until the 1870s that a standard for the modern Beagle was recognized. Since then the breed has remained remarkably popular, at first for hunting and now as a companion dog. This versatile hound has also been used by law enforcement agencies to sniff out drugs, explosives, and other illegal items.

The Beagle's friendly and tolerant nature makes it an excellent pet, provided it has plenty of company and exercise—it does not easily tolerate long periods of solitude, which may lead to behavioral problems. A typical scent hound, this dog is highly active and has a strong instinct for following a trail. Left alone in an inadequately fenced yard, or allowed to run off the lead, a Beagle can disappear swiftly and stay away for hours. The breed has a loud bark and can be noisy, which may irritate neighbors if the barking becomes excessive. Fortunately, Beagles are relatively easy to train, and do best with an owner who combines fondness with firmness and clear leadership. This breed is good with children old enough to understand how to handle a dog, but cannot be considered safe with small family pets.

In the US two sizes are recognized, based on the height of the dog at the shoulders: those under 13in (33cm) and those between 13in and 15in (33cm and 38cm).

PUPPY

SNOOPY—THE SILENT HERO

Snoopy the dog is a cartoon Beagle from the long-running comic strip *Peanuts*, created by Charles M. Schulz. The Beagle is usually drawn sitting on top of his doghouse. Snoopy is shown as having an ironic view of the world and a rich fantasy life, featuring himself in glamorous roles, including World War I flying Ace. In 1969 Schulz depicted Snoopy as an astronaut flying to the Moon—and the real astronauts of NASA's Apollo 10 lunar mission went on to name their lunar module after this famous Beagle.

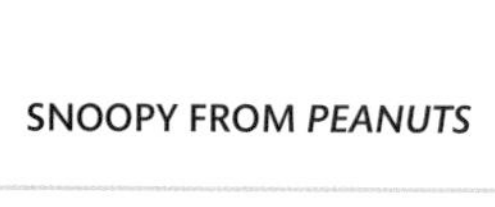

SNOOPY FROM *PEANUTS*

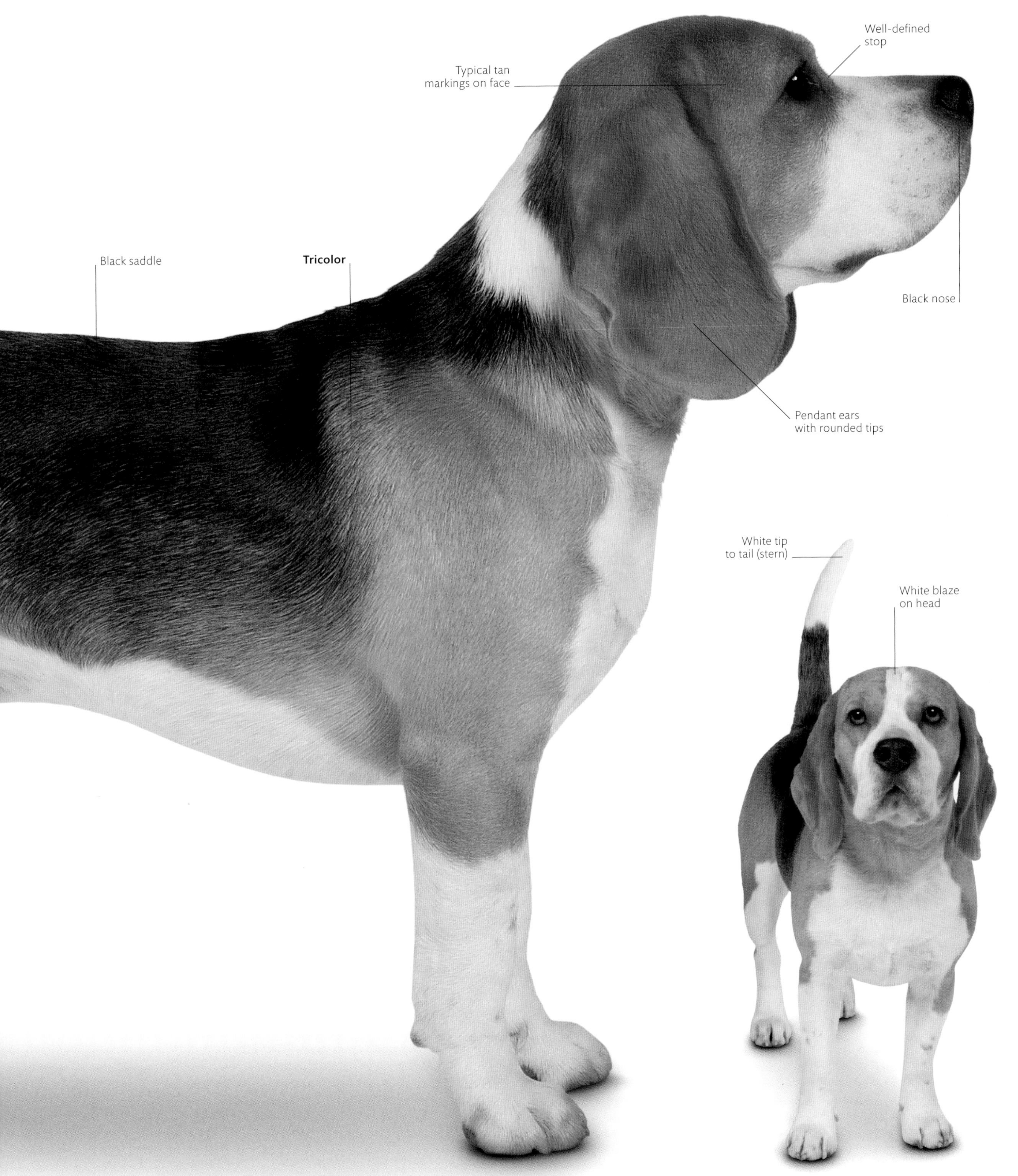
Typical tan
markings on face
Well-defined
stop
Black saddle
Tricolor
Black nose
Pendant ears
with rounded tips
White tip
to tail (stern)
White blaze
on head

Beagle Harrier

HEIGHT 18–20in (46–50cm)
WEIGHT 42–46lb (19–21kg)
LIFE SPAN 12–13 years

Larger than a Beagle (see p.152) but smaller than a Harrier (right), this attractive little hound is thought to have both these breeds in its ancestry. Beagle Harriers are not often seen outside France, where they have been used for hunting small game since the late 1800s. This dog has a pleasant temperament and makes a good family pet.

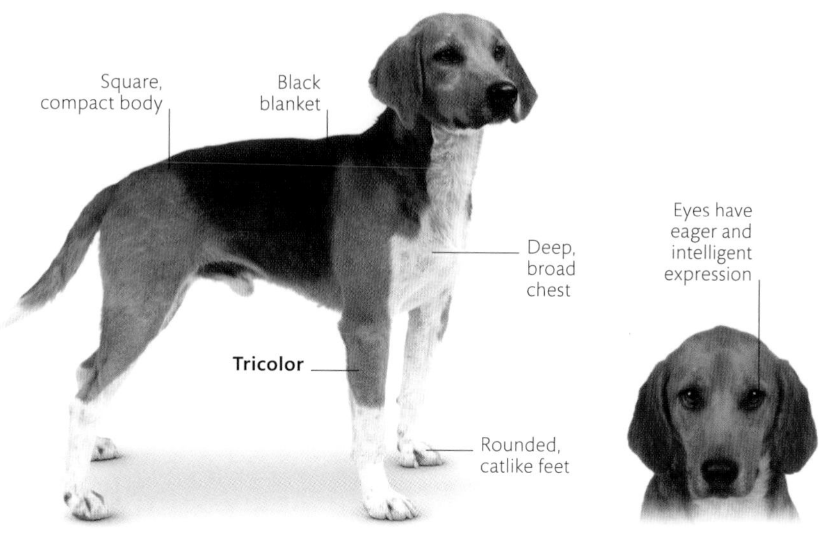

Harrier

HEIGHT 19–22in (48–55cm)
WEIGHT 42–60lb (19–27kg)
LIFE SPAN 10–12 years

Once popular for pack hunting, this handsome, classically proportioned English hound was probably developed as a smaller version of the English Foxhound (see p.158). Originally used to hunt hare with foot followers, Harriers later hunted fox with mounted followers. Today the dog makes a great outdoor companion and agility competitor.

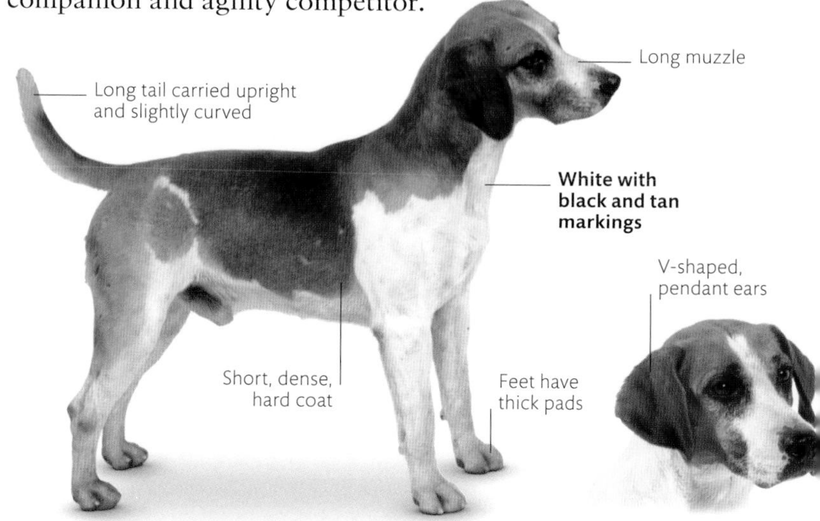

Anglo-Français de Petite Vénerie

HEIGHT 19–22in (48–56cm)
WEIGHT 35–44lb (16–20kg)
LIFE SPAN 12–13 years

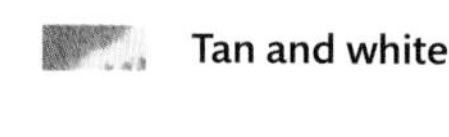
Tan and white

Also known as the Petit Anglo-Français, this hound was developed in France and is the result of crossbreeding between English and French scent hounds a few hundred years ago. The breed is now rare and mostly seen in Continental Europe, where it is still used for small game hunting (to which its name, Petite Vénerie, alludes).

Porcelaine

HEIGHT 21–23in (53–58cm)
WEIGHT 55–62lb (25–28kg)
LIFE SPAN 12–13 years

Possibly the oldest of the French pack hounds, with origins in the Franche-Comte on the French-Swiss border, this breed is named for the distinctive glazelike sheen of its beautiful white coat. It is used primarily for hunting deer and wild boar. If kept as a pet, this hound needs plenty of exercise and tactful training.

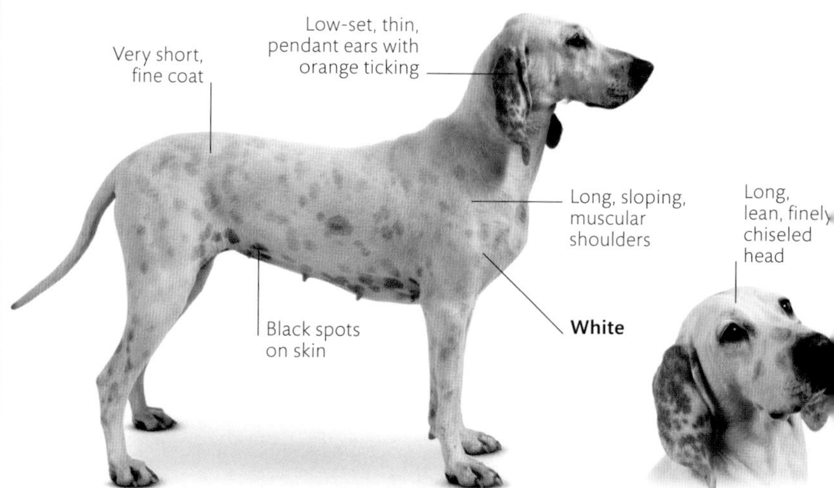

Schillerstövare

HEIGHT 19–24in (49–61cm)
WEIGHT 33–55lb (15–25kg)
LIFE SPAN 10–14 years

rare Swedish breed, the Schillerstövare is much prized for its unting speed and stamina, especially over snow. This dog's thick oat insulates it well from its native climate. It tracks alone, rather ian in a pack, and emits a deep-throated bay to pinpoint the osition of its prey—hare or fox. The breed is named after s breeder, farmer Per Schiller.

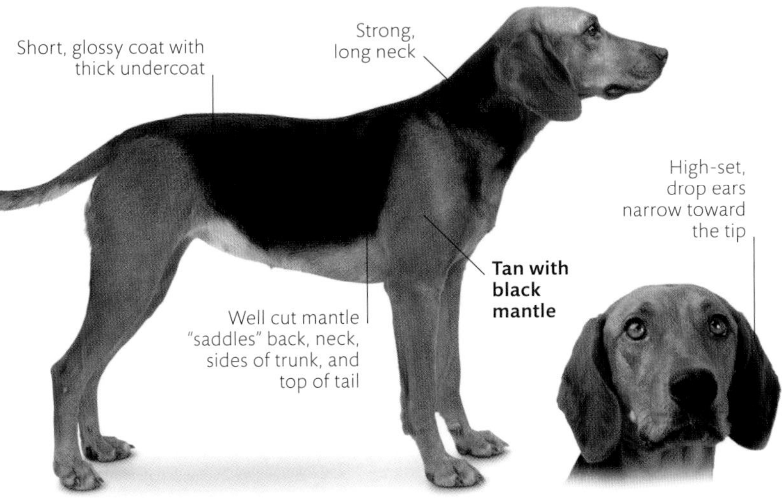

Hamiltonstövare

HEIGHT 18–24in (46–60cm)
WEIGHT 51–60lb (23–27kg)
LIFE SPAN 10–13 years

Developed by Count Adolf Patrick Hamilton, a founder of the Swedish Kennel Club, this handsome, easy-going hound loves to roam fields and flush out small game. The Hamiltonstövare is a mix of English Foxhound (see p.158) stock (it has also been called the Swedish Foxhound) and Holstein Hound, Hanovarian Haidbrake, and Courlander Hound.

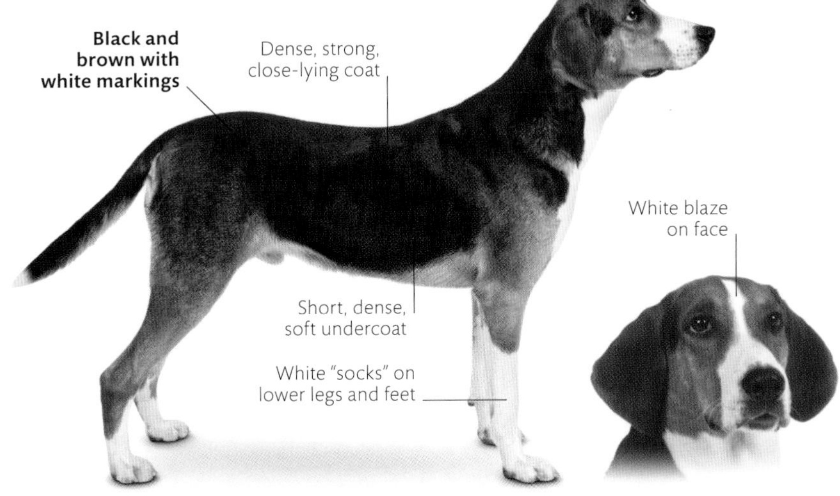

Smålandsstövare

HEIGHT 17–21in (42–54cm)
WEIGHT 33–44lb (15–20kg)
LIFE SPAN 12 years

'his Swedish Hound, also known as the Småland Hound, is hought to date back to the 16th century and takes it name from he dense forest of Småland in southern Sweden where it was sed to hunt fox and hare. It has a distinctive black and tan oat similar to that of a Rottweiler (see p.83).

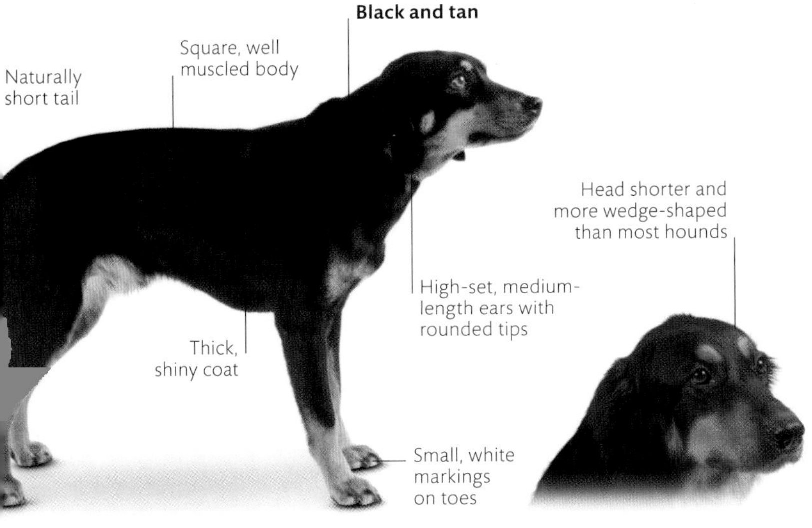

Halden Hound

HEIGHT 20–26in (50–65cm)
WEIGHT 51–64lb (23–29kg)
LIFE SPAN 10–12 years

The largest of the four stovare breeds, this hound loves a speedy chase over snowy open spaces. Like other Norwegian dogs bred as hunting companions, the Halden Hound is not widely known outside its native land. It was developed in Halden in the southeast, by crossing an English Foxhound (see p.158) with a local "beagle."

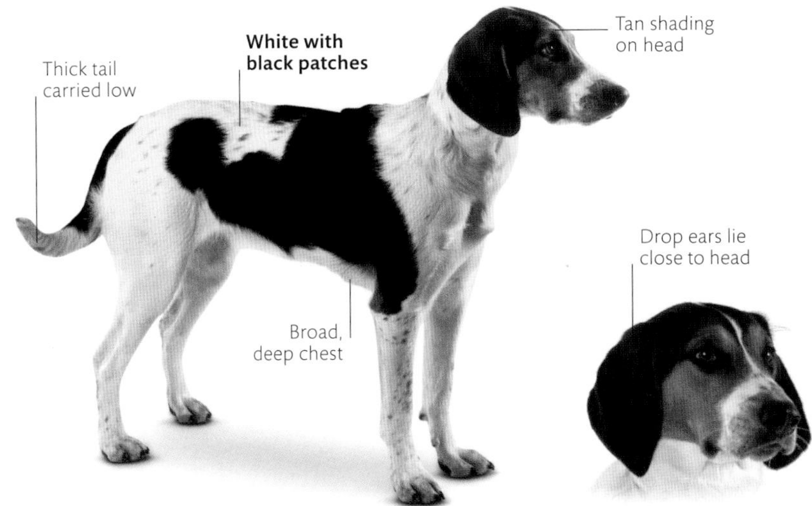

Norwegian Hound

HEIGHT 19–22in (47–55cm)
WEIGH 35–51lb (16–23kg)
LIFE SPAN 11–14 years

Tricolor

Trusting, friendly, and easy to handle when not hunting, the Norwegian Hound, or Dunker, is designed to track rabbits in snow in temperatures as low as -59°F (-15°C). Originally named after Captain Wilhelm Dunker, this hound was bred from other Norwegian and Russian hounds in the early 1800s.

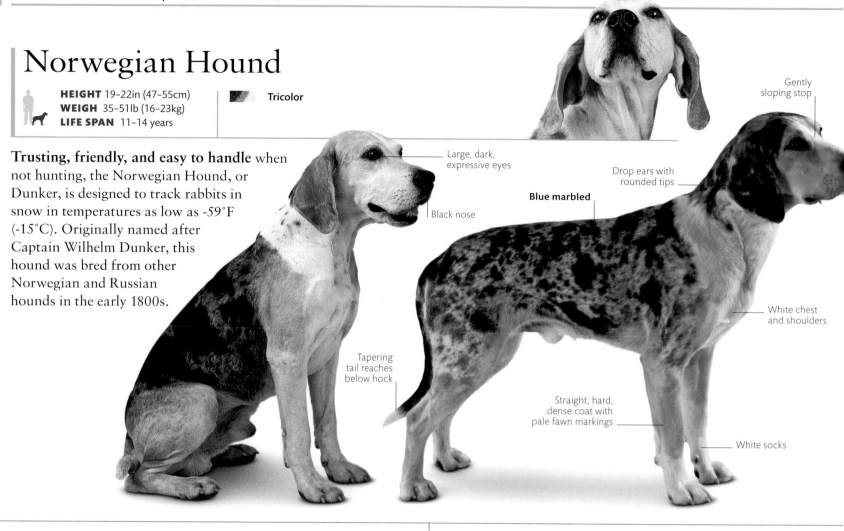

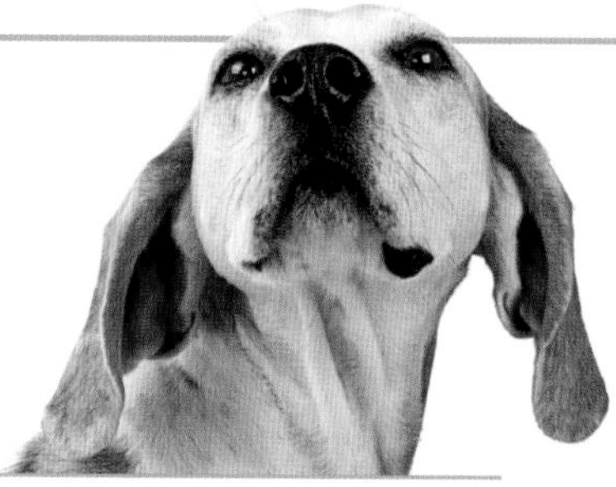

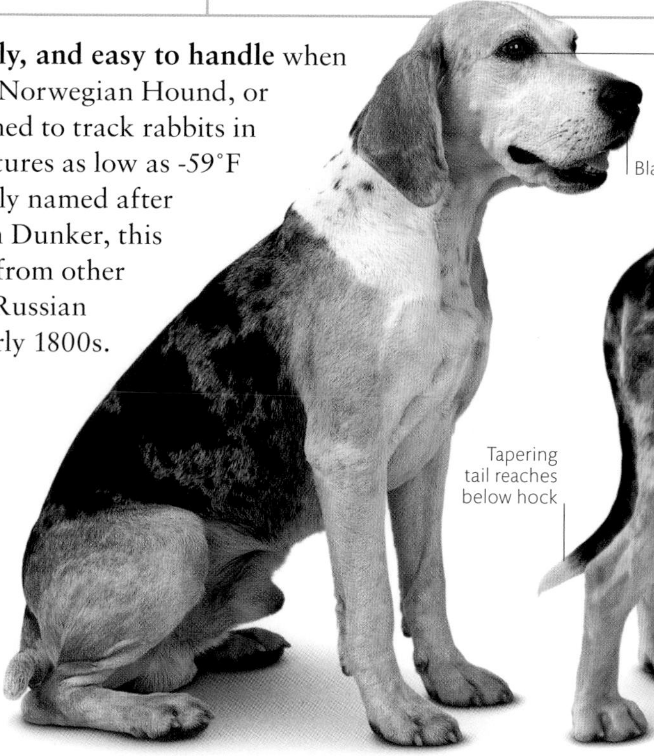

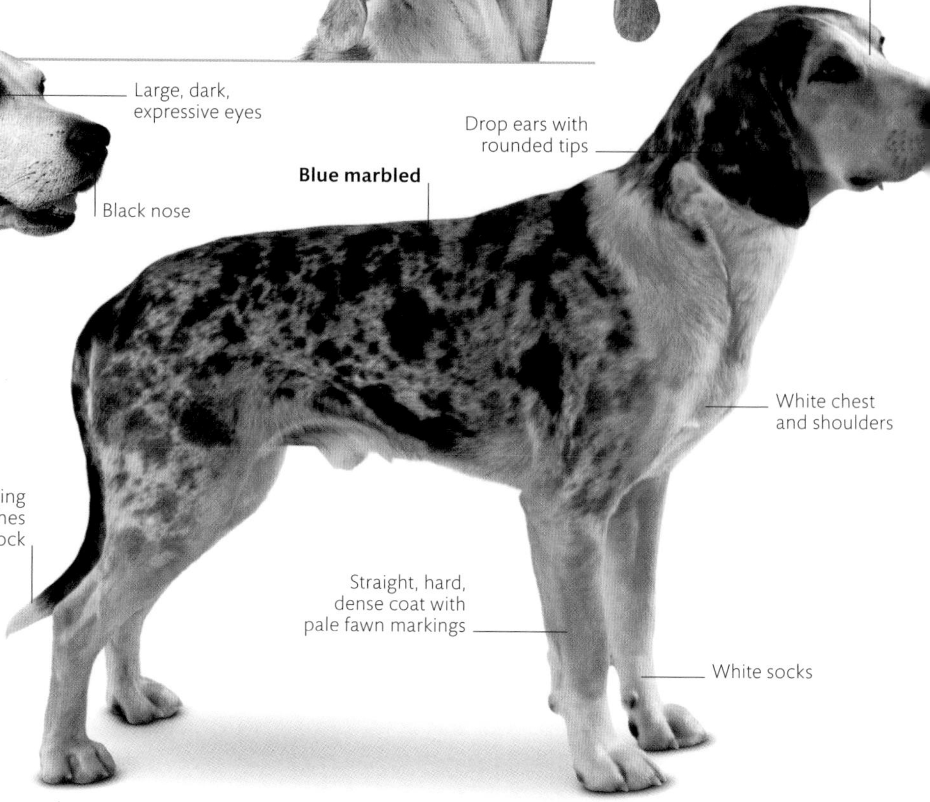

Large, dark, expressive eyes
Black nose
Gently sloping stop
Drop ears with rounded tips
Blue marbled
White chest and shoulders
Tapering tail reaches below hock
Straight, hard, dense coat with pale fawn markings
White socks

Finnish Hound

HEIGHT 20–24in (52–61cm)
WEIGHT 46–55lb (21–25kg)
LIFE SPAN 12 years

By far Finland's most popular hunting dog, this hound is bred to drive rabbits and fox in the country's snowy forests. It hunts with unfailing eagerness, but at home it is an easygoing and manageable pet. Although generally placid, the Finnish Hound can sometimes be shy around strangers.

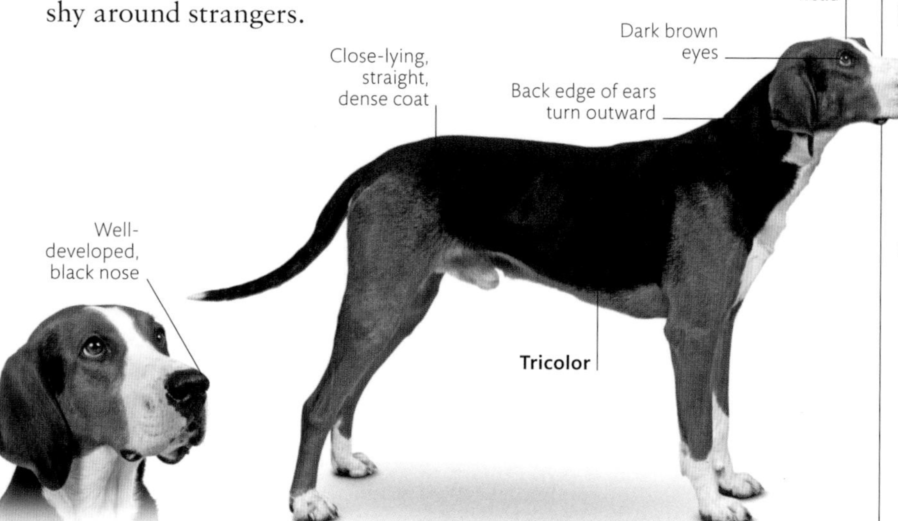

Hygen Hound

HEIGHT 19–23in (47–58cm)
WEIGHT 44–55lb (20–25kg)
LIFE SPAN 12 years

Yellow-red
Black and tan
Yellow-red coats have black shading.

A more lightweight dog than the Norwegian Hound (above), this breed from Ringerike and Romerike in eastern Norway is purpose built for the snowy Arctic expanses and has the stamina to bound through them tirelessly. Compact like the Smålandsstövare (see p.155), this is a quick-thinking hunter that loves long walks.

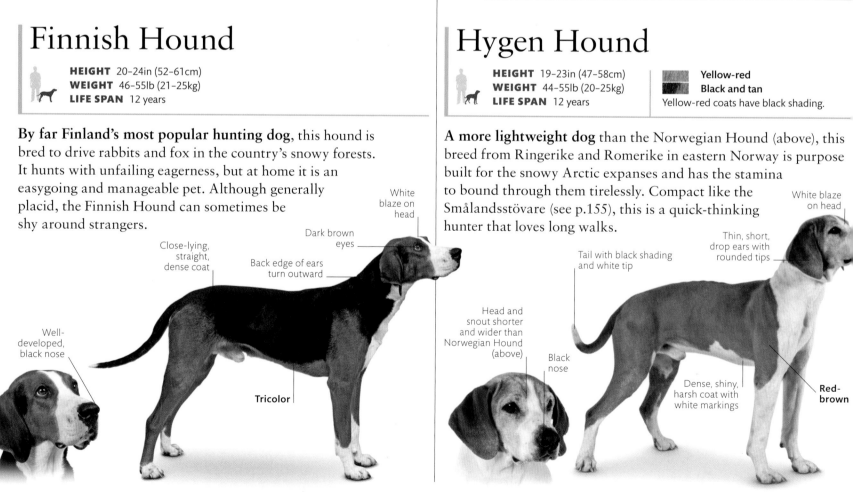

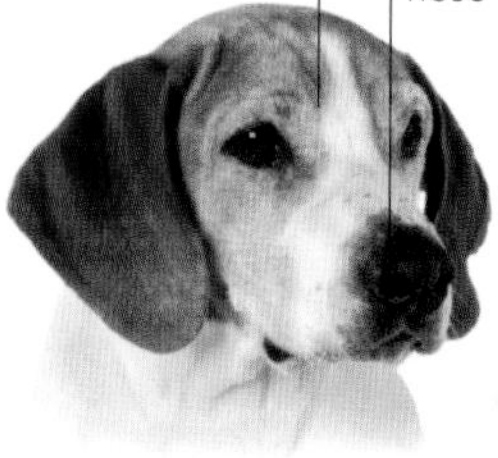

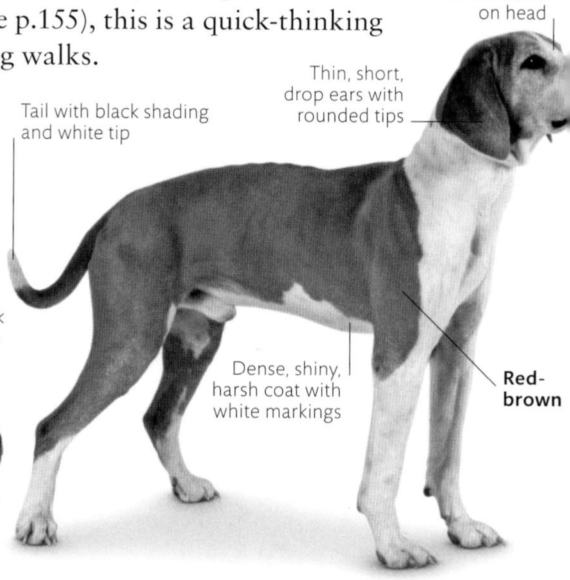

White blaze on head
Thin, short, drop ears with rounded tips
Tail with black shading and white tip
Head and snout shorter and wider than Norwegian Hound (above)
Black nose
Dense, shiny, harsh coat with white markings
Red-brown

Plott

HEIGHT 20–25in (51–64cm)
WEIGHT 40–60lb (18–27kg)
LIFE SPAN 10–12 years

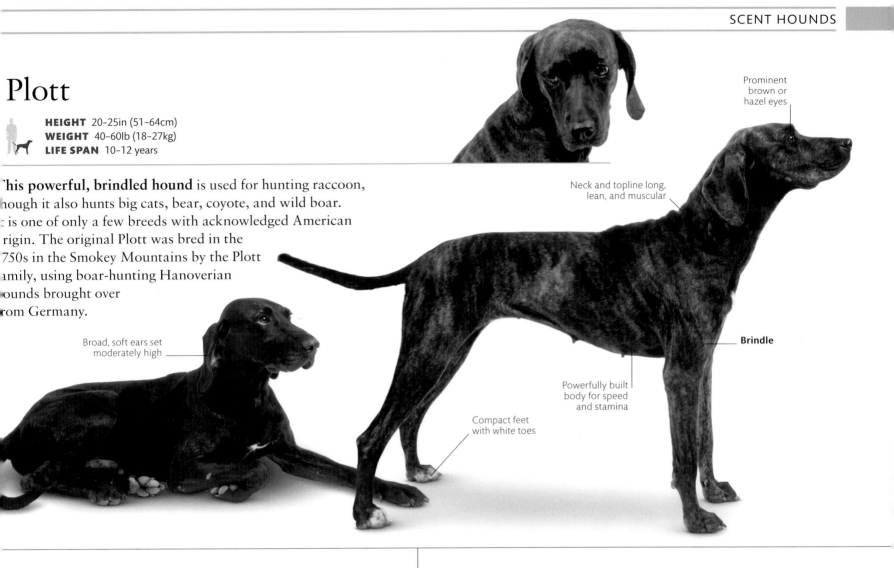

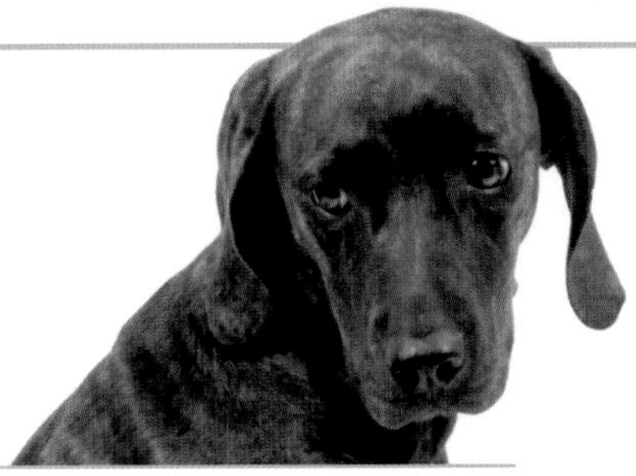

'his powerful, brindled hound is used for hunting raccoon, hough it also hunts big cats, bear, coyote, and wild boar. : is one of only a few breeds with acknowledged American rigin. The original Plott was bred in the 750s in the Smokey Mountains by the Plott amily, using boar-hunting Hanoverian ounds brought over rom Germany.

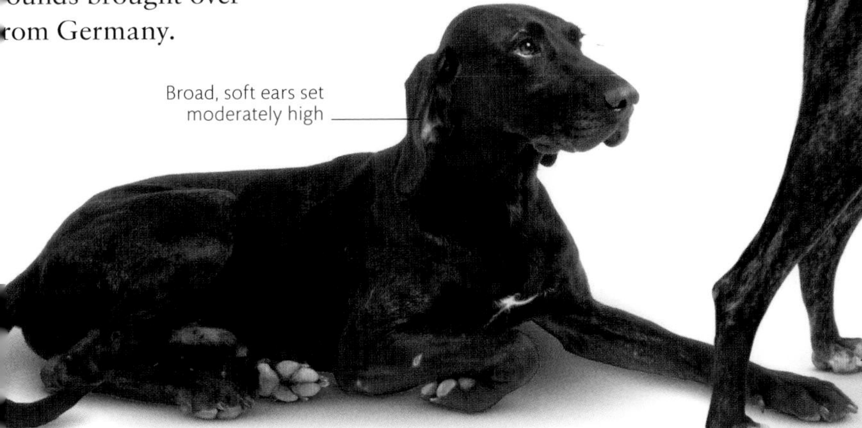

Prominent brown or hazel eyes

Neck and topline long, lean, and muscular

Broad, soft ears set moderately high

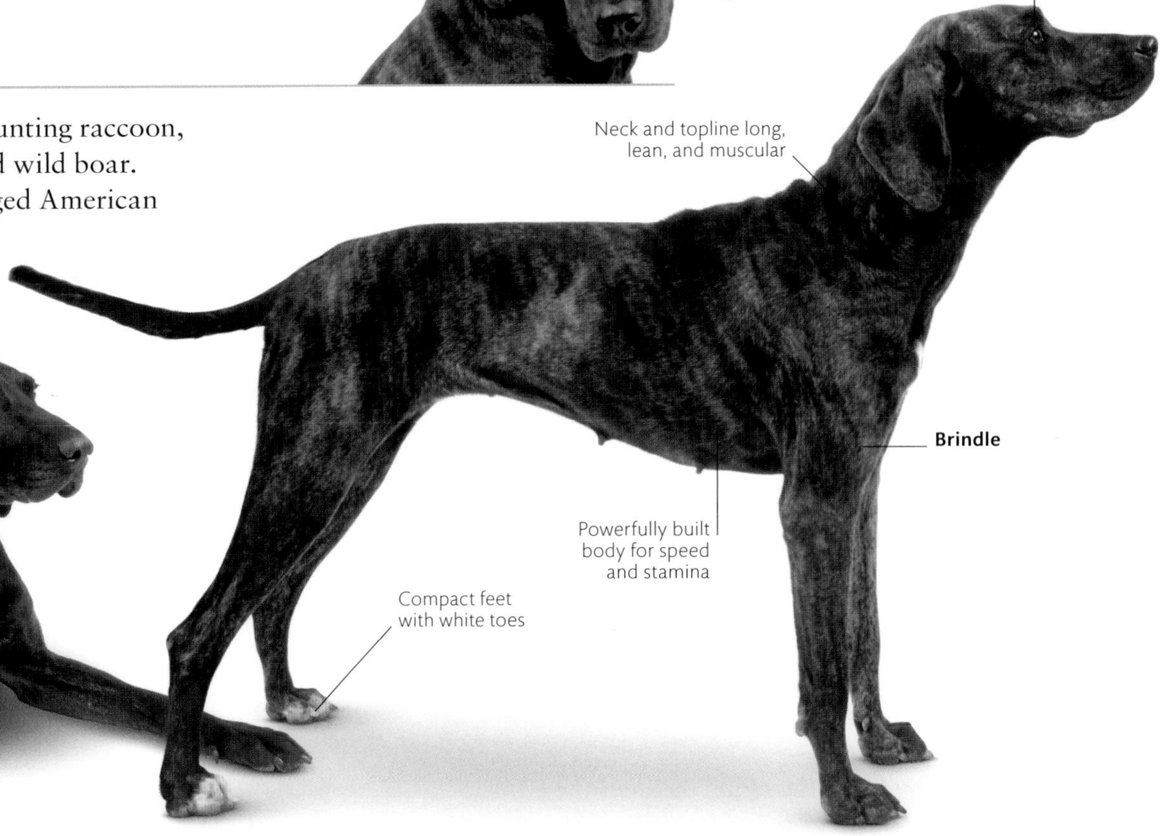

Brindle

Powerfully built body for speed and stamina

Compact feet with white toes

Catahoula Leopard Dog

HEIGHT 20–26in (51–66cm)
WEIGHT 51–90lb (23–41kg)
LIFE SPAN 10–14 years

Variety of colors

This striking-looking Louisiana herding dog and hunter of wild oar and raccoon is a mix of Spanish colonial greyhound, mastiff, nd possibly native Red Wolf. It can work well in swamps, orests, and more open terrain. Named after a parish in ts home state, the Catahoula Leopard Dog is an alert vatchdog, wary of strangers, but calm and dedicated o its household.

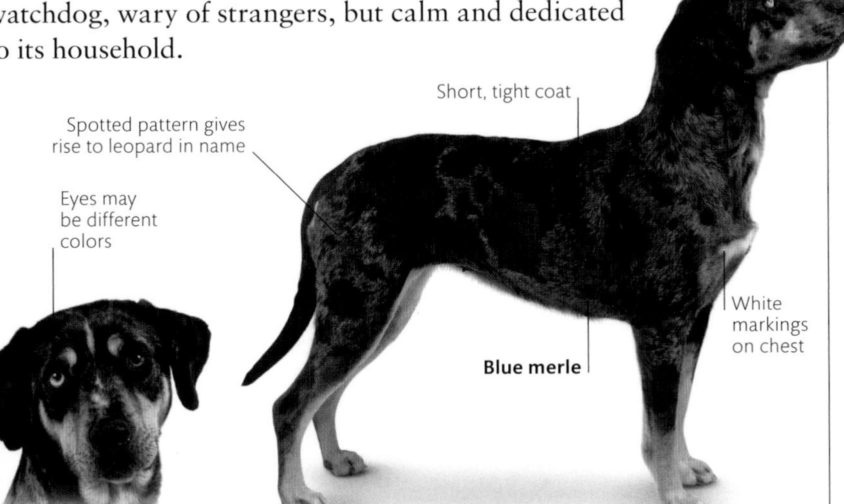

American Foxhound

HEIGHT 21–25in (53–64cm)
WEIGHT 40–66lb (18–30kg)
LIFE SPAN 12–13 years

Any color

These dogs have the most august of patrons—the first president of the United States, George Washington. He bred them from French and English hounds to produce a taller and more athletic, stand-alone breed. American Foxhounds love running in packs, hunting singly, or competing in field trials.

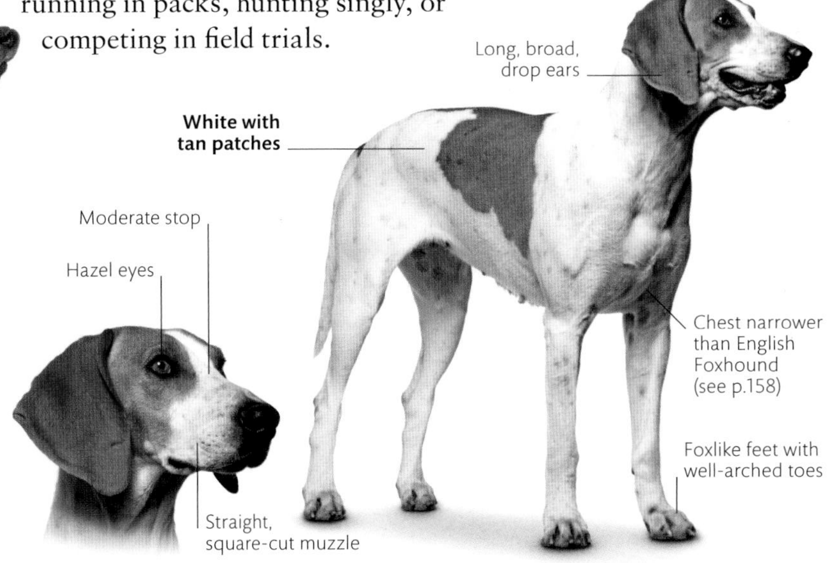

English Foxhound

HEIGHT	WEIGHT	LIFE SPAN	Variety of colors
23–25in (58–64cm)	55–75lb (25–34kg)	10–11 years	Any recognized hound color.

MAN'S BEST FRIEND

The idea of the dog as man's best friend originated in a court case in Missouri, in 1870. Farmer Leonidas Hornsby shot a foxhound named Old Drum for apparently worrying his sheep. The distraught owner, Charles Burden, sued Hornsby. Burden's lawyer, George Vest, made a long speech in praise of dogs; as he said, "The one absolutely unselfish friend that a man can have in this selfish world... is his dog." The listeners were moved to tears; Hornsby's lawyer noted that "the dog, though dead, had won."

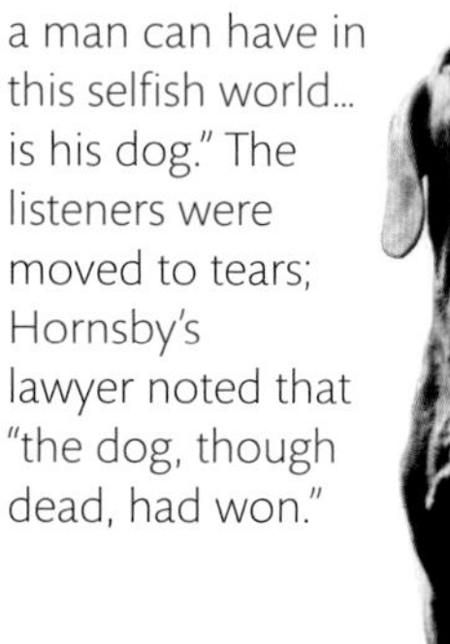

MONUMENT IN MISSOURI, ERECTED AS A TRIBUTE TO OLD DRUM

Good-natured, with a sunny approach to life, this breed needs plenty of activity if it is to adapt to a rural, family life

The ancestry of the English Foxhound is centuries old. The practice of hunting foxes with packs of hounds arose in the late 17th century as deer hunting declined and the English landscape changed from forests to fields. People started to breed foxhounds specifically for the new hunting; the animals needed the nose and stamina to follow a scent for several hours and had to be fast enough to keep up with the fox. By the 1800s more than 200 packs of foxhounds existed in England, and the first breeding records were being kept. The breed was introduced to the US in the 18th century.

This hound is highly responsive to training but can also be stubborn and strong-willed especially when on the scent. Historically kenneled in packs, the English Foxhound retains much of its pack instinct and tendency to bay (howl melodiously).

When kept as a house dog, the breed is very friendly and excellent with children, as long as it has plenty of exercise. It is not suited to city life. People who enjoy running and cycling would make good partners for this dog. These hounds can retain their playfulness, liveliness, and stamina into old age.

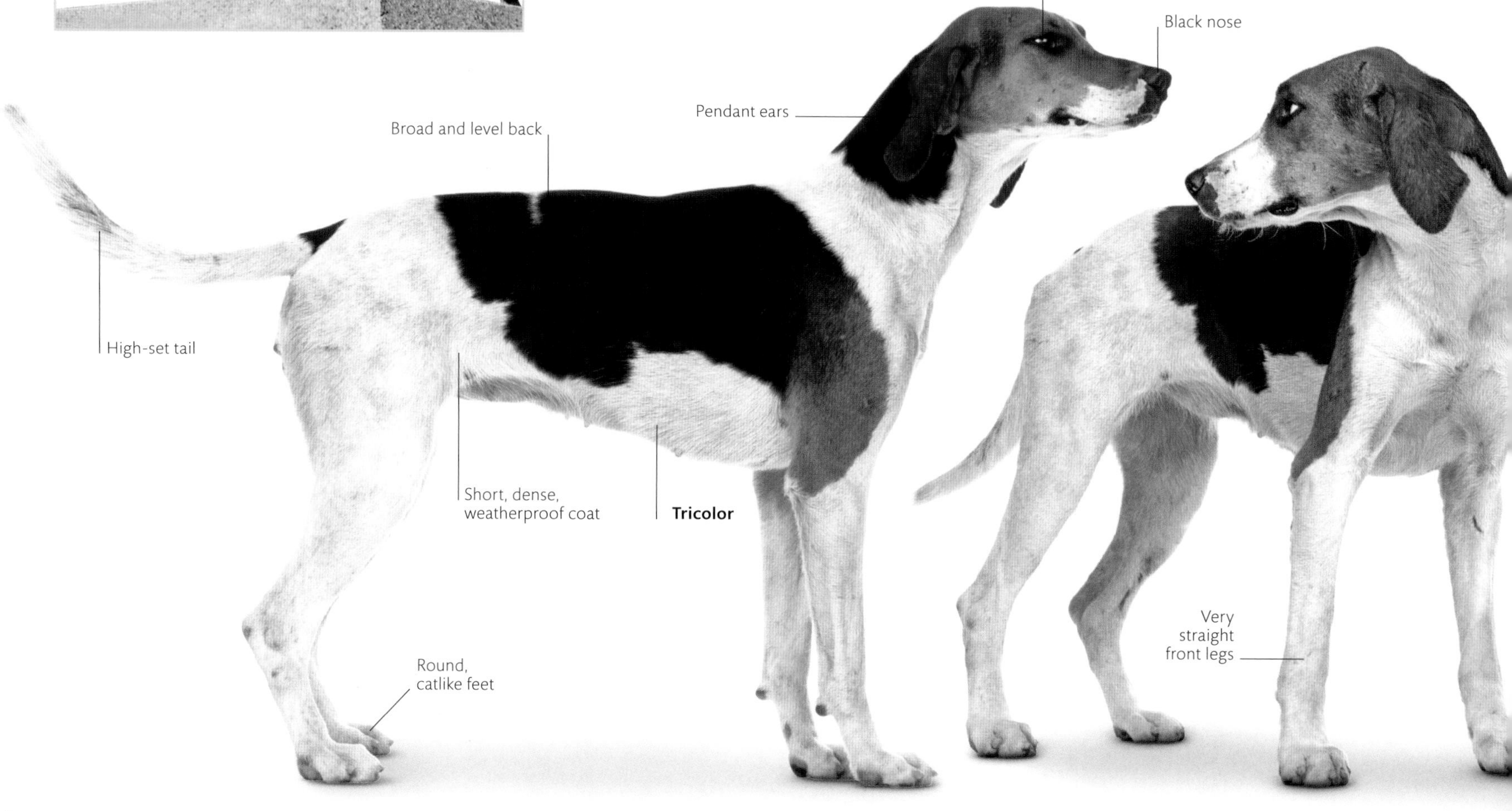

Large eyes with friendly expression

Black nose

Pendant ears

Broad and level back

High-set tail

Short, dense, weatherproof coat

Tricolor

Very straight front legs

Round, catlike feet

American English Coonhound

HEIGHT	WEIGHT	LIFE SPAN
23–26in (58–66cm)	46–90lb (21–41kg)	10–11 years

 Red and white
White and black
 Tricolor ticked
May also have a blue and white ticked coat.

BARKING UP THE WRONG TREE?

Coonhounds have left their mark on the English language as well as on American history. The expression "barking up the wrong tree" is derived from the Coonhound's practice of driving its prey up a tree and then barking until the hunter arrives. Coonhound's treeing drive is so strong, however, that they will stay by one tree, looking up and barking, even if the prey has escaped.

COONHOUNDS TREEING A RACCOON

This American-bred hunter is full of athletic poise and pace and may make an excellent pet when socialized

This energetic and intelligent dog evolved from English Foxhounds (opposite) that settlers brought to the New World in the 17th and 18th centuries. Among those who imported these hounds, known as Virginia Hounds, was President George Washington. From these animals a new dog was bred that was adapted to the harsher climate and rougher terrain, hunting foxes by day and raccoon by night.

The breed first gained recognition in 1905 under the name English Fox and Coonhound. During the 1940s the various Coonhound types were separated further, and the American Kennel Club officially recognized the American English Coonhound in 1995.

The American English Coonhound is still used for hunting and is famed for its speed and stamina. It has an effortless, tireless trot and a strong drive for pursuing prey and for treeing. The breed can work as both a cold nose dog (following an old animal trail for hours) and a hot nose dog (following a fresh, active scent at high speed). It is also used to pursue cougars and bears.

As a pet, the breed requires firm handling but in return will be a devoted companion and good guard dog.

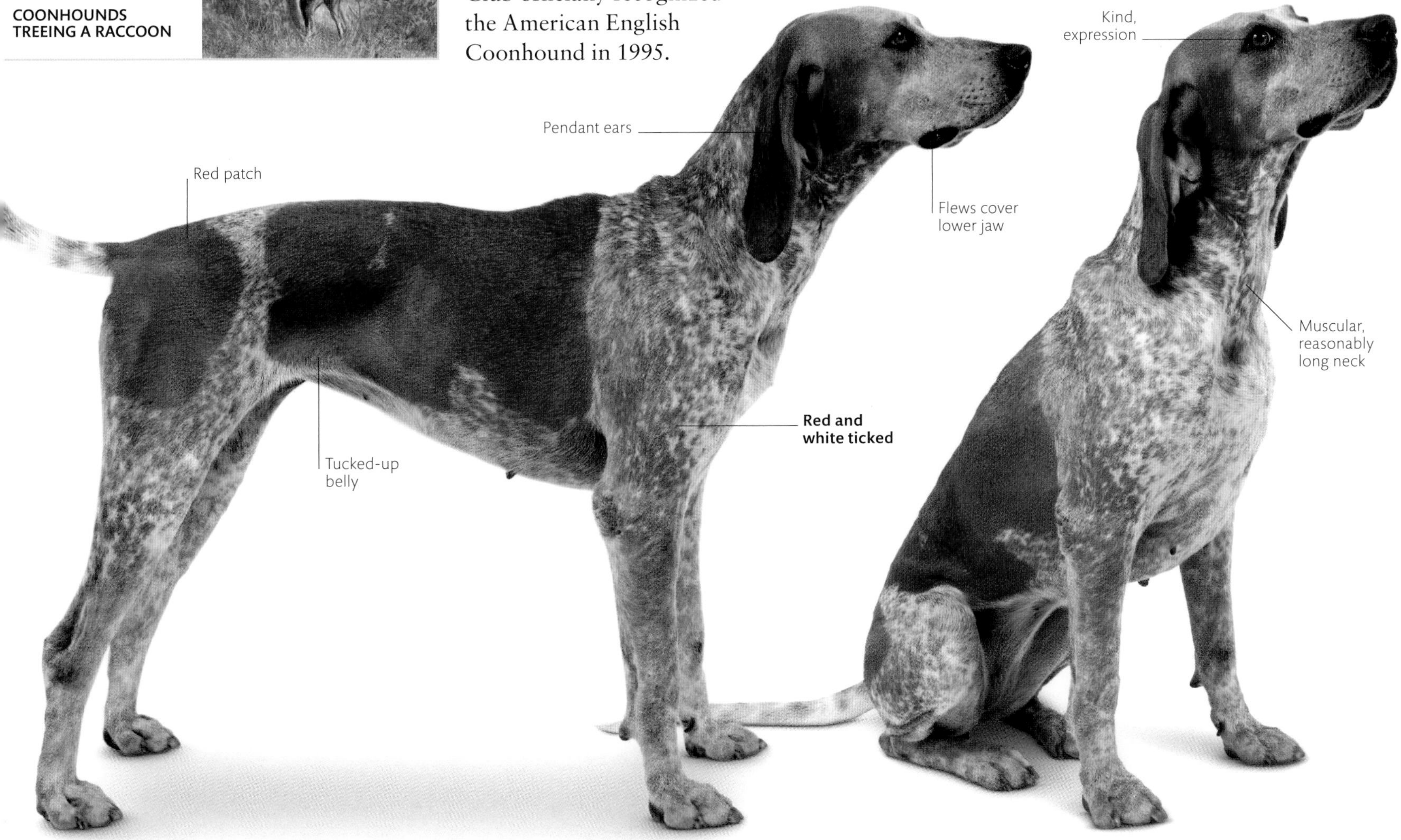

Kind, expression

Pendant ears

Red patch

Flews cover lower jaw

Muscular, reasonably long neck

Red and white ticked

Tucked-up belly

Black and Tan Coonhound

HEIGHT 23–27in (58–69cm)
WEIGHT 51–75lb (23–34kg)
LIFE SPAN 10–12 years

This big American hunting dog probably descends from the Bloodhound (see p.141) and a now-extinct old English breed called the Talbot Hound. Tough and powerful, the Black and Tan Coonhound is a superb tracker of raccoon, opossum, and even cougar, baying loudly when it has chased its quarry up a tree.

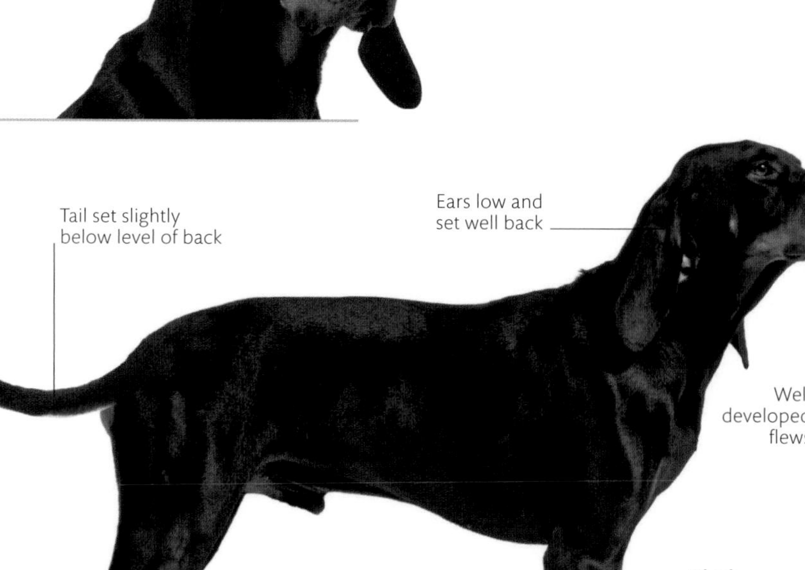

Redbone Coonhound

HEIGHT 21–27in (53–69cm)
WEIGHT 46–71lb (21–32kg)
LIFE SPAN 11–12 years

Bred in the southern states of the US, the handsome, glossy-coated Redbone Coonhound has been a popular hunting dog for over a century. Fast and agile over almost any type of terrain, this hound is well known for its prowess in tracking raccoons, bears, and cougars. Trainable as a companion dog, this coonhound is sociable and affectionate.

Bluetick Coonhound

HEIGHT 21–27in (53–69cm)
WEIGHT 44–79lb (20–36kg)
LIFE SPAN 11–12 years

breakaway breed, originally garded as the English Coonhound, e Bluetick Coonhound has had devoted followers in the US since e 1940s. Although mainly used track raccoon and opossum, is hound also hunts deer and ar. Happiest when working, the luetick Coonhound has proved be highly successful at obedience d agility trials.

Treeing Walker Coonhound

HEIGHT 20–27in (51–68cm)
WEIGHT 51–71lb (23–32kg)
LIFE SPAN 12–13 years

White

White coats have tan or black spots.

his fast and efficient racoon unter has been recognized as a istinct breed since the 1940s. the US this hound is much dmired for its outstanding bilities in coonhound ompetitions. It is a reed that appreciates friendly home nvironment and ves people.

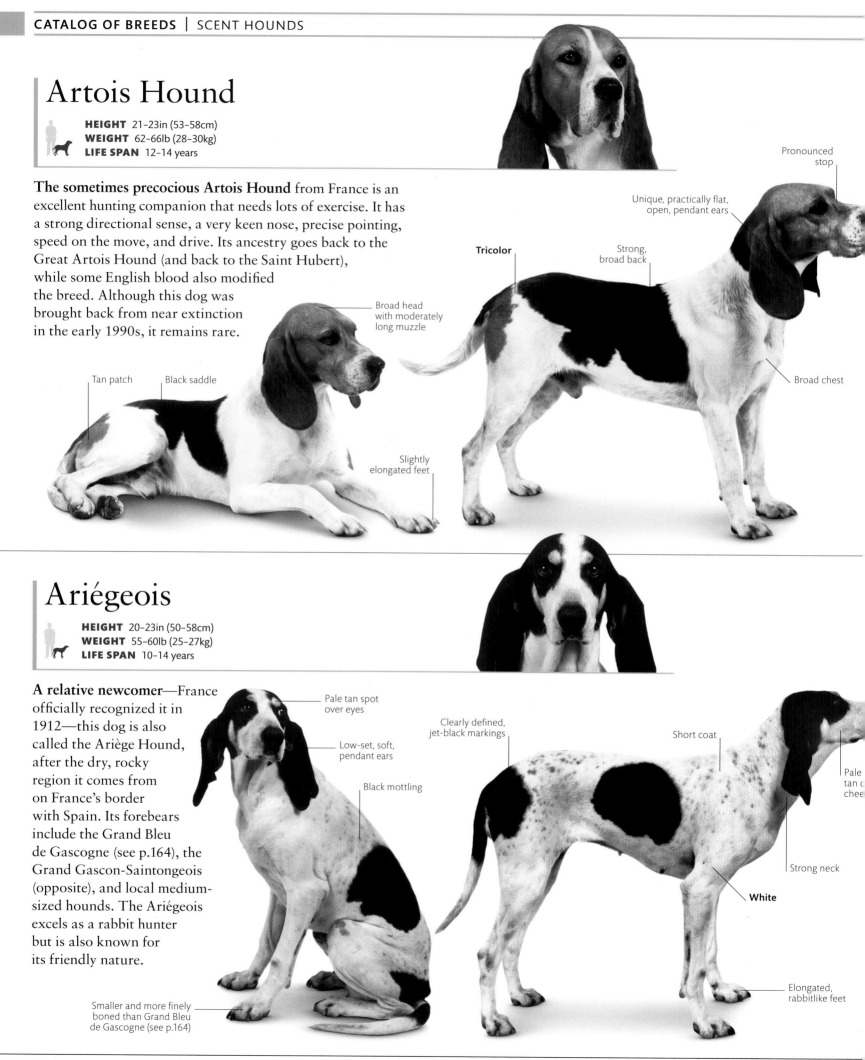

Artois Hound

HEIGHT 21–23in (53–58cm)
WEIGHT 62–66lb (28–30kg)
LIFE SPAN 12–14 years

The sometimes precocious Artois Hound from France is an excellent hunting companion that needs lots of exercise. It has a strong directional sense, a very keen nose, precise pointing, speed on the move, and drive. Its ancestry goes back to the Great Artois Hound (and back to the Saint Hubert), while some English blood also modified the breed. Although this dog was brought back from near extinction in the early 1990s, it remains rare.

Ariégeois

HEIGHT 20–23in (50–58cm)
WEIGHT 55–60lb (25–27kg)
LIFE SPAN 10–14 years

A relative newcomer—France officially recognized it in 1912—this dog is also called the Ariège Hound, after the dry, rocky region it comes from on France's border with Spain. Its forebears include the Grand Bleu de Gascogne (see p.164), the Grand Gascon-Saintongeois (opposite), and local medium-sized hounds. The Ariégeois excels as a rabbit hunter but is also known for its friendly nature.

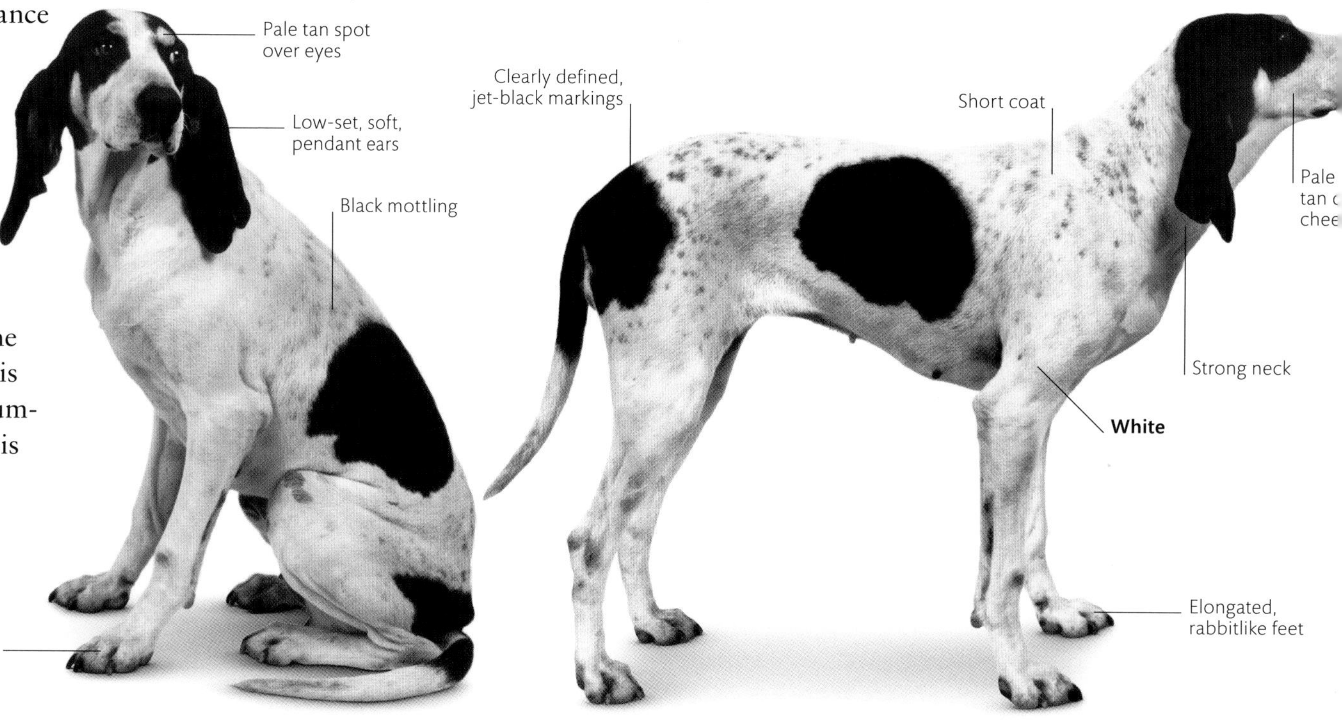

Gascon-Saintongeois

HEIGHT Petit: 21–24in (54–62cm); Grand: 24–28in (62–72cm)
WEIGHT Petit: 53–55lb (24–25kg); Grand: 66–71lb (30–32kg)
LIFE SPAN 12–14 years

This rare breed, from the Gascony area of France, is also known as the Virelade Hound after the Baron de Virelade who crossed the Saintongeois with the Grand Bleu de Gascogne (see p.164), and the Ariégeois (opposite). It is a high-stamina hunter, with a fine-tuned sense of smell. There are two sizes: Petit and Grand.

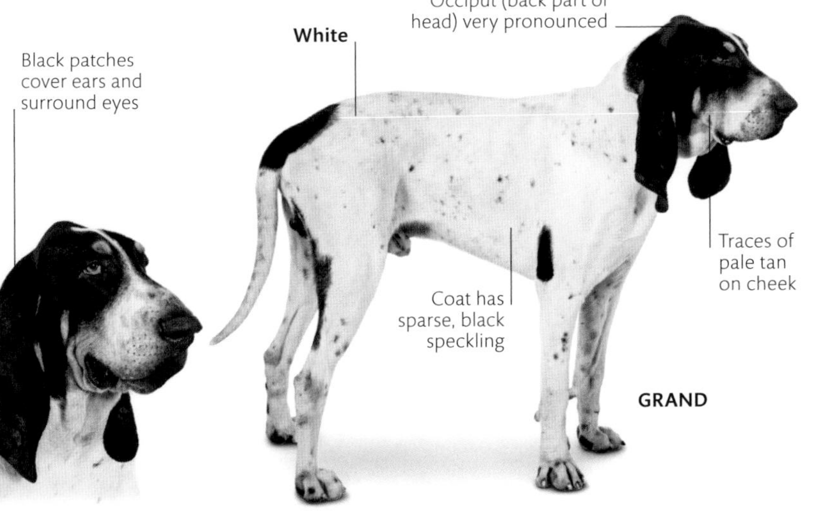

Blue Gascony Griffon

HEIGHT 19–22in (48–57cm)
WEIGHT 37–40lb (17–18kg)
LIFE SPAN 12–13 years

A cross between the Petit Bleu de Gascogne (below) and wire-coated hounds, this French dog has a coarse, shaggy coat that allows it to work in harsh conditions. A comparatively rare breed, it was specifically developed to hunt deer, fox, and rabbit. It has stamina rather than great speed and a remarkably efficient nose.

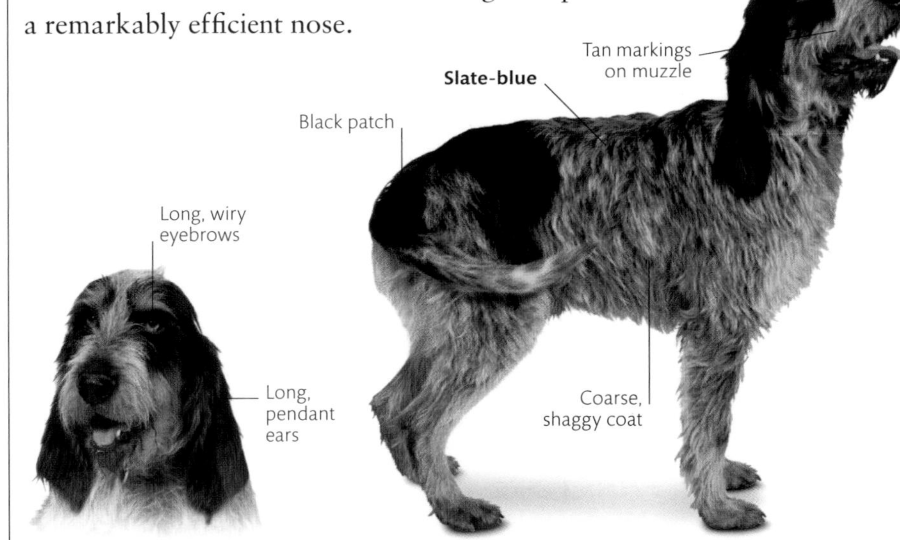

Basset Bleu de Gascogne

HEIGHT 12–15in (30–38cm)
WEIGHT 35–44lb (16–20kg)
LIFE SPAN 10–12 years

In 12th-century France blue hounds of this type were used to hunt wolves, deer, and boar. The modern breed was established in the 20th century. A low-slung dog, it is not fast moving but makes up for lack of speed with great determination, tracking quarry for hours once on the scent. An enthusiastic outdoor companion as well as a fine household pet, this dog takes patience to train and socialize.

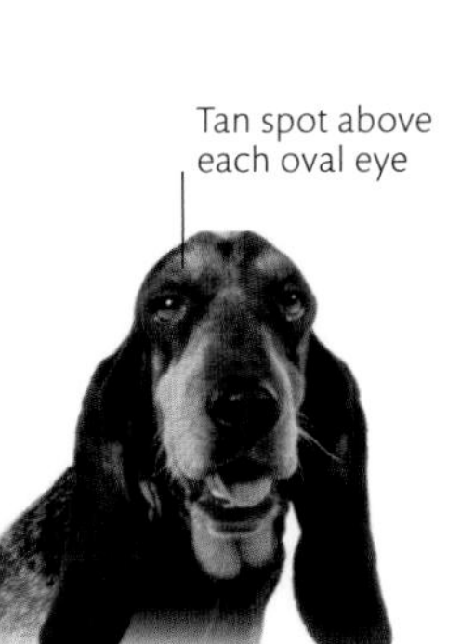

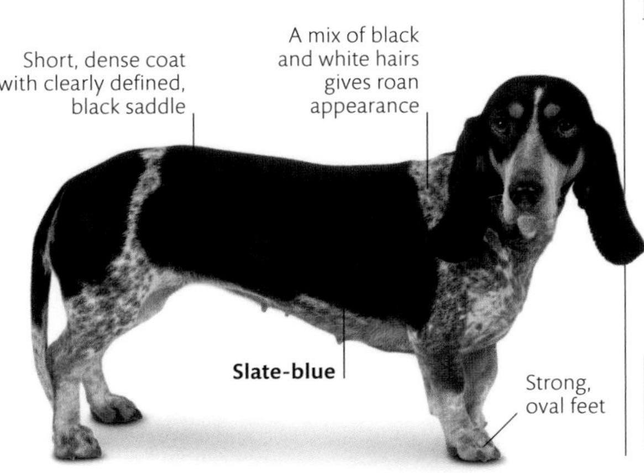

Petit Bleu de Gascogne

HEIGHT 20–23in (50–58cm)
WEIGHT 88–106lb (40–48kg)
LIFE SPAN 12 years

Bred down in size from the Grand Bleu de Gascogne (see p.164), the Petit Bleu de Gascogne was developed in France for hunting rabbit but is also used to pursue larger game. With a fine nose and a musical voice, this hound works well either as an individual or in a pack. If kept as a companion, it needs a firm hand and a lot of exercise.

Grand Bleu de Gascogne

HEIGHT	WEIGHT	LIFE SPAN
24–28in (60–70 cm)	80–120lb (36–55kg)	12–14 years

large working hound with impressive looks that has great tamina and tenacity when following a scent

his French scent hound originated southern and southwestern France, articularly in the area of Gascony. escended from the original hunting ogs of ancient Gaul, and crossed with ogs imported by Phoenician traders, this reed is, in turn, the ancestor of all the cent hounds found in southern France he Midi). The breed is still widespread France today, and has also been ntroduced to other countries, such as ne UK and the US.

The Grand Bleu de Gascogne was riginally employed to hunt wolves, but nce these declined in numbers it was sed in wild boar and deer hunts. Packs f hounds are still used to hunt these nimals today, as well as to hunt hare. he breed's scenting abilities are highly developed and it is single-minded when following a trail. It works at a moderately slow pace but is noted for its endurance and for its powerful, resonant baying voice.

The breed's tall stature and aristocratic bearing have led some people to refer to the Grand Bleu de Gascogne as the "King of Hounds." The elegant appearance is heightened by its coat, which has areas of shimmering bluish color, produced by black mottling over white.

The breed has started to appear in the show ring but, despite its gentle and friendly nature—and the fact that it bonds closely with its owners—its size and energy can make it difficult to live with. The Grand Bleu de Gascogne needs plenty of exercise, which should include training that provides mental as well as physical challenges.

FROM FRANCE TO AMERICA

In 1785 George Washington was given seven Grand Bleu de Gascogne hounds (seen below in a 1907 French print) by General Lafayette. Washington, an avid hunter, found the dogs to be excellent trackers, but they were unaccustomed to pursuing animals that could climb trees, such as raccoon. This was frustrating for Washington, since the dogs often failed to keep their quarry in the tree until it was shot. Coonhounds were later developed for this type of hunting by crossing various breeds, including the Grand Bleu de Gascogne, whose coloring can be seen in the Bluetick Coonhound (see p.161).

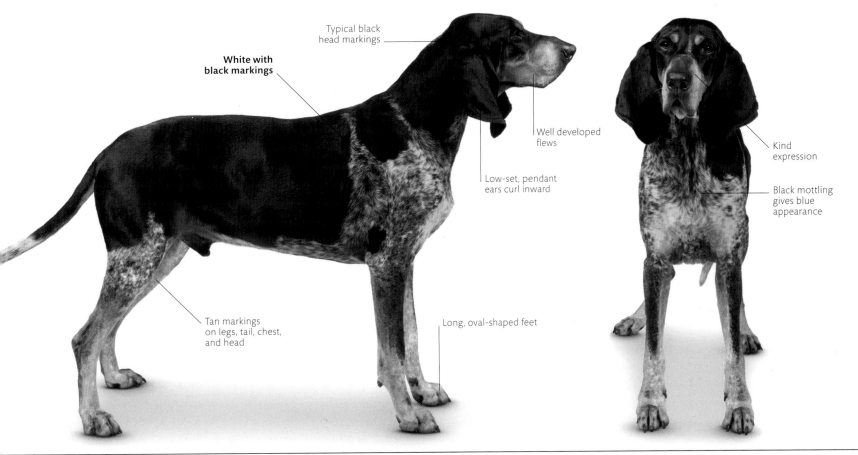

Typical black head markings

White with black markings

Well developed flews

Low-set, pendant ears curl inward

Kind expression

Black mottling gives blue appearance

Tan markings on legs, tail, chest, and head

Long, oval-shaped feet

Poitevin

HEIGHT 24–28in (62–72cm)
WEIGHT 132–146lb (60–66kg)
LIFE SPAN 11–12 years

White and orange

Wolf-colored hair also often occurs.

This big, courageous hound is adept at fast and furious pack-hunting over rough ground, and once hunted the wolves that used to roam the province of Poitou below the Vendée and Brittany in western France. The longest-serving of the French pack hounds, today this powerfully muscled breed shows great prowess and stamina in pursuing wild boar and deer. It can hunt all day and can even follow its quarry through water.

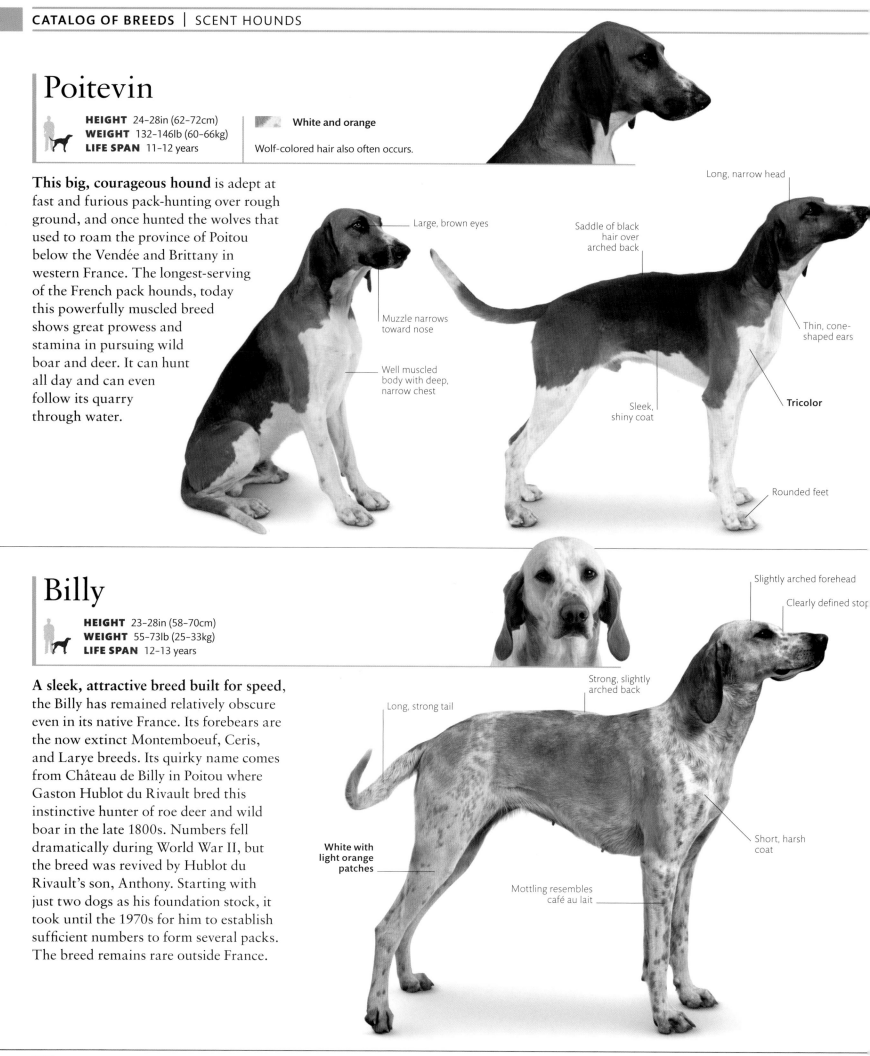

Billy

HEIGHT 23–28in (58–70cm)
WEIGHT 55–73lb (25–33kg)
LIFE SPAN 12–13 years

A sleek, attractive breed built for speed, the Billy has remained relatively obscure even in its native France. Its forebears are the now extinct Montemboeuf, Ceris, and Larye breeds. Its quirky name comes from Château de Billy in Poitou where Gaston Hublot du Rivault bred this instinctive hunter of roe deer and wild boar in the late 1800s. Numbers fell dramatically during World War II, but the breed was revived by Hublot du Rivault's son, Anthony. Starting with just two dogs as his foundation stock, it took until the 1970s for him to establish sufficient numbers to form several packs. The breed remains rare outside France.

French Tricolor Hound

HEIGHT 24–28in (60–72cm)
WEIGHT 75–77lb (34–35kg)
LIFE SPAN 11–12 years

erhaps the most popular hound in France, the French Tricolor Iound was blended from the Poitevin (opposite) and Billy opposite) to try to create a homegrown pack hound ithout English Foxhound (see p.158) blood, though iere is a hint of Great Anglo-French Tricolor Iound (right). Today these rong, well muscled pack ogs hunt game such as eer and wild boar.

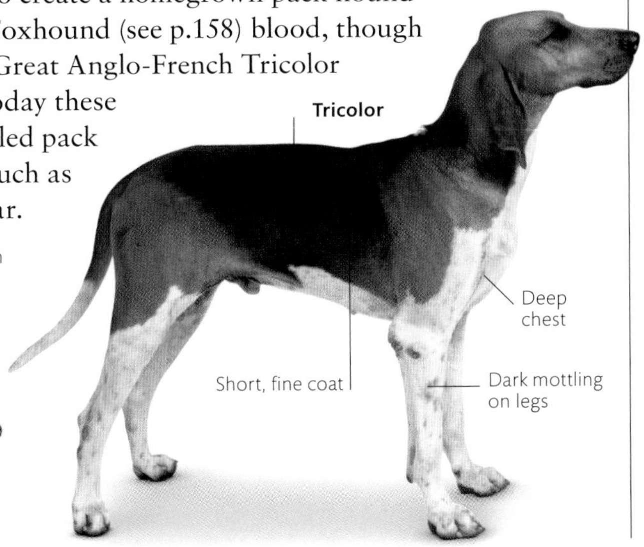

Tricolor
Large, brown eyes
Deep chest
Short, fine coat
Dark mottling on legs

Great Anglo-French Tricolor Hound

HEIGHT 24–28in (60–70cm)
WEIGHT 66–77lb (30–35kg)
LIFE SPAN 10–12 years

Like several French scent hounds, the name says what it is: a tricolored dog with cross-Channel connections—the "Great" refers to the game it hunts, such as red deer, not the dog's size. Its coat and character come from the tricolored Poitevin (opposite), and the powerful muscles and stamina from the English Foxhound (see p.158).

Black blanket
Broad, pendant, tan ears
Tricolor
Short, quite coarse coat
Fairly broad, white chest
Rounded feet

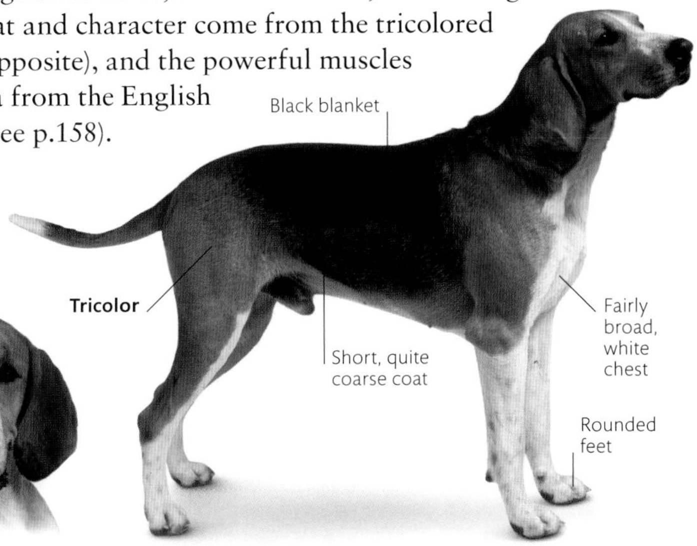

Great Anglo-French White and Black Hound

HEIGHT 24–28in (62–72cm)
WEIGHT 66–77lb (30–35kg)
LIFE SPAN 10–12 years

This Anglo-French scent hound is one of three color-based arieties recognized as separate breeds. It originated in the 1800s rom a mix of Bleu de Gascogne and Gasçon Saintongeois hounds see p.163) crossed with English Foxhound (see p.158). Most live n kennels in France and are used to hunt deer in packs. Very few of these powerful, sturdy hunters re kept as domestic pets.

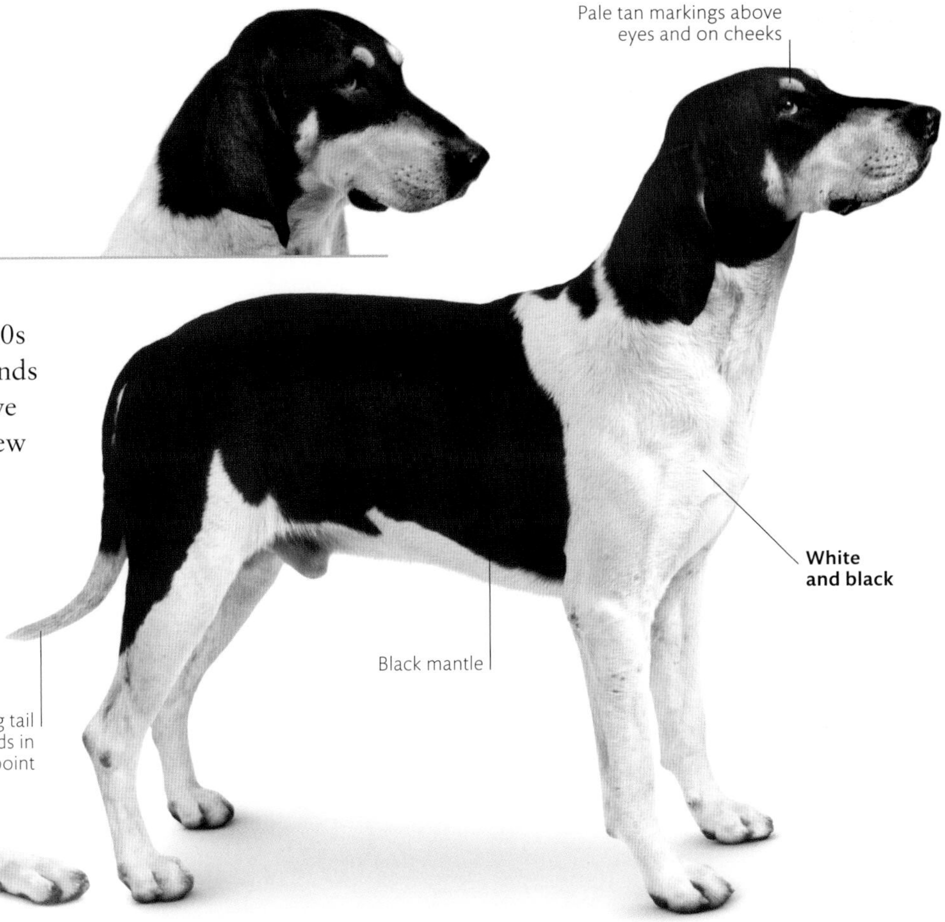

Pale tan markings above eyes and on cheeks
Deep-set, brown eyes
White and black
Long tail ends in sharp point
Black mantle

French White and Black Hound

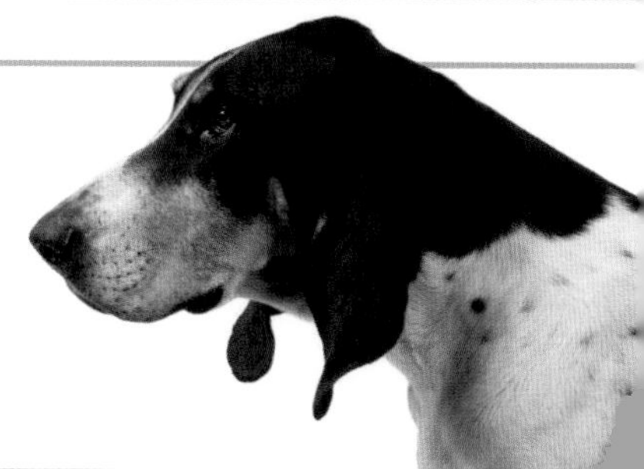

HEIGHT	WEIGHT	LIFE SPAN
24–28in (62–72cm)	57–66lb (26–30kg)	10–12 years

CHIEN D'ORDRE

There are many breeds of hound in France but only a few, such as the French White and Black Hound, are considered to be a Chien d'Ordre. These big dogs, working in packs, hunt large game such as deer. The dogs track by scent and pursue their quarry, under the clear direction of a huntsman, until it is caught and killed. To do this a French White and Black Hound needs courage, stamina, speed, and a good nose.

A swift-footed, stamina-filled hunter of large game that gives endless chase and requires strenuous exercise

This uncommon but striking hound was first developed in France in the early 20th century. The earliest ancestor was the Saintonge Hound, whose own origins are uncertain but which was bred to hunt wolves. The modern French White and Black Hound was developed by Henri de Falandre, who wanted to create a hound with exceptional stamina and endurance. The breed, a mix of Bleu de Gascogne and Gascon Saintongeois breeds (see p.163), was officially recognized by the FCI in 1957. However, in 2009 the FCI recorded no more than 2,000 of these dogs in existence.

The French White and Black Hound is highly valued for hunting deer, particularly roe deer, due to its tenacity and agility. It is usually kept as a working dog and kenneled in packs, rather than as a companion dog. The breed can be a good house dog with the right owner, since it is amiable and gentle with children. It does, however, have a strong pack instinct, so requires firm handling.

It needs a home in the country or one with a large yard, plenty of exercise, and opportunities to express its hunting and tracking drives.

Great Anglo-French White and Orange Hound

HEIGHT 24–28in (60–70cm)
WEIGHT 75–77lb (34–35kg)
LIFE SPAN 10 years

ne of three breeds of the Great Anglo-French pack-hunting ogs produced in the early 19th century, this hound is the result crossing the English Foxhound (see p.158) with a large, French ent hound—the Billy (see p.166). Although trainable and kind-atured, this dog lives to hunt and is too nergetic to be happy in omplete domesticity.

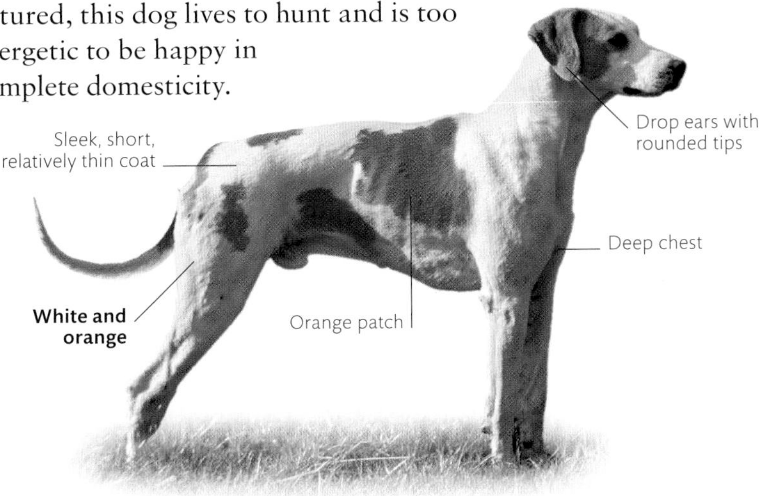

French White and Orange Hound

HEIGHT 24–28in (62–70cm)
WEIGHT 60–71lb (27–32kg)
LIFE SPAN 12–13 years

Rarely seen, the French White and Orange Hound is a relatively new hunting dog—only gaining recognition in the 1970s. Easier to manage than most pack hounds, this dog is usually reliable with children and other dogs but must be supervised around small pets. It loves action and should not be kept in a confined space.

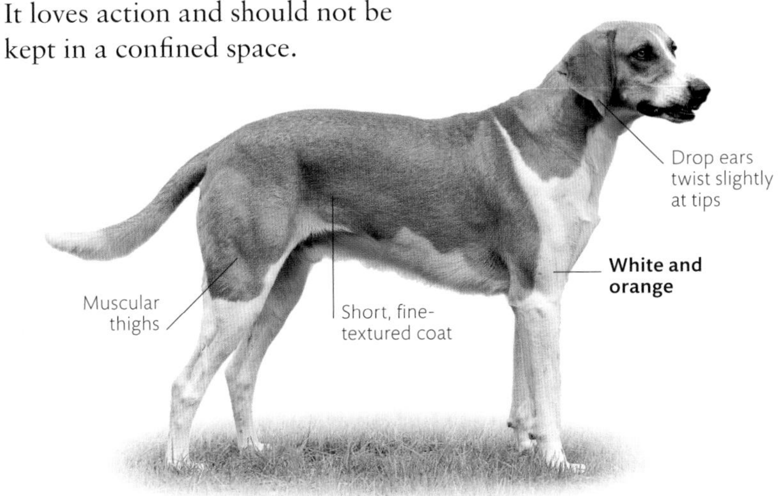

Westphalian Dachsbracke

HEIGHT 12–15in (30–38cm)
WEIGHT 33–40lb (15–18kg)
LIFE SPAN 10–12 years

short-legged version of the German Hound (see p.172), his sturdy little dog was bred to hunt small game in areas too hickly overgrown for larger dogs to penetrate. Playful and heerily good-natured, the Westphalian Dachsbracke makes delightful companion and is well suited to family life.

Alpine Dachsbracke

HEIGHT 13–17in (34–42cm)
WEIGHT 26–49lb (12–22kg)
LIFE SPAN 12 years

Vieräugl (black and tan)

May have white star on chest.

Hunting dogs very similar in appearance to the Alpine Dachsbracke existed hundreds of years ago and may have been the predecessors of this small hound. In the 1930s the modern breed was recognized as one of Austria's top scent hounds. Sturdy, tireless, and bred to hunt, it is not an ideal house dog.

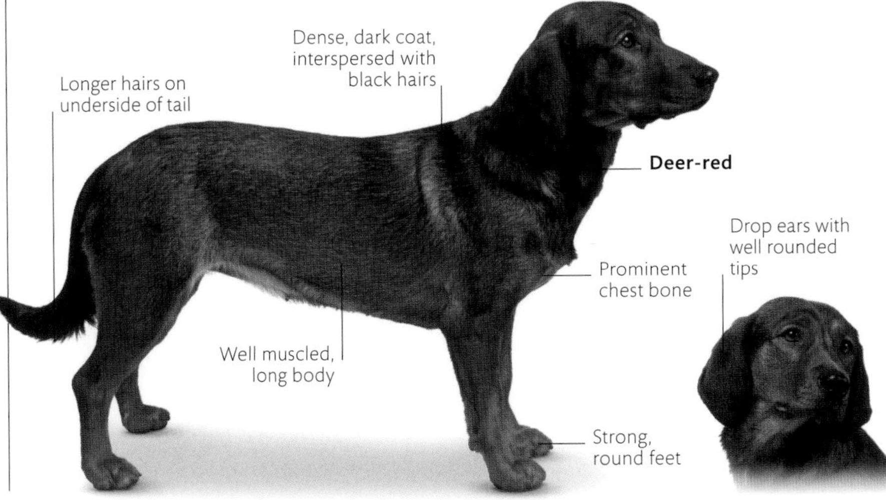

Dachshund

HEIGHT
Miniature: 5–6in (13–15cm)
Standard: 8–9in (20–23cm)

WEIGHT
Miniature: 9–11lb (4–5kg)
Standard: 20–26lb (9–12kg)

LIFE SPAN
12–15 years

Variety of colors

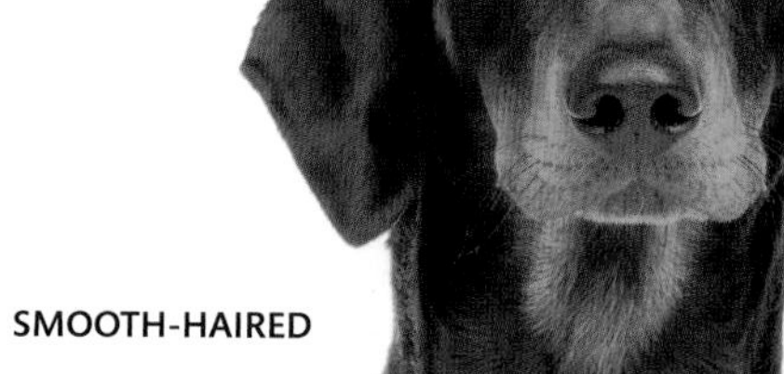

SMOOTH-HAIRED

Inquisitive, brave, loyal, and with a bark that belies its size, this dog is popular as a companion and watchdog

A symbol of Germany, the Dachshund has become popular worldwide and earned the nicknames "sausage dog" and "weiner." The breed originated as a long-bodied, short-legged dog used to hunt ground-dwelling animals such as badgers; the name *Dachshund* means "badger dog" in German. The dogs could trail their quarry by scent as other hounds do, but could also go to ground like terriers, to flush out or kill their prey. In addition to the badger, the dogs hunted rabbit, fox, and stoat, and could even take on wolverines.

The modern Dachshund has even shorter legs than its forebears, and includes crosses from other small or short-legged breeds. During the 18th and 19th centuries different sizes were bred for different types of prey. Also, in addition to the original smooth-haired coat, two other varieties—longhaired and wirehaired—were created. The American Kennel Club recognizes six breeds: standard and miniature sizes, with three coat types for each size. The FCI recognizes the three coat types, plus three sizes—standard, miniature, and rabbit (the smallest)—based on chest circumference.

Some Dachshunds are still used in Germany for hunting, but most are family pets. Despite their small size, Dachshunds need plenty of physical and mental activity. They are clever, bold, and affectionate, but can be strong-willed and tend to ignore commands when following a scent. Dachshunds are protective toward their human family and make good guard dogs, but can be snappy with strangers. Longhaired dogs need daily grooming.

ARTISTS' CHOICE

Three of the world's greatest artists—Pablo Picasso, Andy Warhol, and David Hockney—owned smoothhaired Dachshunds. Both Picasso and Warhol painted pictures of their dogs but only Hockney produced enough canvasses to have an exhibition in which they were the sole subjects. Hockney referred to Stanley and Boogie, his dogs, as "two dear little creatures (that) are my friends"; "food and love dominate their lives."

DAVID HOCKNEY

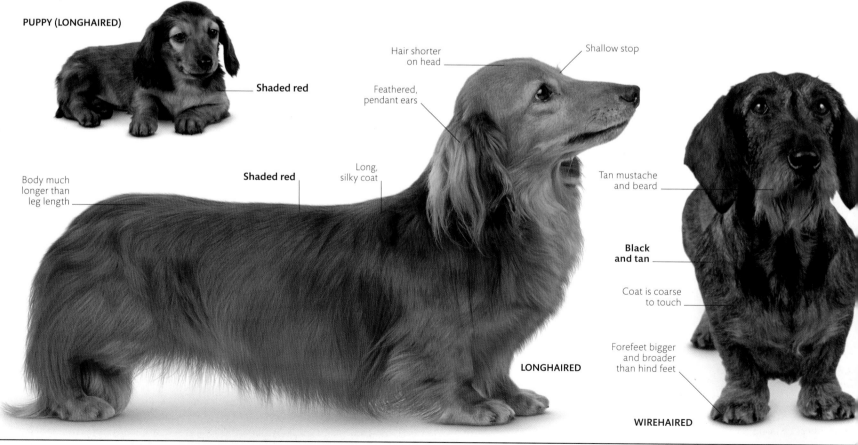

PUPPY (LONGHAIRED)

Shaded red

Body much longer than leg length

Shaded red

Long, silky coat

Hair shorter on head

Feathered, pendant ears

Shallow stop

LONGHAIRED

Tan mustache and beard

Black and tan

Coat is coarse to touch

Forefeet bigger and broader than hind feet

WIREHAIRED

Bundle of fun
Despite its short legs, the Dachshund is a lively, energetic dog that needs plenty of activity and mental stimulation. The breed is well-known for temporarily turning a deaf ear to any commands when it finds an interesting scent to follow.

German Hound

HEIGHT 16–21in (40–53cm)
WEIGHT 35–40lb (16–18kg)
LIFE SPAN 10–12 years

Numerous hunting dogs of the type known as brackes existed in Germany for centuries. Today the German Hound, or Deutsche Bracke, is one of the few to survive. This hound, bred by combining several bracke varieties, is still used mainly for hunting. Although good-natured, the German Hound does not adapt well to life indoors.

Drever

HEIGHT 12–15in (30–38cm)
WEIGHT 31–35lb (14–16kg)
LIFE SPAN 12–14 years

Variety of colors

In the early 20th century a small, short-legged hound from Germany, the Westphalian Dachsbracke, was imported to Sweden. The breed proved popular as a game tracker, and by the 1940s the Swedes had developed their own version, the Drever. Because of its strong hunting instinct, this breed is best kept as a sporting dog.

Laufhund

HEIGHT
19–23in
(47–59cm)

WEIGHT
33–44lb
(15–20kg)

LIFE SPAN
12 years

SCHWYZER

This noble-headed, lean hound with Roman roots has a laid-back attitude to life

Also known as the Swiss Hound, dogs of this type have existed in Switzerland for hundreds of years; a Roman mosaic found at Avenches shows pack hounds resembling the Laufhund. There are four varieties, each named after a Swiss canton and certified by its coat colors—the Bernese (white with black patches), Lucerne (blue), Schwyzer Laufhunds (white with red patches), and Bruno Jura (tan with black blanket; see p.140). (A further variety, the Thurgovia, had died out by the early 20th century.)

The Laufhund is a tireless, strong-nosed tracker that works easily in high Alpine terrain; it is especially well-known for tracking rabbit, fox, and roe deer. The double-layered coat, with its dense undercoat and hard top coat, gives protection in all weather.

These dogs are still used for hunting today. They also make elegant companions; the fine, sculpted head and good proportions lend the Laufhund an air of nobility. At home the breed is relaxed and docile, and is friendly to children. However, it does need a lot of exercise to burn off its energy; it would do well in a country home with an active owner.

THE SAME OR DIFFERENT?

Originally all called Swiss Beagles, these Swiss hunting dogs were split into four breeds based on regional differences in 1881. Although similar in form, the Jura, Schwyzer, Bernese (shown below in a French print from 1907), and Lucerne dogs differ in color, possibly reflecting the different breeds used in their development. The Lucerne, for example, shows a marked similarity to the Petit Bleu de Gascogne (see p.163). In the 1930s the dogs were united once again, under a single FCI breed standard, since Laufhunds with four color varieties. The dogs are, however, assessed and exhibited separately as if they were still distinct breeds.

Slim, elegant, domed head with tan markings

Pendant ears set below eye level

White with black patches

Elegant tail carried hanging down

Firm, straight back

Black marking on head

Blue

Light to dark tan markings on cheeks

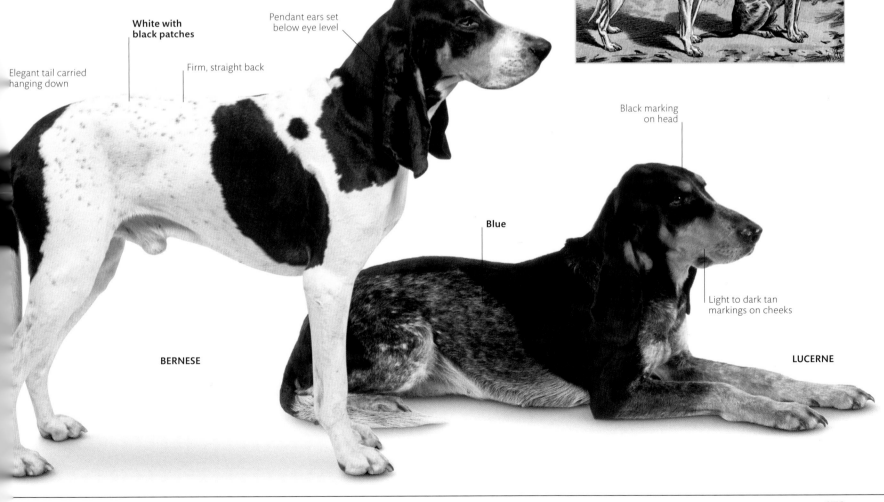

BERNESE

LUCERNE

Niederlaufhund

HEIGHT	WEIGHT	LIFE SPAN
13–17in (33–43cm)	18–33lb (8–15kg)	12–13 years

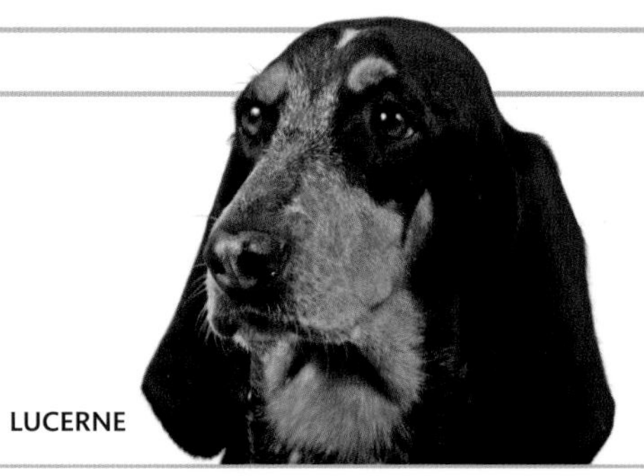
LUCERNE

THE ROUGH-COATED BERNESE

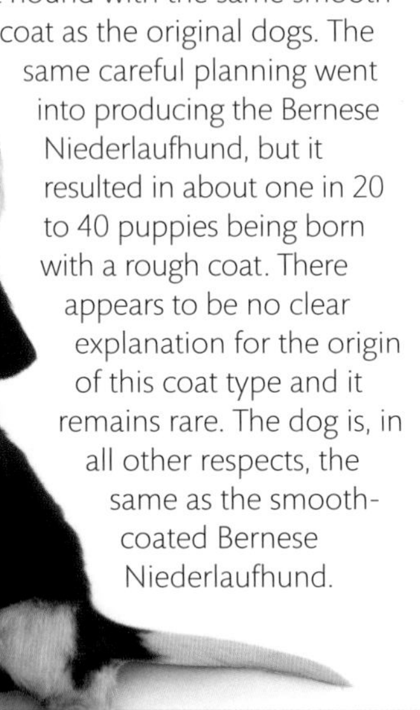

In downsizing Laufhunds to Niederlaufhunds, breeders of the Schwyzer, Lucerne, and Jura varieties produced an identical but smaller scent hound with the same smooth coat as the original dogs. The same careful planning went into producing the Bernese Niederlaufhund, but it resulted in about one in 20 to 40 puppies being born with a rough coat. There appears to be no clear explanation for the origin of this coat type and it remains rare. The dog is, in all other respects, the same as the smooth-coated Bernese Niederlaufhund.

This highly vocal Swiss hound is an excellent hunting dog and a good family pet, when given sufficient exercise

This smaller, shorter-legged version of the Laufhund (see p.173) was developed in the early 20th century. It was bred for use in shooting, specifically to make the most of the Swiss cantons' high-mountain game reserves—the larger Laufhund was thought to move too fast in these enclosed areas. Being slower, the Niederlaufhund can track big game more effectively than its larger cousin. This short-barreled, stocky version has a great nose for game such as wild boar, badger, and bear.

The Niederlaufhund occurs in four varieties, each developed from one of the Laufhund varieties: Bernese, Schwyzer, Jura, and Lucerne. Each has a distinctive coat color, similar to those of their larger counterparts. The Bernese Niederlaufhund comes in a smooth-haired version and a rarer rough-coated version with a small beard. The Schwyzer, Jura, and Lucerne are all smooth-haired.

The Niederlaufhund is still primarily used as a working dog but also makes an excellent family pet, since it has a friendly nature and is good with children. The breed needs firm but positive obedience training, as well as the opportunity to express its strong drive for finding and tracking scents. It is best suited to a rural home where it can be offered plenty of exercise and mental stimulation.

Tan markings over eyes
Long, pendant ears
Long tail carried down when active
White with black patches
Friendly, alert facial expression
White blaze extends on to sides of muzzle
White with orange patches

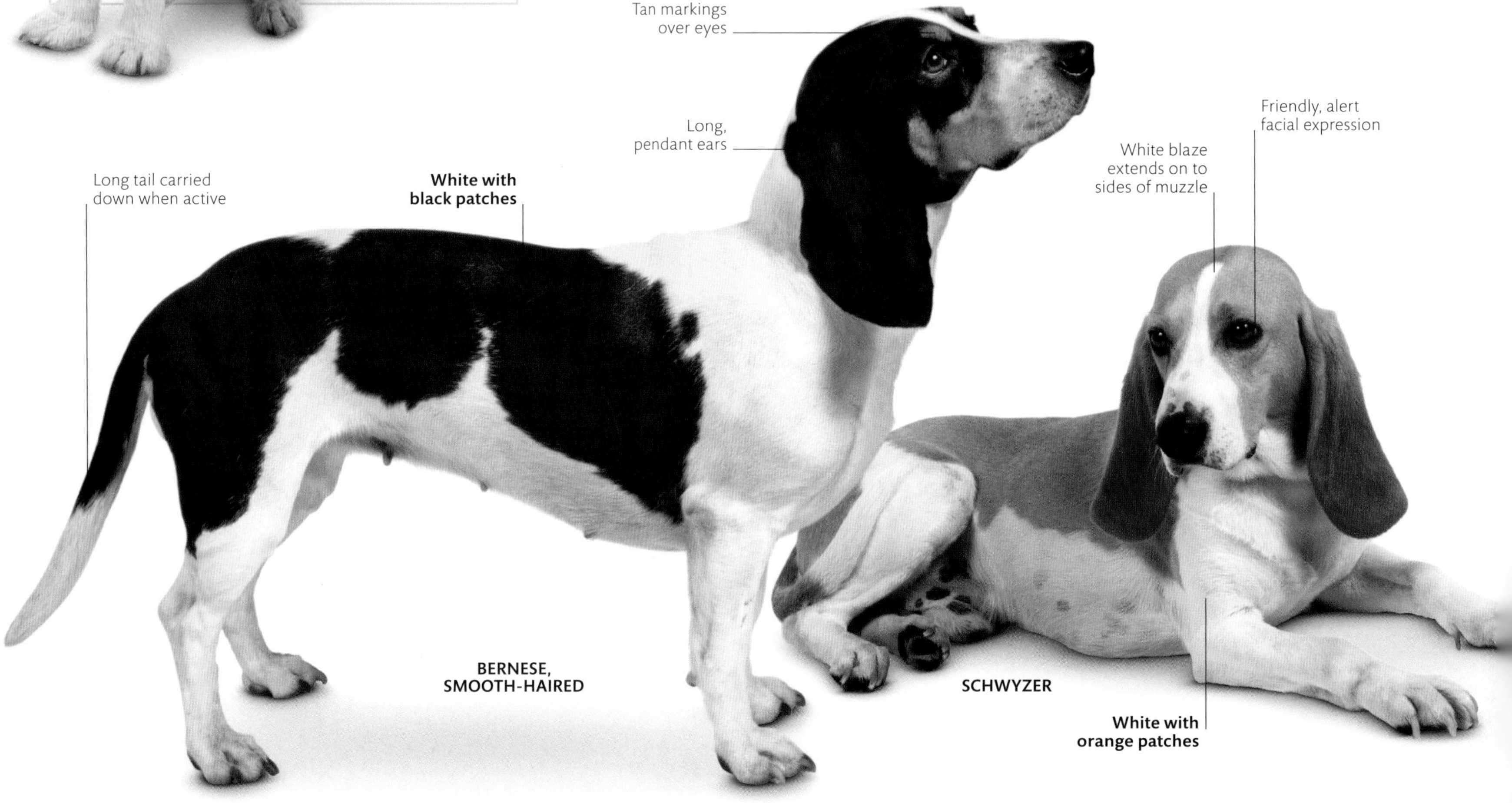

BERNESE, SMOOTH-HAIRED

SCHWYZER

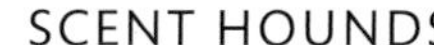

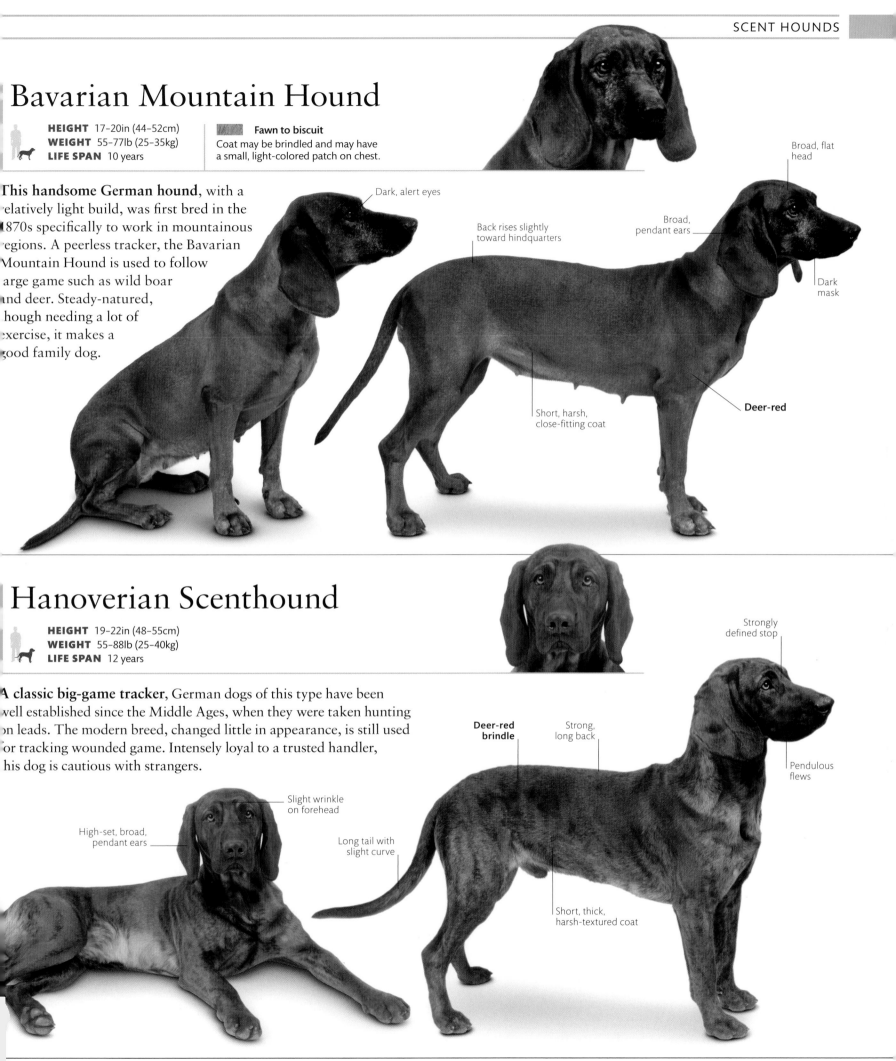

Bavarian Mountain Hound

HEIGHT 17–20in (44–52cm)
WEIGHT 55–77lb (25–35kg)
LIFE SPAN 10 years

Fawn to biscuit
Coat may be brindled and may have a small, light-colored patch on chest.

This handsome German hound, with a relatively light build, was first bred in the 1870s specifically to work in mountainous regions. A peerless tracker, the Bavarian Mountain Hound is used to follow large game such as wild boar and deer. Steady-natured, though needing a lot of exercise, it makes a good family dog.

Hanoverian Scenthound

HEIGHT 19–22in (48–55cm)
WEIGHT 55–88lb (25–40kg)
LIFE SPAN 12 years

A classic big-game tracker, German dogs of this type have been well established since the Middle Ages, when they were taken hunting on leads. The modern breed, changed little in appearance, is still used for tracking wounded game. Intensely loyal to a trusted handler, this dog is cautious with strangers.

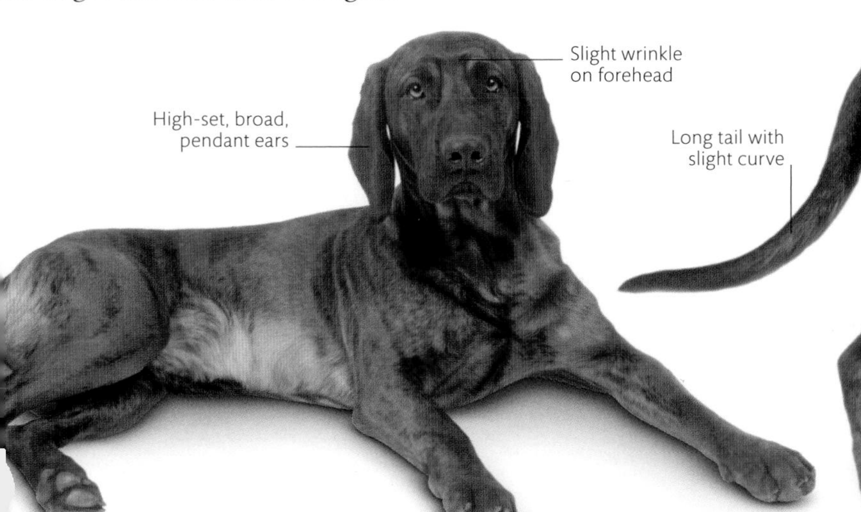

Doberman Pinscher

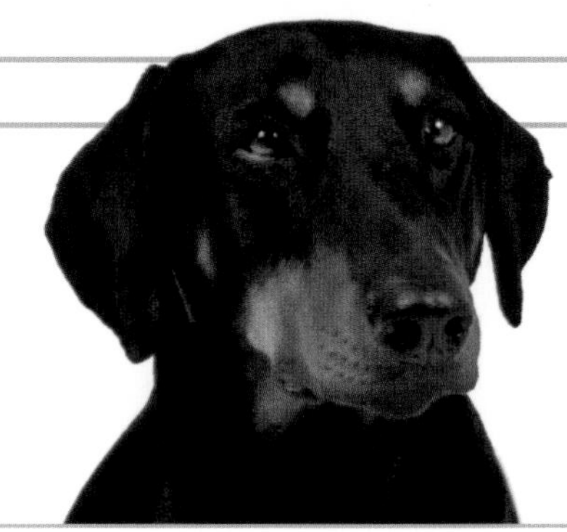

HEIGHT	WEIGHT	LIFE SPAN	
26–27in (65–69cm)	66–88lb (30–40kg)	13 years	 Isabella, Blue, Brown

This strong and graceful dog makes a loyal and obedient pet for an experienced and active owner

This powerful, protective breed was created in the late 19th century by a German tax official named Louis Dobermann who needed a dog to protect him. He developed the breed from the German Shepherd Dog (see p.42) and the German Pinscher (see p.218), which is why the dog is still known as the Doberman Pinscher. Other crosses are thought to include the Greyhound (see p.126), the Rottweiler (see p.83), the Manchester Terrier (see p.212), and the Weimaraner (see p.248). From these breeds, the Doberman Pinscher inherited a collection of admirable traits, including guarding and tracking abilities, intelligence, endurance, speed, and good looks.

The breed was first presented at a dog show in 1876 and was immediately popular. By the 20th century it was in demand throughout the US and Europe as a police dog and guard dog and for use by the military.

Still widely used for police and security work, this breed is also popular as a house dog. In the past Doberman Pinschers have had an unjustified reputation for being aggressive. They do need firm, authoritative handling, but in return they are loving, loyal, and willing to learn. Studies have shown that the Doberman Pinscher is one of the easiest breeds to train. They enjoy being part of family life—the more active the better. In the US and some other countries, the ears may still be cropped to stand upright and the tail may be docked, but these practices are illegal in much of Europe.

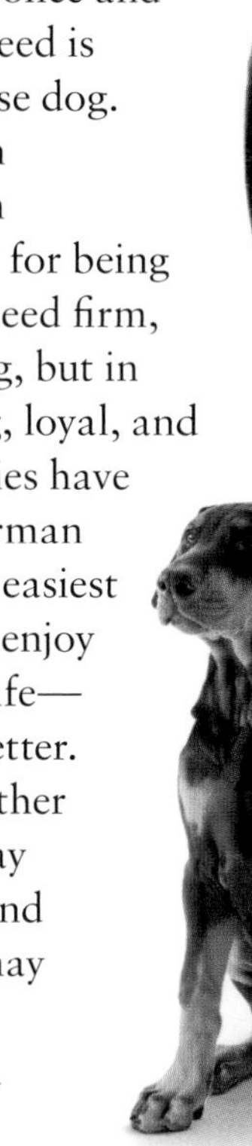

PUPPY

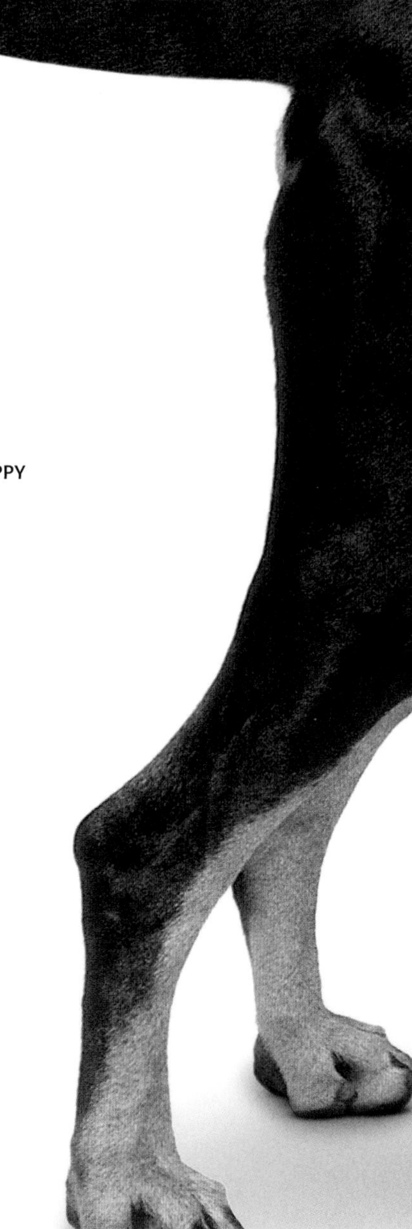

DOBERMANNS IN THE MARINE CORPS

The US Marine Corps first used dogs in World War II, as sentries, scouts, messengers, and to detect enemy troops. Most of the war dogs, nicknamed "devil dogs," were Dobermanns. Seven dog platoons served in the Pacific and their brave actions saved many human lives. In 1994 a statue of a Dobermann was unveiled at the War Dog Cemetery on Guam (right) to commemorate the 25 dogs that died liberating the island 50 years previously. The statue's name, "Always Faithful," is a translation of the Marines' motto, *Semper Fidelis*.

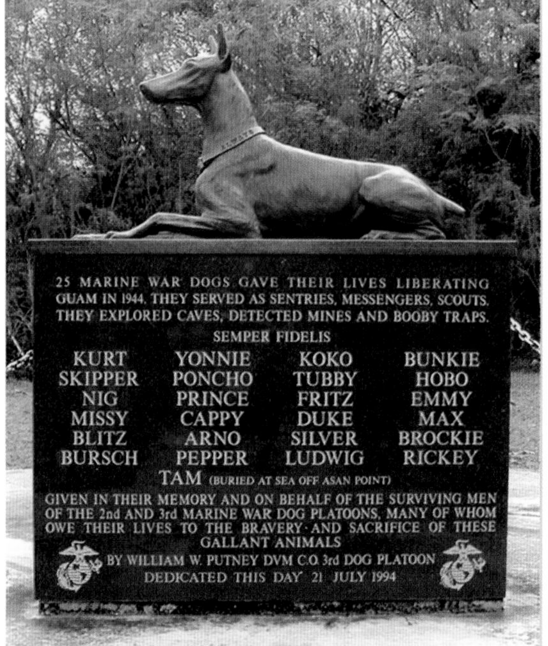

"ALWAYS FAITHFUL" STATUE AT THE MARINE CORPS WAR DOG CEMETERY, GUAM

Long, flat-
topped head
Triangular,
drop ears
Black and tan
ack slopes gently down
oward croup
Typical tan
markings
Smooth,
short coat
Deep chest
Almond-shaped eyes
with tan spot above
Compact,
catlike feet

Black Forest Hound

HEIGHT 16–20in (40–50cm)
WEIGHT 33–44lb (15–20kg)
LIFE SPAN 11–12 years

The Black Forest Hound, or Slovenský Kopov, originated in the foothills and snowy mountain forests of central Eastern Europe. It is used to hunt boar, deer, and other game in small packs or alone. Local hunters like the breed because it can follow a scent for hours through dense thickets, protected by its coarse coat.

Polish Hound

HEIGHT 22–26in (55–65cm)
WEIGHT 44–71lb (20–32kg)
LIFE SPAN 11–12 years

Evolving from a heavier bracke and lighter scent hound, this rare breed emerged as a large game hunter in Poland's thick, mountainous forests. The ancestors of this hound hunted in pack for Polish nobility during the Middle Ages. The Polish Hound displays excellent tracking abilities regardless of how fast it is running.

Transylvanian Hound

HEIGHT 22–26in (55–65cm)
WEIGHT 55–77lb (25–35kg)
LIFE SPAN 10–13 years

Also known as the Hungarian Hound, or Erdelyi Kopó, this hardy hunting dog was once the preserve of Hungarian kings and princes. Then, as now, its keen sense of direction, and hardiness in heavy, snowbound Carpathian forests and climate extremes made it the large game hunter of choice. However, it remains an extremely rare breed.

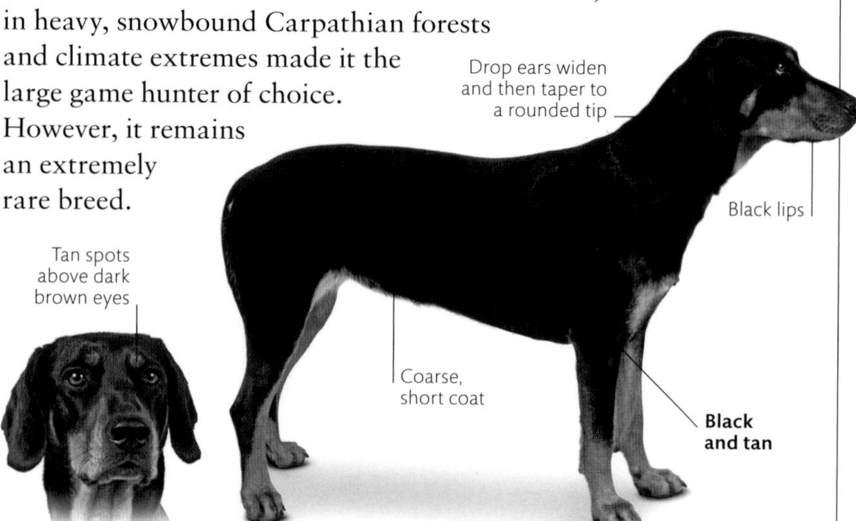

Posavaz Hound

HEIGHT 18–23in (46–58cm)
WEIGHT 35–53lb (16–24kg)
LIFE SPAN 10–12 years

The Croatian name for the Posavaz Hound, Posavski Gonic, can be translated as scent hound from the Sava valley, and its robu build makes it ideally suited to the dense underbrush of the Sava river basin. Passionate in the hunt, this hound is very docile in the home.

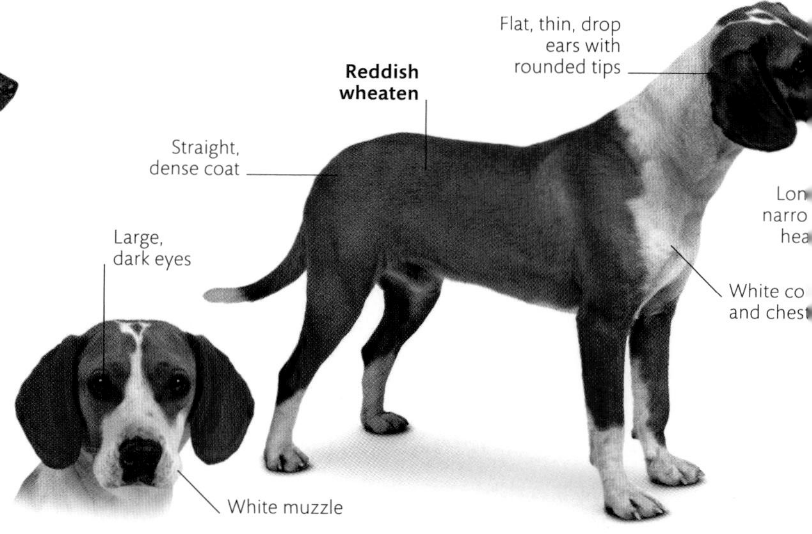

Bosnian Rough-coated Hound

HEIGHT 18–22in (45–56cm)
WEIGHT 35–55lb (16–25kg)
LIFE SPAN 12 years

Tricolor

ormerly known as the Illyrian Hound, ıis breed has been a hunter's ompanion since the 19th entury. A hardy, solidly uilt dog, it has a thick, oarse-haired coat that nables it to work in itterly cold weather nd through thick ndergrowth.

Montenegrin Mountain Hound

HEIGHT 17–21in (44–54cm)
WEIGHT 44–55lb (20–25kg)
LIFE SPAN 12 years

\lso known as the Serbian Mountain Hound, this rare dog from the Planina egion of Serbia has a calm, gentle nature hat is appreciated by nonhunting wners. Nevertheless, it remains a uperb hound for hunting fox and abbit, or even larger animals such s deer and wild boar.

Serbian Tricolored Hound

HEIGHT 17–22in (44–55cm)
WEIGHT 44–55lb (20–25kg)
LIFE SPAN 12 years

Once regarded as a variety of the Montenegrin Mountain Hound (see p.179), this rare breed has striking white markings that distinguish it from its relative. Used to hunt fox and rabbit, or occasionally larger game, it also makes a gentle and devoted family dog.

Pendant ears

Black mantle

Short, abundant, gleaming coat

White legs

White tip to tail

Tricolor

White hair on chest reaches to end of breastbone

Serbian Hound

HEIGHT 17–22in (44–56cm)
WEIGHT 44–55lb (20–25kg)
LIFE SPAN 12–14 years

This pack-hunting dog with a booming voice tracks game of all sizes from rabbit to elk and boar. Away from the hunt, it is sweet-natured and makes a good companion for an active family, especially if there are other dogs around. The Serbian Hound is also a fine watchdog.

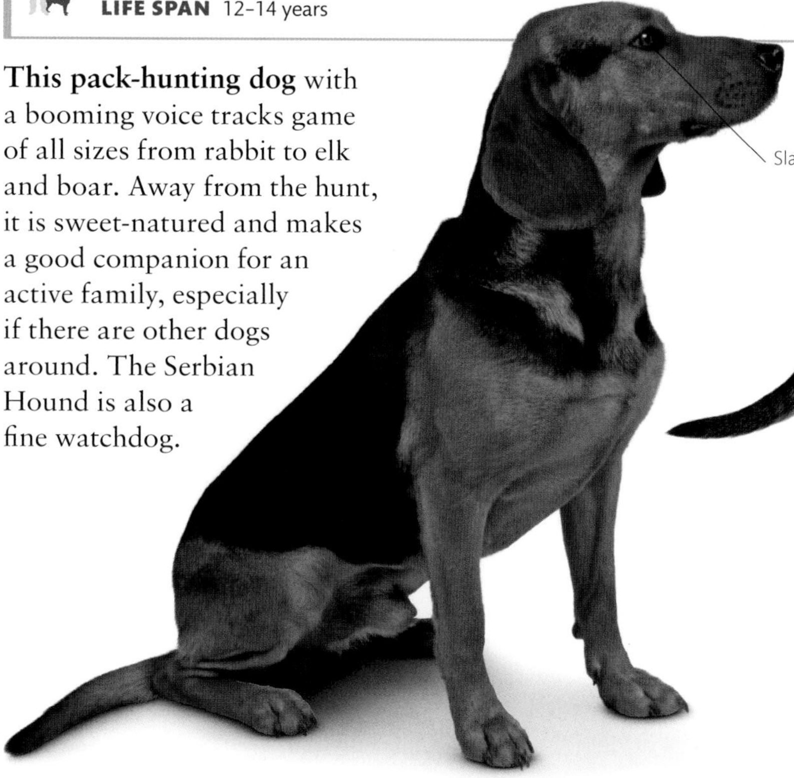

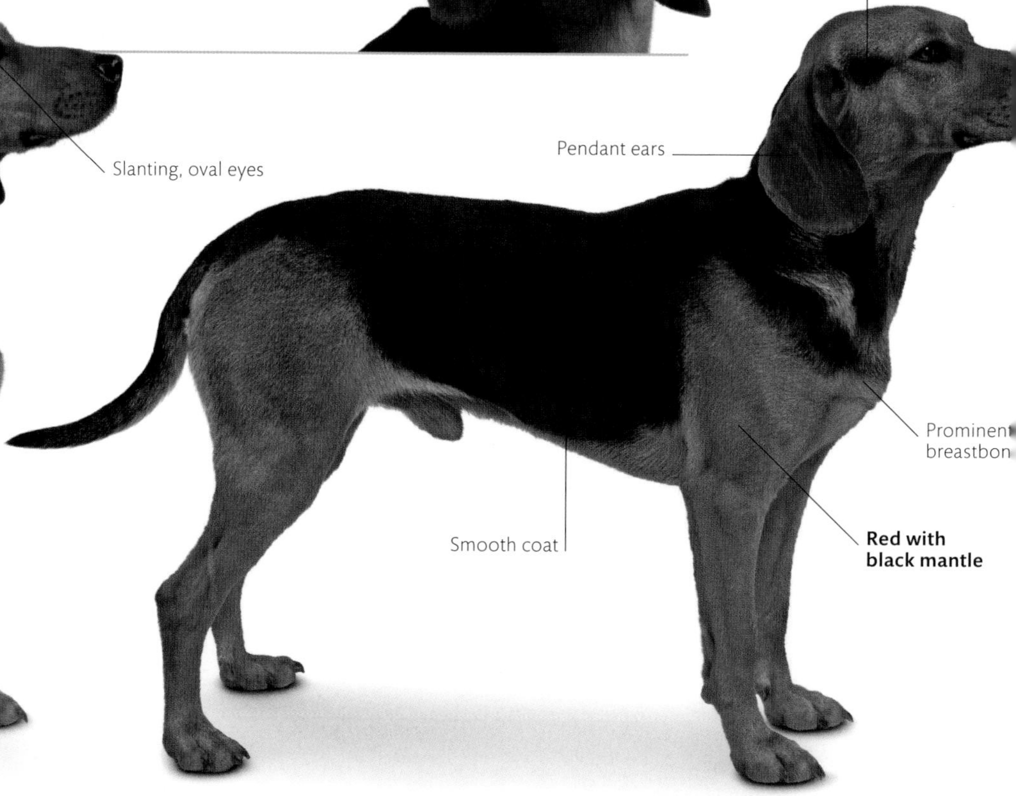

Black markings on either side of temples

Slanting, oval eyes

Pendant ears

Prominent breastbone

Smooth coat

Red with black mantle

Hellenic Hound

HEIGHT 18–22in (45–55cm)
WEIGHT 37–44lb (17–20kg)
LIFE SPAN 11 years

escended from the traditional ent hounds of ancient Greece, e Hellenic Hound has a musical unting voice that carries over ng distances. Once used to unt boar and rabbit, if trained ith care, the breed can be pleasant companion, but ithout plenty of space run in can develop ad behavior.

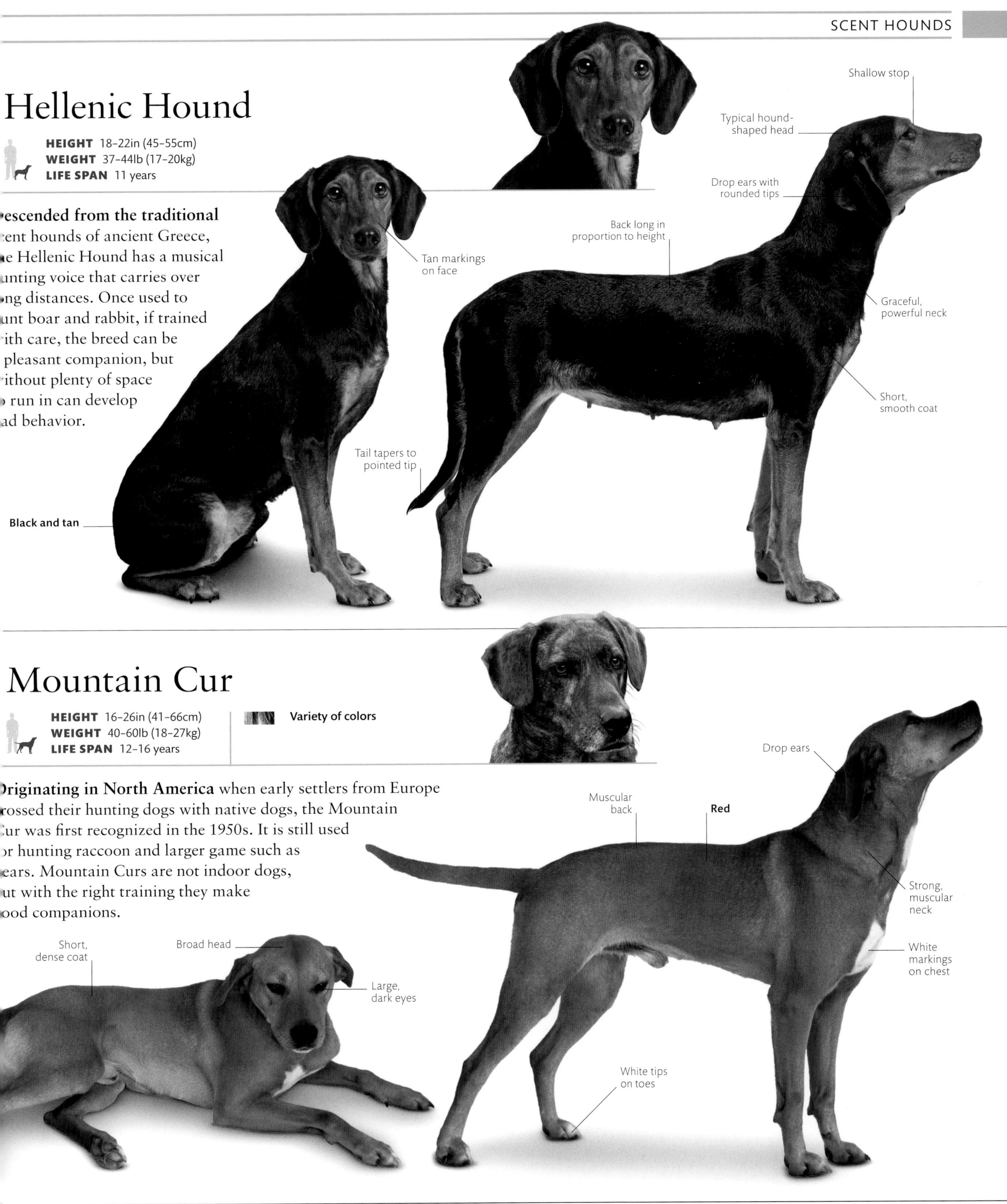

Mountain Cur

HEIGHT 16–26in (41–66cm)
WEIGHT 40–60lb (18–27kg)
LIFE SPAN 12–16 years

riginating in North America when early settlers from Europe rossed their hunting dogs with native dogs, the Mountain ur was first recognized in the 1950s. It is still used r hunting raccoon and larger game such as ears. Mountain Curs are not indoor dogs, ut with the right training they make ood companions.

Rhodesian Ridgeback

HEIGHT	WEIGHT	LIFE SPAN
24–27in (61–69cm)	65–90lb (29–41kg)	10–12 years

oisterous and highly strung, this dog needs an experienced wner and plenty of mental and physical activity

his African hound is instantly recognizable ' the distinctive ridge of hair along its back, owing in the opposite direction from the st of the coat. Native to Zimbabwe ormerly Rhodesia), the breed is descended om dogs that European settlers brought to uthern Africa in the 16th and 17th nturies. These imported dogs were crossed ith the semi-wild, ridge-backed hunting ogs used by the indigenous people. The sulting dogs were introduced to Rhodesia 1870, and the first breed standard for the hodesian Ridgeback was drawn up in 1922.

The breed was used in packs to hunt lion, ith hunters on horseback; for this reason it is sometimes known as the African Lion Dog. It was also used for other quarry, such as baboons. The dogs had the stamina to work all day and could endure the hot days and cold nights in the African bush. They were also used as guard dogs to protect families and property.

The Rhodesian Ridgeback is still used today for hunting and as a guard dog, but it is also increasingly popular as a family companion. Despite the breed's fierce image, it is kind-natured and affectionate, although perhaps too boisterous for small children. It is highly protective toward its human family but reserved around strangers, and needs to be socialized thoroughly from an early age. This intelligent, strong-minded dog does best with an experienced owner who will be a kind but firm pack leader. It needs to be kept occupied, since it may develop behavioral problems if bored or underexercised.

THE "LION DOG"

The Rhodesian Ridgeback inherits its hunting drive from European dogs, including Great Danes (see p.96), Mastiffs (see p.93), and Pointers (see pp.254–58), and the tough, fearless dogs of the Khoikhoi people. Small packs were used to hunt lion; the dogs had the speed and agility to keep up with the quarry, and the courage to hold a lion at bay (below) until the hunter shot it. The breed has also been used in South America to hunt jaguar and in North America to hunt mountain lion, lynx, and bear.

PUPPY

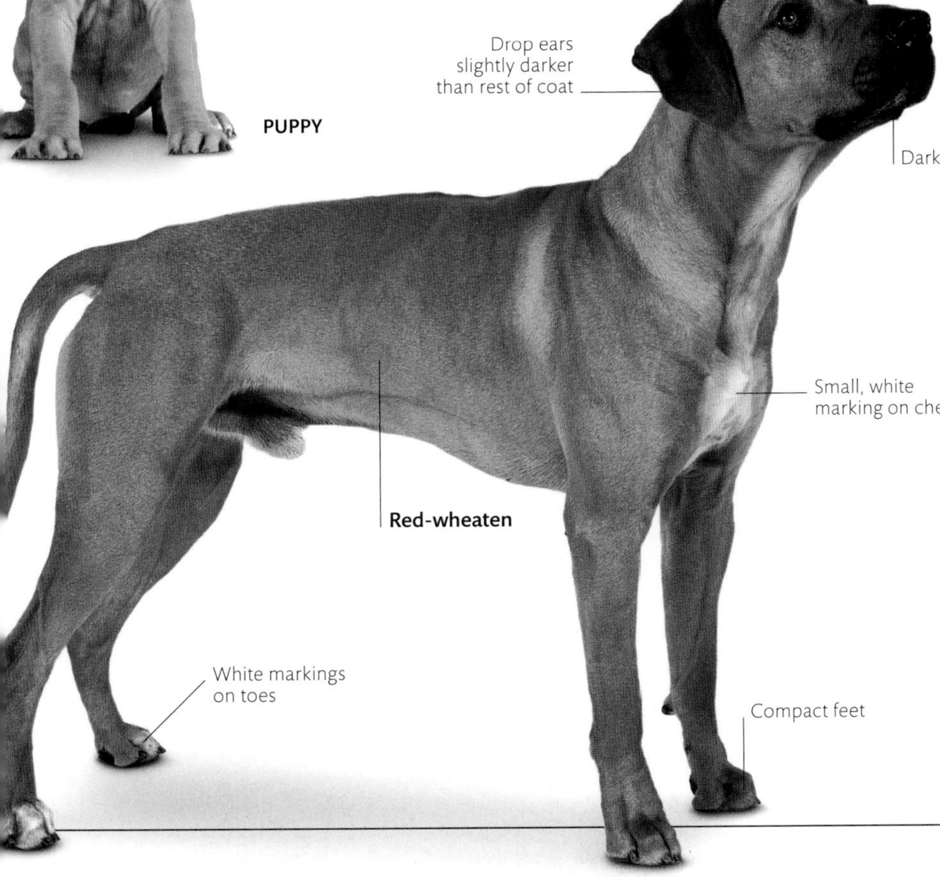

Drop ears slightly darker than rest of coat

Dark muzzle

Small, white marking on chest

Red-wheaten

White markings on toes

Compact feet

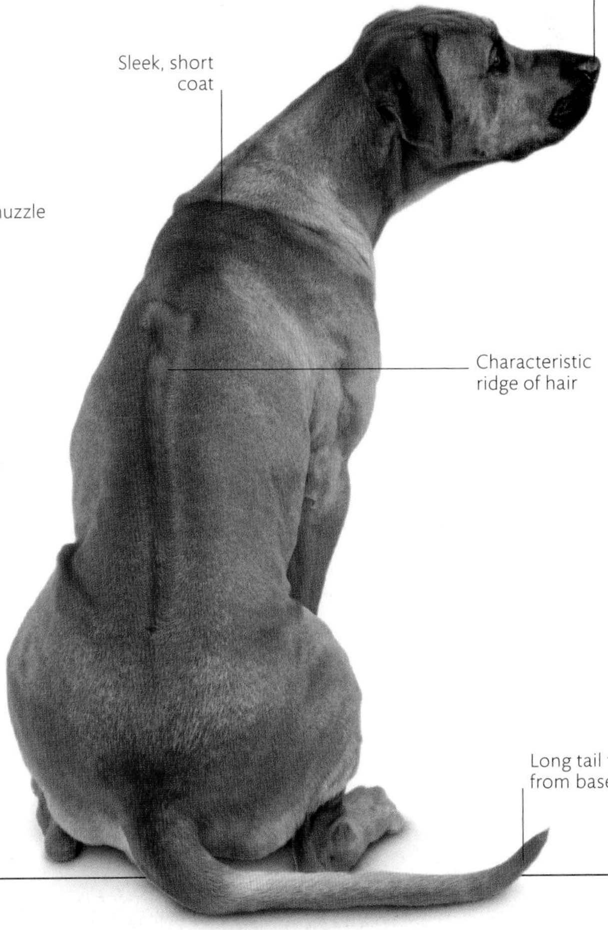

Black nose

Sleek, short coat

Characteristic ridge of hair

Long tail tapers from base

Digging instinct
Intent on his task, this Jack Russell Terrier is doing what comes naturally—excavating a hole. Most terriers are inveterate diggers and tunnelers.

TERRIERS

Tough, fearless, self-confident, energetic—a terrier can claim all of these descriptions, and more. The terrier group takes its name from the Latin word *terra* (soil), referring to the original use of various types of small dog as hunters of underground-dwelling vermin, such as rats. However, some modern terriers are large dogs, bred for different purposes.

Many breeds of terrier originated in the UK, where they were traditionally regarded as hunting dogs for the working man. Some are named after the regions where they were first bred: for example, Norfolk Terrier (see p.192), Yorkshire Terrier (see p.190), and Lakeland Terrier (see p.206). Others are known by the types of animal they were used to hunt: for example, Fox Terrier (see p.208) and Rat Terrier (see p.212).

Terriers are by nature quick to react and show great persistence when on the track of quarry. They possess independent—some would say willful—characters and are ready to stand their ground against larger dogs. The dogs developed for hunting below ground, including the much-loved Jack Russell (see p.196) and Cairn Terriers (see p.189), are small, sturdy, and short-legged. Terriers with longer legs, such as the Irish Terrier (see p.200) and the beautiful Soft-coated Wheaten Terrier (see p.205), were once used for hunting above ground and also as guard dogs for protecting flocks. The largest terriers of all include the Airedale Terrier (see p.198), originally bred for hunting badger and otter, and the impressively built Black Russian Terrier (see p.200), which was specifically developed for military use and guard duties.

In the 19th century a different type of terrier became popular. Crosses between terriers and bulldogs produced such dogs as the Bull Terrier (see p.197), the Staffordshire Bull Terrier (see p.214), and the American Pit Bull Terrier (see p.213), breeds intended for the vicious and now illegal sports of dogfighting and bullbaiting. With their broad heads and powerful jaws, these dogs suggest a close affinity with mastiffs and are, in fact, likely to be related to that group.

Most types of terrier are today kept as pets. Intelligent and usually friendly and affectionate, they make excellent companions and watchdogs. Because of their inherent traits, terriers need to be trained and socialized early to prevent trouble with other dogs and pets. Hunting-type terriers also love to dig and can wreak havoc in a yard if unsupervised. The modern breeds of those dogs historically used for fighting are now largely free from aggression and, when properly trained by an experienced owner, are usually trustworthy with families.

Cesky Terrier

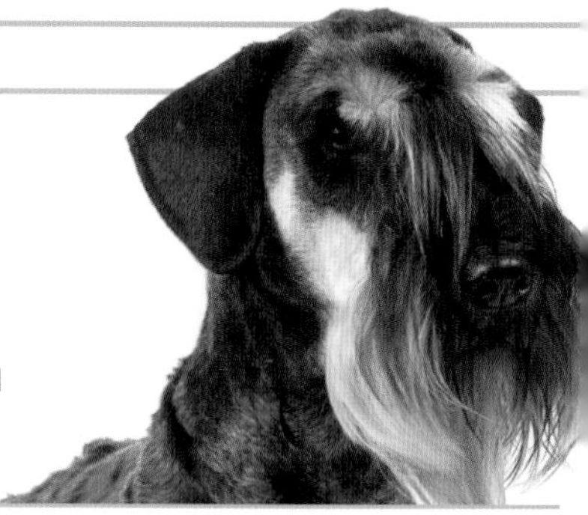

HEIGHT	WEIGHT	LIFE SPAN		
10–13in (25–32cm)	13–22lb (6–10kg)	12–14 years	Liver	Can have yellow, gray, or white markings on the beard and cheeks, neck, chest, belly, and limbs, sometimes with a white collar or a white tip to the tail.

Tough, fearless, and sometimes willful, with patient training this dog makes a cheerful, laid-back companion

Also known as the Czech Terrier or Bohemian Terrier, this breed was created in the 1940s in what is now the Czech Republic. Its founder, Frantisek Horak, already bred Scottish Terriers for hunting, but he wanted to create a smaller dog that could fit into animal burrows and would be easy to handle and keep. He contacted people who owned Sealyham Terriers, and in 1949 crossed these with Scottish Terriers. He made more of these crosses in the 1950s, keeping careful records, to create the Cesky Terrier. Horak's new breed was registered with the Czechoslovakian Kennel Club in 1959 and the FCI in 1963. In the 1980s he made further Sealyham crosses to broaden the breed's genetic base.

The Cesky Terrier is ideally built for hunting fox, rabbit, duck, pheasant, and even wild boar in its native country. It has plenty of stamina and a strong hunting drive, either working alone or in packs. The breed is still used as a working dog and is also a useful watchdog. Though it has spread to Europe and the US, the Cesky Terrier remains rare outside the Czech Republic. For a terrier, this dog has a relatively relaxed, playful character and it is sometimes kept simply as a companion. However, it retains some terrier stubbornness, so needs consistent training from an early age. The coat is softer than that of most terriers; it is typically clipped short on the body and left long on the face, legs, and belly. It needs to be brushed every few days and trimmed every three to four months.

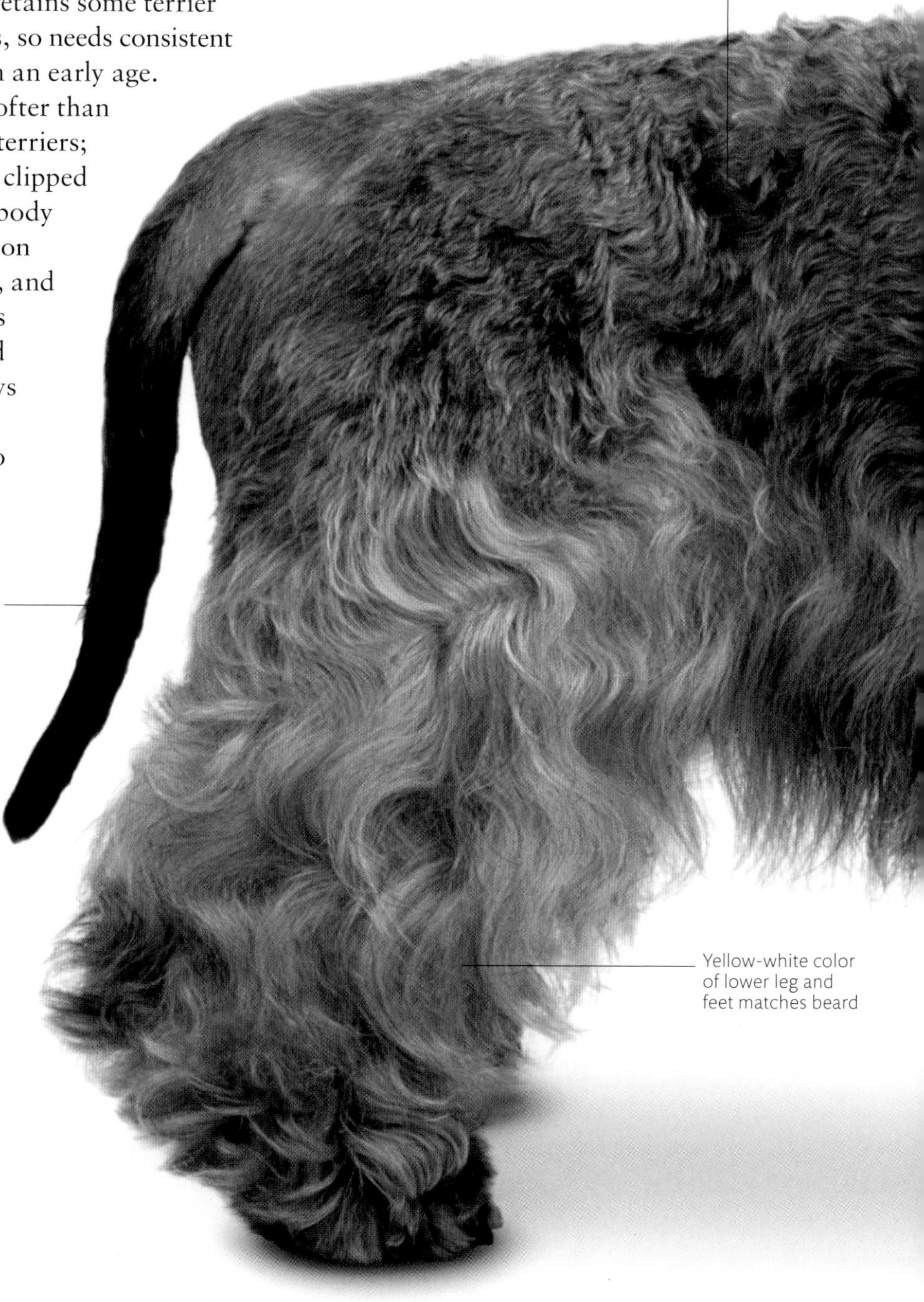

Slightly wavy coat has silky sheen

Tail carried low at rest

Yellow-white color of lower leg and feet matches beard

FOUNDER OF THE BREED

The Cesky Terrier owes its existence to one man: Frantisek Horak (1909–96), who started breeding dogs from the age of nine, and bred his first Scottish Terriers in the 1930s. Once he had begun to develop the Cesky Terrier, from 1949 Horak and his "Lovu Zdar" ("Successful Hunting") kennels became nationally famous, and after the Czech Republic's borders opened in 1989, people came from all over the world to meet him. He lived long enough to see his creation become a national symbol of the country.

A CESKY TERRIER, BOTTOM LEFT, ON A CZECHOSLOVAKIAN POSTAGE STAMP FROM c.1990

Hair left long on front of head
Gray-blue
Long hair forms beard
Triangular, drop ears
Forefeet larger than hind feet

West Highland White Terrier

HEIGHT	WEIGHT	LIFE SPAN
10–11in (25–28cm)	15–22lb (7–10kg)	9–15 years

WESTIE BRANDING

The West Highland White Terrier's white coat, chunky shape, and lively personality have become the distinctive brand for some world-famous products. The most obvious is Cesar™, a brand of dog food made specially for small dogs. Black & White Scotch Whisky highlights its traditional Scottish character with a black Scottish Terrier and a white West Highland Terrier on the labels. The fashion label Juicy Couture features two of the breed in the logo for their fragrances.

Somebody has to be first !
You have only to taste it to know why "Black & White" keeps growing in popularity. Blended in the special "Black & White" way it is a Scotch that is a joy to drink at all times and for all occasions.
BLACK&WHITE
SCOTCH WHISKY
The Secret is in the Blending

ADVERTISEMENT FOR BLACK & WHITE SCOTCH WHISKY

A perky and cheerful character, this terrier can be bossy with other dogs unless socialized as a puppy

One of the best loved of small terriers, the "Westie" was developed in Scotland in the 19th century from Cairn Terriers (opposite). The man most closely associated with developing the breed was Colonel Edward Malcolm, the 16th Laird of Poltalloch. One story has it that Colonel Malcolm decided to breed the white terriers after a reddish brown Cairn Terrier of his was mistaken for a fox and shot; white dogs would not be so easily mistaken for quarry.

The West Highland White Terrier was bred to hunt fox, otter, badger, and rodents such as rats. It had to be strong and agile, able to jump up on to rocks and squeeze into small crevices. It also needed the courage to face foxes at close quarters.

Today most West Highland White Terriers are kept as pets. Intelligent, curious, and friendly, they suit all types of homes. These dogs need plenty of company and activity, otherwise they can become bored and develop bad habits such as excessive barking and digging. Early social training is recommended, since West Highland White Terriers have large egos for their size and can be overbearing with other dogs. The coat needs to be groomed every few days.

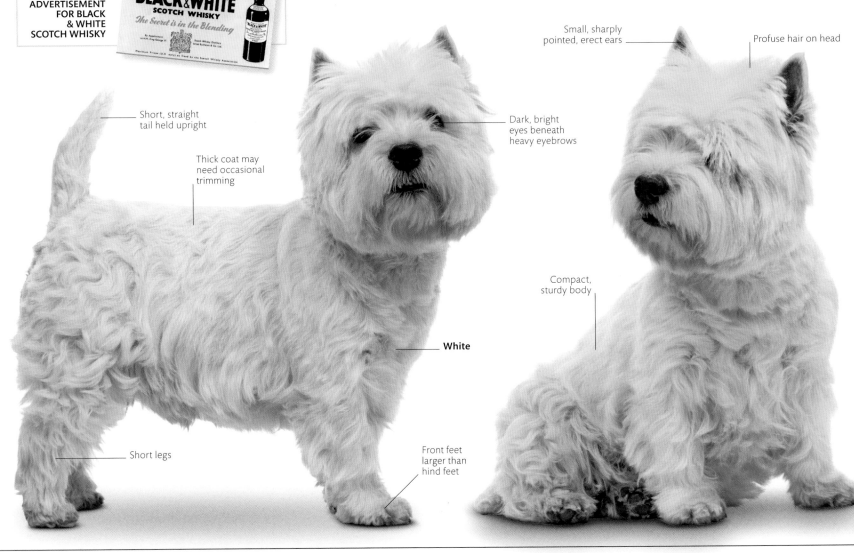

Short, straight tail held upright

Thick coat may need occasional trimming

Small, sharply pointed, erect ears

Profuse hair on head

Dark, bright eyes beneath heavy eyebrows

Compact, sturdy body

White

Short legs

Front feet larger than hind feet

Cairn Terrier

HEIGHT 11–12in (28–31cm)
WEIGHT 13–18lb (6–8kg)
LIFE SPAN 9–15 years

Red
Gray, nearly black
Coat may be brindled.

riginating in the Western Isles of Scotland, the Cairn Terrier as bred for hunting vermin. Amusing and full of character, this urdy terrier is small enough for apartment life and energetic 1ough for romping round a large country home; fits in anywhere. The Cairn Terrier's urge to 1ase everything that oves should be scouraged ırly on.

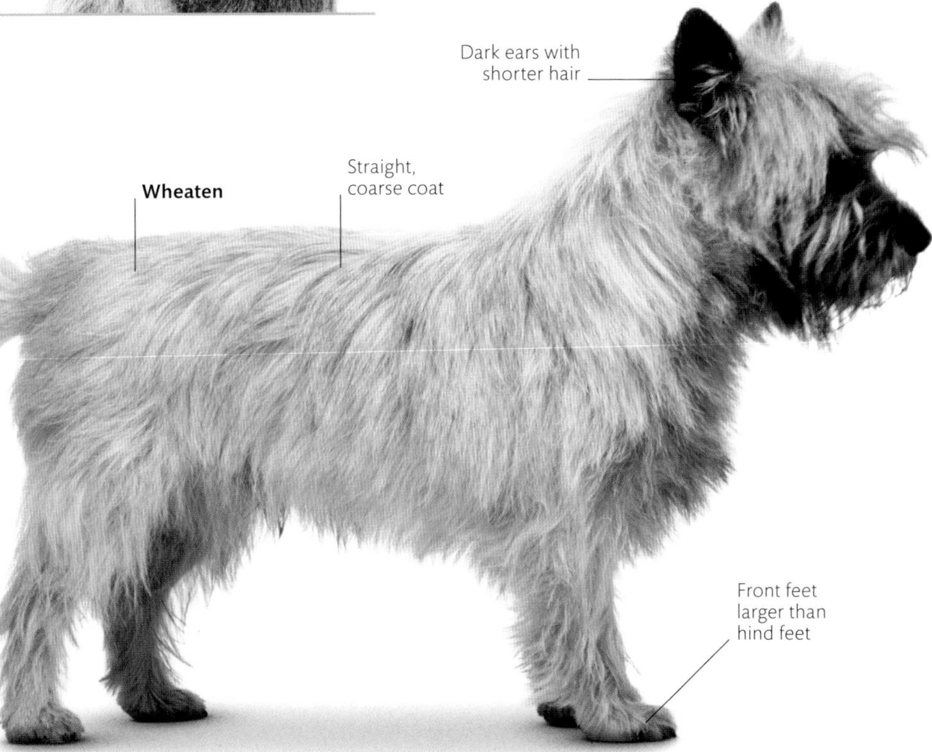

Scottish Terrier

HEIGHT 10–11in (25–28cm)
WEIGHT 20–24lb (9–11kg)
LIFE SPAN 9–15 years

Wheaten
Coat may be brindled.

'his breed was first named in the late 19th century, but dogs f this type existed in the Scottish Highlands much earlier. Powerful nd agile despite their short stature, "Scotties" were bred as vermin-unters like the West Highland White Terrier (opposite) and Cairn 'errier (above). Affectionate and watchful, the Scottish Terrier a good home companion.

Sealyham Terrier

HEIGHT 10–12in (25–30cm)
WEIGHT 18–20lb (8–9kg)
LIFE SPAN 14 years

Originally bred in Wales to tackle badgers and otters, this breed has no working role today but is kept as a pet. Their territorial nature makes Sealyham Terriers good watchdogs, but an innate stubbornness means that persistence in training is required. The show clip is distinctive, but requires regular maintenance.

Yorkshire Terrier

HEIGHT	WEIGHT	LIFE SPAN
8–9in (20–23cm)	Up to 7lb (3kg)	12–15 years

This dog's cute looks and diminutive size belie the feisty temperament typical of terriers

Oblivious to its tiny toy stature, the Yorkshire Terrier has the bravery, energy, and confidence that might be expected of a dog several times its size. An intelligent dog, it responds well to obedience training. However, it is inclined to take advantage of owners who let it get away with behavior that would be unacceptable in a larger dog, and it can become yappy and demanding. With proper handling, this terrier displays its natural character: sweet, affectionate, loyal, and spirited. The Yorkshire Terrier was developed to catch the rats and mice that infested the wool mills and mine shafts in the north of England. It was gradually miniaturized through breeding from the smallest individuals, and over time it became a fashion accessory that was carried around by its lady owner. Such pampering, however, is at odds with the Yorkshire Terrier's dynamic nature and it is much happier when allowed to walk for at least half an hour each day.

The long, glossy show coat is wrapped around paper and secured with rubberbands to protect it outside the show ring. It is very time-consuming to maintain, but the dogs generally love the extra attention.

MR. FAMOUS

One of the first show business celebrities of the canine world was a Yorkshire Terrier named Mr. Famous, who belonged to the movie star Audrey Hepburn. Mr. Famous was inevitably rather spoiled because he was Hepburn's constant companion. He went everywhere with the actress, even appearing alongside her in the 1957 film *Funny Face*. Hepburn launched many trends, from the little black dress to oversized sunglasses, and Mr. Famous may have been the forerunner of present-day "handbag dogs."

YOUNG DOG WITH CLIPPED COAT

Australian Terrier

HEIGHT Up to 10in (25cm)
WEIGHT Up to 15lb (7kg)
LIFE SPAN 15 years

 **Blue with tan**

This terrier is likely to have been the result of crosses between various terriers, including the Cairn Terrier (see p.189), the Yorkshire Terrier (see p.190), and the Dandie Dinmont Terrier (see p.217), which were brought to Australia by British settlers in the 19th century. Diminutive yet spirited, the "Aussie" is an excellent house dog.

Silky Terrier

HEIGHT Up to 9in (23cm)
WEIGHT Up to 9lb (4kg)
LIFE SPAN 12–15 years

This attractive dog was produced from crosses between the Australian Terrier (left) and the Yorkshire Terrier (see p.190) in the late 19th century. A typical terrier, the Silky Terrier has a fondness for digging holes, and its instinct to chase may put other small pets at risk. Regular grooming is needed to keep this dog's long coat tangle-free.

Norfolk Terrier

HEIGHT 9–10in (22–25cm)
WEIGHT 11–13lb (5–6kg)
LIFE SPAN 14–15 years

Red
Black and tan
Coat may be grizzled.

This small terrier was bred from various rat-catching dogs and is an energetic hunter. Because ratters work in packs, this breed is more sociable with other dogs than most terriers, but cannot be trusted with other pets. It makes a good guard dog or companion for families with older children.

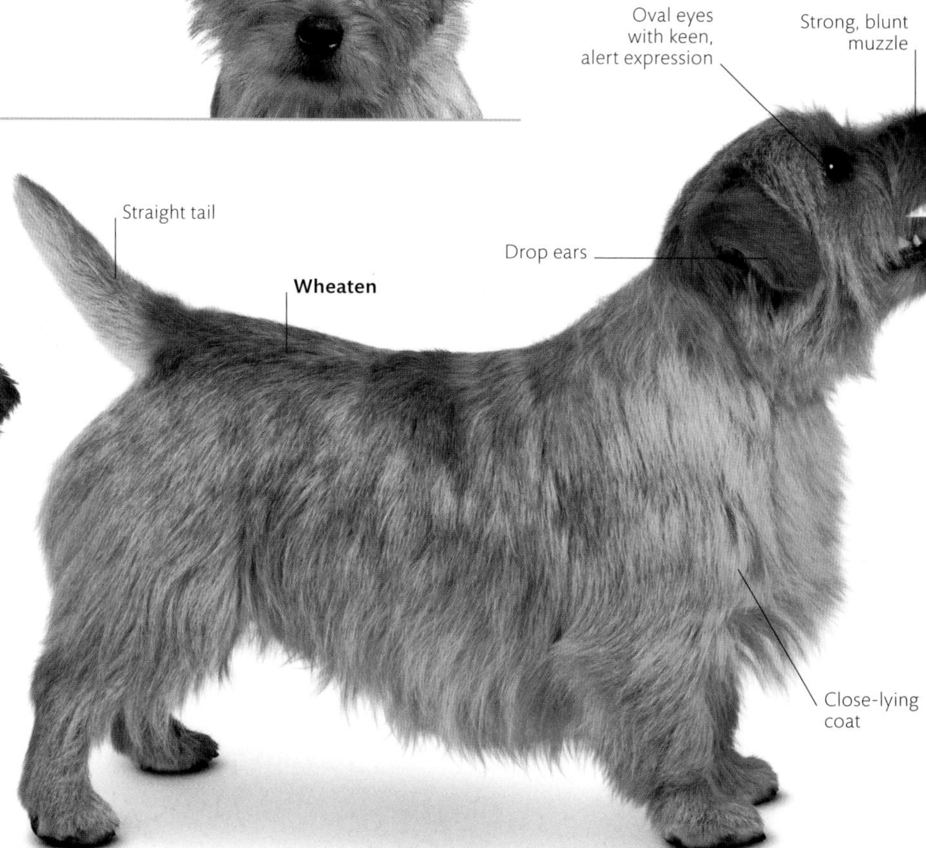

Glen of Imaal Terrier

HEIGHT 14in (36cm)
WEIGHT 35–37lb (16–17kg)
LIFE SPAN 13–14 years

Blue
Brindle

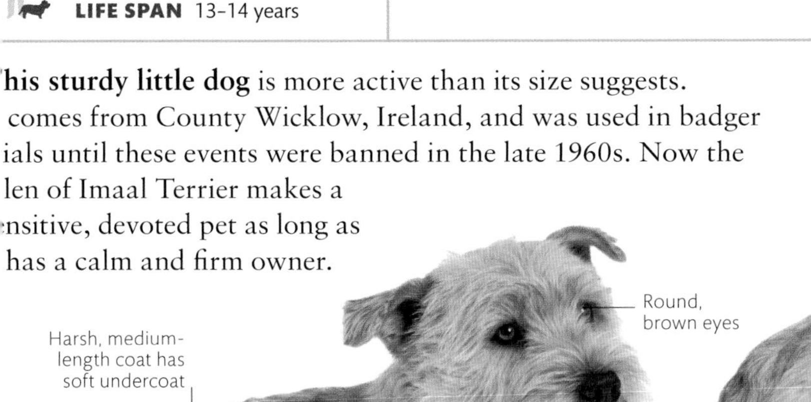

his sturdy little dog is more active than its size suggests. comes from County Wicklow, Ireland, and was used in badger ials until these events were banned in the late 1960s. Now the len of Imaal Terrier makes a nsitive, devoted pet as long as has a calm and firm owner.

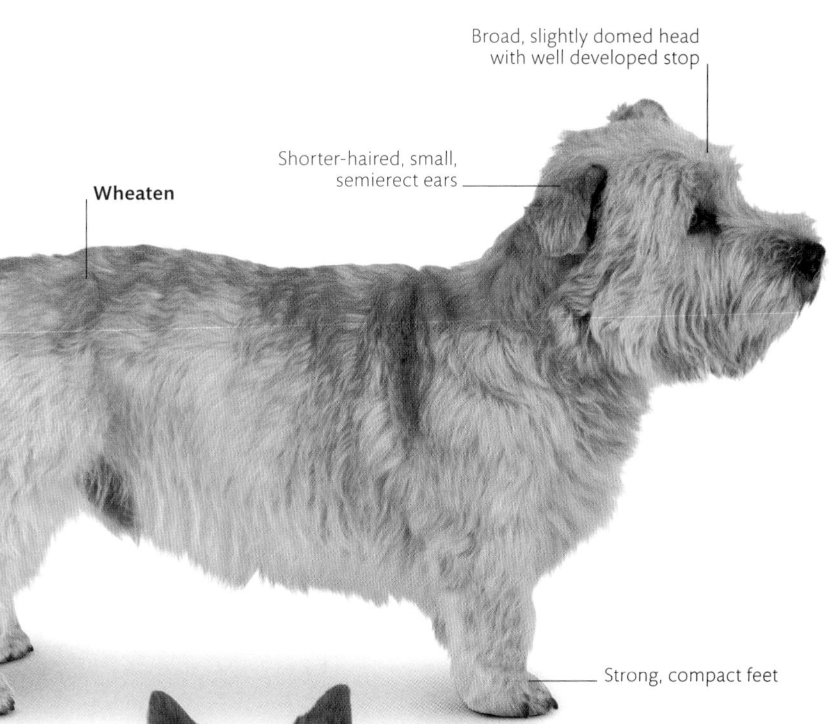

Norwich Terrier

HEIGHT 10in (25–26cm)
WEIGHT 11–13lb (5–6kg)
LIFE SPAN 12–15 years

Wheaten
Red
Red coats may be grizzled.

ne of the smallest working terriers, the Norwich Terrier, ke its cousin the Norfolk Terrier (opposite), strikes a happy alance between courage and gentleness. With its easy-going ature, it is good with children but will bark at strangers. ike all ratting terriers, it is playful and loves to chase.

Parson Russell Terrier

HEIGHT	WEIGHT	LIFE SPAN	White
13–14in (33–36cm)	13–18lb (6–8kg)	15 years	May have black markings.

This energetic dog, with a strong hunting instinct, needs firm handling and an active lifestyle

This foxhunting terrier was one of two strains previously classified together as the Jack Russell Terrier. Today the longer-legged type is known as the Parson Russell Terrier, while the shorter-legged dog retains the name of Jack Russell Terrier (see p.196).

The breed was created in England's West Country in the early 19th century by a cleric, the Reverend John Russell. Like many clergymen in the late 18th and early 19th centuries, he enjoyed hunting. In 1876 Reverend Russell, a founding member of the Fox Terrier Club, helped to write a breed standard for an ideal type of Fox Terrier (see p.208). However, the existing fox hunting terrier with the shape "of an adult vixen" persisted, too, and eventually gave rise to both the Parson Russell Terrier and the smaller Jack Russell Terrier.

After many years of work by Parson Russell enthusiasts, particularly in the 1980s, the UK Kennel Club finally recognized the Parson Jack Russell Terrier as a breed in 1984. The name Parson Russell Terrier was established in 1999.

The modern breed is a workmanlike dog with longish legs and a narrow chest (easily enclosed by average-sized adult hands). Intelligent and high-spirited, the breed needs plenty of company and daily exercise or it will become yappy and destructive. It is good with people and horses, but its hunting drive may make it a risk to small animals.

The weatherproof coat has a dense undercoat and a coarse outer layer, which may be either smooth or rough (broken). Both types are easy to groom.

SMOOTH-HAIRED PUPPY

EARLY HISTORY

While studying at Oxford in 1818, John Russell bought a small, predominantly white terrier bitch with tan markings from a milkman. He wanted a dog that was fast enough to keep up with the horses when hunting but small enough to go down burrows after foxes and flush them out. Named Trump, the terrier became the foundation bitch of the breed. By the 1890s the Jack Russell type was well established and seen in the paintings of the famous English dog artist John Emms (right), but it was not until the 1980s that the Parson Russell Terrier was officially recognized.

A JACK RUSSELL BY JOHN EMMS, 1891

High-set, white tail with tan base

Lower legs short relative to upper legs

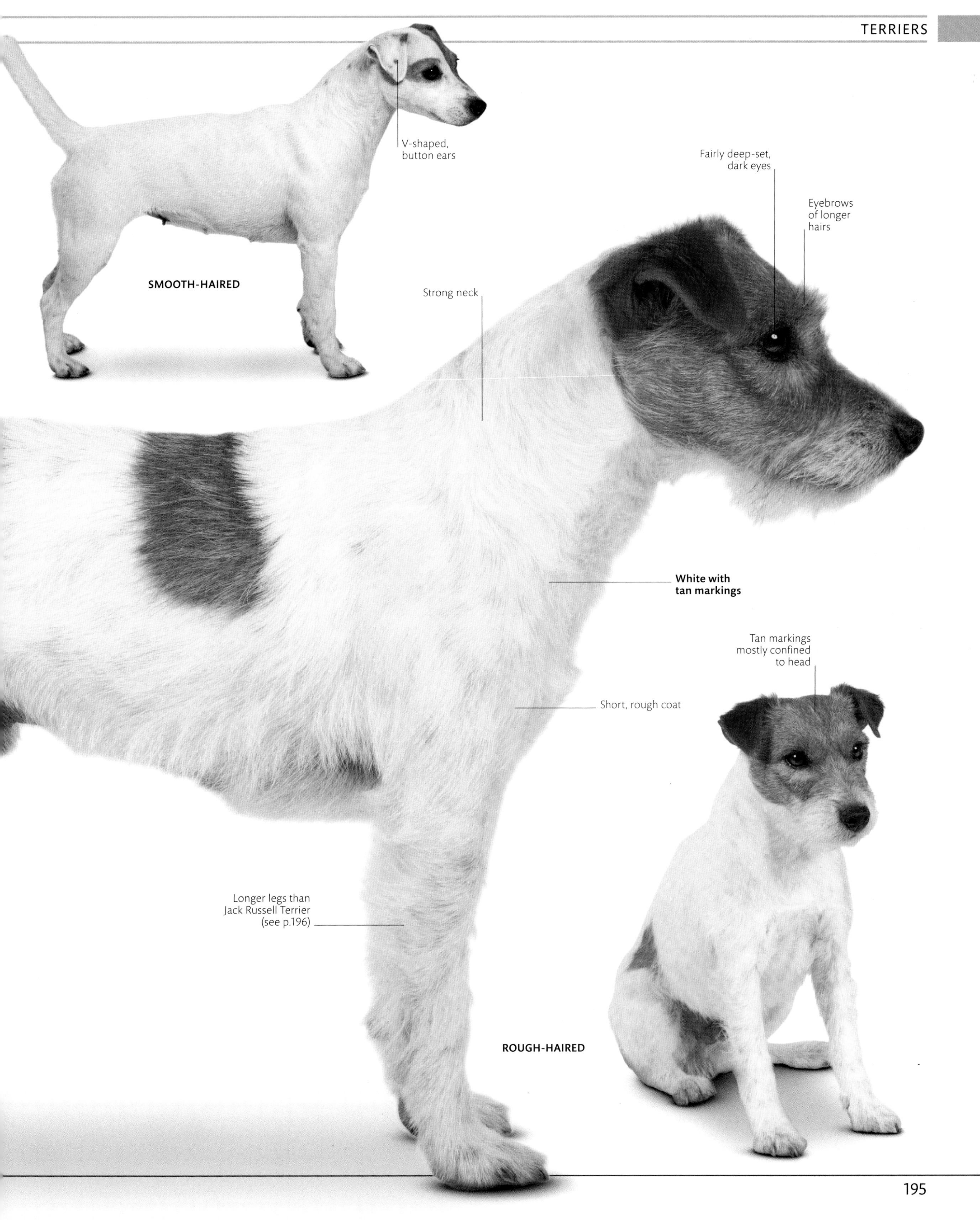
V-shaped,
button ears
SMOOTH-HAIRED
Fairly deep-set,
dark eyes
Eyebrows
of longer
hairs
Strong neck
White with
tan markings
Tan markings
mostly confined
to head
Short, rough coat
Longer legs than
Jack Russell Terrier
(see p.196)
ROUGH-HAIRED

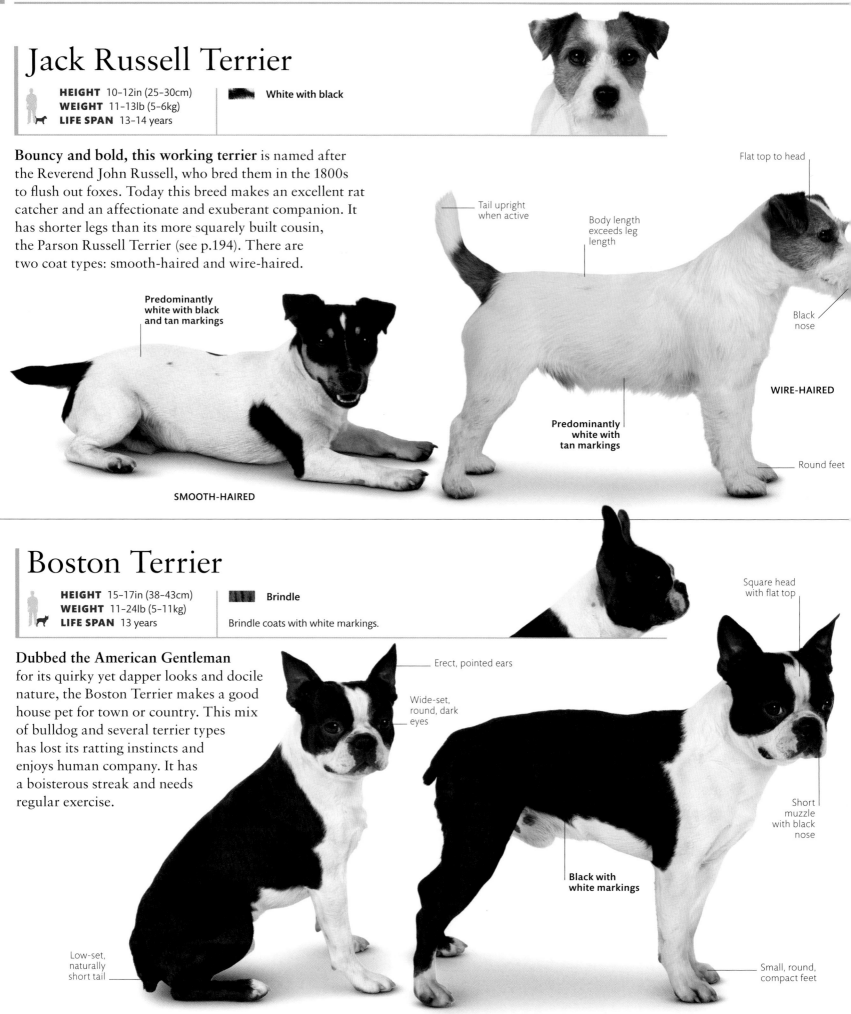

Jack Russell Terrier

HEIGHT 10–12in (25–30cm)
WEIGHT 11–13lb (5–6kg)
LIFE SPAN 13–14 years

White with black

Bouncy and bold, this working terrier is named after the Reverend John Russell, who bred them in the 1800s to flush out foxes. Today this breed makes an excellent rat catcher and an affectionate and exuberant companion. It has shorter legs than its more squarely built cousin, the Parson Russell Terrier (see p.194). There are two coat types: smooth-haired and wire-haired.

SMOOTH-HAIRED

Flat top to head

Tail upright when active

Body length exceeds leg length

Black nose

Predominantly white with tan markings

Round feet

WIRE-HAIRED

Boston Terrier

HEIGHT 15–17in (38–43cm)
WEIGHT 11–24lb (5–11kg)
LIFE SPAN 13 years

Brindle

Brindle coats with white markings.

Dubbed the American Gentleman for its quirky yet dapper looks and docile nature, the Boston Terrier makes a good house pet for town or country. This mix of bulldog and several terrier types has lost its ratting instincts and enjoys human company. It has a boisterous streak and needs regular exercise.

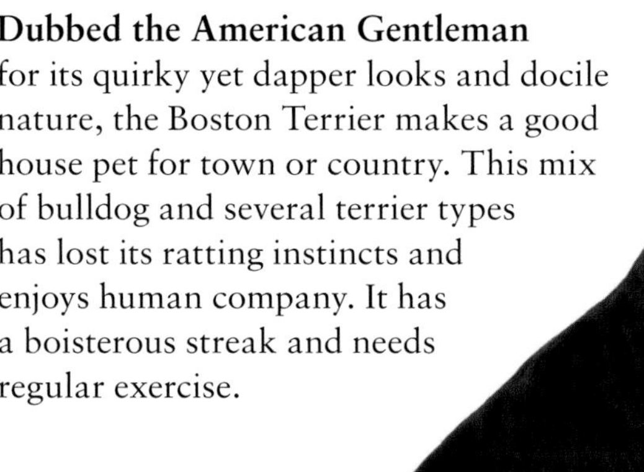

Bull Terrier

HEIGHT 21–22in (53–56cm)
WEIGHT 51–71lb (23–32kg)
LIFE SPAN 10–12 years

Variety of colors

argely the result of crossbreeding etween the Bulldog (see p.95) nd terriers of various types, the ull Terrier was developed for pit-ghting in 19th-century England. failure at vicious sports, this og achieved greater success s a pet. The modern breed normally good-natured nd does well with firm owner.

Miniature Bull Terrier

HEIGHT Up to 14in (36cm)
WEIGHT 24–33lb (11–15kg)
LIFE SPAN 10–12 years

Variety of colors

'his scaled-down version of ne Bull Terrier (above) had lmost disappeared by the 920s. The breed was revived ı the following decades, lthough it is still uncommon. ,ike its larger relative, the Ainiature Bull Terrier eeds early training and ocializing to ensure that is a good family pet.

Airedale Terrier

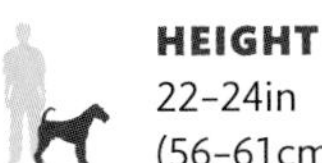

HEIGHT	WEIGHT	LIFE SPAN
22–24in (56–61cm)	40–65lb (18–29kg)	10–12 years

The largest of all terriers, this versatile dog makes a good family pet but may be mischievous and boisterous

The tallest of the terrier breeds, the Airedale Terrier is known as the King of Terriers. This square, strong British breed originated in the valley of the Aire River in Yorkshire. It was first developed in the mid-19th century by local hunters who wanted a robust terrier for catching vermin and larger game such as otters. Breeders therefore crossed black and tan terriers with the Otterhound (see p.142), as well as with the Irish Terrier (see p.200) and possibly the Bull Terrier (see p.197). The crosses produced a dog with a terrier's courage and an Otterhound's skill in the water. The breed was put to work along riverbanks, a practice that gave the dog its alternative name, Waterside Terrier. The Airedale Terrier was officially recognized as a breed in 1878.

The Airedale Terrier became an all-purpose dog that could follow trails and retrieve as well as pursue small game. Farmers used the dog to herd and drive livestock and to guard property. Airedale Terriers also featured in competitive rat hunts along the banks of the Aire River and its tributaries. From the 1880s dogs were exported to the US, where they were used to hunt quarry such as raccoons, coyotes, and bobcats.

The breed's subsequent uses have included guarding, police and military work, and search and rescue, but it is also a popular companion. Friendly, intelligent, and full of terrier character, this dog loves the thrill of the chase and needs plenty of daily exercise. It has a strong personality, so needs kind and assertive handling, but responds well to training.

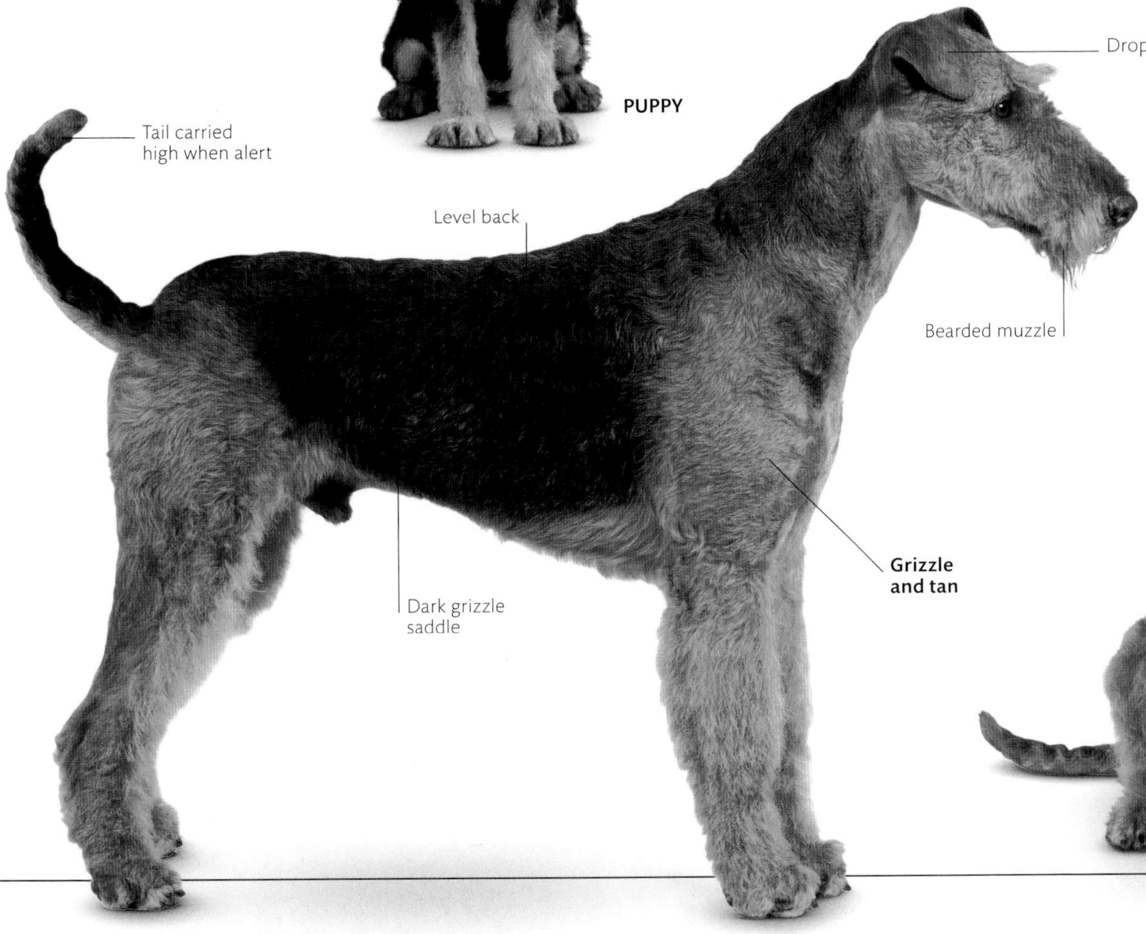

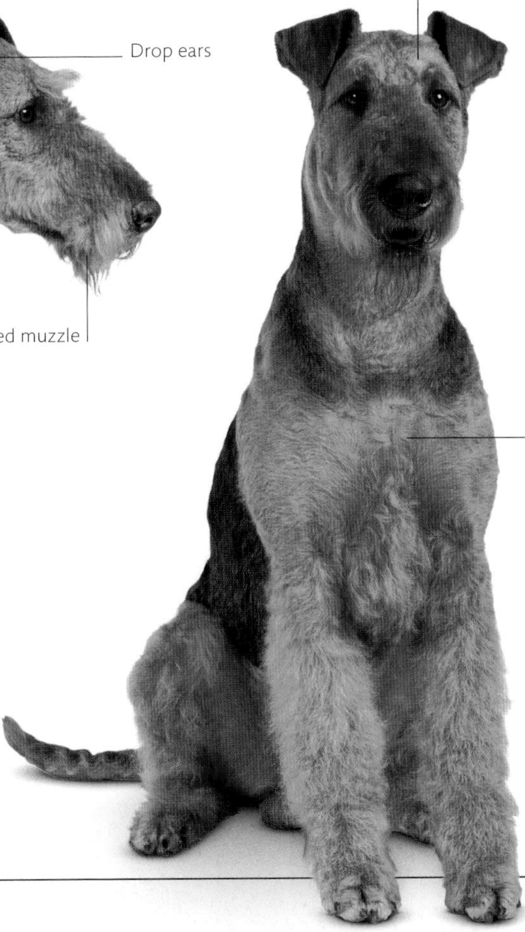

WAR SERVICE

The Airedale Terrier gave invaluable service to the British Army and the Red Cross during World War I. On the battlefield, the dogs were used to carry messages and mail, and to find wounded soldiers. Some endured grave danger and terrible injuries. One dog, named Jack was said to have saved a battalion by carrying a message through a swamp and under artillery fire that broke his jaw and foreleg. He just completed his mission before he died. Jack was posthumously awarded a medal for his gallantry. Airedale terriers were trained for service in World War II, too, seen below at a training camp in 1939.

PUPPY

Tail carried high when alert

Level back

Drop ears

Bearded muzzle

Dark grizzle saddle

Grizzle and tan

Long, flat head

Wiry, wavy coat

Black Russian Terrier

HEIGHT 26–30in (66–77cm)
WEIGHT 84–143lb (38–65kg)
LIFE SPAN 10–14 years

First developed in the 1940s, this massively built and hardy terrier was the special creation of the Soviet Army in the former USSR. The breeders' goal was to produce a large dog suitable for military work and able to withstand the severe cold of Russian winters. Among many breeds used in its development were the Rottweiler (see p.83), the Giant Schnauzer (see p.46), and the Airedale Terrier (see p.198). Although formidable in size and appearance, it can be a friendly and well-adjusted house dog, if handled responsibly.

Irish Terrier

HEIGHT 18–19in (46–48cm)
WEIGHT 24–26lb (11–12kg)
LIFE SPAN 12–15 years

Wheaten

This handsome breed emerged in County Cork in Ireland and is believed to have a long history, although its earliest ancestry is unknown. The Irish Terrier has a delightful temperament and can be trusted with children, but outside the home it is inclined to be belligerent toward other dogs.

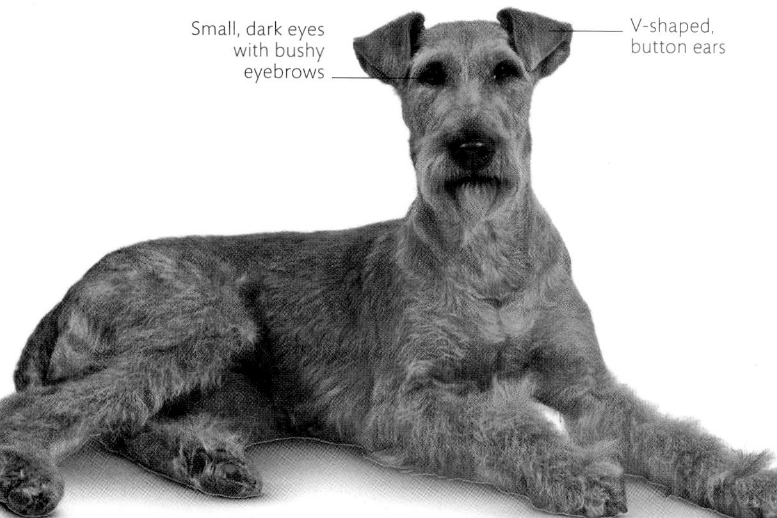

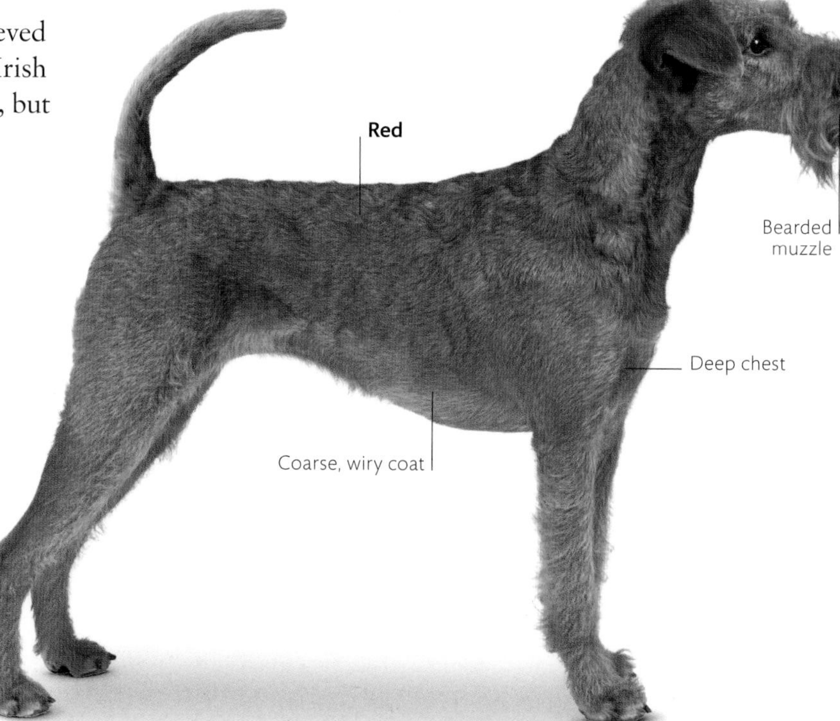

Welsh Terrier

HEIGHT Up to 15in (39cm)
WEIGHT 20–22lb (9–10kg)
LIFE SPAN 9–15 years

Black grizzle and tan

nce used in packs for hunting fox, badger, and otter, e Welsh Terrier was recognized as a breed in the 1880s, and is medium-sized terrier has gained attention as a show dog. lthough lively and energetic, the Welsh Terrier is easier to anage than many other terriers and is a good house dog.

Kerry Blue Terrier

HEIGHT 18–19in (46–48cm)
WEIGHT 33–37lb (15–17kg)
LIFE SPAN 14 years

he national dog of Ireland is born black, but its coat color gradually hanges to blue before the age of two. A versatile farm and guard dog, e Kerry Blue Terrier is intelligent and makes an affectionate and bedient pet as long as it is well trained and handled firmly.

Bedlington Terrier

HEIGHT	WEIGHT	LIFE SPAN	
16–17in (40–43cm)	18–22lb (8–10kg)	14–15 years	Sandy Liver All colors may have tan markings.

)espite its cuddly appearance and short, high-stepping ;ait, this is an eager, swift, and tenacious breed

'he typical terrier spirit lies beneath the ·oolly coat of the Bedlington Terrier, a dog ıat has been described as having "the look f a lamb but the heart of a lion." The breed riginated in Northumberland, in northeast ngland, and was bred by both the upper lasses and working men. It was descended ·om the Whippet (see p.128) and from ther terrier breeds, and used to hunt hare, ıbbit, fox, and badger above ground. It ould also work in water to hunt rat and tter. A national breed association was)rmed for the Bedlington Terrier in 1877, nd the breed became a feature in the show ng as well as in family homes.

Its sight hound ancestry has given the ·edlington Terrier not only great speed nd agility but a more tolerant temper than some terriers. Now usually kept as a companion, the dog is normally quiet, affectionate, and rather sensitive, but if provoked it will defend itself in true terrier fashion. The Bedlington Terrier needs plenty of physical and mental activity to work off its energy and prevent boredom. Owners may need to be vigilant when walking outdoors, to stop the dog from giving in to its strong chasing instinct. It has proved itself in agility and obedience competitions.

The puppies are born dark blue or dark brown. Their coats grow lighter as they mature, and need regular trimming. Show dogs have a unique clip, with long hair on the face and legs and tassels on the ears.

BEDLINGTON HISTORY

The ancestors of the Bedlington Terrier included various terrier types that lived in the area of Rothbury Forest, in Northumberland, England, and were known as Rothbury Terriers. The earliest example of a dog with a Bedlington-like look was born in 1782 and called Old Flint. In 1825, in the town of Bedlington, a man named Joseph Ainsley mated a pair of terriers with this Bedlington "look" and declared the resulting puppy the first of a new breed, the Bedlington Terrier.

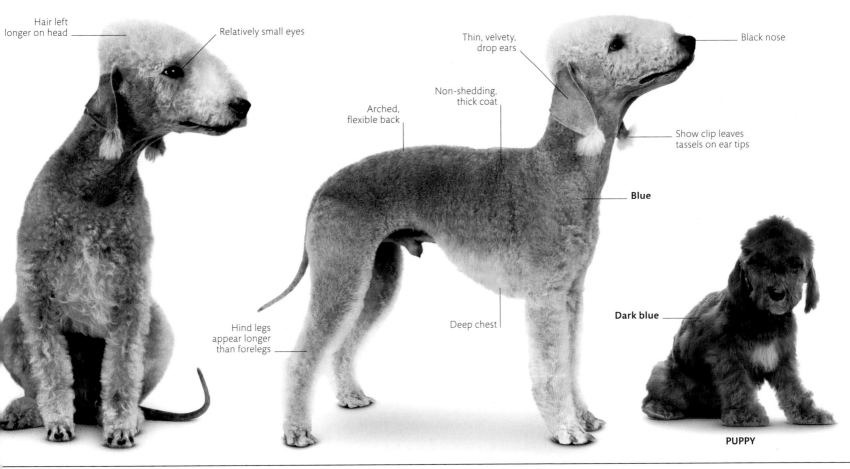

Hair left longer on head

Relatively small eyes

Thin, velvety, drop ears

Black nose

Non-shedding, thick coat

Arched, flexible back

Show clip leaves tassels on ear tips

Blue

Hind legs appear longer than forelegs

Deep chest

Dark blue

PUPPY

German Hunting Terrier

HEIGHT	WEIGHT	LIFE SPAN
13–16in (33–40cm)	18–22lb (8–10kg)	13–15 years

This fearless dog is a tenacious hunter, but can be a faithful companion given sufficient mental and physical activity

This modern hunting dog (Jagdterrier in German) was developed in the early 20th century. It was hardly known outside Germany until the 1950s, when a few of the dogs were brought to the US. The dogs are still widely used for hunting in Germany, and are becoming popular in North America for hunting squirrels and birds.

The German Hunting Terrier is happy to sleep outdoors by night and hunt all day, above or below ground and in all types of terrain. It will also work in water. The breed can be used to pursue quarry that lives underground, such as fox, weasel, and badger; to flush rabbit or wild boar out of thickets; and to track the blood trails from wounded animals such as deer.

A brave, active dog, the German Hunting Terrier needs to work, ideally in the hunting field. Kept active, it can be a loyal family pet as well as an effective guard dog; it is friendly and willing to learn, but needs to be socialized early and have clear leadership. It must have vigorous exercise every day. There are two coat types: rough and smooth.

ALL-AROUND TERRIER

The German Hunting Terrier was created by four Bavarian dog breeders just after World War I to be an all-around, world-class terrier. At that time, Fox Terriers were popular in Germany but were bred more for looks than for utility. The breeders started with four Fox Terriers, which had the desired black and tan coloring but lacked in hunting prowess. They then crossed these dogs with the hunting Wire Fox Terrier (see p.208), old English wire-haired terriers, and the Welsh Terrier (see p.201). The result was a hardy, courageous, multipurpose hunting dog (below).

Black and tan

Small, oval, dark eyes

Long, straight back

Tan markings on chest

Rough, wiry coat

ROUGH-COATED

Triangular, button ears

Strong neck

SMOOTH-COATED

Forefeet often broader than hind feet

Soft Coated Wheaten Terrier

HEIGHT	WEIGHT	LIFE SPAN
18–19in (46–49cm)	35–46lb (16–21kg)	13–14 years

This all-around farm dog, with its happy-go-lucky, affectionate nature, adapts well to family life

Known for more than 200 years, the Soft Coated Wheaten Terrier is probably one of the oldest Irish breeds. It shares ancestry with the Irish Terrier (see p.200) and the Kerry Blue Terrier (see p.201). Despite its history, it only gained official recognition in Ireland in 1937.

The breed began life as a working dog, and the first dogs had to prove themselves in rat, rabbit, and badger hunts in order to become champions. Today it is mainly kept as a pet, but some dogs also work as therapy dogs.

The Soft Coated Wheaten Terrier loves people, being gentler than other terriers, and it is good with children, although it can be too boisterous with toddlers. It retains its "puppy" nature into adulthood but is a highly intelligent dog and responds well to training. It needs plenty of exercise every day.

The breed is named for its coat, which differs from the wiry coat of other terrier breeds. There are two main coat types: the silky, glossy "Irish" coat, and the thicker "English" or "American" coat. Many puppies are born with a dark red or brown coat, which lightens to pale gold as the dogs mature. The coat will need thorough grooming every few days, as well as regular trimming.

THE POOR MAN'S DOG

In England and Ireland, for many centuries, only the nobility were allowed to keep hounds and other hunting dogs. Poorer people kept terriers, which were easy to care for and could do a range of jobs. The Soft Coated Wheaten Terrier (pictured below in a 19th-century painting by Alfred Duke) was used to kill rats and other vermin, and also used to guard property and herd livestock. Later it was taken hunting as a gundog. Perhaps due to its stature and hunting skill, it was known as the "poor man's Wolfhound."

Dutch Smoushond

HEIGHT 14–17in (35–42cm)
WEIGHT 20–22lb (9–10kg)
LIFE SPAN 12–15 years

This former coachman's dog is strong enough to follow a horse and carriage and is also an avid rat catcher. During the 1970s this breed almost became extinct; it is still rare but is now regaining popularity. This dog makes a good watchdog, gets along well with children, and will even accept the family cat. It needs plenty of exercise.

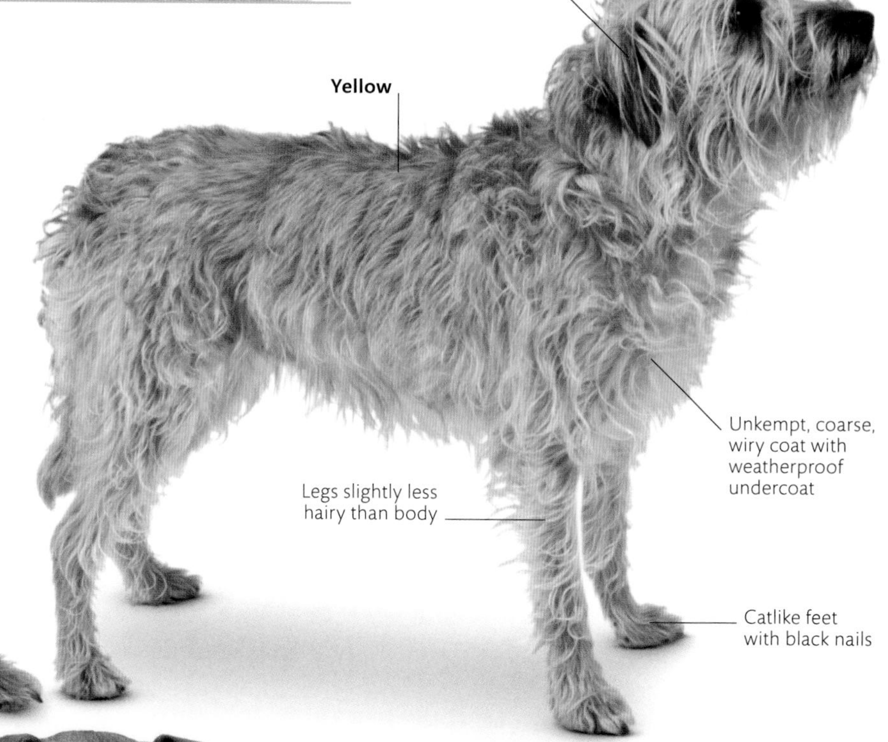

Thin, black-rimmed lips

Lakeland Terrier

HEIGHT 13–15in (33–37cm)
WEIGHT 15–18lb (7–8kg)
LIFE SPAN 13–14 years

Variety of colors

This determined, agile little terrier was bred to chase foxes over hilly terrain and into their burrows, and it retains the tendency to chase anything that moves—regardless of size—and to be aggressive with other dogs. With training, it makes a fearless guard dog and an enthusiastic companion.

Border Terrier

HEIGHT	WEIGHT	LIFE SPAN	
10–11in (25–28cm)	11–15lb (5–7kg)	13–14 years	Wheaten Red Blue and tan

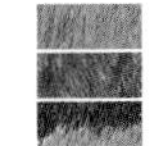

NEW JOBS FOR AN OLD BREED

The traits that made the Border Terrier a good hunting dog also help it to work well in modern-day jobs. One such role is as a therapy dog. The Border Terrier's friendly nature makes it ideal for comforting sick children, highly stressed people, and lonely elderly people. In addition, thanks to its steadiness and courage, the breed has also been used in disasters such as floods or accidents, to reduce stress in victims and emergency personnel.

This energetic and cheerful terrier with a laid-back personality makes a good family pet

This breed, known for its endurance and its distinctive otterlike head, originates in the Cheviot Hills, on the border between England and Scotland. Although the UK Kennel Club only recognized it officially in 1920, the Border Terrier has existed since at least the 18th century; it is thought to be one of the oldest terrier breeds in the UK.

The Border Terrier was initially bred as a working farm dog but became widely used for hunting. It was bred to be fast enough to keep up with horses, but small enough to fit down fox and rat burrows in order to flush out the prey. The breed had courage and the stamina to work all day in all weather. Owners often left the dogs to find their own food, so the Border Terrier developed a strong hunting drive.

This breed still excels in hunting and hunting trials, as well as in agility and obedience contests. It has also become a popular pet, since it tends to be more cooperative and more tolerant of small children and of other dogs than other terriers. It needs daily outlets for its energy, or it may become unhappy and destructive.

Short, strong muzzle

High-set, drop ears

White mark on chest

Short, thick tail

Dense coat has thick undercoat

Grizzle and tan

Tan hair on legs

Typical terrier
Terriers should be ready to spring into action at the slightest provocation. The Wire Fox Terrier here shows this alertness as he playfully grapples with a turned on hose.

Fox Terrier

HEIGHT	WEIGHT	LIFE SPAN	
Up to 15in (39cm)	Up to 18lb (8kg)	10 years	White May have tan or black markings.

TINTIN AND SNOWY

In the comic-book series *The Adventures of Tintin*, the hero Tintin's best friend is Snowy the dog. Tintin's creator, Hergé, modeled Snowy on a Wire Fox Terrier because this breed was popular at the time he was writing. He was also inspired by a Wire Fox Terrier belonging to the owner of a restaurant that he frequented. Snowy is a comic-book character but has the cleverness to rescue his master from danger and the courage to take on enemies much bigger than himself—the quintessential terrier.

This cheerful, affectionate, and fun-loving dog is good with children and enjoys long walks in the country

An energetic and sometimes vocal companion, the Fox Terrier from England was originally kept to kill vermin, hunt rabbits, and tackle foxes that had been run to ground. Its bold and fearless nature and love of digging make early socialization and training essential to prevent snappiness and curb any tendency to dig. If this is achieved, the Fox Terrier makes a wonderful family pet that loves to play and readily reciprocates any affection it receives.

The Wire Fox Terrier's coat needs regular grooming and plucking to remove any shed hair, and more extensive stripping three or four times a year. The coat should never be clipped, because this does not remove shed hair and may cause irritation, and also leads to deterioration in coat texture and color. Much rarer than its wire-haired cousin, the Smooth Fox Terrier's shorter coat requires less grooming.

The Fox Terrier is ancestral to several other dog breeds, including the Toy Fox Terrier (see p.210), the Brazilian Terrier (see p.210), the Rat Terrier (see p.212), the Parson Jack Russell Terrier (see p.194), and the Jack Russell Terrier (see p.196).

PUPPY

Tail carried erect

White with black and tan markings

Very slight stop

Chest deep but not broad

Long, powerful thighs

WIRE FOX TERRIER

Small, V-shaped, semierect ears

Head and muzzle of equal length

Wiry coat with white predominant

Round, compact feet

Wedge-shaped head

Circular, dark eyes

Tan markings

Coat has black flecks

Black patch

Black nose

SMOOTH FOX TERRIER

Japanese Terrier

HEIGHT 12–13in (30–33cm)
WEIGHT 5–9lb (2–4kg)
LIFE SPAN 12–14 years

Black, tan, and white

Also known as the Nippon or Nihon Terrier, this rare breed is strong and athletic for its size. Its ancestors are thought to include the English Toy Terrier (opposite) and the now extinct Toy Bull Terrier. The Japanese Terrier has been kept as a lapdog, ratter, and retriever, and it makes an adaptable family pet as well as a good watchdog.

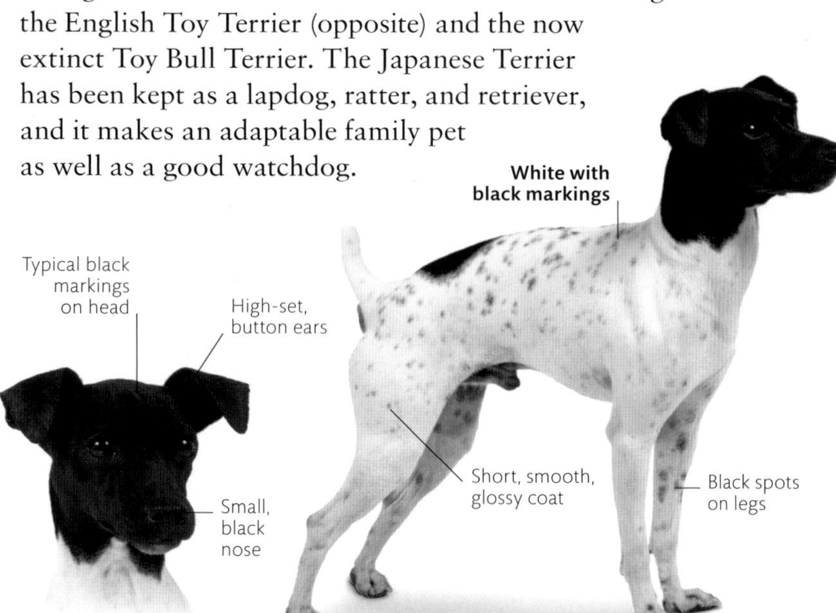

Toy Fox Terrier

HEIGHT 9–12in (23–30cm)
WEIGHT 5–7lb (2–3kg)
LIFE SPAN 13–14 years

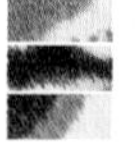

White and tan
White and black
White, chocolate, and tan

Also called the American Toy Terrier, this breed is a cross between the Smooth Fox Terrier (see p.208) and various toy breeds. The result is a dog that is a good ratter but also family-friendly. As with all toy breeds, the Toy Fox Terrier is not recommended as a pet in a home where there are babies and toddlers, but older children will enjoy its zest for life.

Brazilian Terrier

HEIGHT 13–16in (33–40cm)
WEIGHT 15–22lb (7–10kg)
LIFE SPAN 12–14 years

Bred from European terriers crossed with local Brazilian farm dogs, this breed has marked hunting instincts and is eager to explore and dig as well as track, chase, and kill rodents. Like its smaller cousin, the Jack Russell Terrier (see p.196), the Brazilian Terrier needs to know who is boss. It rewards a firm owner with devotion and obedience and makes a protective—and vocal—watchdog. Ever active, it thrives on a long, daily walk, otherwise it becomes restless. When well trained, it makes an excellent family pet.

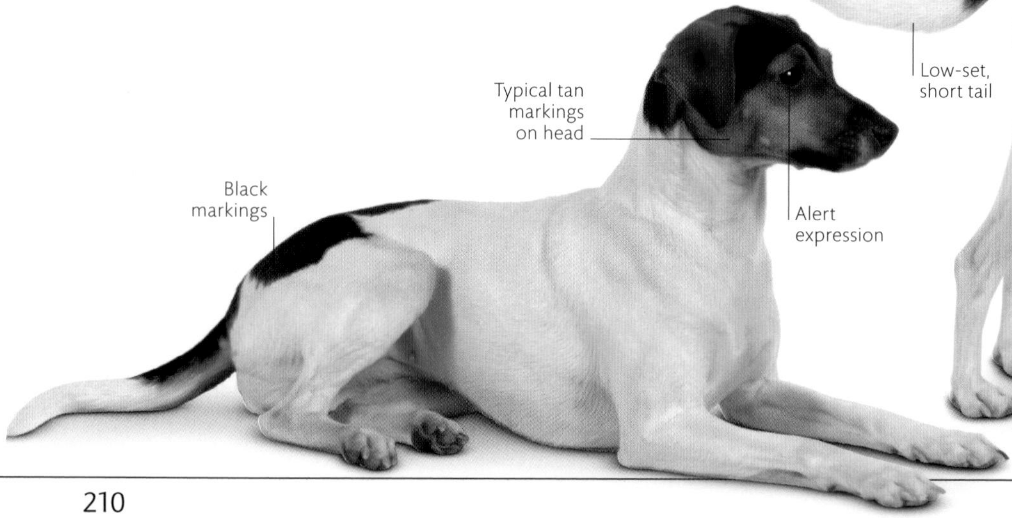

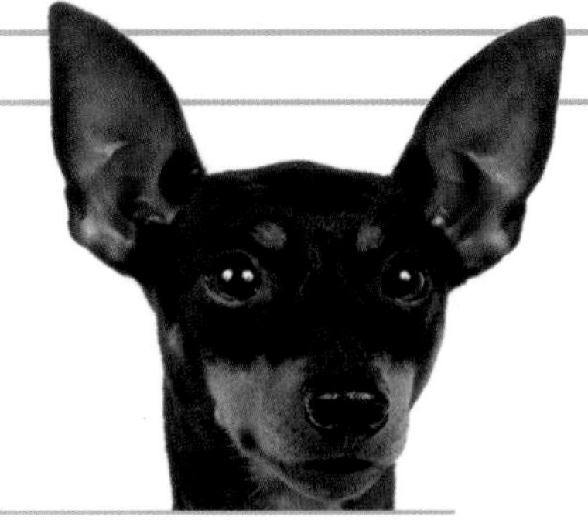

English Toy Terrier

HEIGHT	WEIGHT	LIFE SPAN
10–12in (25–30cm)	7–9lb (3–4kg)	12–13 years

RAT PITS

During the Industrial Revolution in England, using terriers such as the black and tan terriers to kill rats was a necessity in the fast-growing towns. For betting men, it also became a sport. Terriers would be placed in "rat pits" with a certain number of rats (as seen in the 19th century painting, *Rat-catching at the Blue Anchor Tavern*, below), and men would bet on how quickly the dogs could kill all the rats. The idea was to find the smallest dog that could kill the rats in the fastest time. Baiting blood sports were outlawed in 1835 in the UK, but rat baiting continued illegally until around 1912.

This perky, friendly, and confident little companion dog adapts well to either town or country life

The oldest British toy breed, the English Toy Terrier differs from its larger cousin, the Manchester Terrier (see p.212), only in its size and its erect ears. The two have only been classified as distinct breeds since the 1920s.

Black and tan terriers have been known in England since the 16th century, when they were used to kill rats. The terriers became popular as town pets in the 18th century. During Queen Victoria's reign a fashion for breeding them to be increasingly small severely weakened the breed; however, in the late 19th century enthusiasts set up more rigorous standards for the smaller type. This type became known as the Miniature Black and Tan Terrier and from 1960 the English Toy Terrier (black and tan). The breed is rare today and is included on the UK Kennel Club's list of Vulnerable Native Breeds.

The English Toy Terrier has the sharply alert, active nature of the terrier, although it is perhaps more sensitive than other terriers. It bonds with its owner and family and makes a good watchdog; however, it may try to hunt small pets. Its compact size means that this breed needs only limited daily exercise and adapts well to city living.

Almond-shaped, dark eyes

High-set, candle-flame ears

Well-defined, mahogany tan markings

Mahogany tan markings on chest

Jet-black and tan

Thick, glossy coat

Low-set, tapering tail, ends just above hock

Two inner toes longer than outer ones

Manchester Terrier

HEIGHT 15–16in (38–41cm)
WEIGHT 11–22lb (5–10kg)
LIFE SPAN 13–14 years

With its sleek good looks, the Manchester Terrier makes an elegant and lively companion dog, bigger than the related English Toy Terrier (see p.211). It takes its name from the weekly rat-killing contests in England that occurred in the 19th century and at which it excelled. Ruthless with vermin, it is gentle with its owners.

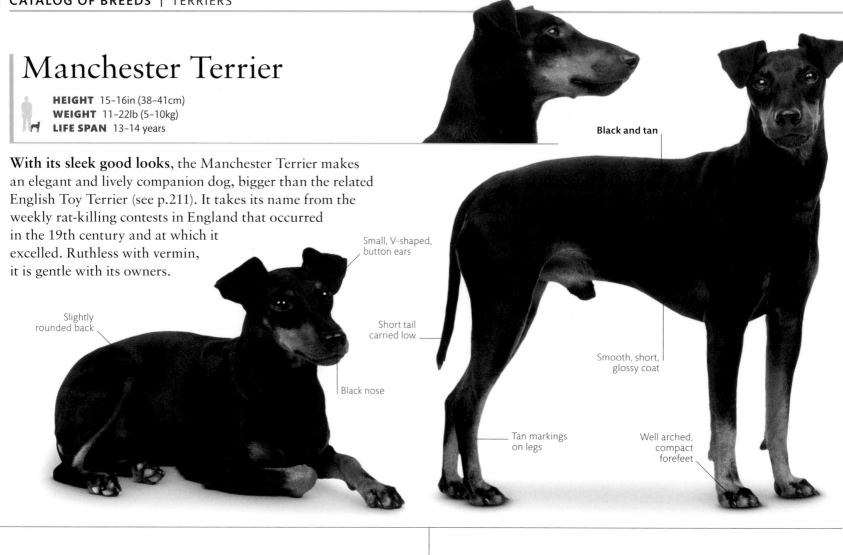

Rat Terrier

HEIGHT Standard: 14–22in (36–56cm)
WEIGHT Standard: 11–35lb (5–16kg)
LIFE SPAN 11–14 years

Variety of colors

Tan markings are common.

This terrier is a phenomenal rat catcher—one dog is reputed to have caught over 2,500 rats in just seven hours. Popular in the US, the Rat Terrier was President Theodore Roosevelt's choice of hunting dog. The Miniature—height range: 8–14in (20–36cm), weight range: 7–9lb (3–4kg)—is a good pet; the Standard suits an energetic owner. There are two ear types: erect and button.

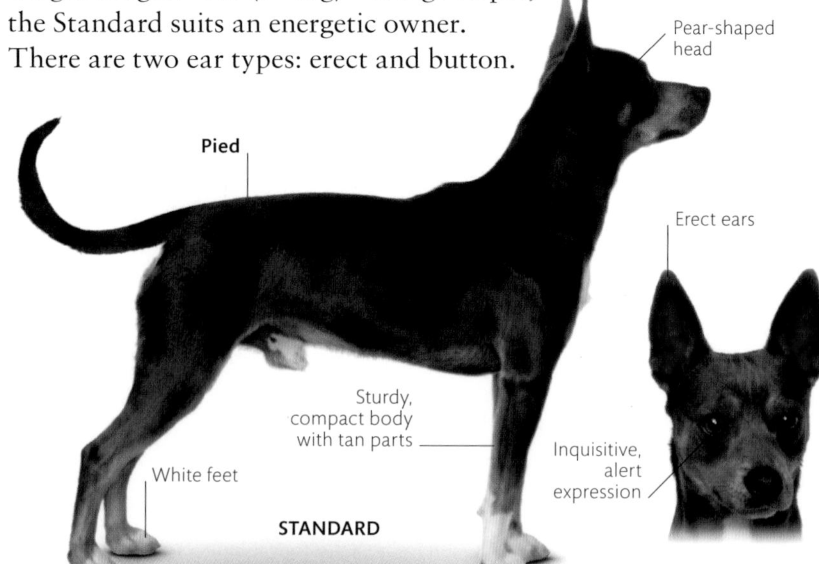

American Hairless Terrier

HEIGHT 10–18in (25–46cm)
WEIGHT 7–13lb (3–6kg)
LIFE SPAN 12–13 years

Any color

The first hairless Rat Terriers (left) were the result of a genetic mutation, but were then bred with each other to produce hairless puppies. Apart from its lack of hair, this is a typical, lively terrier. It needs a coat in winter to stay warm and to avoid sunburn in summer. Ears may be erect, semierect, or button.

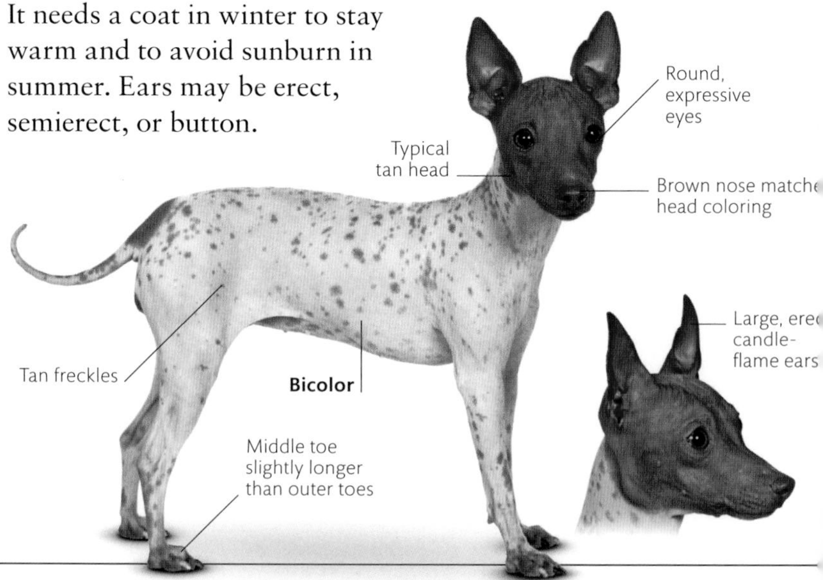

Patterdale Terrier

HEIGHT 10–15in (25–38cm)
WEIGHT 11–13lb (5–6kg)
LIFE SPAN 13–14 years

Red
Liver or bronze
Coats may be grizzled.
Black and tan

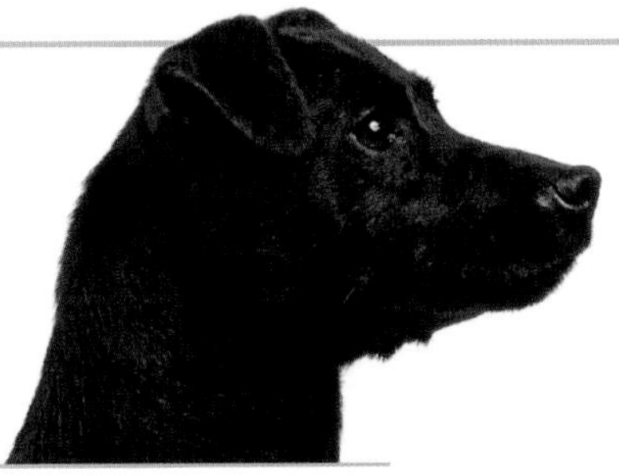

he isolated valleys of the Lake District in the UK ch had their own terrier—this one originates from e village of Patterdale. It remains popular in the UK it has gained favor in the US, too. It makes an cellent hunting companion since never gives up on its prey. here are two coat types: nooth and broken.

Head reflects its Staffordshire Bull Terrier bloodlines (see p.214)
Coarse topcoat
Eyes set wide apart
PUPPY

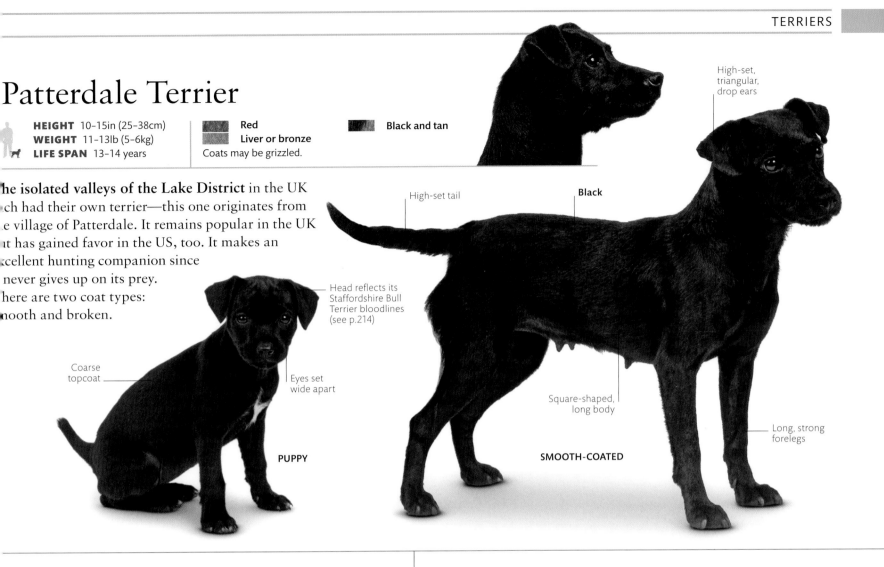

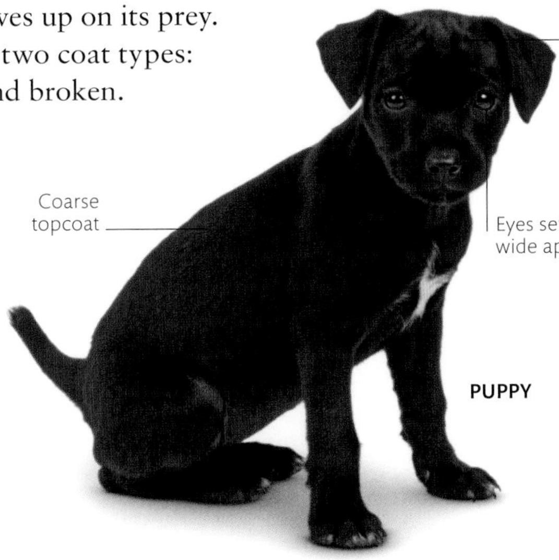

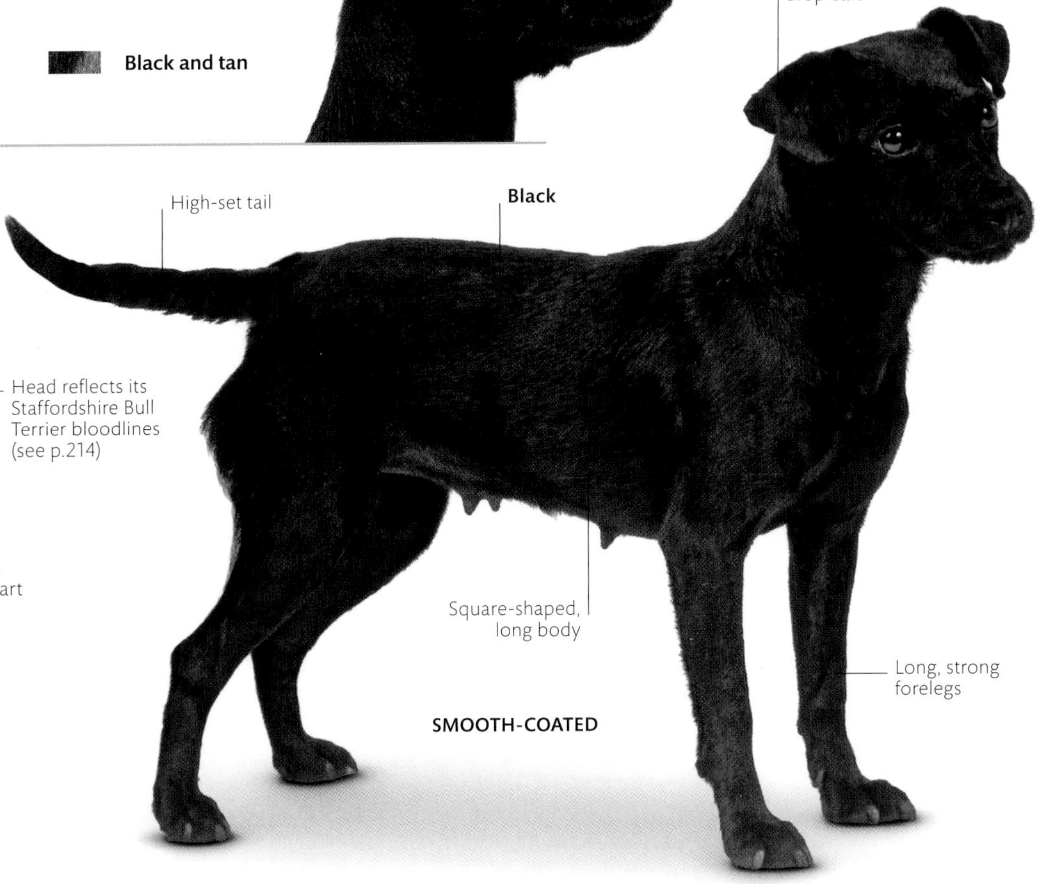

High-set, triangular, drop ears
High-set tail
Black
Square-shaped, long body
Long, strong forelegs
SMOOTH-COATED

American Pit Bull Terrier

HEIGHT 18–22in (46–56cm)
WEIGHT 31–60lb (14–27kg)
LIFE SPAN 12 years

Any color
Merle colors discouraged.

he ancestors of the American Pit Bull Terrier were dogs brought the US in the 19th century by Irish immigrants. Although bred for ghting, this breed became much loved as a working dog or family et. The breed has lately acquired reputation for aggression, which vigorously refuted y its supporters.

Distinctive wrinkles on forehead
Muscular, heavy neck
Short, dense, glossy coat
Deep, moderately wide chest with small, white markings
Red

High-set, semierect ears

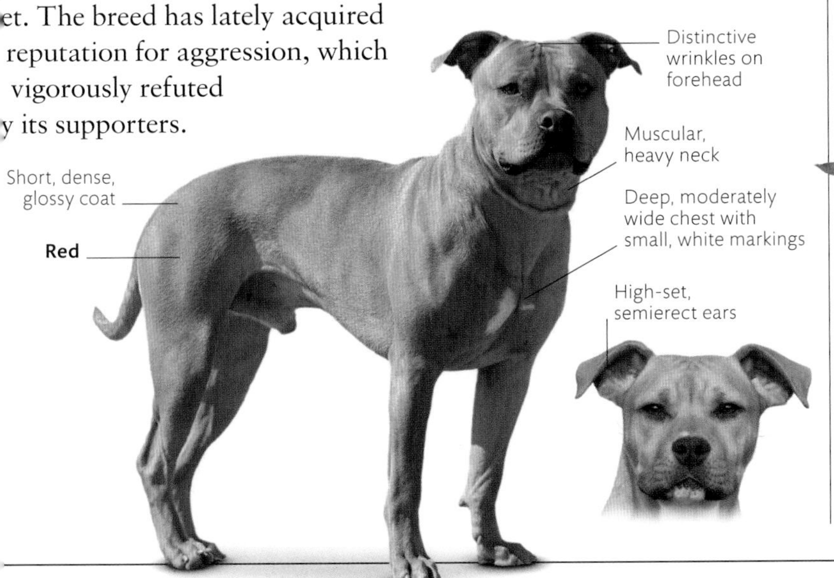

American Staffordshire Terrier

HEIGHT 17–19in (43–48cm)
WEIGHT 57–66lb (26–30kg)
LIFE SPAN 10–16 years

Variety of colors

Developed from the Staffordshire Bull Terrier (see p.214), this dog was recognized as a separate breed in the US in the 1930s. Apart from being more heavily built than its English counterpart, the American Staffordshire Terrier shares all the characteristics of the original Staffie. It is bold and intelligent and makes a loyal family pet.

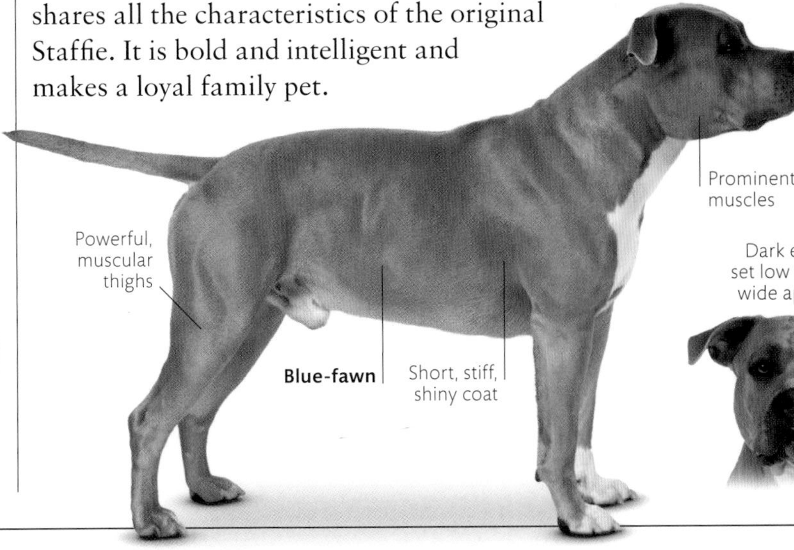

Prominent cheek muscles
Powerful, muscular thighs
Blue-fawn
Short, stiff, shiny coat

Dark eyes set low and wide apart

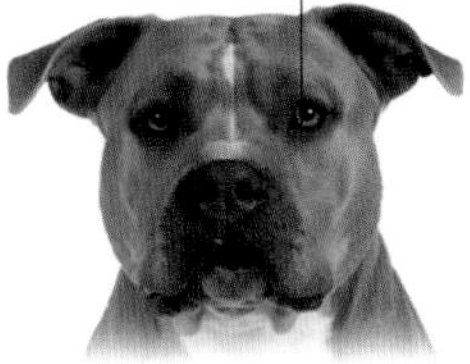

Staffordshire Bull Terrier

HEIGHT	WEIGHT	LIFE SPAN	
14–16in (36–41cm)	24–37lb (11–17kg)	10–16 years	Variety of colors

his fearless dog loves children and can achieve high evels of obedience with correct handling

riginally bred for dogfighting in the 19th ntury, the Staffordshire Bull Terrier was eveloped in the English Midlands from osses between Bulldogs (see p.95) and local rriers. The resulting dog, first known as e Bull and Terrier, was small and agile but rong, with powerful jaws. Although it had show courage and aggression when fighting the dog pit, it needed to stay calm when andled by people. Even when bullbaiting nd other "baiting" sports were banned 1835, clandestine dogfights continued ntil the 1920s.

During the 19th century one group of thusiasts sought to adapt the Bull and errier dog to create an animal more suitable for the show ring and family home. This modified breed, called the Staffordshire Bull Terrier, was officially recognized by the UK Kennel Club in 1935.

The modern "Staffie," as it is affectionately known, is hugely popular in both city and country. This dog is robust and boisterous, and possesses legendary courage. Firm handling and early obedience training are essential, but given an owner who is an effective trainer, the Staffordshire Bull Terrier will be an obedient and rewarding pet. Unfortunately, in recent years the breed has gained an unwarranted reputation as a dangerous dog, which has led to many being abandoned and ending up in animal shelters. Although a Staffordshire Bull Terrier is likely to respond if challenged by an unfamiliar dog, the breed is typically friendly and sweet-tempered with people and has a particular affinity with children.

JOCK OF THE BUSHVELD

Jock was a Staffordshire Bull Terrier belonging to a man named Percy FitzPatrick, who worked in South Africa as a transport rider with a team of oxen in the 1880s. Originally the runt of the litter, Jock (depicted engaging an antelope in the bronze statue at Jock Safari Lodge, Kruger National Park, South Africa, below) grew into a brave, loyal guard and hunter. He and his owner had many adventures in the bush, which FitzPatrick recounted as tales for his children. In 1907 he published the tales as *Jock of the Bushveld,* and it is now a classic in South African children's literature.

PUPPY

Red

lmost raight, apering ail

Dark rims to eyes

Smooth, short coat

Darker hair on muzzle

Powerful, muscular body

White markings on feet

Feet turn out slightly from pasterns

Broad head with distinct stop

Semierect, small ears

Broad chest with white markings

Kromfohrländer

HEIGHT	WEIGHT	LIFE SPAN
15–18in (38–46cm)	20–35lb (9–16kg)	13–14 years

RANDOM ORIGINS

The Kromfohrländer breed originated in the 1940s, from the random mating of a Wire Fox Terrier female (see p.208) and a stray dog named Peter that its owner, a woman named Ilse Schleifenbaum, identified as a Grand Griffon Vendéen (see p.144). The resulting puppies were attractive and uniform in type. Frau Schleifenbaum decided to breed more of these dogs, assisted by a man named Otto Borner. After about ten years the two breeders were ready to present their animals at dog shows as an entirely new breed.

This even-tempered, lovable terrier is good with the entire family but may be shy with strangers

A modern German breed, the Kromfohrländer has only been officially recognized since 1955. The breed takes its name from the Krom Fohr area of Siegerland, in western Germany, where it originated. In 1962 a Finnish woman named Maria Åkerblom began importing Kromfohrländers for breeding in Finland, and this country has now become the second center for the breed. The Kromfohrländer is still rare, however—there are fewer than 1,800 of these dogs in existence worldwide.

The Kromfohrländer's ancestry includes the Wire Fox Terrier (see p.208) and the Grand Griffon Vendéen (see p.144) as well as random-bred local German dogs. The result is an attractive, low-maintenance dog that is eager to please. From the outset, the breed has been developed as a family dog.

While wary of strangers, the Kromfohrländer is gentle and playful with familiar people and dogs. It makes a good watchdog and, like other terriers, is an excellent rat catcher, although it has less of the killing instinct typical of terriers. The breed is easy to train, if rather independent-minded, and some dogs have performed well in agility competitions. There are two coat types: rough-haired (with a beard) and smooth-haired.

White blaze with tan speckles

Triangular drop ears

Typical symmetrical head markings

White with tan patches

Thick coat lying close to body

Feathering on upper thighs

Tan speckling on legs

SMOOTH-HAIRED

ROUGH-HAIRED

Dandie Dinmont Terrier

HEIGHT 8–11in (20–28cm)
WEIGHT 18–24lb (8–11kg)
LIFE SPAN Up to 13 years

Mustard

May have white chest hair.

'his terrier comes from the border country between England nd Scotland, where it was developed to hunt badger and otter. : was named the Dandie Dinmont Terrier after a character vho owned a similar-looking dog in a novel by Sir Walter cott. Fun-loving, sensitive, and intelligent, he Dandie Dinmont Terrier thrives n love and attention.

Skye Terrier

HEIGHT Up to 10in (25–26cm)
WEIGHT 24–40lb (11–18kg)
LIFE SPAN 12–15 years

Cream
Fawn

Black

May have white spot on chest.

\ breed from the Western Isles of Scotland, the Skye Terrier vas originally used for fox and badger hunting. With a long, ow-slung body, the Skye Terrier could easily slip into the narrow ınderground passages used by its quarry. This elegant little dog s active, good-spirited, and makes an excellent family pet. The ong coat, characteristic of the breed, can take several years to ;row to its full adult length.

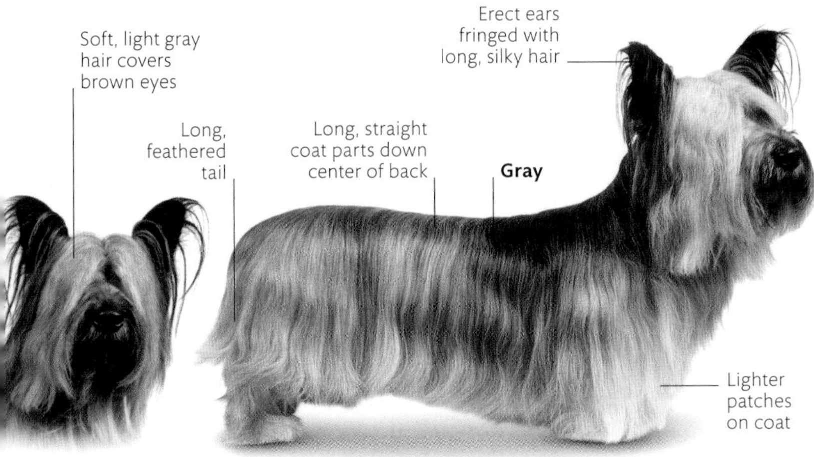

Miniature Pinscher

HEIGHT 10–12in (25–30cm)
WEIGHT 9–11lb (4–5kg)
LIFE SPAN Up to 15 years

Blue and tan
Brown and tan

Bred in Germany and developed from the much larger German Pinscher (see p.218), this sturdy but graceful dog was once used as a barnyard rat hunter. The Miniature Pinscher is quick and lively, moving with a characteristic high-stepping gait. Perfect for a small home, the breed has sharp senses that make it a good watchdog.

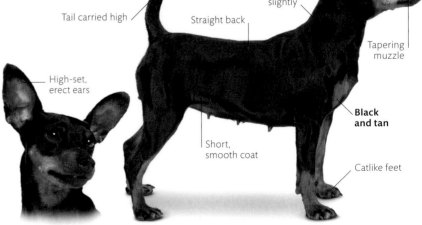

Neck arches slightly
Tail carried high
Straight back
Tapering muzzle
High-set, erect ears
Black and tan
Short, smooth coat
Catlike feet

German Pinscher

HEIGHT 17–19in (43–48cm)
WEIGHT 24–35lb (11–16kg)
LIFE SPAN 12–14 years

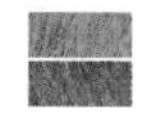

Isabella
Blue

Also known as the Standard Pinscher, this tall terrier started out as an all-purpose farm dog. It makes a protective guard dog, but needs to be well trained so that it does not become overprotective, bark for too long, or behave aggressively toward other dogs. With the right training it is gentle and responsive.

Austrian Pinscher

HEIGHT 17–20in (42–50cm)
WEIGHT 26–40lb (12–18kg)
LIFE SPAN 12–14 years

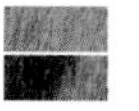

Russet-gold or brownish yellow
Black and tan

Bred as an all-purpose guard and herding farm dog in its native Austria, this breed rewards a confident owner with complete loyalty and devotion. Barking at anything suspicious, it makes an excellent watchdog for isolated locations, but its protective instincts and fearlessness can lead to aggression.

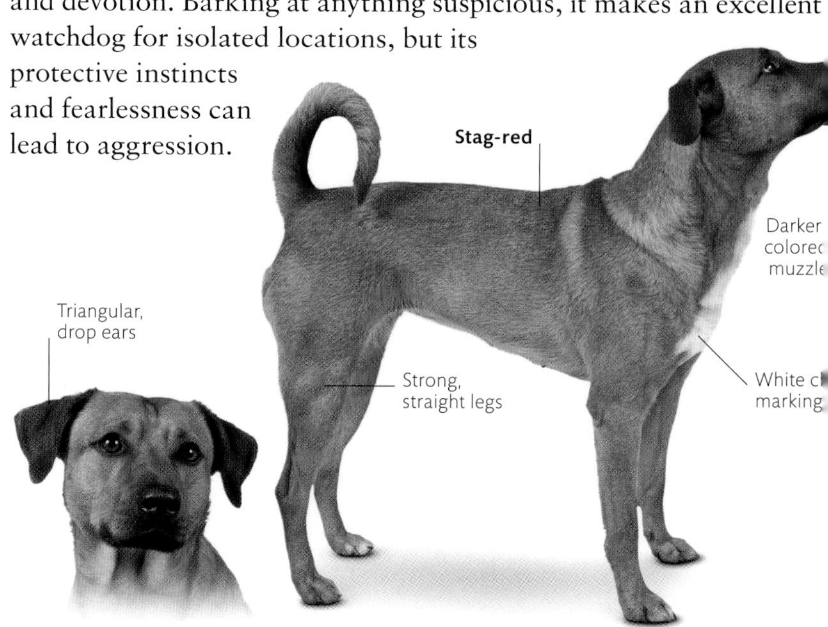

Affenpinscher

HEIGHT 9–11in (24–28cm)
WEIGHT 7–9lb (3–4kg)
LIFE SPAN 10–12 years

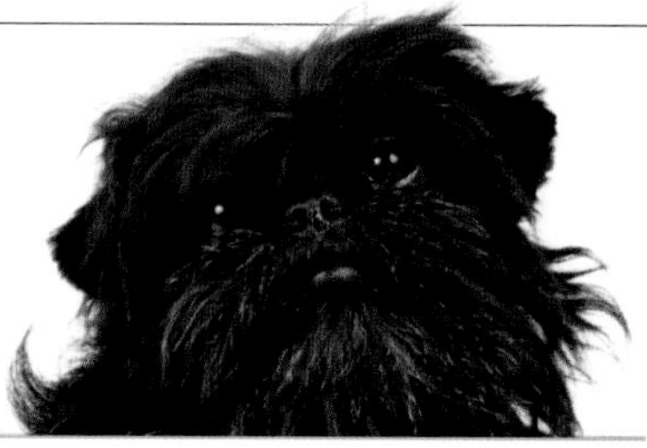

Sometimes called the Black Devil, the Affenpinscher is among the oldest of the European toy dogs. It retains its terrier instincts, though, and is a brave watchdog and ratter despite its size. With its bright, sometimes stubborn personality, this dog learns easily but needs to know who is in charge. It loves to play and gets along well with children who handle it considerately.

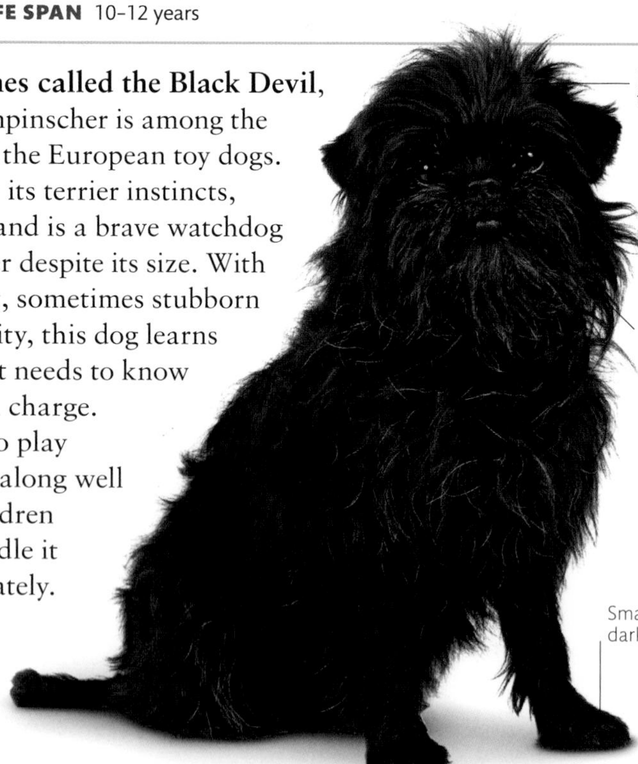

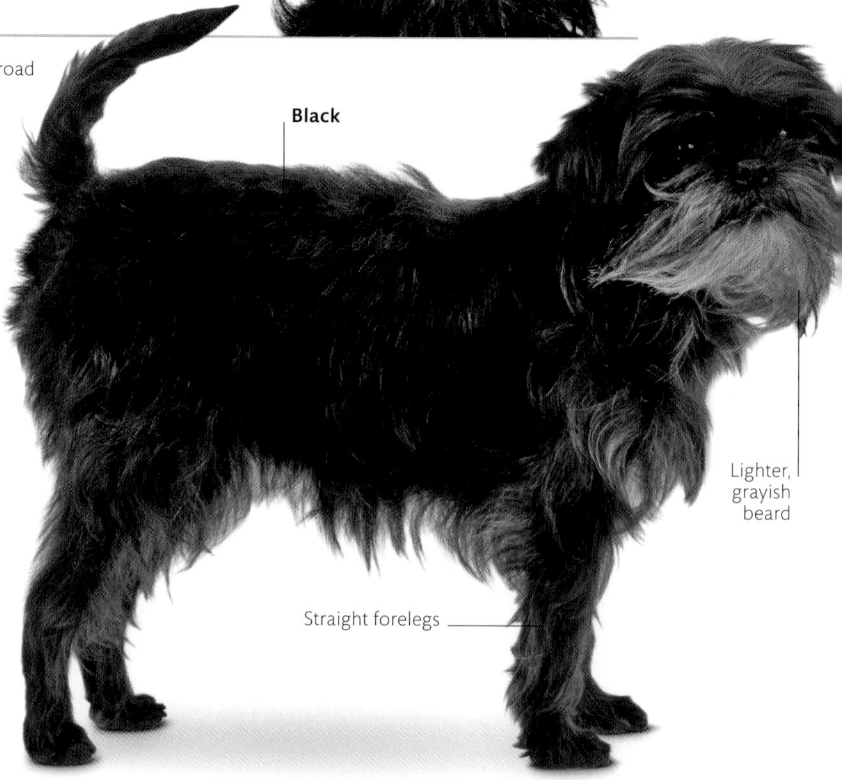

Domed, broad forehead
Blunt muzzle with wide nostrils
Small, round, dark feet
Black
Lighter, grayish beard
Straight forelegs

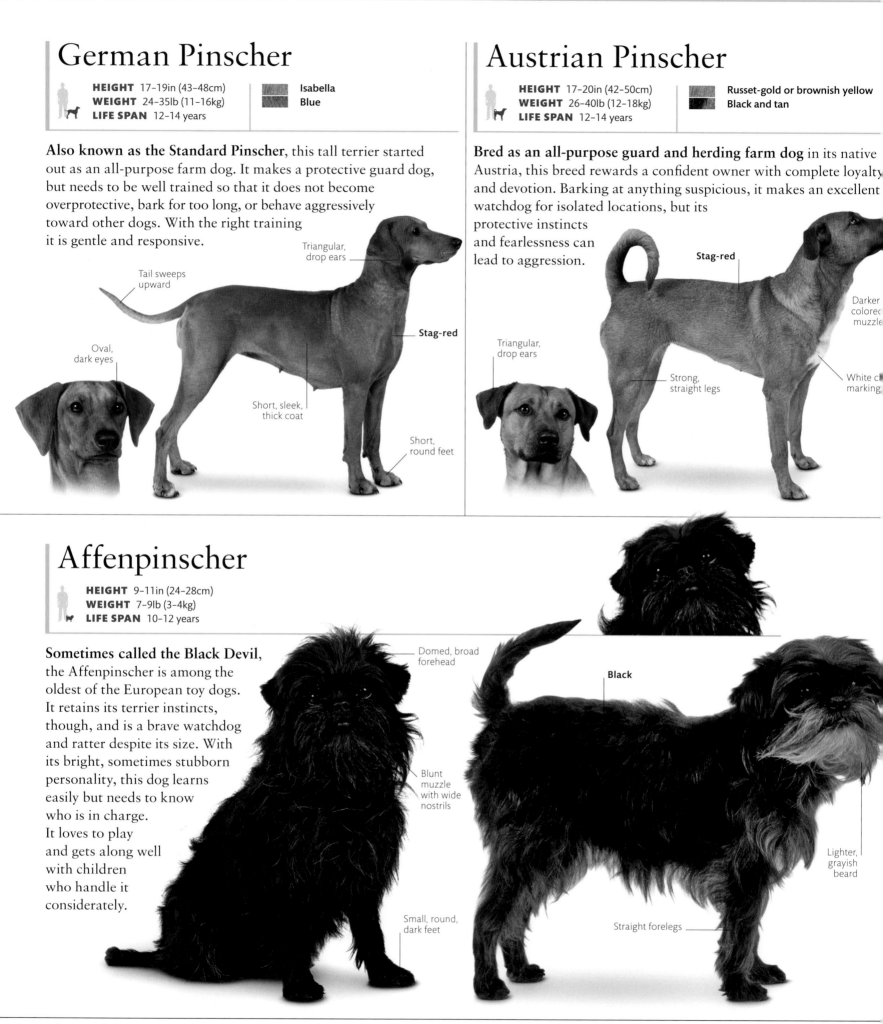

Miniature Schnauzer

HEIGHT	WEIGHT	LIFE SPAN	
13–14in (33–36cm)	13–15lb (6–7kg)	14 years	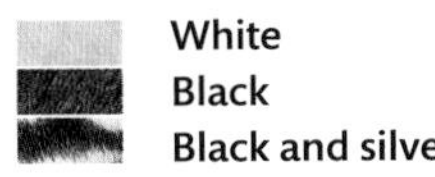 White Black Black and silver

CREATING A MINIATURE BREED

The Miniature Schnauzer (below, left) was created in the 19th century by farmers who wanted a compact version of the Standard Schnauzer (below, right) for hunting vermin as well as for guarding property and livestock. The breeders used small Standard Schnauzers, thus keeping the distinctive Schnauzer look and character. They crossed these dogs with the Affenpinscher (opposite) and possibly also the Miniature Pinscher (see p.217) and the Poodle (see p.276) to produce animals with a compact but strong frame.

This cheerful, friendly, fun-loving dog is a reliable family pet that responds well to training

The Miniature Schnauzer, like the Giant Schnauzer, was developed in Germany from the Standard Schnauzer (see p.45); it is the most recently created but the most popular of the three breeds. They derive their name from one dog named Schnauzer, who was exhibited at a dog show in 1879. All Schnauzers have the distinctive long-bearded muzzle; *schnauze* means muzzle in German.

The first Miniature Schnauzer was exhibited in 1899, but the breed was not recognized as distinct from the Standard Schnauzer until 1933. After World War II the breed became popular internationally, especially in the US.

The Miniature Schnauzer was originally bred by farmers as a ratter, but today it is most often kept as a companion or a show animal. It is playful and protective toward its family and can be a good guard dog. A lively, tough, intelligent dog, the Miniature Schnauzer is quick to learn but strong-minded, and needs firm, patient training. The breed can live happily in urban as well as rural homes, but despite its small size, it needs time to play off the leash as well as a brisk daily walk to keep it healthy and happy.

High-set, semierect ears

Strong, straight back slopes from shoulder to tail

Bushy eyebrows

Salt and pepper

Powerful muzzle with lighter-colored beard

Legs short below hocks

Coarse, wiry coat

Strongly muscled thighs

Multitasking
The German Shorthaired Pointer is one of various gundog breeds that are skilled at multitasking and combine several functions, here "pointing" to show the hunter where the prey is located.

GUNDOGS

Before the advent of firearms, hunters used dogs to help them locate and chase game. With the introduction of guns, a different type of dog was required. Gundogs were developed to carry out specific tasks and to work more closely with the hunters. The breeds fall into several categories based on the type of work they were bred to perform.

The dogs in the gundog group, which all hunt by scent, are classified broadly in three main divisions: the pointers and setters, which locate prey; the spaniels, which flush game out of cover; and the retrievers, which collect fallen prey and bring it back to the hunter. Breeds that combine these functions are known as HPR (hunt/point/retrieve) dogs and include the Weimaraner (see p.248), German Pointer (see p.245), and the Vizsla (see p.246).

Pointers have been used as hunting dogs since the 17th century. They have the extraordinary ability to indicate the location of prey by "pointing"—freezing into position with nose, body, and tail aligned. A pointer remains motionless until the hunter either flushes out the game or instructs the dog to do so. The Pointer (see p.254), which features in many old sporting portraits alongside hunting squires and their "bags" of game birds, is a classic example of the type.

Setters also direct attention to game by freezing. Typically used to hunt quail, pheasant, and grouse, these dogs crouch, or "set," when they pick up a scent. Originally, setters were trained to work with hunters who caught game with nets while their dogs prevented the prey from making an escape on the ground.

Spaniels drive out, or flush, game birds, forcing them to take wing into the line of the guns. They watch where a bird falls and are usually sent to retrieve it. This division includes small, silky-coated, long-eared dogs such as the Springer Spaniel (see p.224) and English Cocker Spaniel (see p.222), used for finding game on land, and less familiar breeds such as the Barbet and the Wetterhoun, which specialize in flushing waterbirds.

The retrievers were bred specifically for retrieving waterfowl. In common with some breeds of the spaniel division, these gundogs often have water-resistant coats. They are renowned for their "soft" mouths, and quickly learn to carry game without damaging it.

Cocker Spaniel

HEIGHT 13–15in (34–39cm)
WEIGHT 15–31lb (7–14kg)
LIFE SPAN 12–15 years

Any color

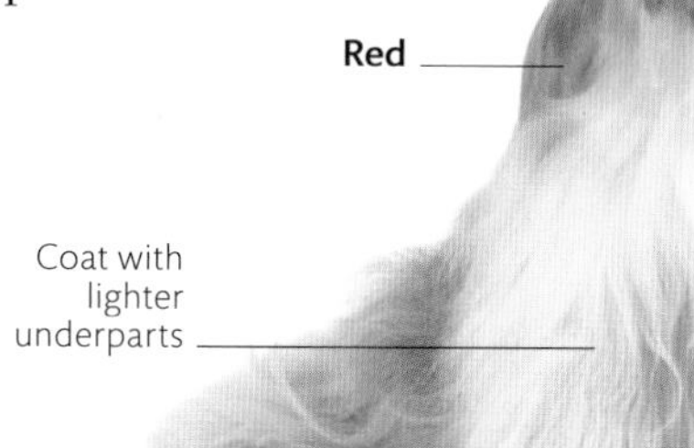

With its sweet, playful nature, the Cocker Spaniel is suited to life as a pet or a working gundog; the breed has speed and stamina and needs plenty of exercise. It also has a tendency toward shyness, so early and regular socialization is important.

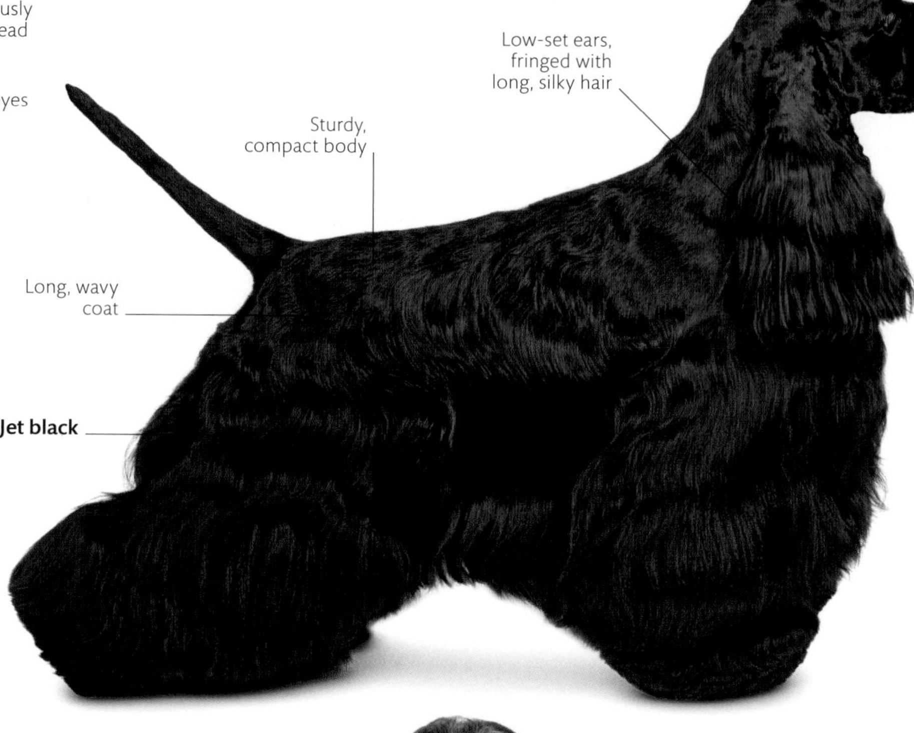

English Cocker Spaniel

HEIGHT 15–16in (38–41cm)
WEIGHT 29–33lb (13–15kg)
LIFE SPAN 12–15 years

Any color

Solid colors should have no white markings.

Originally known as the cocking spaniel and used for flushing woodcock and grouse, the English Cocker Spaniel is one of the most popular spaniel breeds. Smaller than the English Springer Spaniel (see p.224), this dog was developed to work in dense undergrowth. Show dogs are sturdier and heavier than working dogs, but both make excellent pets.

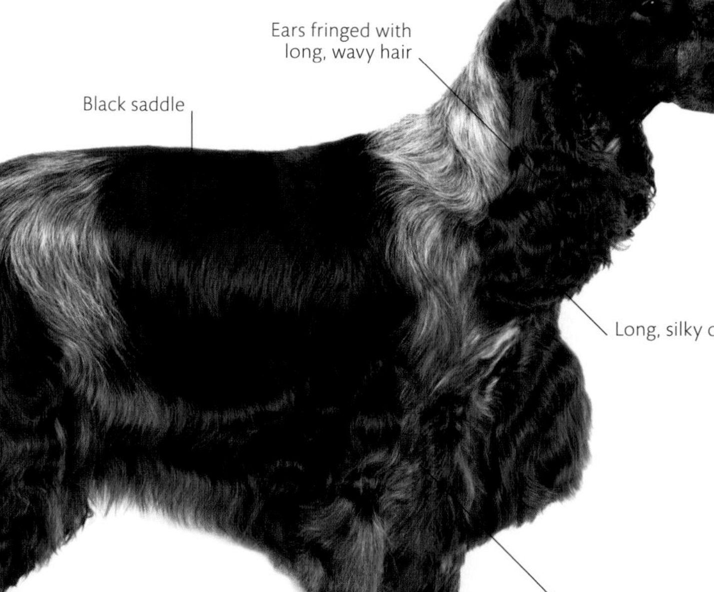

German Spaniel

HEIGHT 17–21in (44–54cm)
WEIGHT 40–55lb (18–25kg)
LIFE SPAN 12–14 years

Red
Brown
Red-roan

An excellent retriever, this dog loves the water. The German Spaniel has masses of stamina and is happiest working, although long, brisk walks will keep it content. This breed will live outdoors, but thrives indoors with a family, and makes a good working gundog and pet.

Short, fine, brown coat on head
Brown-roan
Brown saddle
Medium-brown eyes with kind expression
Lightly feathered drop ears
Dense, wavy coat
Spoon-shaped feet

Boykin Spaniel

HEIGHT 14–18in (36–46cm)
WEIGHT 24–40lb (11–18kg)
LIFE SPAN 14–16 years

Liver
May have white hair on chest and toes.

The official state dog of South Carolina, the Boykin Spaniel is a devoted companion and gets on well with other dogs and children. Its easygoing nature and willingness to work make it an ideal gundog or pet for an active family. The Boykin Spaniel's curly coat requires regular grooming.

Field Spaniel

HEIGHT 17–18in (44–46cm)
WEIGHT 40–55lb (18–25kg)
LIFE SPAN 10–12 years

Black
Roan
May have tan markings.

Originally a cross between the Sussex Spaniel (see p.226) and the English Cocker Spaniel (opposite), the Field Spaniel was used for retrieving from water and heavy cover. This docile but high-energy, medium-sized gundog needs to be kept busy and makes the perfect hunting companion for an active family living in the country.

English Springer Spaniel

HEIGHT	WEIGHT	LIFE SPAN	
18–22in (46–56cm)	40–51lb (18–23kg)	12–14 years	 Black and white May have tan markings.

Full of enthusiasm and affection, this sociable companion is an excellent working dog

This classic gundog is so-called because it was originally used to spring game—startle birds into the air. Spaniels used as gundogs were once classified according to their size: the larger dogs (called Springers, see pp.224–26) were used for flushing game birds, and the smaller ones (called Cockers, see p.222) for hunting woodcock. Until the beginning of the 20th century the English Springer Spaniel was not recognized as an official breed, although it had developed into a distinct type known as the Norfolk Spaniel.

The English Springer Spaniel will work with hunters in the field all day, undeterred by rough terrain or adverse weather conditions, even jumping into freezing water when necessary. This breed is a popular choice with game shooters but its friendly, obedient disposition makes it an excellent family dog, too. It likes company, including children, other dogs, and the household cat. If left alone for too long, it may resort to excessive barking. A nonworking dog needs long, energetic daily walks and will enjoy having a stream to splash in, mud to roll in, or toys thrown for it to retrieve. This breed is bright and willing to learn, and will respond to calm authority. It is highly sensitive, so giving harsh or loud commands is likely to be counterproductive. The English Springer Spaniel's love of the outdoors means that it needs weekly grooming to prevent its thick coat from becoming matted and dirty, and regular trimming, especially of the long feathering on the ears and legs.

There are two types of English Springer Spaniel: working and show. Dogs bred specifically to work in the field tend to have their tails docked and be slightly smaller and of lighter build than dogs produced for showing. Both types make equally good companions.

PUPPY

Well feathered tail, carried below level of back

Liver freckling on legs

SNIFFER DOGS

Although traditionally bred for hunting, the English Springer Spaniel is now also familiar as a sniffer dog (right), used to detect drugs, explosives, money, and even people. The breed's highly acute sense of smell enables it to detect the tiniest traces of explosives, or the smell of drugs in a person's sweat. The English Springer Spaniel has the speed and energy to search large areas quickly; in addition, it is compact and agile enough to work in small spaces such as vehicle interiors.

Pronounced stop
Pendant ears set at eye level
Weather-resistant, thick, wavy coat
Liver and white
Heavily feathered chest
Almond-shaped, dark hazel eyes express kind nature
Body moderately feathered all over
Rounded, compact feet

Welsh Springer Spaniel

HEIGHT 18–19in (46–48cm)
WEIGHT 35–51lb (16–23kg)
LIFE SPAN 12–15 years

A close cousin of the English Springer Spaniel (see p.224) and the English Cocker Spaniel (see p.222), this medium-sized Welsh gundog has a jolly disposition and makes a fine family dog and hunting companion. It is inclined to wander, so early and consistent training is imperative.

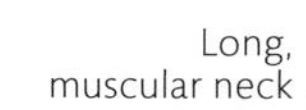

Sussex Spaniel

HEIGHT 15–16in (38–41cm)
WEIGHT 40–51lb (18–23kg)
LIFE SPAN 12–15 years

Although active by nature, this English gundog from Sussex will adapt to life in a smaller household, providing it is exercised sufficiently. Unlike other gundogs, the Sussex Spaniel will bark while working—a trait frowned upon in all other gundog breeds; another distinctive characteristic is the rolling action to its gait.

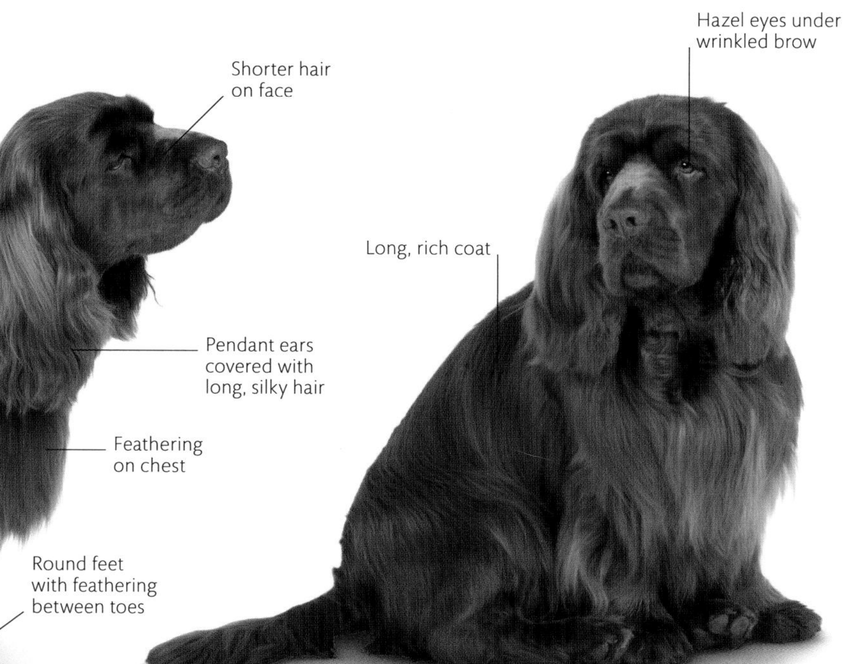

Clumber Spaniel

HEIGHT	WEIGHT	LIFE SPAN
17–20in (43–51cm)	55–75lb (25–34kg)	10–12 years

RETURN TO WORK

The Clumber Spaniel (shown in an engraving from the late 19th century, below) almost disappeared as a working gundog, but since the 1980s shooting enthusiasts in the UK have rediscovered the breed. Although the Clumber Spaniel is slower than other spaniels and may take longer to mature and to train, it is a quiet and thorough worker in all conditions. It can penetrate thick and thorny undergrowth with little difficulty, copes well with water, and can detect the most subtle of scents.

This big, good-tempered, easy-going dog enjoys family life and space in a country home

The Clumber Spaniel takes its name from Clumber Park in Nottinghamshire, in the English Midlands, home of the Duke of Newcastle. Various ancestors for this breed have been suggested, including the old British Blenheim Spaniel, the now-extinct Alpine Spaniel, and the Basset Hound (see pp.146–47). In the late 18th century the second Duke of Newcastle and his gamekeeper bred the first dogs recognized as the modern Clumber Spaniel.

During the 19th and early 20th centuries the Clumber Spaniel was a favorite with the British royal family—first Prince Albert (consort of Queen Victoria) and then kings Edward VII and George V, who bred them at their Sandringham estate in Norfolk. After World War I, however, the breed's numbers declined. It is still uncommon today, and it is included on the UK Kennel Club's list of Vulnerable Native Breeds.

Muscular and low to the ground, this breed is the most solidly built of all the spaniels. Its calm, steady nature has made it a beloved pet and show animal, but there is a resurgence of interest in using it for hunting. Gentle and well behaved, the Clumber Spaniel is easy to train. The breed can be sensitive to heat and needs protection from warm weather.

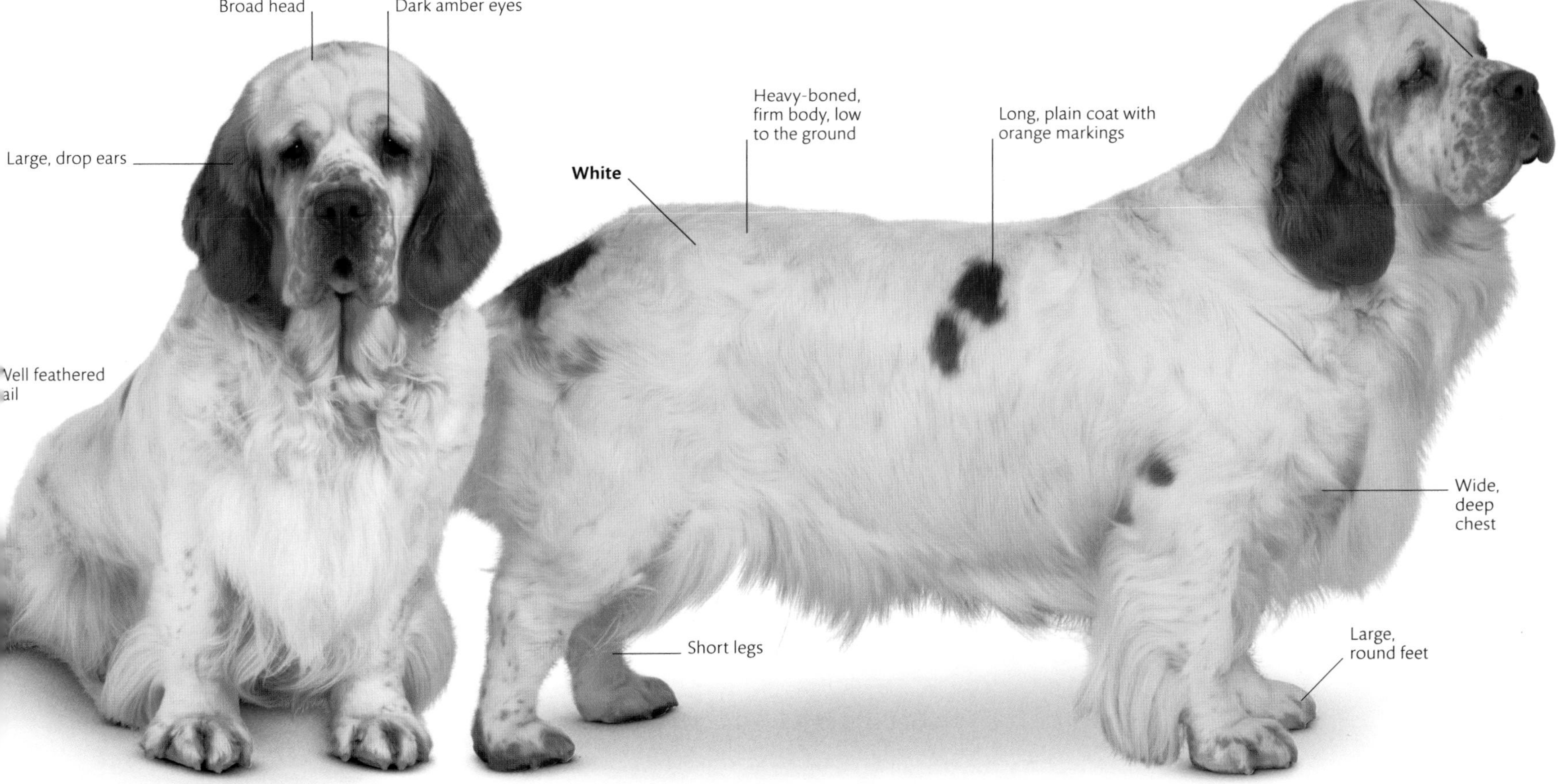

Irish Water Spaniel

HEIGHT 20–23in (51–58cm)
WEIGHT 44–66lb (20–30kg)
LIFE SPAN 10–12 years

This tireless dog is an ideal companion for hikers. Its dark liver coat is virtually waterproof, and the breed's enthusiasm for plunging into ice-cold water earned it the nickname of "Bogdog." Although gentle and faithful, it is slow to mature and can be headstrong, so needs thorough training when young.

Smoother hair on face

Broad, level back

Nose matches coat color

Naturally oily, dense coat

Coat forms dense ringlets

Smooth hair on throat forms V-shaped patch

Smooth tail except at base

Puce-liver

Large, round feet well covered with hair

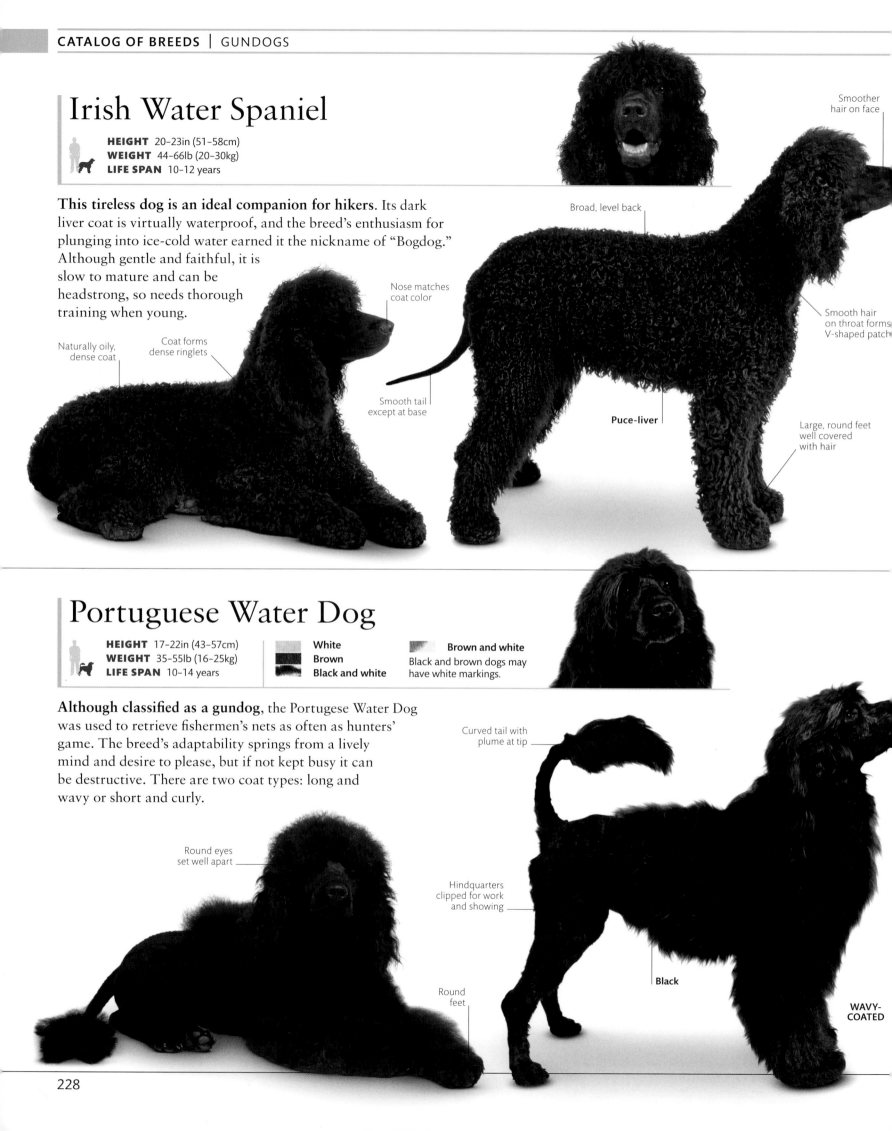

Portuguese Water Dog

HEIGHT 17–22in (43–57cm)
WEIGHT 35–55lb (16–25kg)
LIFE SPAN 10–14 years

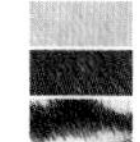

White
Brown
Black and white
Brown and white

Black and brown dogs may have white markings.

Although classified as a gundog, the Portugese Water Dog was used to retrieve fishermen's nets as often as hunters' game. The breed's adaptability springs from a lively mind and desire to please, but if not kept busy it can be destructive. There are two coat types: long and wavy or short and curly.

Curved tail with plume at tip

Round eyes set well apart

Hindquarters clipped for work and showing

Round feet

Black

WAVY-COATED

American Water Spaniel

HEIGHT 15–18in (38–45cm)
WEIGHT 26–46lb (12–21kg)
LIFE SPAN 10–12 years

Chocolate
May have a few white hairs on chest and toes.

)riginally bred as an all-round hunting and water dog in the Great Lakes :gion, the American Water Spaniel's moderate size and lean build allowed it to ork from boats as well as on shore. The breed is still used to flush and retrieve 'aterfowl, but also makes an easygoing companion for an active family. Its ense, curly coat is inherited from ancestors that include ıe Irish Water Spaniel (opposite) and the urly Coated Retriever (see p.262). ome dogs have a less tightly curled oat, called the Marcel coat.

Light brown eyes
Broad head
Liver
Moderate feathering along tail
Ears covered with curly hair
Smooth hair on face
Moderately feathered legs

DULT AND PUPPY

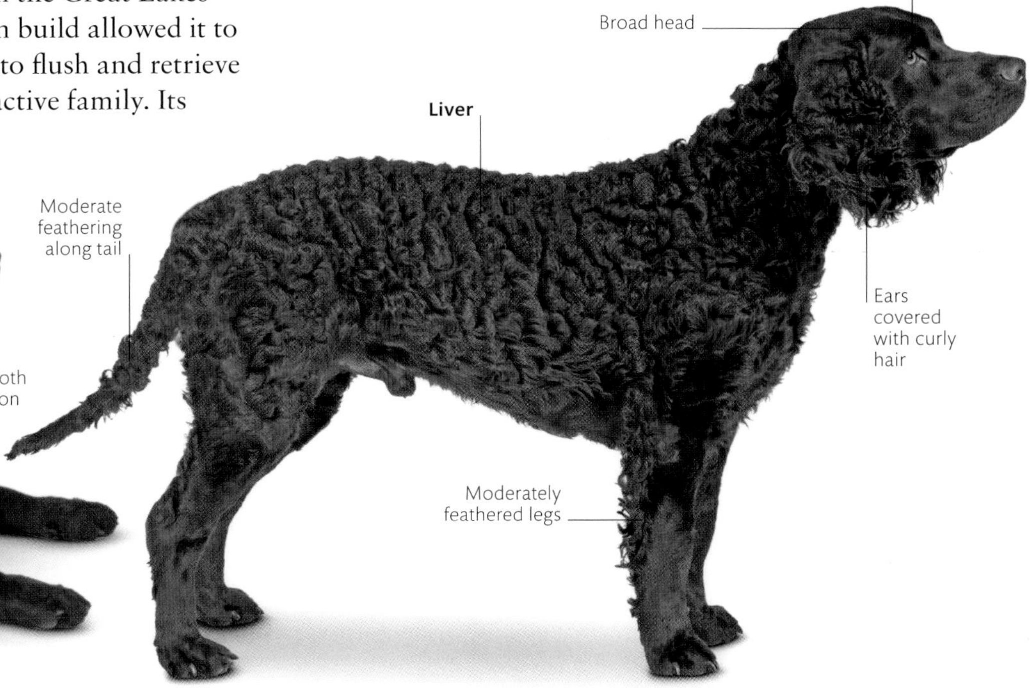

French Water Dog

HEIGHT 21–26in (53–65cm)
WEIGHT 35–60lb (16–27kg)
LIFE SPAN 12–14 years

Variety of colors

)ne of Europe's oldest water dogs, with ancestors dating back) the Middle Ages, the French Water Dog has contributed to ıany other breeds. Its coat is perfect protection for a working og but its high maintenance may be one reason why this breed no longer popular, despite its tolerant, friendly attitude to ıildren and to other dogs.

Poodle

HEIGHT Over 15in (38cm)
WEIGHT 46–71lb (21–32kg)
LIFE SPAN 10–13 years

Any solid color

Claimed by France but probably from Germany, this breed was originally a water dog, and the standard size remains closest to those roots. It is popular for crossbreeding because it is robust, clever, and good-tempered. A simple all-over clipping is easiest to maintain.

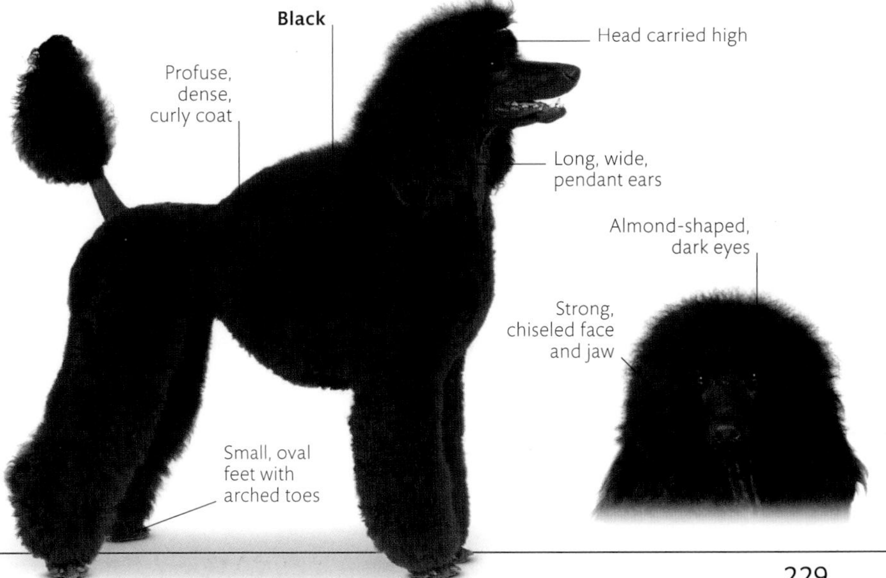

Corded Poodle

HEIGHT 9–24in (24–60cm)
WEIGHT 46–71lb (21–32kg)
LIFE SPAN 10–13 years

Any color

Like other poodles, Corded Poodles have been bred from separate lines of the well-known Poodle (see p.229) for many years but as yet are not recognized as a breed in their own right. Their kind of cording is more often found on herding breeds, offering protection against harsh weather and predators. Coats are corded with a little encouragement and are fairly easy to look after.

Frisian Water Dog

HEIGHT 22–23in (55–59cm)
WEIGHT 33–44lb (15–20kg)
LIFE SPAN 12–13 years

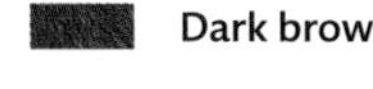

Dark brown

Also known as the Dutch Spaniel or Wetterhoun, this breed was originally used by fishermen to control otters. It is still used for flushing and retrieving, but also as a guard and farm dog. Its independent, slightly suspicious character makes it unsuitable for city living, but it is a reliable and rugged dog for a rural home.

Lagotto Romagnolo

HEIGHT	WEIGHT	LIFE SPAN	
16–19in (41–48cm)	24–35lb (11–16kg)	12–14 years	 Orange Roan Orange and roan coats may have a brown mask.

'his affectionate dog makes a good pet but can be oisterous so is best suited to a country life

nown in its native Italy since at least the 1iddle Ages, dogs of this type are thought) be the ancestor of all the water dog reeds. Originally, the Lagotto Romagnolo orked as a retriever in the marshland of omagna, northern Italy; its name is Italian or "lake (or water) dog of Romagna." From ne late 19th century when the marshes ere drained—and as a result the flocks f waterfowl dwindled the breed was found new job digging for truffles.

By the mid-20th century the Lagotto omagnolo had become a specialized truffle ound. However, it had been extensively rossed with other breeds, and by the 1970s there were very few purebred dogs left. A group of enthusiasts stepped in to save and restore the breed, and it was officially recognized by the FCI in 1995.

Today the Lagotto Romagnolo is bred as often for companionship as for work. It makes an affectionate family pet as well as an effective guard dog. This breed is good-natured and easy to train. It likes to be kept busy with plenty of walks and opportunities for swimming and digging. Its characteristic curly coat needs weekly combing and annual clipping.

FROM DUCKS TO TRUFFLES

For centuries the peasants of the Romagna region used the Lagotto Romagnolo for hunting waterfowl from their flat-bottomed boats, and a few dogs still do this work. The breed is the ultimate water dog. It is an excellent swimmer, aided by webbing between its toes, and its curly double coat enables it to work for hours in cold water. It still retains its swimming and retrieving instincts. In addition, it has a highly developed sense of smell and strong digging drive, making it ideally suited to being trained for truffle hunting (below).

Spanish Water Dog

HEIGHT	WEIGHT	LIFE SPAN		
16–20in (40–50cm)	31–49lb (14–22kg)	10–14 years	White Brown	Black

This adaptable working dog with a no-nonsense attitude can be stubborn, but if well trained it makes a good companion

This distinctive breed has had a variety of roles and names in its homeland, where it is now called the Perro de Agua Español. Records show that Water Dogs with woolly coats have existed in Spain since 1110CE. Their origins are unknown, but it is thought that merchants from North Africa or Turkey may have brought this type of dog to Andalusia. Three separate strains developed in rural Spain: a smaller type in northern Spain; a type with a long, corded coat in the marshes of western Andalusia; and a larger dog in the southern Andalusian mountains.

In the 18th century the Spanish Water Dog was employed to herd sheep on an annual migration from the south of Spain to the north and back again in search of fresh pastures. The breed was also used for hunting, especially in water. In addition, the dogs worked in Spanish ports, traveling with fishermen in their boats and towing ropes to help bring incoming boats to shore.

Today the Spanish Water Dog has become more unified by a standard size and coat type. Until the 1980s it was little known outside southern Spain, and it remains rare today, although efforts are being made to promote the breed.

It is still used as a working dog, as well as being employed in search and rescue work and as a sniffer dog. The Spanish Water Dog is a generally sensible companion but can be impatient with children. The coat should never be brushed but may be bathed as necessary and shorn once a year.

Tail barely reaches hocks

PUPPY

GAINING RECOGNITION

The recent history of the Spanish Water Dog began in 1980 when Antonio Perez recognized a type of dog that he knew well at a dog show in Malaga. It was referred to as an Andalusian and Perez asked show organizers, Santiago Montesinos and David Salamanca, why it was not considered a breed. They too were familiar with the dog and agreed to help Perez get it recognized. In 1983 a breed standard was drawn up, and by 1985 about 40 Spanish Water Dogs had been registered. The FCI finally officially recognized it as a breed in 1999.

Back slopes gently down toward tail
Woolly coat forms cords if left unclipped
Brown and white
Brown nose matches color of coat
Light chest markings
Legs slightly shorter than body length
Round feet covered in hair

Brittany

HEIGHT	WEIGHT	LIFE SPAN
19–20in (47–51cm)	31–40lb (14–18kg)	12–14 years

 Liver and white
 Black, tan, and white
Black and white
Colors may be merged and not clearly defined (roan).

THE BRITISH CONNECTION

The Brittany dog breed, shown below in a French print from 1907, bears a striking resemblance to the Welsh Springer Spaniel (see p.226) and it is possible that there was some crossing between the two. From the mid-19th century Brittany dogs were being crossed with spaniels and English Setters (see p.241) brought over by English huntsmen. Since quarantine laws were already in place, English hunters simply left their dogs in France at the end of the hunting season and some of them were mated with French dogs.

This adaptable and reliable dog is good with children and an ideal companion for an active, rural owner

Formerly known as the Brittany Spaniel, and as the Epagneul Breton in its native France, this breed is now generally referred to simply as the Brittany, and its hunting style is more like that of a pointer or setter (focused on locating game) than a spaniel (which is used to flush out quarry). This quick, agile gundog is used for hunting birds and certain other quarry, such as rabbits; it can retrieve game but is best at simply locating game birds.

A long-established type of hunting dog, the Brittany is named for the region of northwest France where it originated. The first recognizable Brittany types are shown in paintings and tapestries dating from the 17th century. The dog became popular with the French nobility—and its obedience, together with its skill at pointing and retrieving, also made it a useful dog for poachers. The breed was officially recognized in France in 1907.

Today the Brittany is popular both as a sporting dog and as a good-natured, gentle family companion. It is an energetic breed needing plenty of exercise as well as mentally challenging activity, so is more suited to rural homes. Some Brittanys are born tail-less or bobtailed.

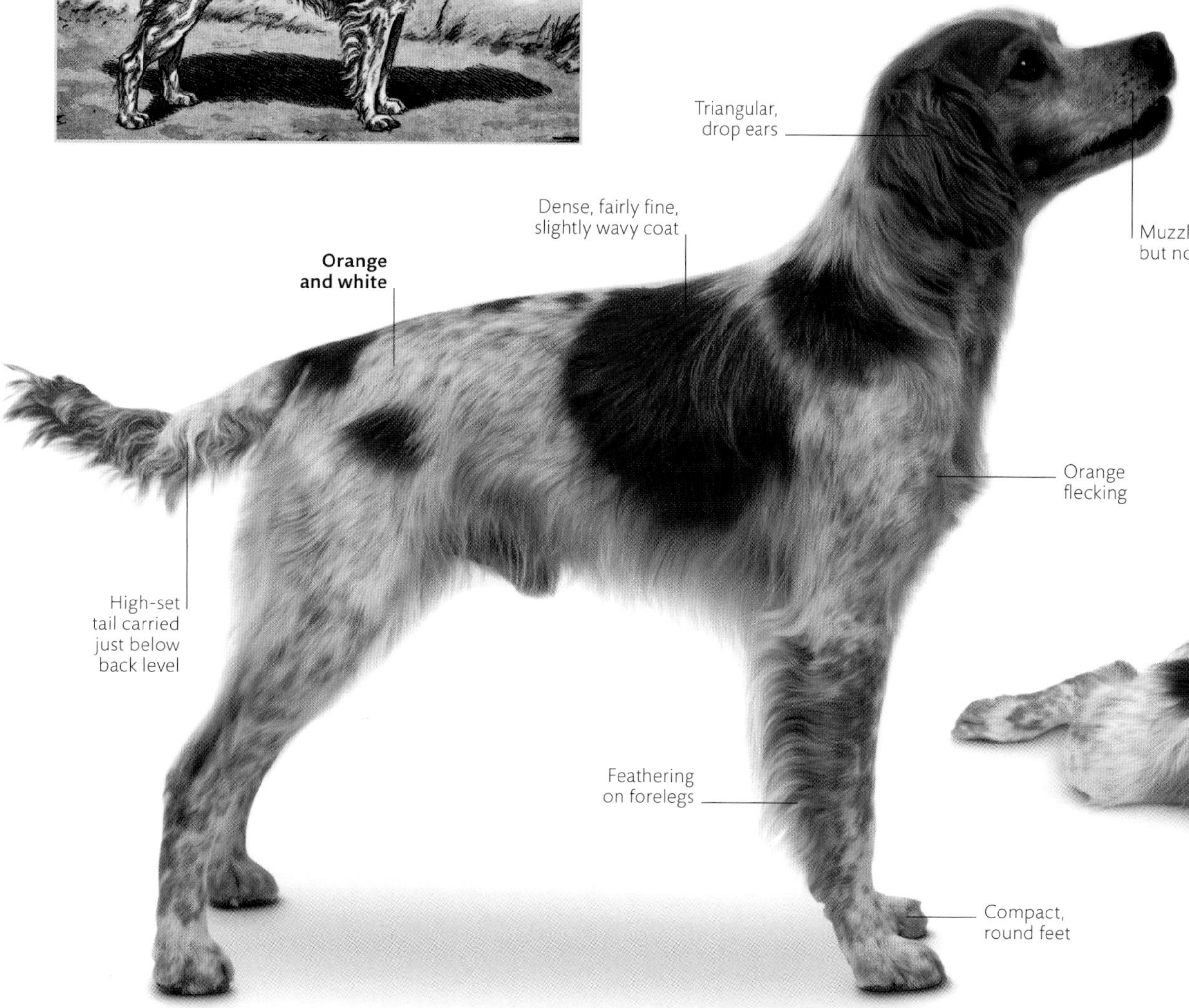

Triangular, drop ears

Muzzle tapered but not pointed

Dense, fairly fine, slightly wavy coat

Orange and white

Oval, dark eyes

Orange flecking

High-set tail carried just below back level

Feathering on forelegs

Compact, round feet

Large Munsterlander

HEIGHT 23–26in (58–65cm)
WEIGHT 65–68lb (29–31kg)
LIFE SPAN 12–13 years

The Grosser Munsterlander, as it is called in Germany, is more closely related to the German Pointer (see p.244) than the Small Munsterlander (below). It is slow to mature, but makes a calm, highly trainable, and versatile gundog. It positively thrives on close human company and is good with children.

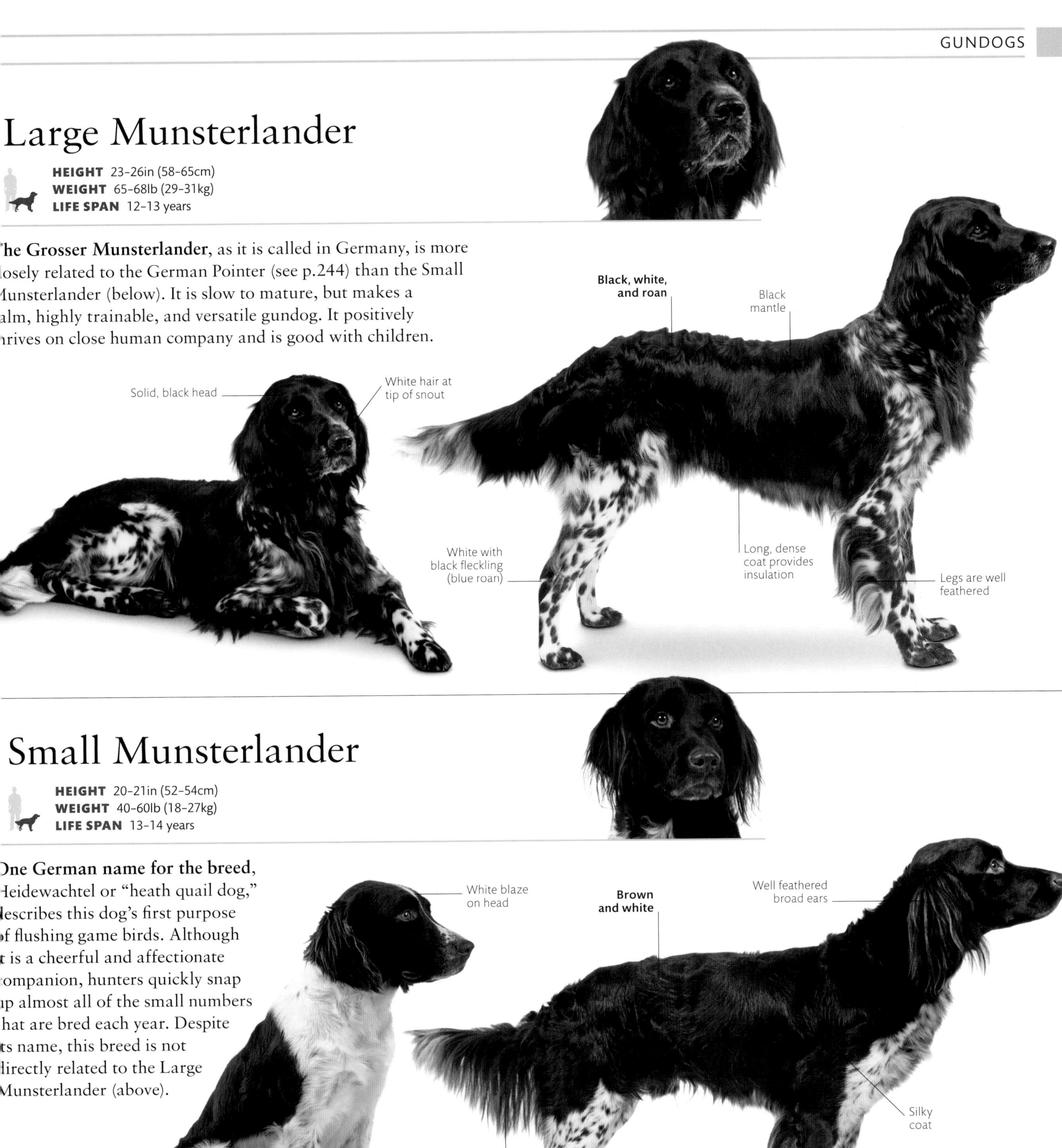

Small Munsterlander

HEIGHT 20–21in (52–54cm)
WEIGHT 40–60lb (18–27kg)
LIFE SPAN 13–14 years

One German name for the breed, Heidewachtel or "heath quail dog," describes this dog's first purpose of flushing game birds. Although it is a cheerful and affectionate companion, hunters quickly snap up almost all of the small numbers that are bred each year. Despite its name, this breed is not directly related to the Large Munsterlander (above).

Pont-Audemer Spaniel

HEIGHT	WEIGHT	LIFE SPAN	
20–23in (51–58cm)	40–53lb (18–24kg)	12–14 years	 Brown

This engaging breed is gentle and relaxed in the home but loves open spaces so is not well suited to city life

This rare French pointer and retriever is a specialist at hunting in water and swampland. The breed is believed to have originated in the 19th century in the marshy Pont-Audemer region of Normandy, in northwest France. It is thought that some of the dogs at that time were crossed with British dogs brought over by English huntsmen and left in France at the end of the hunting season. Many people consider that the breed also includes the Irish Water Spaniel (see p.228) in its early history.

During the 20th century the numbers of these dogs fell so low that concerted efforts had to be made to rescue the breed. It survived in small numbers and is still mainly used for hunting today. The Pont-Audemer Spaniel was traditionally used for flushing small waterfowl. However, it was also trained to be an all-purpose gundog that could point and retrieve, too. While its ancestry predisposes it to working in water, it can also work in woodland and thick undergrowth to hunt rabbit, hare, and pheasant.

Pont-Audemer Spaniels are not often kept purely as pets, but do make amiable family dogs. Its happy, amusing character has earned it the nickname "the little clown of the marshes." It ideally needs a rural home with plenty of space to run freely. The curly, ruffled-looking coat is not particularly difficult to maintain, although it does need to be brushed once or twice a week.

Tail slightly curved with lighter-colored tip

A BREED IN CRISIS

The Pont-Audemer Spaniel (seen below in a French print from 1907) has never been well-known, even in its native France, and by the end of the 19th century its numbers were declining. Breeders worked to revive the breed, but by the 1940s it was almost extinct. In 1949, to relieve concerns about inbreeding, crosses were made with the Irish Water Spaniel, but numbers still remained very low. In 1980 the breed society for the Pont-Audemer Spaniel combined with the societies for the Picardy Spaniel (see p.239) and Blue Picardy Spaniel (see p.239) to make a united effort to save all three breeds from extinction.

Rounded skull with topknot of curly hair
Drop ears covered with long, silky hair
Brown and gray mottled
Long, slightly pointed muzzle
Brown patch
Deep, broad chest reaches elbows
Small, dark amber eyes
Curly, disheveled-looking coat
Round feet with long, curly hair between toes

Kooikerhondje

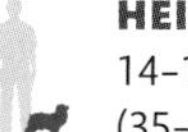

HEIGHT	WEIGHT	LIFE SPAN
14–16in (35–40cm)	20–24lb (9–11kg)	12–13 years

FOILING AN ASSASSIN

In the 17th century Dutch masters depicted similar dogs to the Kooikerhondje in paintings of family groups, such as Jan Steen's painting *The Way You Hear It Is the Way You Sing It* (below). Kooikerhondjes were well regarded as loyal and affectionate companions, and one dog named Kuntze is accredited with saving the life of Prince William II of Orange (1626–50). One night during the war between Holland and Spain, Kuntze woke William to warn him of intruders—and saved him from being assassinated. From that day on the grateful prince kept a Kooikerhondje by his side.

This cheerful, energetic dog makes a friendly pet, but its love of open spaces means it is not suited to city life

This Dutch breed goes by several names, including Kooikerhondje and Dutch Decoy Spaniel, which describe its unusual role. The Kooikerhondje was traditionally used for hunting ducks and other waterfowl. Romping and waving its flaglike tail, never barking, it would attract the attention of waterfowl and lure them into a tunnel-shaped trap on the water, called a *kooi* in Dutch. Hunters could then catch the bird alive.

Dogs of this type have existed since at least the 16th century, but by the 1940s the Kooikerhondje had become almost extinct. A noblewoman named Baroness van Hardenbroek van Ammerstol rescued and restored the breed. Today the Kooikerhondj remains rare, but is becoming more popular in Europe and North America. The dog continues to perform its traditional task of luring waterfowl, but is now used mostly by conservationists working to tag and release birds. Some Kooikerhondjes have also been trained for search and rescue work. The breed makes a playful, good-natured family dog, although it is perhaps too sensitive for life with young or boisterous children. It is dedicated to its owners but can be aloof toward strangers.

Drop ears covered in long, silky hair

Shorter hair on face

Long hair on neck forms ruff

Orange-red patches on pure white

Well feathered tail

Feathering on front legs

Small, harelike feet

Sleek, slightly wavy coat

Alert, almond-shaped, deep brown eyes

White blaze on face

Frisian Pointing Dog

HEIGHT 20–21in (50–53cm)
WEIGHT 42–55lb (19–25kg)
LIFE SPAN 12–14 years

 Orange with white markings

red by farmers, this dog—also known as the Stabyhoun—acks, points, and retrieves alongside hunters. It makes an active nd even-tempered family companion, and is excellent with nildren. This breed, despite efforts to improve its numbers, emains rare even in its native Netherlands.

Drentsche Partridge Dog

HEIGHT 22–25in (55–63cm)
WEIGHT 44–55lb (20–25kg)
LIFE SPAN 12–13 years

Somewhere between a pointer and a retriever, the Drentsche Partridge Dog, or Patrijshond, is a typically versatile European hunting dog related to the Small Münsterländer (see p.235) and the French Spaniel (see p.240). This Dutch breed is a reliable and relaxed family companion as long as it gets enough activity.

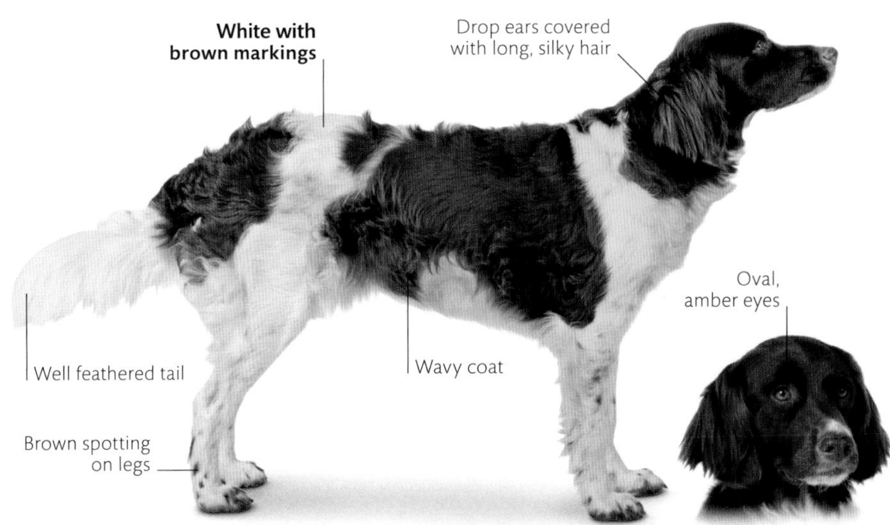

Picardy Spaniel

HEIGHT 22–24in (55–60cm)
WEIGHT 44–55lb (20–25kg)
LIFE SPAN 12–14 years

ne of the oldest spaniel breeds, the Picardy Spaniel is still sed in France to flush birds in woodland and wetland areas. An nthusiastic swimmer, it makes a placid, reliable, and affectionate mily dog that will even adapt to city life if given a reasonable mount of exercise.

Blue Picardy Spaniel

HEIGHT 22–24in (57–60cm)
WEIGHT 44–46lb (20–21kg)
LIFE SPAN 11–13 years

Mainly used as a water dog for pointing and retrieving snipe in marshland, this quiet and easy-going breed is a fun-loving companion and good with children. The Blue Picardy Spaniel's friendly temperament, however, makes it of little use for guarding.

French Spaniel

HEIGHT 22–24in (55–61cm)
WEIGHT 44–55lb (20–25kg)
LIFE SPAN 12–14 years

In its native land the French Spaniel is claimed to be the original of all hunting spaniels. It is still used for hunting at home and abroad, but because it is level-headed and not inclined to bark, it also makes a good city dog, as long as it is given enough exercise and affection.

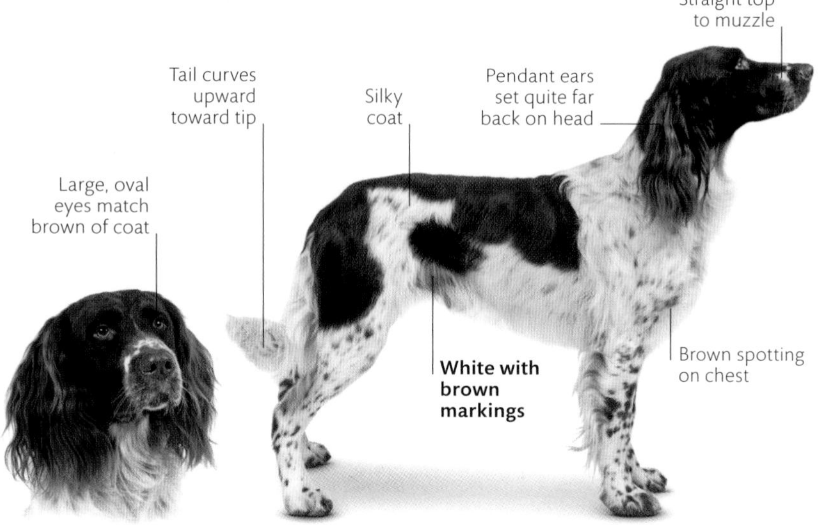

Irish Red and White Setter

HEIGHT 25–27in (64–69cm)
WEIGHT 55–75lb (25–34kg)
LIFE SPAN 12–13 years

This setter has the red and white coloring that is typical of many hunting dogs, but today this dog is more often kept for company. Long overshadowed by the related Irish Setter (see p.242), this intelligent if impulsive breed is slowly gaining the popularity it deserves. Cheerful and energetic, it thrives on attention and firm guidance.

Gordon Setter

HEIGHT 24–26in (62–66cm)
WEIGHT 57–66lb (26–30kg)
LIFE SPAN 12–13 years

Originally employed in Scotland to track game birds and then freeze once it had located them, changes in hunting fashions have seen this breed move from field to fireside. It brings with it a level-headed and loyal nature, but also a need for vigorous daily exercise and a good deal of space.

English Setter

HEIGHT	WEIGHT	LIFE SPAN	
24–25in (61–64cm)	55–66lb (25–30kg)	12–13 years	 Orange or lemon belton Liver belton Liver beltons may have tan markings.

EDWARD LAVERACK

In the 19th century breeder Edward Laverack transformed the traditional English Setter. From two dogs, which he obtained in 1825, Laverack developed a distinct strain that set game birds in a more upright stance than was usual, and that was taller, more lightly built, and more heavily feathered than the earlier dogs. Laverack's dogs formed the basis of the breed standard drawn up in the 1870s. The trading card from around 1890 (below) shows an early example of the English Setter.

The perfect country-house dog in both looks and character, this tireless breed loves wide open spaces

The oldest of the Setter dogs, which date back at least 400 years, this breed takes its name from its habit of setting—stopping and facing the game it has located—that enables the hunter to find the animal. The English Setter's ancestors probably included the English Springer Spaniel (see pp.224–25), the Spanish Pointer, and large Water Spaniels. The result was a dog that was skilled in tracking and finding game on open moorland.

The modern breed was founded by two men. Edward Laverack developed the pure English Setter in the 1820s. In the late 19th century R. Purcell Llewellin used some of the Laverack dogs to breed a distinct strain for field work. His dogs differed in appearance from those of Laverack's and some people referred to Llewellin setters as a separate breed.

The English Setter is still worked today, although different bloodlines are used for hunting and the show ring. The hunting dogs have slightly shorter legs than their Irish and Scottish cousins. An elegant dog, the English Setter has a calm, reliable nature, making it a good family dog. However, it does need lots of exercise and space to run. Show dogs have a longer, more wavy coat than the field type.

Low-set, pendant ears

Square muzzle with slightly pendulous flews

Blue belton

Well feathered tail

Light tan markings on face

Irish Setter

HEIGHT	WEIGHT	LIFE SPAN
25–27in (64–69cm)	60–71lb (27–32kg)	12–13 years

his exuberant, enthusiastic dog is both glamorous nd affectionate but needs a patient and active owner

unting dogs called "setters"—dogs that ould crouch, or "set," near game birds to ıow the birds' location—were first entioned in English texts of the late 16th • early 17th century and were recognized as distinct type in the 18th century. The Irish ›tter was created in the 18th century, ›ssibly from crosses of breeds including the nglish Setter (see p.241), the Gordon Setter ee p.240), and the Irish Water Spaniel (see .228), as well as other spaniels and ›inters. Bred for hunting birds in upland ·eas, it was valued for its speed, efficiency, and keen nose.

The first dogs were red and white like today's Irish Red and White Setter (see p.240), but during the 19th century the deep, rich red color became the standard for the Irish Setter. Even now, however, some dogs are born with small, white markings.

By the 1850s the red Irish Setter had spread through Ireland and the UK, and began to be seen in the show ring. A male named Palmerston, born in 1862, was the first champion show and stud dog and is the ancestor of most modern Irish setters. Today the breed is mainly a show dog or a companion, but some breeders still produce dogs for working ability as well as looks.

The Irish Setter makes a striking, affectionate pet with a love of children and other dogs and a great sense of fun. Slow to mature, it requires firm training from an early age. The breed needs a home where it will have plenty of daily exercise, including chances to run freely.

BIG RED

In North America the Irish Setter's free spirit was made famous by the 1962 Disney film *Big Red*. Set in Canada, the film tells of a champion show dog, Big Red, who makes friends with an orphan boy called René. Big Red becomes more interested in hunting with René than being a good show dog, and as a result his owner gets rid of him. Big Red escapes across country and is reunited with René when the two friends heroically save the dog's owner from a cougar.

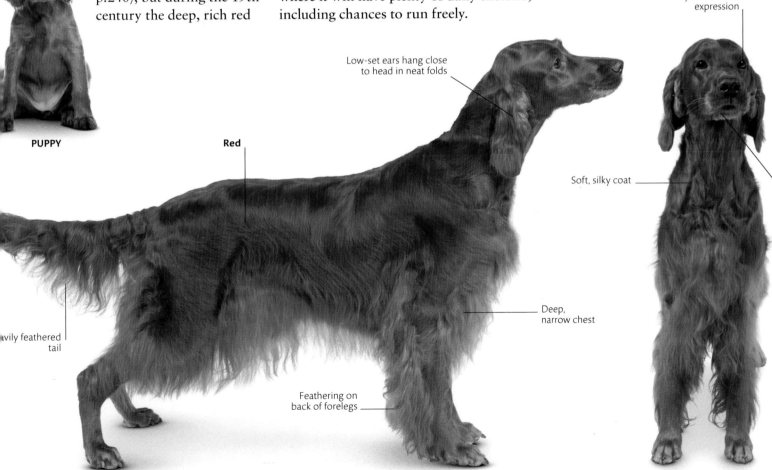

PUPPY

Red

Low-set ears hang close to head in neat folds

ıvily feathered tail

Feathering on back of forelegs

Deep, narrow chest

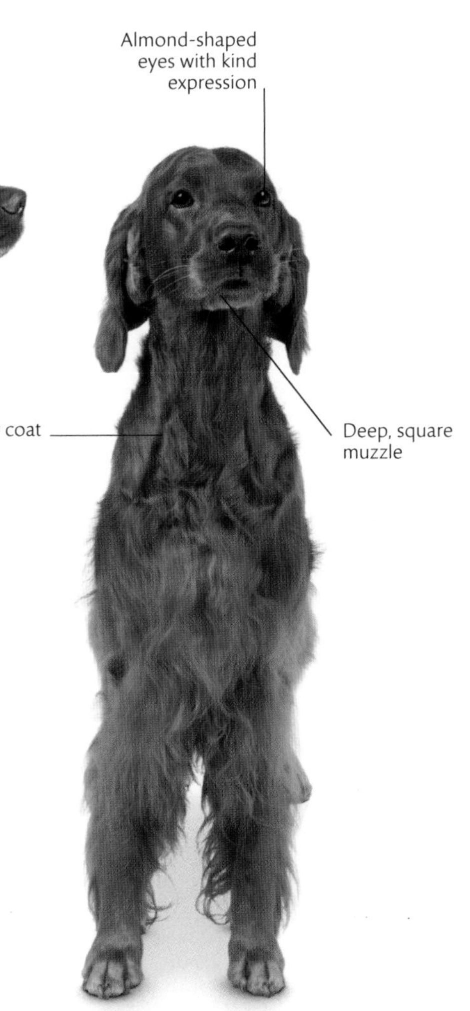

Nova Scotia Duck Tolling Retriever

HEIGHT	WEIGHT	LIFE SPAN
18–21in (45–53cm)	37–51lb (17–23kg)	12–13 years

CUNNING AS A FOX

Tolling is naturally practiced by foxes. One or two foxes will tantalize waterfowl by playing near them at the waterside. The birds will come closer to drive the foxes away and sometimes stray close enough for the foxes to catch them. Native Americans copied this trick by pulling a fox pelt back and forth on a rope to catch ducks. Europeans bred red-coated dogs resembling foxes and trained them to act in the same way. The foxlike coloring and the behavior (below) can be seen in the Nova Scotia Duck Tolling Retriever.

This good-natured, attractive gundog adapts well to family life if given sufficient physical activity

This Canadian breed, also known as the Toller, takes its name from its role in an unusual form of duck and goose hunting. Traditionally, the dog worked with hunters in a hide. The concealed hunter threw a stick for the dog, which would chase it with a great show of activity but no barking, and this activity would lure in, or toll, inquisitive birds. Once the birds were within range, the hunter could shoot them and the dog retrieve them.

The Nova Scotia Duck Tolling Retriever originated in Nova Scotia in the mid-19th century. It is descended from "decoy dogs" brought over from Europe; its tolling method is similar to that of breeds such as the Kooikerhondje (see p.238). These dogs were crossed with spaniels, retrievers, and the Irish Setter (see p.242). The breed acquired its present name when the Canadian Kennel Club recognized it in 1945.

The Nova Scotia Duck Tolling Retriever is compact and agile, with a thick, water-repellent coat and webbing between its toes. The coat is reddish, often with a white chest and tail tip, like a fox's pelt. The dog's playful, quiet, and obedient nature makes it an excellent companion. It is also tireless, so needs plenty of exercise.

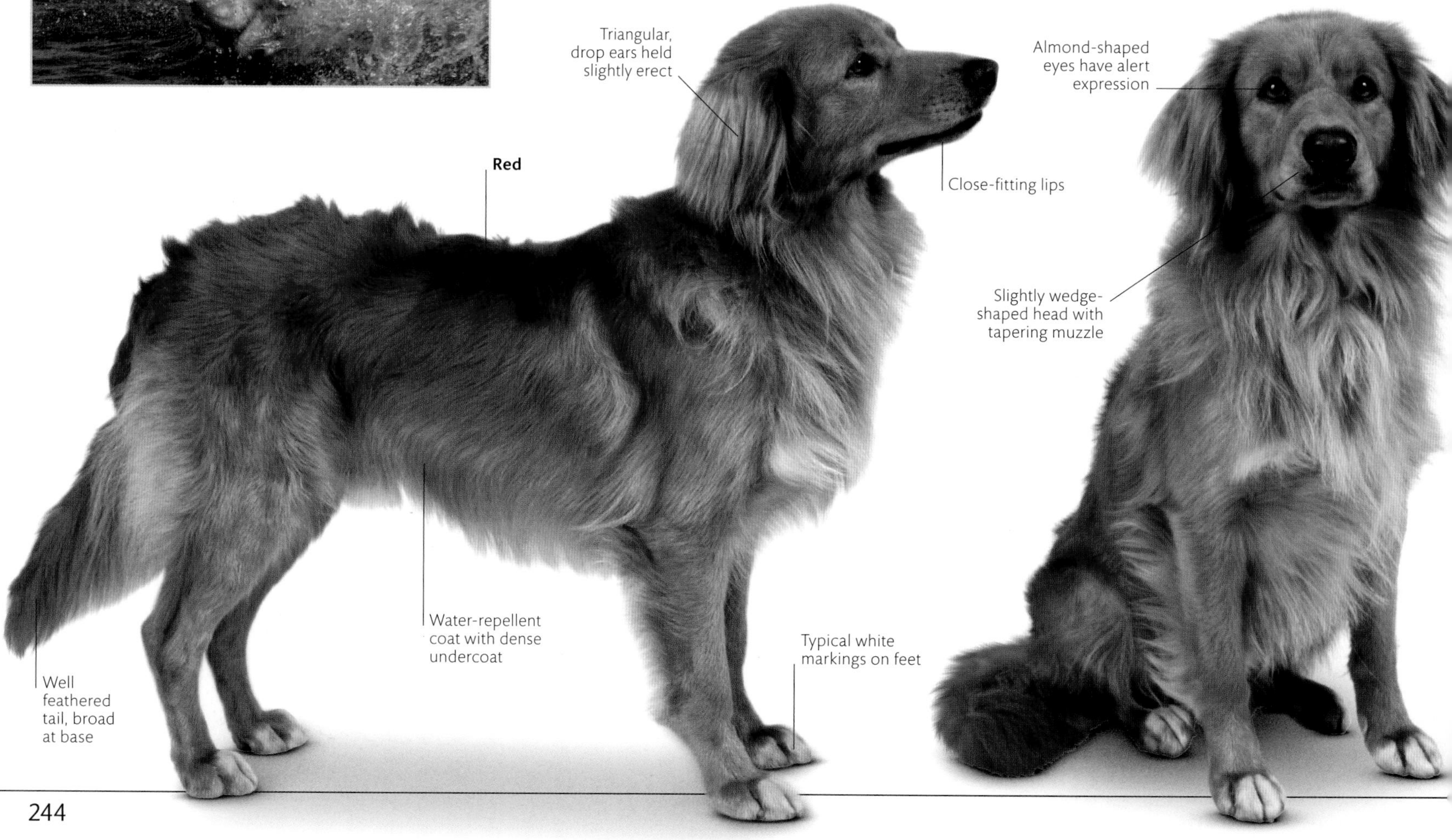

German Pointer

HEIGHT	WEIGHT	LIFE SPAN	
21–25in (53–64cm)	44–71lb (20–32kg)	10–14 years	Liver Brown Black

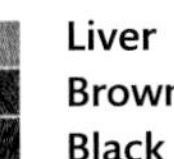

This popular, intelligent breed is genial and gentle if kept busy, so it makes a rewarding family pet for active owners

A superlative all-purpose hunting dog that tracks, points, and retrieves over any terrain from grassland to marshland, the German Pointer originated in the 19th century. Breeders, led by Prince Albrecht zu Solms-Braunfels, crossed German hounds and retriever breeds, including the Schweisshund (a heavy, houndlike dog that could both track game and point), and the Pointer (see p.254) to add speed, agility, and elegance.

There are three varieties of German Pointer. The main variety, and by far the best known, is the German Shorthaired Pointer (Deutsch Kurzhaar), called GSP by British hunters. It dates from the 1880s. This breed has become one of the most popular hunting dogs in the world. The German Longhaired Pointer (Deutsch Langhaar) appeared at about the same time. The German Wirehaired Pointer (Deutsch Drahthaar) was developed slightly later, from the German Shorthaired Pointer.

In its homeland the German Pointer has always been kept for the family as well as the hunt, and it is generally level-headed and reliable with people. This is an energetic dog, however, and needs a lot of exercise each day. It does best with hunters and people who like to run, hike, or cycle.

HPR BREEDS

The German Pointers belong to a group of all-purpose gundogs known as the hunt, point, retrieve (HPR) breeds. HPR breeds originated in mainland Europe, where hunters might only have kept one or two dogs to perform a variety of tasks. Other examples include the Weimaraner (see p.248), the Viszla (see p.246), and the Spinone Italiano (see p.250). By contrast, British breeders focused on producing gundogs for specific tasks and particular types of game, such as the Cocker Spaniel (see p.222), bred for flushing out woodcock.

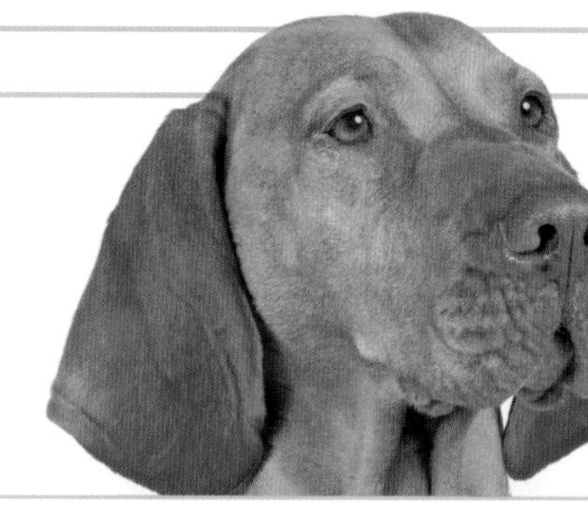

Vizsla

HEIGHT	WEIGHT	LIFE SPAN
21–25in (53–64cm)	44–66lb (20–30kg)	13–14 years

This loyal and gentle dog makes an attractive family companion, but its high energy levels need to be satisfied

Ancestors of the Vizsla, a typical European all-purpose hunting dog, appear in written texts from the 14th century, and may have existed even earlier. Stone carvings dating back 1,000 years show Magyar hunters with falcons and dogs that resembled the Vizsla. For centuries the Vizsla was a favorite with the Hungarian aristocracy, who kept the bloodlines pure; it was known as the "Gift of Kings," presented only to royalty and the most select of foreigners. The breed almost died out after World War II, but Hungarian emigrants brought the dogs to western Europe and the US, where it is now increasingly popular.

In the hunting field the Vizsla has speed and stamina and will work all day in any conditions, on land or in water. It has been used to hunt a variety of game, including duck, rabbit, wolf, and boar. The breed has an excellent nose for tracking and a soft mouth for retrieving. It is intelligent and responds well to training.

Although a hunting dog, the Vizsla has always been a family companion as well; traditionally, it was said that the dog was as much a part of the family as the children. The breed is very loyal and loving but needs plenty of vigorous exercise every day.

There are two varieties: the original short-haired type, also known as the Hungarian Pointer, and the wire-haired variety, which was developed in the 1930s and has a sturdier build.

YOGI—SHOW CHAMPION

In the show ring the most famous Vizsla is a male named Yogi (registered name Hungargunn Bear It'n Mind). Born in 2002 in Australia, he won his first "Best in Show" at the age of only 12 weeks. In 2005 Yogi was brought to the UK, where he has had a dazzling show career. By 2010 he had won 17 UK "Best in Show" titles, breaking a record that had stood for more than 70 years. He went on to win "Best in Show" at Crufts in 2010 (below, with the trophy and his handler, John Thirwell) before being retired to stud.

WIRE-HAIRED PUPPY

Slightly curved tail tapers to pointed tip

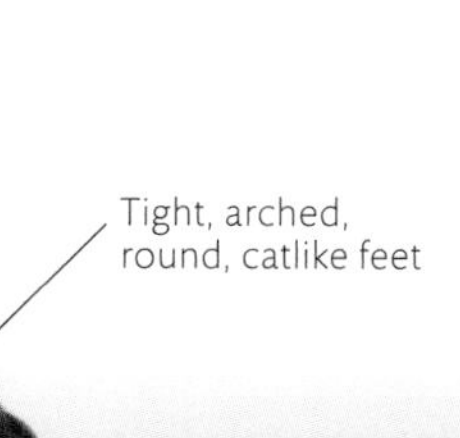

Tight, arched, round, catlike feet

Nose color matches coat
Strong, muscular back
Smooth, arched neck is muscular
Distinctive, sleek coat lacks insulating undercoat
Eyes slightly darker than coat color
Slightly shorter hair on drop ears
Tapering muzzle is square at end
Golden-russet
Long forearms

SHORT-HAIRED

WIRE-HAIRED

Weimaraner

HEIGHT	WEIGHT	LIFE SPAN
22–27in (56–69cm)	55–90lb (25–41kg)	12–13 years

PHOTOGRAPHIC BEAUTY

Since the 1970s American artist William Wegman (pictured below) has used his Weimaraners for inspiration in his photographs and video work, starting with his dog Man Ray (named after the Surrealist artist and photographer). Wegman highlights the beauty of the Weimaraner's body shape and the texture of the fur. He also draws on the breed's otherworldly appearance by showing his dogs posing in odd settings, peculiar costumes, or mysterious films.

This elegant, unusually colored, and intelligent dog has boundless energy so needs plenty of space to explore

Created as an all-purpose hunting, pointing, and retrieving gundog (HPR breed, see p.245), this 19th-century breed is descended from various German hunting dogs. The Weimaraner takes its name from the German Court of Weimar, where it was developed, and for a long time it was mainly kept by the nobility. At first it was used for bringing down big game such as wolves and deer, but later it was used for retrieving birds from land or water.

The Weimaraner has a smooth, powerful gait and great stamina. It is also known as a careful, almost stealthy dog in the field. This style of working, together with the striking silver-gray coat and pale eyes, has given rise to the breed's nickname, the "Gray Ghost." Elegant lines, silver-gray color, and grace in movement have made this breed popular as a show dog and pet as well as a working animal. While the Weimaraner may be reserved with strangers, it is a bouncy family companion and can be too boisterous for small children. The breed needs lots of exercise, including running and exploring, as an outlet for its energy. There are two coat types: short-haired, and the much less common long-haired type.

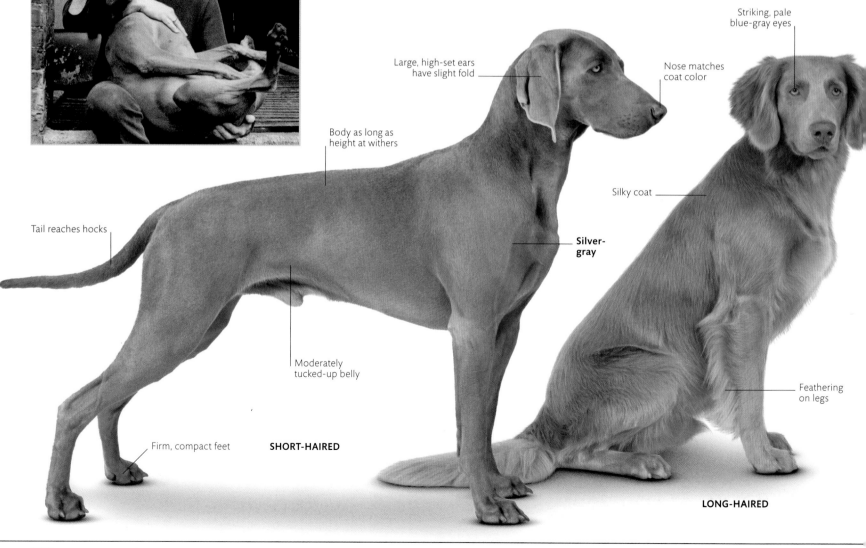

Cesky Fousek

HEIGHT 23–26in (58–66cm)
WEIGHT 49–75lb (22–34kg)
LIFE SPAN 12–13 years

Brown
Brown coats may have ticked markings on chest and lower limbs.

'**his breed, variously claimed** to be of Czech, Slovakian, r Bohemian descent, is still popular in these areas but . rare elsewhere. It is loyal and trainable, and usually entle around people, but is a natural hunter and o may be unreliable with other pets.

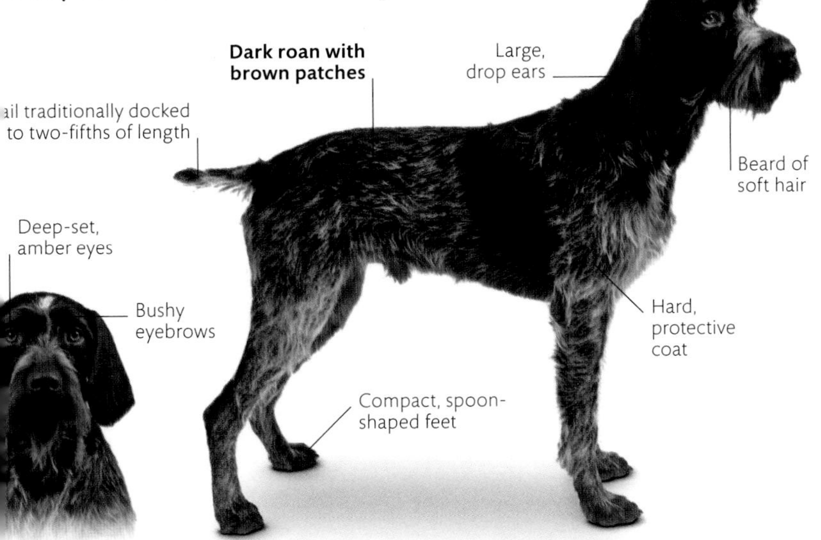

Wirehaired Pointing Griffon

HEIGHT 20–24in (50–60cm)
WEIGHT 51–60lb (23–27kg)
LIFE SPAN 12–13 years

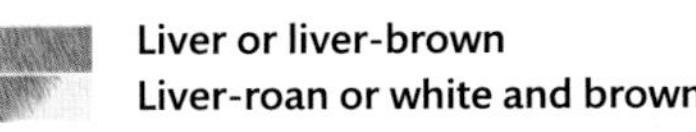

Liver or liver-brown
Liver-roan or white and brown

Related to the German Pointer (see p.245), bred by Dutchman Edward Korthals, and adopted by French hunters, this is a versatile and easy-going breed. It is not the fastest gundog, but it is popular for hunting where obedient, close-working dogs are needed—qualities that also make it a valuable companion.

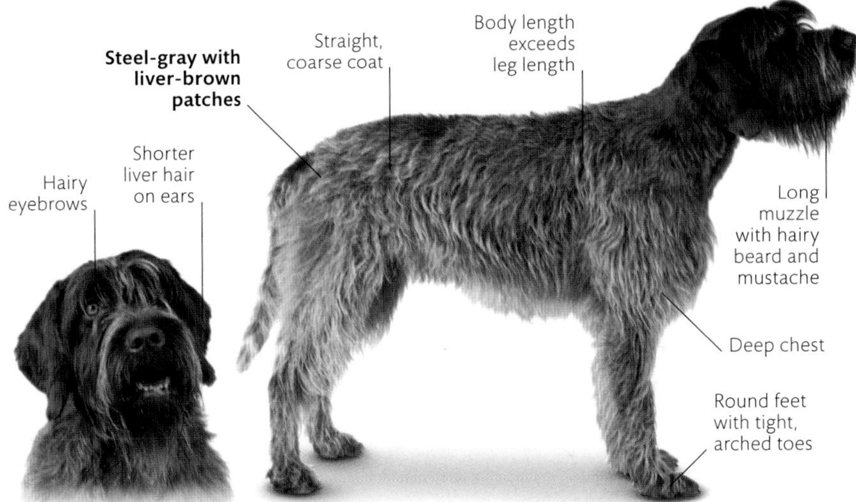

Portuguese Pointing Dog

HEIGHT 20–22in (52–56cm)
WEIGHT 35–60lb (16–27kg)
LIFE SPAN 12–14 years

Also known as the Perdigueiro Português, which literally means the Portuguese partridge dog, this breed was used as a pointer for hunters with falcons or nets. Still worked today, the Portuguese Pointing Dog is level-headed and obedient and so also makes an amenable companion. However, this tenacious hunter needs considerable mental and physical activity every day.

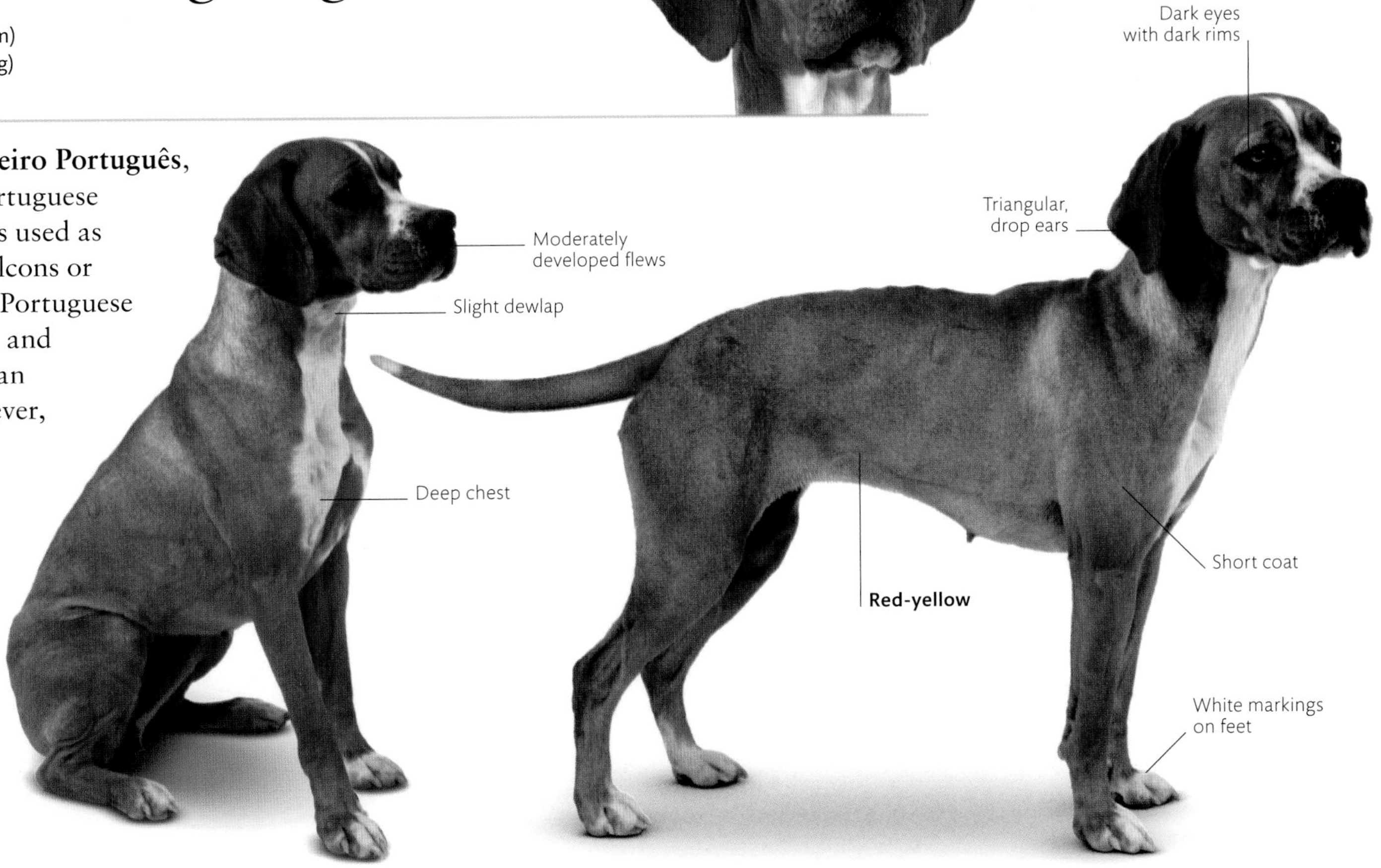

Dark eyes with dark rims

Moderately developed flews

Slight dewlap

Triangular, drop ears

Deep chest

Short coat

Red-yellow

White markings on feet

Spinone Italiano

HEIGHT	WEIGHT	LIFE SPAN	
23–28in (58–70cm)	65–85lb (29–39kg)	12–13 years	White Orange-roan White and brown or brown-roan

This easy-going and relaxed companion can be quickly distracted and is not ideal for house-proud owners

The origins of the Spinone Italiano are unclear, but wire-haired pointer-type dogs have been known in Italy since the time of the Renaissance; one such dog is featured in the mural "The Court of Gonzaga," painted in the 1470s by Andrea Mantegna in the ducal palace at Mantua.

The modern breed originated in the Piedmont region of northwest Italy, and acquired the name "Spinone" in the 19th century. This versatile "hunt, point, retrieve" breed (see p.245) was the region's most popular hunting dog until the 20th century. The Spinone Italiano played a vital role for Italian partisans during World War II, tracking enemy soldiers as well as bringing in food. By the end of the war the number of dogs was very low, so from the 1950s Italian breeders formed a club to save it from extinction.

The Spinone Italiano can follow both airborne and ground scents and will work even in heavy, thorny cover. It tracks quietly and thoroughly, hunting close to its handler and covering the ground in a zigzag fashion, at a long-striding trot. The dog's rough coat protects it even in dense thorn bushes and icy water. The Spinone Italiano is still worked, although the faster Bracco Italiano (see p.252) is now more popular for hunting in Italy.

In recent years the Spinone Italiano has become a popular pet in various countries, prized for its gentle temperament and loyalty. It needs plenty of daily exercise, but its tendency to move at a slower pace than many gundogs makes it a comfortable walking companion. The coat requires little care, aside from occasional brushing and hand-stripping, although it does retain smells.

PUPPY

A THORNY NAME

The breed now known as the Spinone Italiano once had a variety of names, according to the region in which it was bred. One name was Bracco Spinoso, "prickly pointer," thought to refer to the dog's rough, bristly coat. The name "Spinone" links to the word *pino*, the name for a kind of dense Italian thorn bush, because the Spinone, with its tough skin and coarse coat, was one of the few dogs that could push through the thorns to reach its quarry (shown here in a French print from 1907).

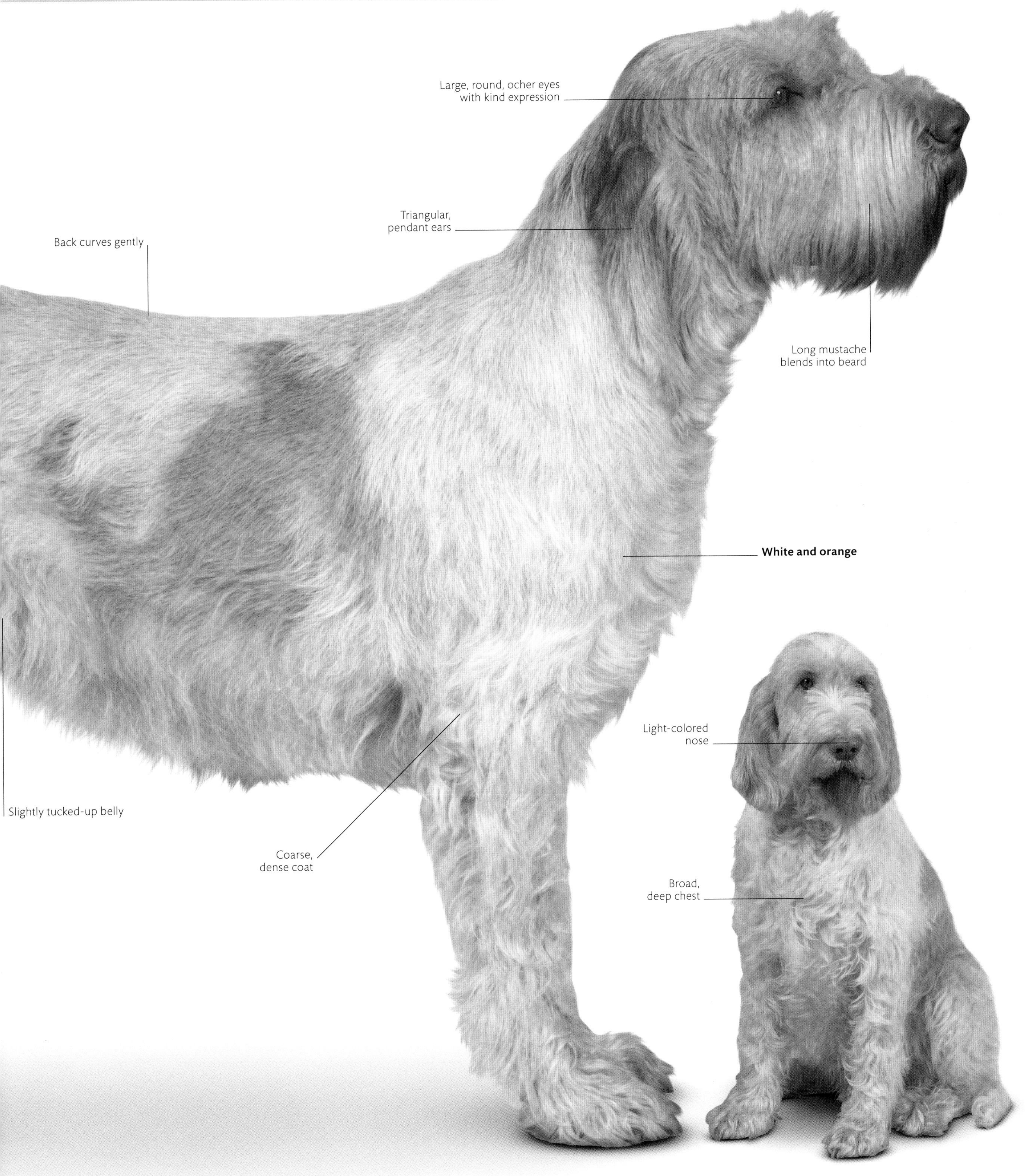
Large, round, ocher eyes
with kind expression
Triangular,
pendant ears
Back curves gently
Long mustache
blends into beard
White and orange
Light-colored
nose
Slightly tucked-up belly
Coarse,
dense coat
Broad,
deep chest

Bracco Italiano

HEIGHT	WEIGHT	LIFE SPAN	
22–26in (55–67cm)	55–88lb (25–40kg)	12–13 years	 White **White and orange, amber, or chestnut**

NOBLE HUNTER

During the Renaissance period dogs like the Bracco Italiano were popular with the Italian nobility. The dogs were used with falcons to hunt game birds. Aristocratic families such as the Medicis and the House of Gonzaga kept breeding kennels and produced dogs that were prized for their hunting skills. In 1527 it was recorded that some chestnut-colored dogs had been given to the Court of France as a present; the Piemontese dogs (seen below in a French print from 1907) were also highly sought after in royal courts across Europe.

This rare gundog is surprisingly athletic for its size, but its level-headedness makes it a suitable family pet

A breed from northern Italy, the Bracco Italiano, or Italian Pointer, has ancestors dating back to at least the Middle Ages. Dogs like this can be seen in paintings from the 14th century, when they were used to drive game birds into nets. Once hunters started using guns, the breed evolved into an all-purpose "hunt, point, retrieve" (HPR) gundog (see p.245).

By the 19th century there were two types: the tall, sturdy Bracco Lombardo from Lombardy, with a white and brown-roan coat, and the lighter, white-and-orange Bracco Piemontese, adapted for working in the mountains. Numbers had declined by the early 20th century but enthusiasts saved the breed, and the Italian Kennel Club drew up a standard for it in 1949. The two types were brought under one name, but the heavier and lighter dogs can still be seen today.

Still used as a working dog, the Bracco Italiano has a distinctive style of following a scent at a long-striding trot, with its nose held high—"led by the nose," as the Italians say. It is very fond of people and makes a calm, gentle companion, although it needs lots of exercise and may have to be walked on a leash to control its strong hunting drive.

Roan with chestnut markings

Pendant ears with rounded tips

Slightly arched muzzle

Nose matches coat color

Well developed flews

Powerful neck has soft dewlap

Oval-shaped feet

Tail tapers slightly

Pudelpointer

HEIGHT 22–27in (55–68cm)
WEIGHT 44–66lb (20–30kg)
LIFE SPAN 12–14 years

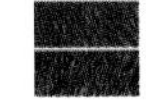

Dead leaf
Black

eveloped for both the field nd home, this cross of oodle and pointer aims o be the best of both: ntelligent, hardy, and ociable, with excellent ll-around working abilities. Aost popular with hunters, ne Pudelpointer is an menable and cheerful ural companion.

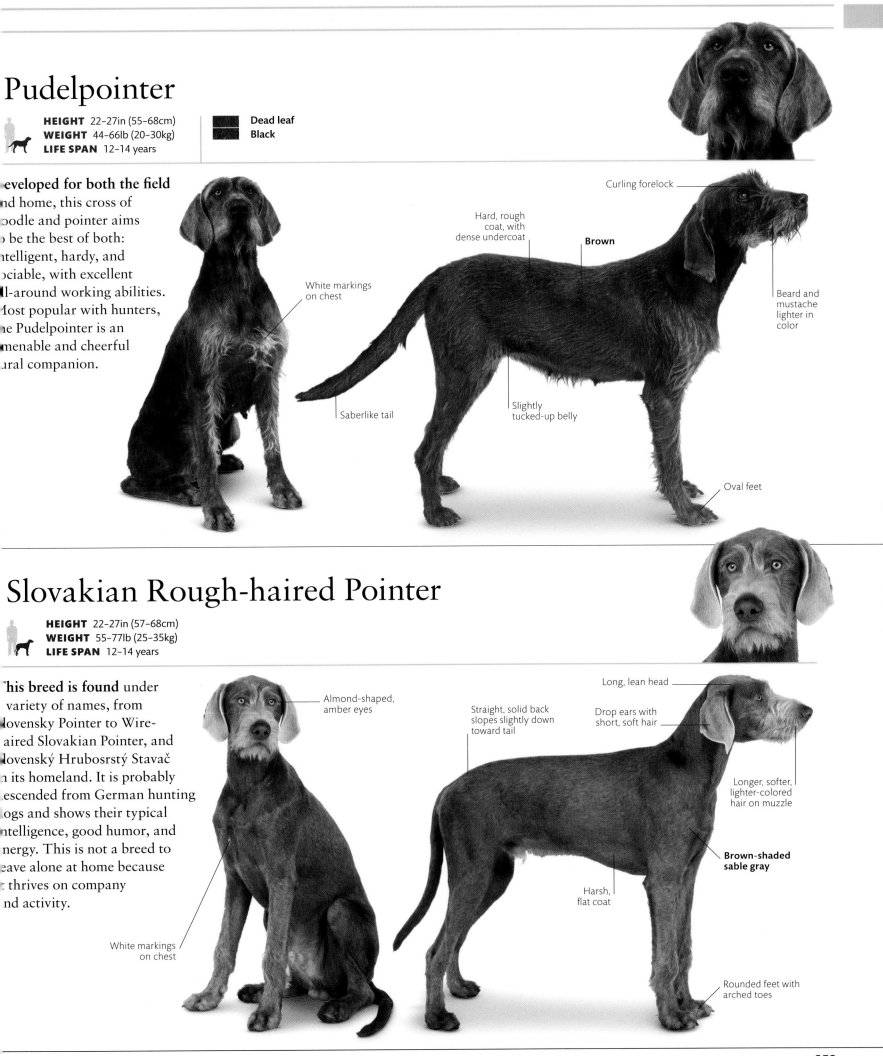

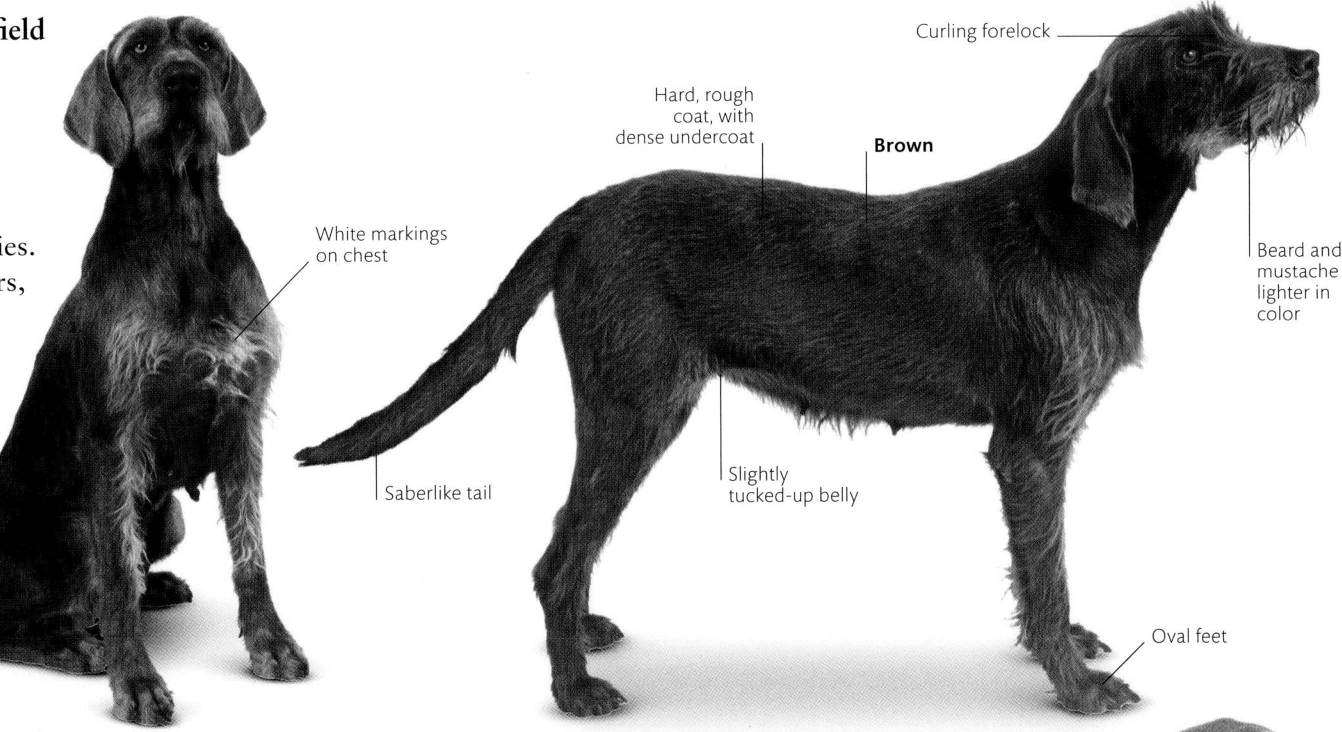

Slovakian Rough-haired Pointer

HEIGHT 22–27in (57–68cm)
WEIGHT 55–77lb (25–35kg)
LIFE SPAN 12–14 years

'his breed is found under variety of names, from lovensky Pointer to Wire-aired Slovakian Pointer, and lovenský Hrubosrstý Stavač n its homeland. It is probably escended from German hunting ogs and shows their typical ntelligence, good humor, and nergy. This is not a breed to eave alone at home because t thrives on company nd activity.

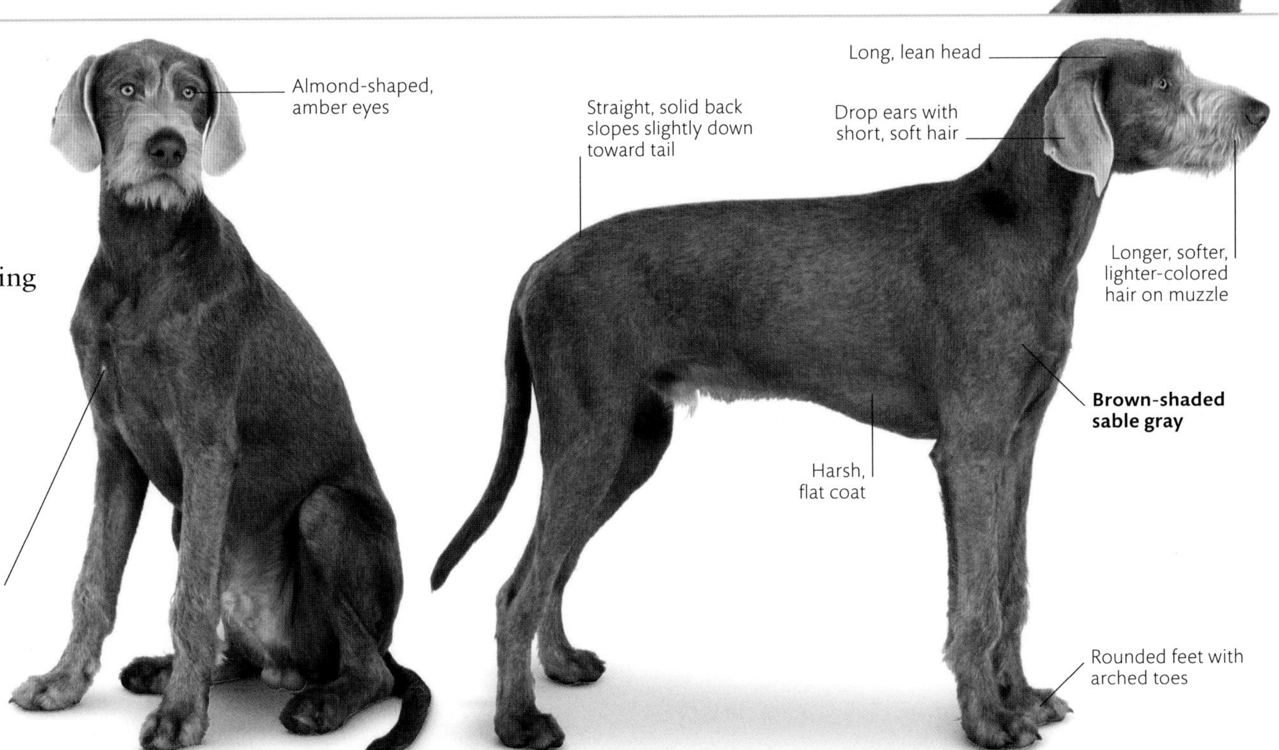

Pointer

HEIGHT	WEIGHT	LIFE SPAN	
21–25in (53–64cm)	45–75lb (20–34kg)	12–13 years	Variety of colors

·riendly and intelligent, this athletic dog needs plenty ·f physical and mental activity if kept as a pet

·ointers are a type of hunting dog ·amed for the stance they assume when they ·nd game: standing still, with one foot ·ised and their nose pointing in the ·irection of the game. These breeds ·eveloped in various European countries at ·e same time. In Britain ancestors of the ·ointer appeared around 1650. These early ·ogs may have resulted from crosses including ·e English Foxhound (see p.158), the Greyhound (see p.126), as well as an old type of "setting spaniel." Later, crosses with the Spanish hunting dogs and with setter breeds were made to improve the breed's pointing skill and trainability.

At first Pointers were used to "point" hare for Greyhounds to pursue, or used for hunting with falcons. From the 18th century, when it became popular to shoot birds on the wing, they were used to locate game birds, especially in upland areas. The breed has excellent air-scenting abilities, which help make it an effective pointer; it is less good at retrieving, although it is sometimes used for this purpose, too. The Pointer is noted for its speed and endurance, and is still used today in hunting and field trials in the US and the UK.

Pointers are gentle, loyal, and obedient. They are affectionate family companions and reliable with children, although they can be a little too boisterous with toddlers. The breed has retained its hunting stamina, so these dogs need plenty of vigorous exercise every day.

PUPPY

LITERARY POINTER

In the 19th century some Englishmen gave their Pointers Spanish names in recognition of the Spanish influence on the breed. One fictional example is Ponto, mentioned in *The Pickwick Papers* by Charles Dickens. The dog features in a tall tale told by the rascally Mr. Jingle; allegedly, during a day's shooting, Ponto stopped still, refusing to move, while staring at a notice saying that the gamekeeper would shoot all dogs in that area. Pointers are intelligent dogs—but reading may be beyond even their abilities!

ILLUSTRATION FROM AN 1837 EDITION OF *THE PICKWICK PAPERS*

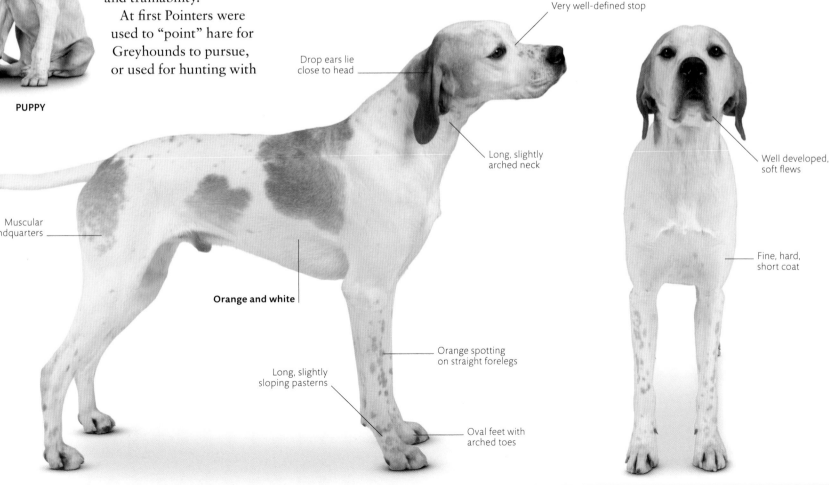

Very well-defined stop

Drop ears lie close to head

Long, slightly arched neck

Well developed, soft flews

Muscular ·ndquarters

Orange and white

Fine, hard, short coat

Orange spotting on straight forelegs

Long, slightly sloping pasterns

Oval feet with arched toes

French Pyrenean Pointer

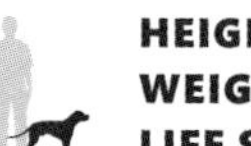

HEIGHT 19–23in (47–58cm)
WEIGHT 40–53lb (18–24kg)
LIFE SPAN 12–14 years

Chestnut-brown

Chestnut-brown dogs may have tan markings.

The most popular of the French pointers, the French Pyrenean Pointer is still rare and mostly used for hunting. A swift and tireless breed, it was created in southwest France to work in mountain terrain. It is gentle and affectionate at home, and makes an ideal companion for the more active owner.

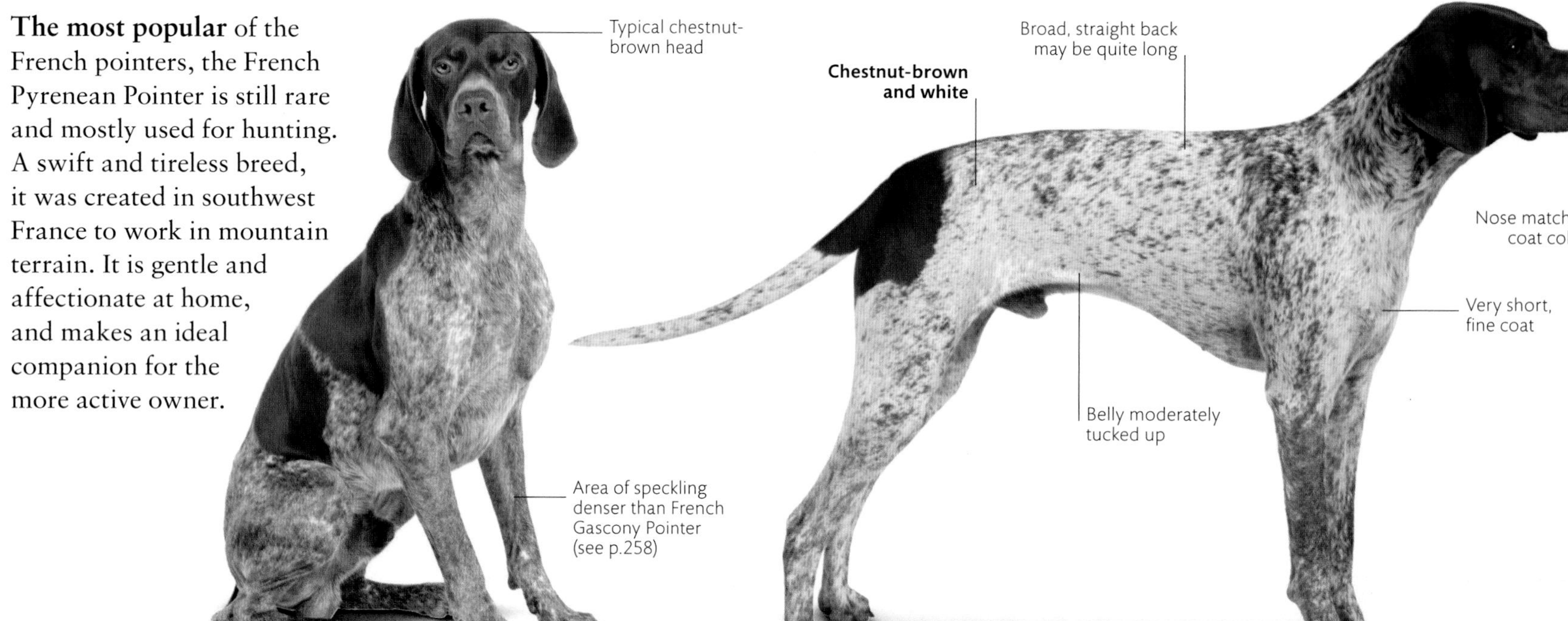

Saint Germain Pointer

HEIGHT 21–24in (54–62cm)
WEIGHT 40–57lb (18–26kg)
LIFE SPAN 12–14 years

Also known as the Braque Saint-Germain, this is a fleet-footed pointer and retriever of birds in field, woodland, and marshland. However, its coat is not sufficiently insulated to make it an all-weather dog. The Saint Germain Pointer is affectionate but sensitive, needing firm yet gentle handling, and adapts surprisingly well to urban family life.

Bourbonnais Pointing Dog

HEIGHT 19–22in (48–57cm)
WEIGHT 35–57lb (16–26kg)
LIFE SPAN 12–14 years

Brown, drop ears
with rounded tips

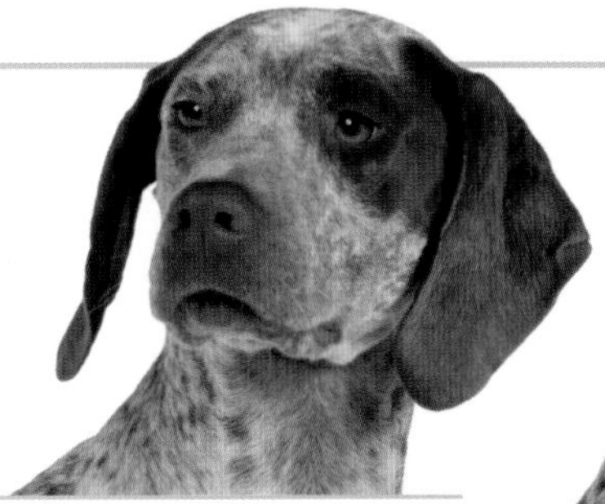

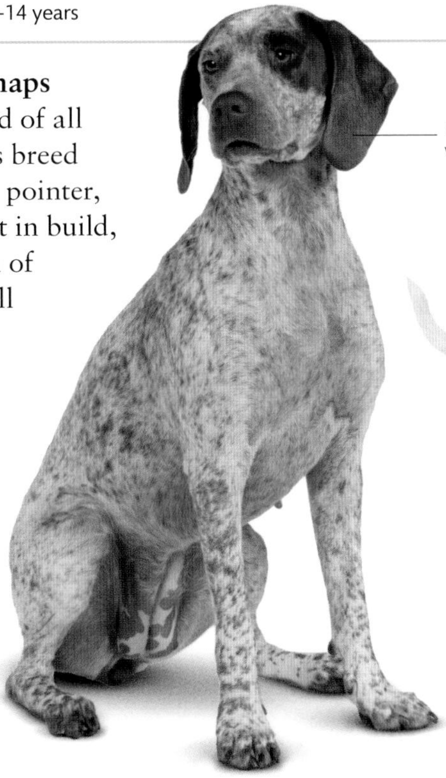

'he oldest and perhaps ıe most level-headed of all ·rench gundogs, this breed a versatile tracker, pointer, ıd retriever. Robust in build, ıving an impression of ower, this dog is full f stamina when ·orking but relaxed ıd affectionate ·hen off duty.

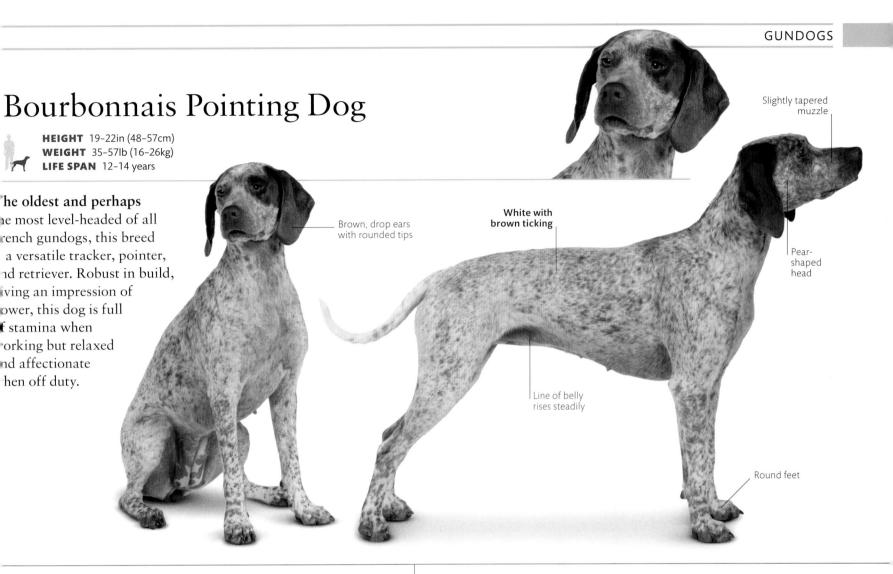

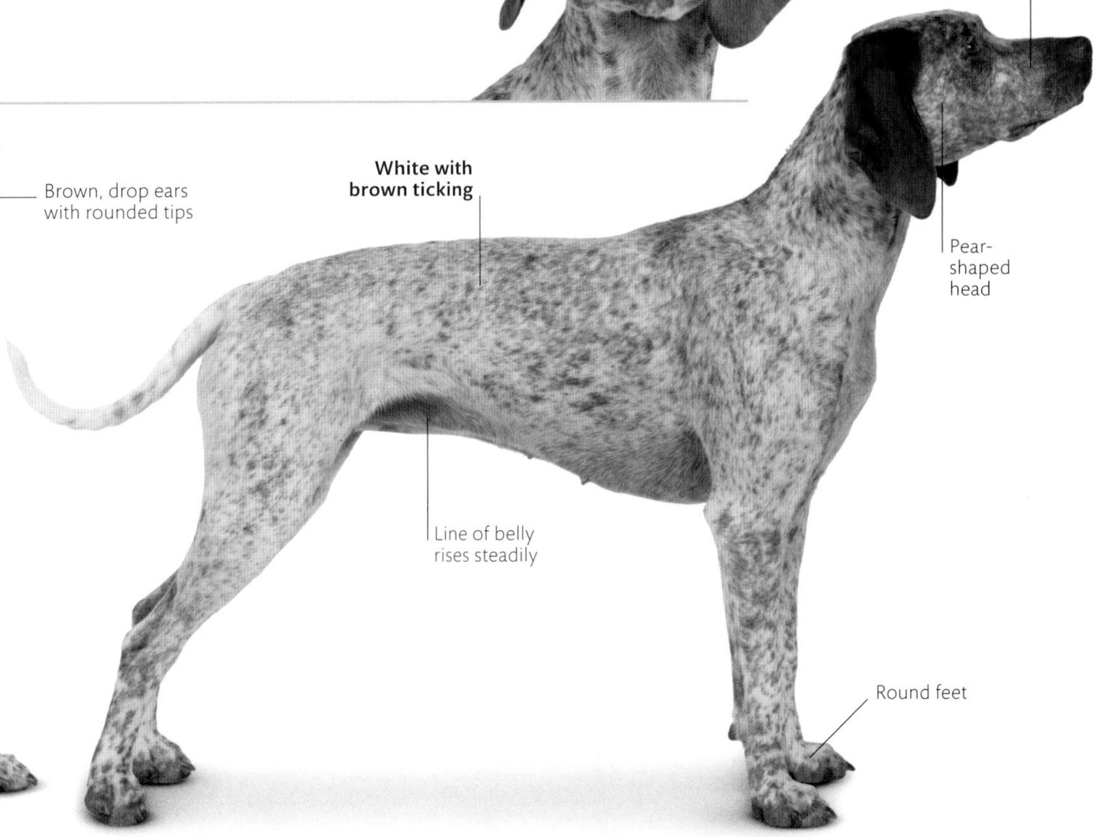

Slightly tapered
muzzle
White with
brown ticking
Pear-
shaped
head
Line of belly
rises steadily
Round feet

Auvergne Pointer

HEIGHT 21–25in (53–63cm)
WEIGHT 49–62lb (22–28kg)
LIFE SPAN 12–13 years

'he Auvergne Pointer, or Braque d'Auvergne, was bred in ·entral France by and for hunters, and it remains a tenacious ll-purpose hunting dog that can work all day over long distances. ·riendly and intelligent, this is a lively, affectionate breed that easily trained and loves company. 'he Auvergne Pointer will thrive ı any active household.

Flews neatly
overlap
lower lip
Black flecking over
white gives coat
blue appearance
White with
black markings

Typical black
markings on
face and ears

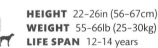

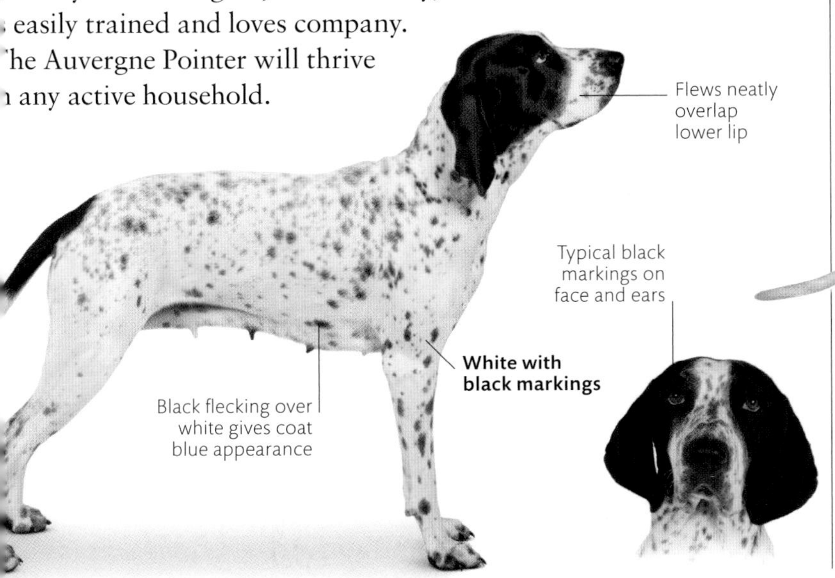

Ariege Pointing Dog

HEIGHT 22–26in (56–67cm)
WEIGHT 55–66lb (25–30kg)
LIFE SPAN 12–14 years

Rare even in its homeland in southwest France, the Ariege Pointing Dog, or Braque de l'Ariège, is used for pointing and retrieving, and has some tracking ability. It is almost exclusively owned by hunters, and needs patient training to settle an enthusiastic nature that can spill over into wildness, and plenty to do if it is not to become destructive.

Tapering tail
Long,
straight
muzzle
White with
fawn ticking
Short,
glossy coat
Compact feet
with well-
arched toes

Fine,
folded,
tan ears

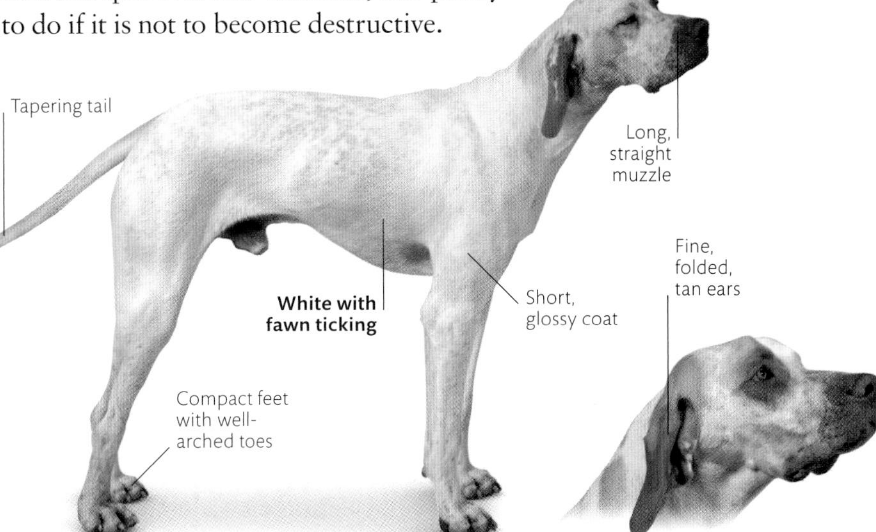

French Gascony Pointer

HEIGHT 22–27in (56–69cm)
WEIGHT 55–71lb (25–32kg)
LIFE SPAN 12–14 years

Chestnut-brown

Chestnut-brown dogs may have tan markings.

One of the oldest pointer breeds, the French Gascony Pointer, from southwest France, is still kept as a hunter's dog as well as a household companion. Loyal and affectionate, it has a sensitive nature that responds best to gentle, consistent training. It is a determined and enthusiastic tracker in the field.

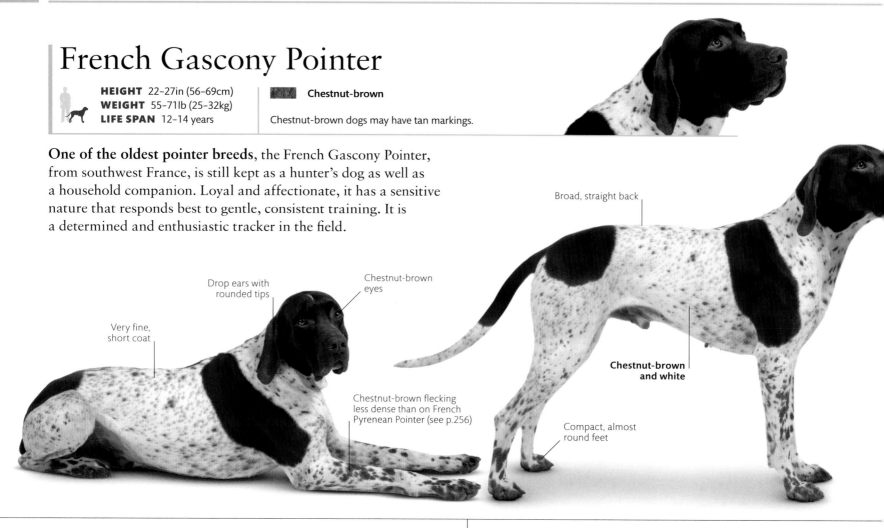

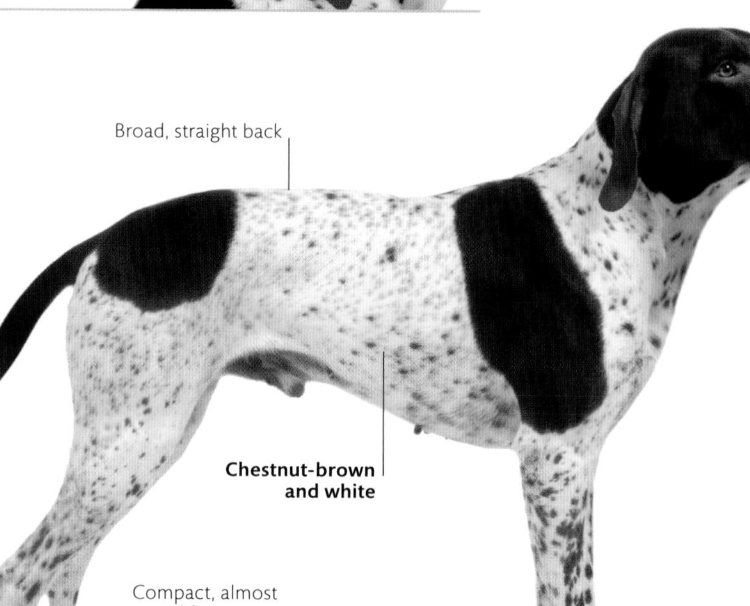

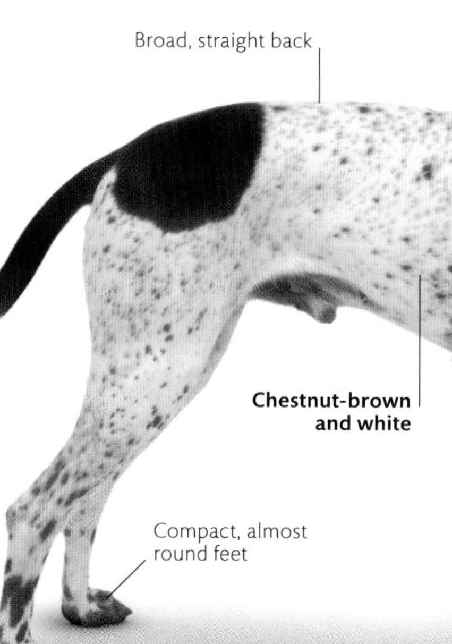

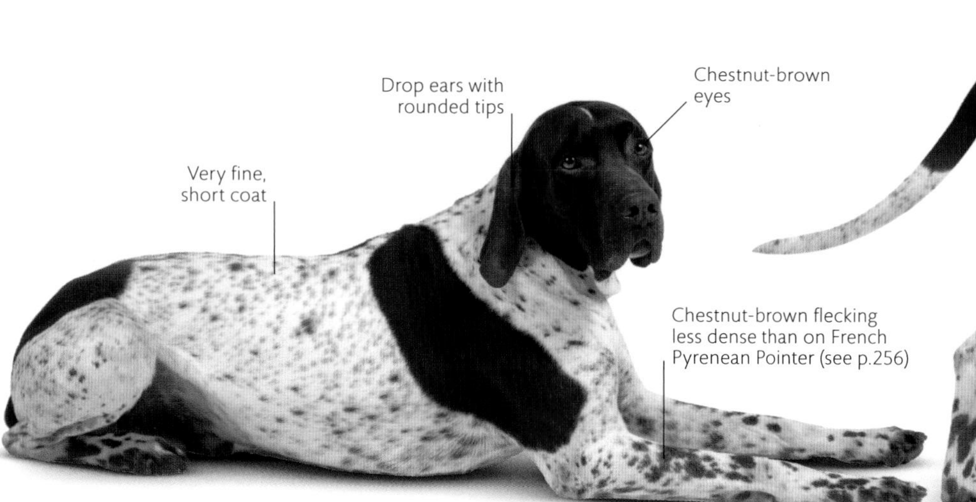

Spanish Pointer

HEIGHT 23–26in (59–67cm)
WEIGHT 55–66lb (25–30kg)
LIFE SPAN 12–14 years

Also known as the Perdiguero de Burgos, this dog was bred to track deer, but is now mostly used for smaller game. It is a reliable, easy-going breed that fits well into family life. Nonetheless, it is an avid hunter—halfway between a scent hound and a pointer—and thrives on work.

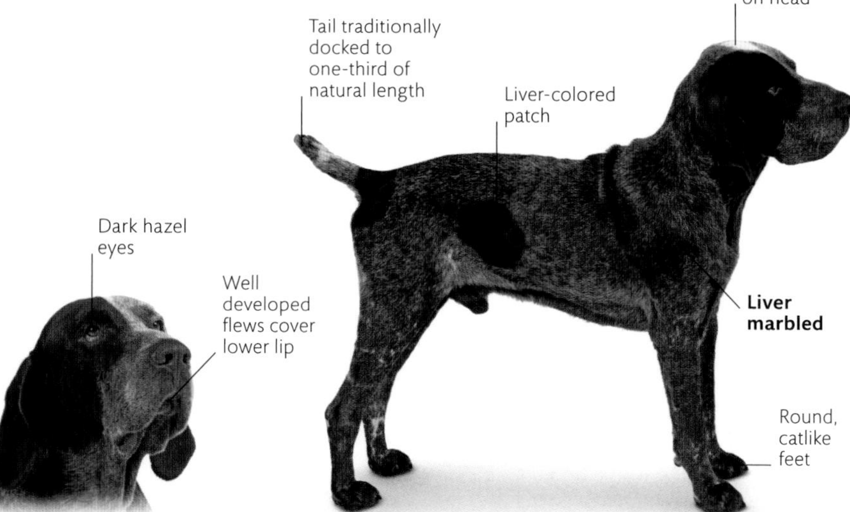

Old Danish Pointer

HEIGHT 20–24in (50–60cm)
WEIGHT 57–77lb (26–35kg)
LIFE SPAN 12–13 years

Its local name, Gammel Dansk Hønsehund, also translates as Old Danish Chicken Dog or Bird Dog. This breed is still used as a determined tracker, pointer, and retriever, and even as a sniffer dog, but it also makes an even-tempered family dog for those willing to give it plenty to do.

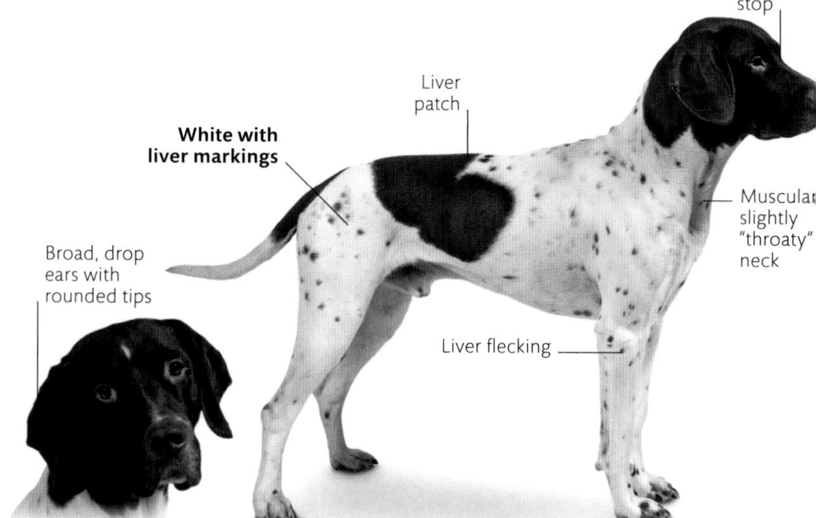

Golden Retriever

HEIGHT	WEIGHT	LIFE SPAN	
20–24in (51–61cm)	55–75lb (25–34kg)	12–13 years	Cream

GUIDE DOGS FOR THE BLIND

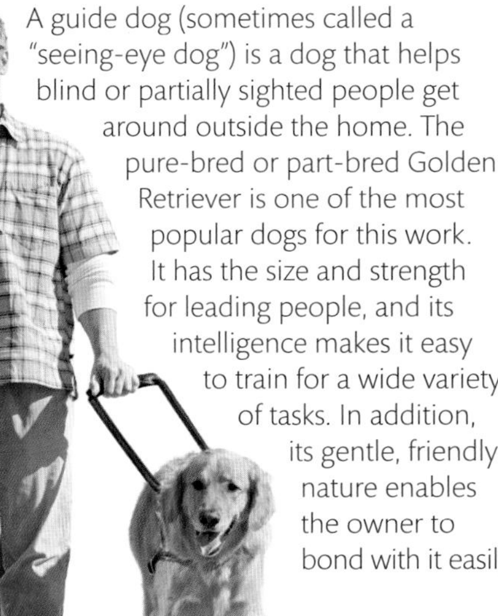

A guide dog (sometimes called a "seeing-eye dog") is a dog that helps blind or partially sighted people get around outside the home. The pure-bred or part-bred Golden Retriever is one of the most popular dogs for this work. It has the size and strength for leading people, and its intelligence makes it easy to train for a wide variety of tasks. In addition, its gentle, friendly nature enables the owner to bond with it easily.

The temperament of this exuberant, easy-going gundog has made it a family favorite in many countries

One of the most popular breeds worldwide, the Golden Retriever originated in Scotland in the mid-19th century, when the aristocrat Lord Tweedmouth crossed his "Yellow Retriever" with the now-extinct Tweed Water Spaniel of the English-Scottish border country. Later crosses were made with the Irish Setter (see p.242) and the Flat Coated Retriever (see p.262). The result was an active, intelligent retriever that could work for long distances in difficult upland terrain, heavy vegetation, and icy water. It was also noted for being easy to train and having a soft mouth when carrying game.

The Golden Retriever is still used by hunters, and competes in field trials and obedience competitions. It is effective in search and rescue and in detecting drugs and explosives. The breed is also employed as a guide dog for blind people, an assistance dog for those with other disabilities, and a therapy dog. Perhaps the only job at which it fails is being a guard dog because it is so friendly. It is enormously popular as a pet. Gregarious, responsive, and even-tempered, this dog's main goal in life is to please. It needs plenty of company and vigorous exercise, and loves games that involve retrieving and carrying things.

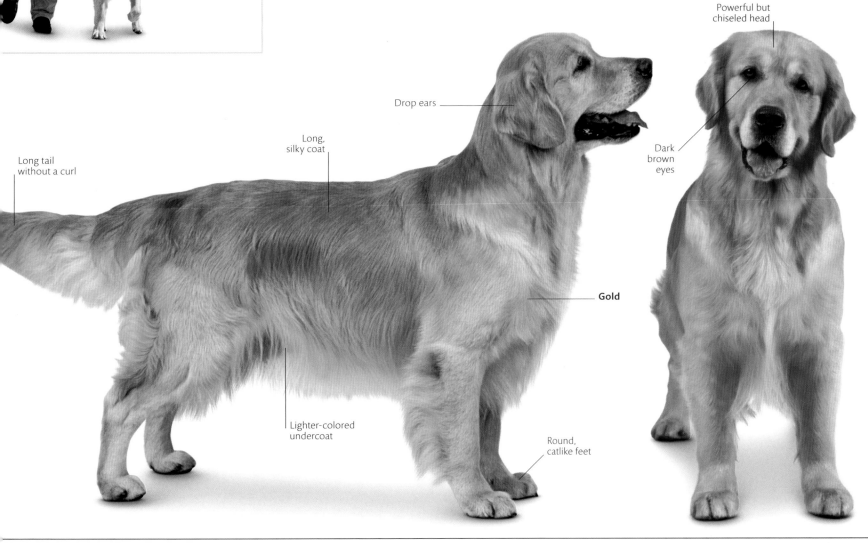

Labrador Retriever

HEIGHT	WEIGHT	LIFE SPAN	
22in (55–57cm)	55–82lb (25–37kg)	10–12 years	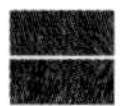 Chocolate Black May have a small, white spot on chest.

This family favorite owes its popularity to its kind and even temperament and its enthusiasm for sports and swimming

One of the most familiar dogs, the Labrador Retriever has been topping popular dog lists for at least two decades. The dogs from which the present-day Labrador Retriever descended were not from the Canadian region of Labrador, as is commonly supposed, but from the province of Newfoundland. Here, from the 18th century onward, black dogs with waterproof coats were bred by local fishermen and used to help tow in catches and retrieve escaping fish. Dogs of this early type no longer exist, but a few were brought to England in the 19th century and these led to the development of the modern Labrador Retriever. By the early 20th century the breed was officially recognized and continued to be much admired by field sportsmen for its excellent retrieving skills.

Today the Labrador Retriever is still widely used as a gundog and has proved efficient at other types of work, such as tracking for police forces. In particular, its steady character makes it a superb guide dog for the blind. However, it is as a family dog that this breed has gained great popularity. The Labrador Retriever is loving and lovable, easy to train, anxious to please, and reliable with children and household pets—but it has too amiable a character to make a good guard dog.

This breed has energy to burn and needs to be kept mentally as well as physically active. Long daily walks are essential, preferably with the chance to have a swim along the way. If this dog sees water, it will plunge straight in. Underexercised and left to its own devices, a Labrador Retriever may be prone to excessive barking or become destructive. It tends to gain weight easily, and lack of exercise combined with its insatiable appetite can lead to weight problems.

THE COTTONELLE PUPPY

For many years the Cottonelle Puppy has symbolized the Cottonelle® brand of toilet paper in the US. This vital but unglamorous item has been given a soft, fluffy, appealing image thanks to the golden Labrador Retriever puppies. The puppy has also become a feature in Australia and more than 30 other countries, where it is known as the Kleenex puppy. Andrex in the UK and Kleenex Cottonelle in Australia now use the puppy to promote charities that train dogs for blind people and others with disabilities.

PUPPY

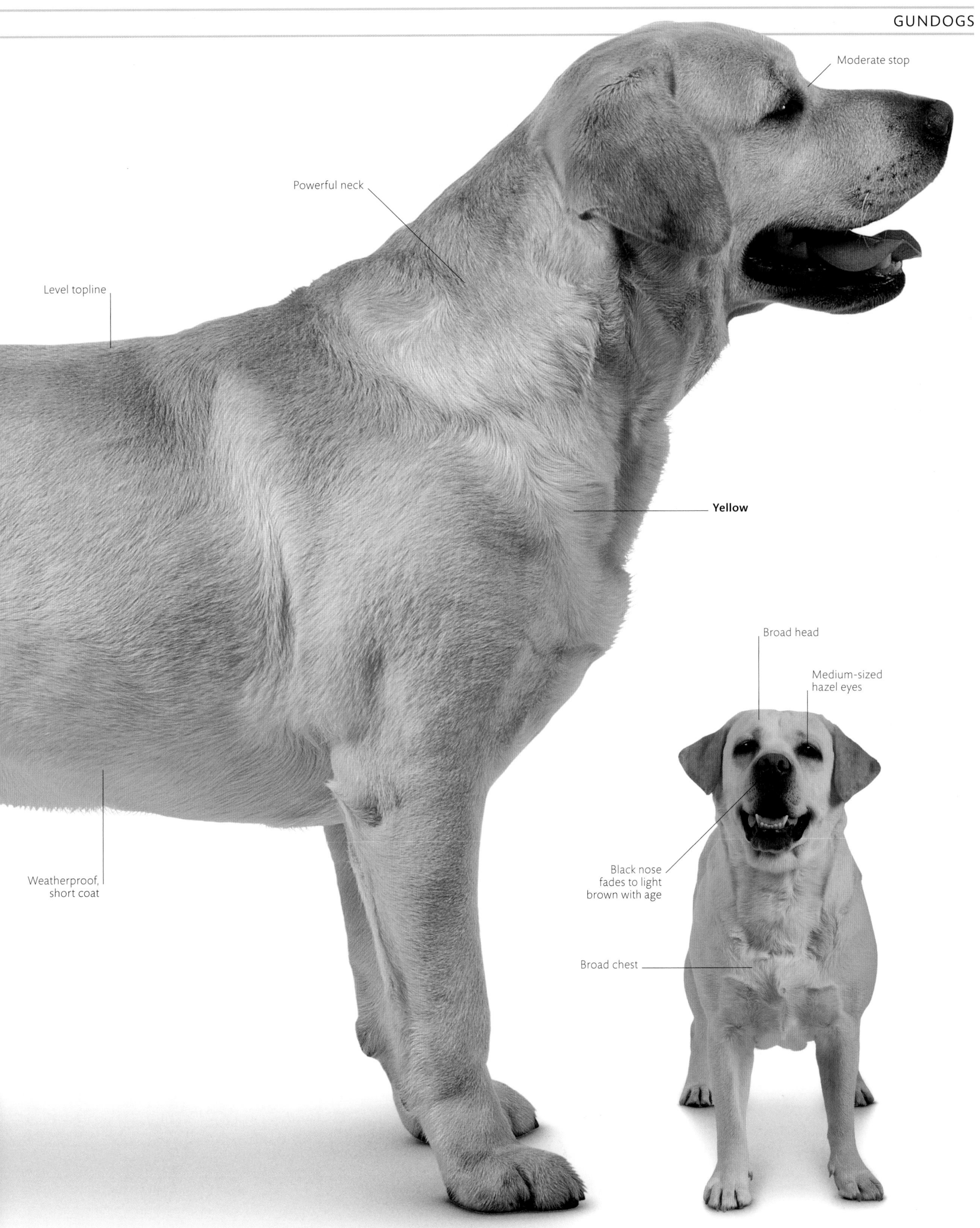
Moderate stop
Powerful neck
Level topline
Yellow
Broad head
Medium-sized
hazel eyes
Black nose
fades to light
brown with age
Weatherproof,
short coat
Broad chest

Flat Coated Retriever

HEIGHT 22–24in (56–61cm)
WEIGHT 55–79lb (25–36kg)
LIFE SPAN 11–13 years

Liver

One of the earliest retriever breeds, this was once a favorite among British gamekeepers. Today it is still worked but is more often found as a good-natured and handsome pet. Lively and brimming with enthusiasm, the Flat Coated Retriever is also level-headed and obedient. It has a deep bark so can make a good guard dog.

Dense coat

Curly Coated Retriever

HEIGHT 25–27in (64–69cm)
WEIGHT 60–71lb (27–32kg)
LIFE SPAN 12–13 years

Bred for hunting waterfowl, this rare British retriever is worked and used as an assistance dog, as well as being kept as an affectionate and level-headed companion. High energy levels and a need for company make this dog more suited to a rural life than to an urban home.

Small, triangular, drop ears

Oval eyes match coat color

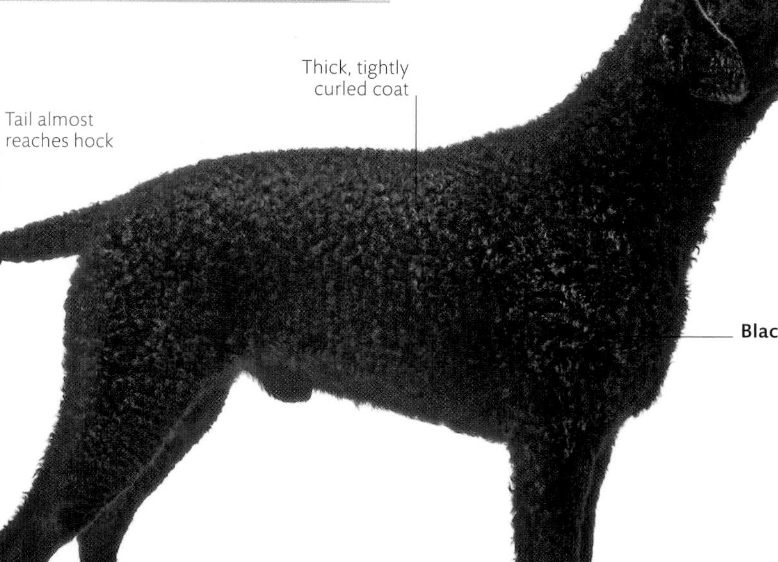

Chesapeake Bay Retriever

HEIGHT	WEIGHT	LIFE SPAN	
21–26in (53–66cm)	55–79lb (25–36kg)	12–13 years	**Straw to bracken** **Red-gold** May have small, white markings.

SHIPWRECK SURVIVORS

The origin of the Chesapeake Bay Retriever dates back to 1807, when two Newfoundland-type pups were rescued from a sinking ship off the coast of Maryland. The pups—a "dingy red" dog named Sailor and a black bitch called Canton (after the ship)—were separated and given to different owners. They proved themselves to be superb waterfowl retrievers—enthusiastically leaping into the water to retrieve shot birds (as below). Crossed with local dogs, including Flat Coated Retrievers (opposite) and Curly Coated Retrievers (opposite), they produced the first Chesapeake Bay Retrievers.

This even-tempered, hardy dog is suited to country life and loves plenty of attention and exercise

This retriever, also known as the Chessie, originated in the state of Maryland. A superb water dog, it was developed to retrieve waterfowl in the cold, rough waters of Chesapeake Bay. During the 19th century the Chesapeake Bay dogs were so admired that a cast-iron manufacturer made and used statues of the founding dogs, Sailor and Canton, as its company emblem. By the 1880s the Chesapeake Bay Retriever had emerged as a distinct type, and the breed was recognized by the American Kennel Club in 1918. The Chesapeake Bay Retriever is now the state dog of Maryland.

With typical retriever gentleness but an alert, determined personality, the Chesapeake Bay Retriever is still used for hunting today. It will work under all conditions, including strong tides and high winds, and will even break ice with its forepaws to reach its quarry. Dogs have been known to retrieve several hundred birds in a day. The Chesapeake Bay Retriever is a superb swimmer, aided by webbing between its toes, and a short, dense, oily coat that is water-repellent. The breed also makes a good companion, although it needs plenty of activity, especially swimming and retrieving, to match its high energy levels.

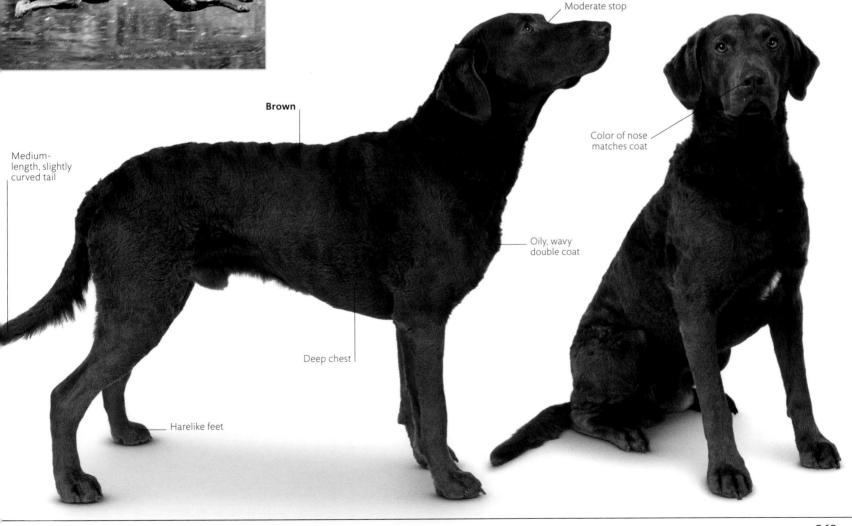

Moderate stop

Brown

Color of nose matches coat

Medium-length, slightly curved tail

Oily, wavy double coat

Deep chest

Harelike feet

Mexican pet
A Chihuahua may fit into a handbag but it is not a fashion accessory. This little breed from Mexico needs exercise as much as any larger dog.

COMPANION DOGS

Almost any dog can provide companionship. Many dogs once used for outside work, such as herding, have moved indoors with the family. Usually, these breeds have been developed for specific tasks and so are traditionally grouped according to their primary function. With a few exceptions, the companion dogs included here are bred solely as pets.

Most companion dogs are small breeds, created primarily to sit on laps, look decorative, and entertain their owners without taking up much room. Some of them are toy versions of larger working breeds. The Poodle (see p.229), for example, once used for herding or for retrieving waterfowl, was bred down in size to a toy dog that could no longer perform that practical function. Other, larger, dogs sometimes grouped with companion breeds include the Dalmatian (see p.286), whose career included a short-lived spell as a carriage escort, as much for prestige as guard duty. Now that this job no longer exists, Dalmatians are rarely used for any working purpose.

Companion dogs have a long history. A number of them originated thousands of years ago in China, where small dogs were kept in the imperial courts as ornaments and a source of comfort. Until the late 19th century companion dogs everywhere were almost exclusively the pampered pets of the wealthy. As such, they often featured in portraits, depicted sitting prettily in the drawing room or with children as a nursery plaything. Some, such as the English Toy Spaniel (see p.279), owe their enduring popularity to the former patronage of royalty.

Appearance has always mattered in the breeding of companion dogs. Over the centuries selective breeding has produced characteristics, some bizarre, that serve no useful function but are designed to appeal—for example, the humanlike flat faces and large, round eyes of the Pekingese (see p.270) and the Pug (see p.268). Some have extravagantly long coats, curly tails, or—in the case of the Chinese Crested Dog (see p.280)—no hair at all, apart from a few tufts on the head or legs.

In modern times companion dogs are no longer a symbol of class. They find a place with owners of all ages and circumstances, in small apartments as well as in large country homes. Although still chosen for their looks, these dogs are also sought after as friends that give and demand affection and adapt happily to family activities.

Brussels Griffon

SMOOTH-HAIRED (PETIT BRABANÇON)

HEIGHT	WEIGHT	LIFE SPAN	
9–11in (23–28cm)	7–11lb (3–5kg)	Over 12 years	 Black and tan Black

This lively, well balanced dog with a terrierlike disposition adapts well to city life but remains rare outside Europe

This little dog originated in Belgium, where it was kept as a stable dog. This dog was related to the Affenpinscher (see p.218), from which it probably inherited its "monkey face." During the 19th century it was crossed with the Pug (see p.268) and the Ruby English Toy Spaniel (see p.279), the latter producing the reddish or black and tan coloring seen in some dogs.

Despite its popularity in the late 19th century, by 1945 the Brussels Griffon had almost disappeared in Belgium. It was only saved by breeders importing dogs from the UK. It is still uncommon today, although these dogs have featured in major movies such as *As Good As It Gets* and *Gosford Park*.

There is a smooth-haired variety known as the Petit Brabançon, and a rough-haired variety with a distinctive beard. In some countries black rough-coated dogs are defined as Belgian Griffons, and all other colors of rough-haired dog as Brussels Griffons.

Bold and confident but affectionate, the breed is an entertaining companion, although it may be too sensitive for homes with small children. It enjoys a good walk and being pampered.

FROM STABLE TO ROYAL PET

The Brussels Griffon is descended from the little rough-haired dogs that were often seen in Brussels streets and known as "little street urchins." The dogs were favorites with the city's hansom cab drivers, who kept them in the stables for catching rats. During the 19th century the breed became popular throughout society as a companion dog. One of the foremost supporters was Queen Marie Henriette of Belgium (right, with her maid of honor), who brought the breed to international fame.

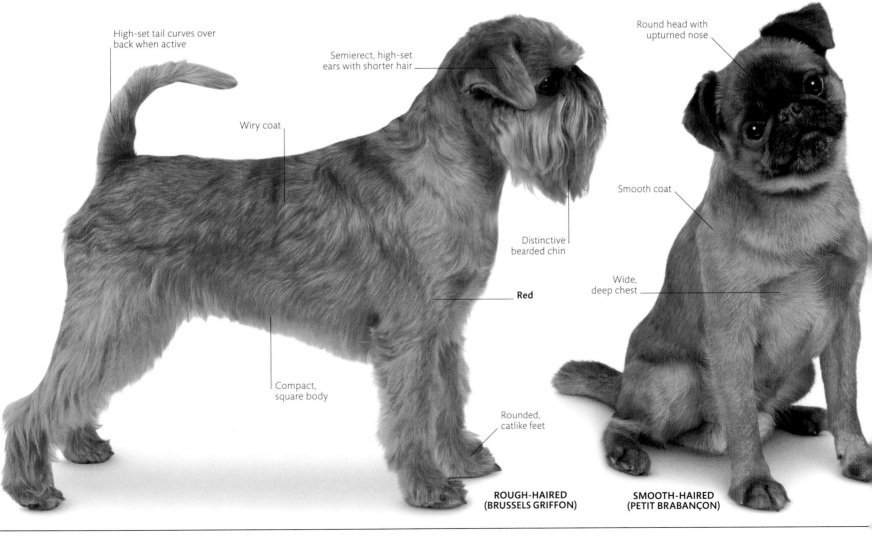

High-set tail curves over back when active

Semierect, high-set ears with shorter hair

Wiry coat

Distinctive bearded chin

Red

Compact, square body

Rounded, catlike feet

ROUGH-HAIRED (BRUSSELS GRIFFON)

Round head with upturned nose

Smooth coat

Wide, deep chest

SMOOTH-HAIRED (PETIT BRABANÇON)

American Bulldog

HEIGHT 20–27in (51–69cm)
WEIGHT 60–125lb (27–57kg)
LIFE SPAN Up to 16 years

Variety of colors

Early English settlers brought the Bulldog (see p.95) with them to the US. Two breeders, John D. Johnson and Alan Scott, used the English variety to develop the American Bulldog, which is taller, more active, and more versatile than its English counterpart. Male dogs are significantly heavier than females.

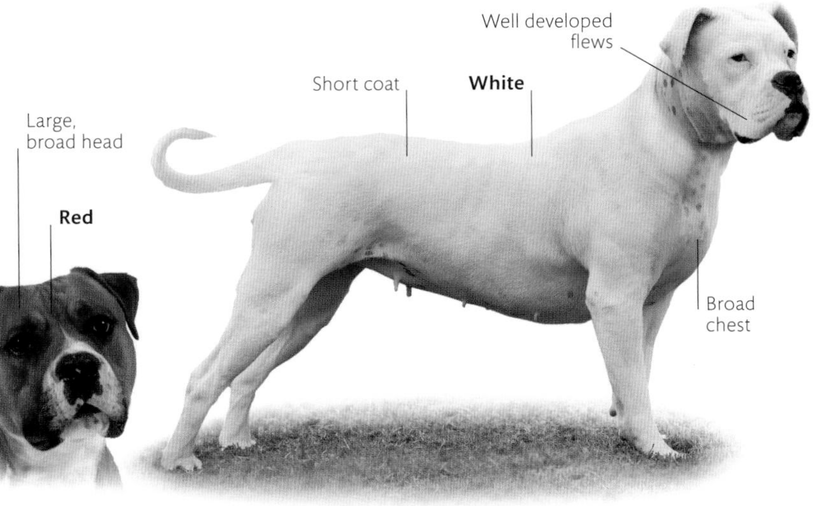

Olde English Bulldogge

HEIGHT 16–20in (41–51cm)
WEIGHT 51–79lb (23–36kg)
LIFE SPAN 9–14 years

Variety of colors

This muscular dog is a re-creation of the original 19th-century Bulldog. It was developed in the US during the 1970s by David Leavitt to eliminate some of the health problems that are now seen in the modern Bulldog (see p.95). Confident and courageous, these intelligent dogs are excellent family companions. However, they benefit from early socialization and training.

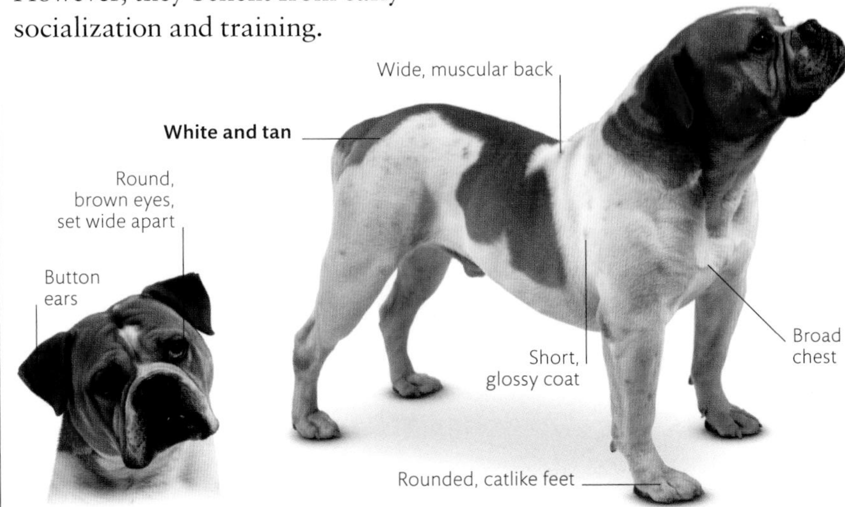

French Bulldog

HEIGHT 11–13in (28–33cm)
WEIGHT 24–29lb (11–13kg)
LIFE SPAN Over 10 years

Black brindle

A sturdy, compact little dog, the French Bulldog makes an excellent companion, but has few boundaries and will want to share its owner's favorite chair. Always ready for fun, the dog may need kind but firm direction. This breed is a descendant of the British Toy Bulldog taken to France in the 19th century.

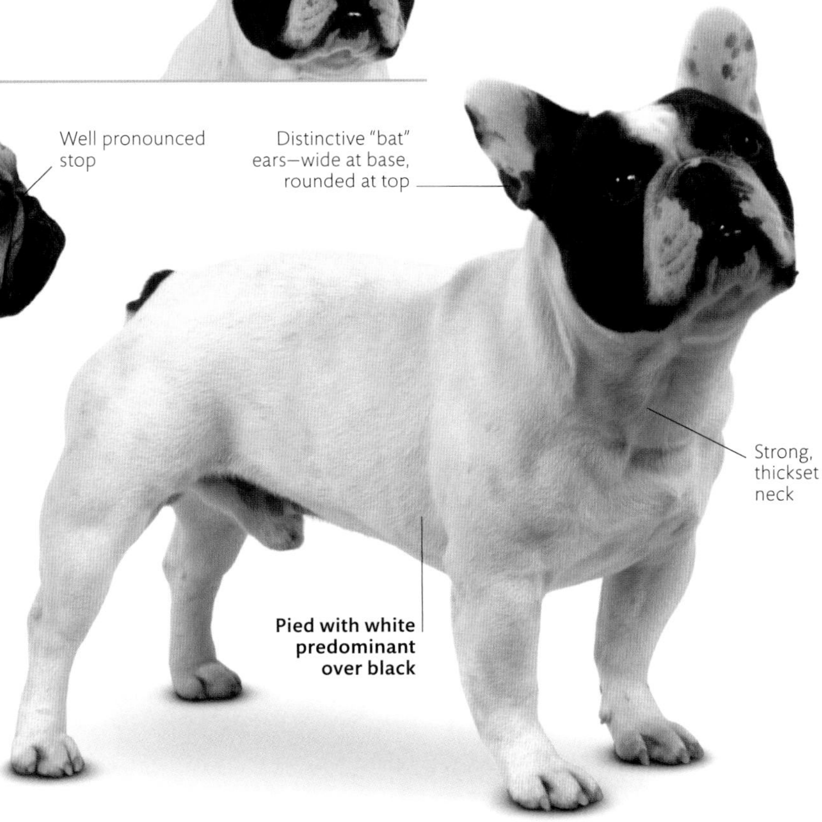

Pug

HEIGHT	WEIGHT	LIFE SPAN	
10–11in (25–28 cm)	13–18lb (6–8kg)	Over 10 years	 Silver Apricot Black

This playful, even-tempered, and intelligent dog loves people but can sometimes be stubborn

mall, stocky, puglike dogs have existed or many hundreds of years, but the ancestry nd origin of the Pug breed remain uncertain. Genetic evidence suggests the Pug is most losely related to the Brussels Griffon and in particular to the smooth-haired Petit Brabançon (p.266). It also has a shared ncestry with both the Pekingese (p.270) nd the Shih Tzu (p.272). It is likely that the Pug is linked with these dogs through the xtinct Chinese Happa Dog (see box p.270).

Puglike dogs were brought to Europe in the 16th century by the Dutch East India Company traders. The dogs became very popular with the Dutch aristocracy and were brought to Britain by William and Mary of Orange when they acceded the British throne in 1689. During the 18th century the dogs' popularity increased further and they appeared in paintings by Francisco Goya (1746–1828) and William Hogarth (1697–1764) (see p.22).

In the 19th century Pugs were imported to the US, where the breed was officially recognized in 1885. Imports of dogs from China to the UK in 1877 introduced a third color—black—which the Kennel Club recognized in 1896.

The Pug's wrinkled, sad-looking, little face belies its cheerful, and often mischievous, outgoing character. Highly intelligent, loving, and loyal, it is good with children and other pets. The breed thrives on regular exercise but does not need a great deal of space.

PUPPY

CHANGING FACES

The appearance of Pugs has changed radically since the 19th century, as can be seen in the 1893 etching below. Pugs at this time had a longer muzzle and lacked the flat face and upturned nose of today's dogs. Their legs were also longer and their bodies more muscular and less square. The features seen in modern Pugs started to appear toward the end of the 19th century. Both of the Pugs below have clipped ears, a common practice that was banned in the UK by Queen Victoria, who considered it cruel.

Fawn

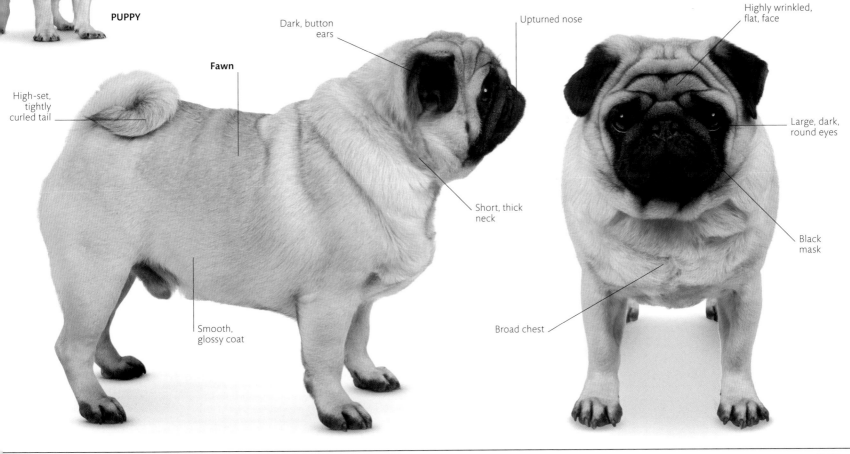

High-set, tightly curled tail

Dark, button ears

Upturned nose

Short, thick neck

Smooth, glossy coat

Highly wrinkled, flat, face

Large, dark, round eyes

Black mask

Broad chest

Pekingese

HEIGHT	WEIGHT	LIFE SPAN	
6–9in (15–23cm)	11lb (5kg)	Over 12 years	Variety of colors

Dignified and courageous yet sensitive, this good-natured dog has a mind of its own, making it difficult to train

Named after the Chinese capital (formerly Peking, now Beijing), the Pekingese has been revealed through DNA analysis as one of the oldest dog breeds in existence. Small, snub-nosed dogs have been associated with the Chinese Imperial Court since at least the Tang dynasty (618–907CE). They were considered sacred because of their resemblance to the lion—an exalted symbol of Buddha—and could only be owned by royalty. Commoners had to bow to the dogs, and anyone caught stealing one was put to death. The smallest individuals were "sleeve dogs," carried as guard dogs in noblemen's billowing sleeves.

By the 1820s breeding had reached its height in China and the best dogs were painted by court artists in "Imperial dog books," which served as a visual pedigree. The dogs reached the West when the British sacked the Imperial Palace in 1860, capturing five of them. Less controversially, in the 1900s the Dowager Empress Cixi gave dogs as presents to some of her European and American guests.

The perfect dog for an apartment, the Pekingese loves exercise but not long walks. It makes a loyal and fearless companion but can be jealous of children and other dogs.

THE LION AND THE MARMOSET

In Chinese legend, the story is told that a lion once fell in love with a marmoset—an impossible love because of their differing sizes. The lion therefore begged Ah Chu, the protector of animals, to shrink his body to the same size as the marmoset, but keep his lion's heart and character. From the union of the two animals, the Fu Lin, or "lion dog" was born (shown below in an illustration from an Imperial Dog Book with a Happa Dog, right).

Long, coarse, straight topcoat

Gold

Lionlike mane around face

Very short muzzle

Lighter-colored undercoat

Bichon Frise

HEIGHT 9–11in (23–28cm)
WEIGHT 11–15lb (5–7kg)
LIFE SPAN Over 12 years

ometimes known as the Tenerife dog, the Bichon Frise—a escendant of the French Water Dog (see p.229) and the Poodle ee p.229)—was allegedly taken from Tenerife to France. This a happy, little dog that loves to be the center of attention and oes not like being left alone.

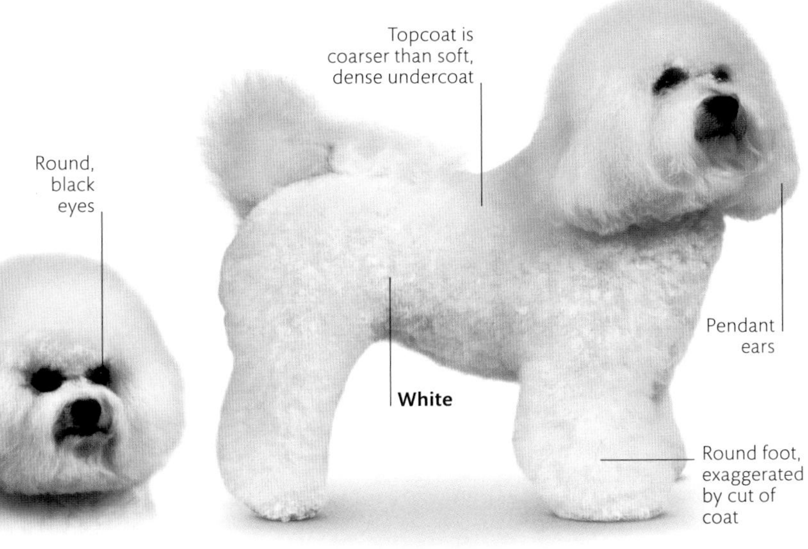

Coton de Tulear

HEIGHT 10–13in (25–32cm)
WEIGHT 9–13lb (4–6kg)
LIFE SPAN Over 12 years

This small, long-haired dog is known for its happy temperament. The Coton de Tulear enjoys the company of humans as well as other dogs and does not like to be left alone. It is sometimes called the Royal Dog of Madagascar, where the dog existed for several hundred years before being introduced to France.

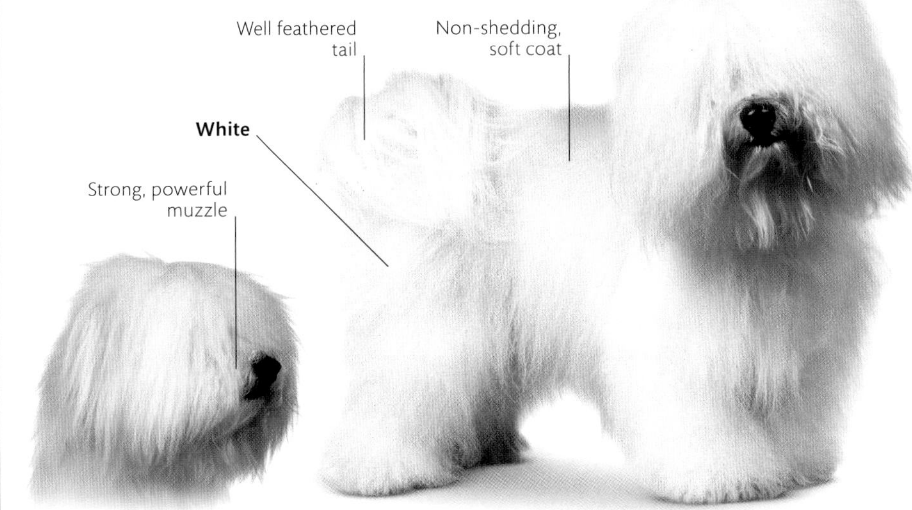

Lhasa Apso

HEIGHT Up to 10in (25cm)
WEIGHT 13–15lb (6–7kg)
LIFE SPAN 15–18 years

Variety of colors

irst bred in Tibet as a watchdog for temples and monasteries, he Lhasa Apso was brought to Europe via India in the 1920s. : is a small, hardy dog that will happily walk for miles. Its ong, flowing coat is not difficult to care for. Very ffectionate, it can also be fairly stubborn.

Shih Tzu

HEIGHT	WEIGHT	LIFE SPAN	
Up to 11in (27cm)	11–18lb (5–8kg)	Over 10 years	Variety of colors

This intelligent, bouncy, and outgoing dog loves being part of the family, making it a popular pet around the world

This sturdy breed is descended from the small, long-haired "lion dogs" that were originally bred in Tibet. Tibetan lamas (spiritual leaders) sent some of these valuable dogs as tributes to the Chinese emperors, and these were then crossed with small dogs imported from the West in previous centuries. Like the Pekingese (see p.270), the Shih Tzu was revered as a holy dog because it resembled the Chinese notion of a lion, which was a holy Buddhist symbol. The breed name means "little lion" in Chinese.

The Shih Tzu was a favorite with royalty. During the late 19th century Dowager Empress Cixi kept breeding kennels for Shih Tzus (as well as Pugs (see p.268) and Pekingese (see p.270), but after her death in 1908 the dogs were dispersed.

After China became a republic in 1912, Shih Tzus were exported overseas. Small groups of imported dogs survived in the UK and Norway, and the English dogs formed the basis of today's Shih Tzu. The breed was officially recognized in the UK in 1934. English Shih Tzus were exported to Europe and Australia and, after World War II, reached the US, too. In their native land, however, numbers had been in decline, and by the time of the Communist revolution in 1949, Shih Tzus had become almost extinct in China. Today the Shih Tzu is one of the world's most popular toy breeds. Despite its dignified carriage, the Shih Tzu makes an affectionate and friendly pet, although it can be strong-willed. The long coat requires daily grooming but sheds little or no hair, making this breed suitable for allergy sufferers.

PUPPY

A NEW DISCOVERY

In 1930 two small black-and-white dogs, a male and a female, were imported to the UK by Lady Brownrigg, an avid dog breeder (right). A second male was taken to Ireland. Descendants of these three dogs were the foundation stock of Lady Brownrigg's kennel and are ancestral to many of the dogs that exist today. When first shown in 1933, in a class for Tibetan dogs, it was immediately apparent that Lady Brownrigg's dogs were different from the Lhasa Apso (see p.271) and the Tibetan Terrier (see p.283) and this led her to form the Tibetan Lion Dog Club and write the first breed standard.

LADY BROWNRIGG WITH SOME OF HER SHIH TZUS

Heavily plumed tail
with white tip
Long, dense
topcoat
Hair grows upward
around muzzle
White blaze
on forehead
Short, muscular legs
hidden by long coat

Löwchen

HEIGHT 10–13in (25–33cm)
WEIGHT 9–18lb (4–8kg)
LIFE SPAN 12–14 years

 Any color

The Löwchen originated in France and Germany. The name *Löwchen* is German for "little lion," hence its other name, the Little Lion Dog. It is a compact dog with a bright expression and a reputation for agility and quickness. The Löwchen's intelligent, outgoing attitude makes it a pleasure to live with. It is highly recommended as a pet and its size and non-shedding coat make it an ideal family dog.

Bolognese

HEIGHT 10–12in (26–31cm)
WEIGHT 7–9lb (3–4kg)
LIFE SPAN Over 12 years

This breed originates from northern Italy; similar dogs were known as far back as Roman times and are represented in many 16th-century Italian paintings. Slightly more reserved and shy than its relative the Bichon Frise (see p.271), the Bolognese loves people and will form a close relationship with its owner. Like the Bichon Frise, it has a non-shedding coat.

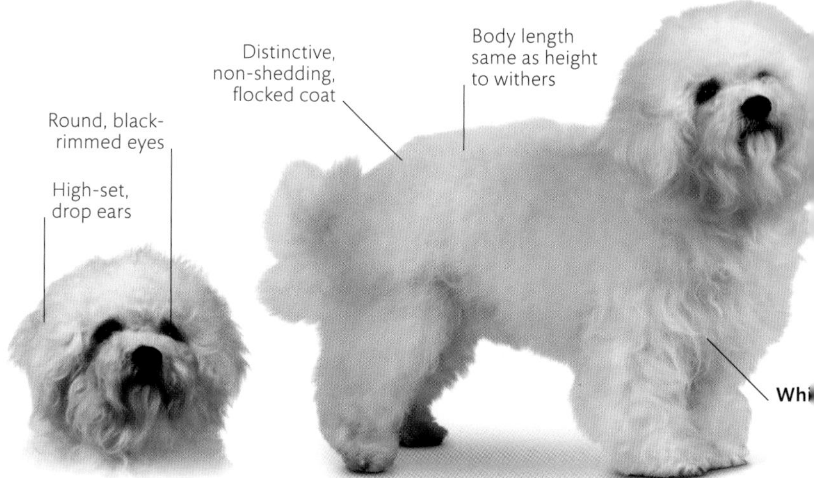

Maltese

HEIGHT Up to 10in (25cm)
WEIGHT 5–7lb (2–3kg)
LIFE SPAN Over 12 years

An ancient dog from the Mediterranean, Maltese-like dogs are mentioned in writings as far back as 300BCE. This is a lively, fun-loving, little dog that belies its chocolate-box appearance. The long, silky coat is a major commitment—it does not shed but requires daily grooming to prevent matting.

Havanese

HEIGHT 9–11in (23–28cm)
WEIGHT 7–13lb (3–6kg)
LIFE SPAN Over 12 years

 Any color

The Havanese is the national dog of Cuba, where it is known as the Habanero. A relative of the Bichon Frise (see p.271), it was probably brought to Cuba by Italian or Spanish traders. The Havanese loves to be at the center of its family, plays endlessly with children, and is also a good watchdog.

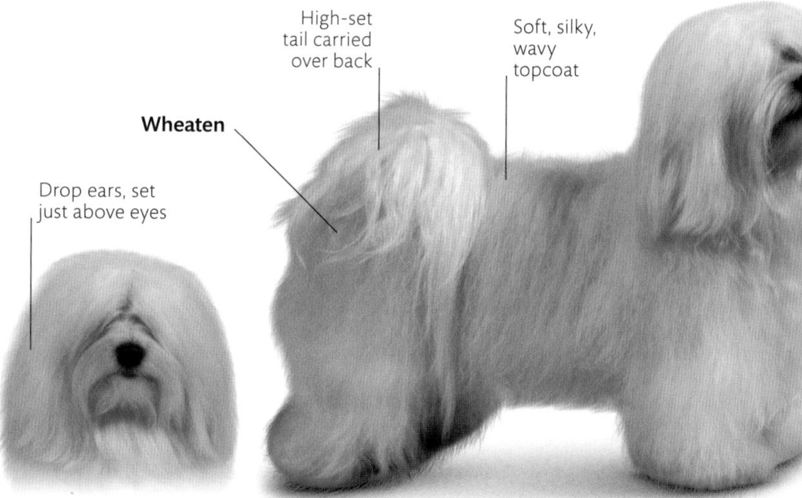

Russian Toy

HEIGHT	WEIGHT	LIFE SPAN	
8–11in (20–28cm)	Up to 7lb (3kg)	Over 12 years	**Red** **Black and tan** **Blue and tan**

TINY TERRIER

Small dogs have always been very popular as pets and many different breeds have been created. One of the most recent is the Russian Toy, which was accepted by the FCI in 2006. It is one of the smallest breeds in the world, and is about the same size as a Chihuahua (see p.282). Despite its small size, two features of this tiny terrier are described as large—its dark, expressive eyes, and its erect, triangular ears.

SMOOTH-HAIRED PUPPY

Small but not delicate, and with a big personality, this lovable dog thrives on human company

Also known as the Russkiy Toy, this miniature dog is descended from English Toy Terriers (see p.211), which were first brought to Russia in the 18th century to indulge the aristocracy's enthusiasm for the English way of life. This association with nobility led to a serious drop in numbers during the Communist Revolution of 1917. Then in the late 1940s the decline was further exacerbated when only dogs with a military function were bred. A few miniature dogs did, however, survive and their descendents became known as the smooth-haired Russian Toy. The long-haired Russian Toy appeared in Moscow in 1958 when a puppy with a silky coat and fringed ears was born to smooth-haired parents.

After the fall of the Soviet Union in the 1980s, numbers of both the long- and short-haired toy terriers declined again, this time due to an influx of Western breeds. Though both types of Russian Toy remain rare, official recognition in Russia in 1988 ensured their survival. Despite its tiny size and fragile appearance, the Russian Toy is active and energetic, and usually has robust health.

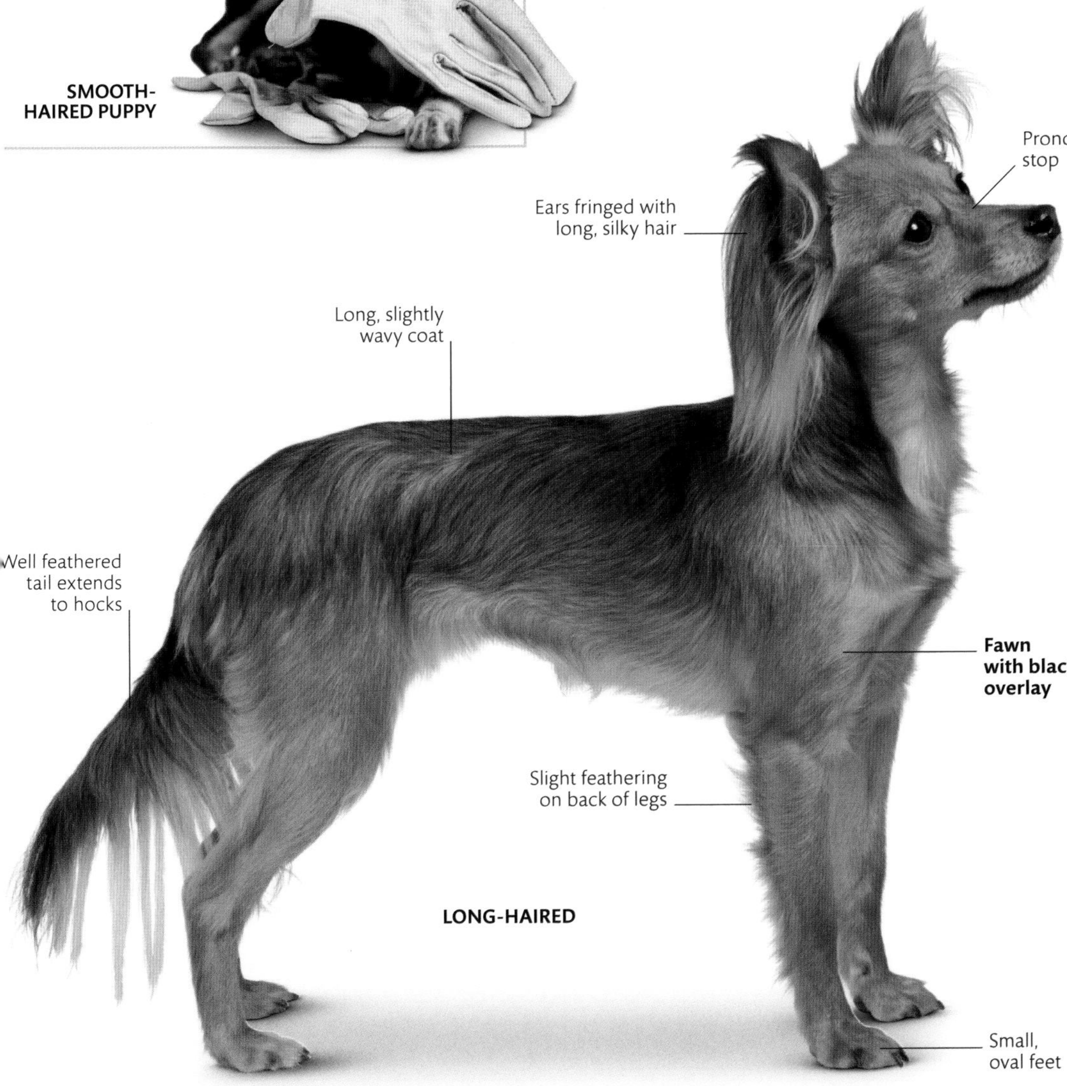

Pronounced stop

Ears fringed with long, silky hair

Long, slightly wavy coat

Well feathered tail extends to hocks

Fawn with black overlay

Slight feathering on back of legs

Small, oval feet

LONG-HAIRED

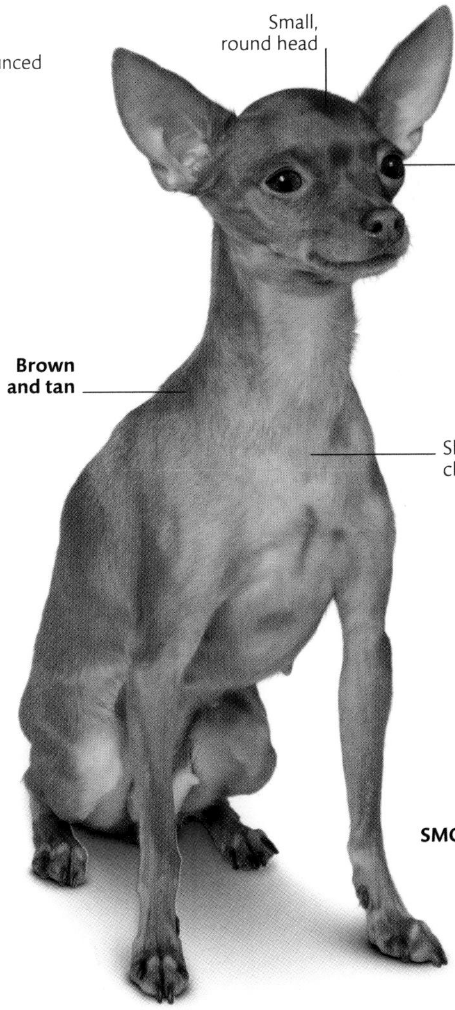

Small, round head

Round, prominent eyes

Brown and tan

Short, close coat

SMOOTH-HAIRED

Poodle

HEIGHT
Toy: up to 11in (28cm)
Miniature: 11–15in (28–38cm)
Medium: 15–18in (38–45cm)

WEIGHT
Toy: 7–9lb (3–4kg)
Miniature: 15–18lb (7–8kg)
Medium: 46–77lb (21–35kg)

LIFE SPAN
Over 12 years

Any solid color

'his highly intelligent, extroverted dog with a natural talent o amuse, is active, agile, and quick to learn

'**he smaller sizes of Poodle** that xist today are based on the Poodle ee p.229), and came into existence only short time after the Poodle emerged, y deliberate downsizing of the larger dogs. oodlelike dogs appear in engravings by ierman artist Albrecht Dürer, from the late 5th to early 16th century. These little oodles have always been companion dogs; ighly popular in the French court between he reigns of Louis XIV and Louis XVI, hey were also favorites in the Spanish court, and entered England in the 18th century. Small poodles were introduced to the US in the late 19th century but did not become popular until the 1950s; however, today they are one of the most well-loved breeds in the US. The most widely recognized of the small Poodles are the Miniature and Toy. Another size, recognized by the FCI, is the Medium Poodle (also known as the Klein Poodle or Moyen Poodle), which is intermediate in size between the Standard and Miniature.

One unusual use for small Poodles has been as circus dogs—their intelligence makes them easy to train for a wide variety of tricks. It has been suggested that circus life as well as the show ring has given rise to the variety of fancy poodle clips.

The Poodle is energetic, intelligent, affectionate, and eager to please. A sensitive dog, it tends to bond most closely with one person. The coat is non-shedding, although it does need regular brushing and clipping.

PUPPY

CLIPPING STYLES

Poodles need to have their coats clipped because they do not shed hair. In most clips, some parts of the coat are left long while others are shaved. The original styles for working Poodles (see p.229) were designed to protect the legs from undergrowth and keep the vital organs warm, while the face, hindquarters, and upper legs were shaved for cleanliness and ease of movement. Showing, performance, and professional grooming have given rise to a number of clips, two of which are shown in the 19th-century engraving below.

MINIATURE

Kyi Leo

HEIGHT 9–11in (23–28cm)
WEIGHT 9–13lb (4–6kg)
LIFE SPAN 13–15 years

Variety of colors

May have tan markings.

A playful, affectionate American breed that is gaining popularity, the Kyi Leo is named after its parents: *Kyi*, Tibetan for "dog," after its Lhasa Apso parent from Tibet; and *Leo*, Latin for "lion," after its Maltese parent, which was once called the Lion Dog. Suited to indoor life, this alert dog makes a good watchdog.

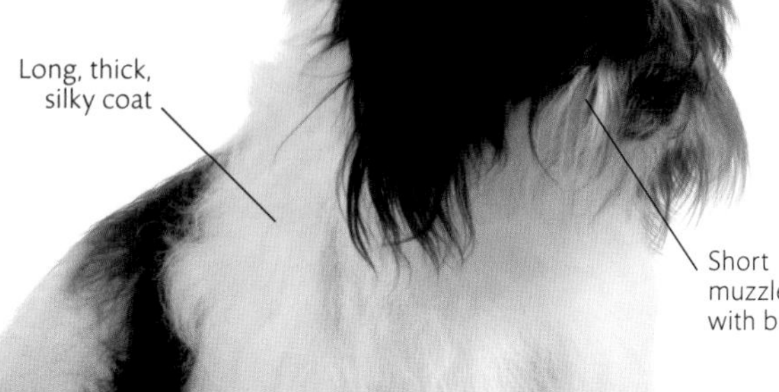

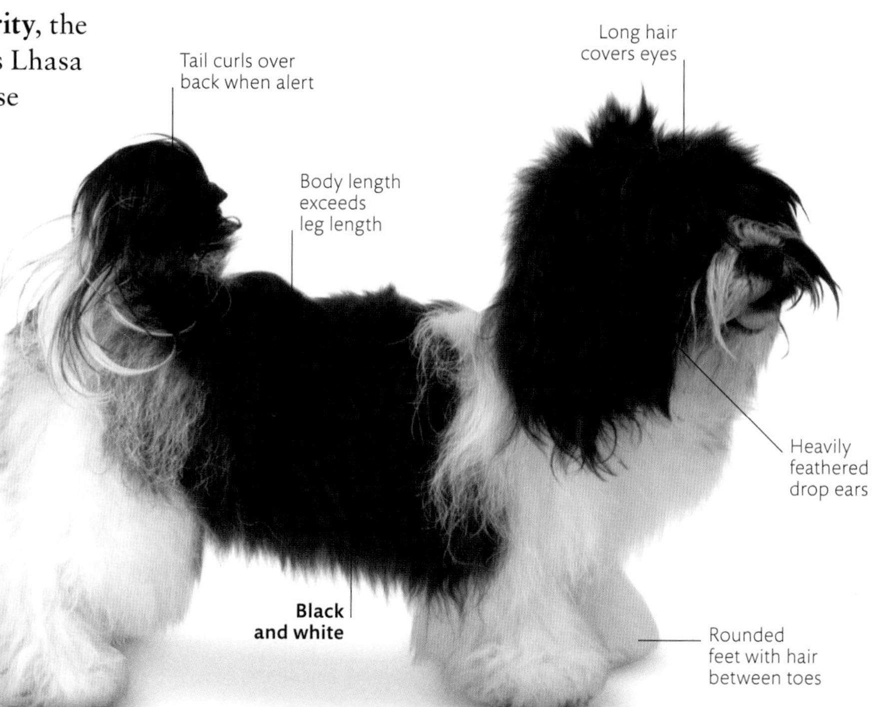

Cavalier King Charles Spaniel

HEIGHT 12–13in (30–33cm)
WEIGHT 11–18lb (5–8kg)
LIFE SPAN Over 12 years

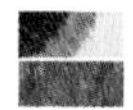

Prince Charles (right)
Ruby

A relative of the English Toy Spaniel (opposite), ancestors of this breed date back centuries. With large, dark eyes, a melting expression, and an ever-wagging tail, the Cavalier King Charles Spaniel is game, easy to train, and loves children—making it the perfect family pet. Its silky coat requires regular grooming.

English Toy Spaniel

HEIGHT	WEIGHT	LIFE SPAN	
10–11in (25–27cm)	9–13lb (4–6kg)	Over 12 years	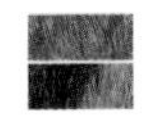 Ruby King Charles

A ROYAL FAVORITE

King Charles II of England (1630–85) doted on his companion dogs, which were allowed to roam all over the palace, even on state occasions. (Anthony van Dyck's painting, below, shows Charles while still a child with two of his siblings and two of the treasured dogs.) The diarist Samuel Pepys noted how much the king loved them—even his "silliness" in playing with his dog instead of attending to business in meetings. The king's strong attachment remains to this day, as the descendants of his dogs are called King Charles Spaniels.

Naturally well behaved and eager to please, this dog makes a gentle and affectionate companion

Also known as the King Charles Spaniel, this British breed is related to the Cavalier King Charles Spaniel (opposite), although the latter is a more recent breed. The ancestors of the English Toy Spaniel were first seen in European and English royal courts in the 16th century, and thought to be descended from small Chinese and Japanese breeds.

The original "comforters" looked like other spaniels, and some were used for hunting. From the late 18th century they were crossed with the Pug (see p.268) to give a fashionably short nose and became exclusively lap dogs. By the end of the 19th century there were four varieties: the King Charles (black and tan in color); the Blenheim (red and white); the Ruby (deep red); and the Prince Charles (white with black and tan markings). All four types were reclassified as one breed—the English Toy Spaniel in 1903.

The modern English Toy Spaniel is a quiet, obedient, but playful dog and makes an excellent family pet. The breed lives quite happily in a small home and needs only moderate exercise. It loves company, so should not be left alone for long periods. The long coat requires grooming every few days.

Ready for action
The alert expression, muscular body, and tail carriage of this Chinese Crested epitomize its playful personality. The long, flowing head crest and fringed ears add to its appeal.

Chinese Crested

HEIGHT	WEIGHT	LIFE SPAN	
9–13in (23–33cm)	Up to 11lb (5kg)	12 years	Any color

GYPSY ROSE LEE

One of the first breeders of the modern Chinese Crested dog was the famous American burlesque performer Gypsy Rose Lee. Lee first encountered the breed when her sister gave her a Chinese Crested dog that she had rescued from an animal shelter. Lee (below, left) included the dog in her act, thus helping to publicize the breed. She also founded the Lee breeding kennels for Chinese Crested dogs in the 1950s, and established one of the two main bloodlines that exist today.

This elegant, intelligent dog attracts attention wherever it goes, but doesn't require a lot of outdoor exercise

Hairlessness is a feature of several dog breeds around the world. It is the result of a genetic mutation that was initially considered a curiosity but then became desirable since the breed did not harbor fleas, shed hair, or have body odor. Although the Chinese Crested requires little grooming, its bare skin is sensitive: in winter it needs a coat to keep it warm, and in summer requires protection from the intense heat of the sun, which can burn and dry out its skin. This delicate skin, combined with the fact that the breed needs little exercise and activity, makes it unsuitable for owners who spend a lot of time outdoors. However, it is an ideal companion dog for older people due to its happy and friendly nature and playful personality.

The variety of Chinese Crested that does have hair—the Powderpuff—has a long, soft coat that needs regular grooming to prevent matting. Both coat varieties can occur in the same litter. Some Chinese Crested dogs are more lightly built than others. These fine-boned individuals are referred to as the deer type, while Chinese Crested dogs that have a heavier build are known as the cobby type.

POWDERPUFF VARIETY

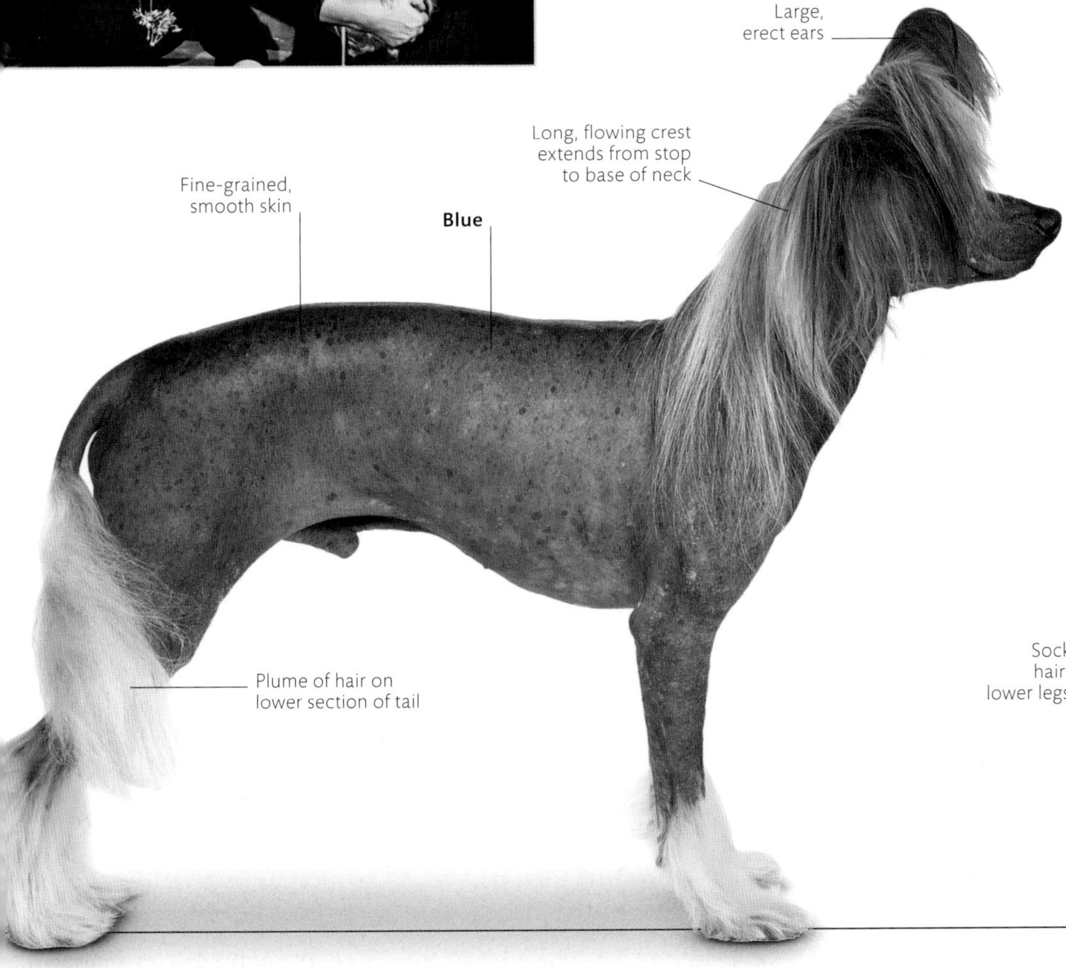

Large, erect ears

Long, flowing crest extends from stop to base of neck

Fine-grained, smooth skin

Blue

Plume of hair on lower section of tail

Distinctive stop

Sock of white hair encircles lower legs and feet

Chihuahua

HEIGHT	WEIGHT	LIFE SPAN	Any color
6–9in (15–23cm)	5–7lb (2–3kg)	Over 12 years	Always a single color—never dappled or merle.

This companionable, intelligent, tiny dog with a large-dog personality makes a devoted pet

The smallest dog breed in the world, the Chihuahua is named after the Mexican state where it was discovered in the 1850s. It is most probably descended from the Techichi, a small, mute dog kept by the indigenous Toltec people (c.800–1000CE) and sometimes eaten or sacrificed in religious rituals.

Little dogs were known to explorer Christopher Columbus and to the Spanish conquistadors by the 15th–16th century. Chihuahuas were first imported to the US in the 1890s, and the AKC recognized the breed in 1904. In the 1930s and 40s stars such as actress Lupe Velez and bandleader Xavier Cugat made the Chihuahua fashionable as a lap dog, and it is now one of the most popular breeds in the US.

The Chihuahua typically has an "apple head" (short nose and rounded skull). There are two main varieties: short-haired and long-haired. Both coats need only minimal grooming.

The breed makes a lovable companion dog and often becomes very attached to its owner. It benefits from short walks and games every day. It is not usually recommended for children; adult owners should take care to treat it as a dog rather than a toy or fashion accessory.

GIDGET—THE TACO BELL DOG

In 1997 a Chihuahua named Gidget was chosen as the mascot for the "Taco Bell" Tex-Mex food chain. Gidget was a female, although the "character" she played in advertisements had a male human voice with a "Mexican" accent. She became a superstar and made the brand hugely popular. Once the advertising campaign ended in 2000, Gidget appeared in further commercials as well as a movie (*Legally Blonde 2: Red, White, & Blonde*). She died in 2009 at age 15.

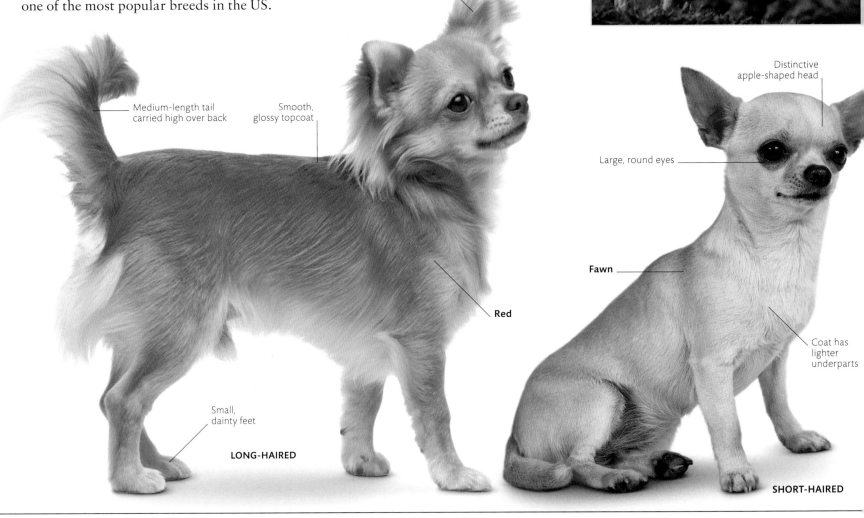

Large, triangular, batlike ears

Medium-length tail carried high over back

Smooth, glossy topcoat

Red

Small, dainty feet

LONG-HAIRED

Distinctive apple-shaped head

Large, round eyes

Fawn

Coat has lighter underparts

SHORT-HAIRED

Tibetan Spaniel

HEIGHT 10in (25cm)
WEIGHT 9–15lb (4–7kg)
LIFE SPAN Over 12 years

Any color

This small dog has a delightful, easy-going temperament. Bred and owned by the monks of Tibet, the Tibetan Spaniel has a long history and was first brought to the UK around 1900 by returning medical missionaries. In spite of its slightly haughty expression, this dog is only too happy to run around a yard and play.

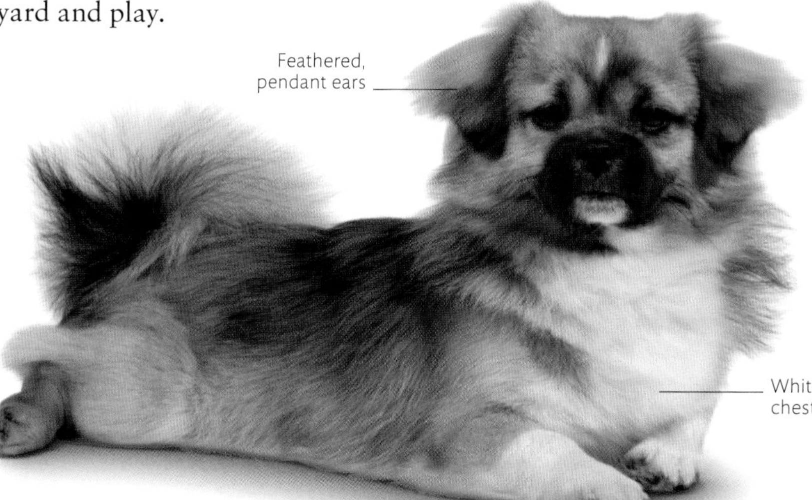

Tibetan Terrier

HEIGHT 14–16in (36–41cm)
WEIGHT 18–31lb (8–14kg)
LIFE SPAN Over 10 years

Variety of colors

Resembling a miniature Old English Sheepdog (see p.56), the Tibetan Terrier was originally bred for herding and was also used as a guard dog for traders journeying to and from China. This medium-sized dog requires a firm hand, but the reward is a loyal, devoted companion. The long coat needs daily grooming.

Japanese Chin

HEIGHT 8–11in (20–28cm)
WEIGHT 5–7lb (2–3kg)
LIFE SPAN Over 10 years

Red and white

Ancestors of the Japanese Chin are thought to have been a royal gift from China to the Emperor of Japan. This dog was bred especially to warm the laps and hands of the ladies of Japan's Imperial Palace. Happy living in a small space, it makes an ideal apartment dog but its profuse coat sheds heavily.

North American Shepherd

HEIGHT 13–18in (33–46cm)
WEIGHT 15–31lb (7–14kg)
LIFE SPAN 12–13 years

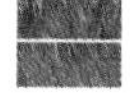
Red merle
Blue merle

Downsized from the Australian Shepherd (see p.68) by American breeders, this dog is sometimes called the Miniature Australian Shepherd. It is highly intelligent, easy to train, and very good with children. The North American Shepherd is eager to please, but can be quite destructive if left on its own for long periods of time.

Danish-Swedish Farmdog

HEIGHT 13–15in (32–37cm)
WEIGHT 15–26lb (7–12kg)
LIFE SPAN 10–15 years

Tricolor

This working dog has historically been used on farms in Denmark and Sweden as a herder, watchdog, and ratter, as well as a companion. Always eager to play, the Danish-Swedish Farmdog is good with children, so can make a great family dog, but it does have a tendency to chase small animals.

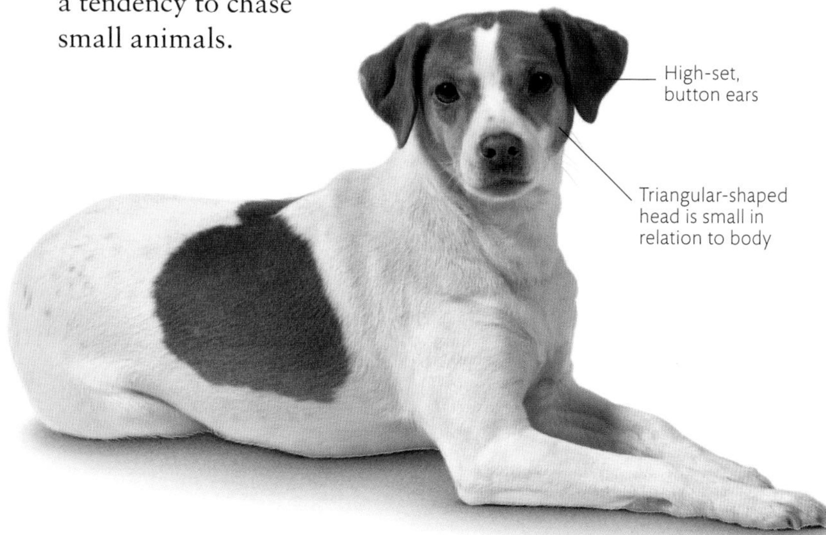

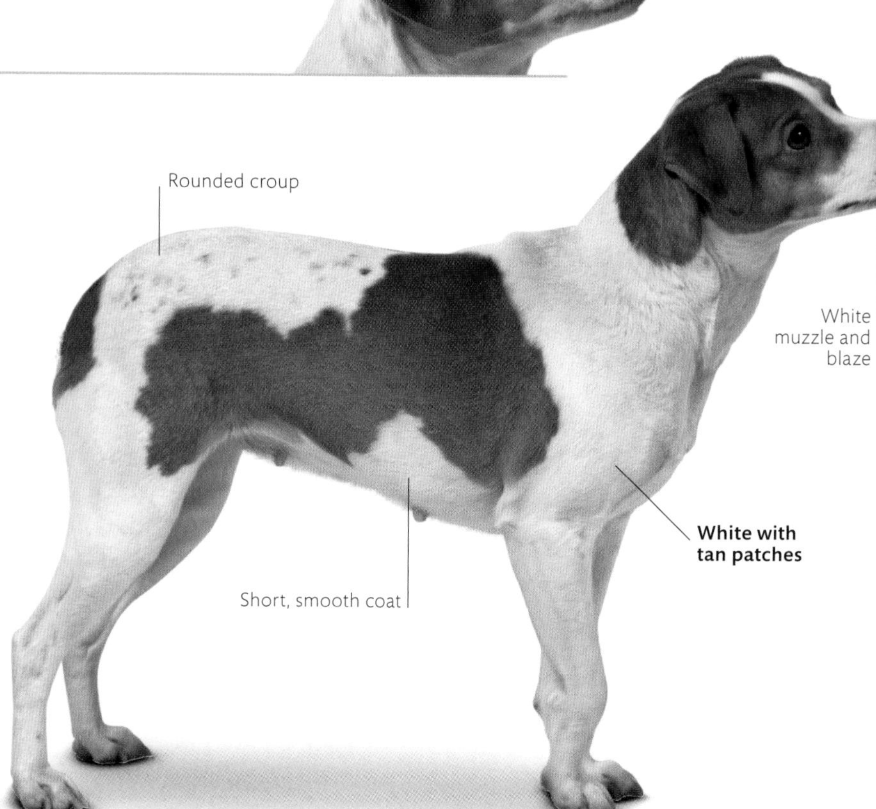

Himalayan Sheepdog

HEIGHT 20–25in (51–63cm)
WEIGHT 51–60lb (23–27kg)
LIFE SPAN 10–11 years

Gold
Black
Black and tan (right)

lso known as the Bhotia, this are dog from the foothills of the Iimalayas is related to the larger ibetan Mastiff (see p.80), but s exact origins and former uses re obscure. This is a powerful og with a strong herding nstinct. Kept as a family pet, t is a good companion and n efficient guard dog.

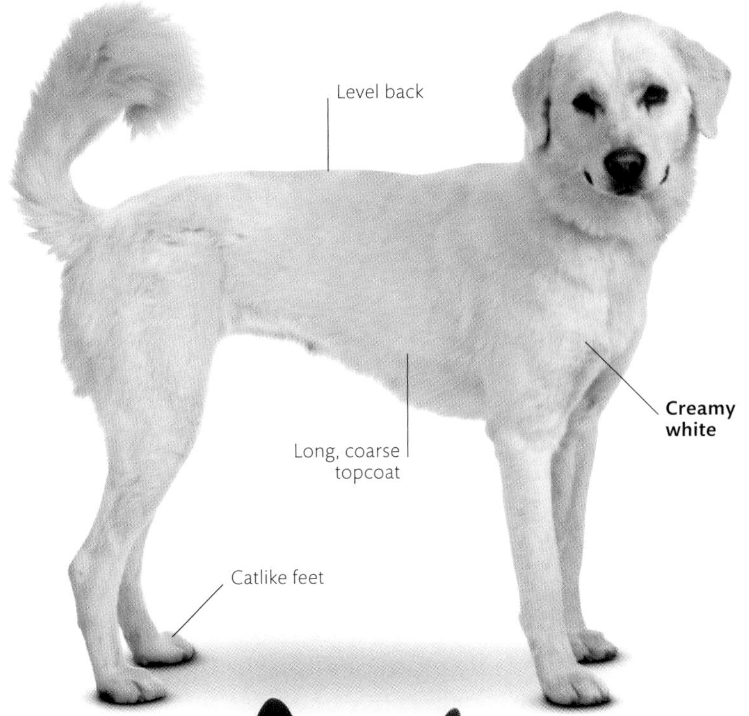

Thai Ridgeback

HEIGHT 20–24in (51–61cm)
WEIGHT 51–75lb (23–34kg)
LIFE SPAN 10–12 years

Isabella
Red
Blue

An old breed and unknown outside Thailand until the mid-1970s, the Thai Ridgeback has since gained recognition in other countries. It was used for nunting, to follow carts, and as a guard dog. Its earlier geographic isolation nas resulted in most of its original natural instincts and drives remaining, since there were few chances for it to breed with other dogs. Today, it is orimarily kept as a companion dog, and is naturally orotective of its home and family. It can make a loyal, loving pet, but is often suspicious of other dogs, and can be aggressive or shy if not properly socialized.

Dalmatian

HEIGHT	WEIGHT	LIFE SPAN	
22–24in (56–61cm)	40–60lb (18–27kg)	Over 10 years	 White with liver spots

This playful and easy-going dog makes a good family pet, but needs plenty of exercise and persistent training

The Dalmatian is the only spotted dog in existence today. Its ancestry is unclear, although spotted dogs have been known since ancient times in Europe, Africa, and Asia. The FCI has defined the breed's area of origin as Dalmatia, a region of Croatia on the eastern coast of the Adriatic Sea.

The breed has had many uses, including as a hunting dog, a dog of war, and a guard for livestock. The Dalmatian was especially popular in the UK during the early 19th century, when it was known as the "carriage dog" because it was trained to run under or beside horse-drawn carriages, often traveling very long distances. As well as looking elegant, it protected the horses and carriage from marauding stray dogs.

In the US the Dalmatian was used as a "fire-house dog," running with the horse-drawn fire engines and barking to clear the way for them. Some fire stations still keep Dalmatians as mascots. The breed is also an emblem of the American Anheuser-Busch beer company, often seen running beside the wagons pulled by the famous Clydesdale horses.

The Dalmatian is intelligent, friendly, and outgoing. It loves human company and still has an affinity with horses. However, it does have a great deal of energy and can be stubborn and aggressive with other dogs, so an owner needs to give it an active lifestyle and dedicate time to training.

The puppies are born pure white, and the black or liver spots only start to appear from about four weeks of age. The white coat sheds a great deal.

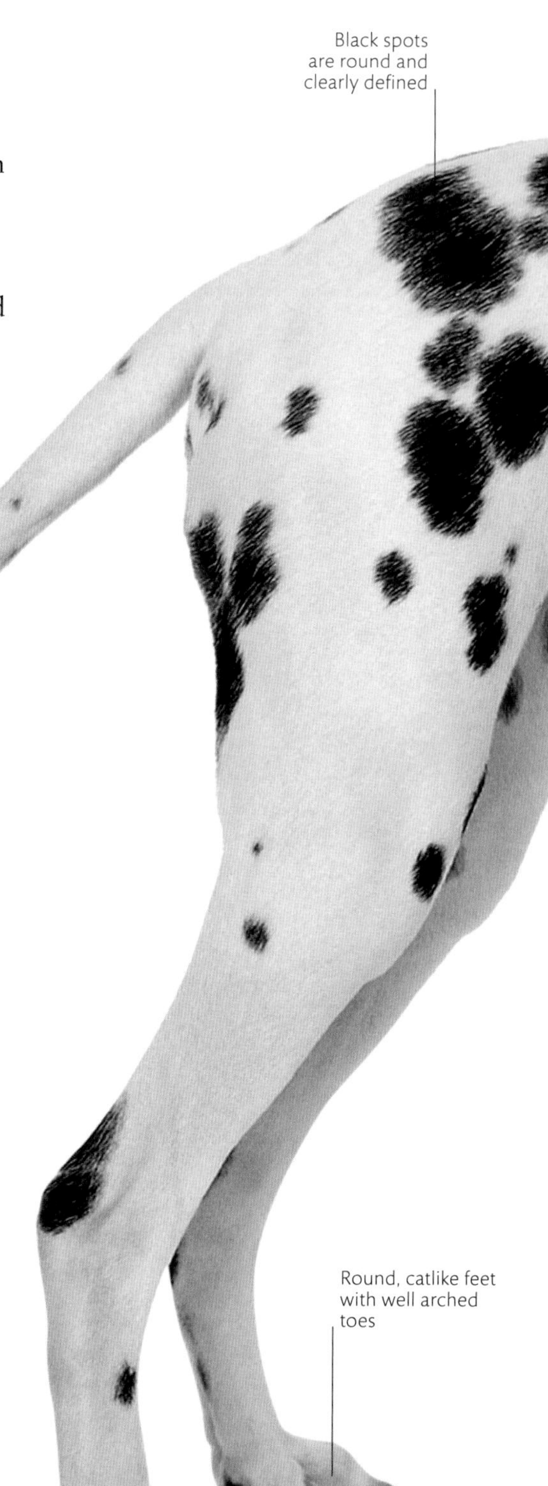

101 DALMATIANS

The 1956 children's book *The Hundred and One Dalmatians* by Dodie Smith tells the story of a litter of Dalmatians that is kidnapped by the evil Cruella De Vil, to be skinned and turned into coats. They are, fortunately, rescued by their parents, Pongo and Perdita. Dalmatians became hugely popular thanks to the two Walt Disney films that followed. However, many new owners lacked the experience to cope with this energetic breed, and countless Dalmatians were abandoned and ended up in rescue shelters.

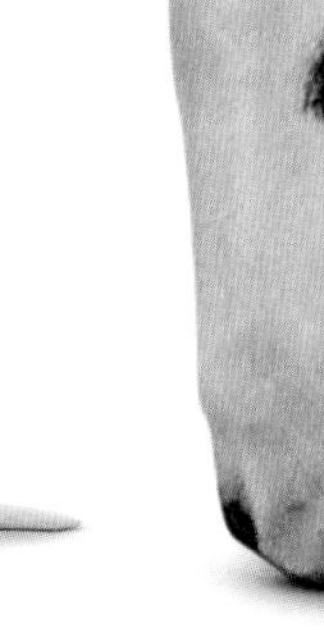

PUPPY

Clearly defined stop
White with black spots
Short, dense, glossy coat
High-set, drop ears taper to rounded points
Black nose

Goldendoodle
This attractive dog is a cross between a Poodle and a Golden Retriever. The characteristics of the Poodle parent are clearly evident.

CROSSBREEDS

ogs of mixed breeding vary from the so-called designer dogs, with purebred parents of two ifferent recognized breeds, to the bit-of-everything type, the result of accidental, random crosses ;ee p.298). Some designer hybrids are now extremely fashionable. They are mostly given whimsical ombination names, such as Cockerpoo (a Cocker Spaniel-Poodle cross).

)ne of the reasons for creating ıodern hybrid dogs was to mix ıe desired characteristics from one reed with the non-shedding coat of nother. A cross of this type currently njoying great popularity is the abradoodle (see p.291), a mixture of abrador Retriever (see p.260) and oodle (see p.229). However, ven when the parents are readily :cognized breeds such as these, it ıay be impossible to predict which ide of the family the puppies will ıvor. Labradoodles, for example, how little consistency from litter) litter, some puppies inheriting ıe curly poodle coat while others re more obviously influenced by he Labrador parent. Such lack of tandardization is common in designer crosses, although occasionally it has proved possible to produce a standard and attempt to breed dogs to type. An example of this is the Lucas Terrier (see p.293), the result of crossing the Sealyham Terrier (see p.189) and the Norfolk Terrier (see p.192). Currently, few such crosses have achieved official breed recognition.

Deliberate mixing of two specific breeds to produce particular characteristics has proliferated since the end of the 20th century, but is by no means a modern trend. One of the best-known crossbreeds, the Lurcher (see p.290), has been around for several hundred years. This dog combines the qualities of speedy sight hounds, such as the Greyhound (see p.126) and Whippet (see p.128), with desirable traits found in other breeds, such as the collie's enthusiasm for work, and the tenacity of the terrier.

Prospective owners of a crossbreed, designer dog should take into account the personalities and temperaments of both breeds involved in the mix. These may be very different and either one might predominate. It is also important to consider both parent dogs' requirements for general care and exercise.

All crossbred dogs are commonly believed to be more intelligent than pedigree dogs, but there is no sound evidence for this. Random breeds are often said to be healthier than purebreds, and it is true that they are at much lower risk of the inherited diseases prevalent in some breeds.

Lurcher

HEIGHT 22–28in (55–71cm)
WEIGHT 60–71lb (27–32kg)
LIFE SPAN 13–14 years

Any color

Famed as a poacher's dog and used to hunt rabbit and hare, Lurchers were traditionally first-generation crosses of a sight hound with a terrier or a herding dog. Today they are also bred with each other and ideally are greyhound size. In the home Lurchers are peaceful and tolerant and make fine family companions.

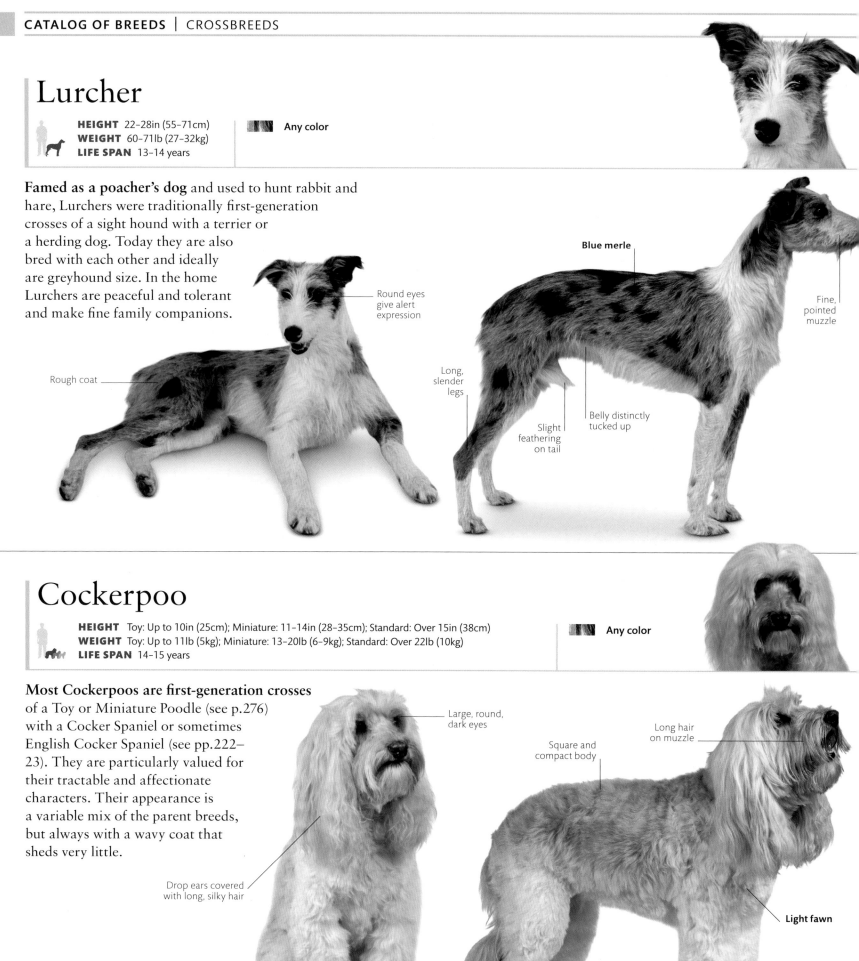

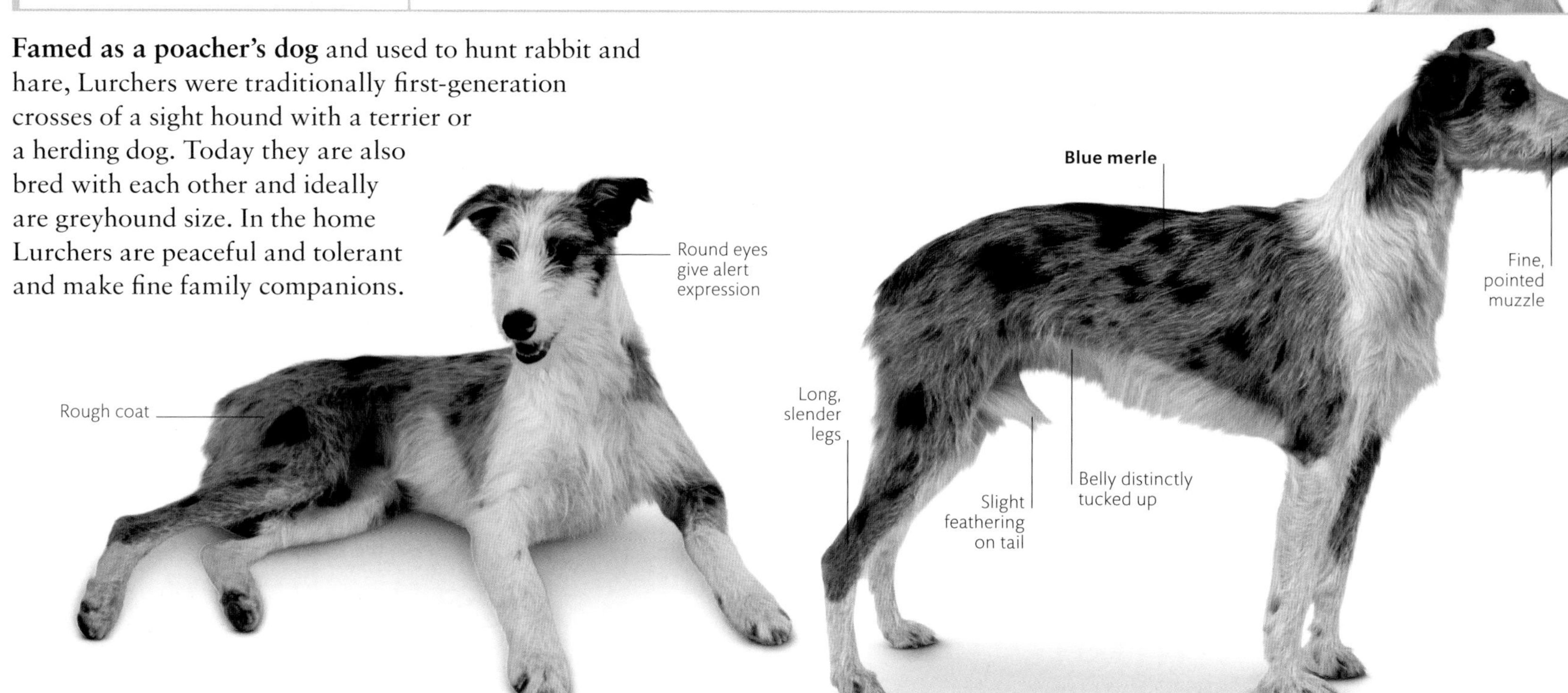

Cockerpoo

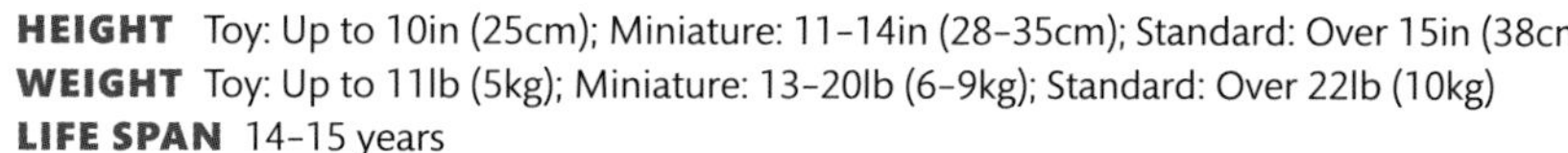

HEIGHT Toy: Up to 10in (25cm); Miniature: 11–14in (28–35cm); Standard: Over 15in (38cm)
WEIGHT Toy: Up to 11lb (5kg); Miniature: 13–20lb (6–9kg); Standard: Over 22lb (10kg)
LIFE SPAN 14–15 years

Any color

Most Cockerpoos are first-generation crosses of a Toy or Miniature Poodle (see p.276) with a Cocker Spaniel or sometimes English Cocker Spaniel (see pp.222–23). They are particularly valued for their tractable and affectionate characters. Their appearance is a variable mix of the parent breeds, but always with a wavy coat that sheds very little.

Labradoodle

HEIGHT	WEIGHT	LIFE SPAN	
Miniature: 14–16in (36–41cm) Medium: 17–20in (43–51cm) Standard: 21–24in (53–61cm)	Miniature: 15–24lb (7–11kg) Medium: 31–44lb (14–20kg) Standard: 51–65lb (23–29kg)	14–15 years	Any color

DONALD CAMPBELL'S DOG

Individual crosses between the Poodle and the Labrador Retriever were known before the founding of the Labradoodle as a "breed." One such dog belonged to Donald Campbell, CBE (below, left), who set land and water speed records in Britain in the 1950s and 60s. In his 1955 autobiography, *Into the Water Barrier*, Campbell referred to his beloved Maxie, a Labrador-Poodle cross born in 1949, as a "Labradoodle"—long before breeder Wally Conron used the name in Australia.

Increasingly popular, this dog's reliably playful, affectionate, and intelligent temperament reflects its parentage

This hybrid dog was founded when Wally Conron of Guide Dogs Victoria, Australia, received a request from a vision-impaired woman in Hawaii who needed a guide dog that would not aggravate her husband's dog allergy. Conron mated a Poodle (a breed with a coat suitable for people with allergies) with a Labrador Retriever guide dog. One of the resulting puppies, a male named Sultan, had the required non-irritating coat and a good temperament. He became the first recognized Labradoodle, a cross between the Labrador Retriever (see p.260) and Poodles (see pp.229, 276).

In Australia the Labradoodle is on its way to becoming a pedigree breed. Elsewhere it remains a crossbreed, with no official status but in huge demand.

First-generation crosses vary in appearance; later Labradoodle-only breedings are more predictable. There are now two main Labradoodle varieties, distinguished by coat type: wool coat (tightly curled like a Poodle's) and fleece coat (long and loosely curled).

The Labradoodle has rapidly gained popularity as a family dog. The dog's friendly, intelligent nature attracts owners as much as its appearance.

Apricot

Long, curved tail

Tucked-up belly

Large, round, dark eyes

Body slightly heavier than a Poodle (see p.229)

Cream underparts

Medium-sized, round feet

STANDARD

Drop ears

Curly coat has little dander

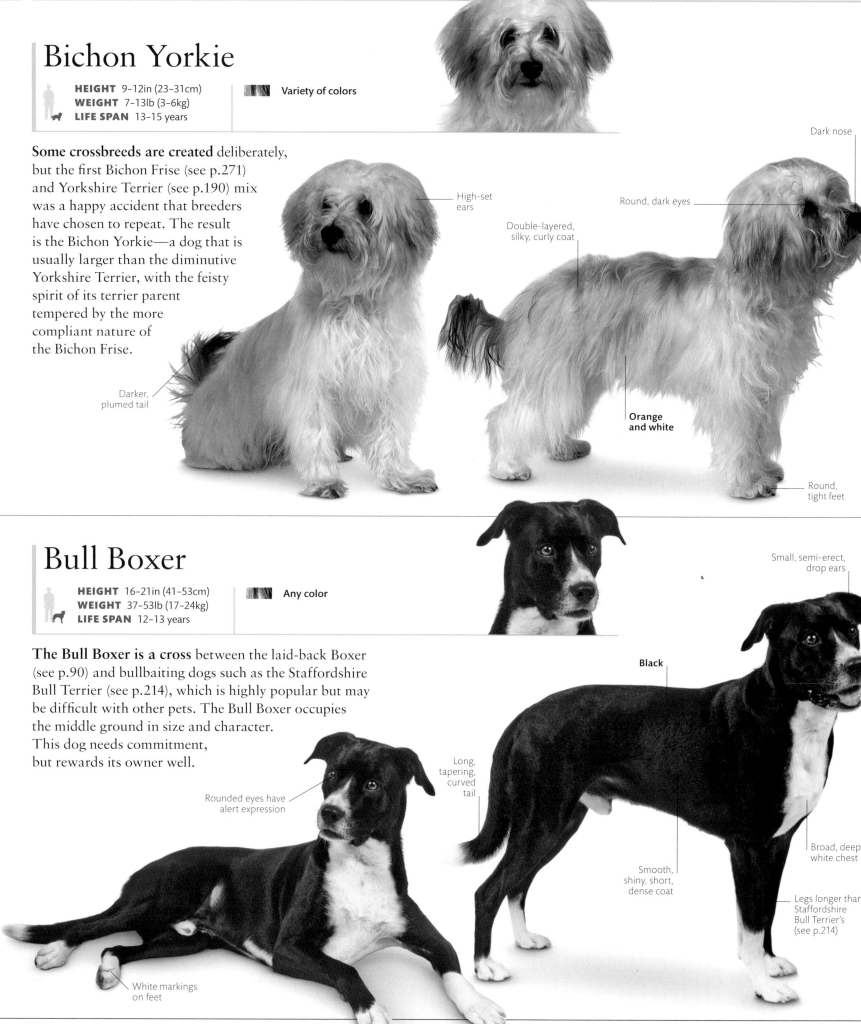

Bichon Yorkie

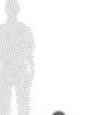

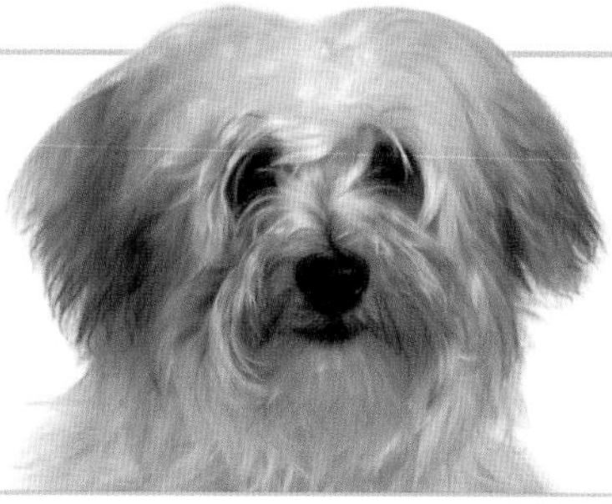

HEIGHT 9–12in (23–31cm)
WEIGHT 7–13lb (3–6kg)
LIFE SPAN 13–15 years

Variety of colors

Some crossbreeds are created deliberately, but the first Bichon Frise (see p.271) and Yorkshire Terrier (see p.190) mix was a happy accident that breeders have chosen to repeat. The result is the Bichon Yorkie—a dog that is usually larger than the diminutive Yorkshire Terrier, with the feisty spirit of its terrier parent tempered by the more compliant nature of the Bichon Frise.

High-set ears
Darker, plumed tail

Dark nose
Round, dark eyes
Double-layered, silky, curly coat
Orange and white
Round, tight feet

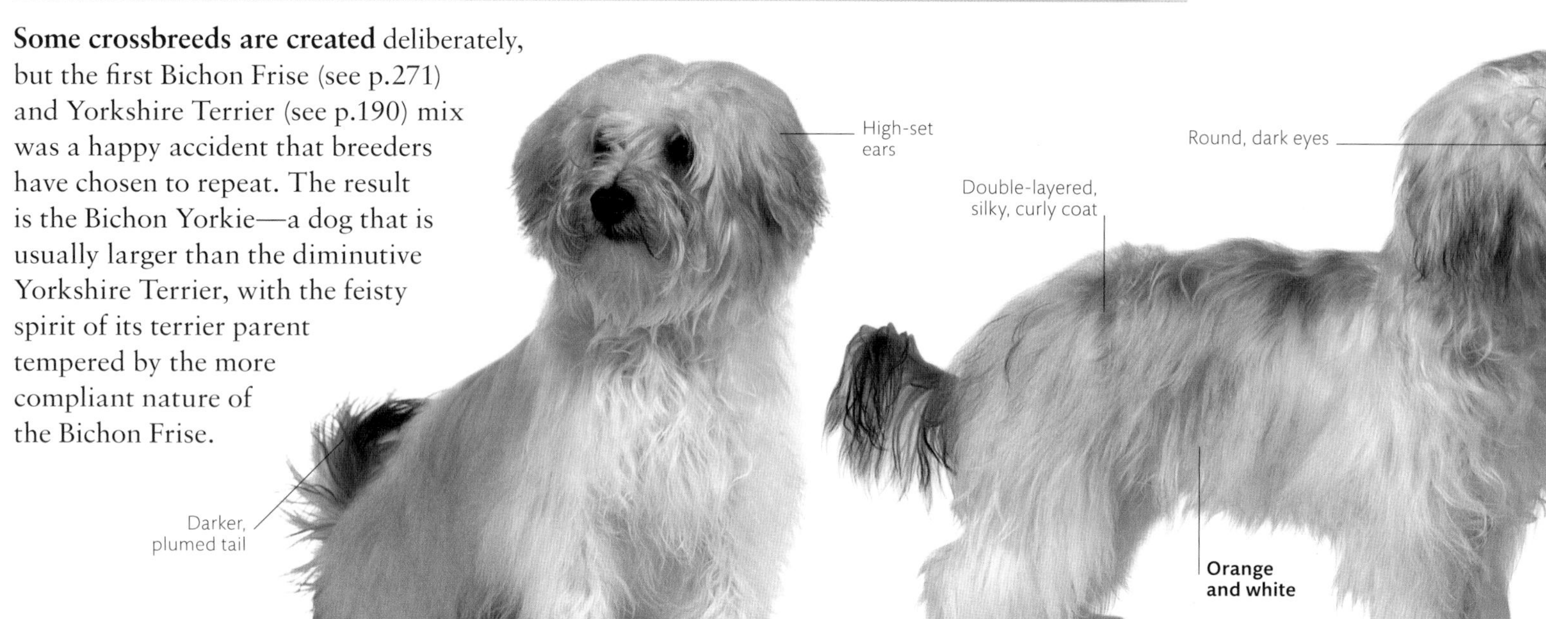

Bull Boxer

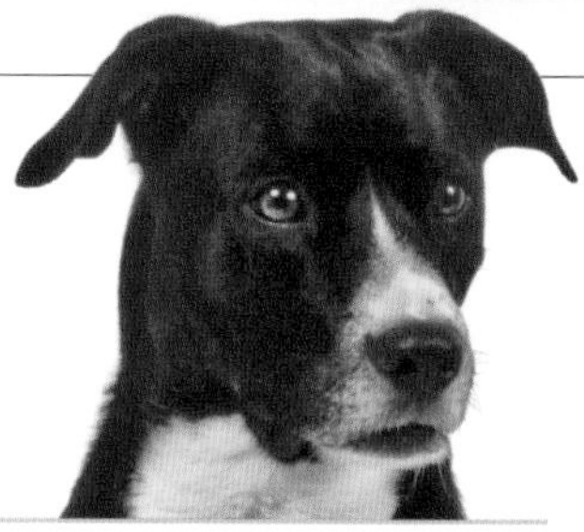

HEIGHT 16–21in (41–53cm)
WEIGHT 37–53lb (17–24kg)
LIFE SPAN 12–13 years

Any color

The Bull Boxer is a cross between the laid-back Boxer (see p.90) and bullbaiting dogs such as the Staffordshire Bull Terrier (see p.214), which is highly popular but may be difficult with other pets. The Bull Boxer occupies the middle ground in size and character. This dog needs commitment, but rewards its owner well.

Rounded eyes have alert expression
White markings on feet

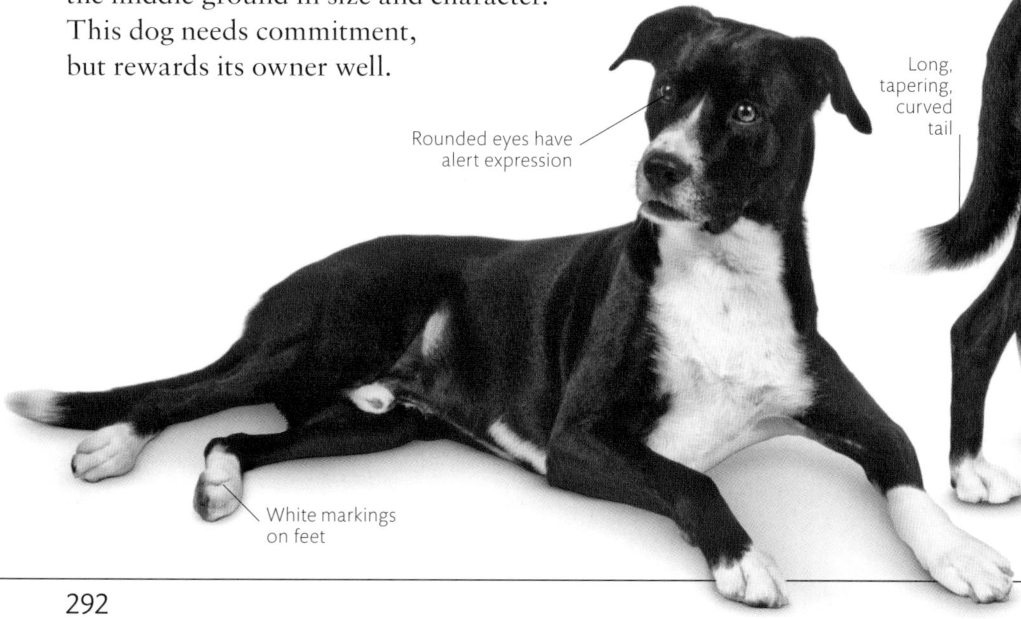

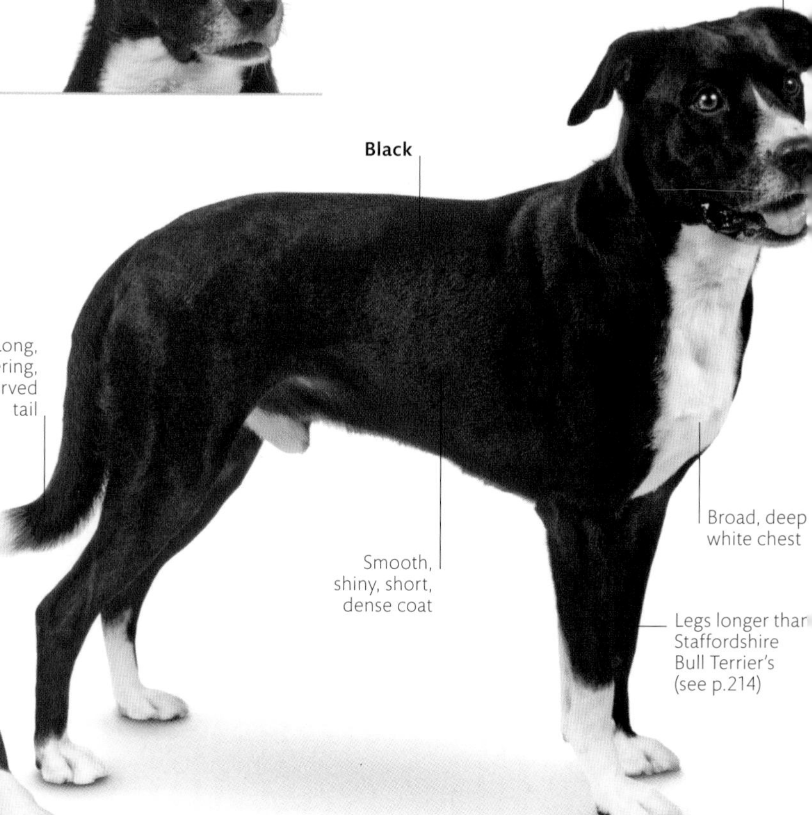

Small, semi-erect, drop ears
Black
Long, tapering, curved tail
Broad, deep white chest
Smooth, shiny, short, dense coat
Legs longer than Staffordshire Bull Terrier's (see p.214)

Lucas Terrier

HEIGHT	WEIGHT	LIFE SPAN	White
9–12in (23–30cm)	11–20lb (5–9kg)	14–15 years	Tan coats may have a black or badger-gray saddle. White coats may be marked with black, badger-gray, and/or tan.

'his friendly, non-yappy terrier thrives on long walks ınd gets along well with children and other pets

'his rare working terrier was produced in ıe 1940s by crossing Norfolk Terriers (see .192) with Sealyham Terriers (see p.189). 'he Lucas Terrier is named after its first reeder, Sir Jocelyn Lucas, a British olitician and sportsman who wanted to evelop a hunting dog that was smaller nd more nimble than the Sealyham 'errier. From the 1960s Lucas Terriers vere also exported to the US, where they roved popular with a variety of people, ıcluding Hollywood stars.

After the death of Sir Jocelyn and his usiness partner, the Hon. Enid Plummer, breed society was set up in the UK in 1987 to promote and improve the Lucas Terrier. The Lucas Terrier Club created a breed standard in 1988 and in recent years has been trying to obtain official recognition—to date unsuccessfully. There are now believed to be around 400 of these dogs in the UK and around 100 in the US.

Today the Lucas Terrier is kept mainly as a companion dog. Biddable, smart, and eager to please, the breed is easy to train. It is also good with children and well behaved in the house, provided it has a vigorous daily walk. It has typical terrier traits, such as enjoying play and loving to dig, but is less inclined to bark than many other terrier breeds.

CREATING A WORKING TERRIER

Sir Jocelyn Lucas was a well-known Sealyham breeder who was unhappy about the increase in size and weight of show dogs. Not only were they no longer suited to the work for which they were bred, but his dogs also sometimes had whelping problems when crossed with show dogs. As a result, he decided to outcross his dogs with Norfolk Terriers when he bred from them for the first time. He was so impressed with the puppies from these matings that he continued breeding them, and in doing so created the Lucas Terrier.

SIR JOCELYN LUCAS WITH MINIATURE SEALYHAM PUPPIES

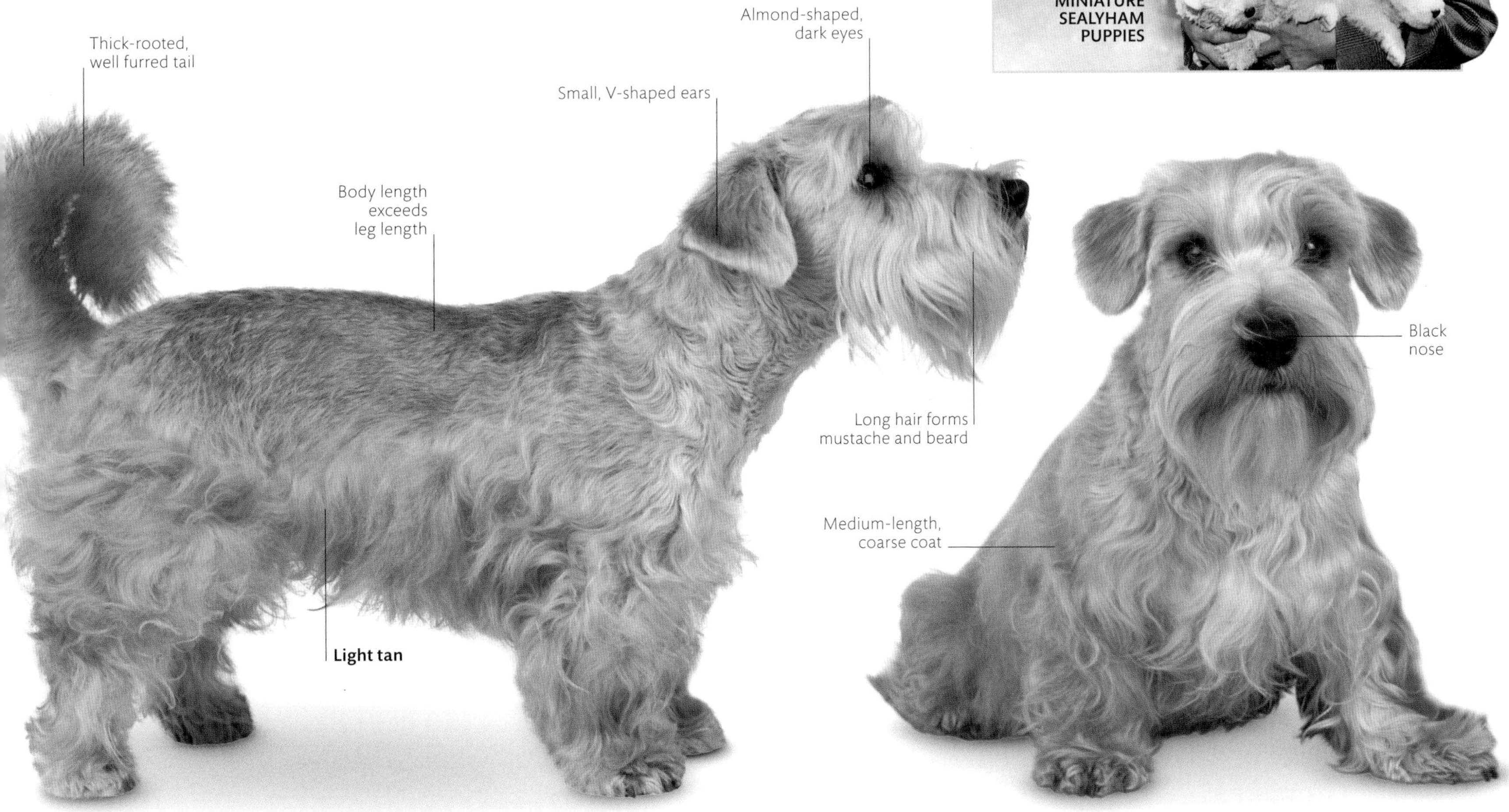

Thick-rooted, well furred tail

Small, V-shaped ears

Almond-shaped, dark eyes

Body length exceeds leg length

Black nose

Long hair forms mustache and beard

Medium-length, coarse coat

Light tan

Goldendoodle

HEIGHT	WEIGHT	LIFE SPAN	Any color
Up to 24in (61cm)	51–90lb (23–41kg)	10–15 years	

ALLERGY SUFFERER'S DOG

The Goldendoodle is often spoken of as a "hypoallergenic" or "non-shedding" dog suitable for people who normally have allergies to dogs. While there is no such thing as a truly hypoallergenic dog (that is, rarely or never causing allergies), Goldendoodles do shed more lightly than other breeds, especially those Goldendoodles with curly or wavy coats, and their skin sheds less dander. This may make them more suitable as pets for people who are known to have allergic reactions to dogs (or dog hair).

A delightful new crossbreed, this dog is sociable and easy to train and a pleasure to live with

One of the newest "designer dogs," this mixture of the Poodle and the Golden Retriever (see p.259) was first bred in the US and Australia in the 1990s. Since then the Goldendoodle's growing popularity has encouraged breeders elsewhere to continue its development. The original "standard" Goldendoodles were crosses between the Standard Poodle (see p.229) and the Golden Retriever, but from 1999 smaller "medium," "miniature," and "petite" Goldendoodles have been bred, with the smaller sizes having Miniature Poodle or Toy Poodle parents (see p.276).

Most of these dogs are first-generation crosses and vary considerably in appearance. Goldendoodles may also be crossbred with each other, or bred back to Poodles. There are three coat types: straight, like a Golden Retriever's coat; curly, like a Poodle's coat; and wavy, with loose, shaggy curls.

Goldendoodles are in demand as guide dogs, assistance dogs, and therapy dogs, and for search and rescue work. They are also hugely popular as pets; in 2012 US musician Usher bid $12,000 for a Goldendoodle puppy at a charity auction. Energetic but gentle, Goldendoodles are usually easy to train. They get along well with children and other pets and love human company.

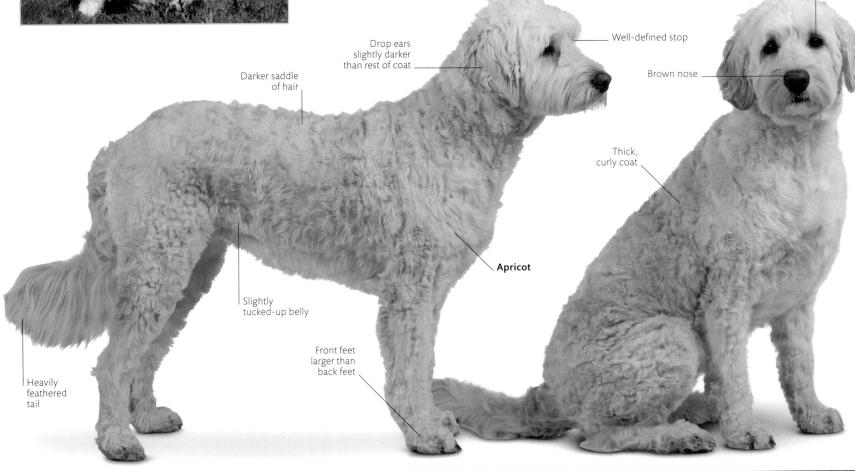

Dark eyes with kind expression
Well-defined stop
Drop ears slightly darker than rest of coat
Brown nose
Darker saddle of hair
Thick, curly coat
Apricot
Slightly tucked-up belly
Front feet larger than back feet
Heavily feathered tail

Labradinger

HEIGHT	WEIGHT	LIFE SPAN	
18–22in (46–56cm)	55–90lb (25–41kg)	10–14 years	Yellow Liver Chocolate

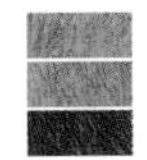

TREO, THE ARMY DOG

A Spaniel-Labrador cross named Treo has become a military hero for his work with the British Army in Afghanistan. Treo was originally given to the army because of his tendency to snap and growl at people. However, he went on to distinguish himself as an arms and explosives detection dog, working with handler Sergeant Dave Heyhoe. On two occasions he detected chains of roadside bombs planted by the Taliban, enabling the bombs to be defused and saving many lives. He was awarded the Dickin Medal—the "Animals' Victoria Cross"—for his bravery.

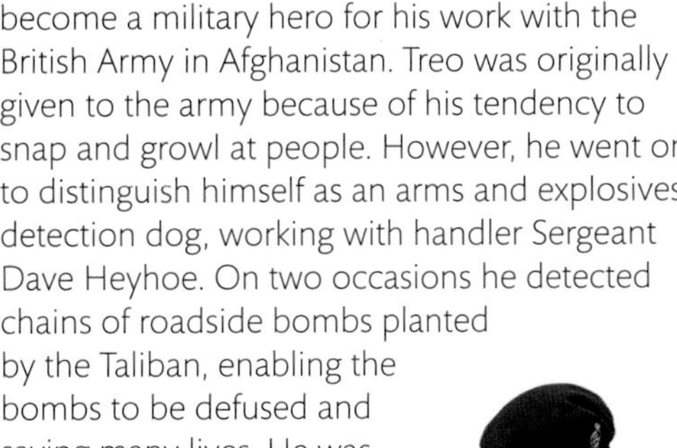

TREO AND HANDLER SERGEANT DAVE HEYHOE POSE WITH DICKIN MEDAL

This attractive all-arounder is suitable as both a gundog and family dog, given sufficient exercise

A cross between the Labrador Retriever (see p.260) and the English Springer Spaniel (see p.224), this dog is also sometimes known as the Springador. Unplanned mixing of these two breeds is likely to have occurred for centuries on traditional country estates where such gundogs were kept. Benefiting from recent interest in "designer" crossbreeds such as the Labradoodle (see p.291), the Labradinger has now acquired both popularity and a name.

Labradingers vary in appearance, but they tend to be smaller and lighter in build than a Labrador Retriever, with a slightly finer-featured head. They are larger than an English Springer Spaniel, with longer legs. The coat may be straight and flat, or a bit longer and more ruffled.

The Labradinger is an excellent gundog that can be trained both to retrieve like a Labrador and to flush game as a spaniel does. It is also proving very successful as a family dog. These dogs are intelligent, fun-loving, affectionate, and highly people-oriented. They need lots of company and plenty of exercise every day, including walks and games, to prevent them from becoming bored and developing behavioral problems.

Puggle

HEIGHT	WEIGHT	LIFE SPAN		
10–15in (25–38cm)	15–31lb (7–14kg)	10–13 years	 Red or tan Lemon Black	Any of these colors with white (particolor). May have black mask.

A sweet-tempered, intelligent dog that makes an ideal family companion if given sufficient exercise

One of the most newly created "designer dogs," the Puggle is a cross between a Pug (see p.268) and a Beagle (see p.152). These dogs were developed in the US in the 1990s. The breeders' original goal was to produce a dog with a Pug's compact size and a Beagle's sweet nature, but without some of the health problems that can afflict Pugs. The new crossbreed is now registered with the American Canine Hybrid Club.

In recent years the Puggle has seen a huge rise in popularity. It was named in the US media as the "Hottest Dog of 2005" and has been an enormous hit with celebrities and Hollywood stars. In 2006 Puggles accounted for more than 50 percent of sales of crossbred dogs. The Puggle is now the most popular crossbreed in the US and in 2013 puppies were sold for as much as $1,000 each.

The Puggle looks like a snub-nosed Beagle, and often has a curly tail and black facial mask like a Pug. Easy to train, it makes a lively and affectionate family dog, bonding easily with its owners and loving human company. It is good with children and readily accepts strangers and other dogs. Because it will easily adapt to living in an apartment, it is particularly popular in urban areas such as Los Angeles and New York. The Puggle needs daily walks, including games, to keep happy. The short-haired coat requires little grooming, aside from a weekly brushing.

A CELEBRITY PET

The Puggle's meteoric rise to fame has been helped by the huge celebrity interest in the dog. Stars such as James Gandolfini, Jake Gyllenhaal, Uma Thurman, and renowned dog-lover Henry Winkler (below) are just a few of those who own a Puggle. In taking the dogs with them to parties, TV shows, and media events, and being photographed with them, celebrities have helped introduce the Puggle to the public. People wanted to know what this unusual dog was and some then went further and purchased one.

YOUNG DOG

Square body

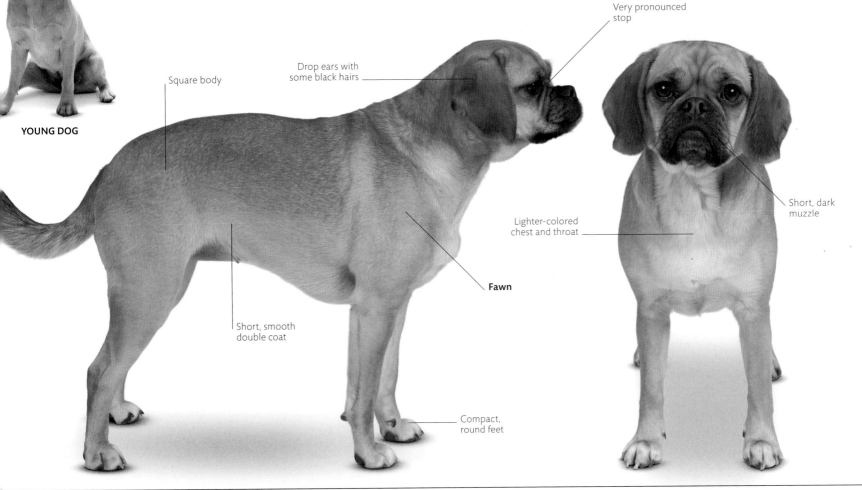

Drop ears with some black hairs

Very pronounced stop

Short, dark muzzle

Lighter-colored chest and throat

Fawn

Short, smooth double coat

Compact, round feet

Random Breeds

DOGS WITH UNKNOWN ANCESTORS

These dogs may lack a pedigree but they can provide love, companionship, and fun

Dogs with random breeding are usually of unknown ancestry, with the parents themselves likely to be the result of accidental mixings. Choosing a random-bred puppy is a bit of a lottery for prospective owners as it is difficult to predict what the dog will look like at maturity. But random-bred dogs tend to be healthier than pedigree dogs as there is less likelihood of an inheritable genetic disorder being passed on. Many rescue centre dogs are random crossbreds; in the majority of cases they make excellent pets.

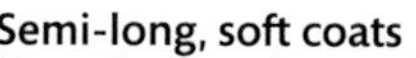

Semi-long, soft coats
Dogs that may have collies or spaniels among their ancestors often have silky coats with feathered legs, and fringed ears that are either semi-erect or hang down close to their heads.

Feathered legs with tan markings

Head is like that of a Labrador Retriever (see p.260)

High-set, drop ears with fringed edges

Silky coat with feathering resembles a spaniel's

Smooth, silky coat like a Border Collie's (see p.51)

Asymmetrical black patches less acceptable in pedigree dogs

Short hair on front of forelegs

Semi-erect ears

Semi-long, wavy coat is typical of a collie

Longer hair on underside of neck and on chest

Wiry and curly coats
Dogs with wiry and curly coats may resemble sight hounds, terriers, or some of the pastoral breeds, but without analysing their DNA it is impossible to be sure of their genealogy.

Short, double coat
These three dogs all have a short double coat but are otherwise quite different in appearance. The black dog has affinities with the Labrador Retriever (see p.260), whereas the dog on the far right is more like a German Shepherd Dog (see p.42).

Short, single coat
The shorter, wider jaws and short, harsh coat of these dogs suggest a link with dogs such as the Staffordshire Bull Terrier (see p.214). The dog on the far right is much smaller than the other two but still has terrierlike qualities.

Short legs
Dogs can be downsized by selective breeding from the smallest dogs but short legs may also occur when dogs breed at random. Short-legged dogs may display achondroplasia (dwarfism), which causes curving of the front leg bones. Dogs with short legs can have any type of coat.

Enjoying life to the full
Given a good home with sufficient mental and physical activity, dogs such as this terrierlike random breed will be just as rewarding to own as a pedigree dog.

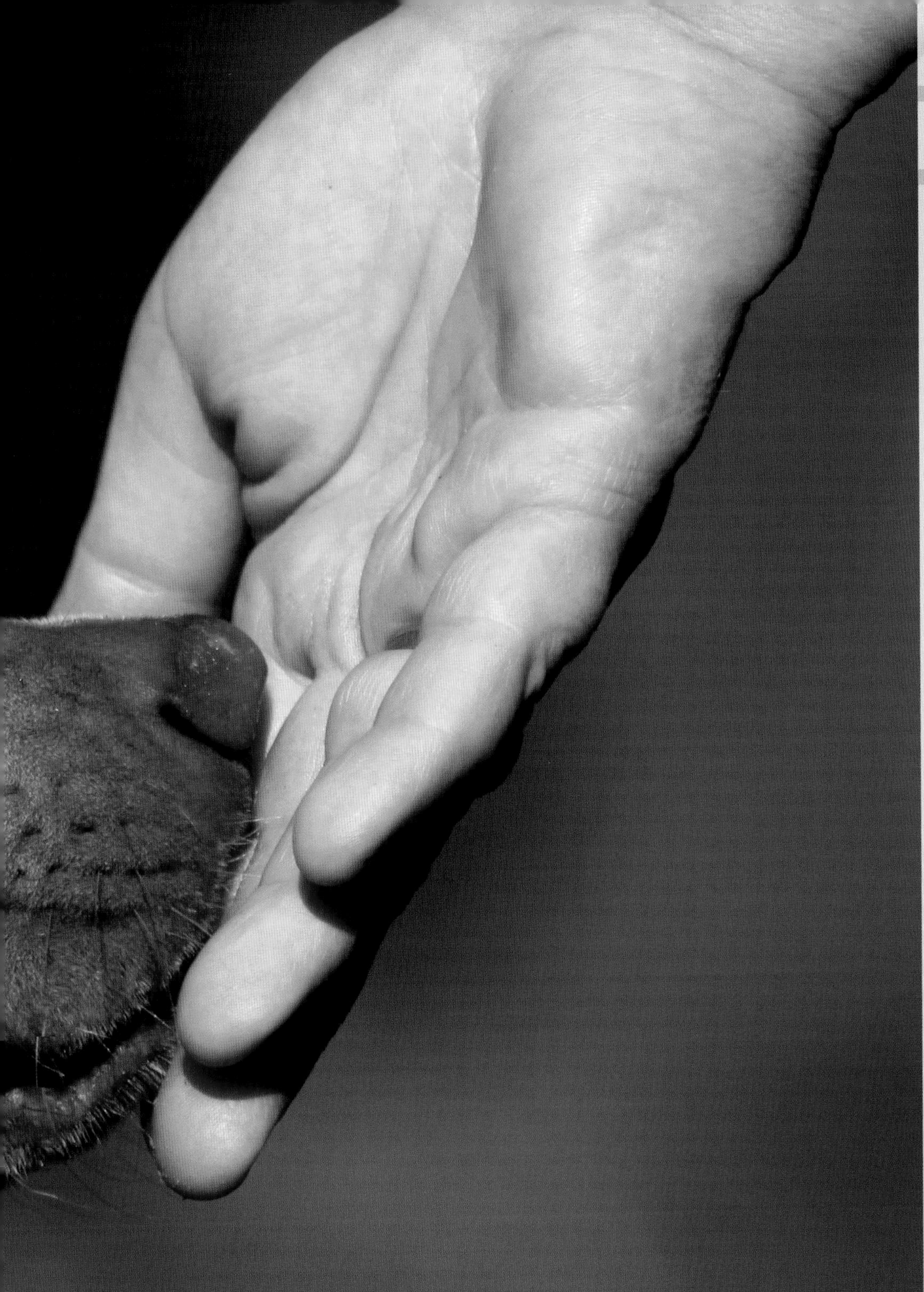

CHAPTER 3

CARE AND TRAINING

Happy beginning
Decide what your needs are—a puppy or older dog, maybe from a rescue shelter, and what size, sex, and breed. Making the right choice beforehand is key to a long and fulfilling partnership.

Becoming a dog owner

. dog can be a wonderful addition to your family, but bringing a new pet into your fe is a responsibility that requires preparation and planning. Consider what kind f dog will best suit your needs and make sure your home is a safe environment.

IRST CONSIDERATIONS

efore buying or adopting a dog, you eed to have a clear understanding of hat you are taking on. A dog can live or up to 18 years and you need to be ommitted to caring for your pet over is entire life span.

Ask yourself some pertinent questions: o you, or anyone else at home, have the me to train and play with a puppy? Can ou afford to keep a dog? Is your home nvironment suitable? Do you have other ets or very young children? Is anyone in our home allergic to dogs?

Think carefully about what kind of og you want by finding out about uitable breeds. Even if you are drawn o a particular breed for its appearance, ear in mind that temperament is more nportant than looks. Could you cope vith an active dog with lots of energy? o you need a dog that is good with hildren? Large dogs often require a lot of are and training and food, all of which an be expensive. Would a smaller dog etter suit your lifestyle and surroundings? Would you prefer a male dog or a bitch? Dogs tend to be more affectionate with people but can be easily distracted during training. Un-neutered dogs can be aggressive. Bitches are often considered calmer with children.

What age is best? A puppy will learn to fit in with your family's routine as he grows up but at first he will need extra care and should not be left alone for long periods. If everyone is out of the house all day, you may be better off adopting an adult dog.

A common way to acquire an adult dog is from a rescue center. Some rescue shelters are run by welfare charities and place dogs of many sizes and ages. Others specialize in particular dog breeds that have special issues, such as greyhounds after the end of their racing career, or dogs with specific care and training needs, such as Dobermanns (see p.176) and Staffordshire Bull Terriers (see p.214). Most breed societies run a breed rescue service.

At a rescue center the dogs' temperaments will have been assessed. Many of their dogs have had difficult experiences, such as being abandoned or neglected, so staff will be eager to see that they go to a loving and protective home. You may have to fill in an application form, attend an interview (possibly with other family members), and have your home inspected by the staff before they allow you to adopt a dog. In return, you can ask questions and meet dogs suitable for your lifestyle. The staff will advise you on care, veterinary, and behavioral issues.

LEGAL POINTS

You are responsible for your pet's welfare and, in many countries, there are laws to ensure that pet owners care for their animals properly. Essential duties include making sure that your dog has a safe place to live, good food, and plenty of company. As a dog owner you also need to make certain that your pet will not cause harm to himself or to other people or animals.

Take out pet insurance before taking ownership of a dog. Insurance is essential for illnesses and injuries, and covers costs if your pet is lost or dies, or if he harms a person, other animals, or property.

CHECKLIST FOR A SAFER HOME

Indoors

- Keep hard floors dry, and towel-dry a wet dog promptly.
- Keep outside doors shut; install a stair gate.
- Block any small gaps behind or between furniture.
- Fix frayed electrical cords.
- Fit child locks to cabinet doors and drawers.
- Use trash cans with secure lids.
- Put cleaning chemicals away and out of reach.
- Keep medicines in the cabinet.
- Get rid of any toxic houseplants.
- Check floors and low surfaces for small or sharp items.
- At holiday times, keep your dog away from fragile decorations and lit candles. Find a safe place for him to hide from fireworks.

Outdoors

- Close off any gaps in hedges or fencing or under gates.
- Move or get rid of toxic plants.
- Make sure your dog has sufficient shade in the yard.
- Keep garage or shed doors shut to keep your dog away from machinery, sharp or heavy tools, or chemicals such as antifreeze, paints, and paint thinner.
- Keep poisons and fertilizers locked up or on a high shelf.
- Keep your dog away from areas where poisons or slug pellets have been used; dispose of dead animals that have eaten poison.
- Never leave your dog alone with a barbecue—hot coals and sharp skewers can cause injury.

Preparing for arrival
Introducing a new dog into your life is an exciting experience, but it comes with big responsibilities. Taking the time to prepare your home and yard will make his arrival safe and enjoyable for you both.

Bringing your dog home

Introducing a new pet into your home will be exciting but also a little nerve-racking—not least for your dog. Prepare as much as possible beforehand so the first days are quiet and calm while your dog settles in.

PREPARING FOR ARRIVAL

It is best to obtain essential equipment before your dog arrives in your home. You will need a bed before anything else. A strong cardboard box may be fine for a puppy, since it can be thrown away if soiled or chewed, or as the dog grows. Alternatively, molded plastic beds are easy to clean and can withstand some chewing. Whichever you choose, it needs to be big enough for him to stretch out and turn around in. Add a soft lining of towels or blankets or use with a foam bed. Foam beds are comfortable and many have machine-washable covers. They are good for elderly dogs with joint issues but not so suitable for younger dogs likely to chew or soil the bed. If you are getting a young puppy, letting him sleep in a box or basket in your bedroom can help him to settle in.

For a new puppy or a dog that needs to feel and be secure, it can help to use a dog crate with wire sides and top and a solid bottom, or an open-topped pen. Set this up somewhere warm and quiet, where he can see and hear people so he will not be lonely. Line the bottom with newspapers in case of accidents and add bedding and toys. This is a good place for him to be until he is housebroken, for short periods alone, or as a safe space if he is hurt or sick, but never leave him in the crate for long periods or lock him inside as a punishment.

The next essential items are bowls for food and water. Both need to be cleaned every day and food bowls cleaned before each meal. Ceramic bowls are sturdy enough even for large dogs; however, they are often straight-sided, with hard-to-reach corners. Stainless-steel bowls are easy to use and keep clean. The best are non-tip with a rubber rim around the bottom to keep them still during use. Plastic bowls are better suited to puppies and smaller dogs. Collect any diet sheets and initial supplies from the breeder or shelter and have at least a week's supply of food.

Your dog will also need a collar. Use a soft, fabric one for a puppy, fastened so you can slip two fingers between it and the puppy's neck, and check every week that it is not getting too tight. For adult dogs, use fabric or leather collars, or a harness for a strong dog.

You will also need a basic grooming kit (see p.319), even for short-haired dogs. For clearing up dog feces outdoors, carry small biodegradable bags. Vets and pet stores sell bags specially for this purpose.

In addition to equipment, you need to have a name ready. Choose a name of one or two syllables since this will be easy for the dog to learn, but avoid any names that could be confused with words you might use to train the dog, such as "stay" or "no."

Essential equipment
Stable, easy-clean food and water bowls, a comfortable fabric collar with a name tag, and a sturdy leash are all important items to obtain before your new dog arrives.

DOG TOYS

Toys enable a dog to express natural behavior such as chasing and chewing. You can buy special dog toys like the ones shown here, or improvise your own using items such as an old ball or a length of rope. Choose toys made from a substance that will not splinter or choke your dog and that are large enough not to get stuck in his throat. To prevent bad habits, do not use old clothes or shoes.

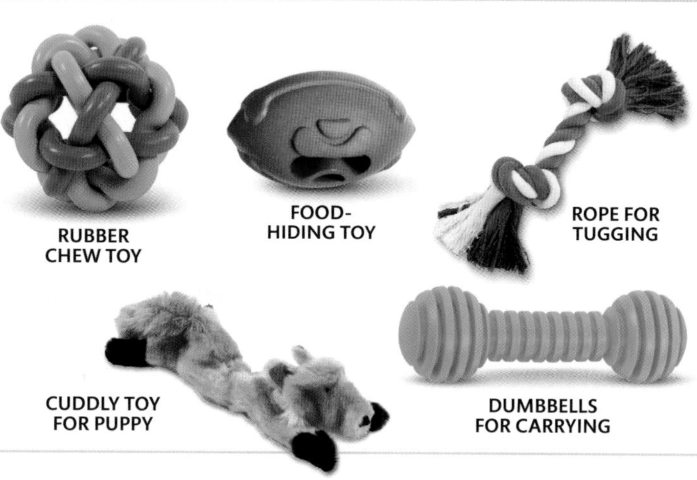

DOG-PROOF HOME

Before bringing a new dog into your home, you will need to check for anything that ma cause him harm (see p.305). Get down to "dog level" to assess for possible hazards such as escape routes. A dog can dart through doors, under gates, or down stairs and run into the street. Make sure you place sharp objects out of reach, and remove chewable items such as balloons, which can cause blockages. Some human foods such as chocolates and grapes or raisins can harm dogs (see p.344) so clear them away, too.

As soon as you get home with your dog or puppy, take him into the yard or outdoors,

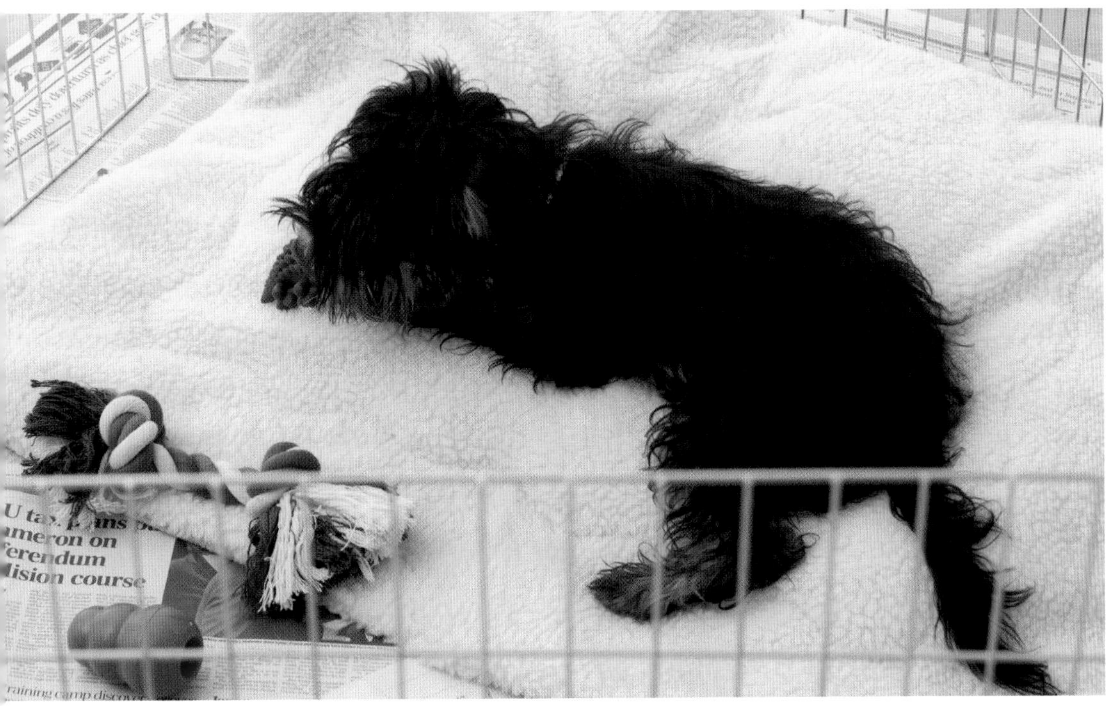

uppy pen
ut the pen in a warm, draft-free area where your puppy an see you and other members of the family during the ay. It should be large enough for him to move around in.

Introducing a young child
Let your dog meet your child once he has settled in. Demonstrate how to stroke the dog gently, then let your toddler try.

ince he may need to relieve himself. Then et your dog into your house and let him xplore. For the first day at least, keep your et in his den area so he can get used to the ome gradually. A puppy will tire quickly o allow him to sleep whenever he wants.

IRST INTRODUCTIONS

ntroduce your dog to everyone in the family. f you have children, supervise them for the irst few days while they and the dog get sed to each other. Explain that your new log may be feeling a bit nervous so they need o be quiet around him. Ask the children to ome into the room with your dog, sit down quietly, and offer him treats. They will need o keep play sessions short for the first few lays so that your dog does not get tired or overexcited. They must not grab him or pick him up suddenly because he could get rightened and bite them.

Let your new dog meet other pets one at a time after the first day or so, once he has settled in. Introduce resident dogs to the new one in "neutral territory," such as the yard, so there is room to escape if one of them gets nervous. Make a fuss of your resident dog before paying attention to the new one to reduce any risk of jealousy.

To introduce a cat, choose a large room and hold on to the dog while the cat comes to meet him. Make sure the cat has an easy escape route. Never feed cats and dogs together because the dog may steal the cat's food.

EARLY ROUTINES

Establish a routine from day one and ask everyone to keep to it. Feed your dog and take him outside to relieve himself at regular times. Set ground rules for what your dog is allowed to do and where he can go.

Developing a routine will help avoid accidents while housebreaking. Take your puppy outside after eating, after a nap, just before bedtime, and just after any exciting event (such as meeting a new person). You may need to take a young puppy out about once an hour. Watch for signs such as sniffing the ground, turning in circles, and squatting, and take him out immediately. Stay outdoors with your dog until he relieves himself, then give him lots of praise.

Household appliances such as the vacuum cleaner and washing machine are noisy and potentially frightening so let your dog be present while the machine is running—but at a comfortable distance with an "escape route." If he looks nervous, speak to him in a gentle tone, or distract him with a toy.

Being alone is stressful for a dog, and he will need to learn that he will be safe on his own and trust that you will return. To begin training, choose a time when he is calm or sleepy and leave him in his pen or a room for a few minutes. Come back in, but don't make a fuss of him; stay nearby quietly until he calms down. Extend the periods gradually until he can be left for several hours. When leaving your dog at home alone, make sure he has access to his bed and a bowl of water. Leave him with some favorite toys, including one with food hidden inside it to keep him occupied for a while after you have left.

Making friends
If you have rabbits or other small animals in your home or yard, keep them separated from your dog and supervise the dog whenever he is around them.

At home and away

Your dog will need to get used to people, cars, other pets, and the outside world. Having a well socialized dog will make it easier when going on vacation, whether you travel with him or leave him behind.

LOCAL WALKS

Once your puppy has been inoculated, and ideally microchipped, too, he can be taken for walks. It is important to expose puppies to as many different situations as possible in the first 12 weeks, after which their attitude becomes more guarded; if they encounter something strange, their first instinct will be to run away. For older dogs, walks are about letting them get to know their "territory." Even so, there may be things that your dog has not encountered before, such as livestock and wild animals.

CREATING CONFIDENCE

When your dog first ventures into the wider world, the experience can be overwhelming for him. Some new sights may be frightening, such as cars and trucks. Others may be powerful distractions: for example, a child on a bicycle or skateboard, or lambs in a field. Your dog needs to learn confidence, and you need to be sure you can depend on him to behave in all situations.

Introduce your pet to anyone who wants to meet him. If you have children, meet them from school with your puppy so that he gets used to seeing other children.

When acquainting your dog with other dogs, start with those you already know: for example, go out for walks with someone who has an easy-going dog. You could also attend puppy socialization classes.

It is best to always keep your dog on a leash around livestock and wild animals—even for a quiet dog, the temptation to chase can be sudden and irresistible. In many countries, dog owners are required by law to prevent their animals from harassing livestock.

TRAVELING BY CAR

As a dog owner you have a legal duty to transport your dog in a way that keeps the dog and other passengers safe. If you have a large car, you could install a dog guard behind the rear seats; this should be sufficient for short trips under one hour. For long trips or in a larger vehicle, put your dog in a dog crate. If your dog is traveling on the back seat of your car, a dog harness that links in with the seat belt system will restrain him safely. To help prevent travel sickness, make sure your dog has a nonslip surface to stand on in the car.

Start travel training by teaching your dog to sit in the car for a few minutes with the engine off and the doors open. Graduate to sitting in the car with the doors closed and the engine on for a few minutes. Then start taking short journeys of a few minutes, building up to longer trips. When traveling, don't let your dog stick his head out of the

Meeting new dogs
Allow your dog to meet strange dogs when walking, but if he is upset by them, walk away or ask the owners to hold their dogs or put them on the leash while you pass.

GETTING USED TO TRAFFIC

- Introduce your dog to startling or distracting sights such as noisy cars by getting him to sit at a comfortable distance while the vehicle goes by.
- Crouch down and hold him so he does not try to chase, and praise him when he sits quietly.
- Reward him with a treat once the object has passed.
- Gradually get him used to being closer to these objects but at a safe distance from fast traffic.
- Be patient—let him take his time.

:omfortable trips
/lake sure your dog has space to lie down and turn ɾound comfortably in a car. If using a dog crate, put in blanket or pillows to make him comfortable.

xercising safely
ome dogs are not fond of others. Let your sitter or kennels now if your dog will accept being exercised with other ogs, and whether he is particularly shy or strong-willed, ʋhich could affect how he gets along with strange dogs.

ʋindow because he could risk head or eye njuries. For long journeys, carry water and bowl and stop at least every two hours for our dog to have a drink and to get out and elieve himself. On warm days switch on the ir-conditioning if your car has it, and never eave your dog alone inside a car even with he windows open—on a hot day or in lirect sunlight, heat stroke can kill a dog in s little as 20 minutes (see p.345). Watch for ny signs of travel sickness such as drooling or panting. Excessive barking or chewing on he car's interiors are other signs of distress.

ƷOING ON VACATION

Traveling with your dog can be enjoyable—ʋith a bit of prior organization. Your dog eeds to be controllable in public places nd trained for car travel. He must be nicrochipped and wear an ID tag. Check n advance that your destination will be log-friendly. If you plan to travel abroad with our dog, find out what regulations apply in ach country regarding car travel with dogs; nimal welfare organizations may have nformation. Also arrange travel insurance or your dog and check if you need to have iim vaccinated for any diseases. Find out ɩow the airline or ferry company usually ransports dogs; some airlines may require your dog to travel in a special crate. Take a supply of your dog's usual food and familiar items such as food bowls. Keep to your routine of feeding, walks, and bedtimes as much as possible to minimize stress.

LEAVING YOUR DOG BEHIND

If you do not plan to take your dog with you on vacation, there are several options for care while you are away. Whichever you choose, you need to be sure your dog is used to being separated from you (see p.307).

You could ask a relative, friend, or neighbor to "pet sit," or employ a registered pet sitter who will look after your dog in his or her home. If you can, arrange a few visits to the pet sitter's home in advance so that it becomes a familiar place to your dog. Make sure your dog wears an ID tag at all times. Leave a good supply of his food with the sitter, plus notes on feeding, walking, bedtimes, and emergency contact numbers for you and for the vet. If you plan to use a registered sitter, ask your vet or fellow dog owners for suitable recommendations, and ask the sitter for references.

Family kennels
If you have two dogs, check that the boarding kennels can house both together. It will reassure your dogs to stay together and help them settle into the new environment.

Another option is to use boarding kennels. Your vet or other local dog owners should be able to suggest a good one. Remember to book well in advance, especially before busy times of the year. Staying in kennels can be more stressful for your dog than staying in a home environment so it is wise to visit the kennels before using them to see whether they are suitable.

A balanced diet

Dogs need more than just meat–they need a healthy, balanced diet and the right quantity for their size. Most people buy preprepared dog food, but you can make your own if you prefer.

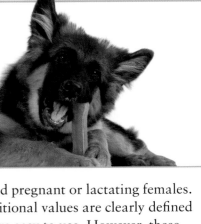

ESSENTIAL ELEMENTS

A good diet should provide all of the nutrients that a dog needs and must contain these elements:

■ Proteins—the "building blocks" of cells, proteins help to build muscles and repair the body. Lean meat, eggs, and cheese are good sources of proteins.

■ Fats—high in energy and making food more tasty, fats also contain essential fatty acids that help to maintain cell walls and aid growth and wound healing in your dog. They are the source of vitamins A, D, E, and K, and are found in meat, oily fish, and in oils such as linseed oil and sunflower oil.

■ Fiber—found in potatoes, vegetables, and rice, fiber helps to bulk out food and slow your dog's digestion, allowing more time to absorb nutrients and making it easier for him to pass feces.

■ Vitamins and minerals—these help to maintain your dog's body structures, such as skin, bones, and blood cells, and support the chemical reactions that turn food into energy or enable vital body functions such as blood clotting.

■ Water—as with humans, water is essential for your dog's life. Make sure your dog has access to fresh water by refilling his bowl two or three times a day.

COMMERCIAL FOODS

These foods can be moist, semimoist, or dry. Dry food can help keep teeth and gums healthy but check that they have wholesome core ingredients. You must provide plenty of water, too, since dogs that are fed dried food drink more. Moist food has a lot of moisture content along with higher fat and protein components.

The main advantage of using commercial foods is that they come in a wide choice of varieties specially adapted for puppies, seniors, and pregnant or lactating females. Their nutritional values are clearly defined and they are easy to use. However, these foods can contain ingredients such as preservatives and flavorings that may disagree with some dogs. Check the labels.

NATURAL FOODS

Instead of feeding your dog on a packaged diet, you can prepare a homemade natural diet in the form of raw meat. You will also need to add cooked vegetables and starchy foods such as rice to provide fiber. Check with your vet to find out if you need to add vitamin supplements.

This diet is closer to how a dog might eat in the wild, and there are no preservatives or other hidden extras. However, natural foods need to be carefully balanced and it can be difficult to ensure consistent nutritional quality or to adapt the diet to different energy needs of dogs. Preparation of fresh food on a daily basis can also take a lot of time.

DOG CHEWS

Chews help keep your dog busy, preventing him from chewing household items or biting your hands. They are especially good for puppies during teething and also play an important role in keeping your dog's teeth clean and his jaws in good condition.

DOG TREATS

Many dog owners give extra-tasty foods when training to reward good behavior or simply as a treat. Dogs prefer smelly, meaty, and soft treats, so try out different ones to see which yours likes best. Treats with chicken and cheese in them are usually popular. Some treats can be high in fats so if you give them to your pet regularly make sure you reduce his main meals to prevent overfeeding. A few treats a day are enough for all dogs. You can buy ready-made treats or prepare your own at home.

BITE-SIZED TREATS

COOKED SAUSAGE

CHEESE CUBES

MEATY TREATS

MOIST TREATS

Varieties of food
The choice of food available for dogs has greatly expanded. This ranges from specially developed commercial foods—moist, dry, or semimoist—to natural food that can be prepared at home.

MOIST FOOD

DRY FOOD

NATURAL FOOD

A good choice
Begin feeding your dog a healthy and balanced diet from a young age, to ensure that he receives all the nutrients he needs as he grows.

Changing diets

Dogs at different stages of life have particular nutritional needs–whether growing puppies, nursing mothers, sports dogs, or older pets. It is important that your dog has the right nutrients for his age to optimize his well-being.

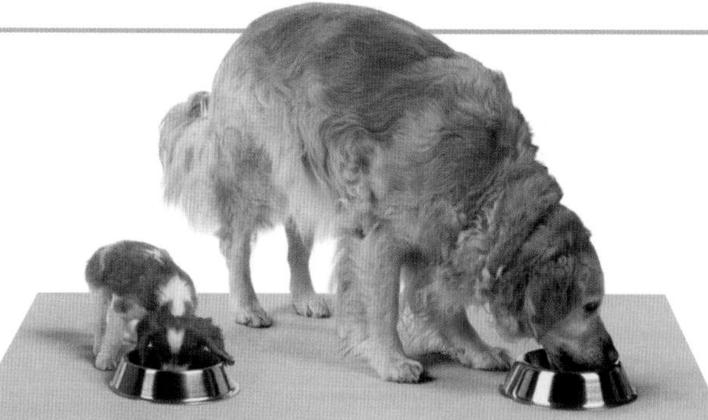

PUPPIES

Once puppies are weaned, they need to be fed little and often—four times a day at first, reducing to three times a day from about six months. Puppies grow fast, so they need high-energy food; ask your vet if you are unsure of the right quantity to feed your puppy based on his size. Increase the amount slowly as he grows but avoid overfeeding. It may be best to feed commercial puppy food to make sure he gets the right balance of nutrients.

If you bought your puppy from a breeder, he may supply a sample of the food that the puppy has been eating. Stick to this food in the beginning, introducing changes gradually.

ADULT PETS

Two meals a day (morning and evening) is often enough. Neutered dogs need fewer calories than un-neutered ones; otherwise, feed according to your dog's size and activity level, and monitor his weight (see pp.314–15).

WORKING DOGS

Working or sports dogs should have high-protein, energy-dense, easily digestible foods to maximize their strength and stamina. However, the volume of food given to a working dog should be no more than for a normal adult dog. Dogs engaged in short, sharp bursts of work, such as racing or agility shows, need a moderately increased fat intake. For endurance work such as sledding, hunting, or herding animals, high fat foods with extra protein are required.

NURSING MOTHERS

A pregnant bitch can stay on her usual diet until the last two to three weeks of pregnancy; from this point until whelping, her energy needs will increase by 25–50 percent. She may lose her appetite as birth approaches, but it will soon return after the puppies are born. A bitch producing milk will need two or three times as many calories as normal in the first four weeks when the puppies' milk needs are at their highest. Feed her energy-dense food specially formulated for lactating bitches, and feed little and often. When the puppies begin weaning (six to eight weeks), the mother will still need extra calories. Only when she stops producing milk should her diet be changed.

Growing up
Always provide your puppy with a balanced diet to build a strong body. Be sure to choose food that is specially formulated for puppies, and change to an adult formula as your puppy matures.

CONVALESCENT DOGS

A sick dog needs easily digestible, extra-nutritious food such as boiled chicken and rice or special commercial foods; your vet can give you guidance. Feed your dog little and often and make sure that the food is at body temperature so it will be more tempting. Keep a note of how much he is eating, and report any loss of appetite to the vet.

OLDER DOGS

From about age seven onward, dogs start to need more nutrients but fewer calories. Many do well on a normal adult diet, slightly reduced in quantity and with vitamin and mineral supplements. You can buy "senior" formulas that are softer, with higher protein, lower fat, and extra vitamins and minerals. You may need to adjust feeding to three times a day. A slower metabolic rate makes older dogs more prone to obesity. Keeping a healthy weight can improve the quality and length of your dog's life.

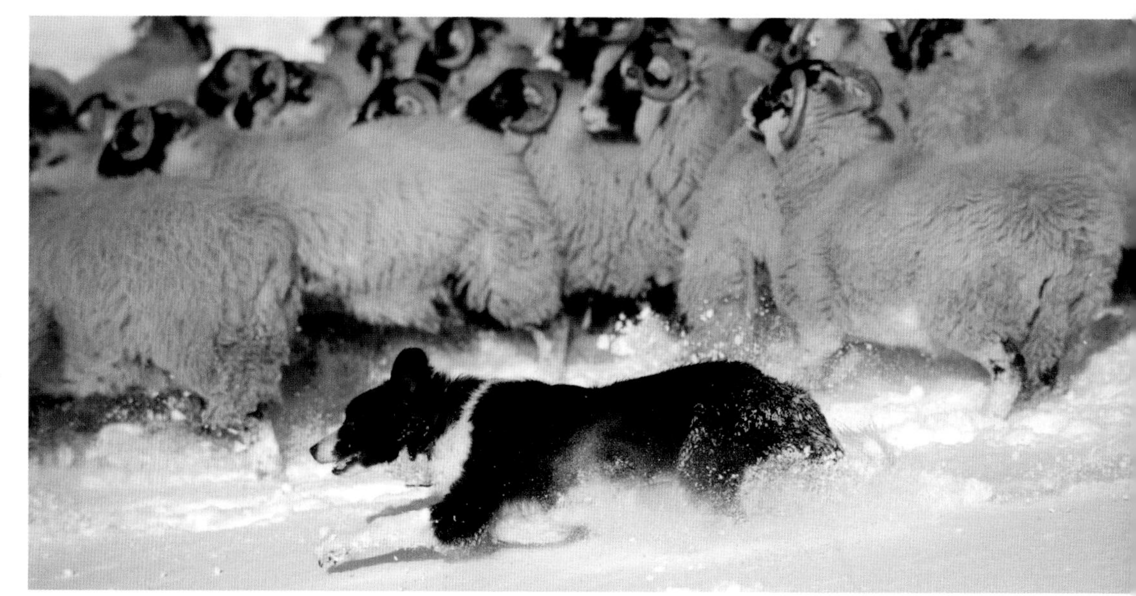

Climate considerations
Dogs in colder climates or those living in outdoor kennels need more energy than those in warmer regions in order to keep their body temperature stable. Regular meals that are high in fat calories can fulfill their additional energy needs.

Nursing needs
The nutritional requirements of a nursing bitch are even more than that of a growing dog. Her calorie needs will steadily increase as the puppies grow and she has to produce more milk to feed them.

Monitoring feeding levels

As with humans, animals can develop health problems due to overeating or a poor diet. Make sure your dog eats the right amount of good-quality food to maintain an optimal weight for his breed or size.

GOOD FEEDING HABITS

Adopting good habits from the start will do much to help you avoid feeding issues as your dog grows. Follow these guidelines:

- Set regular meal times.
- Check that fresh drinking water is available at all times.
- Make sure you wash the food bowls before every use.
- Clear away food bowls when your dog has finished eating, especially if feeding moist canned or homemade foods.
- Don't feed your dog the same things that you eat—his needs are different, and some foods for humans, such as chocolate, can be poisonous to dogs (see p.344).
- If you alter your dog's diet, make changes gradually to avoid stomach upsets.

EATING TOO FAST?

It is natural for your dog to eat fast because in the wild this would stop other pack members from stealing his food. Try using an anti-gorge bowl. This has lumpy protrusions in the base that your dog has to work around as he eats, slowing him down. This can help prevent digestive problems such as gas, vomiting, and indigestion.

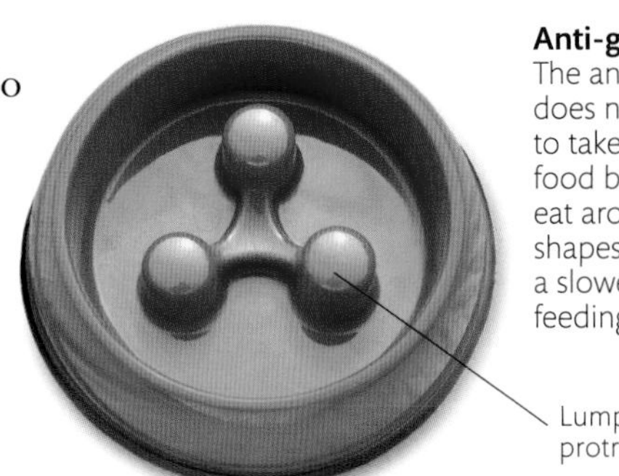

Anti-gorge bowl
The anti-gorge bowl does not allow dogs to take large bites of food because they must eat around the molded shapes. This results in a slower, more relaxed feeding time.

PREVENTING OBESITY

Dogs are scavengers and tend to eat whatever is placed in front of them because they do not know when they might next find food. For pet dogs with regular access to plentiful food, this natural trait has led to a high incidence of excess weight gain. Some dog breeds are prone to put on weight, such as the Basset Hound (see p.146), Dachshund (see p.170), and Cavalier King Charles Spaniel (see p.278). However, any dog can get fat with too much high-energy food and too little exercise. Overfeeding your dog can lead to heart problems, diabetes, and painful joints. In particular, for breeds that have large bodies and thin legs (such as the Rottweiler (see p.83) or the Staffordshire Bull Terrier (see p.214)), weight coupled with exercise can cause ligament problems.

To prevent weight problems in your dog:

- Feed for your dog's age, size, and activity level (see pp.312–13).
- Be extra vigilant about feeding titbits to your dog; don't feed scraps from the table, and never give in if he begs for food.
- Weigh smaller dogs at home on bathroom scales. If your dog is large, ask to have him weighed at your vet's office.
- Keep an eye on your dog's body shape—this can be just as helpful as weighing him. If you are concerned, take a snapshot each week to monitor changes in his shape.
- Ask your vet about a balanced diet for weight loss if your dog becomes fat.

A healthy weight
You need to check your dog's condition regularly to ensure that he is not too fat or too thin. Body shapes differ between breeds, so find out what is normal for your dog's breed. If you are not sure about the right quantity to feed, ask your vet.

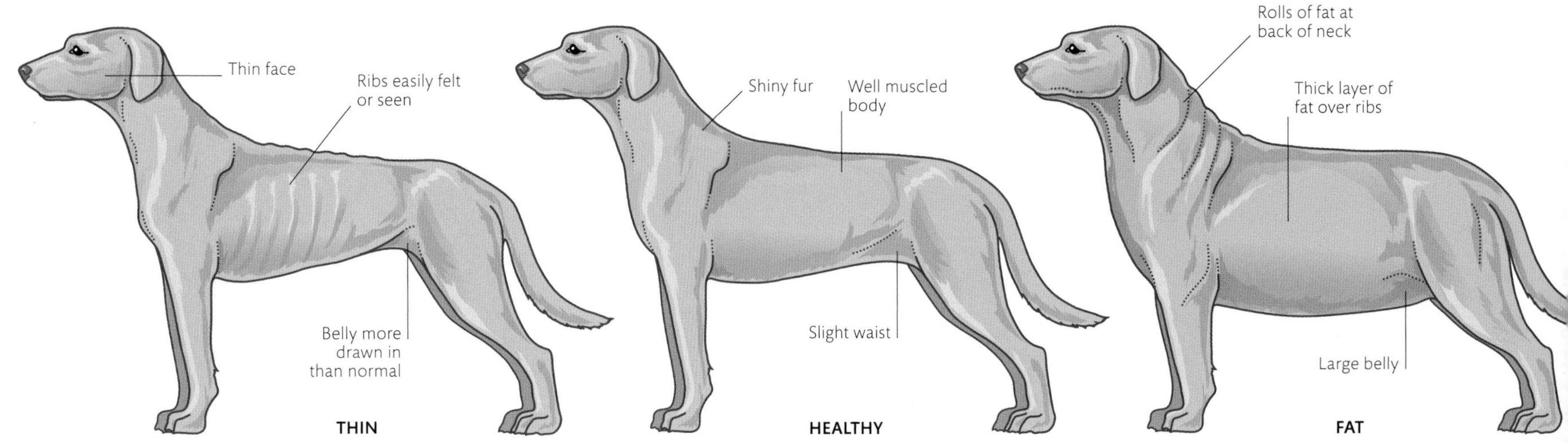

At the vet's
Vets have animal-friendly weighing machines. Tell your dog to sit on the tray so that you and the vet can accurately record the reading.

Exercise

All dogs need exercise to prevent them from becoming bored and frustrated. Regular exercise and play will help your dog burn off excess energy and stay calmer at home, as well as help you to build a close relationship with him.

WALKS AND GAMES

Dogs require regular, daily exercise. For puppies, this will help to build their strength and reinforce learning, while for older dogs gentle activity can help to prevent problems such as obesity and painful joints.

Dogs that are bred for hunting and working have higher energy levels than other breeds; two half-hour walks might be plenty for a Yorkshire Terrier (see p.190) or a Pug (see p.268), but a Dalmatian (see p.286) or Boxer (see p.90) might need at least an hour-long walk or run plus a play session.

Your dog's need for exercise will change through the course of his life. Young puppies can be taken on short walks once they have been inoculated. For adult dogs, long walks and runs and energetic games are ideal. Pregnant bitches, or sick or convalescent dogs, need only gentle exercise for a short time. Older dogs appreciate shorter, gentle walks, but may still enjoy learning new games.

If your dog is under-exercised, he can gain weight and develop behavioral problems—he may become hyperactive and agitated and find it difficult to settle. He may also find alternative, destructive outlets for his mental and physical energies, such as chewing up household furniture, barking excessively, or running off to look for entertainment.

Exercising your dog can be built into your daily activities: for example, taking him with you when you pick up your children from school or walking him when you run errands. Look for open areas where your dog can play, or allow him to exercise in your yard. The following tips will help to keep him comfortable when exercising:

- Watch that your dog does not get too tired: have "warming-up" and "cooling-down" periods such as ten-minute slow walks at each end of the exercise session.
- On hot days carry water with you and exercise when it is cooler—in the early morning or evening.
- In cold weather consider using a dog jacket for short-haired or elderly dogs to help keep their muscles warm.
- Don't let your dog run on hard surfaces if he is not used to it because he could hurt the pads of his paws. Similarly, avoid hard surfaces if they are very hot or cold.
- Take your dog's favorite toy or ball out on walks with you to encourage fun and energetic games of chase. These games are also good mental exercise for your dog.
- Try to keep sessions at around the same time each day so that your dog gets used to the routine and learns to rest in between.

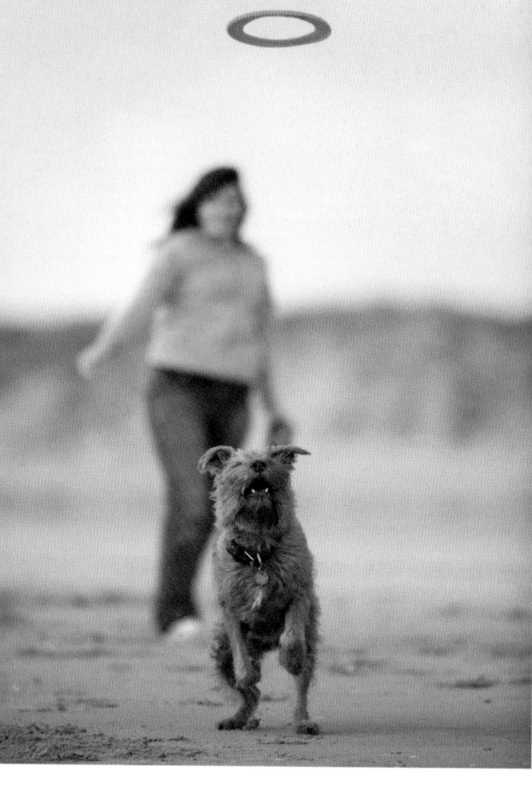

Fetch that!
For games of fetch, take toys with you rather than using sticks. Playing "fetch" also encourages your dog to come to you when called.

Family fun
Exercising your dog with the whole family is good for all of you and will help all family members build a strong bond with your pet.

Active life
Dogs with high energy levels need plenty of exercise and play to stay calm and happy. They need open areas where they can run freely, especially when they are young.

WALKING AND JOGGING

For his own safety and that of others, your dog needs to be able to walk calmly on a leash (see p.326), and once that training is complete, walking can be done almost anywhere. Jogging with your dog will help you both to keep in shape. Remember to carry biodegradeable bags with you to collect and dispose of feces.

FREE RUNNING

Running in open spaces is especially good exercise for high-energy or racing dogs such as Whippets (see p.128) and Greyhounds (see p.126). First, in order for you to trust your dog to run a long distance from you, he needs to be trained to come reliably when you call him (see p.328). Find a large space such as a field or beach without crowds, and check that there is no livestock to disturb. Make sure that you are allowed to let your dog run freely in that area—many urban parks don't allow dogs off leashes in certain places.

To ensure that your dog keeps you in mind while he is running around, play a few games of "hide-and-seek" or "fetch" with him. Agility games such as jumping over and running through obstacles can also be lots of fun for your dog.

CHILDREN AND PLAY

Dogs and children can become the best of friends, but they need time to get habituated to one another. Children can be a bit too rough while playing, so all interaction should be supervised. Avoid a situation where your dog is forced to retaliate, and be ready to step in to help when required. Explain to children that they must not tease a dog because this will upset him and he may bite, and that puppies tire easily and must be allowed to sleep if they want to. Dogs do not like to be disturbed while they are eating, so don't let children play with or near a dog's food or water bowl. Only an adult should feed a dog.

PLAYTIME

Games allow your dog or puppy to express his natural instincts in a fun way. Puppies that learn to play with other dogs are less likely to be timid or aggressive. Keep sessions short and varied so your dog does not get tired or overexcited. Make sure you decide when the play session starts and ends—this subtly reinforces your control. Never encourage your dog to chase people—humans should be friends and leaders, never "prey."

Fetch

This is an excellent way for your dog to burn off energy. By bringing the toy back to you, the dog learns that he will get another chance to chase it—and in the process he learns retrieval skills. Use toys rather than sticks—your dog could injure his mouth by catching or grabbing a stick.

Tug-of-war

Use special "tug" toys (see p.306). Make sure you win more often than the dog does. Remember that all toys are yours—your dog should always give up toys when asked. If he takes hold of your clothes or skin, stop playing immediately and quietly turn away from him. Never let your dog jump up at people or grab things from them.

Hide-and-seek

This game satisfies a dog's food-seeking instincts. Hide a bit of food inside a toy, so your dog has to scrabble and sniff around to find it. You could also play with two people: one takes the dog's "fetch" toy and hides with it, while the other holds the dog. The "hider" calls the dog, and the other person lets the dog go. When the dog finds the hider, this person throws the toy for him. This game is also a good way to teach your dog to come when called.

Squeaky toys

Toys that squeak are especially appealing to chase and catch. Your dog may even try to bite the toy to pieces until it stops squeaking, so be ready to take it away from him, because if he finds the squeak inside he runs the risk of choking on it.

Grooming

No matter what type of dog you have, regular grooming and occasional bathing are essential to his well-being. They will help to keep a dog's skin and coat healthy, and keep dirt, smells, and hair shedding to a minimum.

GROOMING ESSENTIALS

All dogs benefit from regular grooming, so dog owners should build time into their schedule to do it. In addition to removing dead hair, grooming is good for the skin, and reduces the likelihood of your dog getting parasites such as fleas and ticks. The process is also a good opportunity to check for any new lumps, bumps, or injuries that might need veterinary attention. Grooming is relaxing for dogs and helps to strengthen the bond between dog and owner.

Although short-haired breeds can be groomed as little as once a week, longer-coated dogs naturally require more regular attention—some breeds may even need daily brushing. Knots and tangles that form in long coats, for instance, on spaniels, are painful and difficult to remove once they have set in. Similarly, a buildup of dirt should be avoided, because it can quickly cause skin irritation.

When grooming a dog, special attention needs to be paid to the groin, ears, legs, and chest, where body parts rub across one another. These areas are prone to knots and tangles. You will also need to focus closely on the underside of your dog's feet and tail, where dirt can easily build up.

While grooming is essential, it is important not to get too carried away. Be careful when using any tool with metal teeth—being heavy-handed or staying in one place too long can cause cuts called brush burns. Brushing is finished when all the loose hair has been removed—typically when it becomes difficult to remove more than half a brush-full of hair.

Always approach grooming in a calm, relaxed fashion and without any force. If your dog is uncomfortable for any reason, take your time and use treats to help him through the experience. Using force may get the job done quickly, but future grooming sessions will become much more difficult because your dog will associate grooming with being uncomfortable and try to avoid it.

COMBS AND CLIPPERS

There are many grooming tools available, and each boasts features to make grooming more effective. For example, combs are available in a variety of lengths, with and without handles. It is important to select a brush appropriate for your dog's coat type. Brush heads also come in a range of shapes and sizes. Take some time to select equipment that you are comfortable handling and that is appropriate for the size of your dog. Clean your equipment after each use to reduce the risk of contamination.

Grooming your dog
Whatever breed of dog you own, you should make sure you groom him regularly to remove dead hair and to check for parasites.

ong-haired dogs
ogs with long coats should be groomed daily to stop ıngles. To make grooming easier, use a de-matting comb ɔ break the mats into small sections.

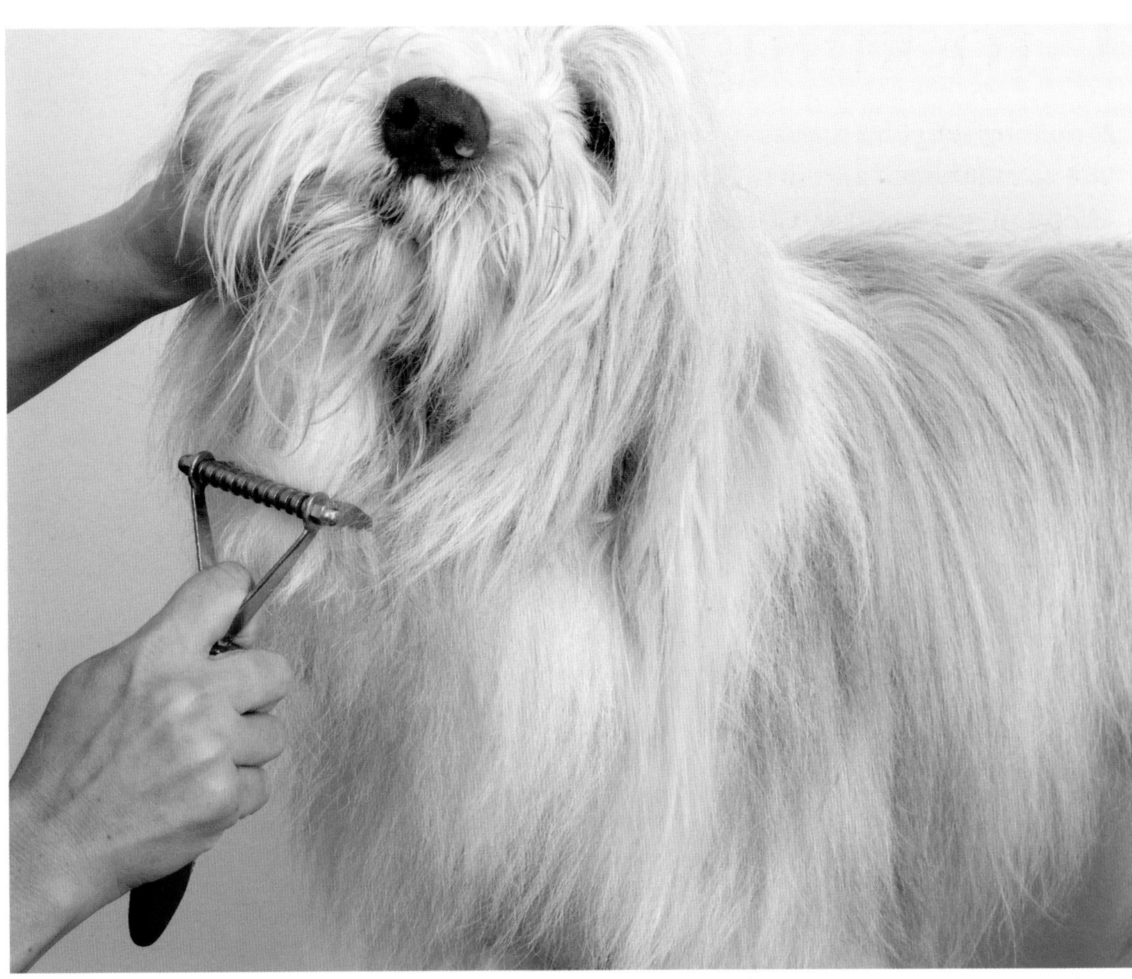

VASHING YOUR DOG

Iow often you need to bathe your dog lepends on what type of coat he has. ome long-haired dogs have a "double coat" vith a warm undercoat and thick guard ıairs on top. The guard hairs make louble-coated dogs naturally dirt repellent, o they don't need to be bathed often—wice a year is enough. Single-coated, hort-haired dogs should be bathed more requently—about once every three months. Curly-coated breeds like Poodles do not hed and may need to be bathed more egularly, even as often as once a month. It s important not to wash any dog too often, ince overwashing causes the coat to compensate by producing extra oils, vhich leads to an increase of natural odor. f your dog gets muddy after a walk, he does ıot necessarily need a bath—wait until the nud dries and then brush it off.

BATH TIME Make bath time a pleasant experience for your dog—feed him treats before you get him wet, have everything you need within easy reach so that you don't have to leave him unattended, and check that he is comfortable and happy throughout the process.

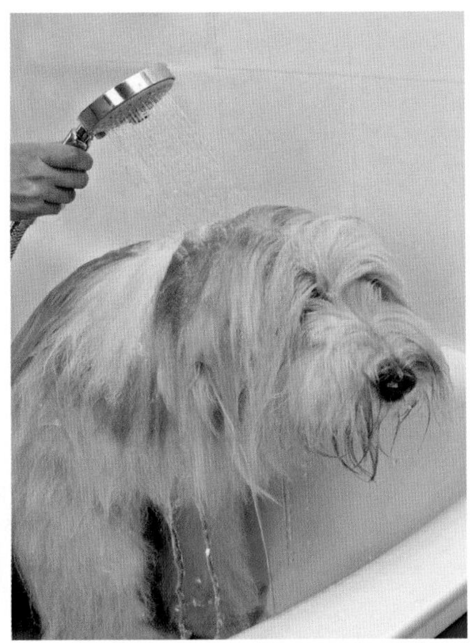

1 Test the water temperature before you wet your dog—it should be warm, but not hot. Beginning at the head, wet him fully from head to tail. Be careful not to get water in his eyes, ears, or nose.

2 Apply a specially formulated dog shampoo and then massage it thoroughly into your dog's coat, right down to his skin.

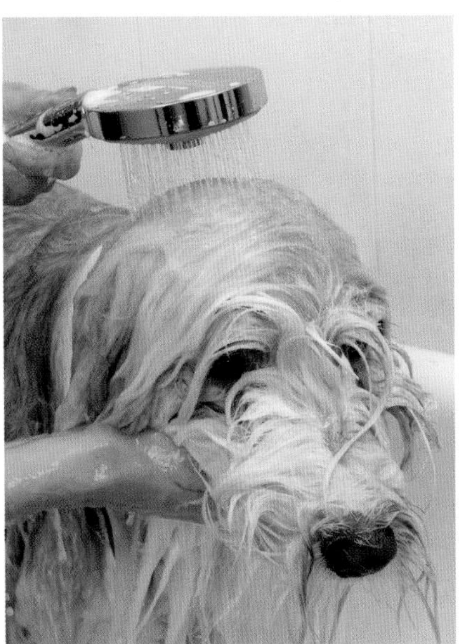

3 Use warm water to rinse all the shampoo out of your dog's coat. Any shampoo residue left in the coat will cause skin irritation.

4 Squeeze the excess water out of his coat by hand, then towel him all over, so that he is nearly dry. Finish by drying him fully with a hair dryer on low heat (as long as he isn't worried by the noise), brushing as you go.

Grooming checks

Grooming is a good time to accustom your dog to routine checks in which you examine each part of his body. It is not just your dog's coat that needs attention—his teeth, ears, and nails also need to be attended to regularly.

ROUTINE CHECKS

From early puppyhood, get your dog accustomed to regular grooming so that you can use this time to carry out health checks as well. Noticing the slightest change could allow early diagnosis of a health problem, and potentially a better outcome.

While grooming and examining each part of your dog's body, talk to him to put him at ease and use commands such as "teeth" and "ears." Look first for any obvious changes in body shape and stance, then go over him in more detail, searching for cuts, lumps, and external parasites. Run your hands over and under his head and body, down all four legs, and along the length of his tail. Part the fur in places, especially over his rump; there should be no evidence of fleas or flea dirts, little or no debris, and the coat should feel and smell pleasant. Stroking your dog should be a good experience for both of you.

Check his eyes to make sure there is no excessive tear production or sticky discharge A little "sleep" is normal—simply wipe it away, using a separate damp cotton ball for each eye. Gently lower the bottom eyelids to check that the lining and the white around the irises are not inflamed and red.

Look under the tail at the anus for soiling and swellings, and in a female check the vulva for swelling and discharges. Examine the penis of a male dog for injuries and excessive discharge or bleeding from the tip.

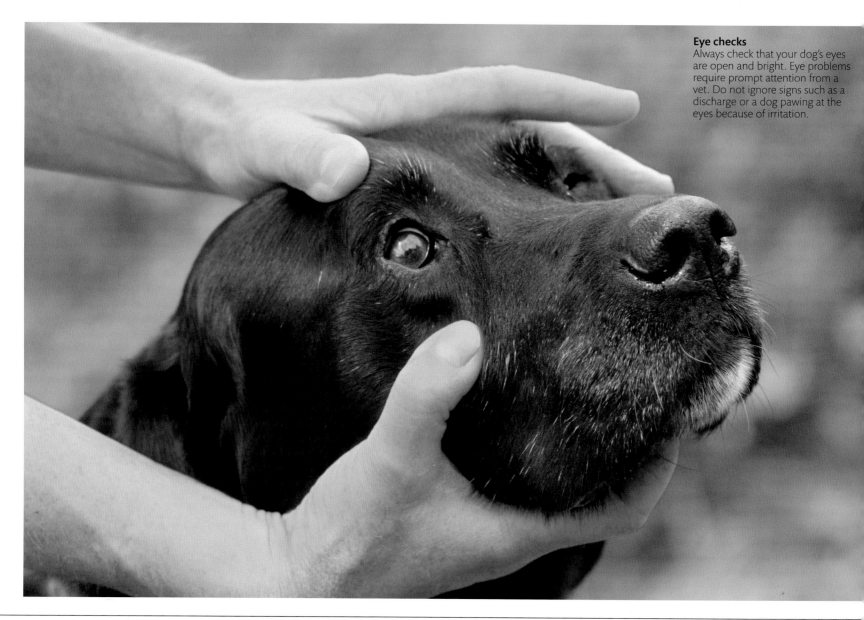

Eye checks
Always check that your dog's eyes are open and bright. Eye problems require prompt attention from a vet. Do not ignore signs such as a discharge or a dog pawing at the eyes because of irritation.

eeth cleaning
se a toothbrush or fingerbrush to clean your dog's teeth, king care not to apply too much pressure. Use this time o check that his teeth, gums, and mouth are healthy.

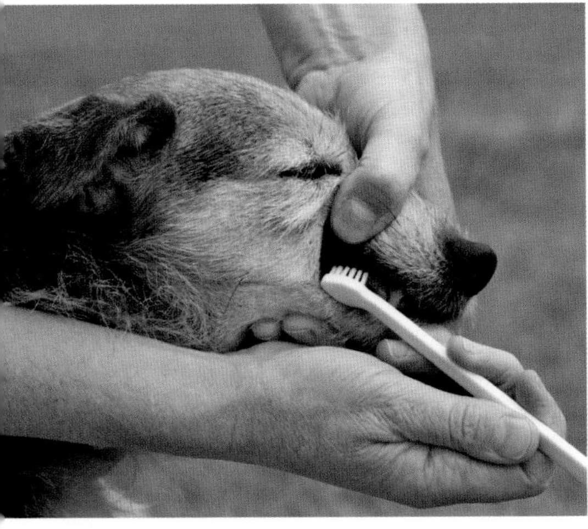

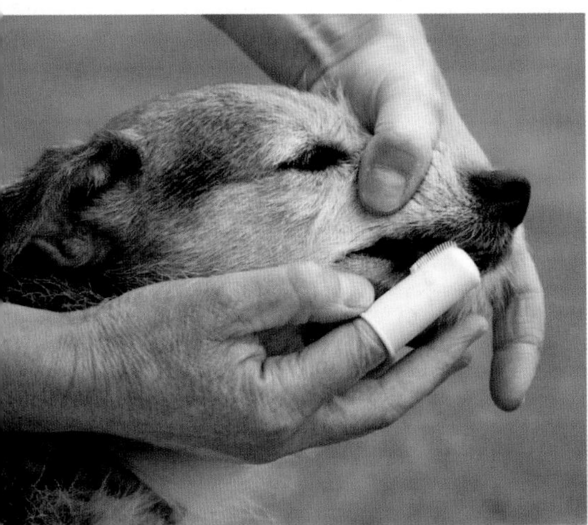

Nail trimming
When trimming your dog's nails, make sure you clip below the quick. Trim only small sections at a time to prevent cutting through the quick. Check your dog's paws for swellings and his claws for breaks or splits.

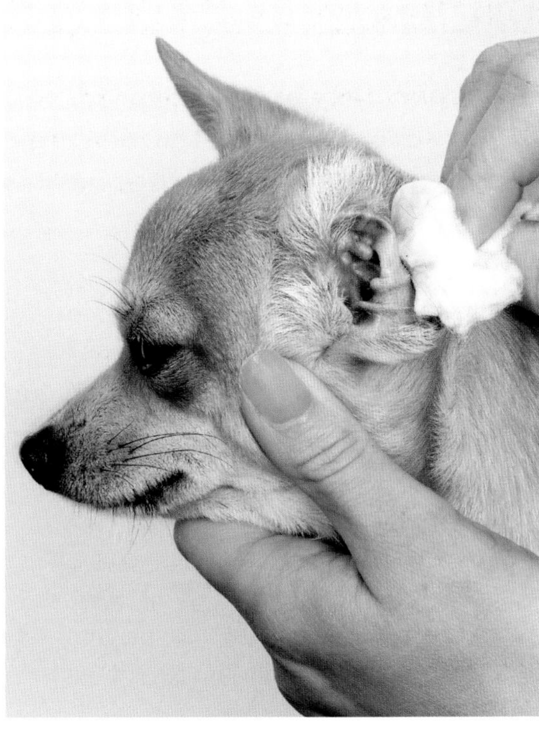

Ear cleaning
Check that your dog's ears are not swollen and do not smell unpleasant. Antiseptic ear cleaner can be applied to cotton balls and used to wipe the visible areas of your dog's ears. Do not insert cotton balls or any other object into the ear canal.

TEETH CLEANING

Your dog can be taught to accept you looking n his mouth and brushing his teeth. First, get him used to the feel of having your hand resting across the bridge of his nose, with your thumb held under his chin to keep his mouth closed. Once he is comfortable with this, use your other hand to lift his top lip gently to reveal the outer surfaces of the teeth. Ideally, these should be white, but light brown tartar may accumulate along the gum line. The gums should be moist and pale pink, and the breath smell pleasant. A toothbrush can be inserted inside the cheek, f your dog remains calm. The most important places to brush are along the gum line and the outside surfaces of the teeth. Move the brush gently in a circular motion rather than scrubbing from side to side.

Dog's teeth benefit from weekly brushing, using only dog-specific products. You might find it easier to use a fingerbrush—a hollow plastic tube that fits over your finger and has built-in bristles. This can be a lot easier to maneuver around your dog's mouth and prevents you from applying too much pressure.

Teeth cleaning will be a strange experience for your dog at first, so use treats at each stage to put him at ease and encourage good practice in future. If he shows signs of aggression or anxiety during the process, stroke him slowly and gently for several minutes before trying again.

NAIL TRIMMING

Train your dog from a young age to allow his feet to be lifted up and examined. Look between the toes for grass awns and bright orange harvest mites. Check for swellings and broken or overly long claws; when the feet are fully weight-bearing, the claws should just touch the ground.

How often you will need to trim your dog's nails depends on the breed and his lifestyle; monthly trimming should be sufficient for most dogs. Nails need to be trimmed back as far as the "quick," which is where the blood vessels and nerves are. The quick is much easier to see on dogs with white nails than on dogs with black nails. It is a two-tone pink area in the center of the nail. If you cut the nails too short, you will sever the quick, which will cause the nail to bleed copiously. Hold your dog's foot firmly to avoid him moving at the moment of cutting. Place the nail clippers just below the quick and cut the nail swiftly in one smooth movement. If you do cut the quick, remain calm and apply a small amount of styptic powder to the nail to help stem the bleeding, and apply firm pressure until the bleeding stops.

EAR CLEANING

Your dog should not find it painful to have his ears touched. There should be no swelling of the flaps, and the ears should be pleasant smelling and clean as far down as you can see.

Inspect your dog's ears regularly for any signs of discharge, unpleasant odor, redness, inflammation, or ear mites. Any of these symptoms may signal an infection, for which you should seek veterinary help. Monthly ear cleaning will maintain the health of the ears and prevent infections. This is particularly important with pendant-eared dogs such as spaniels.

Being in charge

Having a well behaved dog depends on building a good relationship with him. Learning to communicate the rules in a clear and calm way that your dog understands will ensure he responds positively to your requests.

SETTING RULES

Dogs are pack animals and, like humans, they seek out social companionship and build strong relationships. Because their ancestors once lived in packs, dogs look up to a leader they can respect and follow. Without a strong leader they can turn unruly. They are not naturally disobedient—in fact, they crave rules and boundaries—but puppies are not born knowing what the rules are, and even an older dog may not yet have learned all the rules you would like him to follow.

Decide upon a set of rules you feel are important, then enforce them consistently through training methods such as reward-based training (see pp.324–25). Act quickly to stop any behavior that breaks your rules; your dog will soon learn which behaviors are acceptable and which are not.

There is no need to prove your physical strength or dominance. If he senses you are angry or distracted, he may become fearful or withdrawn. A good owner is calm, fair, and likeable—it is important to help your dog understand when he makes mistakes, without getting angry and shouting at him. Giving approval through praise and affection is the best way to make your dog feel secure and loved.

Building a relationship with your dog based on mutual respect will make both you and your dog happier. Your dog will gladly follow commands given by you as long as he understands what he needs to do. When training problems occur, it is usually because of poor communication between you and your dog. Since dogs have different motivations and needs than humans, taking time to understand how your dog learns and what signals he can follow will help set realistic expectations.

Staying focused
Don't get angry if your dog gets distracted by something in his environment. Instead, do something to turn his attention back to you. Using treats or a toy, or even a game of chase, will all help to engage him again.

VOICE AND HAND COMMANDS

Your voice is a useful training tool but it is easy to forget that dogs cannot understand spoken language. Your dog is capable of remembering what certain words sound like and what he should do when he hears them but only after repeated training and only if those words always sound the same. Asking your dog to "sit" one day and "sit down" the next will confuse him and make training more difficult. The tone of your voice is also very important. Your dog will use your tone to gauge whether he is doing the right thing or not, so it is important always to keep your voice cheerful when teaching new words.

Your dog will also look at your body posture to work out the context of a situation and what you are asking him to do. However, just as dogs have no concept of language, they do not understand that by pointing at something you are trying to direct their attention to somewhere other than the end of your hand.

Dogs, and especially puppies, find learning hand signals easier than learning voice commands, because only a small part of their brain can process verbal information. Once your dog has learned the hand signal and is responding reliably to it every time, add a voice command ahead of the hand signal. Eventually, after plenty of repetitions, your dog will respond to the voice command alone.

Remember, your dog can only concentrate on one thing at a time. Be patient while training, and make sure that your dog has fully learned one command before trying to teach him a new one.

Happy together
A healthy relationship is one in which your dog is at ease because he knows what is expected of him, and in return you enjoy the company of a dog that does as he is asked.

Avoid confusion
If you give a voice command at the same time as a hand signal, your dog will tend to learn the hand signal but ignore the voice command.

Basic training

Training should be an enjoyable experience for both you and your dog. The following pages introduce some basic commands and will help to get you started, but if you are unsure, always seek the help of a professional dog trainer sooner rather than later.

WHEN TO TRAIN

There are many things to consider while training, but the most important is to choose the right time. Aim to train for a few minutes several times a day, since this will produce much better results than a longer training session once a day. Choose times when you are not stressed or in a rush, otherwise your dog will sense your tension and be far more likely to get things wrong in his attempts to please you.

Equally important is to consider your puppy's mood. Trying to train an overexcited puppy that hasn't had much exercise will be difficult. And a puppy that has just eaten a large meal will feel sleepy and will not be particularly motivated by food treats. Maximize your training success by limiting his choices and thus preventing him from making the wrong decision. Start training him in a quiet, distraction-free environment such as your living room, especially when attempting to teach new or difficult commands. When you do move training outside, start somewhere quiet and enclosed, far from other dogs and people. You can then build up to training in high-distraction environments such as a local park, but do not attempt this until your puppy has had plenty of practice already and has been inoculated.

REWARD-BASED TRAINING

Training your dog involves creating a situation where he is rewarded for certain behaviors instead of others. Any behavior that is consistently rewarded will be repeated more often. This also means that bad behavior, which is not rewarded, will soon disappear and be replaced by behavior that is rewarded. For your dog to understand how you want him to behave, give him the reward as soon as he has behaved in the way you would like. Reward can include food treats, games with toys, simple praise and affection, or even playing with other dogs. Remember that not all dogs find the same rewards appealing. Spend some time discovering what really motivates your dog and use that as a reward.

One of the easiest reward-based ways of training is to use a food treat to lure your dog into the position you want him to be in. Food treats should be small, soft, and smelly. They work best when they can be given quickly during training sessions and do not take your dog several minutes to eat. More complicated behaviors can be

SIT Dogs naturally sit of their own accord and it can be easy simply to reward them as and when it happens. However, taking the time to teach your dog to sit on command ensures that he sits quickly and reliably in the face of any distraction. It is one of the easiest commands to teach and one that any dog will readily learn.

1 Dog in a stand Hold a treat in front of your dog's nose when he is standing in front of you. Lure him by moving the treat back over his head so that he raises his nose.

2 Feed treat and praise When your dog folds into the sit, release the treat and praise gently. Continue to praise and feed him treats if he remains sitting for longer.

3 Introduce hand signal Once your dog learns to sit, teach him to respond to a clear hand signal—an upward motion with a flat hand and palm facing up. After several repetitions, say "sit" a moment before the hand signal.

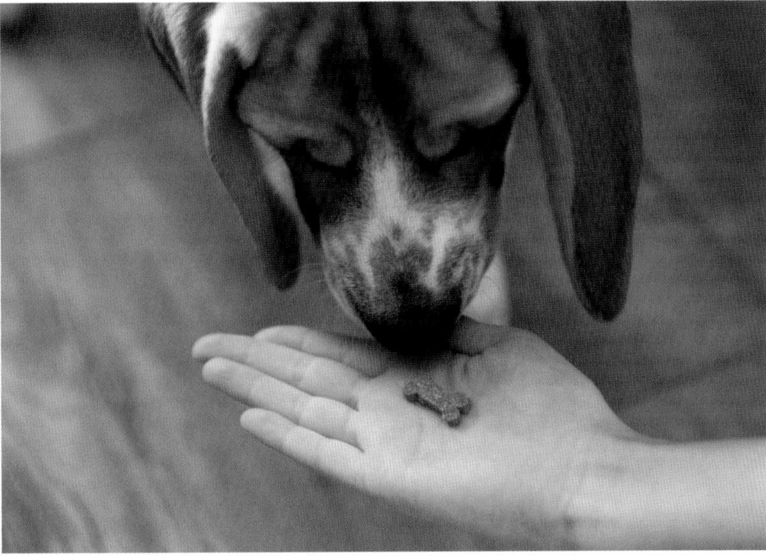

andout
ffering your dog a treat on the at of your hand prevents him om accidentally nipping you with s teeth. Using a variety of treats eeps your dog motivated during aining and allows you to create a ierarchy of rewards.

roken down and ewarded in stages, n a method called shaping." So if you vant your dog to sit, very time he moves loser to the ground and ou reward him, he will realize what he is eing asked to do. Getting rewarded for ach small effort will make him repeat it.

There is also a lot of equipment, such as ollars, leashes, and harnesses, that can help ou during training. Choose equipment that s comfortable for both you and your dog to se and ask a professional to help you fit and se it correctly. However, avoid relying on ools too heavily—if you forget the equipment or it breaks, it will be the good training you have done that will prove most important.

Keeping your training sessions short, and ending with a fun game, will ensure your dog stays engaged and is eager to continue next time. If he is having trouble learning a new task, it is important to be patient. Try breaking the task into smaller chunks and do not progress to the next stage of training until your dog is confident.

DOWN

After your dog has mastered the sit and stay, gradually teach him "down" (below). From a sitting position, first lure him by bringing the hand with the treat in it all the way to the floor so that your dog follows it. As soon as his elbows are both on the ground, reward him immediately. Once he is reliably going straight down, introduce a clear hand signal—a downward motion with palm facing down—and again lure him into the down position. The next step is to train him to respond to your voice. Say "down" and then give your hand signal.

STAY Once your dog has learned to sit on command, teach him to "stay," with your hand flat and palm facing down. Both "sit" and "stay" commands help control unwanted behaviors. Unlike most basic training, teaching your dog to stay for long periods is best practiced when he is tired, since he will be happy to rest in one position and more likely to remain still.

1 Ask for sit Ask your dog to sit, then hold your palm face down and say "stay." Praise him immediately but take your time to reward him.

2 Insert movement When your dog has learned to stay reliably, slowly move away from him by taking a step back and leaning your weight on to your back leg.

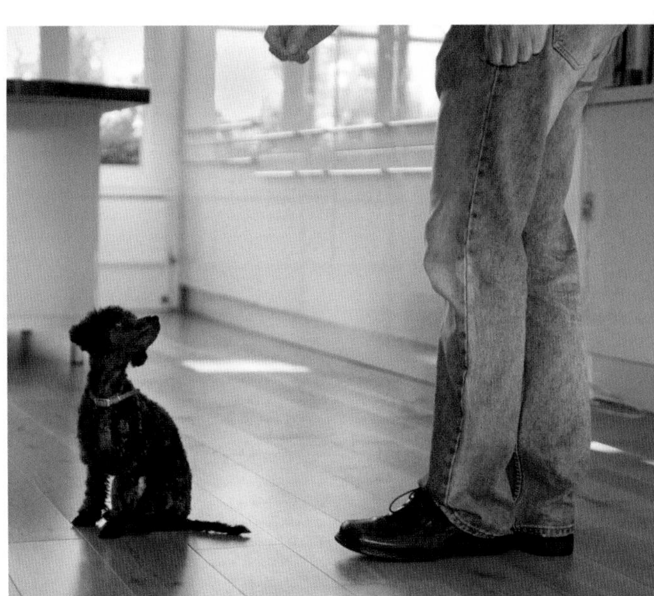

3 Add distance Move around your dog while he is sitting. If he moves to you, calmly reposition him and repeat. Gradually build up the distance between you and your dog.

GOOD PRACTICE IN TRAINING

All dogs need to be walked on a leash at least some of the time to ensure their safety. Teaching your dog to do this without pulling will make going for a walk a more pleasant experience for you both. However, no matter when you start the training, it is crucial to set rigid ground rules. Each new environment is likely to prove challenging for your dog so start each training session by rewarding one step at a time. As he improves and is walking nicely for a few paces, progress to working with distractions in the distance, such as other dogs. If he starts pulling or loses attention entirely, he probably isn't ready for this stage yet. Move the training to a quieter area and go back one stage.

Never become angry with your dog if he makes mistakes. Teaching him to walk without pulling takes time and you should plan longer walks to allow for the many stops you will have to make. Some dogs, especially older rescue dogs, are really dedicated "pullers," and basic training may be unsuccessful. In such cases it is best to seek the help of a professional dog trainer.

Resist the urge to use collars that tighten around your dog's neck. They do not teach your dog anything and have the potential to cause him serious damage.

It may not be necessary for your dog to walk precisely to heel at all times, as long as he does not pull on his leash. However, sometimes it is useful to keep your dog close—for example, when walking past people on the sidewalk. Use a similar method to that used to teach your dog to walk on a leash (below), keeping him in a closer position by using a treat. Once you can rely on your dog walking close to you, gradually phase out the treat but continue to praise.

New places
When training in a new environment for the first time, use special treats that your dog finds particularly tempting.

WALKING ON A LEASH Teaching a puppy to walk on a leash without pulling is easier than teaching an adult dog, which may have developed bad habits. As soon as your dog pulls, stop walking and help him into the correct position next to your leg. This can be frustrating to begin with, since you will be stopping every few paces, but following the steps below will help you both get it right.

1 Position the dog Lure your dog into position using a treat in your left hand. Keep the treat low so that he doesn't jump up, and the leash short so that he can't wander off.

2 Step forward Keep your dog's attention by saying his name cheerfully, and hold him in position against your leg, either sitting or standing, with the treat.

3 Treat in position Take a step forward, stop and let your dog have the treat while he is in the correct position. If he stays by your side, take anothe step forward and reward him again.

4 Practice With each session, gradually increase the number of steps you take before rewarding your dog. If he moves away from you or gets distracted, lure him back into the correct position.

TRAINING CLASSES

No matter how much experience you have training dogs, classes are advisable for any new dog—whether it be a puppy or an older, rescued dog. The benefits dogs receive from taking part in a group class are significant and it is also a useful way to hone your skills. In training classes you will meet other like-minded people and learn about the facilities your local area has to offer dog owners. All dogs are different and will benefit from slightly varied approaches in their training. Furthermore, having an experienced trainer on hand will prevent you from making mistakes. It is also much easier to keep motivated when training as part of a group.

Training classes should be well organized and enjoyable for all the owners and dogs present. A happy, confident dog will move in a relaxed manner during these classes. Any sign of tension, evident in a stiffening of the body, is a warning that he feels uncomfortable. Nervous dogs and those that are aggressive toward people or other dogs are not suitable for group classes. These types of behavioral problems are often aggravated in a class situation and can become more pronounced. Quite often these dogs are better starting off in a one-to-one training session, with someone who is qualified in dealing with behavioral problems, before progressing into a group class. If you have any concerns, ask before enrolling your dog. All training classes teach the basic skill of getting your dog to walk to heel. If you can keep your dog by your side in a controlled environment you will soon be able to walk him in public spaces with confidence.

WHERE TO TRAIN

There are likely to be several classes running in your area. Try to get recommendations from other dog owners or your vet. Choose a trainer who is recognized by an official organization such as the American Kennel Club. Before you choose a class, take the time to visit and watch a training session take place. Even if you have no experience of training classes, you will quickly get a feel for a good class. Aim for classes with relaxed dogs and happy owners. Avoid hectic and noisy environments and classes. A knowledgeable and experienced trainer will take charge in a friendly and effective manner.

WHAT TO LOOK FOR IN A CLASS

- Small classes with only a few dogs.
- High trainer-to-dog ratio.
- Positive training methods utilizing praise, food, and toys.
- No choke chains.
- No aggressive training.
- A relaxed environment.

COME WHEN CALLED Training your dog to come when called should not be started on walks because there are simply too many temptations that may cause your dog to ignore you. However, by practicing the following simple steps at home or in your yard, your dog will learn that coming back to you is always the better choice.

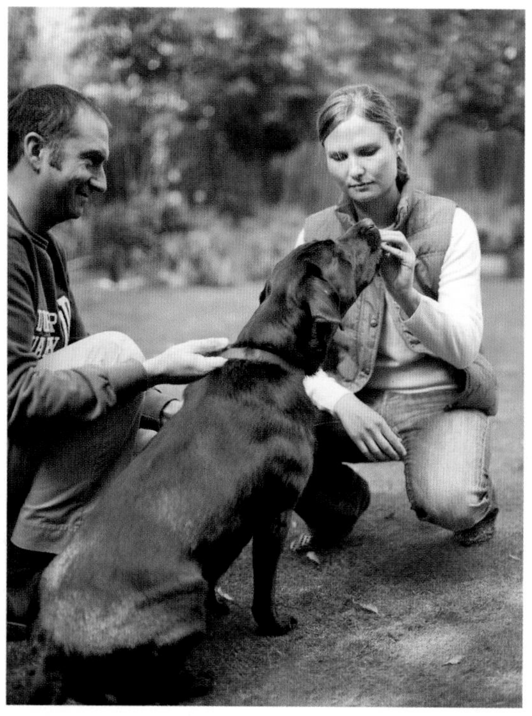

1 Show the treat to tempt him Get your dog focused on you by tempting him with his favorite treat. Let him sniff the treat but have a friend gently hold his collar so that he can't eat it.

2 Call him Keep your dog's attention on you and take a few paces away from him. Then crouch down to your dog's level, throw your arms wide open, and call him with an enthusiastic "come." As you do this, your friend can let go of your dog's collar.

3 Encourage him with a treat As soon as your dog is within two feet of you, hold out the treat as a lure and tempt him to come right up to you. Play with him a bit with the treat—you don't want him to grab the treat and run off.

4 Reward and praise As you give him the treat, gently take hold of his collar with your other hand and pat him or tickle his chin. Praise him and feed him some more treats so he learns that coming back to you is really worthwhile.

Behavioral problems

Most dogs that are trained in basic rules from a young age happily integrate into their household. However, some dogs may develop unwanted behaviors that require further training or specialized help.

DESTRUCTIVE BEHAVIOR

Chewing is a natural behavior in puppies and dogs, but when it becomes excessive or is targeted toward something inappropriate it can quickly become a source of tension between owner and dog. Sometimes dogs exhibit destructive behavior as an outlet because they are experiencing physical pain or suffer from separation anxiety—a condition characterized by extreme distress during the absence of their owner. Dogs can be affected by anxiety disorders, however supportive and happy their homelife. You should seek your vet's advice or consult a professional behaviorist if your dog suffers from anxiety.

Occasionally, destructive behavior such as chewing or digging can become a problem in otherwise healthy, adult dogs. This is often a sign that the dog is not being sufficiently stimulated, and it may help to provide him with an acceptable outlet for this natural behavior—such as allowing him to dig for treats in a sandpit. This will only work in dogs where all of their other needs, such as physical exercise, nutritional requirements, and social interaction, are met.

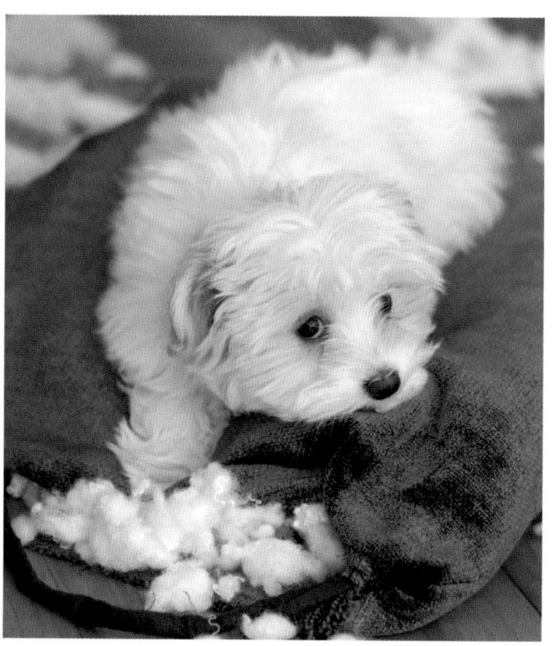

Dealing with chewing
Puppies naturally use their mouths to investigate their environment, especially when teething, but you should never punish them for this or they will learn to hide from you when they are chewing.

The first stage of training is to put the desired behavior on cue, by associating a command word with the behavior. For example, a dog that chews furniture can be taught to chew special toys containing food instead. Offer your dog a toy with treats hidden inside and praise him as he begins to investigate it, telling him "good boy, chew" in a clear voice. It is vital that you make some temporary changes to restrict your dog's opportunities to perform the unwanted behavior, such as preventing chewing by using a bitter spray to make the furniture taste unpleasant.

When you have made a good association between the cue word and the correct behavior, you have a channel of communication when your dog misbehaves. Do not punish your dog, since he is not being bad—he is displaying a natural behavior. If you catch him chewing the furniture, simply interrupt him (for example, with a hand clap) and hand him his chew toy, saying "good boy, chew."

EXCESSIVE BARKING

Barking is a completely normal dog behavior; however, excessive barking can quickly become a problem within a household. Bear in mind that dogs sometimes bark when shut in a room or in the yard for long periods, and allowing more freedom will often result in reduced barking.

The easiest way to control problem barking is to train your dog to bark on command and follow this with teaching "be quiet" on command as well. Start by doing something that would normally cause your dog to bark, such as waving a toy. Insert the command to "speak" just before he barks. Praise him for barking and then approach him and hold a treat in front of his nose to stop him from barking. Then simply say the word "quiet" and feed him the treat. Incorporate training sessions into play, and end with a fun game of tug-of-war or something similar. Don't use this training, however, if your dog is barking out of aggression; in this case, a professional behaviorist will need to be involved.

Don't pay attention
Do not give your puppy any fuss or attention if he jumps up. Only praise him when he has all four paws on the floor again.

JUMPING UP

A common complaint from dog owners, and the one problem they are most guilty of creating themselves, is their dog jumping up at people. Puppies naturally try to get closer to people's face and hands, which they recognize as sources of human affection. It is natural for people to encourage this because it seems cute and fun when puppies do it. However, problems develop when this behavior continues in adult dogs. Teaching young puppies not to jump up from the very first day you bring them home can help you prevent this.

However, if you have an older dog that already habitually jumps up at people you will need to train him that this is unacceptable. This can be as simple as following the instructions to teach a "sit" (see p.324) so that he cannot jump up. If the urge to jump up is irresistible to your dog, it may be necessary to set up specific training sessions. To do this, put him on a short leash and get a friend to walk slowly toward you. When your dog is sitting obediently, your friend can approach and give him praise but must move away again if he gets overexcited and jumps up. As training progresses, you should be able to take off the leash but your dog will still need to be reminded to "sit." Make sure that everyone enforces the rule or your training will fail. Do not become complacent about praising your dog for sitting obediently or he is very likely to jump up as a way of getting attention again.

RUNNING OFF

All dogs love to run freely and play, so it is important that your dog will return to your call when off his leash—you may meet someone who isn't confident around dogs, or another dog that is unfriendly.

Begin recall training in a distraction-free environment such as your home or yard. Start by practicing "come when called" at home (see p.328). Once your dog will return to you quickly, move the training outside. Walk your dog on his normal leash, but have a light, long-line attached as well and tuck it away in your pocket. When you get to a safe, open space you can make a big show of taking off your dog's leash. He will assume he is off the leash, but in fact you have hold of the end of the long-line. Leave the line dragging along the ground and don't pull it taut. Now call your dog's name, followed by "come," stand up tall and wave your arms with a big smile on your face. Your dog should always want to come back to you, because he knows he will get treats or praise every time he does. Keep the training varied—ask your dog to recall a number of times and be totally unpredictable about when you call him. Make sure that you always reward the recall in some way.

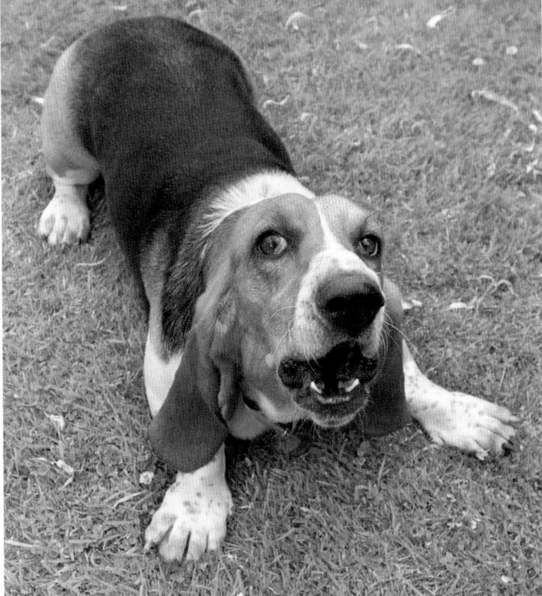

Stages of aggression
Dogs show a whole range of signs before they resort to biting. Only if these signs are ignored will the dog feel the need to escalate his response.

AGGRESSION

A natural canine response when a dog is not comfortable in a situation is to become aggressive. However, for pet dogs to be trustworthy in all situations they must understand that aggression is not an acceptable response toward humans or other dogs. A good owner needs to take note of when a dog is becoming distressed and help him be more comfortable in that situation, to reduce the risk of an aggressive response. Most happy and socialized dogs are not aggressive other than in rare cases where they are in pain or surprised while sleeping. Never challenge an aggressive dog. If a dog is growling at you, he is telling you that he is unhappy and wants you to move away. Any harsh treatment will only result in the dog becoming more aggressive over time as he feels the need to defend himself.

Do not attempt to remedy an aggression problem without professional help. First ensure you put control measures in place, such as keeping your dog muzzled and on a leash when out, and then speak to your vet about getting a professional, accredited dog behaviorist to assist you.

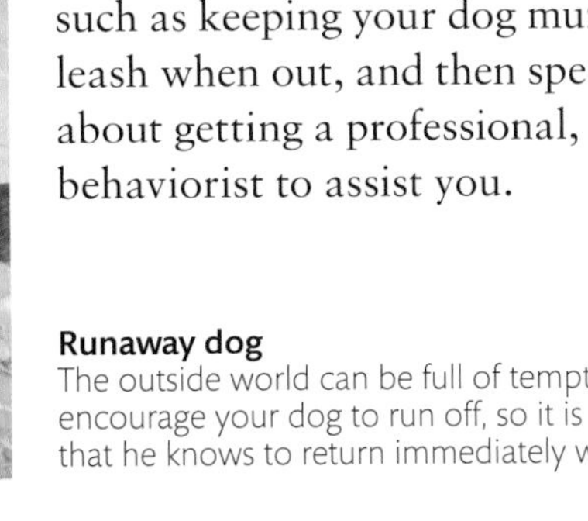

Runaway dog
The outside world can be full of temptations that might encourage your dog to run off, so it is important that he knows to return immediately when you call.

Visiting the vet

Your dog will need veterinary check-ups throughout his life, from early puppyhood to old age. Regular health check-ups of your dog will help pick up hidden problems and minor issues before they become major worries.

FIRST PUPPY HEALTH CHECK-UP

Take your puppy for his first veterinary check-up as soon as it is convenient. Unless he is already vaccinated, carry him into the office and keep him off the floor. He should wear a collar and leash in case he jumps out of your arms. Alternatively, use a pet carrier. There may be other animals in the waiting room and it can be noisy, so reassure your puppy.

Vets enjoy meeting puppies, and you are likely to receive a warm welcome. The vet will ask you for details of your puppy's early life: his date of birth; the size of the litter; where and how the pups were reared; what worming and flea treatments were done; and the results of any screening tests for the breed. If your puppy has been vaccinated, show the vet the certificate. Your puppy will be weighed, and the vet will make a detailed examination, including checking his ears with an auroscope and listening to his heart.

The vet will also scan your puppy to check that he has been microchipped. Implanting a microchip under the skin between your puppy's shoulders—a procedure somewhat like giving a vaccination—ensures that he can always be identified. Scanning the chip reveals a unique number against which any contact information you have provided is recorded in a central database.

If a vaccination is required, it will be given now. You may need to make some follow-up appointments to complete the vaccination course and to allow the vet to monitor your puppy's progress. Before you leave, the vet should offer advice on diet, flea control, neutering, socializing, training, and traveling in the car. Do not hesitate to ask if you need any further information.

FOLLOW-UP PUPPY CHECK-UP

The veterinarian may suggest that you take your puppy for another check-up when he is four or five months old, to ensure that he is growing well and developing both physically

Meeting the vet
Your puppy should be relaxed and enjoy his first appointment at the veterinary practice. Reassure him while the vet examines him so that he remains calm.

VACCINATIONS

Protecting your dog against infection is one of the best things you can do for him. Vaccination has greatly reduced the incidence of major canine diseases, such as parvovirus and distemper, and prevents other infections, including rabies and leptospirosis. During pregnancy a bitch (provided her vaccinations are up to date) passes immunity on to her puppies. This protection lasts for a few weeks after birth, after which the puppies should be vaccinated. Your vet will recommend when boosters should be given. Some vaccines can give up to three years' protection against certain diseases, following a booster 12 months after the initial course.

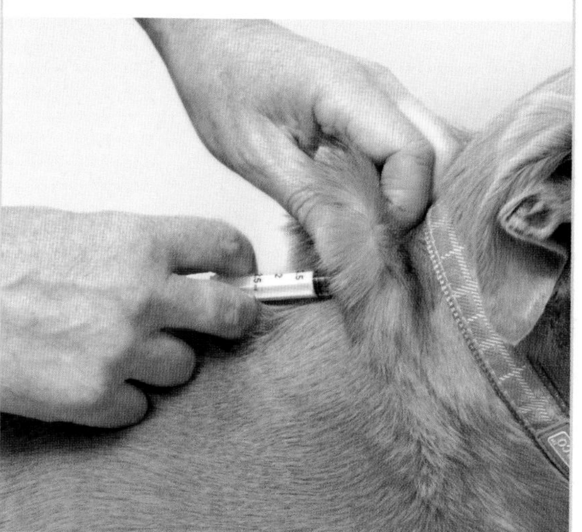

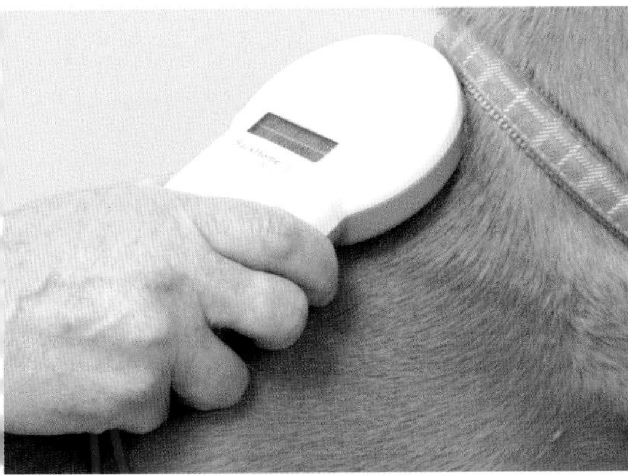

Scanning a microchip
Checking that the microchip can be identified by a scanner is very important. Remember to keep the contact information that is registered against the chip number up to date.

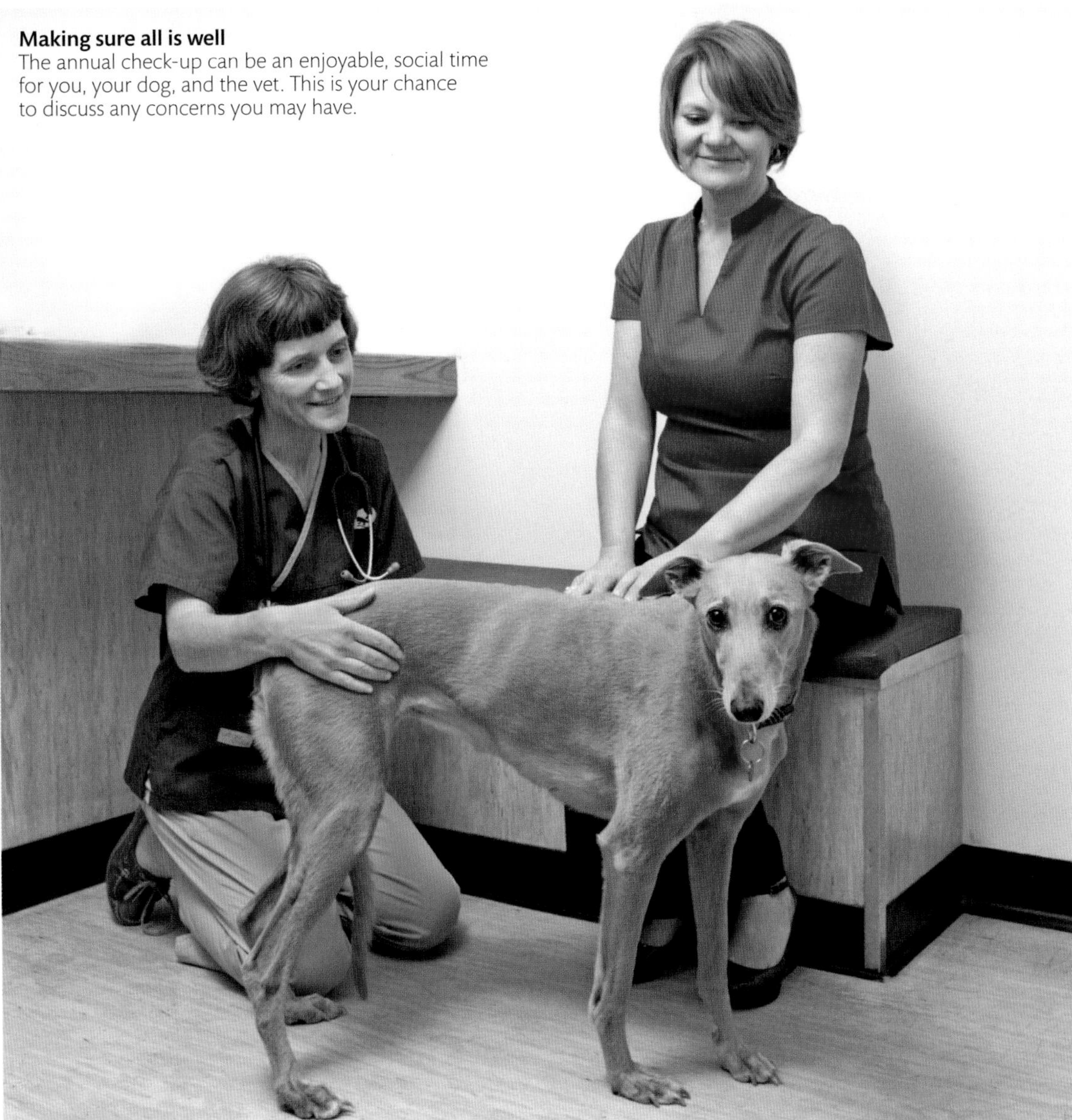

Making sure all is well
The annual check-up can be an enjoyable, social time for you, your dog, and the vet. This is your chance to discuss any concerns you may have.

and socially. This will also give you the chance to build on the advice given at the first puppy appointment. At the follow-up check-up, the vet will look for any puppy teeth that were not shed as the adult versions came through. This is important because the baby teeth may need to be removed to allow the adult teeth to take up the right position within the mouth and ensure the correct bite.

ANNUAL CHECK-UP

In addition to the regular check-ups you do at home (see pp.320–21), you should also make an appointment for an annual vet check-up. The vet will examine your dog from head to tail and ask various questions—for instance, about his thirst, appetite, diet, toilet habits, and exercise. If there is any cause for concern, detailed diagnostic tests may be recommended. You may be asked to bring a sample of your dog's urine, particularly if your pet is a senior, since this will provide additional important information about the kidneys and bladder. The sample should be collected early that morning into a suitable container. Your vet will also be able to advise on general health matters such as weight, body and coat condition, and control of worms, fleas, and other parasites. Other routine procedures may include clipping the nails if they are overgrown and giving booster vaccinations to maintain protection against infectious diseases.

Some dogs do not like being examined. If this is the case, the vet may suggest muzzling your dog, or he may ask you to go out of the room and have a veterinary nurse assist because some dogs are braver and better behaved away from their owners.

Some veterinary practices run specific clinics, such as those dealing with weight issues. If your dog's weight is recorded at a regular clinic, any gain or loss will be identified and treated at an early stage.

DENTAL CHECK-UP

A healthy mouth not only enables your dog to enjoy eating his food, but it is also important for his general well-being, since decayed teeth and infected gums can lead to diseases in other parts of the body. The teeth will be examined at annual check-ups and any interim visits, but you may want to consider taking your dog to a regular dental clinic. Such clinics can give you advice on home dental hygiene techniques and will monitor your progress. They will also provide support if your dog has to undergo a dental procedure such as a scale-and-polish.

ASKING ABOUT NEUTERING

If you decide to have your dog neutered, as the majority of owners do, an early puppy health check-up is a good opportunity to ask for advice. Your vet will explain what the procedure involves for either a dog or a bitch, and suggest when neutering is best carried out. Veterinary opinions differ as to the ideal time for dogs to be neutered, with the recommended age ranging from a few weeks to a few months. Most commonly, the operation is performed after puberty. Many owners worry about the after-effects of neutering and any concerns you may have can also be discussed at your puppy's first health check-up.

Signs of health

A healthy dog is easy to recognize by the way he looks and behaves, allowing for individual variation, breed, and age. Once you get to know your own dog, you should have no difficulty in judging if all is well.

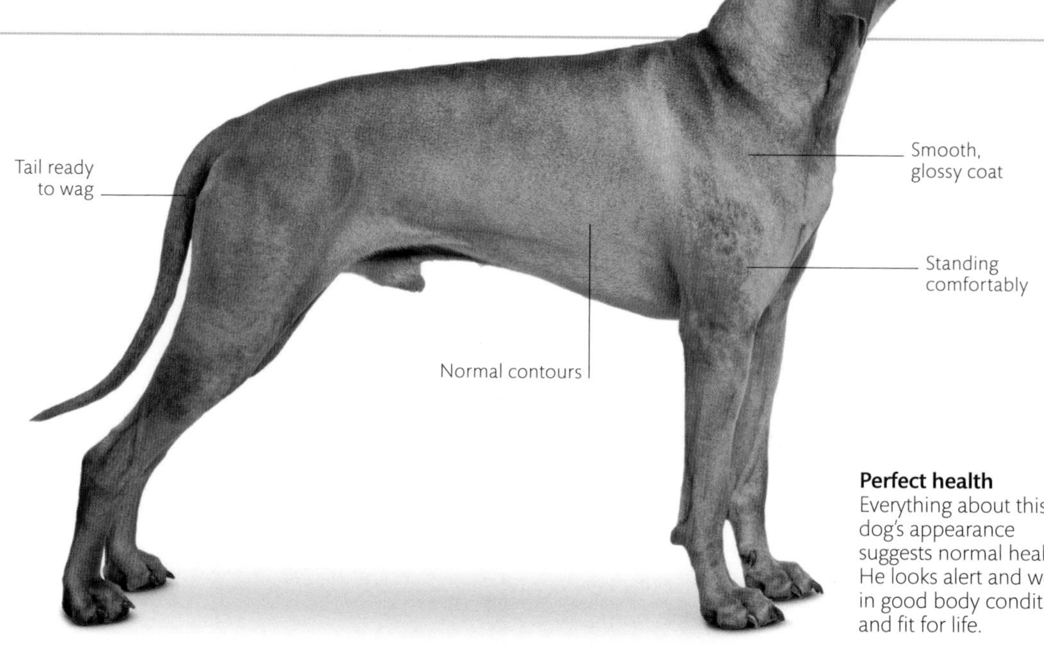

Perfect health
Everything about this dog's appearance suggests normal health. He looks alert and well, in good body condition, and fit for life.

HEALTHY APPEARANCE

Bright eyes, a glossy coat, and a cold, wet nose are often cited as classic signs of good health in a dog, but these are not invariable indicators. A dog's bright eyes may dim with age, even if he stays perfectly fit; his coat will not look glossy if he is wire-haired; and a healthy dog can often have a warm, dry nose.

Perhaps more useful health indicators are your dog's body shape and weight, which should stay consistent: strange swellings, sudden loss of weight, and abdominal bloating are all possible early health warnings. You can monitor weight gain and growth in a young dog by weighing him weekly and plotting the weight on a graph; back up this data by taking regular photographs as he matures.

Changes in health are also revealed in a dog's feces and urination habits, which can be markedly different from one dog to another. Your dog should urinate and defecate to his normal pattern. As you clear up after your dog, it will become obvious what is normal for him in terms of frequency, consistency, and color.

A healthy dog should appear bright and alert, and interact readily with the family and other dogs and pets. He should move around freely, without stiffness, be eager for physical exercise, and not be unduly tired afterward. A normal interest in food, and drinking the expected amount of water, are also signs that he is in good health.

Fit and healthy
A dog in good health will have a hearty appetite and show an obvious enjoyment of exercise. He should appear bright, inquisitive, and playful, too.

SIGNS OF A PROBLEM

- Unwillingness to exercise; lethargy, tiring unexpectedly on a walk
- Loss of coordination or bumping into objects
- Altered breathing pattern or an abnormal sound during respiration
- Coughing or sneezing
- Open wound
- Swelling or unusual bump
- Pain, swelling, and heat in a joint
- Swollen eyes or eyelids
- Blood: from a wound; passed in urine (which will appear pink or contain blood clots); in feces or in vomit
- Limping or stiffness
- Shaking head
- Unintentional weight loss
- Weight gain, particularly if the dog has developed a distended abdomen
- Reduced appetite or refusing food altogether
- Voracious appetite, or a change in what the dog will eat
- Vomiting, or regurgitation of food shortly after eating
- Diarrhea or difficulty passing a motion
- Bloated abdomen
- Crying with pain when passing feces or urine
- Itchiness: rubbing at mouth, eyes, or ears; dragging rear along the ground ("scooting") or washing excessively in that area; or all-over bodily itching
- Abnormal discharge: from any orifice (such as the mouth, nose, ear, vulva, prepuce, or anus) from which there is not usually a discharge, or because the normal smell, color, or consistency has altered
- Coat changes: dull with a greasy texture, or excessively dry; debris in the coat, such as flea dirts, actual fleas, scabs, or scales
- Excessive hair loss resulting in areas of baldness
- Change in coat color (may occur so gradually that it is noticed only when compared with an old photograph)
- Changes to gum color—becoming paler or yellowing; or a bluish tinge to gums; or grey discharge at gum line
- High temperature

RECOGNIZING A PROBLEM

Any change in your dog may be a warning of poor health. The most trivial sign, such as a droopy eyelid, should not be dismissed, since it could be significant. Your dog may have an internal problem such as an upset stomach, an external problem affecting the coat and skin, or a combination of the two. You may notice only vague signs, such as your dog sleeping more or exercising less readily, or something obviously wrong, such as your dog limping, or shaking his head because a grass awn is trapped in his ear.

Many common disorders are minor and easily treated, especially if they are recognized early. Always speak to your vet before attempting any home treatment. What might seem an appropriate course of action for humans could be harmful to a dog. It may be sufficient to act on advice given by your veterinary practice over the telephone, although often the vet will need to examine your dog to be certain of how best to proceed. If there is no simple explanation of a problem, your vet will work through the possible causes in order of likelihood.

After taking a dog's history and examining him fully, the vet may still need to perform further investigations, such as blood tests and imaging. Sometimes a dog may be diagnosed with a serious disorder that needs hospitalization and even surgery, followed by a long convalescence—but, fortunately, common ailments really are common. An itchy dog is more likely to have fleas than an obscure problem with his nervous system.

Remember, both you and your vet are aiming for your dog to lead as long and healthy a life as possible. If you need more advice or information, your vet will also be ready to help.

Recognizing the warning signs
It is helpful to understand what is normal in your dog. You will then be able to recognize anything unusual, such as lack of interest in food or exercise, that may be due to ill health.

ABNORMAL THIRST

A dog spending more time than usual at his water bowl, or a source of water outside, may have an abnormal thirst. Measure the volume of water he drinks over 24 hours by emptying all his bowls and recording how much you add (in ounces); 24 hours later, measure how much is left and subtract that from the total. Divide that figure by your dog's body weight in pounds—if it is around 1oz per lb then your dog's thirst is normal, but contact your vet if the figure is more than 2oz.

Inherited disorders

An inherited disorder is one that is passed on from one generation to the next. Such disorders appear more often in pedigree dogs and may be breed-specific. Some common examples are described below.

THE RISK OF DISEASE

Smaller gene pools and widespread inbreeding in the past have made pedigree dogs more likely than crossbreeds to be affected by inherited disorders. However, although crossbred dogs may be at reduced risk, they still have a chance of inheriting disease-causing genes from either parent.

HIP AND ELBOW DYSPLASIA

These two conditions occur mainly in medium-sized and large breeds. In dysplasia, structural defects either of the hip or the elbow cause a joint to become unstable, resulting in pain and lameness. Diagnosis is based on the dog's history, together with joint manipulation and radiography.

Treatment may consist of pain relief, reducing exercise, and maintaining ideal body weight. Various surgical options are also available, including total hip replacement for hip dysplasia. After a set age (generally more than one year old), susceptible breeds can be screened for hip and elbow dysplasia.

AORTIC STENOSIS

A congenital defect, present from birth, aortic stenosis is a narrowing of the aortic valve in the heart. There may be no signs, the disorder being detected as a murmur when a vet listens to the heart with a stethoscope at a puppy check. It may be investigated further (with radiography, ultrasound, and ECG) or simply monitored, as only a few dogs can be treated surgically. Some dogs with aortic stenosis go on to develop congestive heart failure.

BLOOD CLOTTING DISORDERS

The most common inherited clotting disorder (in both dogs and humans) is hemophilia, in which lack of an essential factor for blood clotting results in recurrent bleeding. The faulty gene responsible is passed on by affected males to their female offspring, who remain unaffected themselves but can be carriers of the gene. Hemophilia can occur in both pedigree and crossbred dogs.

Another inherited blood clotting disorder is Von Willebrand's disease, which affects many breeds of either sex. DNA tests are available for some breeds.

EYE PROBLEMS

Dogs can be affected by several inherited eye conditions, including some that are easily visible, such as entropion (right), and others that need internal examination of the eye using specialized equipment. An eye disease that can occur in any breed and also in crossbred dogs is progressive retinal atrophy (PRA). In this disorder, there is degeneration of the retina—the layer of light-sensitive cells at the back of the eye—leading to loss of vision. An owner may become aware of PRA when a dog begins to display sight problems, which at first may be only at night. PRA is diagnosed from examining the retina with an ophthalmoscope, and the vet may recommend more specialized investigations. There is no treatment and loss of vision is permanent. DNA screening is available for some breeds.

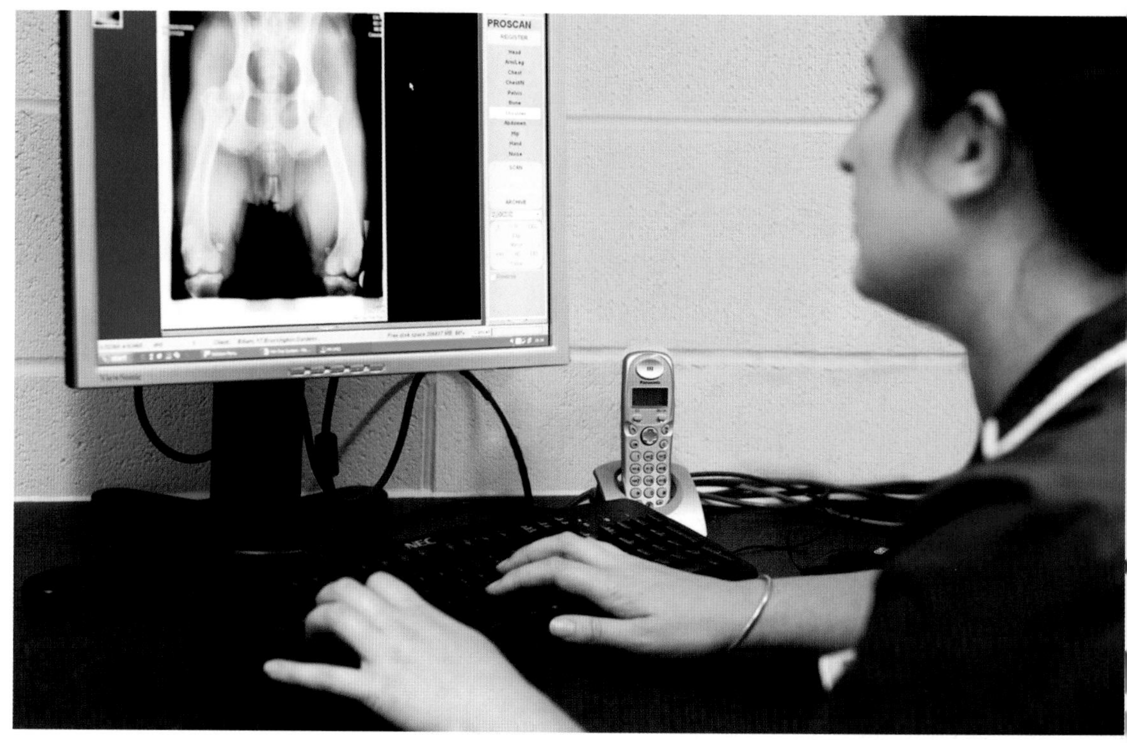

Radiograph of hip
Screening is advisable before using a dog for breeding when hip dysplasia is known to occur in the breed. This involves submitting a radiograph of the dog's hips for scoring (see box below).

HIP SCORING

The hips are radiographed with the dog lying on his back, hind legs extended straight out. For best results, the dog may be given sedation to keep him in the right position. Each hip joint is given a score for six factors, covering conditions from normal to severe. This gives a maximum score of 53 for each hip—the ideal is for as low a score as possible. Adding the two scores together gives a total. When selections are being made for breeding purposes, it is best to choose a dog whose total score is less than the current average for that breed.

Eye problems in the Shar Pei
Entropion, a painful inrolling of the eyelids, is common in the Shar Pei, usually developing in very young puppies. Both upper and lower eyelids may be affected.

Inherited blood disorders
Many breeds, including the German Shorthaired Pointer, can be affected by Von Willebrand's disease, an inherited blood clotting disorder.

Various breeds of collie (Smooth and Border Collies, Shetland Sheepdog, and Australian Shepherd) and some other breeds are affected by a disorder known as collie eye anomaly (CEA), in which there are abnormalities in the choroid, a layer of tissue at the back of the eye. CEA can be detected from birth, so puppies are examined before they are three months old. The mildest form of CEA has little effect on sight, but the most severe form can cause blindness. DNA screening is available.

SCREENING FOR DISEASE

Routine screening is important in reducing the incidence of inherited diseases. For hip and elbow dysplasia, dogs are screened by having radiographs taken (see box opposite). In the past, eye conditions such as PRA and CEA could be identified only by examination, but the advent of DNA screening has improved the chances of detecting both these and many other inherited diseases.

Collie eye anomaly (CEA)
Collies such as the Australian Shepherd must be checked as puppies for CEA, because early signs can be masked as the dog matures.

Parasites

Even the most well-groomed dog is susceptible to invasion by skin parasites, and it is common, too, for worms to live inside your pet. Prevention of parasites, rather than having to treat an infestation and its effects, is the ideal.

FLEAS

You need to take year-round preventive action against fleas. Running a flea comb through your dog's coat, especially over the rump, may catch fleas, which you can kill by squashing them against the teeth of the comb with a finger. You are more likely to find flea dirts, which show up as black debris. Treatment includes spot-on products (applied at the back of the neck), tablets, and collars. Alternatively, you can spray, wash, or powder your dog. Treat all other pets at the same time as your dog. Fleas pass most of their life cycle in carpets and furniture, so you may need to use separate products to eradicate them from the home.

TICKS

A seasonal problem, occurring mostly in spring and fall, ticks can attach themselves to your dog and may transmit diseases. Some ticks carry the bacterium *Borrelia burgdorferi*, acquired from mammals such as rodents and deer, which causes Lyme disease in humans and dogs.

Swift removal of a tick reduces the risk of infections. Using tweezers or a tick hook, hold the tick close to the dog's skin but without squeezing its body. Gently twist to remove it. If the head is embedded try to remove it, too. Mouthparts left behind can cause a reaction and a lump may develop, but treatment is not usually needed and the lump will vanish. If you live in or are traveling to an area known for ticks, take preventive measures such as spot-on treatments and collars.

MITES

Demodex mites are probably passed from mother to puppies at birth. They affect the skin on the head and around the eyes, and can appear elsewhere, causing fur thinning, bald areas, and a musty smell. These mites may be found in skin scrapings from healthy dogs but they particularly occur at times of stress or illness when a dog's immune system is weakened. Mild demodectic mange resolves without treatment. Severe cases need specific treatment to kill the mites, which is continued until several skin scrapings are clear; antibiotics may also be needed if there is an associated skin infection.

The spiderlike *Sarcoptes* mite is commonly passed on to dogs from foxes. It causes the highly contagious sarcoptic mange with intense itchiness, hair loss, and skin sores. Your vet will recommend the best treatments.

The bright orange, nonparasitic harvest mite may be picked up by a dog running in fields in summer. It tends to be found on the skin of the toes, ears, and around the eyes. These mites rub off easily and usually cause no reaction, but they may be linked to a serious disorder called seasonal canine illness.

LICE

A dog that has lice will scratch frequently. The lice can be seen in the coat and on the skin, with nits (eggs) attached to hairs. The entire life cycle of a louse takes place on an

Itchy skin
Fleas are the most common cause of skin irritation in dogs. If fine-combing fails to detect them, ask your vet to check your dog for other possible problems.

Iealthy family
.oundworm prevention for these puppies started before ıey were born, since their mother was treated during ›regnancy. They should be wormed regularly throughout life.

Danger in snails
ungworm can be picked up if a dog eats an infected snail r slug, either intentionally or accidentally if, for example, ıere is one on a toy or bowl left outside.

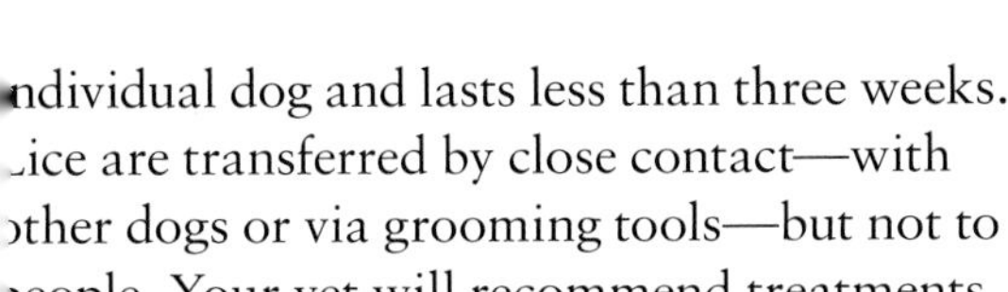

ndividual dog and lasts less than three weeks. ice are transferred by close contact—with ›ther dogs or via grooming tools—but not to ›eople. Your vet will recommend treatments.

ROUNDWORM

The adult worms, which look like strands of spaghetti, live in the intestines, producing ggs that pass out of the body in the feces ınd mature for one to three weeks before ›eing infective to others, including humans. This is why carefully disposing of your dog's ces is so important. A dog can acquire oundworms from the soil or by eating other arriers such as rodents. Puppies can be nfected in the womb by roundworm larvae ›assed on from their mother.

Prevention of roundworms starts with reating the pregnant bitch and continues ıfter birth, both with the puppies and their nother, and at regular intervals throughout ife. Ask your vet about which product to ıse, as well as the worming schedule to follow as your puppy grows up.

TAPEWORM

The eggs of the commonest tapeworm species, *Dipylidium caninum*, are carried by fleas, and your dog can become infected by licking fleas off his coat and swallowing them. The adult flat, segmented worm develops within the gut, and sheds egg-containing segments, which you may see as wriggly "rice grains" around your dog's anus or in his feces. They cause itching, and your dog may "scoot" his bottom along the ground. Treatment comprises tapeworm-specific medication, together with flea control.

Your dog may pick up other tapeworm species from eating offal, raw meat, wild animals, or roadkill. Some tapeworms are a serious health risk to humans.

LUNGWORM

Also known as French heartworm, this parasite (*Angiostrongylus vasorum*) is picked up by a dog eating snails and slugs, which can carry the worm larvae. Worms develop in the right ventricle (chamber) of the heart and in the pulmonary artery. The females lay eggs containing first-stage larvae, which are carried in the bloodstream to the lungs. Here they hatch, burrowing into lung tissue and causing damage. The dog coughs them up and swallows them, passing them out in feces as a source of further infection to slugs and snails.

Lungworm can be hard to diagnose. Various symptoms may include lethargy, a cough, anemia, nose bleeds, weight loss, poor appetite, vomiting, and diarrhea. The dog may also display behavioral changes. Diagnostic tests include examining a tracheal wash and feces, as well as radiography and blood tests. Your vet will recommend drugs for treatment and prevention of lungworm. Pick up dog feces promptly (and fox feces, too, if you find them). Lungworm cannot be passed directly to other pets or to humans.

HEARTWORM

This parasite (*Dirofilaria immitis*) is transmitted by the bite of an infected mosquito. Heartworms live in the dog's heart, lungs, and surrounding blood vessels, and can cause death if left untreated. Owners in high-risk areas should seek prompt veterinary attention if their dog develops a cough or becomes lethargic during the mosquito season. Diagnosis is by blood test and treatment is risky, requiring the dog to rest for several weeks afterward. Year-round prevention with heartworm medicines is usually effective.

PREVENTING WORMS

Routine worming reduces the likelihood of infestation. Your vet will advise you on the best treatment for your puppy or dog. The ideal program depends on the perceived risk, which may be high if, for example, you walk your dog in public places, he is an avid scavenger of dead rodents, or he lives with small children. Strict flea control is the key to tapeworm prevention. You must weigh your dog, especially if he is still growing, so that you give the correct dose.

Nursing a sick dog

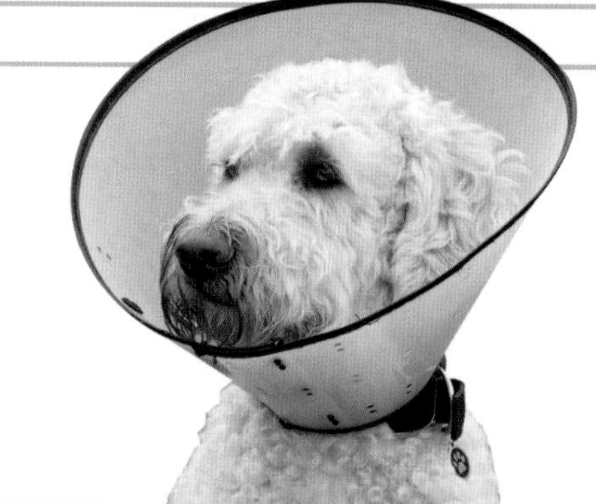

There may be times when your dog needs to be nursed because he is sick or recovering from surgery and cannot manage things he usually does on his own. Follow your vet's instructions and ask for advice if in doubt.

HOME CARE AFTER SURGERY

Dogs are rarely kept in overnight after routine operations such as neutering. Your vet will give you advice on any specific care that is needed, and your dog may be discharged with medication such as pain relief. If he remains uncomfortable then contact the vet.

Contrary to popular belief, a dog does more harm than good if he licks at an undressed wound, which will become sore and infected. Most dogs accept wearing an Elizabethan collar (or E collar)—a large, cone-shaped plastic collar that fits around the neck and head (above right). Anti-lick strips can also deter an inquisitive tongue and stop dogs from removing dressings on paws and legs.

Keep dressings clean and dry by covering with a boot or plastic bag when you take your dog outside to relieve himself. If he worries at a dressing excessively, or it becomes smelly or soiled, then seek your vet's advice as soon as possible.

GIVING MEDICATION

Prescribed medication should be given as directed by your vet, and only by an adult. Make sure other pets do not ingest a drug accidentally, especially if it is given in food.

Giving tablets and liquid medicine
Adding medicine to food is an easy way to administer it. Check the directions first: some medications need to be taken on an empty stomach, or must not be crushed. If the prescribed medication is a suspension, shake the bottle to mix well. Remove the dose and give to your dog directly into his mouth or with food.

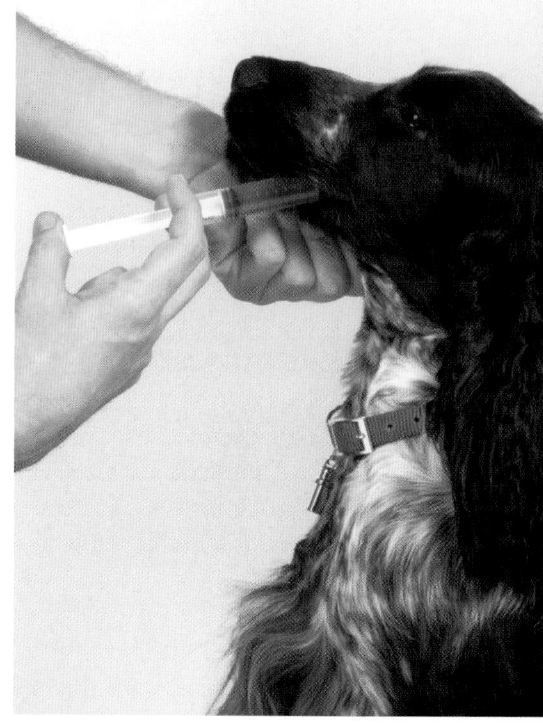

If your dog is prescribed an antibiotic, it is important that he completes the full course. A liquid medication may need to be shaken to ensure thorough mixing before the dose is given.

Giving medication directly by mouth is ideal, since you will be sure that your dog has swallowed it. Speak to your vet if this is difficult, since some medications can be hidden in food or a treat (although not if they must be taken on an empty stomach). Unless the tablet is palatable, avoid crushing and mixing it with food, since your dog may then refuse to eat and will not receive the medication. If your dog develops symptoms such as an upset stomach (vomiting or diarrhea) while on medication, then discontinue the treatment until you have spoken to a vet.

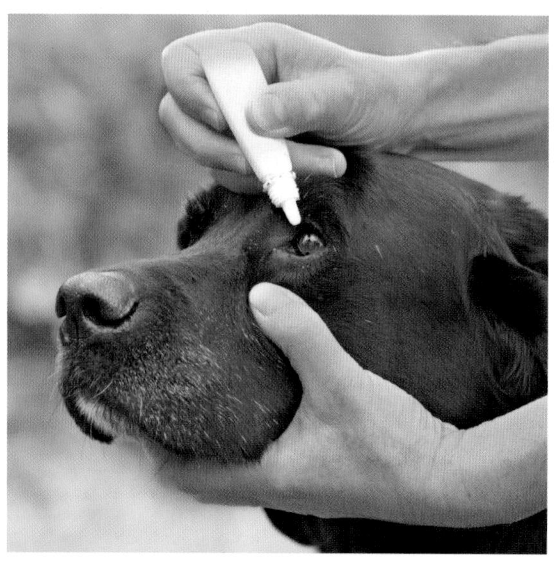

Administering eye drops
When applying eye drops, hold the dropper between your thumb and forefinger and squeeze the drops on to the front of the eye. After applying the drops, gently hold your dog's eyelids closed for a few seconds, and praise him.

FOOD AND WATER

Make sure your dog can reach his food and water bowls comfortably, perhaps raising them off the ground so he has no need to reach down. You may be given a prescription diet to help your dog's recovery, but if he will not eat it ask your vet about alternative suitable foods. A similar problem may occur with your dog refusing to drink recommended rehydration fluids. In this case, encourage him to drink cooled, boiled water, which is better than taking no fluids at all, or mix some water in with his food.

REST AND EXERCISE

A postoperative dog needs to rest in a quiet place at a warm, not hot, temperature with comfortable bedding. He may prefer to sleep away from the family, or he may seek company. Exercise immediately after surgery should be restricted unless you are advised otherwise. Short, slow walks around the yard are important to keep the joints, bladder, and bowels functioning.

Sleeping it off
Following surgery your dog will probably spend more time asleep than usual. Find him a cozy place where he can let his body recover.

First aid

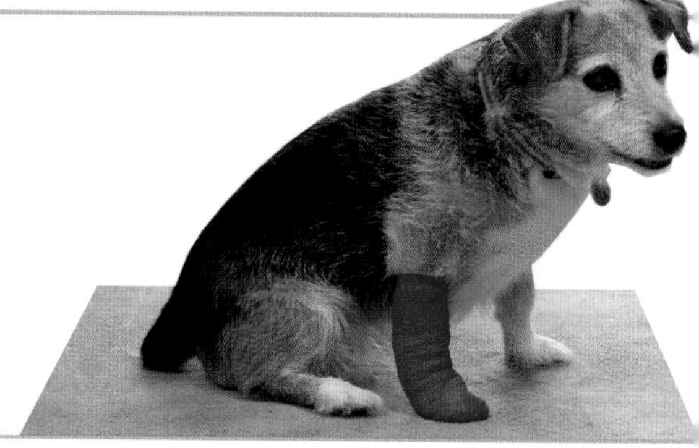

Dogs are inquisitive by nature and do not understand danger the way we do. It is impossible to prevent accidents from happening, so be prepared to provide emergency care if your dog is suddenly injured.

HELPING AN INJURED DOG

Minor injuries can often be treated at home, but if your dog suffers a serious accident he must be examined by a veterinarian. If you know the basic rules of first aid, you will be able to provide help until the vet arrives or, alternatively, the dog can be transported to the vet's practice.

When attending to an injured dog, you may need to muzzle him; if he is in pain and frightened, he may snap. Move him only if absolutely necessary.

In the case of bleeding, try to stem the flow of blood from any major wounds with direct pressure, carefully raising the injured area above the level of the heart, if possible.

If an injured dog is unconscious, put him in the recovery position. To do this, remove his collar and place him on his right side, with his head and neck in line with his body. Gently pull his tongue forward to let it hang out of the side of his mouth.

WOUNDS

Never leave a wound to heal itself—even the smallest injury can become infected, especially if a dog licks it. If your dog has a severe wound, seek veterinary help as soon as possible. Similarly, if a wound is caused by another dog or pet, then it should be attended to by a vet as soon as possible, since it may become infected.

A small, clean wound can be treated at home. Gently flush the wound with saline solution (preprepared, or a teaspoon of salt dissolved in two cups of warm water) to remove any dirt or debris. Apply a dressing or a bandage, if possible, to prevent the dog from licking at the wound. Use appropriate materials if you have them on hand, or improvise with socks or pantyhose to cover a wound on a limb, or a T-shirt for wounds on the chest or abdomen. Use adhesive tape rather than safety pins to hold a bandage in place. Be careful not to apply the bandage too tightly, keep it dry, and change it regularly to check on the wound. Always seek advice if you notice an offensive smell or if a discharge seeps through the bandage.

A deep or extensive wound requires urgent veterinary attention because stitches may be needed. Apply a temporary bandage as best you can to stem the bleeding. If the wound is on a limb, raise it and apply direct pressure via bandages or other padding, and bandage the pad in place. A tourniquet is not advised. Take great care if a foreign body is stuck in the wound: make sure not to push it in more deeply and do not attempt to remove it yourself.

For a wound on the chest, apply bandages soaked in warm saline solution or cooled, boiled water and hold them in place with bandaging or a T-shirt. A wound on the ear flap will spray blood whenever your dog shakes his head. Cover the wound with a bandage and secure the ear flap to his head.

Aftercare will depend on the nature of the wound. Bandages need to be changed every 2–5 days, as advised by your vet. All bandages must be kept dry, so cover with a waterproof layer when your dog goes outside.

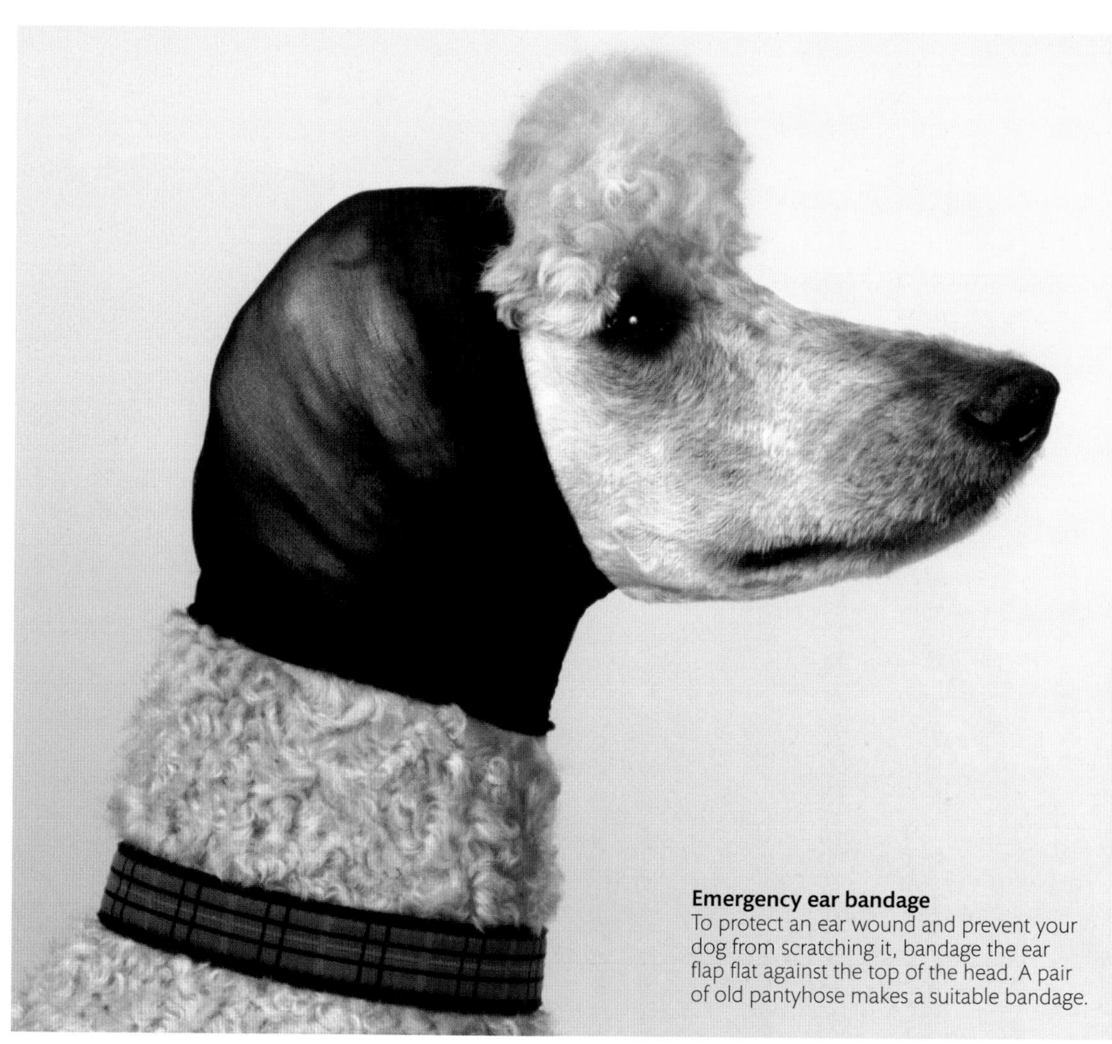

Emergency ear bandage
To protect an ear wound and prevent your dog from scratching it, bandage the ear flap flat against the top of the head. A pair of old pantyhose makes a suitable bandage.

HOW TO BANDAGE A PAW

Apply a sterile dressing. Run a soft conforming bandage down the front of the leg, over the paw, up behind, then back to the paw and up the front again.

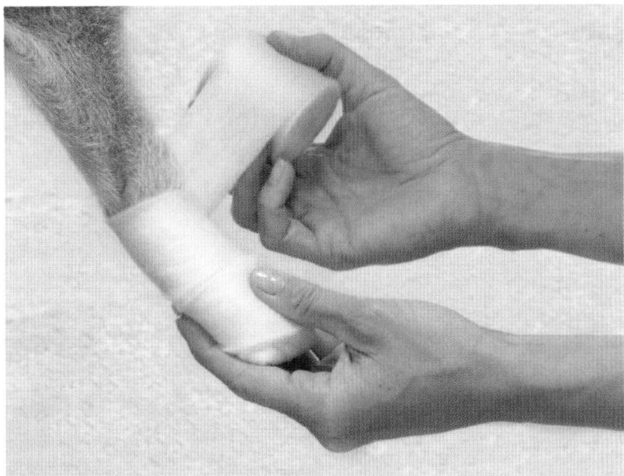

Wind the bandage around the leg down to the paw and then back up the leg. Repeat the earlier steps with an elasticated gauze bandage.

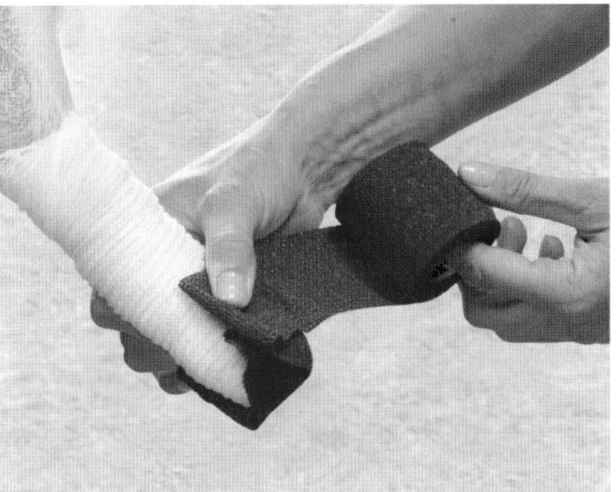

Repeat with a final cohesive layer, running it up on to the fur to secure it. Zinc oxide tape can also be used to secure the top of the dressing.

BURNS

Painful and sometimes severe damage to the skin can be caused by contact with heat, electricity, or chemicals. Burns caused by fire or a hot object such as an iron, or scalding with hot liquid are treated in the same way. Remove your dog from the source of the injury without endangering yourself, then contact your vet for advice; a burn or scald can be very serious, with hidden damage to deep tissues. Keep the dog warm and still while taking him to the vet. He will be given some pain relief and may also require treatment for shock if the area affected is extensive.

CAR ACCIDENTS

Take every precaution to protect your dog from traffic accidents—always keep him on a leash when on or near a road. If your dog is involved in an accident, keep him warm until help arrives. Do not put yourself at risk to tend to him.

Electrical burns to the mouth sustained by biting a power cable are common. Turn off the power at source before handling your dog. Urgent veterinary attention and care will be needed for pain relief and also because an electric shock can cause dangerous complications.

If your dog has been burned by chemicals, be careful not to contaminate yourself while handling the dog. Identify and note down the substances that have caused the burns and contact your vet immediately.

RESUSCITATION

If a dog needs to be resuscitated, it is important for you to stay calm. Call a vet for advice or, ideally, ask someone else to make the call while you place the dog in the recovery position.

If the dog is not breathing, start artificial respiration. Place your hands one over the other on the chest wall, just behind the shoulders. Apply a sharp downward movement every 3–5 seconds, allowing the chest wall to spring back in between each thrust, until voluntary breathing begins.

Check for the dog's circulation by feeling for a pulse (on the inside of the thigh) and a heartbeat (on the side of the chest just behind the elbow). If the heart has stopped, begin cardiac massage. For small dogs, place the fingers and thumb of one hand around the chest just behind the elbow and squeeze them together twice per second while your other hand is supporting the spine.

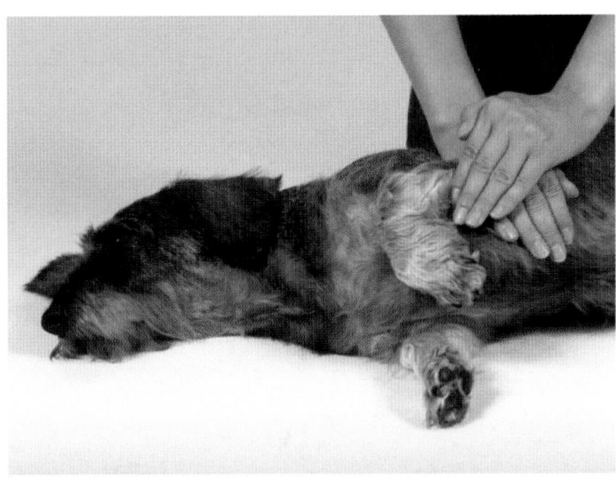

Resuscitation
If a dog's heart has stopped beating, his chances of recovery depend on resuscitation being started within a few minutes. Cardiac massage to keep the circulation going is a simple technique that can be life-saving.

For medium-sized dogs, place the heel of one hand on the dog's chest just behind the elbow; place your other hand on top and press down on the chest approximately 80–100 times per minute.

If the dog is large or overweight, lay him on his back with his head slightly lower than his body, if possible. Place one hand on his chest over the lower end of the breastbone with your other hand on top and apply compressions directed toward the dog's head, approximately 80–100 times per minute.

Check for a pulse after 15 seconds of applying compressions. If the heartbeat is still absent, continue with cardiac massage until you feel a pulse. If someone else is with you, they can give artificial respiration at the same time.

CHOKING AND POISONING

It is in a dog's nature to chew or eat anything that looks promising, but this can get him into trouble, and you will need to act quickly if it does. A dog can choke on all kinds of objects, including bones, rawhide chews, and children's toys. He may drool or paw frantically at his mouth if the object is wedged in his mouth, and may have difficulty breathing if it is obstructing his airway.

Only attempt to retrieve the object from your dog's mouth if you will not be bitten or there is no risk of pushing it farther into the throat. Putting something across your dog's jaw to prevent him from closing his mouth is a good idea if it does not make it harder to retrieve the object. Ideally, use something rubbery or a pad of material to keep from damaging his teeth; never use a muzzle.

If you cannot remove the object, or are concerned that your dog's mouth has been damaged, take him straight to a vet.

If you see your dog swallow something he should not, contact your vet for advice. Very small objects may pass through the dog without causing a problem. A larger object may need to be removed, preferably from the stomach before it enters the intestines.

The most common way for a dog to be poisoned is by scavenging something not meant for him. If you are worried that your dog may have eaten harmful substances, or he has persistent vomiting or diarrhea, keep any packaging and immediately contact your vet for advice.

Take preventive action by always storing anything remotely edible out of reach. This includes all medication, both veterinary and human; antifreeze (ethylene glycol), which has a sweet taste but will cause kidney failure; weed killers and slug bait, which are easily found in the yard; and household cleaners (even if you keep them in an inaccessible cabinet, remember that your dog may drink from a toilet that has a chemical released into the water when flushed).

Bait to control rodents should be used and stored well out of your dog's reach. Many rat poisons interfere with the action of vitamin K, which is essential to the body's blood-clotting process. This causes internal bleeding, which will not become immediately apparent. If you know or suspect that your dog has eaten rat poison, or a poisoned rodent, take the dog straight to the vet and bring along any relevant packaging.

Chocolate is highly appealing to a dog but is toxic if it has a high cocoa-solid content. Onions and their relatives, including leeks, garlic, and scallions, are also poisonous. Generally, the smaller the dog, the smaller the amount of toxin needed to have an effect. However, this is not the case with grapes, both fresh and dried (raisins, golden raisins, and currants), which are recognized as potential poisons.

BITES AND STINGS

Dogs are naturally inquisitive, exploring with their noses, so bites and stings from venomous animals or insects tend to be on the head and legs.

Bees and wasps are a common risk to dogs both indoors and outdoors. If your dog is stung, move him quickly to prevent further stings. Check for insects trapped in your dog's coat and look for the site of the sting. Bees leave their stinger behind, so remove it carefully with tweezers if you can do this without squeezing the poison sac. Wasps can sting repeatedly. Bathe the area with baking soda dissolved in water (for bee stings) or with vinegar (for wasp stings), then apply antihistamine cream. Cover the area to prevent the dog from licking it. If your dog is in pain or his condition worsens, take him to the vet. It is an emergency if your dog has been stung in the mouth or develops a severe allergic reaction (opposite).

Your dog may encounter poisonous toads, which release venom from the skin glands. If your dog licks the toad or picks it up, he may ingest the venom and will react by salivating

Raiding the garbage
A dog's dietary indiscretions include raiding the garbage can. Use containers such as pedal-operated or mechanical push-opening trash cans that will not yield to a dog's questioning nose.

Dangerous bones
A bone can pose a choking hazard if it is small enough to become wedged across the roof of the mouth or between the teeth, or if shards are swallowed and become stuck in the gullet.

Lurking in the undergrowth
Stinging insects, poisonous snakes, and other dangers can remain hidden in long grass until disturbed by an exploring nose. If your dog is bitten or stung, attend to him quickly and keep him calm.

ANAPHYLACTIC SHOCK

Occasionally, a dog may have an extreme reaction shortly after exposure to something to which he is acutely sensitive—for example, bee venom, especially if he has had multiple stings. This severe allergic reaction, which is known as anaphylactic shock, can be a life-threatening situation. Initial signs of anaphylactic shock include vomiting and excitability, rapidly leading to breathing difficulties, collapse, coma, and death. Immediate treatment is needed at a veterinary practice if the dog is to survive.

excessively and appearing anxious. Carefully flush out his mouth with water and seek advice from your vet if you are concerned.

Venomous snakes are encountered worldwide. Their toxicity depends on the species, the amount of venom injected relative to the dog's size, and the site of the bite. The effects of a snake bite develop rapidly within two hours. You can often see the puncture wounds from the bite, and painful swelling develops. A bitten dog may become lethargic and show other signs of poisoning, including rapid heart rate and panting, overheating, pale mucous membranes, excessive salivation, and vomiting. In severe cases, the dog may go into shock or a coma. Speed is of the essence, so take your dog to a vet without delay.

HEAT STROKE AND HYPOTHERMIA

If a dog overheats he cannot cool down again by sweating like humans do. If confined in a car on a hot day or shut in a sunroom at home, especially if there is no drinking water available, your dog can rapidly develop heat stroke. This is a risky condition in which the body's temperature-regulating mechanism breaks down. Without urgent veterinary attention, a dog can die within as little as 20 minutes. Signs include panting, distress, and reddening of the gums, rapidly leading to collapse, coma, and ultimately death. The priority is to move the dog from the hot place to somewhere cool. Cover him with wet sheets or towels, put him in a bathtub of cold water, or run a steady stream of water over him from a garden hose. Ice packs or a fan can also be used.

Heat stroke is often caused by leaving your dog in the car. It is not enough just to leave the windows open, even if you have parked in the shade. The risk is higher if there are several dogs in the car, or the dog is hot and panting from recent exercise.

The reverse of heat stroke is hypothermia, when the body's core temperature falls to dangerously low levels. A dog can develop hypothermia if kept in a drafty kennel, left in an unheated car or room, or if he goes into a pond or lake in the winter. Puppies and older dogs are the most vulnerable. A dog with hypothermia may shiver or move stiffly and appear lethargic. He needs to be warmed up gradually with a blanket until taken to a vet. The vet will give him warm fluids directly into a vein and treat him for shock.

Danger of overheating
Even with the window down, a car quickly becomes an oven, even at only moderately warm temperatures. Left shut in, this dog would be at risk of heat stroke.

CONVULSIONS

Convulsions are caused by abnormal activity in the brain. In a young dog, the cause is likely to be epilepsy; in an older dog, the reasons may vary but could include a brain tumor. If your dog has a seizure, make a note of when it occurred and any other relevant details, such as whether the television was on, or whether your dog had just eaten or come back from a walk.

Convulsions classically occur when a dog is dozing, and signs may be trembling and twitching, or your dog may lie on his side with his legs paddling as if running. A convulsion lasts from only seconds to a few minutes. Your dog may be aggressive during a convulsion or while in recovery.

A dog may have more than one convulsion within a few hours or days of each other. More worryingly, he may have a run of seizures, where he is not fully conscious between each episode. This is called status epilepticus and is a real emergency that requires urgent veterinary attention.

There are various drug options for treating epilepsy, and regular monitoring is needed to ensure that the drug is at the correct level to control the seizures.

Breeding

Making the decision to breed from your dog should not be taken lightly. Not only is it an expensive and time-consuming process, but it can also result in adding to the enormous surplus of dogs without homes.

CONSIDER THE REASONS

Before you breed from your dog, it is important to think long and hard about your reasons for wanting to have a litter of puppies. It is easy to get carried away with thoughts of cute puppies playing around your home, but the reality is that rearing a litter is extremely hard work. Do lots of research and plan everything carefully, and speak to a reputable professional breeder. If you decide that you don't want to breed from your dog, it is best to have it neutered.

PREGNANCY AND PRENATAL CARE

Dogs are pregnant for 63 days, but puppies can be born a few days on either side of this. Let your vet know early on that you have had your bitch mated. The vet will be an invaluable source of advice throughout your bitch's pregnancy and will advise on measures to keep your bitch parasite-free so that she doesn't pass infestations on to her puppies.

There is no need to increase the amount of food your bitch eats in the early stages of pregnancy. However, from around six weeks the food needs to be increased by about 10 percent each week. At this time your dog's exercise requirements are also likely to change. Shorter, more frequent walks that avoid very energetic activities are best.

Whelping area
Spend time making sure that your dog feels relaxed in the whelping area and get her used to you going in with her. Keep her favorite toys or blanket in the box to make it more inviting.

WHELPING

Long before your dog is due to have her puppies, set up a whelping area. The location of this is vital. It should be in the house so that your dog feels comfortable and the puppies get used to everyday household noises. However, it also needs to be in an out-of-the-way place where few people will need to walk once the puppies are born. It should be warm, dry, quiet, and draft-free. The whelping box itself can be either shop bought or homemade.

Whelping can be a daunting prospect; however, it normally occurs without any problems. The key to a smooth whelping is preparation so you know what to expect and what to do if things start to go wrong.

Individual bitches vary drastically in their behavior, but there are some telltale signs that whelping is imminent. Approximately 24 hours before whelping she may become restless because of the discomfort she will feel as her uterus prepares to expel the puppies. She may also refuse food, pant very deeply, and scratch and dig at the bedding of her whelping box—you can provide her with paper to rip up. Your bitch will be visibly calm just before the arrival of the first puppy and you should see the muscles around her abdomen contract as she makes efforts to push the first puppy out. The time to wait until the next puppy is passed can vary greatly. During that time the newborn puppies should be encouraged to suckle and your bitch urged to tend to them. If some time has passed and the bitch appears relaxed and is attentive to her puppies, the whelping process is over.

POSTNATAL CARE

With the worries of the whelping process now behind you, all your focus must switch to making sure that your bitch has everything she needs and that her puppies get the best possible start in life.

Natural birth
After giving birth your bitch will strip off the membrane from the amniotic sac and sever the umbilical cord with her teeth. You should only intervene if she appears to be biting the cord too closely or pulling too vigorously.

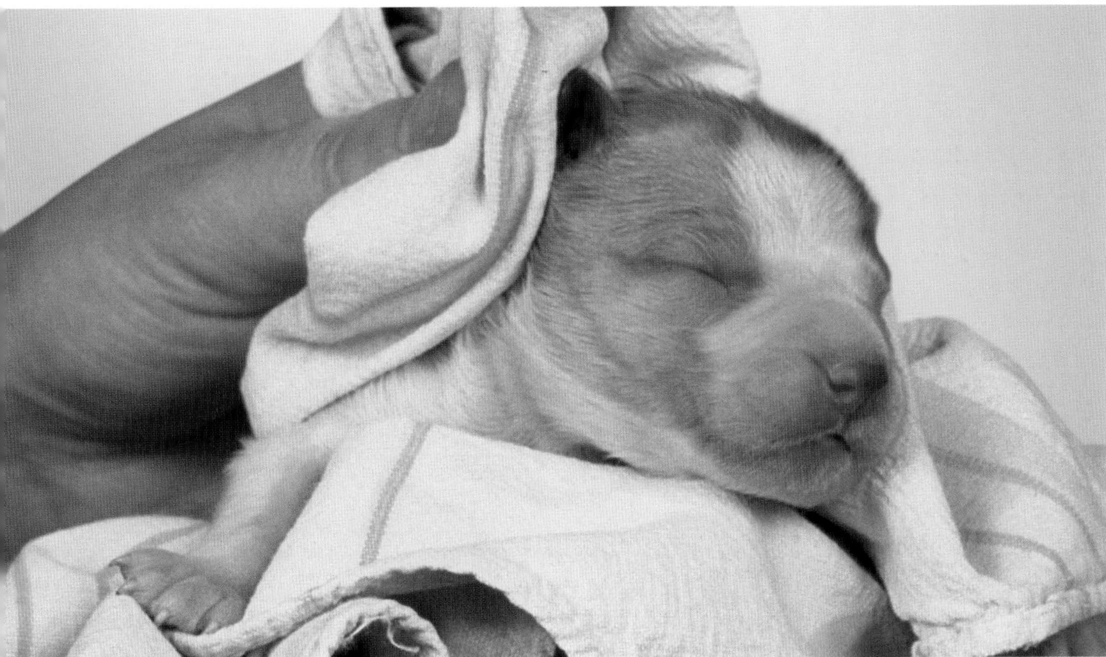

Handling a newborn puppy
Take a moment to check each newborn puppy over and rub it dry with a clean towel. Then return the puppy to the mother without delay.

Housebreaking
Accidents will happen but you will be making it easier for the new owners to complete the training if you get puppies habituated to using newspaper when relieving themselves.

As lactation requires a huge amount of energy, your bitch will need about twice the number of calories she was consuming prior to whelping, and the meals need to be little and often. She will also require lots of water. As she will be reluctant to leave her puppies, feeding her in the whelping box is advisable. She certainly won't need any exercise and will only need to be taken out for short visits to relieve herself a few times a day.

The natural maternal instincts your bitch has means that you will not need to do anything with the puppies initially. They should not be interfered with, other than to be checked over to ensure they are healthy and are putting on weight, and that they drink some of the bitch's first milk. Called colostrum, this initial milk provides the puppies with essential antibodies and is vital to their health. Within a couple of weeks you will need to trim the puppies' nails to prevent them scratching their mother's skin as they suckle.

EARLY PUPPY CARE

By the time the puppies are a few weeks old, their care becomes a full-time job. This is the most important time of the puppies' lives and there is much to prepare them for.

The puppies will soon begin to develop teeth, at which point their diet should consist of solid food as well as plenty of chew toys to help the teething process. Introduce solid food slowly and in tiny quantities at first so that the puppies get used to digesting it. Make sure you buy specially formulated puppy food, which is high in energy with the correct balance of nutrients.

Teaching a few simple rules in the breeder's home can make the difference between a confident and well-adjusted puppy and one that is likely to develop behavioral problems. It is entirely possible to train puppies before they go to their new homes so that they only relieve themselves on newspaper. This makes it much easier for the new owners to complete their housebreaking. In addition, spending a few minutes with each puppy every day gets them used to being handled, and will allow you to train them to do some basic behaviors on command, such as sit.

The most important factor of training is to expose your puppies to a range of everyday experiences. It is important to include them in family activities and help them socialize with people of all ages. Most puppies go into a home environment and, therefore, during these early weeks, getting them used to the sorts of sights and noises that accompany the daily comings and goings of a household is imperative. When they are only a few weeks old, puppies will happily accept new experiences with minimal reassurance. If a puppy has had good early socialization with the breeder, he will emerge a confident youngster.

NEW HOMES FOR PUPPIES

After investing so much time in the planning and rearing of the puppies, you will be very attached to them. Your next responsibility is to ensure that you send them to the best possible homes.

- Contact breed societies and the American Kennel Club to place advertisements; you can also place an ad at your veterinary practice.
- Spend time getting to know each puppy's future owner so that you can start preparing your puppy for its new lifestyle.
- Encourage prospective owners to visit often and give them as much information as possible to prepare them. Inform them about general and breed-specific care and training.

Glossary

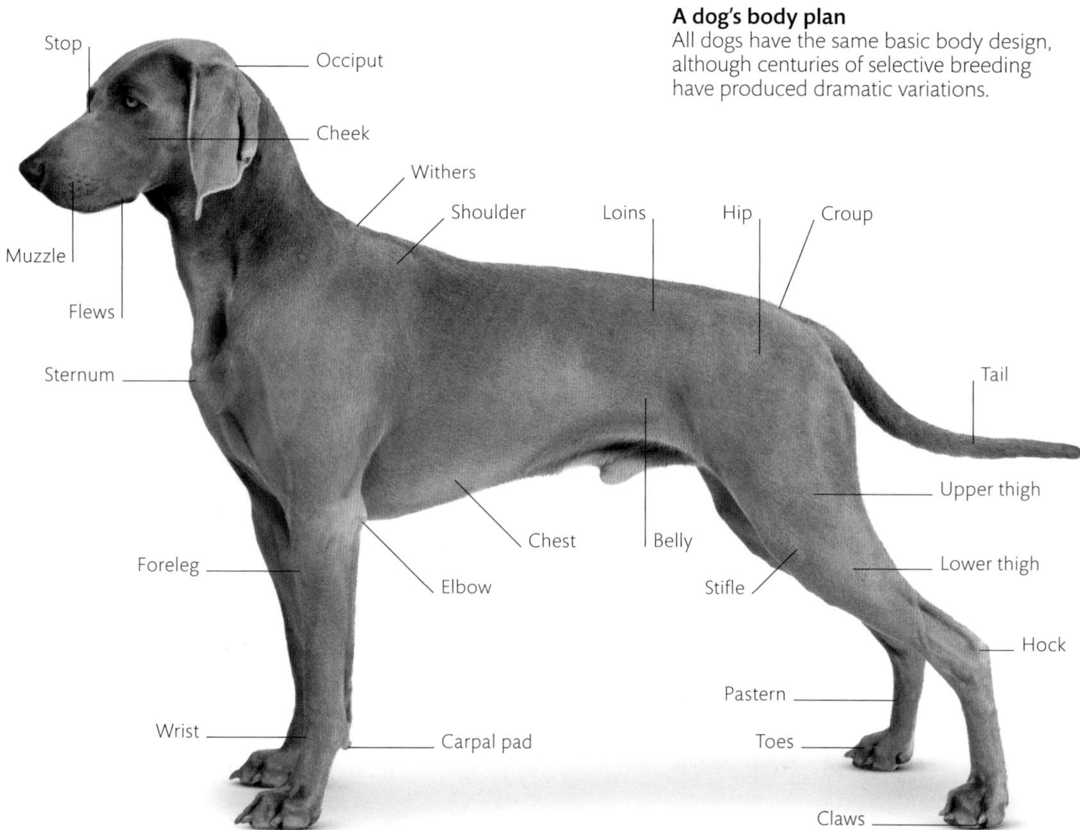

A dog's body plan
All dogs have the same basic body design, although centuries of selective breeding have produced dramatic variations.

ACHONDROPLASIA A form of dwarfism that affects the long bones of the limbs, causing them to bow outward. It is a genetic mutation that has been selectively bred for, resulting in short-legged breeds such as the Dachshund.

ALMOND-SHAPED EYES Oval eyes with slightly flattened corners that are present in breeds such as the Kooikerhondje and the English Springer Spaniel.

BEARD Thick, sometimes coarse and bushy hair around the lower facial area. Often seen in wire-haired breeds.

BELTON A coat pattern that is a mix of white and colored hairs (roan) that may have a flecked or ticked appearance.

BICOLOR Any color combined with white patches.

BLACK AND TAN A coat color with clearly defined areas of black and tan. The black color is usually found on the body and the tan color on the underparts, muzzle, and perhaps as spots above the eyes. This pattern also occurs in liver and tan and blue and tan coats.

BLANKET, BLANKET MARKINGS Large areas of color over the back and sides of the body; commonly used to describe hound markings.

BLAZE Broad, white marking running from near the top of the head to the muzzle.

BRACHYCEPHALIC HEAD A head that is almost as wide as it is long due to shortening of the muzzle. The Bulldog and Boston Terrier are examples of breeds with this head shape.

BRACKE A term used for Continental hounds that specialize in running down small game such as rabbit or fox.

BREECHES Fringing of longer hair on the thighs, which is also known as culottes or pants.

BREED Domestic dogs that have been selectively bred to have the same distinctive appearance. They conform to a breed standard drawn up by a breed club and approved by an internationally recognized body, such as the Kennel Club, FCI, or American Kennel Club.

BREED STANDARD The detailed description of a breed that specifies exactly how the dog should look, the acceptable colors and markings, and the range of height and/or weight measurements.

BRINDLE A color mix in which dark hairs form a striped pattern on lighter background of tan, gold, gray, or brown.

BRISKET The breastbone.

BUTTON EARS Semierect ears in which the top part folds down toward the eye covering the ear opening. They are seen on breeds such as the Smooth Fox Terrier and Wire Fox Terrier.

CANDLE-FLAME EARS Long, narrow, erect ears that are shaped like a candle flame. They are seen on breeds such as the English Toy Terrier.

CAPE Thick hair covering the shoulders.

CARNASSIAL TEETH Cheek teeth (upper fourth premolar and lower first molar) that are used, rather like a pair of scissors, to slice through meat, hide, and bone.

CATLIKE FEET Round, compact feet with the toes grouped closely together.

CONFORMATION The general apearance of a dog that is determined by the development of individual features and their relationship to one another.

CROUP An area of the back just above the base of the tail.

CROPPED EARS Ears that are erect and pointed due to surgical removal of part of the ear cartilage. The procedure, which is illegal in many countries, is normally carried out when puppies are about 10–16 weeks old.

DANDER Small scales of dead skin shed from the body.

DAPPLE A spotted coat of darker markings on a lighter background. Usually used as a description for short-haired breeds only; merle is used to describe the same coloring in long-haired dogs.

DEWCLAW A non-weight-bearing toe on the inner side of the foot. Some breeds, such as the Norwegian Lundehund, have double dewclaws.

DEWLAP Loose, hanging skin that falls in folds on the chin, throat, and neck of some breeds: for example, the Bloodhound.

DOCKED TAIL A tail cut to a specific length, according to the breed standard. The procedure is normaly done when puppies are only a few days old. The practice is illegal in parts of Europe, except on working dogs such as the German Pointer.

DOLICHOCEPHALIC HEAD A long, narrow head with an imperceptible stop, as seen in the Borzoi, for example.

DOUBLE COAT Coat consisting of a thick, warm underlayer and a weatherproof top layer.

DROP EARS Ears that hang down from their base. Pendant ears are a more extreme form of drop ears, being longer and heavier.

ERECT EARS Upright or pricked ears with pointed or rounded tips. Candle-flame ears are an extreme type of erect ears.

ESTRUS A period of about three weeks in the reproductive cycle during which a female dog can be mated. Primitive breeds tend to come into estrus once a year (as do wolves); in other breeds it is usually twice a year.

FEATHERS, FEATHERING Fringes of hair that may be found on the ear margins, belly, backs of legs, and the underside of the tail.

FLEWS The lips of a dog. Most commonly used to describe the fleshy, hanging upper lips in dogs of the mastiff type.

FORELOCK Lock of hair on the forehead that falls forward between the ears.

FURROW A shallow groove, seen in some breeds, that runs from the top of the head down to the stop.

GAIT Movement or action.

GRIFFON (Fr.) Referring to a coarse or wire coat.

GRIZZLE Usually a mixture of black and white hairs, which gives a blue-gray or iron-gray shading to the coat. It is seen in some breeds of terrier.

GROUP Dog breeds are classified into various groups by the Kennel Club, FCI, and American Kennel Club. The groups are loosely based on function but no two systems agree. The number and names of the groups differ, as do the breeds that are recognized and included in them.

HACKNEY GAIT Dogs with this type of action, such as the Miniature Pinscher, raise the lower part of the leg particularly high as they walk.

HARLEQUIN A color pattern comprising irregularly sized patches of black on white; seen only in the Great Dane.

HOCK Joint on the hind leg; equivalent to the human heel; in dogs this is elevated because they walk on their toes.

ISABELLA A fawn color found in some breeds, including the Bergamasco and Dobermann.

MASK Dark coloration on the face, usually around the muzzle and eyes.

MERLE A marbled coat with darker patches or spots. Blue merle (black on a bluish-gray background) is the most common variation.

MESATICEPHALIC HEAD Head shape in which the base and width are of medium proportions. The Labrador Retriever and Border Collie are examples of breeds with this type of head shape.

NEUTERING A surgical procedure that prevents dogs from breeding. Male dogs are castrated at about six months and female dogs spayed about three months after their first estrus.

OTTER TAIL A thickly furred, rounded tail that has a broad base and tapers to the tip; the hair on the underside is parted.

PACK Usually used to describe a group of scent or sight hounds that hunt together.

PASTERN Lower part of the leg, below the carpals (wrist bones) of the foreleg or the hock on the hind leg.

PENDANT EARS Ears that hang down from their base; an extreme form of drop ears.

PENDULOUS LIPS Full, loosely hanging upper or lower lips.

ROSE EARS Small, drop ears that fold outward and backward so that part of the ear canal is exposed. This type of ear is seen in Whippets.

RUFF A long, thick collar of stand-out hair around the neck.

SABLE A coat color in which hairs tipped with black overlay a lighter background color.

SADDLE A darker colored area that extends over the back.

SCISSORS BITE The normal bite of dogs with mesaticephalic and dolichocephalic heads. The upper incisors (front teeth) are slightly in front of but in contact with the lower incisors when the mouth is closed. The other teeth interlock with no gaps and form the cutting edge of the "scissors."

SEMIERECT EARS Erect ears in which only the tip is inclined forward, as seen in breeds such as the Rough Collie (right).

SESAME A coat color comprising an equal mixture of black and white hairs. In black sesame, there are more black hairs than white; red sesame is a mixture of red and black hairs.

SICKLE TAIL Tail that is carried in a half circle over the back.

SPOONLIKE FEET Similar to catlike feet but more oval in shape because the middle toes are longer than the outer toes.

STOP The indentation between the muzzle and the top of the head, in between the eyes. The stop is almost absent in dolichocephalic breeds, such as the Borzoi, and very pronounced in brachycephalic and dome-headed breeds, such as the Cocker Spaniel and the Chihuahua.

TEMPERAMENT The character of a dog.

TOPCOAT Outer coat of guard hairs.

TOPKNOT Long tuft of hair on the top of the head.

TOPLINE The outline of the dog's upper body from ears to tail.

TRICOLOR A coat of three colors in well-defined patches, usually black, tan, and white.

TUCKED UP Referring to the belly, an upward curve to the abdomen toward the hindquarters, typically seen in breeds such as the Greyhound and the Whippet.

UNDERCOAT Underlayer of hair, usually short, thick, and sometimes woolly, that provides insulation between the topcoat and the skin.

UNDERSHOT Facial conformation in which the lower jaw protrudes beyond the upper jaw, seen in breeds such as the Bulldog.

UNDERSHOT BITE The normal bite of brachycephalic breeds such as the Bulldog. Because the lower jaw is longer than the upper jaw, the incisor teeth do not meet and the lower incisors are in front of the upper ones.

WITHERS The highest point of the shoulder, where the neck meets the back. A dog's height is measured vertically from the ground to the withers.

Index

The dog breeds listed in this index may be followed by any combination of the initials KC (Kennel Club), FCI (Federation Cynologique Internationale—the World Canine Organization), and AKC (American Kennel Club). The initials indicate which of these three international organizations recognizes the breed. Occasionally the KC, FCI, and AKC recognize the same breed but use a different name from the one used in this book. This alternative name is also listed along with the initials of the organization that uses it. Some breeds have been granted provisional acceptance by the FCI and these are indicated here as FCI*.

Other breeds have no initials following their name but may be recognized by other kennel clubs in their country of origin and be in the approval process of one of the organizations listed here.

Numbers in **bold** refer to main entries

I

J

K

L

R

S

T

U

V

W

X

Y

Z

Acknowledgments

The publisher would like to thank the following people for their assistance with the book:
Vanessa Hamilton, Namita, Dheeraj Arora, Pankaj Bhatia, Priyabrata Roy Chowdhury, Shipra Jain, Swati Katyal, Nidhi Mehra, Tanvi Nathyal, Gazal Roongta, Vidit Vashisht, Neha Wahi for design assistance; Anna Fischel, Sreshtha Bhattacharya, Vibha Malhotra for editorial assistance; Caroline Hunt for proofreading; Margaret McCormack for the index; Richard Smith (Antiquarian Books, Maps and Prints) www.richardsmithrarebooks.com, for providing images of "Les Chiens Le Gibier et Ses Ennemis," published by the directors of La Manufacture FranÂaise d'Armes et Cycles, Saint-Etienne, in May 1907; C.K. Bryan for scanning images from Lydekker, R. (Ed.) The Royal Natural History vol 1 (1893) London: Frederick Warne.

The publisher would like to thank the following owners for letting us photograph their dogs:
Breed name: owner's name/dog's registered name "dog's pet name"
Chow Chow: Gerry Stevens/Maychow Red Emperor at Shifanu "Aslan"; English Pointers: Wendy Gordon/Hawkfield Sunkissed Sea "Kelt" (orange and white) and Wozopeg Sesame Imphun "Woody" (liver and white); Grand Bleu de Gascognes: Mr. and Mrs. Parker "Alfie" and "Ruby"; Irish Setters: Sandy Waterton/Lynwood Kissed by an Angel at Sandstream "Blanche" and Lynwood Strands of Silk at Sandstream "Bronte"; Irish Wolfhound: Carole Goodson/CH Moralach The Gambling Man JW "Cookson"; Pug: Sue Garrand from Lujay/Aspie Zeus "Merlin"; Puggles: Sharyn Prince/"Mario" and "Peach"; Tibetan Mastiffs: J.Springham and L.Hughes from Icebreaker Tibetan Mastiffs/Bheara Chu Tsen "George" and Seng Khri Gunn "Gunn." Tibetan Mastiff puppies: Shirley Cawthorne from Bheara Tibetan Mastiffs.

PICTURE CREDITS
Dorling Kindersley would like to thank the following for their kind permission to reproduce their photographs:
(Key: a-above; b-below/bottom; c-center; f-far; l-left; r-right; t-top)

1 Dreamstime.com: Cynoclub. **2-3 Ardea:** John Daniels. **4-5 Getty Images:** Hans Surfer / Flickr. **6-7 FLPA:** Mark Raycroft / Minden Pictures. **8 Alamy Images:** Jaina Mishra / Danita Delimont (tr). **Getty Images:** Jim and Jamie Dutcher / National Geographic (cr); Richard Olsenius / National Geographic (bl). **9 Dorling Kindersley:** Scans from Jardine, W. (Ed.) (1840) The Naturalist's Library vol 19 (2). **Chatto and Windus:** London (br); Jerry Young (tr/Grey Wolf). **14 Dreamstime.com**: Edward Fielding (cra). **16 Dreamstime.com**: Isselee (tr). **20 Alamy Images**: Mary Evans Picture Library (bl). **Dorling Kindersley:** Judith Miller (tr). **21 Alamy Images**: Susan Isakson (tl); Moviestore collection Ltd (bl, crb). **22 Alamy Images**: Melba Photo Agency (cl). **Corbis:** Bettmann (tr). **Getty Images:** M. Seemuller / De Agostini (bl); George Stubbs / The Bridgeman Art Library (crb). **23 Alamy Images**: Kumar Sriskandan (br). **Getty Images:** Imagno / Hulton Archive (tl). **24 Dreamstime.com**: Vgm (bl). **Getty Images:** Philippe Huguen / AFP (tr); L. Pedicini / De Agostini (c). **25 Getty Images:** Danita Delimont / Gallo Images (t). **26-27 Getty Images:** E.A. Janes / age fotostock. **28 Alamy Images**: F369 / Juniors Bildarchiv GmbH. **31 Alamy Images**: Mary Evans Picture Library (cra). **Fotolia:** Farinoza (br). **34 Alamy Images**: T. Musch / Tierfotoagentur (cr). **36 Corbis:** Kevin Schafer (cr). **37 The Bridgeman Art Library:** Meredith J. Long (cr). **38 Corbis:** Alexandra Beier / Reuters. **43 Getty Images:** Hulton Archive / Archive Photos (cra). **46 Fotolia:** rook76 (cr). **47 Corbis:** Bettmann (cl). **51 Alamy Images**: Greg Vaughn (cra). **52 Alamy Images**: Moviestore Collection (bc). **53 Alamy Images**: Petra Wegner (tl). **54 Corbis:** Havakuk Levison / Reuters (cl). **56** The Advertising Archives: (cl). **59 Corbis:** Bettmann (cr). **Fotolia:** Oleksii Sergieiev (c). **63 Getty Images:** Jeffrey L. Jaquish ZingPix / Flickr (br). **66 Dreamstime.com**: Anna Utekhina (clb). **67 Corbis:** National Geographic Society (cr). **68 Dreamstime.com**: Erik Lam (tr). **70 Corbis:** Gianni Dagli Orti (cl). **73 Alamy Images**: Juniors Bildarchiv GmbH (cr). **74 Alamy Images**: Rainer / blickwinkel (br); Steimer, C. / Arco Images GmbH (crb). **75 Animal Photography**: Eva-Maria Kramer (cra, cla). **76 Alamy Images**: Glenn Harper (bc). **77 Dreamstime.com**: Isselee (cla). **81 Corbis:** REN JF / epa (cr). **83 Fotolia:** cynoclub (cr). **84 The Bridgeman Art Library:** Eleanor Evans Stout and Margaret Stout Gibbs Memorial Fund in Memory of Wilbur D. Peat (bc). **Dreamstime.com**: Dmitry Kalinovsky (clb). **86 Alamy Images**: elwynn / YAY Media AS (bc). **Flickr.com**: Yugan Talovich (bl). **87 Alamy Images**: Tierfotoagentur / J. Hutfluss (c). **Animal Photography**: Eva-Maria Kramer (cla). Jessica Snäcka: Sanna Södergren (br). **88 Alamy Images**: eriklam / YAY Media AS (bc). **Animal Photography**: Eva-Maria Kramer (bl). **90 Alamy Images**: Juniors Bildarchiv GmbH (cb). **Getty Images:** David Hannah / Photolibrary (bc). **92 Alamy Images**: AlamyCelebrity (cl). **93 Getty Images:** Eadweard Muybridge / Archive Photos (cr). **95 Alamy Images**: Mary Evans Picture Library (cr). **97 Dorling Kindersley:** Lights, Camera, Action / Judith Miller (cra). **Fotolia:** biglama (cl). **98 Corbis:** Alaska Stock. **100 Getty Images:** Universal Images Group (cra). **101 Corbis:** Lee Snider / Photo Images (cra). **103 Alamy Images**: North Wind Picture Archives (cr). **Fotolia:** Alexey Kuznetsov (clb). **104** Brian Kravitz: http://www.flickr.com/photos/trpnblies7/6831821382 (cl). **106 Corbis:** Peter Guttman (bc). **Fotolia:** Eugen Wais (cb). **109 Alamy Images**: imagebroker (cra). Photoshot: Imagebrokers (ca). **111 Alamy Images**: Alex Segre (cr). **113 Dreamstime.com**: Waldemar Dabrowski (cl). **Getty Images:** Imagno / Hulton Archive (cr). **115 Corbis:** Mitsuaki Iwago / Minden Pictures (fcla). Photoshot: Biosphoto / J.-L. Klein & M (cla). **116 akg-images:** (cr). **118 Alamy Images**: D. Bayes / Lebrecht Music and Arts Photo Library (bc). **Dreamstime.com**: Linncurrie (c). **123 The Bridgeman Art Library:** Giraudon (br). **124 Dreamstime.com**: Nico Smit. **126 Corbis:** Hulton-Deutsch Collection (cra). **127 Alamy Images**: Personalities / Interfoto (cr). **128 TopFoto.co.uk**: (bl). **129 Alamy Images**: Petra Wegner (cl). **130 Dorling Kindersley:** T. Morgan **Animal Photography** (cb, bl, br). **131 Dorling Kindersley:** Scans from Lydekker, R. Ed.)The Royal Natural History vol 1 (1893) London: Frederick Warne. (cra). **132 Corbis:** (cl). **135 Alamy Images**: Wegner, P. / Arco Images GmbH (cl); Robin Weaver (cr). **136 Corbis:** Seoul National University / Handout / Reuters (cl). **138 Alamy Images**: Edward Simons. **141 Alamy Images**: Mary Evans Picture Library (cr). **142 Dorling Kindersley:** Scans from Lydekker, R. Ed.)The Royal Natural History vol 1 (1893) London: Frederick Warne. (bl). **144 Dorling Kindersley:** Scans from "Les Chiens Le Gibier et Ses Ennemis", published by the directors of La Manufacture Française d'Armes et Cycles, Saint-Etienne, in May 1907. (cl). **146 Alamy Images**: Antiques & Collectables (cr). **147 Fotolia:** Eugen Wais. **150 Alamy Images**: K. Luehrs / Tierfotoagentur (bc). Photoshot: Imagebrokers (bl). **151 Alamy Images**: Lebrecht Music and Arts Photo Library (cl). **152 Alamy Images**: Interfoto (bc). **Dreamstime.com**: Isselee (cb). **158 TopFoto.co.uk**: Topham Picturepoint (cl). **159 Getty Images:** Edwin Megargee / National Geographic (cl). **165 Dorling Kindersley:** Scans from "Les Chiens Le Gibier et Ses Ennemis", published by the directors of La Manufacture Française d'Armes et Cycles, Saint-Etienne, in May 1907 (cr). **168 Corbis:** Hulton-Deutsch Collection (cl). **169 Animal Photography**: Eva-Maria Kramer (bc, bl, cra). Photoshot: NHPA (cla). **170 Getty Images:** Anthony Barboza / Archive Photos (cr). **171 Fotolia:** Gianni. **172 Animal Photography**: Sally Anne Thompson (tr, cra, ca). **173 Dorling Kindersley:** Scans from Jardine, W. (Ed.) (1840) The Naturalist's Library vol 19 (2). **Chatto and Windus:** London (cr). **176 Fotolia:** Kerioak (cr). **TopFoto.co.uk**: Topham / Photri (bc). **181 Dreamstime.com**: Joneil (cb). **183 Corbis:** National Geographic Society (cr). **184 Alamy Images**: R. Richter / Tierfotoagentur. **186 Alamy Images**: DBI Studio (bc). **188 Alamy Images**: Lebrecht Music and Arts Photo Library (cl). **190 Corbis:** Bettmann (bl). **194 The Bridgeman Art Library:** Bonhams, London, UK (bc). **Getty Images:** Life On White / Photodisc (c). **197 Alamy Images**: K. Luehrs / Tierfotoagentur (bc). **Fotolia:** CallallooAlexis (cla). **199 Alamy Images**: Juniors Bildarchiv GmbH (c). **Getty Images:** Fox Photos / Hulton Archive (cra). **201 Dreamstime.com**: Marlonneke (bl). **203 The Bridgeman Art Library:** (cra). **Fotolia:** Eric Isselée (br). **204 Alamy Images**: B. Seiboth / Tierfotoagentur (cr). **205 The Bridgeman Art Library:** Christie's Images (cr). **207 Dreamstime.com**: Marcel De Grijs (cl/BG). **Getty Images:** Jim Frazee / Flickr (cl/Search Dog). **208 Alamy Images**: tbkmedia.de. **209 Dreamstime.com**: Isselee (c). Photoshot: Picture Alliance (cl). **211 The Bridgeman Art Library:** Museum of London, UK (cl). **213 Corbis:** Eric Planchard / prismapix / ès (bc); Mark Raycroft / Minden Pictures (bl). **215 Alamy Images**: Paul Gregg / African Images (cra). **216 Alamy Images**: Juniors Bildarchiv GmbH (cl). **219 Alamy Images**: S. Schwerdtfeger / Tierfotoagentur (cl). **220 Getty Images:** Nick Ridley / Oxford Scientific. **223** Pamela O. Kadlec: (cra). **224 Alamy Images**: Vmc / Shout (bc). **Fotolia:** Eric Isselée (cb). **227 Dorling Kindersley:** Scans from Lydekker, R. Ed.)The Royal Natural History vol 1 (1893) London: Frederick Warne. (cl). **231 Alamy Images**: Grossemy Vanessa (cr). **232 Alamy Images**: Sami Osenius (bc); Tim Woodcock (cb). **234 Dorling Kindersley:** Scans from "Les Chiens Le Gibier et Ses Ennemis", published by the directors of La Manufacture Française d'Armes et Cycles, Saint-Etienne, in May 1907. (cl). **236 Dorling Kindersley:** Scans from "Les Chiens Le Gibier et Ses Ennemis", published by the directors of La Manufacture Française d'Armes et Cycles, Saint-Etienne, in May 1907. (bl). **238 Corbis:** Francis G. Mayer (cl). **241 Corbis:** Swim Ink 2, LLC (cl). **243 Alamy Images**: AF Archive (cra). **Fotolia:** glenkar (clb). **244 Alamy Images**: D. Geithner / Tierfotoagentur (cl). **245 Corbis:** Dale Spartas (cl). **246 Fotolia:** biglama (bc). **Getty Images:** Dan Kitwood / Getty Images News (bl). **248 Corbis:** Christopher Felver (cl). **250 Dorling Kindersley:** Scans from "Les Chiens Le Gibier et Ses Ennemis", published by the directors of La Manufacture Française d'Armes et Cycles, Saint-Etienne, in May 1907. (bc). **Fotolia:** quayside (c). **252 Dorling Kindersley:** Scans from "Les Chiens Le Gibier et Ses Ennemis", published by the directors of La Manufacture Française d'Armes et Cycles, Saint-Etienne, in May 1907. (cl). **255 Alamy Images**: R. Richter / Tierfotoagentur (cl). **Getty Images:** Hablot Knight Browne / The Bridgeman Art Library (cra). **259 Getty Images:** Image Source (cl). **260** The Advertising Archives: (bl). **263 Corbis:** C / B Productions (cl). **264 Corbis:** Yoshihisa Fujita MottoPet / amanaimages. **266 Mary Evans Picture Library:** Grenville Collins Postcard Collection (cra). **267 Alamy Images**: Farlap (cla). **269 Dorling Kindersley:** Scans from Lydekker, R. Ed.)The Royal Natural History vol 1 (1893) London: Frederick Warne. (cr). **Dreamstime.com**: Isselee (cl). **270 Mary Evans Picture Library:** (cr). **272 Dreamstime.com**: Isselee (c). **Mary Evans Picture Library:** Thomas Fall (bc). **275 Dreamstime.com**: Metrjohn (cl). **276 Alamy Images**: Petra Wegner. **277 Alamy Images**: Petra Wegner (bl, br). **Dorling Kindersley:** Scans from Lydekker R. Ed.)The Royal Natural History vol 1 (1893) London: Frederick Warne. (cr). **Fotolia:** Dixi_ (cl). **279 akg-images:** Erich Lessing (cl). **280 Dreamstime.com**: Petr Kirillov. **281 Corbis:** Bettmann (cl). **282 Getty Images:** Vern Evans Photo / Getty Images Entertainment (cr). **286-287 Getty Images:** Datacraft Co Ltd (c). **286 Alamy Images**: Moviestore collection Ltd (bl). **Getty Images:** Datacraft Co Ltd (tr). **287 Getty Images:** Datacraft Co Ltd (br, fbr). **288 Getty Images:** Photos by Joy Phipps / Flickr Open. **291 TopFoto.co.uk**: Topham Picturepoint (cl). **293 Getty Images:** Reg Speller / Hulton Archive (cr). **294 Fotolia:** Carola Schubbel (cl). **295 Getty Images:** AFP (cl). **297 Alamy Images**: Donald Bowers / Purestock (cl). **Getty Images:** John Shearer / WireImage (cr). **298 Dorling Kindersley:** Benjy courtesy of The Mayhew Animal Home (cr). **Dreamstime.com**: Aliaksey Hintau (br); Isselee (cl, c). **299 Dreamstime.com**: Adogslifephoto (cl); Isselee (tr, bl); Vitaly Titov & Maria Sidelnikova (c); Erik Lam (cr, br). **300 Dreamstime.com**: Cosmin - Constantin Sava (cr); Kati1313 (tc); Isselee (tr, c, bl); Erik Lam (bc, crb, br). **301 Alamy Images**: Daniela Hofer / F1online digitale Bildagentur GmbH. **302-303 FLPA:** Ramona Richter / Tierfotoagentur. **304 Getty Images:** L. Heather Christenson / Flickr Open. **306 Dreamstime.com**: Hdconnelly (cb). **Fotolia:** Eric Isselee (tr). **309 Fotolia:** Comugnero Silvana (br). **Getty Images:** PM Images / The Image Bank (tr). **310 Getty Images:** Arco Petra (tr). **311 Alamy Images**: Ken Gillespie Photography. **312 Alamy Images**: Wayne Hutchinson (br). **Getty Images:** Andersen Ross / Photodisc (ca). **313 Corbis:** Alan Carey. **314 Alamy Images**: F314 / Juniors Bildarchiv GmbH (tr). **316 Getty Images:** Datacraft Co Ltd (bl). **318 Alamy Images**: Diez, O. / Arco Images GmbH (bl). **Fotolia:** ctvvelve (cb/ Clipper). **Getty Images:** Jamie Grill / Iconica (cr). **330 Dreamstime.com**: Moswyn (tr). **Getty Images:** Fry Design Ltd / Photographer's Choice (bl). **331 FLPA:** Erica Olsen (tr). **332 Fotolia:** Alexander Raths (tr). **335 Getty Images:** Anthony Brawley Photography / Flickr (cr). **337 Corbis:** Cheryl Ertelt / Visuals Unlimited (cb). **Getty Images:** Mitsuaki Iwago / Minden Pictures (t); Hans Surfer / Flickr (br). **338 Fotolia:** pattie (br). **339 Corbis:** Akira Uchiyama / Amanaimages (tr). **Getty Images:** Created by Lisa Vaughan / Flickr (cla). **341 Getty Images:** R. Brandon Harris / Flickr Open. **346 Dreamstime.com**: Lunary (tr). **347 FLPA:** Gerard Lacz (tl). **Getty Images:** Datacraft Co Ltd (br)

All other images © Dorling Kindersley
For further information see: www.dkimages.com